Knowledge Engineering for Software Development Life Cycles:

Support Technologies and Applications

Muthu Ramachandran
Leeds Metropolitan University, UK

Information Science
REFERENCE

Senior Editorial Director:	Kristin Klinger
Director of Book Publications:	Julia Mosemann
Editorial Director:	Lindsay Johnston
Acquisitions Editor:	Erika Carter
Development Editor:	Joel Gamon
Production Coordinator:	Jamie Snavely
Typesetters:	Keith Glazewski and Natalie Pronio
Cover Design:	Nick Newcomer

Published in the United States of America by
Information Science Reference (an imprint of IGI Global)
701 E. Chocolate Avenue
Hershey PA 17033
Tel: 717-533-8845
Fax: 717-533-8661
E-mail: cust@igi-global.com
Web site: http://www.igi-global.com/reference

Library of Congress Cataloging-in-Publication Data

Knowledge engineering for software development life cycles: support
technologies and applications / Muthu Ramachandran, editor.
     p. cm.
  Includes bibliographical references and index.
  Summary: "This book bridges the best practices and design principles
successfully employed over last two decades with modern Knowledge Engineering
(KE), which has provided some of the most valuable techniques and tools to
support encoding knowledge and experiences"--Provided by publisher.
  ISBN 978-1-60960-509-4 (hardcover) -- ISBN 978-1-60960-510-0 (ebook) 1.
Software engineering. 2. Artificial intelligence. I. Ramachandran, Muthu.
  QA76.758.K67 2011
  006.3--dc22
                                2010054422

British Cataloguing in Publication Data
A Cataloguing in Publication record for this book is available from the British Library.

Table of Contents

Section 1
Requirements Engineering and Knowledge Engineering

Detailed Table of Contents

Section 1
Requirements Engineering and Knowledge Engineering

Chapter 1

Ali Dogru, Middle Eastern Technical University, Turkey
Pinar Senkul, Middle Eastern Technical University, Turkey
Ozgur Kaya, Middle Eastern Technical University, Turkey

The amazing evolution fuelled by the introduction of the computational element has already changed our lives and continues to do so. Since its earlier days the audience was attracted to the notion of 'electronic brain' that potentially could aid, replace, and even improve human-level intelligence. Initially, the fast advancement in hardware partially enabled an appreciation for software potency. This meant that engineers had to have a better command over this field that was crucial in the solution of current and future problems and requirements. However, software development has been reported as not adequate, or mature enough.

Chapter 2

A. Egemen Yilmaz, Ankara University Faculty of Engineering, Turkey
I. Berk Yilmaz, Ankara University Faculty of Engineering, Turkey

Requirement analysis is the very first and crucial step in the software development processes. Stating the requirements in a clear manner, not only eases the following steps in the process, but also reduces the number of potential errors. In this chapter, techniques for the improvement of the requirements expressed in the natural language are revisited. These techniques try to check the requirement quality attributes via lexical and syntactic analysis methods sometimes with generic, and sometimes domain and application specific knowledge bases.

Chapter 3

In recent years there has been acceleration in the use of computing. The process applies equally to the products used in day-to-day lives (household electrical goods, cars…) and industrial products (industrial monitoring, medical equipment, financial transactions, railway systems…). When computing is introduced into complex systems a higher level of rigor is required.

Chapter 4

Wikis have been widely used as knowledge management tools. However, most of them do not support the conversion process of knowledge in an appropriate way. Specifically, they do not support brainstorming and creativity techniques, which are needed to convert tacit knowledge into explicit. This chapter presents how a wiki tool called the Spatial Hypertext Wiki (ShyWiki) can be used for supporting collaborative requirements elicitation following the knowledge creation spiral of Nonaka. The knowledge conversions in the spiral (socialization, externalization, combination, and internalization) and the knowledge types in each conversion are related to different activities in requirements elicitation, which can be performed through ShyWiki. ShyWiki allows stakeholders to collaborate by creating, brainstorming, structuring and reorganizing requirements contained in notes. In this way, the requirements negotiation and prioritization process can be done through the wiki pages which are seen as virtual boards that hold hypertext notes.

Knowledge management refers to acquisition, creation, dissemination, and utilization of knowledge. Knowledge is becoming an important resource for today's organisations, and enterprises are keen to deploy this resource to improve their products, services, and processes as well as ensure delivery on demand. Through knowledge management, businesses aim to increase efficiency, reduce costs, and most importantly, retain customers. Enterprises in the electronic commerce arena are already aware of the importance of understanding customer attitudes and their buying habits and are, therefore, taking huge strides to ensure that they employ appropriate techniques to manage the information at hand. This chapter discusses the variety of approaches that business enterprises have adopted for the acquisition of customer information and its deployment and outlines the processes relevant to knowledge management in the context of electronic commerce.

Chapter 6

The software process consists of knowledge-intensive procedures, involving various profiles, which handle a wide range of information. The adoption of a solution that satisfies the knowledge demands related to software engineering is not a trivial task. Despite all the investment made by research institutions and software development organizations in automated environments to support the software process, the quality levels and the productivity rates they need has not been reached. In software engineering, the experience, which helps avoid mistakes of the past and improve decision making, still lies mainly in the organization collaborators. This chapter intends to contribute to software engineering by proposing a new approach to support the capture, packaging, storage, mapping, maintenance and retrieval of the knowledge related to the software process. The approach will support the software process through the creation of a knowledge management model to assist the development of intelligent agents that can (i) realize the knowledge needs, (ii) interact with the Information Systems and (iii) support executing the software developers' tasks. In other words, the chapter proposes creating a multiagent system to manage knowledge related to the execution of software development processes. This system will be the result of implementing the knowledge management models for supporting software process that will also be proposed in this chapter. It will consist of an Information System integrated with a knowledge base related to the implementation of software development processes.

Section 2
Design Patterns, Components, Services and Reuse

There are a number of avenues of articulating experiential knowledge, including patterns. However, the mere availability of patterns does not lead to their suitable use, if at all. In order to establish a systematic approach for using patterns, a pattern stakeholder model and a general, process environment-neutral and domain-independent pattern usage model are proposed, and the relationships between them are underscored. The underlying essential and accidental concerns in putting patterns into practice by pattern stakeholders are highlighted and, in some cases, possible resolutions are suggested. In particular, challenges in acquisition, selection, and application of patterns are discussed.

The reliance on past experience is crucial to the future of software engineering. There are a number of avenues for articulating experiential knowledge, including patterns. It is the responsibility of a pattern author to ensure that the pattern is expressed in a manner that satisfies the reason for its existence. This chapter is concerned with the suitability of a pattern description for consumption by both humans and machines. For that, a pattern description model (PDM), and a pattern stakeholder model (PSM) and a pattern quality model (PQM) as necessary input to the PDM, are proposed. The relationships between these conceptual models are highlighted. The PDM advocates the use of descriptive markup for representation and suggests the use of presentation markup for presentation of information in pattern descriptions, respectively. The separation of representation of information in a pattern description from its presentation is emphasized. The potential uses of the Semantic Web and the Social Web as mediums for publishing patterns are discussed.

Isabelle Mirbel, Université de Nice Sophia-Antipolis, France
Pierre Crescenzo, Université de Nice Sophia-Antipolis, France
Nadia Cerezo, Université de Nice Sophia-Antipolis, France

Scientists who are not proficient in computer science and yet wish to perform in-silico experiments and harness the power of Service Oriented Architecture are presented with dozens of daunting technical solutions: scientific workflow frameworks. While these systems do take care of complex technical aspects such as Grid technologies, little is done to support transfer of service composition knowledge and know-how. The authors of this chapter believe the problem lies in the scientific workflow models which are too low-level and too anchored in the underlying technologies to allow efficient reuse and sharing. This chapter's approach, called SATIS, relies on a goal-driven model, that has proven its worth in requirement engineering, and the Semantic Web technologies to leverage the collective knowledge and know-how in order to bridge the gap between service providers and end-users.

Rosario Girardi, Federal University of Maranhão, Brazil
Adriana Leite, Federal University of Maranhão, Brazil

Automating software engineering tasks is essential to achieve better productivity in software development and quality of software products. Knowledge engineering can address this challenge through the representation and reuse of knowledge of how and when to perform a development task. This chapter describes a knowledge-based approach for automating agent-oriented development whose main components are a software process (MADAE-Pro) and an integrated development environment (MADAE-IDE). MADAE-Pro is an ontology-driven process for multi-agent domain and application engineering which promotes the construction and reuse of agent-oriented application families. MADAE-IDE is an integrated development environment which assists developers in the application of MADAE-Pro, allowing full or partial automation of its modeling tasks through a set of production rules that explores the semantic representation of modeling products in its knowledge base. The approach has been evaluated through the development of a multi-agent system family of recommender systems supporting alternative (collaborative, content-based and hybrid) filtering techniques. Some examples from these case studies are presented to illustrate and detail the domain analysis and application requirements engineering tasks of MADAE-Pro.

Chapter 11

The current trend of open source development and outsourcing industry heavily banks upon the reusability of software for achieving consistency in quality and optimization of cost. Hence, software developers require excellent support in the assessment of the reusability levels of the software that they are trying to develop. This chapter introduces a method which will analyze the object oriented software design and calculate the possible reusability level of that software module. It measures the structural properties of software using design metrics and transforms those measures to reusability levels associated with that package. This scheme brings out a novel data driven-methodology, which can predict the reusability of a software system at its design phase itself and provide a feedback to the design architect to improve the design appropriately to achieve better reusable and cost effective software products.

Section 3
Testing, Metrics and Process Improvement

Chapter 12

Software testing is one of the most important processes in Software Development Life Cycle (SDLC) to ensure quality of software product. A large number of approaches for test data generation and optimization in software testing have been reported with varying degrees of success. In recent years, the application of artificial intelligence (AI) techniques in software testing to achieve quality software is an emerging area of research. It combines the concepts of the two domains AI and Software Engineering and yields innovative mechanisms that have the advantages of both of them. This chapter demonstrates the development of a novel software test sequence optimization framework using intelligent agents based graph searching technique. To ensure the quality, a set of test adequacy criteria such as path coverage, state coverage, and branch coverage have been applied in the approach discussed in this chapter, while achieving optimization.

Chapter 13

Internet security is paramount in today's networked systems, especially when they provide wireless application access and enable personal and confidential data to be transmitted across the networks. Numerous tools and technologies are available to ensure system security, however, external threats to computer systems and applications are also becoming more and more sophisticated. This chapter presents a framework that consists of two components: (1) an assessment model to look at the existing security infrastructure of an organisation to determine its security maturity level; and (2) a process improvement maturity model to suggest an improvement mechanism for the organisation to progress from one maturity level to the next higher level. The intention is to provide a framework to improve the organisation's Internet and network security so that it becomes more efficient and effective than before. The improvement process model is a 5-stage framework, which has the potential to be established as a standard maturity model for assessing and improving security levels in a manner similar to other software process improvement framework such as CMMI. Preliminary results, based on looking at the existing security measures of one particular organisation, reveal that there is indeed a need for an appropriate model such as the one being proposed in this chapter.

Chapter 14

Gopalakrishnan T.R. Nair, Research and Industry Incubation Centre, Dayananda Sagar Institutions, India
Selvarani R, Research and Industry Incubation Centre, Dayananda Sagar Institutions, India

As the object oriented programming languages and development methodologies moved forward, a significant research effort was spent in defining specific approaches and building models for quality based on object oriented measurements. Software metrics research and practice have helped in building an empirical basis for software engineering. Software developers require objectives and valid measurement schemes for the evaluation and improvisation of product quality from the initial stages of development. Measuring the structural design properties of a software system such as coupling, inheritance, cohesion, and complexity is a promising approach which can lead to an early quality assessment. The class codes and class diagrams are the key artifacts in the development of object oriented (OO) software and it constitutes the backbone of OO development. It also provides a solid foundation for the design and development of software with a greater influence over the system that is implemented. This chapter presents a survey of existing relevant works on class code / class diagram metrics in an elaborate way. Here, a critical review of the existing work is carried out in order to identify the lessons learnt regarding the way these studies are performed and reported. This work facilitates the development of an empirical body of knowledge. The classical approaches based on statistics alone do not provide managers and developers with a decision support scheme for risk assessment and cost reduction. One of the future challenges is to use software metrics in a way that they creatively address and handle the key objectives of risk assessment and the estimation of external quality factors of the software.

This chapter discusses knowledge management (KM) aspects of how software process and software process improvement (SPI) is practiced within very small entities (VSEs) in the context of Irish software development industry. In particular, this study is concerned with the process of software development knowledge management in supporting the SPI. In order to understand the support process, the authors of this chapter have studied how KM processes are practiced within VSEs which includes communication, learning, sharing, and documentation process. This study also focuses in detail on the issues of the knowledge atrophy problem in VSEs. The findings explain how KM has been practiced and influenced the software development process and process improvement in VSEs. This result indicates that KM processes in VSEs are being undertaken in a very informal manner and also in indirect way. This is due to a small team size, autonomous working and macro-management style and caused VSEs to be more informal in their KM processes specifically and SPI generally. In addition, the results have indicated that the informal environment and culture helped VSEs to easily create and share knowledge between staff members and also assisted VSEs to mitigate the knowledge atrophy problem in their organization.

This chapter describes a methodology to support the management of large scale software projects in optimizing product correction effort versus initial development costs over time. The Software Process Model (SPM) represents the implementation of this approach on a level of detail explicitly developed to meet project manager's demands. The underlying technique used in this approach is based on Dynamic Bayesian Networks (DBNs). The use of Bayesian Networks (BNs) enables the representation of causal relationships among process and product key performance indicators elicited either by data or expert knowledge. DBNs provide an insight into various aspects of SPM over time to assess current as well as predicting future model states. The objective of this chapter is to describe the practical approach to establish SPM as state of the art decision support in an industrial environment.

Preface

INTRODUCTION

Software Engineering (SE) is a disciplined and engineering approach to software development and management of software projects and complexity. Today, software exists in each and every product, from toys, powered tooth brushes, electric shavers (have 10,000 lines of embedded software code), TV and entertainment systems, mobile computers, portable devices, medical systems, and home appliances, and to large scale software such as aircraft, communication systems, weather forecasts, Grid computing, and much more. Current success in software development practices are based on some of the best practices and good design principles which have been employed over last two decades. On the other hand, Knowledge Engineering (KE) has provided some of the best techniques and tools to support encoding knowledge and experiences successfully. Therefore, it is the main aim of this book to bridge those two successes for the purpose of enhancing software development practices.

Software guidelines have been with us in many forms within Software Engineering community such as knowledge, experiences, domain expertise, laws, software design principles, rules, design heuristics, hypotheses, experimental results, programming rules, best practices, observations, skills, and algorithms, all of which have played major role in software development (guidelines based software engineering). Also, there has been a significant development in new software paradigms such as components, agile aspects, and services. How can we best use those 30 years of best practices in solving software related problems? There has been little evidence of automated approaches to the development of large scale systems and software reuse. The demands of Software Engineering imply a growing need for using Artificial Intelligence and Knowledge Engineering (KE) to support all aspects of the software development process. This book aims to provide insights into the application of knowledge based approaches to the development of software systems, agile software development, software product line, software components, software architecture, automated code generators, automated test case generations, intelligent systems supporting software reuse and productivity, domain-specific software modelling, automated requirements and semantic knowledge capturing techniques, intelligent software intensive devices, and applications. In recent years, there has been significant application of neural networks and genetic programming applied to software development for a variety of applications.

This book also aims to identify how software development best practices captured as software guidelines can be represented to automated software development, decision making, and knowledge management. Therefore, a book of this nature can bring industry and academia together to address the need for the growing applications and supporting knowledge based approaches to software development.

KNOWLEDGE ENGINEERING FOR SOFTWARE DEVELOPMENT LIFE CYCLES

Software development remains costly and laborious as it depends largely on human talents. For faster productivity and to reduce cost in the current knowledge economy, we need to strive for quality; we need to capture best practices and problem solving techniques in all aspects of software development activities. There have been many successful software development life cycles ranging from a water fall model, spiral model, to win-win model, and many more. All of them have proposed a set of activities to be performed and to be checked for maintaining the desired quality and standards. Therefore, it is quite possible to capture and encode those required activities as knowledge, and hence, save us from repetitive tasks that are costly and time consuming. Also, there have been several techniques on modelling and several programming languages, all which require highly skilled people to develop systems. This learning process can be saved by using a number of automated knowledge based activities supported by those emerging technologies. In addition, most of the existing and legacy systems often need to be transformed into those newer technologies due to business competition and enterprise system integration. These activities can also be automated, thus saving cost and effort and at the same time maintaining expected quality.

RESEARCH ISSUES

Interplay between Software Engineering and Knowledge Engineering will dominate the current and further research in the areas such as large scale software development, global software project management, knowledge management practices for software services, and automated technologies. Some of the specific areas of research are:

- Best practice software guidelines
- Efficient programming techniques supporting large scale reuse
- Knowledge engineering support for software reuse
- Knowledge engineering support for code generation
- KE support for requirements, architecture, components
- KE support for software process improvement
- KE support for software testing, quality and metrics
- Intelligent software intensive applications
- Knowledge Management (KM) for software product line
- KE for agile and aspects-oriented software development
- KE for web services and SOA
- Requirements engineering and knowledge management
- Automated code generation techniques from requirements and design
- Automated support for software project management and process improvement
- Automated support for reusability, extensibility, and refactoring
- Automated support for reusable requirements, design, and test scripts

BOOK ORGANISATION

Software development and knowledge engineering process and related technologies are the key to today's globalisation which would not have occurred without integrating these two disciplines. New technologies and concepts are being developed, prompting researchers to find continuously new ways of utilizing both older and new technologies. In such an ever-evolving environment, teachers, researchers and professionals of the discipline need access to the most current information about the concepts, issues, trends and technologies in this emerging field. This book will be most helpful as it provides comprehensive coverage and definitions of the most important issues, concepts, trends and technologies in *Software Engineering and Knowledge Engineering*. This important new publication will be distributed worldwide among academic and professional institutions and will be instrumental in providing researchers, scholars, students and professionals access to the latest knowledge related to information science and technology. Contributions to this important publication will be made by scholars throughout the world with notable research portfolios and expertise. The book chapters are organised into three sections:

- **Section 1. Requirements Engineering and Knowledge Engineering:** This part provides chapters on AI support for Software Engineering in compositional era, Natural Language, Requirements and Knowledge Management.
- **Section 2. Design Patterns, Components, Services and Reuse:** This part consists of chapters on approaches to conceptual modelling for software patterns, web services, and software reuse.
- **Section 3. Testing, Metrics and Process Improvement:** This part consists of chapters on knowledge based approaches to software testing, framework for security improvement, KE supporting software process improvement and models.

REFERENCES

Orwant, J. (2000). EGGG: Automated programming for game generation. *IBM Systems Journal, 39*(3&4).

Rich, C., & Waters, C. R. (1991). *Knowledge intensive software engineering tools.* (Mitsubishi Electric Research Laboratories, Technical Report 91-03).

Ramachandran, M. (2009). Knowledge Engineering support for software requirements, architecture, and components . In Vadera, S., & Meziane, F. (Eds.), *AI support for SE*. Hershey, PA: IGI Global Publication.

Ramachandran, M. (2008). *Software components: Guidelines and applications*. New York, NY: Nova Publishers.

Ramachandran, M., & Ganeshan, S. (2009). Commonality analysis: Implications over a successful product line . In Ramachandran, M., & de Carvalho, R. A. (Eds.), *Handbook of software engineering and productivity technologies: Implications for globalisation*. Hershey, PA: IGI Publishers.

Acknowledgment

This book would not have been possible without the cooperation and assistance of many people. The editors would like to thank Joel Gamon at IGI Global for his expertise in organizing and guiding this project. We thank all the authors who contributed to this book; without their willingness to share their knowledge, this project would not have been possible. Many of them also served as reviewers of other chapters; therefore we doubly thank their contribution. We would like to thank the book's Advisory Board for their suggestions and help reviewing the chapters. I also thank colleagues at Leeds Metropolitan University for providing support.

Muthu Ramachandran
Leeds Metropolitan University, UK

Section 1
Requirements Engineering and Knowledge Engineering

Chapter 1

Modern Approaches to Software Engineering in the Compositional Era

Ali Dogru
Middle Eastern Technical University, Turkey

Pinar Senkul
Middle Eastern Technical University, Turkey

Ozgur Kaya
Middle Eastern Technical University, Turkey

ABSTRACT

The amazing evolution fuelled by the introduction of the computational element has already changed our lives and continues to do so. Initially, the fast advancement in hardware partially enabled an appreciation for software potency. This meant that engineers had to have a better command over this field that was crucial in the solution of current and future problems and requirements. However, software development has been reported as not adequate, or mature enough. Intelligence can help closing this gap. This chapter introduces the historical and modern aspects of software engineering within the artificial intelligence perspective. Also an illustrative example is included that demonstrates a rule-based approach for the development of fault management systems.

INTRODUCTION

Since its earlier days the audience was attracted to the notion of 'electronic brain' that potentially could aid, replace, and even improve human-level intelligence. Expectations from such artificial intelligence, in improving the daily life, now had to be extended to aid the very techniques that would develop the artificial intelligence. Software Engineering could definitely benefit from such leverage while software demand has grown exponentially as ever and corresponding offer – i.e. software development, could never catch up with. Fortunately, before the end of its half a century long quest, after experimenting with improvised

DOI: 10.4018/978-1-60960-509-4.ch001

Figure 1. Semantic gap

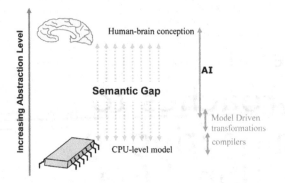

Our History in the AI Perspective

Manifesting itself after the introduction of the modern computer, the older dated field of Computer Science (CS) surfaced with the goal to reduce the "semantic gap". This was simply to convert problem representations from the conventional ways we developed for human understanding, to another, that computers could understand (execute). Figure 1 depicts the semantic gap concept.

This clearly states the main issue as that of Knowledge Representation (KR). KR in return, is a fundamental AI notion. In other words, the computation field is basically trying to enact AI. Among the many sub-fields only these that concern the higher-level regions of the semantic gap are somehow regarded as related to AI. One lowest level tool, covering the bottom region of the gap is the compiler. Neither a compiler, nor an embedded software that drives a dishwasher for example, are considered as artificially intelligent. When the behavior of the artifact mimics human intelligence, then it seems to earn the "intelligent" attribute.

However, when human-level intelligent activities are compared to the Central Processing Unit (CPU), the shier amount of intellectual activity does not seem to be sufficient in differentiating them on the basis of intelligence: It is easy for a human to recognize the face of another, among thousands of faces. While such a capability is very difficult to attain by the computers, multiplying millions of pairs of floating point numbers in a second is easy and yet that is unthinkable for the human brain. Yet the brain is intelligent and the CPU is not. Both require computational power. Repetitive execution of smaller granularity actions does not qualify as intelligence, unless they are organized around a structure to combine the massive calculations towards deducing a higher-level result such as recognizing a face. Otherwise, if even they required the same amount of operations, one-million independent floating point multiplica-

notions the inevitable incorporation of intelligence is in the process of being established.

It is desirable to replace the human in the software process, as much as possible. Linear improvements through better techniques but still targeting the addition of the next single block at a time, to build a huge system, are not sufficient. The development technique needs to be automated and automation is an open invitation to Artificial Intelligence (AI). Software engineers are under pressure for addressing organized ways for utilizing new approaches such as Component Orientation, Service Orientation, Aspect Orientation, Software Product Line Engineering, Model Driven Development, and related approaches. If not due to a conscious planning that is aware of the necessity and the opportunities, this consideration is at least being motivated by such technologies getting more and more popular. Such approaches assume the role of "enabling technologies" for the "Compositional Era". Today's software engineer should expect to deliver a system through locating and integrating sub-solutions in contrast to creating them. AI will help the engineer in automating the search and integration of the sub-solutions. Consequently, our methodologies that are aligned towards defining the code to be written and eventually writing it one line at a time, are changing towards locating and integrating blocks. AI will help the paradigm shift from code writing to composition.

tions conducted within a second do not deserve the intelligence attribute.

The AI filed has gained and lost popularity few times in the relatively short history of CS. Nevertheless, there have been very satisfactory applications. Success of expert systems has been operationally proven even in the medical domain where doctors use them for diagnosis etc. If we were to make some approximation to accept all computer applications as Artificially Intelligent, ignoring the common perception for their identification as discussed above, it will not be wrong to state that AI is now being used to develop AI. Software Engineering discipline is now in an effort to utilize AI for organizing the way to build software. AI applications are software therefore we are in the era where AI is developing AI.

History of Software Engineering

Software Engineering (SE) started as a fruit of frustrations in not being able to respond to the demand. Earlier attempts to manage the complex process were mostly improvised techniques. Primitive tools and even the fast-improving hardware were not adequate to relieve the software engineer from such low-level constraints so that new methodologies could be designed within a relaxed atmosphere that allows to freely think about what is the ideal way, rather than what can we do with the current infrastructure. Thanks to the fast pace in the maturing of the field, we are in much a better position today. Actually, conditions are mature to discuss the inclusion of AI in the SE approaches and this chapter will investigate such an avenue. Nevertheless, it may be useful to look at the history of SE at a time when a quantum leap is expected to affect the current progress of the history.

Infancy

Programs were being developed through artistic talents. The earliest programming practice was

through "wiring" one bit at a time! Almost immediate reaction to early felt agony in such incapacitating environments paved the road for inventing facilitating means to type programs. Also, the exponentially growing demand on software first pushed the programmers to invent programming languages that were higher in abstraction-levels. The instruction codes that were basically numbers corresponding to operations soon left their room to somewhat meaningful words. Instructions that were register-level in the assembly languages, improved into those that enabled writing statements almost like functions written by mathematicians. FORTRAN and COBOL were the earliest high-level languages. Better languages kept appearing as the only leverage against the demand. It took decades before we realized that a discipline transcending programming was needed to engineer software.

The development process was then being managed. The artists approach to programming needed to be preceded by formulating the problem, and then designing the solution. Testing, integration of the modules, and even maintenance after delivery were dealt with. Software monster was now understood better, with modeling techniques for various cross-sections of the artifact.

Still behind the demand, and further frustrated with failure stories, Software Engineers started to look for more suitable tools for human cognition in an effort to defeat the complexity. That was a sign of the later to come evolutions in the maturing of the field that would ever continue.

Evolutions

All the improvement in our approaches converges to two dimensions: Process, that is how we order the necessary activities, and notation, that is how we represent our models and programs. After the initial assumption that requirements could be completely and correctly specified, the industry quickly shifted to evolutionary processes. It was found that the wicked problems of software could not be completely specified until completely solved. The newer processes allowed, even forced to re-visit earlier phases of activities such as problem specification, during development.

Notation on the other hand, changed the way we formulize the conceptions. With less impact at the programming languages level, their effects in the modeling of our designs changed our views to software drastically. The three dimensions of design, implicitly stated by Pressman in relatively the past (Pressman, 1997) were almost orthogonal. Yet our formulations shifted across those dimensions during this evolution, in terms of the primary emphasis our models dedicated. Somehow, the paradigm shift in processes happened once and stayed basically the same. That was from linear (or phased) to evolutionary. However, the change in notation sustained an amazing progress.

It is easier today to look back and classify what the industry was doing in the past. If the Design dimensions of Pressman are taken as reference, amazingly we can observe that they have been dominating the modeling understanding, one at a time, and in an order (Dogru, 2006). The early days with many different 'structured' approaches,

resulted with an assessment of the programs as networks of 'functions.' That is dimension number one, chronologically. Then comes 'data' that was taken as the central element in object orientation, again after lingering for decades. This quest continued with 'structure' gaining emphasis in the component based approaches that suggested acquiring a piece of structure (i.e. a component) and connecting it with others to compose a system. Figure 2 depicts the emphasis shift among design dimensions by time.

The interesting development shown in Figure 2 is the looping of the curve, back on to the function dimensions. Of course, having improved on the way, the curve comes back with extended capabilities. Traditional approaches were viewing the programs as a statically defined set of functions. Now, functional elements are treated as executable units, not for development but for using in composition. Also, their activation order is addressed in the well supported 'orchestration' domain. Actually we want to refer to this new trend as process orientation, rather than function. That is one way to explain the enhanced re-visiting of the function dimension. Since the tradi-

Figure 2. Modeling emphasis changing along design dimensions

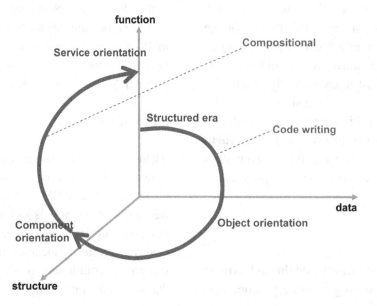

tional era, functions have been referred to as procedural units, suggesting similarity between those two terms. However, the definition of a process as an ordered set of tasks, suggests an emphasis on the 'ordering' capability of a process, in contrast to the isolated assessment of a function. In service orientation, a system is composed by ordering the service activations, where composition is modeled as a process. The modern approach certifies the usage of 'process' that can be regarded as an advanced point on the function dimension.

The initial conscious effort for providing building blocks to enable the "build by integration" paradigm was for the introduction of components (Szyperski, 2002). Depending on the assumption that algorithmic level solutions will be readily available therefore the problem of converting a system definition to working software will be that of locating and integrating sub-solutions. Later referred to as compositional approaches, earlier implementations had to consider components that are structural units, as the building blocks. These prefabricated sub-solutions needed to be found, negotiated, carried to the development environment as executable units, and finally integrated into the solution. Development had to revolve around the structural dimension: the solution would be modeled as a decomposition of structural units that satisfied functional requirements. It was not however late before services replaced components, in the literature and the industry. There is more demand for composing a system using web-services rather than components: solutions no longer had to be composed of physical units moved into the product, they could be 'hired' from the organization that could offer them as their competent artifacts, in a manner that allowed the software enabling the service, transparent to the developer. The units satisfying functional requirements now can reside at remote servers and their maintenance does not bother the developer or the user.

The current position for the practitioners of the compositional approaches is to decompose

Figure 3. Composition with respect to the process view (adopted from Manzer & Dogru, 2007)

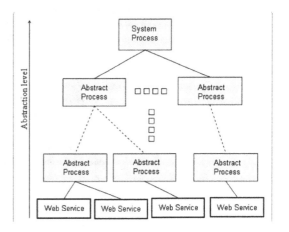

with respect to the function dimension: model the composition of elementary functions in a process model (that in turn is also regarded as a super function – a web service). The solution space is modeled as a hierarchy of procedural or functional units as shown in Figure 3. At the lowest level, these units are web services, and at the higher levels, they are process models, executable also as web services that account for 'orchestration'. This is the jargon of the Service Oriented Architecture (SOA) which is currently widely attractive. Even for the heterogeneous integration of services and processes that cannot execute together, a more abstract process modeling is referred to as choreography in this jargon. A tool support for the hierarchical organization of various compositional process models and web services is provided in (Akbiyik, 2008).

Current Maturity

Certainly methods employed today are substantially more capable, for developing software. The compositional paradigm supports the construction of products of enormous sizes in relatively shorter times. Many techniques rely on software architecture leverage for managing complex systems. All can benefit from AI. Some current approaches

Figure 4. Procedural hierarchy in Service Oriented Architecture (adopted from Akbiyik, 2008)

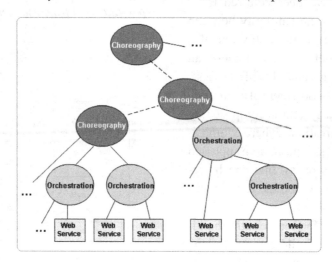

are listed below, together with possible AI support for their enhancements:

Model Driven Development

A very promising approach that once could not gain popularity when referred to as transformational approaches due to the immature infrastructure of then. The philosophy is to provide intellectual control over the complex software, through elevating the abstraction level of the specification activity. Rather than shaping the behavior through programming, more abstract models should be the workspace for the developers. The approach suggests to start with more abstract models and transform to lower levels, preferably automatically. The important factor to render Model Driven Development (MDD) effective is the automation in transferring a higher-level model to lover level models and eventually, to code.

The set of models inherit the characteristics of basic abstraction/refinement relations. It is desirable to manipulate the specification through higher-abstraction models. Details, however, cannot be handled. For that, in MDD, lower-level models need to be worked on, which we try to avoid as much as possible. Consequently, details need to be input to the system of models for the completion of the product. If the environment is mature enough to accept high-level specifications and fill in the details automatically, we have the perfect MDD support. Automatic insertions of intended details is the intelligent component crucially MDD should depend on. So far, as islands of success in automatic code generation exemplifies, such determination of details have been possible in limited domains for solution spaces. Where, expected detail information can be captured in the knowledgebase, since required knowledge size is manageable for narrow domains.

Figure 5 depicts the need for inserting details, and the source of required information. An example is the Graphical User Interface design environ-

Figure 5. Providing the required detail during enhancement

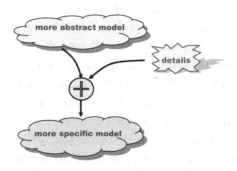

ments that have long been a successful automatic code generation domain. When a developer drags and drops a 'push button' automatically its color is set to gray, because in this limited domain, it is easy to suggest some default details due to the established patterns.

Software Product Lines

Software Product Lines (SPL) conducts planned reuse, exploiting the situation where similar software products are expected to be developed. Such a family of products has many common parts. SPLs need to model the common and variable parts of the family of products. To benefit from SPLs, the organization must undertake the tedious task of domain engineering. However, once the domain is ready, creating consecutive products becomes easier. Especially increased number of developments increases the return on investment, considerably. Significant impact should be sought through more effective management of the variability: Theoretically a comprehensive specification of the variabilities should be the only necessary definition leading to the automatic generation of a product.

There are problems with configuring the variations to define the new product. Every decision in shaping the product has consequences: they may conflict with the previous specifications, and limit the future specifications to come. Intelligence will be very much in demand to resolve the large space of interdependent decisions on variations. Also, some variability may be desired to be resolved dynamically, through the software that can analyze the environment and take actions in an autonomous manner.

Service Oriented Architecture

Targeting loosely coupled distributed systems, Service Oriented Architecture (SOA) seems to offer the best alternative for most of the current architectural needs. Developers would enjoy employing this architecture and yet they still want to be able to locate any web services they need in an assisted manner and integrate them to deliver a product, without hassles. Locating the right web service for a functional requirement is an important task, whereas developers are also concerned with many other issues related with depending on a service deployed and maintained by remote organizations. For a given functional requirement, there could be alternatives that also include non-functional issues in the selection of a web service.

The effective AI application in this most current scenario is through appending semantics to the mechanism for locating the necessary web service. It is a wide research area to append semantically enriched definitions to the web service descriptions that currently are based on syntactic definitions. Similar knowledge will prove useful in the automatic integration of the web services, after they are located to compose the final product. Once again, negotiation among the conflicting constraints will invite intelligent approaches.

Component oriented development would benefit from an intelligent support very similar to service orientation would. Locating of components and integration are the two main areas that are in need for such an aid. The minor difference when incorporating components instead of services is about the way units will be integrated, however, on the business end there are different issues such as licensing a component versus billing for web service usage.

Aspect Oriented Development

This approach is facilitating the separation of concerns, in developing software. A frequently used concern is confined to a localized definition, and hence isolated from the involved units of functional code. The more is such isolation, the better – meaning that concerns are more separated. Currently, through aspect fortified languages the 'functional' units even if not including statements related to the isolated aspect (concern), have to somehow hint about a request for 'weaving' with the aspect through mechanisms such as a substring embedded in the function name. Then, a preprocessor finds such hints and embeds (weaving) the aspect related code in the unit. This simplest approach to aspect oriented programming is fundamentally based on macro expansions and that is not an ideal mechanism. The ideal mechanism would call for intelligence, preferably embedded in the run-time environment, that determines when and which aspect to activate.

The brief discussion about the current maturity will be ended here. It is possible to summarize the investigation with a statement that assesses the awareness to be present, witnesses some AI participation, and points to the need for much more. Next section will expand on the usage of ontologies for intelligent search and integration in the web services world. That is probably the best area to present among the others, due to the fact that there is quite some existing foundation and this area promises the soonest to see results. Another section will introduce an interesting mixing of SPLs, rule based systems, and Domain Specific inference to provide the background for the case study on fault management that follows later.

ONTOLOGY GUIDED SEARCH AND INTEGRATION

The vision in the compositional era for developing software systems requires well established foundations for finding required software units and for integrating them. Currently most promising approach for both requirements is the utilization of ontology. Despite many difficulties in the commercial-range use of this tool, the extent of research towards this goal is interesting.

If every developer could use exactly the same 'name' for a web service that satisfies a universally defined function, there would not be a search problem. Today, the problem is due to

the difficulty of semantic matching between the specification to be presented in the query and the specification defining an existing service. Both advertising of a service and the searching party should speak the same 'language'. There is usually not a high probability to succeed by only matching two strings: the names used at both ends will not exactly match, for many cases. If one of the parties have used a different string to mean a similar functionality, an automatic mechanism to deduce that both parties mean similar semantics will help in the search. Ontology is the tool such an automation mechanism will utilize. Defined as a semantic net built over the terminology of a domain, an ontology can be referred in relating semantically close terms. The simplest case is where synonyms are used by the two parties. For the cases where the pairs of strings correspond to meanings that are slightly different than the same concept, the ontology can help to determine the degree of similarity between the pair. It is therefore possible for a search tool to propose a list of possible matches, with a decreasing similarity measure.

The current experience shows that it is highly unlikely to build a universal ontology that includes most of the concepts (entities) to be used by any software development. Rather, narrow domains of similar applications are preferred scopes for different ontology models. Even then, for a specific domain there are different ontology models that do not agree among themselves. Ontology matching is a practical problem with ongoing research.

Also missing is association mechanisms between ontologies and web services. The above mentioned matchmaking can be possible through an ontology that is associated with a set of web services. Current candidates to ontological matching are the names of the web services, names of the methods within such services, and their input and output parameters. A sophisticated (for today!) match would make use of all these information, as components of the software unit's definition. Early work on semantic description of web services included information to further help in the description of what a function really does, by formally expressing the pre-condition, post-condition, and the invariant constituents of the function. Yet there is no commonly accepted list of what kind of information to include in the semantic definition so that an automatic match can be aided. However, there are practical research examples with limited demonstration about the feasibility of the idea (Fensel, 2002; Martin, 2007; McIlraith, 2001; Medjahed, 2003; Paolucci, 2002; Sirin, 2003; Kardas, 20070.

OWL-S [Owl-S] is one of the most established attempts for describing a web service semantically. It is an upper ontology for services telling about not only input and output of a service, but also the functionality and the structure as atomic or composite and the components, each of which is a simpler web service. Main parts of an OWL-S description are service profile, service model and service grounding. Service model is the part where the structure of the service is described. Service profile and service grounding definitions carry information on what service does and how it is accessed, respectively. From discovery and integration point of view, service profile includes valuable information, including service name, service description and parameters, which facilitate the automation of these tasks.

In considerable number of service discovery and composition studies, it is assumed that the services are described in OWL-S. Once this assumption is accepted, an important step forward is complementing OWL-S and UDDI [uddi]. UDDI was initiated as an XML-based business registry for publishing service listings and enabling potential business partners to discover each other's services. UDDI registry structure supports querying based on mostly syntactic, keyword matching. Actually it includes semantic information in the form of a standard taxonomy denoting the industrial categories. However this much semantic information is quite limited for accurate querying on the registry. Therefore, in [Paolucci 2002b],

it was attempted to integrate OWL-S and UDDI in order to provide semantic search capability on UDDI service registries This simply involves defining a mapping between OWL-S concepts and UDDI registry records. However, this approach is still limited with the registry record structure.

There are also attempts that propose their own service ontology models as in (Mejahed, 2002). The reason behind such a choice is basically to be able to carry more information that OWL-S provides, such as quality of service. Although there are other ontologies for such additional needs, such as QoSOnt (Dobson, 2005), they are not yet mature enough to be a standard.

Once it is assumed that web services are semantically annotated, by either OWL-S or some other ontology model, the basic approach followed is employing semantic matching between two entities. For service search, it is used for matching the semantically described service query, which is actually an abstract target service, against concrete services. For composition and integration, it is applied on the semantically annotated parameters (inputs and outputs) of the service. One of the basic semantic matching approaches for web service capabilities is presented in (Paolucci, 2002). It defines various degrees of similarity on the basis of the inheritance relation in the ontology model. This matching algorithm is further extended in (Karani, 2007) with a more detailed comparison on properties of the concepts. In addition to employing semantic matching (Skoutas, 2008), other common tools used in semantic service discovery and composition include using ontology mediators (Verma, 2005 and Sivashanmugam, 2004) and logic-based semantic reasoners (Sirin, 2002).

In service composition or integration, the main issue is to have collection of services that can fulfill a target goal when they work in coherence. With the use of web services platform dependency and interoperability is no longer a major problem. Now the problem transforms into checking whether a service can be called with the data at hand (Verma, 2005; Karani, 2007; Bleul, 2006). This is actually a semantic matching task. The difference from the service discovery task is a subtle point that input provided for the composite system at the beginning is to be combined with the outputs collected so far from other services in the composition, which constitute the data at hand.

Although we have come a long way in automating the service discovery and composition, the proposed techniques are still semi-automated, requiring human supervision and approval before execution of the service.

DOMAIN SPECIFIC INFERENCE

This section introduces a recent approach to SPL, where the suggested reference architecture combines Domain Specific Engines (DSE) to be configured for implementing variants and accepts rules as input, to do so. The rules are stated complying with the syntax of a Domain Specific Language (DSL). The DSEs are responsible for every aspect of execution of the final system that includes the interpretation of the rules requiring some inference power.

Actually, DSEs are part of Domain Specific Kits (DSK) as proposed in the Software Factory Automation (Altintas et al., 2007) and they also are supported with Domain Specific Tools

(DST). The environment supports the development of artifacts on DSEs that can be combined to form the Software Assets that are reusable across products, and even across domains. The idea builds on the capability to quickly specify the variations through DSLs and interpret the DSLs through DSEs to shorten the "build" cycles. Specification of a domain problem is expected to take shorter development times, if done at higher levels of abstraction, corresponding to the jargon of the domain experts. The idea was inspired after similar flexible manufacturing cells used in the hard engineering domains. Figure 6 presents a runtime view of the architecture.

Eventually this approach is expected to mature to a position where business domains can be addressed by the DSLs. Today, mostly technological domains are practically incorporated. The report generation field, or relational databases can be domains. The DSL for the database case, is SQL, the DSE is the engine in any database management system.

The approach has been implemented in mostly banking and finance domains, utilizing relatively higher-level domains and technological domains. Another field is e-government where the experience is finding its way to develop domain specific assets based on such DSKs. A wider application area may result with the increased popularity of

Figure 6. Building blocks of the reference architecture

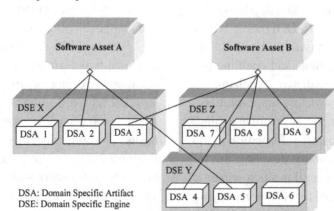

domain specific inference through the Software Factory Automation approach.

Interventive Systems

There has been enhancements on the expert systems, that usually employ rule-based mechanisms. One popular growth has been towards machine learning. Another interesting avenue is discussed here that points to a new class of capabilities. An expert system that listens to the changes in the environment, and updates its facts accordingly but also, through executing the actions in the rules, changes the environment is referred to here as an interventive expert system.

A general rule-based inference has the potential to lock up between the rules and the facts; each changing/triggering the other, now has a further feedback level that is the environment. Thus while making the chain of dependencies for potential deadlocks more complicated, interventive systems offer more power in the control mechanisms. Figure 7 depicts the extended potential deadlock loop.

There are many cases where it may be appropriate to model the problem as an intervention application. Fault management is one such domain where there is a functional system and the fault management system - both influencing each other. Also, it is convenient to program such systems using high-level and domain-specific rules rather than using general programming languages. Another example is robot assisted

cardiac surgeries (Yeniaras et al., 2010) where most of the control is with the surgeon but some security related concerns can be imposed through constraining the robot arms by rule-based instructions. Here, the robot arm will operate in the heart while it is still pumping blood. Hence mutual influence is valid in this case also.

Application: Fault Management Domain

The example domain selected for demonstration in this chapter is concerned mostly with software faults in mission critical systems. A Fault Management (FM) infrastructure is desired to be modified and adapted to various application environments. Thus it is important to manage the variance among the different adaptations that will resume the role of different products of the same family. SDKs were proposed as the important constituents of a reference architecture to support it's Software Product Line. SDKs contain domain specific inherence engines. The solution framework suggests a layered organization for the functional areas of fault domain such as fault monitoring, fault detection, fault diagnosis, fault prediction, fault correction, and other auxiliary services that are also important but have already been extensively used in other domains, such as logging and messaging. There are also points inside the functional system that communicate with the FM system. These points are referred to as Monitoring Points. They could have varying capability levels, as a design issue for the reference architecture. We selected them not to carry intelligence, but to have configuration capabilities.

Figure 8 depicts the overall architecture of the FM system, connected with the functional system. The top part of the diagram is dedicated for the layers of the FM where as some of this concern is also represented in the bottom-most layer that is the application. Here is the application containing monitoring points that can be considered as part of the fault management system.

Figure 7. Interventive Inherence

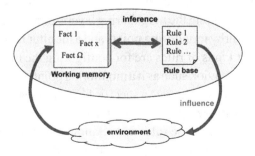

Figure 8. Architecture of the Fault Management system

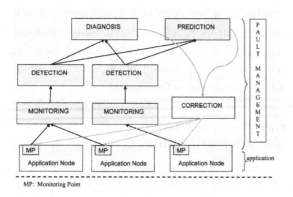

MP: Monitoring Point

The flow arrows in the diagram correspond to messages that are responsible for carrying information and control. In general, after the start-up configuration, information continuously flows from the application towards the higher-level functions, through monitoring and detection. When a corrective action is required, the flow is reversed, from the higher-level functions towards the application: Diagnosis or Prediction functions decide about the corrective action to be taken and dispatch this command to the Correction unit. Actually most of the functional units can be repeated in a distributed manner, based on the nature of the application.

Fault Prediction

Usually fault management considers the "fault" situation, meaning that an error in the software code lines have created an unwanted outcome, during the execution. In other words, the damage has been done and if the FM approach was designed correctly, the system will have backup for the information that is loss-prone, or even backup for the faulty unit to be replaced all together. In case there was a redundant copy of the (software) unit that is not functioning right, or not functioning at all, a switchover should be conducted: The faulty unit will be disconnected and a replacement will

be connected. Depending on the hot or cold reboot requirements, state may need to be loaded from a backup storage. To be able to reload the state, of course, in a proactive manner, it must have been saved foreseeing such faults.

In some cases however, it may be too costly to accept, to wait until fault happens and to try to correct the faulty unit. Predicting the near future fault and hence taking precautions before the fault happens may prove a more economical solution for the processing power, memory, or bandwidth - all may be precious resources depending on the environment. Therefore it may be useful for example to monitor certain values on some parameters, and a less critical value of a parameter could trigger a preventive action while a more severe value or a known fault condition will trigger the diagnosis and correction of a fault that has already happened.

Rule Based Adaptability

The reference architecture should be specialized for a specific application, considering the distributed allocation of the nodes. Then, FM nodes corresponding to different FM domains (diagnosis, prediction, detection, monitoring etc.) need to be programmed using a domain specific input that is the rule-based specification. We came up with three DSLs for a satisfactory configuration of a modest FM configuration. The three languages are very similar in structure, and represent more inference inviting rules for the diagnosis and the prevention domains, than the monitoring domain.

Some of the rules are declarative for configuring the message parameters that are exchanged mostly among the neighboring layers, or between the nearby monitoring points and a monitor node. Other kinds of rules are for configuring the message behavior, such as if a monitoring point should periodically generate a specific kind of a message (e.g. CPU temperature notification) or upon request. Finally the rules that result with reasoning about determining the next action are the most powerful ones. The decision in determining the next action considers what has happened before, the configuration parameters, and the current information input as a triggering event.

To implement an inference-capable platform, many existing shells can be found that have rule-based infrastructures. For a DSL with a narrow domain, it is not very difficult to also develop an interpretive engine that includes inference. Unless efficiency requirements dictate, using a well-known shell has its known advantages. Nevertheless, for critical systems, there is an important trade-off decision at every step. We have decided to implement sequential rules where time criticality was important. At lower functional levels of diagnosis, this kind of an approach finds quite some applicability. Otherwise, general rules can be unpredictable with respect to the time they will use during inference that is dependent on the inference algorithm. The other extreme is hard coding of the rules in a programming language and execute the system after compilation. This last resort is for the extreme time constraints and should not be preferred due to its lacking of agility.

The Domain Specific Language

Configuring the FM for any new member of the product family is desired to be conducted through high-level programming. That is through a rule-based approach. However, the target domain has its critical requirements and efficiency and dependability are of considerable importance. Also, the sequential characteristics of particular embedded and real-time domains require special care. The Rex language (Prasad et al., 1994) has been a good example of such environments where classical rule structures prove to be ineffective.

Considering the above mentioned constraints, the DSL (Kaya et al., 2010) designed for this research had to include rule and procedural structures for the combined expression capability. Rules, having a condition and an action part, are stimulated when their action parts evaluate to "true."

In this respect, every rule is independent and they can be activated in parallel. However, for more predictable sections of the program specification, a procedural structure is designed that is actually a compound rule: A condition statement is similar to those of the elementary rules. The action part is a procedural block where statements look similar to the rules for consistency but they cannot be stimulated independently. Once the execution starts for this procedural block, it has to follow the sequence dictated by the statements.

The procedural blocks can have parallel execution defined within their bodies. The "after" keyword, with a similar semantics to the similar keyword in Rex, can be thought of starting a timer. When the timer expires, it should be able to signal the process, suggesting that meanwhile other activities could be performed. For such needs, the synchronicity of each instruction in the procedural blocks is specified as Asynchronous or Synchronous. Asynchronous means the action part of the statement can start, without blocking the rest of the procedure – after it starts the next instruction can also be activated without having to wait for the end of the current instructions execution. Synchronous is the opposite, displaying a standard sequential behavior that suggest finishing the current statement before others can start. Example instruction sets are discussed in the Case Study section.

Case Study

In this section, examples from the staging of a FM system are presented. Rule based sections of the DSL are provided as well as procedural blocks. We tried to select more representative sections for demonstrative purposes. Mostly, the rules and procedural blocks are selected from the higher-level tiers related to Diagnosis or Prevention. Also, statements for the configuration are presented.

A brief architecture was presented in Figure 8. It is also helpful to remember that any block in this architecture is a candidate for a DSE. Depending

Figure 9. General flow of operations for the Fault Management System (Adapted from Kaya et. al, 2010)

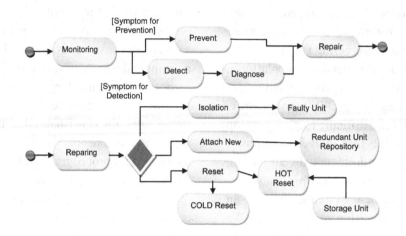

on what tier any specific block is, it is going to be configured through one of the DSLs. A general flow of operations can be traced on the activity diagram presented in Figure 9. Currently, the correction tier is implicitly handled in the action parts of the rules. A separate DSL may be required to be developed as future work, together with its DSE for interpretation.

First Case: Configuration for a Specific Heart-Beat Message

The inference of the FM system is investigated for a scenario where a monitored point seems to be inactive for a suspicious period of time. Heartbeat messages are a mechanism to periodically check if a unit is working good enough to be able to send a message – often deciding on the time to send due to periodical requirements. This example will utilize the heartbeat messages and try to find the cause of the problem, if the heartbeat message has not been received on time. Before the scenario can be executed, some configuration needs to be assumed: A monitor node has sent a configuration messages to a monitoring point to produce a heartbeat message every 50 milliseconds:

Configure (CPUHeatMonitoringAgent, Heart-BeatMessage, Periodic, 50ms, returnAddress).

Also the monitoring point inside, configures itself to wake up to a timer, every 50 milliseconds

to look for the specific message from the specific monitoring point. Once the monitor tries to locate the received message and cannot find it, a 'fact' should be generated that triggers the rules defined below:

1. Find another message source sharing the same node
2. Ask for any available kind of a message to be sent from that neighbor
3. if the neighbor cannot respond, the fault is with the communications channel
4. else the original message source is diagnosed to be faulty.

Sequential Procedure Block with Synchronization Capabilities

This example illustrates the efficient reasoning with sequential statements as the action part of a compound rule that differentiates between different possible causes for a fault. There could be longer sequences with even different decision results. In another scenario where a message about high CPU heat warns the FM system and a series of intervene, monitor, diagnose iterations are conducted, for a different cause at each iteration. Here in the following code section, sequential dependency is hinted by the 'else' keyword where the previous rule delivers a decision.

1. If CPU Heat > critical value then switch to another processor board, signal for hardware maintenance
2. {Else} if fan is down then start the fan
3. if fan is down then switch to another processor board, signal for hardware maintenance
4. {Else} Wait for 1 minute
5. if temperature decreased then send message, exit rule-block
6. {Else} if CPU frequency > critical value then reduce CPU frequency, wait for 1 minute
7. if temperature decreased then, exit rule-block
8. {Else} if CPU voltage > normal value then reduce CPU Voltage, wait for 1 minute
9. if temperature decreased then exit rule-block
10. {Else} if Processor Load > 90% then kill some processes, wait for 2 minutes
11. if temperature decreased then exit rule block
12. {Else} if CPU Heat > Critical Value then unknown error, log, exit rule block.

The above scenarios have displayed sequential statements. In a blackboard style usage of facts, independent rules would only be triggered by the facts that correspond to the 'if' parts of the rules. In such a case, some rules should be dedicated to altering the facts in such a way that facts can model the state that corresponds to a step in a sequence. For example, after starting the fan, 60 seconds have passed and the temperature still has not decreased is a partial scenario that leads to a fault decision. For a single rule to test all these conditions in its "if part," a specific fact should indicate that 60 seconds have passed, after the fan was started. We cannot treat the two events without a time dependency: 5 minutes passed and fan has started. We simply cannot guess the order of these events. Such cases as 'fan started and 5 minutes passed' need to be formulated into one fact or some combination of facts that can carry the same meaning, for classic rules to be able to process this information correctly. Table 1 presents the action part of such a compound rule,

which corresponds to a procedural block where sequence is important.

There are however, further problems with a strict sequence. In this example, time delays will result in the climb-up of the CPU temperature therefore there is no tolerance to wait for different attempts. In case the root cause was the last suspicious factor, that is the process load on the CPU, an additional 3-minute delay would be imposed by this diagnosis procedure. A better approach is represented in Table 1, where different suspects can be tried in parallel. All the corrective actions are started in sequential statements, almost parallel, only the instruction execution time is the delay. They all start a timer, and upon the completion of the timers' period, the instructions indicate which statement to proceed. This way no corrective action will delay any other except for few clock cycles that is probably nano seconds. Such non-blocking instructions need to be indicated as asynchronous as shown in Table 1.

Although Rete algorithm is a widely used solution to the sequential dependency, it requires too much space and careful analysis. All possible branches from the beginning state are modeled in Rete, and when events bring the state to a specific position on one of the paths, that state triggers only the related rules. The effort to converge with minimal rule executions hence is minimized.

The intervention property of our rules for our application domain further renders the sequential processing as a modeling option that is easier to understand. We found this approach to be safer and yet efficient when mission critical systems are managed for faults.

Rules for Independent Activation

This section presents more conventional rules that are activated only based on their condition clause. These rules do not depend on other rules for any sequential ordering mechanism. They all can be thought of mutually exclusive actors. Preliminary research on similar rules for FM has been reported in (Tekkalmaz et al., 2009). The representation in

Table 1. A composite rule example for managing CPU heat related symptoms

Statement Number	Async *	Condition	Condition True		Condition False	
			Action	Next stmt	Action	Next stmt
1		Cpu_heat > 85	Warning message			Exit
2	A	Fan_speed < TH$_{fs}$	Speed_up_fan	(After 1 min) 6	Message (Fan OK)	
3	A	Cpu_Voltage > V_critical	Decrease_Voltage	(After 1 min) 7	Message(Freq OK)	
4	A	Cpu_Frequency > F_critical	Decrease_Frequency	(After 1 min) 8		
5	A	Cpu_load > TH$_{ld}$	Decrease_load	(After 2 min) 9	Message (CpuLoad OK)	10
6		Cpu_heat >84	Message(risky CPU heat)	Exit	Msg (corrected: fan speed)	Exit
7		Cpu_heat >84	Message(risky CPU heat)	Exit	Msg (corrected: Cpu Voltage)	Exit
8		Cpu_heat >84	Message(risky CPU heat)	Exit	Msg (corrected: Cpu Frequency)	Exit
9		Cpu_heat >84	Message(risky CPU heat)	Exit	Message (corrected: Cpu Load)	Exit
10		Cpu_heat >84	Message(risky CPU heat)	Exit	Message(intermittent CPU heat)	Exit

* Async field denotes an asynchronous statement with "A" that can trigger the action and without waiting for its termination, allow the next statement to execute. Otherwise, statements are synchronous: blocking until finished.

Table 2 is intended for easier reading. Such visual aids in the composition of rules are found to be easier and more reliable in the programming of FM components. Explanations of the rules that are also provided after Table 2 accompanied with a lower-level representation style.

Explanations of the rules represented in Table 2 suggest one general idea: considering the tiered architecture presented in Figure 8, the outcome of a rule in a lower-level tier is generally treated as an input condition for a rule in a higher-level tier. The actions are always implemented as messages. What the message causes is a different story; it could be changing a fact in the working memory besides notifying some party.

The explanations about the rules are provided below where a rule number corresponds to the number in the left-most column of Table 2. First a rule is presented in a C language like syntax, followed by further comments:

RULE_1: If Condition (Symptom (process_load >= %85) & (Symptom (Source_ID (1), 4) | disk_space >= %90) & (Symptom (Source_ID (1, 5), 6) > 50)) → Action(Failure (Source_ID (2), 6))

In this Rule, the action:

"Failure (Source_ID (2), 6)" is an action that can be a message or a condition for next level tier e.g. Diagnosis.

Whereas the condition:

"Process_load >= % 85 " actually is not only a message coming from monitoring point but also is a condition for the Detection tier.

In condition "Symptom (Source_ID (1), 4)", 1 represents ID number of the source and 4 is type

Table 2. Examples for independent activation rules

	Condition				Operation			
	Type	Source_ID	Symptom		Warning	Action		
						Type	Source	Tier
1	Process 4 Disk 6	P_1 1 D_1 1,5	(Load>=%85) (Load>=%90) >50	& | &	NO	 6	 2	 Monitoring & Detection
2	6 Cpu 8 Fan	2 C_1 2 F_2	(Heat>=80) (Fan_Speed<TH_{fs})	& | &	NO	2	0	Diagnosis
3	2 1 Cpu Cpu	0 2,8 C_1 C_1	(Cpu_Freq>=F_{max}) (Cpu_Load>%95)	| & &	NO	4	5,2	Diagnosis
4	4 Process Memory Cpu_Heat	5,2 P_3 M_1 C_1	(HeartBeat=False) (Memory_load>%90) (Cpu_Heat>%90)	| & &	YES	7	9,6	Repair
5	7 4 2	9,6 5,2 0		& |	Shutdown_Source(0)	8	0	

of the symptom. That means the source 1 gives a symptom identified with number 4. The "harddisk_space >= % 90 " shows another symptom coming from the Monitoring tier.

Examples from the rules in the Diagnosis Tier:

RULE_2: If Condition (Failure (Source_ID (2), 6) & Symptom (Cpu_heat >= %80)) | Symptom (Source_ID (2), 8) & (Fan_speed < TH))) → Action (Failure (Source_ID (0), 2)))

RULE_3: If Condition (Failure (Source_ID (0), 2) | Failure (Source_ID (2, 8), 1))) & Symptom (Cpu_Freq >= F_{max}) & (Cpu_Load > %95))) →Action(Failure (Source_ID (5, 2), 4))

RULE_4: If Condition (Failure (Source_ID (5,2), 4) | Symptom (HeartBea t= False)) & Symptom ((Memory_load > %90) & (Cpu_Heat > %90)) → Action (Failure (Source_ID (9, 6), 7)))

Examples from the rules in the Repair Tier:

RULE_5: If Condition((Failure(Source_ ID(9,6),7)) & Failure(Source_ ID(5,2),4))) | Failure(Source_ID(0),2)) → Action(Repair(Source_ID(0),8))

With a combination of conventional rules and composite rules that incorporate sequence and parallel execution capabilities, the complex functionalities expected from a FM system can be represented. Also the tiered architecture helps in the structuring of the complexity that in return organizes the rules by categorizing them with respect to the tiers in the architecture.

Comparison of the Different Approaches

The specific property of the case study presented in this chapter is its practical considerations for the mission critical systems. Powerful representations of rule-based languages needed to be combined with practical and efficient runtime support. Also, asynchronous statements require threads under programmer control. Our environment required this combination that is very hard to find in the general purpose mechanisms. Within our approach, conventional rules offer independent activation, that is a powerful capability, whereas composite rules include procedural statements that cannot be independently activated, which in return offer time management and sequential ordering of activities – that is sometimes a critical requirement in the intervention-heavy segments of the introduced domain specific languages.

CONCLUSION

We discussed the importance of intelligence in the software engineering concerns of the contemporary era of approaches. The historical evolution has been consistent with what is being experienced today. There has always been a struggle for using intelligence in one of the most demanding fields of engineering history. Some conscious efforts were utilized while some others improvised their ways towards incorporating more intelligence, without an outset with the intelligence focus. Improvement recently became impressive, with more ambitious goals such as locating and integrating partial solutions into complex systems instead of developing them line-by-line. There are many sophisticated categories of software intensive systems that are on their way to receive guidance from intelligent components. Some examples were demonstrated that utilize intelligence in modern approaches for developing complex software.

In the specific research presented in this chapter, we experienced the convenience of configuring a complex fault management system, through the tiered architecture with specific Domain Specific Languages and corresponding interpretive engines (Domain Specific Engines). Every tier in our case was considered as a 'Domain' while designing

these languages. The specific mission critical focus in our project scope included embedded and real time applications. We found the mentioned approach suitable for both dependability and efficiency. For that, procedural blocks of statements were incorporated in the action clauses of our 'composite rules' with the capabilities to initiate parallel threads to avoid dangerous delays for activities that could run in parallel.

Our initial experimentation has been encouraging. There is however, so much to achieve for better utilization of the idea. Tool support will be of utmost importance, especially in the construction of the rules and statements, to offer more dependable Fault Management configurations. Also, the rules and statements to define repair activities are not completed yet. Some of the ideas are being tested in defense related applications, without completely implementing the capabilities offered in our research. The thread constructs for the composite rules are not yet tested in the real word. We are hopeful for more impressive applications that will provide the opportunity to eliminate such deficiencies through further work.

REFERENCES

Akbiyik, E. K. (2008). Service oriented system design through process decomposition. MS thesis, Computer Engineering Department, Middle East Technical University, Ankara, Turkey.

Altintas, N. I., Cetin, S., & Dogru, A. (2007). Industrializing software development: The factory automation way. *LNCS, 4473*, 54–68.

Bleul, S., Weise, T., & Geihs, K. (2006). *Large-scale service composition in semantic service discovery*. The 8th IEEE International Conference on e-Commerce Technology and The 3rd IEEE International Conference on Enterprise Computing, E-Commerce, and E-Services (CEC/EEE'06), (p. 64).

Dobson, G., Lock, R., & Sommerville, I. (2005, August). *QoSOnt: A QoS ontology for service-centric systems*. In Proceedings of the 31st EUROMICRO Conference on Software Engineering and Advanced Applications, (pp. 80-87).

Dogru, A. H. (2006). *Component oriented software engineering*. Grandbury, TX: The Atlas Publishing.

Dogru, A. H., & Tanik, M. M. (2003). A process model for component-oriented software engineering. *IEEE Software, 20*(2), 34–41. doi:10.1109/MS.2003.1184164

Fensel, D., & Bussler, C. (2002). *Semantic Web enabled Web services*. International Semantic Web Conference (ISWC'2002), vol. 2342.

Kardas, K., & Senkul, P. (2007). *Enhanced semantic operations for Web service composition*. International Symposium on Computer and Information Sciences, Ankara, November 2007.

Kaya, O., Hashemikhabir, S. S., Togay, C., & Dogru, A. H. (2010). *A rule-based domain specific language for fault management*. SDPS 2010: Transformative Systems Conference, Dallas Texas, June 6-11.

Klaus, P., Günter, B., & van der Linden, F. (2005). *Software product line engineering: Foundations, principles, and techniques*. Berlin: Springer-Verlag.

Manzer, A., & Dogru, A. H. (2007). Process integration through hierarchical decomposition. In Lam, W., & Shankararaman, V. (Eds.), *Enterprise architecture and integration: Methods, implementation, and technologies*. New York: Information Science Reference. doi:10.4018/9781591408871.ch005

Martin, D., Burstein, M., McDermott, D., McIlraith, S., Paolucci, M., & McGuinness, D. (2007). Bringing semantics to Web services with OWL-S. *World Wide Web (Bussum), 10*(3), 243–277. doi:10.1007/s11280-007-0033-x

McIlraith, S., Son, T. C., & Zeng, H. (2001). Semantic Web services. *IEEE Intelligent Systems, 16*(2), 46–53. doi:10.1109/5254.920599

Medjahed, B., Bouguettaya, A., & Elmagarmid, A. K. (2003). Composing Web services on the Semantic Web. *Very Large Data Bases Journal, 12*(4), 333–351. doi:10.1007/s00778-003-0101-5

OWL-S. (2004). *Semantic markup for Web services*. Retrieved in October 2009, from http://www.w3.org/Submission/OWL-S/

Paolucci, M., Kawamura, T., Payne, T. R., & Sycara, K. (2002). *Importing the Semantic Web in UDDI*. International Semantic Web Conference, (pp. 225-236).

Paolucci, M., Kawamura, T., Payne, T. R., & Sycara, K. (2002a). *Semantic matching of Web services capabilities*. International Semantic Web Conference, (pp. 333-347).

Prasad, B. E., Tolety, S. P., Uma, G., & Umarani, P. (1994). An expert system shell for aerospace applications. *IEEE Expert, 9*(4). doi:10.1109/64.336148

Pressman, R. S. (1997). *Software engineering: A practitioner's approach* (3rd ed.). McGraw Hill.

Sirin, E., Hendler, J., & Parsia, B. (2003). *Semi automatic composition of Web services using semantic descriptions*. In Web Services: Modeling, Architecture and Infrastructure Workshop in conjunction with ICEIS.

Sivashanmugam, K., Miller, J., Sheth, A., & Verma, K. (2004). Framework for Semantic Web process composition. *International Journal of Electronic Commerce, 9*(2), 71–106.

Skoutas, D., Sacharidis, D., Kantere, V., & Sellis, T. (2008). *Efficient Semantic Web service discovery in centralized and P2P environments*. 7th International Semantic Web Conference (ISWC), (pp. 583-598), Karlsruhe, Germany, October 26-30.

Szyperski, C. (2002). *Component software: Beyond object oriented programming.* New York: Addison-Wesley.

Tekkalmaz, M., Gurler, E., & Dursun, M. (2009). *Görev Kritik ve Gömülü Sistemler için T5D Uyumlu Bir Hata Yönetimi Altyapısı Tasarımı ve Gerçeklemesi.* Ulusal Yazılım Mühendisliği Sempozyumu (UYMS – Turkish National Software Engineering Symposium), İstanbul, October 2009.

Verma, K., Sivashanmugam, K., Sheth, A., Patil, A., Oundhakar, S., & Miller, J. (2005). METEOR-S WSDI: A scalable infrastructure of registries for semantic publication and discovery of Web services. *Journal of Information Technology Management, 6*(1), 17–39. doi:10.1007/s10799-004-7773-4

Yeniaras, E., Navkar, N., Syed, M. A., & Tsekos, N. V. (2010). *A computational system for performing robot assisted cardiac surgeries with MRI guidance.* Presented in the SDPS Conference, June 6-10, 2010, Dallas, Texas.

Chapter 2
Natural Language Processing Techniques in Requirements Engineering

A. Egemen Yilmaz
Ankara University Faculty of Engineering, Turkey

I. Berk Yilmaz
Ankara University Faculty of Engineering, Turkey

ABSTRACT

Requirement analysis is the very first and crucial step in the software development processes. Stating the requirements in a clear manner, not only eases the following steps in the process, but also reduces the number of potential errors. In this chapter, techniques for the improvement of the requirements expressed in the natural language are revisited. These techniques try to check the requirement quality attributes via lexical and syntactic analysis methods sometimes with generic, and sometimes domain and application specific knowledge bases.

INTRODUCTION

System/software requirement quality is one of the most important drivers for the success of a final system/software related product. A study showed that the user involvement is the most important factor for the success of the software development projects (Standish Group, 1995). Moreover, even in the cases where the user involvement

is sufficient, the success is dependent on clear statement of the requirements, which appears as the third most important factor on the list. In addition, another study showed that the underlying reason for 85% of the software errors is nothing but the requirement defects (Young, 2001). On the other hand, if such defects could not be fixed at the early phases of the projects, the cost of fixing the error would dramatically increases at each phase of the development life cycle as seen in Table 1 (Young, 2001). Defects detected dur-

DOI: 10.4018/978-1-60960-509-4.ch002

Table 1. Relative cost of fixing an error (Young, 2001)

Phase in which the Error is Found	Relative Cost
Requirements Analysis	1
Design	3-6
Coding & Unit Test	10
Development Testing	15-40
Acceptance Testing	30-70
Operation	40-1000

ing requirement analysis and design phases could reduce the rework effort between 40% and 50% (Boehm, 1981; Boehm & Basili, 2001; Gause & Weinberg, 1989).

All the above studies support that, effective customer interaction and defect-free requirement engineering processes are the key factors for successful system/software development.

Pohl's requirement engineering process model (Pohl, 1994), depicted in Figure 1, might be considered as a reference for the improvement the software requirement quality. Pohl's model suggests focusing on the three dimensions seen in Figure 1. Stakeholders of the requirement engineering process should perform a progress on the specification, representation and agreement dimensions. Hence, tools supporting progress in any of those three dimensions would increase the success rates of software development projects.

The applicability of natural language processing techniques is best understood via the following two-phase requirement engineering model. Figure 2 depicts a high level representation of these two stages.

The first phase, which can be referred to as "Perception of the domain", is a set of activities performed in order to understand the domain components and their relationships. Engineers embark upon to this stage at the very early phases of the development. This cognitive stage is usually followed by the representation of the information learned so far, where this representation is required to guarantee the correctness and completeness.

The second phase includes the "Expression of the requirements" in terms of visual and verbal statements. Those statements are used for understanding the rest of the domain; they are also important for achieving a better understanding among the end user, the buyer (if different than the end user), and the development team(s). Both

Figure 1. Pohl's requirement engineering model (Adapted from Pohl, 1994)

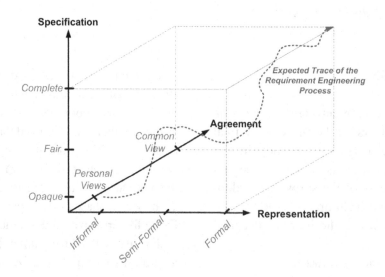

Figure 2. Requirementengineering phases

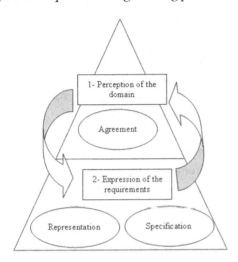

the specification and representation qualities are important in order to deliver the right 'message(s)' from the end user to the developers; and in order to implement the appropriate functionalities for the end user by the developers.

According to Hooks and Kristin (2001), the distribution of all requirement-related defects is as follows:

- 49% of the requirement-related defects are due to wrong assumptions and wrong requirements,
- 29% of them are due to missing requirements,
- 13% of them are due to inconsistent requirements,
- 5% of them are due to ambiguous requirements

Wrong assumptions and missing/ omitting requirements can be encountered in the "Perception of the domain" phase. On the other hand, the most common mistakes made during the "Expression of requirements" phase consist of inconsistent, unclear and ambiguous statements. When proceeding in the 'specifications' dimension of the Pohl model, such defects can be detected while the natural language requirements are being analyzed.

In this chapter, we will try to discuss and present the applicable natural language processing techniques for requirement engineering, and revisit the existing studies in this area. Covering different aspects from requirement classification to requirement error detection and correction, we will try to give the main essences of the existing studies in the open literature and existing relevant commercial-off-the-shelf tools. At each item, we will try to identify the level of the required analysis (syntactic or lexical) and what sort of a knowledge base is necessary. Meanwhile, we will try to present the outputs and work products of our own ongoing research in this subject, which constitutes a superset of existing studies and tools in many aspects. In the conclusion, we will try to present our ideas on the future directions of the requirement analysis tools with natural language processing functionality.

To our belief, the chapter will give the main ideas to the reader; and serve as a bibliographic resource portal to more interested individuals for their upcoming research activities.

REQUIREMENT ENGINEERING PROCESS AND APPLICATION OF NATURAL LANGUAGE PROCESSING TECHNIQUES

In the requirement engineering process, customer interaction is established via verbal and visual communication channels. This interaction is generally conducted in two ways to define requirements; using formal languages or using natural languages (NL) (Liu, Subramaniam, Eberlein & Far, 2004). There are numerous methods developed on formal language requirements (Cockburn, 2000; Bois, Dubois & Zeippen, 1997; Li, Liu & He, 2001; Abrial, 1996; Rumbaugh, Jacobson & Booch, 1999; Spivey, 1992), however NL is widely used for requirements definition since formal languages are difficult for non-experts to understand, which limits their practical application (Lami, 2005). A recent study indicated that 71.8% of the requirement documents are written in natural languages, but non-textual representations are also important in those documents (Mich, Franch & Inverardi, 2004).

Unfortunately, using NL in requirement specifications may lead some problems in requirement engineering activities. The vague nature of the NL sometimes creates misunderstanding or misinterpretation of the expressions present in a requirement set. On the other hand, NL requirements are verbal texts that can be analyzed with syntactic and semantic methods using some supportive tools.

NL Requirements should be analyzed to provide a degree of quality in a requirement set. In order to write good NL requirements, there are some quality indicators and text analysis approaches to be considered. NL Requirements processing methods generally use these indicators and approaches to guarantee a degree of quality in a requirement set. All of these should be analyzed in a NL requirement text to achieve a Mature Requirement set. The whole set of activities, which is depicted in Figure 3, can be specified as a three-step process:

- Lexical and syntactic analysis in order to identify the vague incomplete and inconsistent requirements.
- Statistical and semantic techniques in order to identify the similar or duplicate requirements, and to detect the interdependencies among the requirements.
- Lexical and semantic analysis methods in order to identify the non-functional requirements and to classify them according to functionality (functional /Non-functional) and for non-functional ones to sub-functionality (security, usability, adaptability etc.).

These three dimensions in NL requirement processing and the related work conducted in every dimension are described in the upcoming section. Until now, these three dimensions of NL requirement processing have been carried out independently by various authors but the combinations of these three dimensions have not been applied to the NL Requirement documents yet. We believe, for a complete NL Requirement analysis all three dimension should be applied. Hence in our own research studies, we focus on hybridization of all

Figure 3. NL requirement quality analysis process (Yilmaz, 2010)

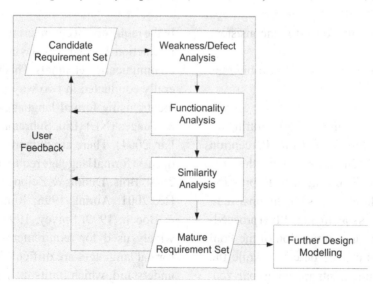

techniques and development of a tool supporting the analysis of NL Requirement texts.

• Weakness/Defect Analysis

As summarized in Figure 3, the very first step of the process followed in requirements engineering is based on collecting all requirement related data and to come up with a 'candidate requirement database'. This database contains a set of functional descriptions for the system/software to be developed. This step can be automatized by detecting the sentences and phrases being a potential requirement after an analysis whether the sentence is strong enough. The meaning of the strength here can be summarized as follows: a requirement should contain a "shall" statement about the specification of a system. Hence, at this initial step, candidate requirements can be selected by a lexical analysis; i.e. if the phrase contains the auxiliary verb "shall", then it is considered as a requirement.

After this initial step for shall analysis, the main body of requirement quality analysis (which includes weakness/defect, functionality and similarity analyses) begins.

Linguistic analysis. Linguistic analysis is the basic analysis for a requirement to provide certain quality attributes so that the particular requirement can be assessed a non-defective one. This step begins with the selection of the defect types by the user (i.e. the analyst) in order to analyze the pre-filtered requirements database. During the defect type selection, the user can define some specific Lexical and Syntactic Analysis Attributes. Based on the defect type selection and a rule set, the analysis takes shape.

A straightforward approach for this purpose would be using some predefined lexicons/dictionaries for some certain defect types, and applying a lexical analysis in the course of those lexicons/dictionaries. No matter how the initial candidate requirement database is constructed (either by direct editing, or recording and performing speech recognition from a meeting, or scanning and performing optical character recognition from informal hand-written meeting notes), by means of dictionaries including the pre-defined rule sets and lexicons, a lexical or syntactic analysis can be applied in order to detect the requirement defects. For classification of the defects, first, the requirement quality attributes shall be considered.

Requirement quality attributes and defect types. So far, numerous quality attributes have been defined in order to measure/describe some aspects/features of the requirements, particularly the ones expressed in natural language. DOD MIL-STD-490A (DoD, 1985), IEEE Std 830-1993 (IEEE, 1993) and ISO/IEC 9126-1:2001 (ISO, 2001) are the most prominent quality attributes used to construct a quality attribute set and to create defect types, accordingly. The major requirement quality attributes can be listed as correctness, unambiguity, completeness, priority ranking, verifiability, modifiability, consistency and traceability.

In order to comply with those attributes, reviews are the most common methods; and the main goal of these reviews is to detect the existing defects. The types of those defects have previously been discussed in numerous publications (Hooks, 1993; Rolland & Proix, 1992; Hanks, Knight & Strunk, 2001a, 2001b; Ambriola & Gervasi, 1997; Macias & Pulman, 1993; Firesmith, 2003). The defect types defined and being used in this study are listed below:

• **Optionality:** The requirement statement contains optional words such as "if needed, if possible, if case, possibly".
• **Subjectivity:** The requirement statement contains personal opinions such as "similar, better, worse, take into account".
• **Vagueness:** The requirement statement contains ambiguous words, which do not have quantifiable meanings, such as "easy, strong, good, bad, efficient, useful, fast, significant, adequate, recent".

Table 2. Requirement defect types and affected quality attributes (Kizilca & Yilmaz, 2008; Yilmaz & Kizilca, 2009)

Requirement Engineering Stage	Requirement Defect Type	Quality Attribute
Perception of the domain	Incorrect perceptions about the context and the concept	Correctness
	Omitted /Neglected domain needs	Completeness
Expression of requirements	Optionality	Consistency
	Subjectivity	Verifiability
	Vagueness	Verifiability
	Implicity	Verifiability
	Incompleteness	Verifiability
	Weakness	Verifiability
	Multiplicity	Verifiability
	Under-Referencing	Consistency Verifiability
	Under-Specification	Consistency
	Over-Specification	Verifiability

- **Incompleteness:** The requirement statement contains indefinite terms such as "to be determined, to be defined".

- **Implicity:** Such requirements imply generic phrases rather than specific. The statement contains implicit/referential demonstrative adjectives (e.g. "this, these, that, those"), pronouns (e.g. "they, it"), adjectives (e.g. "previous, next, following, last") or prepositions (e.g. "above, below").

- **Weakness:** The requirement statement contains weak main verb such as "can, could, may, might".

- **Multiplicity:** Such a requirement has more than one main verb, or more than one direct/indirect complement specifying its subject.

- **Under-Referencing:** The requirement statement contains references to unknown, undefined terms.

- **Under-Specification:** The requirement statement contains terms, which are not defined in the software requirement specification.

- **Over-Specification:** The requirement statement contains phrases regarding the design decisions.

The relationship between requirement defect types and affected requirement quality attribute are depicted in Table 2. Here, "perception of the domain" related defect types and quality attributes are not taken into consideration.

Requirement defect types introduced during the "Expression of requirements" phase are inspected in by means of lexical and syntactical analysis techniques.

Based on these discussions, detection of requirement defects by means of lexical and syntactical analysis techniques via predefined lexicons and rule sets has particularly been applied by the researchers who developed the tools ARM (Wilson, Rosenberg & Hyatt, 1997), RAST (Noh & Gaida, 2003), QuARS (Fabbrini, Fusani, Gervasi, Gnesi & Ruggieri, 1998a, 1998b; Fabbrini, Fusani, Gnesi & Lami, 2000, 2001a, 2001b;

Fantechi et al., 1994; Fantechi, Fusani, Gnesi & Ristori, 1997; Lami, 1999, 2005, 2009; Lami, Gnesi, Fabbrini, Fusani & Trentanni, 2001), and TIGER Pro (Kasser, 2002).

There are also other studies identifying the necessity of ambiguity resolution in the natural language requirements, which have not evolved to stand alone professional tools such as the aforementioned ones. In a very detailed study, Berry, Kamsties and Krieger (2003) identified the probable mistakes made during the expression of the requirements together with their possible misinterpretations and results. Particularly, they have identified when and how to use the words such as "every", "each", "all", etc. Moreover, they have classified the ambiguity types according to their causes (such as misuse of relative clauses, etc.). Gervasi and Nuseibeh (2002) proposed a practical and lightweight systematic for the control and validation of natural language requirements.

Lexical analysis focuses on individual words by means of predefined dictionaries; while syntactical analysis focuses on the phrasal and grammatical structure of the requirement statement.

It should additionally be noted that some of the defects (such as optionality, subjectivity, vagueness, implicity, incompleteness, weakness, multiplicity, and over-specification) are defined for individual requirements.

Table 3. Defects and required analyses for their detection (Kizilca & Yilmaz, 2008)

Requirement Defect Type	Required Analysis Type	
	Lexical	Syntactical
Optionality	√	
Subjectivity	√	
Vagueness	√	
Implicity		√
Incompleteness	√	
Weakness	√	
Multiplicity		√
Under-Referencing	√	
Under-Specification		√
Over-Specification	√	

Namely, for the detection of a defect, analysis over the relevant requirement statement is sufficient. On the other hand, some defects (such as under-referencing and under-specification) are defined for the whole requirement set. This means that for detection of such defects, complete set of requirements has to be analyzed. Moreover, as seen in Table 3, it is sufficient to perform lexical analysis in order to detect some defect types; on the other hand, some types require syntactical techniques.

Readability, although not being a sufficient condition about the clarity or understandability

Table 4. Examples of statements with defects

Requirement Defect Type	Example Detected Phrases
Optionality	The system shall perform the target detection or classification.
Subjectivity	The system shall report the analysis results explicitly.
Vagueness	The system shall respond to the configuration changes in a timely manner.
Implicity	The system shall conform to the standards listed below:
Incompleteness	The system shall complete the interrogation operation in TBD milliseconds..
Weakness	The system can be modifiable.
Multiplicity	The system shall perform the IFF interrogations of suspect tracks and saturation alleviation in order to increase the performance.
Over-specification	Target information shall be provided by the tactical display module.

of a text, can be regarded as a necessary condition for such attributes. With a similar argument, the readability analysis, which will be performed on the candidate requirements database, might give an idea about the understandability of the requirement set.

Since readability of a requirement specification document can be considered as a quality measure (even an additional quality attribute), it is common practice to perform such an analysis over the requirement statements.

In Table 4, a simple set of examples detected by the tool is given. For defect types for which the whole requirement set should be analyzed (i.e. under-referencing and under-specification), it is difficult to give the relevant examples explicitly.

STEP 2: FUNCTIONALITY ANALYSIS

Functionality analysis is based on eluting functional requirements from non-functional one. Here it is important to note that non-functional requirements (NFRs) should not be interpreted as "bad" requirements as its name may imply; those are the requirements that do not express a function of a product, but the quality characteristic to be expected from a product, instead. Hence, NFRs can be defined as the quality requirements of a software item. There is a strong relation between functional requirements and NFRs, where NFRs constrain or set some quality attributes upon a functional requirement (Cysneiros, Leite & Neto, 2001).

NFRs are important for a system since they are quality standards and operation conditions to be expected for a product therefore, Stakeholders are increasingly demanding non-functional requirements (Cysneiros et at., 2001). Recent work in the requirements engineering field has shown the necessity of conceptual models that take NFRs into consideration (Dardenne, van Lamsweerde & Fickas, 1993; Mylopoulos, Chung, Yu & Nixon, 1992).

Underestimating the role and the necessity of the NFRs may cause to much due to a system. One of the prominent example is the well-known case of the London Ambulance System (LAS) (Finkelstein & Dowell, 1996). The LAS was deactivated, soon after its deployment, because of several problems, many of which were related to NFRs such as performance and conformance with standards (Breitman, Leite & Finkelstein, 1999).

Cleland-Huang, Setimi, Zou and Solc (2007) applied a lexical analysis (so-called "keyword classification method" by the authors themselves) for the classification of the non-functional requirements. For this purpose, they have constructed a lexicon set containing string patterns (not separate words, but their string subsets), which indicate the words that are highly probable to be encountered. In that study, the authors have applied a simple taxonomy of non-functional requirements. More advanced non-functional taxonomies (such as those in (Cysneiros et al., 2001) or (Chung, Nixon, Yu & Mylopoulos, 2000) shall also be applied, and results with more granularity might be achieved, as well.

SIMILARITY ANALYSIS

In practice, requirement analysis activities are usually carried out in spreaded intervals of time. This yields the individuals in the projects to be substituted by others. Even a particular individual might have difficulties to recall his/her earlier statements. Another point is that, unlike most other steps in the software development life cycle, requirement analysis is the one where all stakeholders feel more free and responsible to participate. All of these factors increase the probability of repetition of the same requirement with exactly same or slightly different statements. Hence, detection and identification of the duplications and the similarities in the candidate requirement set is another cruical step in order to achieve a more mature requirement set.

Figure 4. The desired requirement management tool of the 21ˢᵗ Century (Adapted from Yilmaz & Kizilca, 2009)

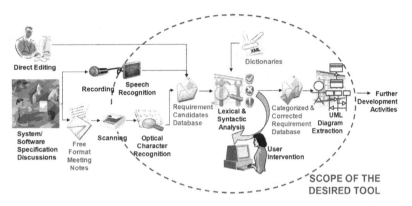

Natt och Dag, Regnell, Carlshamre, Andersson and Karlsson (2001) conducted a study in order to identify the similarities among the phrases in a requirement set. Based on Jaccard, Dice and Cosine similarity metrics, they identified similar statements for a given requirement set, successfully. Certainly, ideally, similarity analysis shall perform a very advanced hybridization of lexical and syntactical analysis techniques due to the following reasons:

- Usage of synonyms (or words with close meanings) shall also be captured during the analysis
- Usage of different sentence structures (the placement of the object, subject, and the verb; the usage of definite/indefinite relative clauses, etc.) shall also be captured during the analysis.

Moreover, most of the similarity metrics are based on the number of identical whole/isolated words. Hence, suffixes and prefixes also create problems during the similarity analysis. Natt och Dag et al. (2001) identified the difficulties caused by the suffixes and prefixes in English. Considering agglutinative languages (such as Korean or Turkish), where a single root word might take upto 4,000 different forms by agglutination, similarity

analysis strongly require syntactical analysis in addition to lexical analysis.

RESULTS AND PROBABLE FUTURE DIRECTIONS

Requirement analysis is one of the most important (but unfortunately the most ignored and underestimated) steps in the software development process. Despite the existence of a considerable amount of formal languages or methods for expression of the requirements, it is (and it will) still common practice to state the requirements in natural language in order to increase the understanding and participation of all stakeholders (with different technical capabilities and domain knowledge). Hence, some formalized methods (and commercial tools implementing those) for the improvement of the software requirement quality. Even though there exist numerous commercial tools for the requirement management activity with advanced features (such as relational databases to satisfy traceability, scripting interfaces for data extraction, etc.), the market still lacks of a powerful commercial tool with customer support, which performs requirement management activity with the three-step quality improvement perspective presented in Section 2.

As stated before, there have been individual activities existing in the literature; but most of them have been conducted as academic research, and their outputs have been bounded. Regarding that almost all steps in the software development life cycle have so far been more or less automated somehow; in our opinion, the future direction of the requirement management shall also be in terms of searching some ways or methods to ease and automate the construction of the requirement set. Moreover, means of automatic transition to the design phase (i.e. extraction of mode, state diagrams, use cases from the requirement statements by means of natural language processing techniques) shall also be investigated and studied. Figure 4 illustrates our desire and dream about the requirement management tool of the 21st century.

REFERENCES

Abrial, J. R. (1996). *The B book-assigning programs to meanings*. Cambridge, UK: Cambridge University Press. doi:10.1017/CBO9780511624162

Ambriola, V., & Gervasi, V. (1997). Processing natural language requirements. *Proceedings of the 12th IEEE Conference on Automated Software Engineering (ASE '97)*.

Berry, D. M., Kamsties, E., & Krieger, M. M. (2003). *From contract drafting to software specification: Linguistic sources of ambiguity–a handbook (version 1.0). Technical report*. Ontario, Canada: University of Waterloo – Computer Science Department.

Boehm, B. (1981). *Software engineering economics*. Englewood Cliffs, NJ: Prentice-Hall.

Boehm, B., & Basili, V. R. (2001). Software defect reduction top 10 list. *IEEE Computer, 34*(1), 135–137.

Bois, P. D., Dubois, E., & Zeippen, J. M. (1997). On the use of a formal RE language-the generalized railroad crossing problem. *Proceedings of the Third IEEE International Symposium on Requirements Engineering*, (pp. 128–137).

Breitman, K. K., Leite, J. C. S. P., & Finkelstein, A. (1999). The world's stage: A survey on requirements engineering using a real-life case study. *Journal of the Brazilian Computer Society, 6*(1), 13–37. doi:10.1590/S0104-65001999000200003

Chung, L., Nixon, B., Yu, E., & Mylopoulos, J. (2000). *Non-functional requirements in software engineering*. Dordrecht, The Netherlands: Kluwer Academic Publications.

Cleland-Huang, J., Setimi, R., Zou, X., & Solc, P. (2007). Automated classification of non-functional requirements. *Requirements Engineering, 12*, 103–120. doi:10.1007/s00766-007-0045-1

Cockburn, A. (2000). *Writing effective use cases*. Boston, MA: Addison-Wesley.

Cysneiros, L. M., Leite, J. C. S. P., & Neto, J. M. S. (2001). A framework for integrating non-functional requirements into conceptual models. *Requirements Engineering, 6*, 97–115. doi:10.1007/s007660170008

Dardenne, A., van Lamsweerde, A., & Fickas, S. (1993). Goal directed requirements acquisition. *Science of Computer Programming, 20*, 3–50. doi:10.1016/0167-6423(93)90021-G

Fabbrini, F., Fusani, M., Gervasi, V., Gnesi, S., & Ruggieri, S. (1998a). Achieving quality in natural language requirements. *Proceedings of the 11th International Software Quality Week*.

Fabbrini, F., Fusani, M., Gervasi, V., Gnesi, S., & Ruggieri, S. (1998b). On linguistic quality of natural language requirements. *Proceedings of 4th International Workshop on Requirements Engineering: Foundations of Software Quality (REFSQ '98)*.

Fabbrini, F., Fusani, M., Gnesi, S., & Lami, G. (2000). Quality evaluation of software requirement specifications. *Proceedings of Software & Internet Quality Week*.

Fabbrini, F., Fusani, M., Gnesi, S., & Lami, G. (2001a). An automatic quality evaluation for natural language requirements. *Proceedings of the 7th International Workshop on Requirements Engineering: Foundation for Software Quality (REFSQ'01)*, 2001.

Fabbrini, F., Fusani, M., Gnesi, S., & Lami, G. (2001b). The linguistic approach to the natural language requirements quality: Benefits of the use of an automatic tool. *Proceedings of 26th Annual IEEE Computer Society - NASA Goddard Space Flight Center Software Engineering Workshop*.

Fantechi, A., Fusani, M., Gnesi, S., & Ristori, G. (1997). *Expressing properties of software requirements through syntactical rules. (Technical Report: IEI-CNR)*. Italy: Pisa.

Fantechi, A., Gnesi, S., Ristori, G., Carenini, M., Vanocchi, M., & Moreschini, P. (1994). Assisting requirement formalization by means of natural language translation. *Formal Methods in System Design*, *4*(3), 243–263. doi:10.1007/BF01384048

Finkelstein, A., & Dowell, J. A. (1996). Comedy of errors: The London ambulance service case study. *Proceedings of the Eighth International Workshop on Software Specification and Design*, (pp. 2–5).

Firesmith, D. (2003). Specifying good requirements. *Journal of Object Technology*, *2*(4), 77–87. doi:10.5381/jot.2003.2.4.c7

Gause, D. C., & Weinberg, G. M. (1989). *Exploring requirements: Quality before design*. New York, NY: Dorset House Publishing.

Gervasi, V., & Nuseibeh, B. (2002). Lightweight validation of natural language requirements. *Software, Practice & Experience*, *32*, 113–133. doi:10.1002/spe.430

Hanks, K. S., Knight, J. C., & Strunk, E. A. (2001a). Erroneous requirements: A linguistic basis for their occurrence and an approach to their reduction. *Proceedings of Software Engineering Workshop - NASA Goddard Space Flight Center*.

Hanks, K. S., Knight, J. C., & Strunk, E. A. (2001b). *A linguistic analysis of requirements errors and its application*. (Technical Report CS-2001-30), University of Virginia Department of Computer Science.

Hooks, I. (1993). Writing good requirements. *Proceedings of the 3rd International Symposium of International Council of Systems Engineering*.

Hooks, I. F., & Kristin, A. F. (2001). *Customer-centered products: Creating successful products through smart requirements management*. New York, NY: AMACOM.

Institute of Electrical and Electronics Engineers. (1993). *IEEE Std 830-1993: Recommended practice for software requirements specifications*. Piscataway, NJ: IEEE Standards Association.

International Organization for Standardization. (2001). *ISO/IEC 9126-1-2001: Software engineering–product quality*. Geneva, Switzerland: ISO Publications.

Kasser, J. (2002). A prototype tool for improving the wording of requirements. *Proceedings of the International Symposium of Systems Engineering*.

Kizilca, H., & Yilmaz, A. E. (2008). Natural language requirement analysis methods and their applicability for Turkish. *Proceedings of the First Software Quality and Software Development Tools Symposium (YKGS 2008)*, (pp. 69–77).

Lami, G. (1999). *Towards an automatic quality evaluation of natural language software specifications*. (Technical Report B4-25-11-99: IEI-CNR), Pisa, Italy.

Lami, G. (2005). (QuARS: A tool for analyzing requirements). (Technical Report CMU/SEI-2005-TR-014 ESC-TR-2005-014), Carnegie Mellon University Software Engineering Institute, Software Engineering Measurement and Analysis Initiative.

Lami, G. (2009). Analytic effectiveness evaluation of techniques for natural language software requirements testability. *International Journal of Computer Systems Science and Engineering, 29*(2).

Lami, G., Gnesi, S., Fabbrini, F., Fusani, M., & Trentanni, M. (2001). An automatic tool for the analysis of natural language requirements. *Proceedings of the 7th International Workshop on RE: Foundation for Software Quality (REFSQ'2001).*

Li, X., Liu, Z., & He, J. (2001). Formal and use-case driven requirement analysis in UML. *Proceedings of the 25th Annual International Computer Software and Applications Conference (COMPSAC2001)*, (pp. 215–224).

Liu, D., Subramaniam, K., Eberlein, A., & Far, B. H. (2004). *Natural language requirements analysis and class model generation using UCDA.* (LNCS 3029*)*, (pp. 295–304).

Macias, B., & Pulman, S. G. (1993). Natural language processing for requirement specifications. In Redmill, F., & Anderson, T. (Eds.), *Safety-critical systems: Current issues, techniques and standards.* London, UK: Chapman-Hall.

Mich, L., Franch, M., & Inverardi, P. N. (2004). Market research for requirements analysis using linguistic tools. *Requirements Engineering, 9,* 40–56. doi:10.1007/s00766-004-0195-3

Mylopoulos, J., Chung, L., Yu, E., & Nixon, B. (1992). Representing and using non-functional requirements: A process-oriented approach. *IEEE Transactions on Software Engineering, 18*(6), 483–497. doi:10.1109/32.142871

Nattoch Dag, J., Regnell, B., Carlshamre, P., Andersson, M., & Karlsson, J. (2001). Evaluating automated support for requirements similarity analysis in market-driven development. *Proceedings of the Seventh International Workshop on Requirements Engineering: Foundation for Software Quality.*

Noh, S.-Y., & Gadia, S. K. (2003). *RAST: Requirement analysis support tool based on linguistic information.* (Technical Report 03-08), Iowa State University Department of Computer Science.

Pohl, K. (1994). The three dimensions of requirements engineering: A framework and its application. *International Journal of Information Systems, 19*(3), 243–258.

Rolland, C., & Proix, C. (1992). A natural language approach for requirements engineering. *Proceedings of the 4th International Conference on Advanced Information Systems Engineering.*

Rumbaugh, J., Jacobson, I., & Booch, G. (1999). *The unified modeling language reference manual.* Boston, MA: Addison-Wesley.

Spivey, J. M. (1992). *The Z notation: A reference manual.* London, UK: Prentice-Hall.

Standish Group. (1995). *Chaos report.* Boston, MA: The Standish Group International Inc.

U. S. Department of Defense. (1985). *DOD MIL-STD-490A specification practices.* Washington, DC: United States Federal Government.

Wilson, W. M., Rosenberg, L. H., & Hyatt, L. E. (1997). Automated analysis of requirement specifications. *Proceedings of the 19th International Conference on Software Engineering.*

Yilmaz, A. E., & Kizilca, H. (2009). A tool for improvement of the software requirement quality. *Proceedings of the 2nd Engineering and Technology Symposium*, (pp. 270–276).

Yilmaz, I. B. (2010). *Quality improvement of the software requirements written in natural language by means of linguistic analysis techniques*. MSc Thesis, Ankara University, Turkey.

Young, R. R. (2001). *Effective requirements practices*. Boston, MA: Addison-Wesley.

KEY TERMS AND DEFINITIONS

Requirement: A singular documented need of what a particular product/service should be/perform.

Natural Language Requirement: Requirement statement expressed in spoken/written language without any auxiliary tool or syntax.

Requirements Analysis: The set of tasks for determining the needs or conditions to meet for a new or altered product, taking account of the possibly conflicting requirements of the various stakeholders.

Non-Functional Requirement: A requirement specifying criteria for judgment about the operation of a system rather than its specific behavior.

Lexical Analysis: Analysis based on sequence of characters regardless of meanings.

Syntactical Analysis: Analysis based on the sentence structures and meanings.

Stakeholder: Entity having an interest on completion of a project.

Chapter 3
Requirement Management and Link with Architecture and Components[1]

Jean-Louis Boulanger
CERTIFER, France

ABSTRACT

In recent years there has been acceleration in the use of computing. The process applies equally to the products used in day-to-day lives (household electrical goods, cars...) and industrial products (industrial monitoring, medical equipment, financial transactions, railway systems...). When computing is introduced into complex systems a higher level of rigor is required.

INTRODUCTION

There is a specific group of systems, known as dependable safety-critical systems, which are characterized by the fact that a failure may have catastrophic results for human lives, finance and/or the environment. The design of such systems involves the application of standards, which cover quality control, the design process and risks. These standards require studies to be made with regard to the design of the system and the demonstration of safety.

In the European railways standards (CENELEC EN 50126, 1999; EN 50128, 2001; EN 50129, 2000) and in the new automotive ISO standard (ISO 26262, 2009), it is required to obtain evidence of safety in system requirements specifications. In the railway domain, safety requirements are obviously severe and in the new automotive standard similar objective exist.

It is very important to keep requirements traceability during software development process even if the different used models are informal, semi formal or formal. This study is integrated into a

DOI: 10.4018/978-1-60960-509-4.ch003

larger one that aims at linking an informal approach (UML notation) to a formal (B method) one.

This paper shows the requirements engineering from specification to the basics components. It describes phases of elicitation, modeling and traceability, verification and validation, and accompanied tools. The methodology concerns other aspects like safety, real-time, variability, or model transformation that will not be addressed here.

Our research addresses the model-based methodology that emphasizes the requirements verification/validation and traceability. We focus on the development of system requirements specifications with respect to fulfilling demands of standards (Railways: CENELEC EN 5012x, Automotive: ISO 26262).

We investigate how the Unified Modeling Language (UML) and/or OMG SysML (2006), can be used to formally specify and verify critical systems. A benefit of using UML is it status as an international standard, normalized by the Object Management Group (OMG), and its widespread use in the software industries. The reader interested by more details in syntax and semantic aspects can refer to the reference guide of UML (OMG UML, 2006).

Even if UML notation is a language in which models can be represented, it doesn't define the making process of these models. Nevertheless, several dedicated tools have strengthened the popularity of UML. These tools allow graphic notation and partial generation of the associated code and documentations. The UML notation is known by most computer scientists and is now used in several domains. Using UML class diagrams to define information structures has now become standard practice in industry. Recently, the critical application domains have used the notation and several questions exist around this use. In order to give a solution to this problem, we propose a method named BRAIL more information in Bon, Boulanger and Mariano (2003) and Boulanger, Bon and Mariano (2004), which proposed a

transformation of an UML model into a formal specification (B model in our case).

We present a state of art for requirement management (methods, principles and tools) and propose some enhancements for improve the process (SysML, model based approach, ...). Some examples from automotive and railway domains are used for help the understanding.

STANDARDS AND OBLIGATION

It is well known that a failure in safety-critical systems such as nuclear, railway, aeronautics or automobile may endanger human life or the environment. This is especially true when more and more electronics are embedded in these systems. For this reason, many standards were conceived to normalize the systems design, implementation and exploitation. Examples of these standards are CEI 880 in nuclear system, CENELEC EN50126, EN50128 and EN50129 in railway system in Europe, and DO-178 and DO-254 in aeronautic system. Above all these standards are the general CEI 61508 (2000), which covers all systems, based on electric, electronics and programmable electronics.

The standard CEI 61508 (2000) covers aspects concerning the safety of the electrical/electronic/programmable electronic systems (E/E/PESs). It aims for use in many different sectors of industry (see Figure 1). The objective is that it shall suit all contexts where electrical, electronic or programmable electronic systems are included.

As a particularly important example, systems known as safety critical are systems, which can in case of failure cause important damage to people and by extension to the goods or the environment. For this class of systems, it is necessary to perform analyses in order to demonstrate the absence of failures scenarios, whatever are the causes of elementary faults involved in these scenarios (physical, environment, development, interaction...), which could lead to this kind of

Figure 1. CEI 61508 and its derivation in different sectors

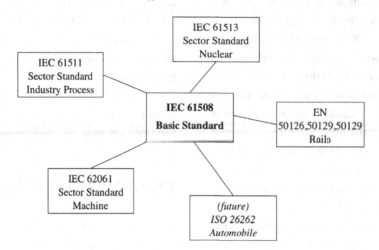

consequences. All systems sharing not the same criticality level, there are scales, which make it possible to define levels, which are associated to safety targets. The standard CEI 61508 (2000) defines four Safety Integrity Levels (SIL) in function of the probability of failures. From these levels, adequate requirements in software design and coding are recommended.

The SIL makes it possible to quantify the safety level of a system and consequently to evaluate criticality. It can take the following values 0 (system without impact on the safety of people), 1 (system which can cause light wounds), 2 (system which can cause serious wounds), 3 (system which can cause the death of a person: individual accident) and 4 (system which can cause the death of a whole of people: collective accident). Design of SIL 3 or 4 systems (that one finds in many fields related for example to transport, energy production, as in many sectors of industrial production) is subjected to the respect of technical reference frames.

Railway Domain

The safety requirements have always been taken into account in the railway transport system development. Nowadays, contractual obligations on performances, led industrials to a total control of parameters acting on Reliability, Availability, Maintainability and Safety (RAMS) in the field of railways. The choice of standards to be used is the designer's and the manufacturer's responsibility. But to have this done in openness and in a non-discriminatory manner, it is necessary that each State prescribes safety requirements (e.g. safety target) and that national railway networks recommend standards reference systems. Moreover, interoperability of railway equipments within European Union is a major concern, which leads to increasing needs of standardizations. Laws and standards aiming to define and achieve a certain level of RAMS requirements usually govern the safety of railway projects.

On one hand, the legislation is, at the present time, most often national: for example in France depending of the type of railway activity (urban

Table 1. Link between THR (Tolerable Hazard Rate) and SIL

Probability of failure (by hour)	SIL
$10^{-9} <= \ldots < 10^{-8}$	4
$10^{-8} <= \ldots < 10^{-7}$	3
$10^{-7} <= \ldots < 10^{-6}$	2
$10^{-6} <= \ldots < 10^{-5}$	1

Figure 2. Scope and application areas of CENELEC standards

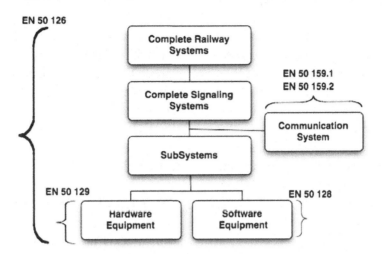

guided transit, or intercity transit), the relevant regulations are:

- Decree 2006-1279 relating to safety of railway traffic and to interoperability of railway system (19 October 2006)
- Decree 2003-425 relating to safety of public guided transit (9 May 2003)

For high-speed railway traffic however, the existence of the European Council Directive 96/48/EC on the interoperability of the trans-European high-speed rail system (23 July 1996), is noticeable. The Technical Specification for Interoperability of the rolling-stock subsystem 2002/735/EC (30 May 2002) can also be mentioned.

On the other hand the reference standard are most often European (CENELEC reference system: EN50126, EN50129 and EN50128), indeed International (CEI 61508 2000). The later one (applicable to all type of electrical/electronic/programmable electronic safety-related system) is furthermore the founding one: many aspects of EN50126, EN50128 and EN50129 are railway applications of CEI 61508 prescriptions.

The purpose of the CENELEC reference system is to:

- Provide a common reference frame in Europe to support the widening of railway components markets, the interoperability, the inter-changeability and the "cross acceptance" of railway components,
- Meet the specificities in the railway domain.

Facing the complexity of new systems, the RAMS requirements are an essential point in the project development of railway transportation systems.

The assessment of such a product (whole system, subsystems, control/command equipments generally including software) consists of evaluating the product's conformity in relation to a reference system (generally a standard, a part of a standard or a set of standards), according to the method used. The assessment procedure consists of five main processes:

a. Planning the Assessment,
b. Specifying the Requirements of the Assessment,
c. Assessing the Process used to develop the Product,
d. Assessing the Product,

e.   Documenting the Findings in a Report.

The assessor will produce both the Assessment Plan and the Assessment Requirements Specification. The Assessment Requirements Specification will be produced in close consultation with the Transport Organizing Authority, which will be required to authorize the final document. Finally, the assessment report is a mandatory part of the different safety files required by regulations and which are transmitted to State Authorities (Representative of the technical department of the Ministry of Transportation).

Automotive Domain

Up to now, there is no legal requirement for certification of compliance of automotive E/E/PE systems with CEI 61508 (2000). Moreover, when applying on automotive system, CEI 61508 have many inconvenient, e.g. not adapted to real-time system and automotive lifecycle development, not requirements for manufacturer and supplier relationship.

The ISO 26262 (2009) is an adaptation of CEI 61508 (2000) in automotive industry. ISO 26262 (2009) addresses hazards caused by safety related E/E/PE systems due to malfunction, excluding nominal performances of active and passive safety system. ISO 26262 also provides automotive specific analysis methods to identify the four Automotive Safety Integrity Levels (ASIL) associated with each undesired effects then provides ASIL- dependent requirement for the whole lifecycle of hardware and software components. The draft ISO 26262 is in the circulation and planned to be in use from 2010 as a worldwide automotive standard.

Impact on Requirement

In the standard for railways domain, the management of requirement (identification, contains,

verification and testability) is mandatory on the complete V cycle (from system to piece of code).

In the automotive domain like CEI 61508 2000 or the future ISO 26262 (see Siemens 2006) now impose that each requirement must be traceable from specification to the validation and must be tested by test case.

CASE STUDIES

Case 1: Level Crossing

Rail systems are complex, particularly when they perform safety-related functions (signaling, automatic driving, etc.). Modeling them is also complex. We have decided to consider the case of the level crossing, which is a safety-critical subsystem. Level crossings are locations where road traffic intersects with rail traffic and in spite of protection systems they are still responsible for serious accidents, which justifies our decision to give them special attention. The term "level crossing", in general a crossing at the same level, i.e. without bridge or tunnel, is especially used in the case where a road crosses a railway; it also applies when a light rail line with separate right-of-way crosses a road; the term "metro" usually means by definition that there are no level crossings.

Firstly, a single-track line, which crosses a road in the same level, is modeled (figure 3).

For conciseness, this paper will only describe the context of the study and not the Functional Specification. Those readers interested in greater detail should refer to (Jansen & Schneider, 2000), as we have used the functional specification proposed by these authors as an initial informal specification. This functional specification features software distribution and real time constraints for a level crossing, which is entirely controlled by software. Although it is theoretical, it has the advantage that it is familiar to the relevant research community and features a degree of complexity, which marks it out from most case studies.

Figure 3. Single-track line level crossing

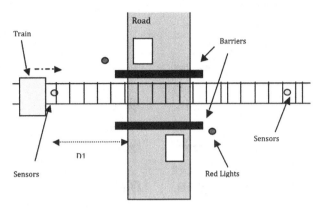

The crossing zone is named danger zone. The most important security rule is to avoid collision by prohibiting road and railway traffic simultaneously on level crossing. The railway crossing is equipped with barriers and road traffic lights to forbid the car passage.

Two sensors appear on the railroad to detect the beginning (train entrance) and the end (train exit) of the level crossing protection procedure. The level crossing is not in an urban zone; this implies a sound signalization.

Traffic lights consist of two lights: one red and one yellow. When they are switched off, road users (drivers, cyclists, pedestrians,…) can cross. When the yellow light is shown road shall stop at the level crossing if possible. In the other case, the level crossing is closed and railway traffic has priority. The yellow and red light never must be shown together.

Case 2: Engine Knock Controller

In a four-stroke gasoline engine, air and vaporized fuel are drawn in the first stroke (intake). In the second stroke, fuel vapor and air are compressed and ignited (compression). Fuel combusts and piston is pushed downwards in the third stroke (combustion) and exhaust is driven out in the last stroke (exhaust).

The cycle can be seen in the left of the Figure 4. In practice, ignition usually occurs before the end of the second stroke in order to maximizing power and fuel economy and minimize exhaust emission. Under some circumstances, when the temperature and pressure of the unburned air/fuel mixture exceeds a critical level, a second auto-ignition occurs as shown in the right of the figure 4. The two-flame crossing produces a shock wave with rapid increase in cylinder pressure. The impulse caused by the shock wave excites a resonance in the cylinder at a characteristic frequency. Damages to piston, ring, and exhaust valves can result if sustained heavy knock occurs.

An appropriate anti-knock control, represented in Figure 5, is applied to each cylinder at every engine cycle from low engine speed up to the highest engine speed. A knock control system consists of one or several noise sensors, and a controller, which acquire the noise through the sensors, and computes the correction during the combustion phases of the cylinders. The controller can detect knocks using spectral analysis techniques M. Zadnik, F. Vincent, R. Vingerhoeds and al. (2007). The controller decided to advance or retard the ignition to correct.

Figure 4. Illustration of the desired combustion (left) and knock phenomenon (right) in a 4-cycle gasoline engine

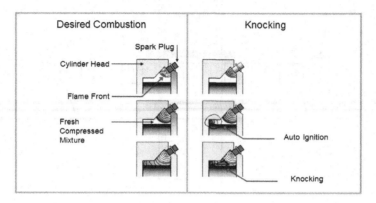

REQUIREMENT

The V-Model

We use the V-model in the figure 6 to illustrate the requirements engineering phase by phase. It begins with the requirement elicitation from the specification document. Then requirement are represented in models from architecture level to design level down to the code. Verification and validation (V&V) are present along the requirement engineering, showing V&V activities in each phase and for each requirement.

Requirement

At the start of a project, the informal specification describes, in natural language, the requirements, which the computerized system must meet. It therefore describes what is expected of the unit that is to be designed, in terms of the services and the conditions under which these are provided. In a design process, requirements must be validated and verified.

On the one hand verification means that the designer must ensure, at the different abstraction levels, that the requirement has been taken into account, and give raise to a model element. Verification is of particular importance in an assessment process. On the other hand validation means that

Figure 5. Knock controller description

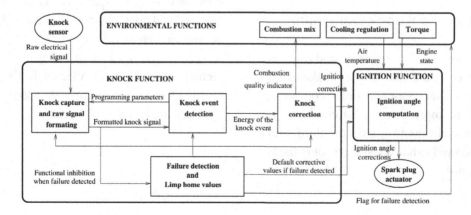

Figure 6. Verification and validation activities in V-model development

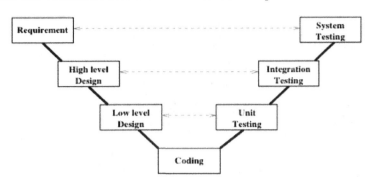

the designer must ensure at the different abstraction levels, that the model satisfies the requirements.

Some research initiatives are providing to transform the expression of needs (natural language, drawing, …) into a set of requirements. A simple description of a requirement is not fully sufficient to define it. There are other status information that each requirement must carries. The requirements must be tagged to provide such information.

In order to produce a system which complies with the stated requirements, it is necessary to model what the system must achieve, that is to say create a prescriptive model. It is very useful, in order to model the system (or subsystems) to possess a graphic representation that can perform the acquisition of concepts and the different aspects

of a system, and the OMG UML, 2006 notation is an interesting candidate for this.

But it remains indispensable to be able to reason and analyze behaviours, as in order to resolve a problem, it is not sufficient merely to model a system, it must also be possible to show that the model is correct (traceability, consistency of behaviours) and that the modelled system possesses certain properties (safety, correct behaviour, reachability, absence of famine, absence of blockage…). To achieve this, we propose to generate a formal model from the UML model and for this purpose we have selected the B method (Abrial, 1996), which appears to provide the rigour which is required for the design of safety-critical systems.

Figure 7. The SysML Requirement stereotype (left) and MeMVaTEx Requirement stereotype (right)

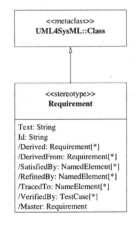
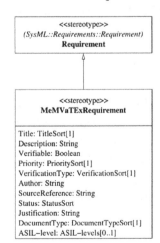

Table 2. Requirements in the knock controller case study

ID	Requirement
VL-F-2	Motor Unit shall produce torque upon feature request.
VL-F-9	Engine Control shall manage knock phenomenon.
VL-NF-A-1	Engine Control shall report diagnosis results in order to identify failures.
AL-F-10	Knock control function shall know the piston position in order to measure and correct the knock on the right cylinder.
AL-F-12	Knock correction sub-function shall be triggered each time the knock value is greater than a threshold.
AL-NF-S-1	Knock function shall not generate a knock noise stronger than the previous one.
DL-F-1	The capture must end when the Knock Acquisition Window Duration (expressed in cranksaft angular degree) has elapsed.
DL-NF-P-3	The sub-function Filtering must be performed in X ms

Some tools like DOORS, REQTIFY or RTM handle the traceability management. The OMG SysML (2006) UML profile allows now the designer to consider requirements as first class concepts in UML for system level design.

The SysML Requirement stereotype as defined by the standard contains a description "Text", an identifier ("Id") and links to other requirements, design element, and test case for each requirement (see Figure 7, left). When taking into accounts other aspects of analysis, verification, and validation, this definition is not detailed enough. In order to better support the requirements engineering, we have interest in extending this SysML Requirement stereotype by adding new fields. These fields are described in details in A. Albinet, S. Begoc, J-L. Boulanger and al., 2008. We call the new stereotype called MeMVaTEx Requirement (see fFigure 7, right).

Requirement Elicitation

This phase consists of a list of requirements that can be exploited during the next phases. System engineers, safety experts, and time are needed to build a complete and consistent list of requirement. Most of project's failure is due to insufficient attentions in this phase, as reported in I.F. Alexander and R.Stevens, 2002.

In MeMVaTEx project, EAST-ADL levels classify requirements. At each level, requirements are numbered and structured in functional (F) and non-functional (NF). Non-functional requirement are classified by categories such as performance (P), safety (S) and availability (A). Note that the respects of regulation in automotive domain introduce safety requirements at each level, resulting more complexity in the design and test. It also led us to extent the SysML Requirement stereotype to a particular MeMVaTEx Requirement stereotype

Table 2 gives some examples of requirements of the case study: the knock controller. Requirements are actually stored in tabular applications like Word or Excel.

Table 3 gives some examples of requirements for the second case study: the level crossing.

REQUIREMENT ANALYSIS: KNOCK CONTROLLER

Modeling and Traceability

This phase consists of selecting requirements from an upper level and links it to one or many requirements from the lower levels using one of four stereotypes defined above. Doing that correctly guarantees the bidirectional traceability

Table 3. The requirement table corresponding to the model in the Figure 7

Name	Txt	Derived	Derived From	Refines	Refined By	Satisfied By	Verified By
VL-F-9	Engine Control shall manage Knock phenomenon.		«requirement» AL-F-12 (Requirements ::AL) «requirement» AL-F-11 (Requirements ::AL)			«block» Controller (Requirements)	«Use Case» Analyze requirement (Requirements)
AL-F-11	If no knock is detected, base value shall be restored.	«requirement» VL-F-9 (Requirements ::VL)					«Activity Diagram» BaseValueSettingTest (Requirements) «Operation» BaseValueSetting (Testing ::BaseValueSetting)
AL-F-12	Knock correction sub-function shall be triggered each time the knock value is greater than a threshold.	«requirement» VL-F-9 (Requirements ::VL)		«requirement» DL-F-7 (Requirements ::DL)		«block» KnockFunction (Requirements)	
DL-F-7	To calculate the knock energy EGY_LNL, the knock threshold is calculated for each cylinder separately and depends on the cylinder individual noise value.				«requirement» AL-F-12 (Requirements ::AL)	«block» ThresholdCalculation (Requirements)	

from requirement to design and code. We show an example of requirement modeling from the Vehicle level to design level in Figure 8.

Requirements are classified by EAST-ADL~2 levels. In the diagram, the requirements traceability from Vehicle Level to Design Level is shown: AL-F-12 is a functional requirement at the Analysis Level. It is derived from the requirement VL-F-9 at Vehicle Level, and then refined to DL-F-7 at Design Level. The three requirements are respectively satisfied by KnockCorrection, EngineControl, and ThresholdCalculation blocks.

The basic design of KnockFunction block is sketched in a Block Definition Diagram in the Figure 9. It show blocks involved and its item flows. Each block in the KnockFunction can be detailed by using Internal Diagram Block (IBD).

Verification and Validation

The V&V is an important phase in software development. V&V activities concern two aspects:

- Verification of the realization, i.e. did we build the product right? It is the analysis of the works that have been done, generally document analysis, code inspection and review, unit and integration testing.
- Validation of the application, i.e. did we build the right product? This is a test phase whose objective is to show that intended services are fulfilled. This test phase is realized on the product.

In MeMVaTEx project, it is needed that V&V activities must link to and test each requirement

Figure 8. Requirement modeling in reference to EAST-ADL levels: Screenshot from ARTiSAN Studio

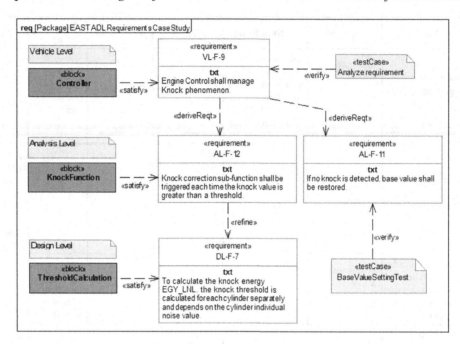

as requested by safety regulations. We show a test case, represented by an activity diagram in the Figure 9, planned for the requirement like DL-NF-1 "The capture must end when the Knock Acquisition Window Duration has elapsed". In this case, the internal structure of the capturing

block and how it works may be known by the tester. This kind of test is called white-box testing.

There are also functional requirements such as AL-F-10 "Knock control function shall know the piston position in order to measure and correct the knock on the right cylinder". In this case, tester may have no knowledge of the internal structure

Figure 9. SysML Block Definition Diagram

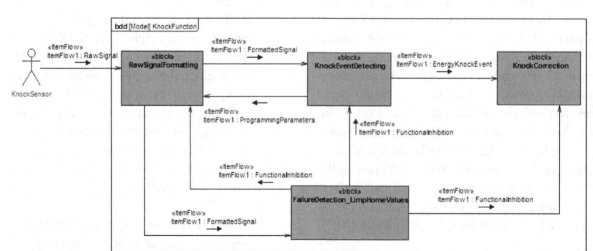

Figure 10. A test case realized with an activity diagram

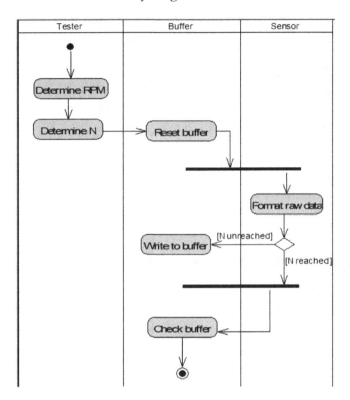

of the knock control block. This kind of test is known as black-box testing. Input data is sent to the structure and the output is compared to expected output, giving the verdict. This test can be resumed in the Figure 11.

Framework Tools

Tools are listed in refer to the V-model. On the left branch, requirement management (RM) tools like DOORS, RequisitePro, or Reqtify are used in projects with large number of requirement. They have the capacities of managing and tracing requirement and support team's corporation.

Major modeling tools such as Telelogic Rhapsody Rhapsody, IBM Rational, or ARTiSAN Studio support UML/SysML and have the capacities to import specific profiles. It can also export models into an interchangeable format.

Simulink is a prime tool at the implementation level. Simulink gives the most details descriptions of a functional block. Simulink and its tool suite can generate code and test cases, and verify the design by simulation.

On the right branch, the validation can be reinforced by running software on simulator (software-in-the-loop, SIL) or by injecting code on dedicated hardware then running simulation (hardware-in-the-loop, HIL) see for example dSPACE (2007). Finally, a prototype testing validates the product. The validation is enterprise and proprietary solution.

In the MeMVaTEx project, there are about many hundreds requirements for the knock controller. It can be managed using only Office applications like Word and Excel. The use of RM like Reqtify or DOORS is planned for future use when the number of requirements is big enough.

Figure 11. A test case realized with a sequence diagram

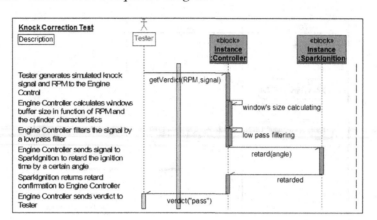

Figure 12. Tools accompanying the methodology represented in V-model

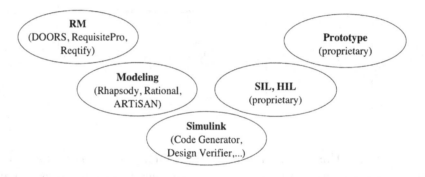

Modeling is done using ARTiSAN Studio. For particular purpose, we need EAST-ADL profile and MARTE (2007), another UML profile for real-time modeling. These profiles are imported into ARTiSAN Studio. ARTiSAN can connect to RM tools to import requirements from or export traceability or requirement tables as seen in Table 3.

At implementation level, ARTiSAN introduces integration with Simulink models that will give systems engineers the ability to define and simulate function block diagrams in Simulink and export them into a SysML model in ARTiSAN for ongoing development and maintenance.

For now, test cases are generated manually and the use of many validation tools is under consideration.

REQUIREMENT ANALYSIS: LEVEL CROSSING

The way of this section is structured reflects the stages of our proposed methodology:

a. Stage 1 deal with requirement acquisition. The aim is to extract from the specification the user requirements, which must be taken into account in development (design, verification and validation) and in the demonstration of the safety of the system.

b. Stage 2 describes the environment of the system, which is the starting point of safety analyses: identification of failures and their effects, analyses of risks, etc.

c. Stage 3 breaks the system down into subsystems (and/or sub equipments). The UML notation has been used until this stage.

d. Stage 4 describes the transformation of the UML notation into a B model, which provides an opportunity to prove that the requirements have been correctly implemented.

The conclusion assesses the work that has been performed and considers the outlook.

UML Notation

The UML (Unified Modeling Language) notation was the result of the merger of the dominant object-oriented methods. It was then standardized in 1997 by the OMG group2, rapidly acquiring the status of an indispensable industrial standard for the object-oriented modeling of software applications. Modeling is performed with diagrams of several types, each making a specific contribution (Muller, 2001). Readers requiring further information on the syntactic and semantic aspects may refer to the UML 2 reference guide (OMG, 2007).

The UML notation was not responsible for the development of object-oriented concepts but it provides a more formal definition and a more methodological dimension, which the object-oriented approach previously lacked. The definition of the Object Constraint Language (OCL) within the UML notation is an important development, which makes it possible to define constraints during system design. These constraints may be either safety properties or liveness properties.

Although the UML notation is a model representation language, the model development process is not specified. The authors of the UML notation (Booch et al., 1999) nevertheless recommend using an iterative and incremental approach, which is guided by the needs of users and centered on the software architecture.

As the UML notation does not impose a specific working method, it can be integrated in a transparent manner within any process of software or system development. It should therefore be regarded as a toolbox, which provides a means of gradually improving working methods while retaining domain-specific modes of operation.

The popularity of the UML notation has been increased by a large number of tools, such as computer-aided software engineering (case) tools with which the notation can be implemented graphically and which also assist the development

Figure 13. From input document to user's requirement

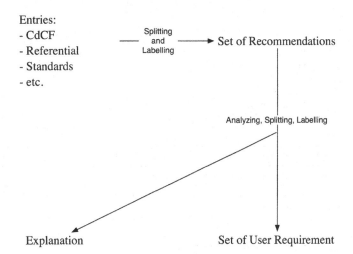

Table 4. Some recommendations (the complete set contain 21 CdCF)

ID	Requirement
CdCF-01	The problem chosen for the reference case study is a decentralized radio-based control system for a railway level crossing, where a single-track railway line and a road are crossing at same level.
CdCF-02	The intersection area of the road and the railway line is called danger zone, since trains and road traffic must not enter it at the same time to avoid collision.
CdCF-03	The railway crossing is equipped with barriers and road traffic lights. Traffic lights at the level crossing consist of a red and a yellow light. When the yellow light is shown road users (drivers, cyclists, pedestrians etc.) shall stop at the level crossing if possible. The red light means that the level crossing has been closed for road traffic and must not be entered.
…	…
CdCF-15	The level crossing control system is able to detect the occurrence and repair of failures of traffic lights and vehicle sensor. It immediately reports such an event to the operations centre. This does not imply that train operation is suspended on the affected part of track for the time up to repair.
…	…
CdCF-21	CENELEC EN 50126, EN 50128 and EN 50129 are applicable.

process by permitting partial code generation, the generation of documentation and reverse engineering. In addition to being supported by all the information processing stakeholders, the UML notation is today used in every domain and has recently been introduced into the field of safety-critical applications.

Table 5. Some user recommendation (the complete set contain 84 UR)

ID	Requirement
UR1	We want to developed a decentralized radio-based control system
UR2	The future system managed a level crossing (named LC)
UR3	The LC is necessary when a single track railway line and a road crossing at same level
UR4	Train run on railway line.
UR5	The intersection area of the road and the railway line is called danger zone.
UR6	Since trains and road traffic must not enter in the danger zone at the same time to avoid collision.
…	…
UR50	List of potential failures: - failures of the yellow, - failures of the red TL, - failures of the HAB, - failures of the VS, - failures of the transmission delay, - loss of telegrams on the radio network (MRC).
…	…
UR54	The LCCS is able to detect the occurrence and repair of failures of TL and vehicle sensor.
UR55	The LCCS immediately reports such an event to the OC.
UR56	TL and vehicle sensor failure don't imply that train operation is suspended on the affected part of track for the time up to repair.
…	…
UR84	The train may be assumed to always run in the same direction.

Table 6. Traceability matrix

User requirement	Recommendation
UR1 + UR2 + UR3	CDCF-01
UR4 + UR5 + UR6	CDCF-02
…	
UR54 + UR55+ UR56	CDCF-15
…	
UR83 + UR84	CDCF-20

Table 7. Some user recommendation dedicated to external users

ID	Requirement
UR7	The LC is equipped with barriers.
UR8	The LC is equipped with road traffic lights.
UR9	The TL consists of a red and a yellow light.
UR10	Road user are drivers, cyclists, pedestrian, etc.

Stage 1, Requirement Acquisition

This first stage is an important phase in the methodology as it consists of extracting the system design requirements from the functional specification, which is written in natural language. It breaks down into three stages.

Identification of User Requirements

The customer functional specification, or any other input document provided by the client, has various components, for example functional requirements, comments, assessments, recommendations, etc.

These are written from the client's point of view and may be incomplete, over specifying, under specifying, erroneous and/or redundant. It is therefore necessary to select the requirements that relate to the user's needs, obviously with the latter's agreement.

The common input documents (functional specification, standards, system specification…) are then broken down into recommendations, each of which is labeled. A second textual analysis is then performed in order to break down, or clarify, the recommendations to obtain a set of labeled user requirements (UR). Any abandonment of a recommendation from the client must imperatively be justified. In Figure 13 present the elicitation of user requirement.

When this process was applied to the case of the level crossing, we obtained a list of twenty one recommendations, partially set out in Table 4, from which we derived a list of eighty-four user requirements, partially presented in Table 5.

The traceability matrix that links the finally selected user requirements to the initial recommendations (Table 6) allows us to verify that

Figure 14. Contextual diagram

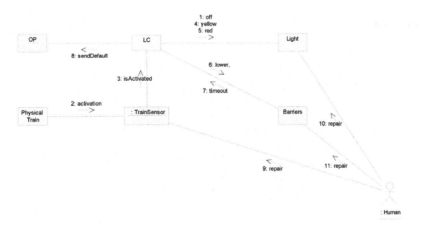

nothing has been overlooked at this level. These user requirements are also submitted to the client for approval.

This section is not a complete course of requirement management; you can found more information in Hull, E., Jackson, K., Dick, J., 2005, A. Albinet, S. Begoc, J-L. Boulanger and al. 2008 and/or I.F. Alexander and R. Stevens 2002. It is often difficult to understand requirements if they are stated as a list. For that reason, functional requirements (and even some non-functional requirements) can be expressed by using some "use cases".

A use case analysis involves the following steps:

- Determine the actors, i.e. any outside entities (people, systems, etc.) that interact with the system.

Figure 15. Collision

- Identification of Use Cases (name, purpose, goal, pre- and post-condition, …).

A use case diagram describes and traces the functional requirements of the system and describe how the system can and will be used. The use case diagram gives an overview of the model.

Identification of Risks

According to EN 50129, 2000 risk analysis essentially consists of four steps:

- System definition;
- Identification of operational hazards;
- Consequence analysis;
- Risks assessments.

The operational risks may be identified by an analysis of the user requirements (UR) and/or by classical risk analysis. User requirement UR6 (see Table 5) describes the collision between a train and a road user (motorist, cyclist, pedestrian…) in the danger zone.

We define the first risk:

R1: When trains and road users enter at the same time in LC a collision is possible.

The collision is therefore the major risk. If the UML notation is used, this requirement may be

Figure 16. System view

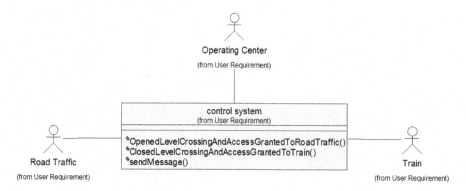

Figure 17. Sequence diagram for authorizations of access to danger zone

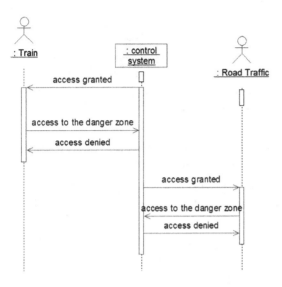

Table 8. Our "world"

	Component	Description
Environment	lc	Level Crossing
	op	Operation center
	tl	Traffic Light management
	Barrier	Barrier for protect the access to "danger zone"
	Light	One light (red or yellow)
	Captor	Captor for detect the entry of a train in the "danger zone"
Sub-system	lccs	Sub-system for controlling locally the level-crossing
	tcs	Sub-system for controlling one train
	mcr	Sub-system for communication

In our model, failures of yellow or red traffic lights (to be separately), barriers, the vehicle sensor and the delay or loss of radio network are considered.

Identification of Services

Three system level services have been identified from analysis of user requirements and the risk of collision. They are: the opening of the level crossing, which allows road traffic to pass through; closure of the level crossing, which restricts the passage to rail traffic; the sending of messages (to trains and the operations centre).

This breakdown has been introduced into the UML model as a class diagram (Figure 16), which provides a visual representation of the actors in the system and the interactions with the system under design. A set of sequence diagrams can be added to this diagram in order to describe the interactions (sending of messages) between the different interlocutors (actors and/or class and/ or object), with time being modeled by vertical bars (life lines), which are associated with the interlocutors. Figure 17 shows the sequencing of authorizations of access to the hazard zone.

The system states, as identified in the requirements, can also be added. The level crossing is

modeled by a use case, which connects the actors (system users) to the situations (slices of life). The use case links a graphical form (Figure 15) to a textual description.

The system design team and the team whose responsibility is to demonstrate its safety can therefore both use a common model. Consequently, it is possible at an early stage to take account of operating safety requirements and improve the traceability of these requirements while also avoiding the mixing of responsibilities.

During safety analysis, we can introduce some new risk, for example:

R2:   Road users enter by the exit lanes when the waiting times is long

The user requirement gives information concerning the failures and their direct effects on the system.

UR42: Possible failure conditions have to be taken into account for a safe control of the level crossing and the train.

Table 9. Functional requirement

ID	Requirement	UR
FR1	LC is a decentralized radio-based control system	1
FR2	LC is equipped with traffic light	8, 9, 11, 12
FR3	LC is equipped with barriers	7
FR4	When the train has completely passed the level crossing area the LC may be opened for road traffic.	22
FR5	The LC will be opened upon receipt of the deactivation order from TC	67
…	…	

either closed (authorization for train traffic) or open (authorization for road traffic). The states and changes of state are modeled by a "state and transition" diagram. A fallback state must be provided for use in the event of a failure.

Stage 2, Environment and Risk Analysis

Identification of the Environment

The purpose of this second stage is to model the environment and the interactions between the environment and the system. Our "world" is identified on the basis of an analysis of user requirements. This "world" consists of two groups of components (Table 8), the environment (operations center (OC), the barriers, the luminous signals and sensors) and the subsystems (level crossing control subsystem (LCSS), the on-board train

control system (TCS) and the communications system (MCR)

Description of our "World"

Starting once again from the user requirements in Table 4, the component or components that are appropriate for describing the environment are taken from each and combined to produce functional requirements (FR). Table 9 shows a list of some of the functional requirements that describe the behavior of the level crossing and their traceability with the URs in the last column.

It is vital to show that all the URs have been taken into account in this way. For this purpose an FR/UR traceability matrix is drawn up (Table 10), similar to the traceability matrix in Table 6. Some user requirements may be abandoned. For example, UR2 has been abandoned because it has already been included in the description of this "world" as it is the system itself.

Some functional requirements, such as FR1, highlight the importance of the distributed nature of the software architecture. This distribution is based on the idea that the management of a level crossing must be the outcome of an interaction between the level crossing and the trains that pass through it. It is risky to keep a level crossing closed too long as drivers may become impatient and drive through the half barrier. An analysis of these requirements gives rise to an initial interface diagram (Figure 18).

It should be pointed out that the operations centre supervises the whole line and that the main

Table 10. UR/FR

UR	FR
UR1	FR1
UR2	-
UR3	FR13 + FR14
…	

Figure 18. Distributed architecture

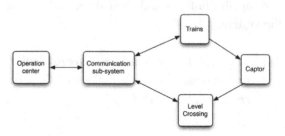

Figure 19. Sub-system view

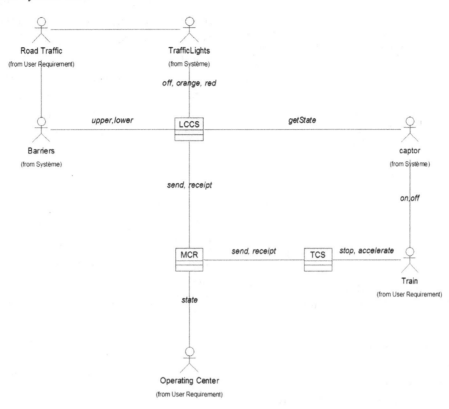

objective of the communications is to transmit information about detected failures with a view to launching remedial maintenance operations. After the analysis of the functional requirements, which must be performed for each component in the universe, the subsystem architecture can be described with a class diagram that characterizes the interactions between the equipments (Figure 19). The different components in our "world" (Table 8) are shown with the interactions between them.

Failure in the Environment

The safety demonstration must identify potential failures and show that the system remains in a safe state for each. The actors, which interact with the sub systems, are a source of failures (sensor malfunction, loss of messages, excessive delays, loss of electrical power and damage to

physical equipment). This is why analysis of the URs must provide an initial identification of the failures. If this is not the case, the failures must be identified as soon as possible by referring to the knowledge of professionals. The specification at our disposal was sufficiently complete for a considerable number of failures to be identified from the URs extracted from it. Nevertheless, some of them, such as failures D8, D9 and D10 in Table 11, were impossible to deduce from the analysis of requirements and had to be added.

The safety studies can be started on the basis of the risks identified in Figure 15 and this first list of failures. A preliminary risk analysis (PRA) can then be performed which reveals new safety-related requirements, which will be added to the functional requirements. The primary risk of a collision between a train and a road vehicle is obtained by implementing a failure tree analysis (FTA), which is a method that identifies the causes

Table 11. Failure

ID	Description	UR
D1	Failures of the yellow traffic light	37, 38, 43, 45
D2	Failures of the red traffic light	37, 38, 43, 45
D3	Failures of the barriers	37, 38, 43, 45
D4	Failures of the vehicle sensor	37, 38, 43, 45
D5	Failures of the transmission delay	37, 38, 43, 45
D6	Loss of telegrams on the radio network	37, 38, 43, 45
D7	Failure of the system itself	41, 43
D8	Bad human behavior	

of potential problems affecting a product, a process or a service.

We derive safety requirement by using FTA (Fault Tree Analysis). A FTA is a graphical technique that provides a systematic description of the combinations of possible occurrences in a system, which can result in an undesirable outcome (for more information see International standard CEI 61025, 1990). This method can combine hardware failures and human failures. For safety-critical systems, the root node of the tree will often represent a system-wide, catastrophic event taken from a preexisting hazards list.

Figure 20 is a limited version (with only the OR gates) of the failure tree for the risk of a collision between a train and a road vehicle. Sub tree D deals with human failures. Sub tree C is linked to the fundamental property of our software system. The system must not admit trains and road vehicles simultaneously into the danger zone.

The first FTA is split in some part. The D part concerns some human errors. The C part introduces the principle property for the system: "The system does not granted access in same time to train and road traffic".

The two sub trees A (shown in Figure 21) and B result from equipment failures (barriers, road traffic lights, communication, train presence sensor). In a model in UML notation, the failure tree in Figure 20 can be partially modelled by a use case diagram, which introduces the link Consequence on (Figure 22).

The above analysis must be completed by an analysis, which ascends from failures to degraded situations so that no situation that might cause an accident is ignored. This type of analysis is represented on Figure 23 for barrier failures.

Use case of Figure 24 is an example where we model some communication failures. Operational scenarios can be specified by means of sequence diagrams of UML (see Figure 25).

This type of analysis, which descends from risks to dangerous situations, may reveal new requirements, for example the need to verify that physical objects (lights, signals, sensors) are always present and in good condition. These require-

Figure 20. Fault tree analysis

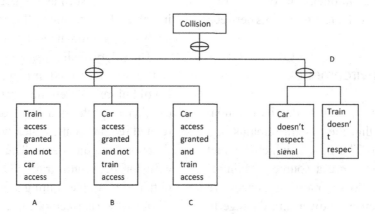

Figure 21. Fault tree analysis continue

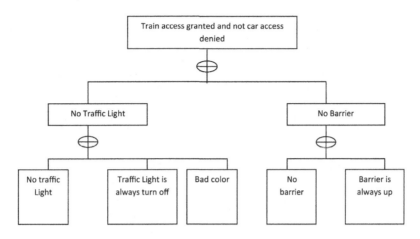

Figure 22. Link between failure and consequences

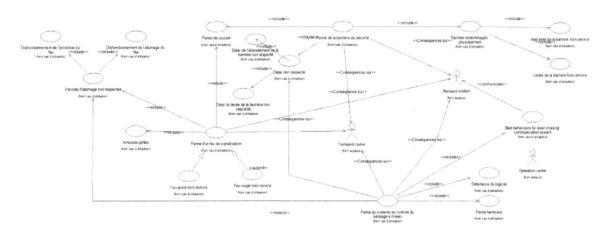

ments must be taken into account by the system and exported to installation procedures, then maintenance procedures. Table 12 gives some examples of safety-related functional requirements (SFR).

The above analysis must be completed by an analysis, which ascends from failures to degraded situations so that no situation that might cause an accident is ignored. This type of analysis is represented on Figure 23 for barrier failures and Figure 24 for the road traffic lights.

Impact on the Environment

Sequence diagrams are constructed in order to describe the impact of a situation on the system. The one in Figure 26 describes the nominal operation of the protocol for the passage of a train through the level crossing. To begin with, the road traffic lights are illuminated in order to stop the road traffic. If the zone is not sensitive to noise (i.e. no dwellings in the vicinity), bells also ring simultaneously. After a warning period, the barriers are lowered. If this has been performed correctly, that is to say within the relevant time

Figure 23. Failures of barriers

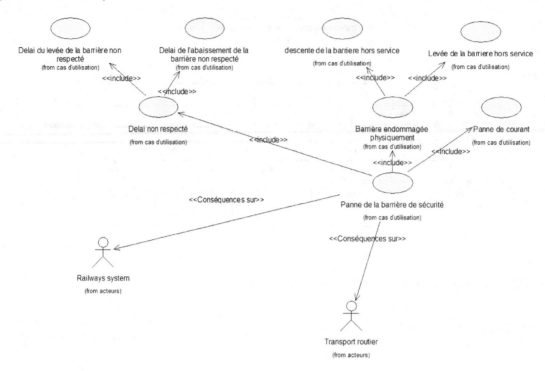

limits, the system is said to be in safe mode and the train is allowed to pass through the level crossing. Once the train has passed through, the barriers are raised, the traffic lights are turned off and any bells are stopped.

Figure 24. Use case for modeling some failures

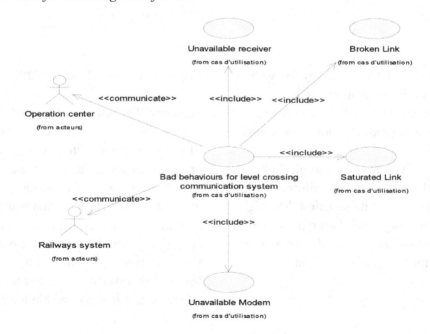

Figure 25. Operational scenarios

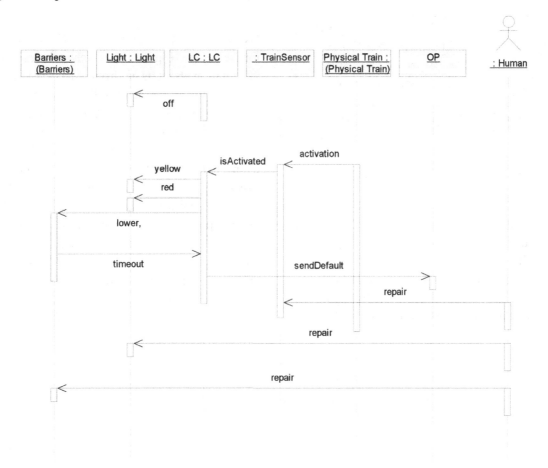

Sequence diagrams of this type may be used to describe the impact of degraded situations on the system. In the case where the train receives no confirmation from the level crossing that it is in a safe state, two behaviours are possible: the train can either brake and stop or the driver can decide to take control and proceed cautiously. Figure 27 shows the sequence diagram for passing through the level crossing in this way (manual mode).

Maintenance

The consideration of the actions of maintenance (repair of barriers, repair of lights) has to be made during a phase of identification of the actions realize and effects on the system. These actions can

be introduced into the model in the form of case of use, diagram of sequence and complement in the diagram of class.

The introduction of the actions of maintenance in the model allows to encircle the impact on the system and to make the link with the exported requirements. The link can even go to the procedure to be operated.

Stage 3, the Breakdown into Components

Selection of Requirement

The previous section has shown how it is possible to set up a risk analysis process. This process allows us to find the functional requirements

Table 12. Safety functional requirement

ID	Requirement
SFR1	The road users have to respect the traffic lights.
SFR2	Train drivers have to respect the railway signaling.
SFR3	Train drivers have to indicate degradation, which they observe.
SFR4	Sensors to detect train should be placed at the point under design.
…	…
SFR12	Trained persons must realize the maintenance.

and the safety requirements for each subsystem. While this is not able to formalize the process, it justifies the choice of requirements. Table 13 corresponds to the LCCS subsystem. Traceability with the functional requirements (FR) is covered by a specific matrix, similar to that in Table 10.

Architecture

We are able to propose a functional architecture for the system (Figure 28), which includes all the information about its environment (list of actors, complete list of interactions, list of failures, etc.). This class diagram shows the physical actors (Physical train managers, sensors, road traffic lights and barriers) and the interactions between them. As an example, we have shown a link between the class Physical train manager and the class Physical sensor manager, which signifies that the physical components are in interaction. Readers should note that the Sensor manager class possesses a state named failure, which expresses the fact that the sensor may break down.

Figure 26. Nominal operational scenarios

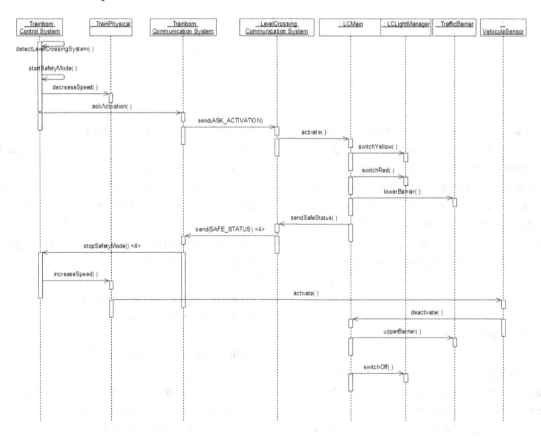

Figure 27. Operational scenarios in manual mode

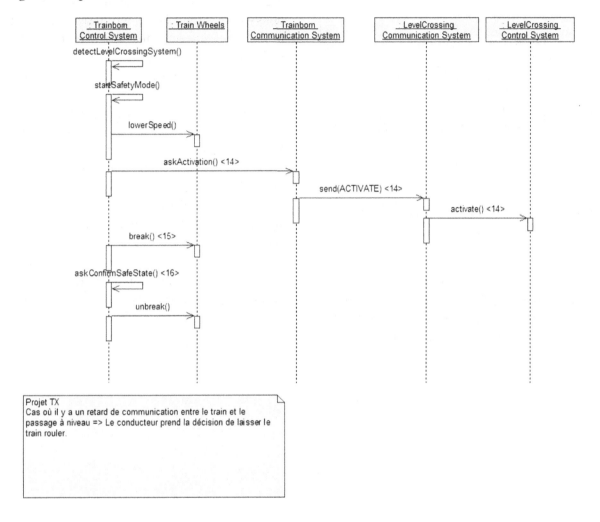

Behavior

If the state and transition diagrams are associated with a class, they can characterize its behaviors by describing the possible states for the objects in the class and the transitions by which they can pass from one state to another. For a given object, a transition connects a possible origin state to a possible destination state. It is characterized by the event, which triggers the passage from one state to another, and by a condition and by an action, which will be performed when the state changes (Figure 29). Using state and transition diagrams,

we shall describe the behavior of the level crossing control system and the on-board system.

Table 13. System functional requirement for LC

ID	Requirement
SFS86	Road Users are stopped in two phase: yellow and red
SFS87	LC authorise Road user to enter by switch off TL
SFS88	The maximum closure time for the LC is fixed (finite/known)
SFS89	LC manage the maximum closure time (C_WAIT_ TIME)
SFS90	When the LC is open then road user can enter in the CA
SFS91	When the LC is close then train can enter in the CA
SFS92	LC report all failures (TL, VS, HAB) to the OC

Table 14. System functional requirement for LCCS

ID	Requirement
SFS99	LCCS will be activated when a train is approaching the CA
SFS100	LCCS will be deactivated when the train has completely the CA
SFS101	They exist some rules for late arrival
SFS102	When the train approaching, rules for late arrival must be apply
SFS103	When the train running on the LC, rules for late arrival must be apply
SFS104	In the activated mode, the LCCS performs a sequence of actions in order to safely close the LC
..	…

The barriers, the road traffic signals and the sound signal are managed by the level crossing control system, which is activated as soon as the arrival information is generated. This activation triggers an ordered sequence of conditioned actions whose purpose is to empty the level crossing in time and guarantee that it is closed to road traffic. Figure 30 presents the state and transition diagram, which characterizes the behavior of the LCCS.

The train's on-board system performs a series of actions in the approach to a level crossing. When the train passes the level crossing trigger, it asks the level crossing control system for a signal that confirms that the lowering of the barriers has been initiated. After it has received this signal, the on-board system places itself in a wait state and starts to brake in order to give the barriers time to close. When the waiting period is over, the level crossing control system communicates its state to the on-board system. If the level crossing is in safe mode, the on-board control system overrides the braking instruction and

Figure 28. Class diagram

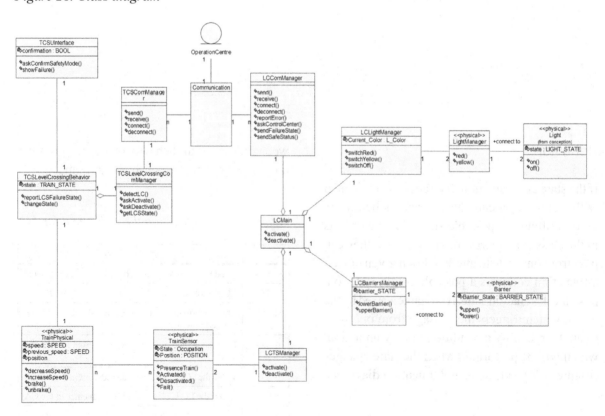

Figure 29. LCCS behavior

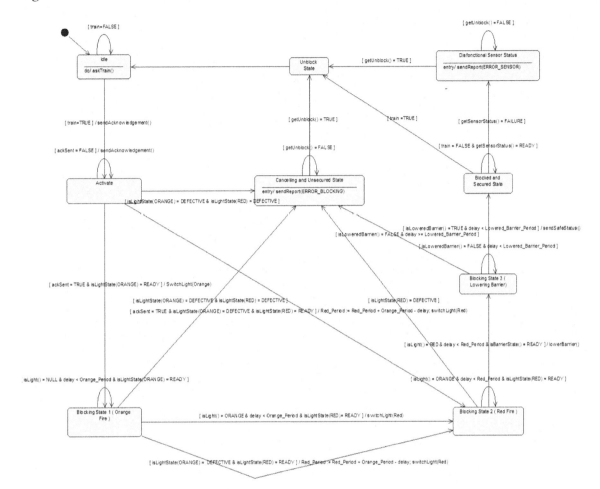

the train returns to its initial speed. An end of passage sensor (that belongs to the sensor manager class) detects when the train leaves the level crossing and triggers the raising of the barriers and the deactivation of the road traffic light.

Figure 30 shows the state and transition diagram that characterizes the behaviour of the on-board software.

Stage 4, Translation into a B Model

B Method

The benefits of formalization and the use of formal methods, which allow a definitive decision

to be made about whether a model has satisfied a requirement have been demonstrated in the fields of rail and air transport. The decision in question allows design faults to be detected at a very early stage thereby limiting the test phases.

The use of formal methods is highly recommended for the development of railway software (CENELEC EN 50128 2001).

The B method, which was developed by Jean-Raymond Abrial, 1996, is a formal model-oriented method like Z and VDM but differs in that it integrates the concept of refinement which makes incremental development from the specification to the code possible in a single formalism, that of the abstract machine language. Proof obligations

Figure 30. TCS behavior

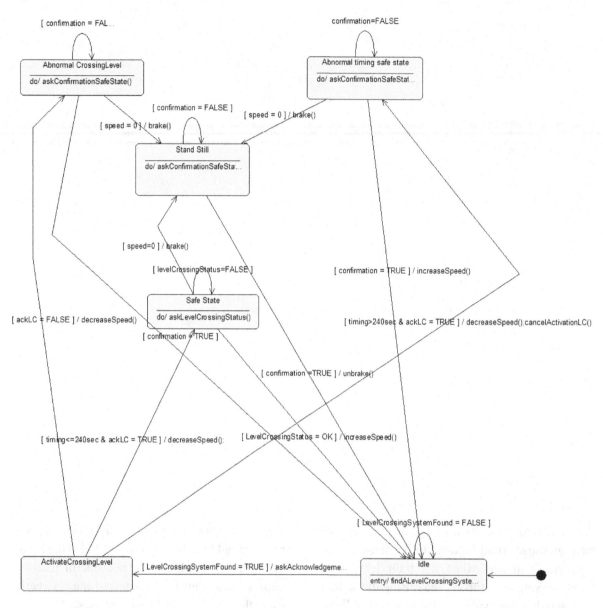

are generated at each stage of the B development process in order to guarantee the validity of the refinement and the abstract machine.

The use of formal methods, the B method in particular, is becoming increasingly widespread in the French rail sector for the development of safety-critical systems. The software for these systems must meet very strict quality, reliability and robustness criteria. One of the first applica-

tions of formal methods was made a posteriori on the SACEM3.

More recent projects, such as SAET-METE-OR4, the VAL5, which is operating at Roissy-Charles-de-Gaulle Airport (April 2007) or the automatic system on Line 1 of the Paris metro (currently at the design stage) have used the B method throughout the development process (from specification to code generation).

The UML notation subset which we used to model our systems in view of its benefits is only semi-formal and we undertook the translation of the UML model into B language: as verification with the B method is regarded as a proof, it will therefore be possible to demonstrate that requirements have been met. We are currently verifying the state and transition diagrams with regard to this. We still have to translate the ocl constraints into B.

B Model Presentation

At this stage, what we have is a model of our case study and we shall translate this into a B model, which will allow us to verify the requirements. The B-RAIL project was not intended to describe a new code generation process but to propose a comprehensive methodology for accurate requirement acquisition using existing B model generation techniques. By combining various pieces of research in this area, we have proposed an initial process for generating B models from UML models, which is based on class diagrams and state and transition diagrams (Bon et al., 2003).

The abstract machine known as *TCS_LevelCrossingBehavior_0* defines the current state, which is *belongs to STATE* and introduces an operation known as *change_state*, which de-

scribes the changes in the state of the subsystem managing the level crossing (Figure 31). This component is not deterministic as it uses the substitution *list_var:(predicat)* to describe the operation *change_state*. This substitution means that all the variables become *such as* (tel que) the predicate is true. Figure 32 is an extract of the *TCS_LevelCrossingBehavior_n* installation, which faithfully reproduces in B language the state and transition diagram in Figure 30.

B-RAIL: Conclusion

The objective of the B-RAIL project is to specify a methodology for developing rail systems which are subject to very strong operating safety constraints as shown by the cenelec standards which govern the design of both software and hardware for rail systems (cenelec, 2000, 2001 and 2003).

The proposed methodology combines the UML notation, which is used to identify the requirement and describe the system, and the B method. The essentially graphic nature of the UML notation makes it easier to understand models and facilitates discussions between the different actors involved in the project (client, developer, checker, validator…). The B method is a formal language, which expresses properties and detects inconsistencies in the context of a proof activity.

Figure 31. Machine. TCS_LevelCrossingBehavior_0

```
MACHINE TCS_LevelCrossingBehavior_0
SETS  STATES ={        Idle,
                       SafeState, ActivateCrossingLevel, StandStill,
                       AbnormalTimingSafeState, AbnormalCrossingLevel}
CONCRETE_VARIABLES              current_state
INVARIANT                       current_state : STATES
INITIALISATION                  current_state := Idle
OPERATIONS
change_state =
BEGIN
 current_state :( current_state :STATES
 &((current_state$0= Idle)
        =>current_state:{ActivateCrossingLevel,Idle})
 ...
 &((current_state$0= StandStill)
        => current_state/:{SafeState, AbnormalTimingSafeState})
 )
END
END
```

Figure 32. Implementation. TCS_LevelCrossingBehavior_n

```
IMPLEMENTATION      TCS_LevelCrossingBehavior_n
REFINES            TCS_LevelCrossingBehavior_0
INVARIANT (current_state = StandStill) => (brake = TRUE)
  &   (current_state /= StandStill) => (brake = FALSE)
INITIALISATION      current_state := Idle
OPERATIONS
change_state =CASE current_state OF
        EITHER  Idle THEN
        VAR bb IN
            bb <-- detectLevelCrossingSystem;
            IF    ( bb = TRUE ) THEN
            BEGIN
                current_state := ActivateCrossingLevel
            ;   AskAcknowledgement
            END
            ELSIF  ( bb = FALSE) THEN current_state := Idle
            END
        END
        ....
        END
END
```

Using the example of a level crossing, we have demonstrated the feasibility and advantages of transforming a model in UML notation into a B model, although admittedly the transition process from one to the other requires refinement. For this purpose, we shall conduct a thorough analysis of the processes proposed in the literature (Abrial, 1996), (Ledang, 2001), (Ledang and Souquières, 2002), (Marcano and Lévy, 2001), (Marcano et al., 2004).

The study presented in this paper has highlighted three factors.

- Conducting an analysis of risks during the system design phase guarantees traceability throughout the process.
- It is possible to use the UML notation to formalize a complex system and safety requirements.
- It is essential to highlight the requirements and their traceability throughout the design cycle. Although the UML notation has proved its value for problem representation and acquisition, the consistency of this model with the initial need must still be demonstrated.

Improvements are in progress (Ossami et al., 2007). We are thus in the process of introducing SySML (OMG, 2006) into our translation into a B model in order to model requirements and traceability links with the components in the UMLmodel. In addition, in the framework of the rt3-tucs project, we are attempting to identify a subset of the UML 2 notation (OMG, 2007) that can model a dependable safety-critical system. We are also considering the generation of test scenarios based on the sequence diagrams and the use cases in order to tackle the problem of functional validation.

CONCLUSION

Actual context in developing software for embedded electronics raises challenges of managing the complexity of software while still guaranteeing the quality and productivity.

Automotive industry introduces many standards as a base from which automotive actors will compete on implementing software using proper process and methodology. The main difficulty to specify railway case study is the less of harmonization between the different European railways systems. The level crossing modeling presented here gives a first step to a computerized management of level crossing.

In this paper, we purpose a method for modeling a safety railways application. But the precondition to use UML diagrams for system specification, which is usable for formal correctness proofs and refutation checks, is that the UML has to be used with a precise semantics. This is possible by definitions of translation rules for the conversion of UML notation in a formal language.

Our global project purposes to transform a semi formal modeling (UML model) to a formal specification (B method, for more information see Abrial, 1996).

REFERENCES

Abrial, J. R. (1996). *The B book assigning programs to meanings*. Cambridge, UK: Cambridge University Press. doi:10.1017/CBO9780511624162

Albinet, A., Begoc, S., Boulanger, J.-L., et al. (2008). *The MeMVaTEx methodology: From requirements to models in automotive application*. ERTS 2008, Toulouse, France.

Albinet, A., Boulanger, J.-L., Dubois, H., et al. (2007). Model-based methodology for requirements traceability in embedded systems. In *Proceedings of ECMDA*, June 2007.

Alexander, I. F., & Stevens, R. (2002). *Writing better requirements*. Addison-Wesley.

André, C., Malet, F., & Peraldi-Frati, M.-A. (2007). A multiform time approach to real-time system modeling: Application to an automotive system. In *Proceedings of IEEE Industrial Embedded Systems*, July 2007.

Bon, P., Boulanger, P.-L., & Mariano, G. (2003). *Semi formal modeling and formal specification: UML & B in simple railway application*. ICSSEA 2003, December 2-4 2003.

Boulanger, J.-L. (2008). RT3-TUCS: How to build a certifiable and safety critical railway application. 17th International Conference on Software Engineering and Data Engineering, SEDE-2008, June 30-July 2, 2008, Los Angeles, (pp. 182-187).

Boulanger, J.-L. (2009). Requirements engineering in a model-based methodology for embedded automotive software. In Ramachandran, M., & Atem de Carvalho, R. (Eds.), *Handbook of software engineering research and productivity technologies: Implications of globalization*.

Boulanger, J.-L., Bon, P., & Mariano, G. (2004). From UML to B-a level crossing case study. [May. Dresden, Germany.]. *Oral Presentation to COMPRAIL, 2004*, 17–19.

Boulanger, J.-L., & Dao, V. Q. (2007). A requirement-based methodology for automotive software development. In *Proceedings of MCSE*, July 2007.

Boulanger, J.-L., & Dao, V. Q. (2008a). *An example of requirements engineering in a model-based methodology for embedded automotive software*. 17th International Conference on Software Engineering and Data Engineering, SEDE-2008, June 30-July 2 2008, Los Angeles, (pp. 130-137).

Boulanger, J.-L., & Dao, V. Q. (2008b). *Requirements engineering in a model-based methodology for embedded automotive software*. July 13-17, 2008, IEEE RIVF 2008, IEEE International Conference on Research, Innovation and Vision for the Future, Ho Chi Minh City, Vietnam, (pp. 263-268).

Boulanger, J.-L., Rasse, A., & Idani, A. (2009). Models oriented approach for developing railway safety-critical systems with UML. In Ramachandran, M., & Atem de Carvalho, R. (Eds.), *Handbook of software engineering research and productivity technologies: Implications of globalization*.

Boulanger, J.-L., & Schön, W. (2007). Certification and safety assessment in railway domain. LT 2007, Sousse, Tunisie, 18-20 November 2007.

CEI 61025. (1990). *Fault Tree Analysis (FTA)*. (International Electrotechnical Commission Std. 61025).

CEI 61508. (2000). *Functional safety of electrical/electronic/programmable electronic safety-related systems*. (International Electrotechnical Commission Std. 61508).

CENELEC EN 50126. (1999). *Railways application–the specification and demonstration of Reliabilty, Availibility, Maintenabiliy and Safety (RAMS)*.

CENELEC EN 50128. (2001). Railways application–communication, signaling and processing systems–software for railway control and protection systems.

CENELEC EN 50129. (2000). *Railways application–safety related electronic systems for signaling*. dSPACE. (2007). *ECU testing with hardware-in-the-loop simulation*.

Einer, S., Schrom, H., Slovák, R., & Schnieder, E. (2002). A railway demonstrator model for experimental investigation of integrated specification techniques. In Ehrig, H., & Grosse-Rhode, M. (Eds.), *ETAPS 2002-integration of software specification techniques* (pp. 84–93).

Hull, E., Jackson, K., & Dick, J. (2005). *Requirement engineering*. Springer Verlag.

Idani, A., Boulanger, J.-L., & Philippe, L. (2009). *Linking paradigms in safety critical systems*. Revue ICSA.

Jansen, L., & Schneider, E. (2000). *Traffic control systems case study: Problem description and a note on domain-based software specification*. Institute of Control and Automation Engineering, Technical University of Braunschweig, 2000.

MeMVaTEx. (2008). *Méthode de modélisation pour la validation et la traçabilité des exigences, Continental AG and ANR*. Retrieved from www.memvatex.org

OMG. (2004). *Unified Modelling Language version 2.0*. Report 2004.

OMG. (2006). Unified Modeling Language: Infrastructure, version 2.0, March 2006, (OMG document formal/05-07-05).

OMG SysML. (2006). *The Systems Modeling Language, Object Modeling Group std*. July 2006. Retrieved from http://www.sysml.org

Siemens. (2006). (Introduction to future ISO 26262, Siemens VDO internal presentation).

KEY TERMS AND DEFINITIONS

ASIL: Automotive Safety Integrity Levels

AUTOSAR: AUTomotive Open System Architecture (AUTOSAR (http://www.autosar.org), another initiative from automotive industry which standardizes software architecture and interfaces for ECUs.

B Method: A formal method developed by J.R Abrial and based on the properties proof.

CERTIFICATION: Certification refers to the confirmation of certain characteristics of an object, person, or organization. This confirmation is often, but not always, provided by some form of external review or assessment.

ECU: Electronic Control Unit

Formal Method: Formal methods are particular kind of mathematically-based techniques for the specification, development and verification of software and hardware systems.

MDA: Model Driven Architecture

MeMVaTEx: Modeling methodology for the validation and the traceability of requirement.

REQUIREMENT: A requirement is a singular documented need of what a particular product or service should be or do.

RAMS: Reliability, Availability, Maintainability and Safety

SAFETY: Is the state of being "safe", the condition of being protected against physical, financial, environmental or other types or consequences of failure, damage, error, accidents, harm or any other event which could be considered non-desirable.

SIL: Safety Integrity Levels
SSIL: Software Safety Integrity Levels
SysML: Systems Modeling Language
UML: Unified Modeling Language

ENDNOTES

[1]   This work is supported by the French regional project RT3-TUCS (2005-2008) dedicated to UML technology for complex systems certification, the French national project ANR-ACI-SEFECODE (2005-2008) about safety components design and the French national project ANR-MEMVATEX (2005-2009) about modelling, validation and traceability of requirement.

[2]   Object Management Group: http://www.omg.org/

[3]   SACEM is a cab signalling technique, which is installed on the rolling stock on line A of the Paris Rapid Urban Rail (RER) network (Georges, 1990).

[4]   SAET-METEOR (Chaumette and Le Fèvre, 1996) is the software-based automatic system, which manages line 14 of the Paris metro, which was commissioned in October 1998. The safety software was developed using the B method (Boulanger *et al.*, 1999), (Boulanger, 2001).

[5]   The VAL is an automatic electronics-based metro, which initially operated in Lille. The VAL that was subsequently installed at Roissy-Charles De Gaulle Airport has a computerized system which can manage traffic 24 hours a day 7 days a week even when maintenance work is being performed on part of the track.

Chapter 4
Managing Requirements Elicitation Knowledge using a Spatial Hypertext Wiki

Carlos Solis
Lero, Ireland

Nour Ali
Lero, Ireland

ABSTRACT

Wikis have been widely used as knowledge management tools. However, most of them do not support the conversion process of knowledge in an appropriate way. Specifically, they do not support brainstorming and creativity techniques, which are needed to convert tacit knowledge into explicit. This chapter presents how a wiki tool called the Spatial Hypertext Wiki (ShyWiki) can be used for supporting collaborative requirements elicitation following the knowledge creation spiral of Nonaka. The knowledge conversions in the spiral (socialization, externalization, combination, and internalization) and the knowledge types in each conversion are related to different activities in requirements elicitation, which can be performed through ShyWiki. ShyWiki allows stakeholders to collaborate by creating, brainstorming, structuring and reorganizing requirements contained in notes. In this way, the requirements negotiation and prioritization process can be done through the wiki pages which are seen as virtual boards that hold hypertext notes.

INTRODUCTION

Knowledge Management is composed of the activities, methods, processes, and software that validate, evaluate, integrate, and disseminate information for learning and decision making (Rhem, 2005). A Knowledge Management System (KMS) is an information system that improves the organizational process of creating, storing, retrieving, transferring, and applying knowledge (Leidner & Alavi, 2001).

DOI: 10.4018/978-1-60960-509-4.ch004

One of the most accepted models for knowledge management is the knowledge creation spiral of Nonaka and Takeuchi, which describes how knowledge is converted into different types of knowledge (Nonaka and Takeuchi, 1995). The diversity of existing types of knowledge such as tacit, explicit, unstructured and structured force organizations to use several knowledge management approaches in order to deal in an effective way with the conversion between the types of knowledge (Leidner & Alavi, 2001). The concept of tacit knowledge was defined by Polanyi (1967) as knowledge that cannot be easily shared, and is composed of intuitions, unarticulated mental models, or technical skills. Explicit knowledge is the one that is documented and can be processed by computers (Nonaka & Takeuchi, 1995).

In any project, Requirements Elicitation (RE) is a critical phase due to the fact that most software project failures are caused from inadequate requirements (Hofmann & Lehner, 2001). The RE phase is the first step in the requirements engineering process, where the requirements or the needs of a system are discovered (Sommerville & Sawyer, 2004). Requirements elicitation is a creative process in which all stakeholders collaborate in the creation of the needs that describe a new system (Robertson, 2001). The stakeholders involved in the requirements elicitation process must understand a domain, and the problems that the different stakeholders want to solve using a software system. Some of the proposed needs will become system requirements after their negotiation and prioritization (Sommerville & Sawyer, 2004). In requirements elicitation, diverse methods are used such as interviews, workshops, brainstorming, and protocol analysis (Davis *et.al.*, 2006).

Tacit knowledge is related to undocumented work practices that workers use to take decisions. When stakeholders try to express their requirements of a system, they are converting part of their tacit knowledge into explicit knowledge. From this point of view, requirements elicitation is a knowledge intensive process which involves converting, managing and sharing different types of knowledge among different stakeholders.

Recently, wikis have emerged as an effective hypertext technology for enabling organizations and individuals to manage knowledge. The advantage of using wikis, is that the knowledge management tasks such as capturing, searching, and sharing knowledge can be performed in an open, collaborative, incremental and distributed way (Decker *et.al.*, 2007), (Leuf & Cunningham, 2001). Wikis are based on the principles of easy of use, incremental content creation, open structure for editing and evolution, and self organized structure (Cunningham, 2006). The content in a wiki page is defined by using a simple markup language, which allows the user to format the content and create hyperlinks. In this way, users do not have to be technical experts in the edition and design of hypertext. However, most wikis do not support the conversion process of knowledge in an appropriate way. Specifically, they do not support brainstorming and creativity techniques, which are needed to convert tacit knowledge into explicit. This is an important characteristic that would improve and extend the use of wikis in requirements elicitation.

This chapter presents the use of the Spatial Hypertext Wiki (ShyWiki), a wiki which uses spatial hypertext for representing its content (Solis and Ali, 2008a, 2008b), for supporting requirements elicitation through the knowledge creation spiral of Nonaka. In ShyWiki, each wiki page can be seen as a virtual board composed of a set of notes. ShyWiki provides a flexible hypertext model that can represent the different types of knowledge involved in the knowledge creation spiral, and supports iterative knowledge creation. ShyWiki users are able to capture tacit knowledge by brainstorming using the virtual board, and represent explicit knowledge which they can incrementally structure by using spatial hypertext. The later is supported by allowing stakeholders to add, move, or group notes, and by defining templates and their instances.

The remaining sections of this chapter are structured as follows: First, we explain the knowledge creation spiral of Nonaka and Takeuchi. In the next section, we describe how the knowledge creation spiral can be used in requirements elicitation. Afterwards, we present how ShyWiki can be used to support requirements elicitation through the knowledge creation spiral. Then, we present related work to ours. Finally, conclusions and further work are given.

THE KNOWLEDGE CREATION SPIRAL

In this work, the taxonomy of knowledge types proposed by Nonaka and Takeuchi (1995) is followed. Knowledge is classified into two types: tacit and explicit. Tacit knowledge is composed of intuitions, unarticulated mental models, or technical skills (Polanyi, 1967). Tacit knowledge is personal, context specific and hard to communicate to others. Tacit knowledge has individual cognitive elements such as mental maps, beliefs, paradigms, viewpoints, concrete technical elements (know-how), and context specific skills (Leidner & Alavi, 2001).

Explicit knowledge is articulated, codified, and can be communicated in natural or symbolic languages (Nonaka & Takeuchi, 1995). Explicit knowledge can be processed by computers. Explicit unstructured knowledge does not have a structure which explicitly indicates the correspondences to the concepts and relations in a domain, e.g., plain text and images are unstructured. On the other hand, structured knowledge can be represented by using logic or models. The most common way for representing structured knowledge is through a graph where nodes correspond to facts or concepts, and arcs correspond to the relations between concepts. Both nodes and links are usually typed (Sowa, 1991).

Organizational knowledge is created by a dynamic process called the knowledge creation spiral. The spiral has four types of knowledge conversion: socialization, externalization, combination and internalization (Nonaka & Takeuchi, 1995).

The process can start from any of the four knowledge conversions. In socialization, tacit knowledge of an individual is shared with a group or another individual. Socialization is a conversion from tacit knowledge to tacit knowledge, and is the acquisition of knowledge and experience directly from person to person.

Externalization is the knowledge conversion where tacit knowledge is articulated into explicit knowledge by capturing ideas and experiences of experts in order to solve a particular problem. Externalization is essential in the knowledge creation spiral because new concepts are created, and documented for the first time. Externalization is supported by groupware systems that allow users to brainstorm or create arguments (Nonaka *et.al.*, 1996).

Combination is a knowledge conversion from explicit knowledge to explicit knowledge. In combination, explicit unstructured knowledge is transformed into systemic explicit knowledge. Combination is a process of improving explicit knowledge by organizing it in more logical ways, and combining different knowledge sources.

Combination is supported by systems that permit to refine and combine different knowledge sources. For example, documents with unstructured text and images can be organized or classified into more detailed themes or topics using collaborative document editors (Nonaka *et.al.*, 1996; Schmidt, 2005), or they can be annotated and mapped to concepts and relations in a domain (Uren, 2006). The objective is both to enable people to better understand the knowledge, and to allow systems to process it.

Internalization is the knowledge conversion from explicit knowledge to tacit knowledge. Internalization is basically learning from documented explicit knowledge and in training activities. In this way, previous explicit knowledge can become

Figure 1. Knowledge creation spiral (Adapted from Nonaka & Takeuchi, 1995)

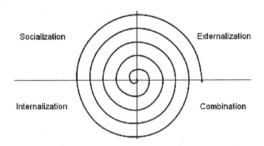

part of the individual tacit knowledge. Internalization is supported by means of e-learning and knowledge repositories.

There are many knowledge management models other than the spiral model of Nonaka et al. All of them have described different knowledge types and activities. For example, the model proposed by Boisot (1998) classifies knowledge into codified or uncodified, and diffused or undiffused. Other models, such as the one proposed by Jordan and Jones (1997), view knowledge management tasks as: acquisition, problem solving, dissemination, ownership, and storage. Although Nonaka's categories and KM tasks do not reflect all knowledge types and tasks encountered in organizations, it has the advantage of viewing knowledge management as a dynamic and recursive process of knowledge creation. Therefore, Nonaka's model has been widely accepted by the Knowledge Management community.

THE REQUIREMENTS ELICITATION KNOWLEDGE SPIRAL

Requirements elicitation is a knowledge intensive activity which can be performed following the knowledge creation spiral approach. In this way, the elicitation process consists of requirements socialization, requirements externalization, requirements combination, and requirements internalization.

Socialization is a continuous process in requirements elicitation which happens when stakeholders communicate, and collaborate to understand each other and learn about each others needs, wishes and expectations (Apshvalka et.al., 2009). In socialization, stakeholders can gain trust among them and get to know who has the expertise and owner of specific knowledge. Socialization begins from the initial stages of software development which can start from the kick off meetings of the project and through the requirements elicitation process methods such as interviews, workshops, or brainstorming sessions.

In requirements elicitation, the concepts that are created in externalization are requirements, which are usually externalized as a result of interviews and brainstorming sessions. The use of creativity techniques is indispensable in the requirements elicitation process, because creative stakeholders can think in an innovative way (Maiden *et.al.*, 2004a). Creative stakeholders are an important factor in the innovation of the companies (Ya & Rui, 2006). That fact has been confirmed by researches that have applied the creativity techniques during the elicitation process (Maiden *et.al.*, 2004b). According to Mich *et.al.* (2005), brainstorming is the most used creativity technique for requirements elicitation (see the next subsection).

Requirements combination happens when accepted requirements are specified with more detail in order to have more complete descriptions that become specifications or when they are integrated and referenced in the artefacts of further development steps. For example, accepted requirements can be specified using a requirement template, and can be referenced in other activities such as task assignation.

The discovered requirements should be stored in digital repositories that provide document management characteristics. In this way, stakeholders can search, consult or edit the requirements and the domain language concepts definitions.

In the following section, we are explaining more in depth how brainstorming can be used in requirements externalization.

Requirements Externalization through Brainstorming

A technique commonly used for externalization is the Kawakita Jiro (KJ) method (Kawakita, 1982) which is used by Japanese companies to brainstorm, evaluate and organize knowledge (Nonaka *et.al.*, 1996). The KJ method is a three phase brainstorming session. In the first phase, ideas are generated and written on adhesive cards or post-it notes without any evaluation or critique. In the second phase, ideas are grouped. If the ideas are related, they can be placed near each other. The goal of the third phase is to create a consensus about the solution to be adopted. In this phase, the groups of ideas are evaluated, i.e., ideas of a group are considered to be the best solution, then the second, and so on. In addition, the participants can vote about the risks in the realization of the ideas.

The WinWin method (Boehm, 1996) is a requirements negotiation approach where each stakeholder expresses her or his system needs as a list of winning conditions. WinWin provides principles and practices for finding winwin conditions shared among stakeholders of the project. In WinWin, when a winning condition of a stakeholder has conflicts with the winning conditions proposed by other stakeholders, a win-lose situation happens (Boehm and R. Ross, 1989). A conflict among winning conditions of different stakeholders is called an issue. An issue is associated with the conflicting winning conditions, and includes a description of the conflict. For solving an issue, the stakeholders propose alternative solutions which are called options. Then, the stakeholders have to evaluate the options and select or reject some of them. After several iterations over the options list, the stakeholders can have an agreement about the solution to be

adopted. During the negotiation process, domain terms appear in the descriptions of the winning conditions, issues, options and agreements. These domain terms have to be defined in a glossary, and structured in a domain taxonomy.

EasyWinWin (Gruenbacher, 2000) is a light-weight WinWin method that has lower entry barriers for stakeholders. EasyWinWin has many similarities with the KJ-Method for brainstorming, and provides a set of concepts and relationships that facilitate the negotiation and prioritization of requirements. In EasyWinWin, stakeholders define their winning conditions through brainstorming. The stakeholders collaboratively define their winning conditions in an electronic brainstorming tool. In this way, they can share and view the different available winning conditions. The win conditions that are similar to others can be merged. As a result, a new win condition is created. The previous brainstorming statements are attached to the winning condition in order to preserve the rationale. In addition, the winning conditions can be organized in a taxonomy. For instance, a winning condition can be a refinement of others.

In the next step, the stakeholders prioritize the winning conditions in order to define their importance. The prioritization has two perspectives: the business perspective, and the ease of realization. The first one defines the importance of the conditions for the business organization, and the second one defines the perceived difficulty of achievement. The difficulty and importance of achievement are subjective because each stakeholder has a different perception of them, e.g. a developer can view difficulty of achievement as the difficulty of implementing a requirement in a specific programming language, whereas a user can view it as the difficulty of expressing conceptually the tasks she does. Both perspectives are measured in the scale from 1 to 10, being 1 unimportant and difficult, and 10 very important and easy. After the prioritization step, it can be observed which tasks are important and easy to accomplish, which are important and hard, which are easy to do but without importance, and which tasks will not be performed for being difficult and without importance.

SUPPORTING THE REQUIREMENTS ELICITATION SPIRAL WITH A SPATIAL HYPERTEXT WIKI

This section explains how the Spatial Hypertext Wiki permits supporting the knowledge creation spiral in the requirements elicitation process. First, an overview of ShyWiki is presented and later we explain how the different knowledge conversions in the knowledge creation spiral are supported in the requirements elicitation.

Overview of ShyWiki

Document centred hypertext is based on using hyperlinks for connecting documents. However, using this kind of navigation in large networks of documents, users can get lost in the hyperspace (Bernstein *et.al.*, 1991). A way to solve such problem is by using map based hypertext, which shows explicitly the relations among hypertext documents (Strauss, 1990). Another way is by using implicit relations.

Spatial hypertext (Marshall & Shipman, 1995) is a kind of hypermedia that is based on using visual and spatial characteristics to define relations among hypertext elements, which are seen as "sticky notes" that can hold hypermedia content. Spatial hypertext can represent implicit hypertext structures, which are interpreted depending on the note's spatial context (Marshall & Shipman, 1993). In this way, the relations that are explicit in the map based approach are represented implicitly by using visual and spatial characteristics. Therefore, hyperlinks become implicit. Spatial hypertext systems have special facilities in their user interface. For example, users can handle and move notes from one place to another in a

hypertext document, or can change their visual properties or their size.

ShyWiki (Solis and Ali, 2008a, 2008b) is a wiki which uses spatial hypertext for representing its content. It is designed to support users in creating, storing, editing, and browsing information and knowledge structures. ShyWiki manages a network of wiki pages. Each page is a hypermedia document that is identified by its name and is made up of an unordered set of named attributes called notes. The main function of notes is to define the attributes that characterize the concept represented by a wiki page.

The content of wiki pages is spatially organized. Notes may be placed in different regions of the page, and can be moved around. Notes can have different sizes or colors. The notes can contain a mix of text, hyperlinks, or images. Composite notes can be created from simpler ones, helping in organizing information hierarchically. Figure 2 shows a ShyWiki page. It is composed of notes that are organized spatially, and that are of different sizes. In Figure 2, it is also observed that there are two composite notes.

The components of the ShyWiki Hypertext Model are summarized in Figure 3. The root of a ShyWiki document is the ShyWikiWeb, which is composed of knowledge stored in WikiPages which are connected by hyperlinks. The WikiPages are composed of notes. The AbstractNote class includes the properties which are common to other types of notes: ContentNotes, TranscludedNotes, and MapNotes. ContentNotes can contain text, images, video and hyperlinks, and can be composed of other ContentNotes.

Transclusion is the inclusion of notes already defined in other wiki pages by reference, i.e., without duplicating them in the including note. A TranscludedNote is a note whose content is defined by another note. MapNotes are used to draw graphs. A MapNote represents a concept, and it is a node in the graph. The arrows in the graph represent the typed hyperlinks that connect two wiki pages.

Figure 2. A wiki page in ShyWiki

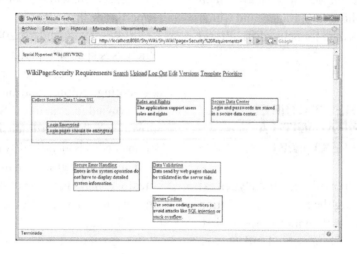

A template is a wiki page abstract type, and it is also a wiki page. One of the purposes of templates is the classification of other wiki pages. A wiki page can be an instance of one or many templates. If a wiki page instantiates a template, the notes in the template are created in the wiki page.

In the edit mode, a user can perform the following actions to create or modify wiki pages:

- **Create wiki pages.** When a wiki link is navigated for the first time, a new wiki page in the ShyWiki web is created.
- **Create notes.** The user can add new notes to the wiki page. The note types that can be added are content, transcluded or map notes.

- **Edit notes.** The content of notes can be changed anytime. The content of the notes is described using the ShyWiki mark-up language.
- **Move notes.** Notes can be moved freely in the interface by dragging and dropping them. In this way, the user can organize the knowledge as she or he desires.
- **Group notes.** The user can group the notes to create aggregations. In this way, a note can be dragged and dropped inside another note, and the note becomes a part of another one. Once notes
- are grouped, a user can manipulate a set of notes together.
- **Transclude notes.** Users can transclude a note inside another wiki page by indicating

Figure 3. ShyWiki hypertext model

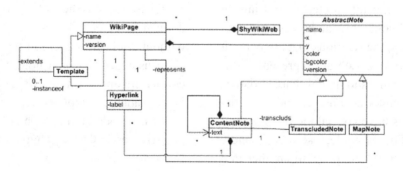

the source document and the note identifier. The position of the transcluded note can be changed, but the other properties can only be modified if the original note is edited.

- **Label hyperlinks.** Hyperlinks in ShyWiki can be typed. A label indicates the meaning or type of the association represented by a hyperlink.
- **Create a template.** This action allows the user to define a new template. A template defines a set of notes which are inherited by wiki page instances, and associations between a template and others.
- **Instantiate a template.** This operation is used to indicate that a wiki page is an instance of a template. As a result, the notes defined in a template are added to the current wiki page.

Requirements Socialization

Socialization takes places in any moment when stakeholders communicate during the development of a project. Requirements elicitation is an intensive stage where needs are collected from the different customers and stakeholders. The initial step in the elicitation is the identification of the participant stakeholders. The identification of stakeholders helps participants to understand

Figure 4. Project setup interface

the social context in which the project will take place. ShyWiki provides a setup page that builds a wiki page for the project, a wiki page with the stakeholders list, a wiki page for each stakeholder, a wiki page with the initial requirements categories, and a glossary wiki page (see Figure 4). The wiki page for each stakeholder can contain a stakeholder's contact information, his or her interests in a project and his or her expertise. This aids stakeholders to socialize by knowing to whom they have to contact or interact.

Requirements Externalization

ShyWiki supports converting tacit knowledge of the individuals into explicit knowledge in a collaborative way. ShyWiki is an idea processing system because its elements are similar to adhesive notes. In this way, a brainstorming session is easily supported. ShyWiki has advantages over blackboard or paper based brainstorming. For example, ShyWiki can support different brainstorming sessions in parallel, one for each team working on a particular problem, the versions of the brainstorming session are stored, and notes can have hypermedia content which can be interconnected among them through hyperlinks.

The three phases of the KJ method can be developed inside ShyWiki. The participants can easily enrich other notes: by adding new content to the original ones, or by adding annotations to them. The drag and drop facilities aid in grouping ideas by using relations of proximity or covering one note with another. The grouping of ideas can also be done by creating container notes. In addition, ideas can be classified by using background or border colours. As a result, the relations that can be expressed among ShyWiki notes are richer and easier to manipulate than the blackboard or paper based techniques. For example, Figure 2 shows a brainstorming session about the security requirements of a web application. If a new requirement has to be added to the board, the stakeholders have to add a new note of type requirement.

Figure 5. Prioritization of a set of requirements

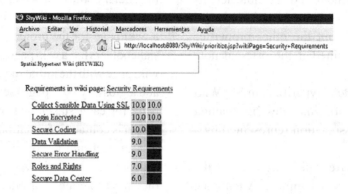

ShyWiki allows stakeholders to vote about the importance and difficulty of a requirement, similarly to the EasyWinWin requirements prioritization approach (Gruenbacher, 2004). A stakeholder can assign a value from 1 to 10 to them.

In ShyWiki, any wiki page has a hyperlink that permits visualizing the priority of the notes that it contains. As a result, a web page that shows the list of requirements contained in the wiki page ordered by their priority is available (see Figure 5). The list is ordered according to the requirements importance to the business, and by their difficulty. The importance and difficulty of a requirement is calculated by the average of all the stakeholders' votes. If the importance or difficulty is greater than 5, then the requirement is shown in green colour. Otherwise, it is shown in red.

An important part of the externalization of requirements is the capture of domain language. Stakeholders might use the same word with different meanings. The definition of an accurate meaning of terms helps in reducing ambiguity, misunderstandings and miscommunication. In this way, the different stakeholders can be aware of the terms, and can speak a common domain language.

Stakeholders have to add the new terms to the project glossary wiki page. The definition of the new terms is explained with detail in the wiki page corresponding to the term name. The open nature of wikis permits any stakeholder to participate in the definition of a term. In addition, the versioning capability of the wiki allows the stakeholders to observe the evolution of the definition. The definition of the terms can be performed incrementally. In the post-it notes of the brainstorming sessions, some terms of the domain language are mentioned. For each term in the domain language, a wiki link has to be added. For example, in Figure 1 the note about secure coding has hyperlinks to the terms SQL injection and stack overflow.

Requirements Combination

In ShyWiki, requirements combination is supported through knowledge types: unstructured and structured. They are explained in the following.

Combination using Unstructured Knowledge

Wikis capture explicit unstructured knowledge in the content of their wiki pages as hypermedia. Users are not able to interact with the wiki in order to reorganize knowledge. However, this is possible in ShyWiki. Users can reorganize knowledge by moving and grouping notes. In this way, requirements written in notes can be grouped with other requirements. For example in Figure 2, the Login Encrypted requirement forms part of the

Figure 6. Logic, set and cardinality relations

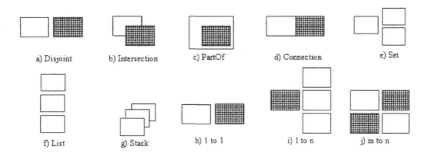

Collect Sensible Data Using SSL requirement. Stakeholders have defined them in different notes and moved the Login Encrypted requirement note into the Collect Sensible Data Using SSL.

The knowledge can be the one captured in the content of notes or the one captured in the relationships among notes that are represented implicitly using visual and spatial properties. They are implicit graphic knowledge structures that can express some logic and set relations (Francisco-Revilla & Shipman, 2005). The following logic relations can be expressed graphically: disjoint, intersection, part of, and connection (see Figure 6). The set relation is expressed by means of proximity, visual properties, and alignment. A group of elements can form sets, lists, and stacks (see Figure 6). In ShyWiki, it is possible to represent implicit relations with different cardinalities: e.g., one to one (see Figure 6). The different ways of expressing graphic relations can be combined to form complex graphic relations.

Combination using Structured Knowledge

In ShyWiki, structured knowledge is captured by means of named notes, typed hyperlinks, and templates. ShyWiki hypertext can have arbitrary node and hyperlink types. Any note in a wiki page can be optionally named. A named note is a property of the concept represented by a wiki page. A named note is a type of annotation to the content, and serves to describe it. Therefore, it can

annotate texts, links, images or a mix of them. The graphic knowledge relations can be used together with named notes. In this way, a wiki page can represent relations among notes that represent specific properties of a concept.

A typed hyperlink is a relation which has a meaning or type that is indicated by a label. Any hyperlink can be labelled by users. The semantic net representation in ShyWiki is straightforward: the name of a wiki page indicates the concept represented, and the labelled hyperlinks give the semantics to the relations. In ShyWiki, the syntax for labeling a link is the following: [[wiki page name | label]]. The first part indicates the name of the target wiki page of the hyperlink, and the second part is the label of the hyperlink. The interpretation given is that the wiki page where the link appears is related to the target wiki page through a named relation, and the name of the relation is the hyperlink label. The relations represented with typed hyperlinks can be drawn in the web interface (Solis & Ali, 2008a) or consulted using SPARQL Protocol and RDF Query Language (SPARQL) interface (Solis & Ali, 2010).

A ShyWiki template is an abstraction which represents a set of concepts that share common properties and relationships. A template has an identifier, which is a unique template name. A template defines the properties and relationships shared by its instances. A template permits the definition of 1 to 1 and 1 to N relationships.

The refinement of a requirement, represented by a note, can be performed in the wiki page as-

Figure 7. Requirement template

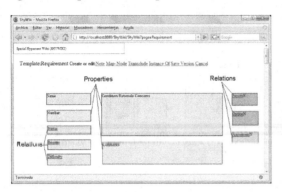

Figure 8. Requirement instance

sociated to a note. In this step, the requirements are defined with more precision and detail, which is often called requirements modeling (Hofmann & Lehner, 2003). We have defined a set of templates for refining requirements which includes: requirement, project, stakeholder, option, agreement, status, priority and difficulty templates. In the requirements model that we have defined, a requirement has a status, a difficulty, a priority, and belongs to a project. A requirement is related to n stakeholders, agreements, and options. The status template has the instances accepted, rejected, and pending. The priority and difficulty templates have the instances low, medium and high.

Figure 7 shows that the user has defined a template called Requirement. Each note is defined by giving it a name, a colour and optionally indicating if it represents an association (relationship) of type 1 to N (by default it is a 1 to 1). When a note represents a property, only the name and colour have to be defined. In Figure 7, the notes Name, Number, Comments are properties. Notes Status, Priority, and Difficulty are 1 to 1 relationships. Notes Person (stakeholder), Option, and Agreements are 1 to N relations. Figure 8 also shows that the Stakeholder relation is defined. The note's name Stakeholder defines the name of the relation, and the associated concept Person is selected from the template list. The content of the note shows the definition of the relation: [[Person | Stakeholder]]N.

The instantiation of a template is performed in the following way: when a new wiki page is created, the user has the option to make it an instance of a set of templates. If the user chooses a wiki page to be an instance of a template, the instance includes the properties and relations defined in the template. If the user edits a note which corresponds to a one to one relation, a select box of the instances of the associated template is presented, and the user can select one of these instances. The user can also type a name that is not included in the select box. As a result, the wiki page indicated is declared an instance of the associated template. The definition of 1 to N relationships is similar to the definition of 1 to 1 relationships. When a note corresponding to a 1 to N association is edited then a select box of the possible associated instances and a text box to define a new one are presented. Also, an operation for removing the instanceof relation is provided. The result of this operation is the removal of the instance of relation between the template and the instance, but it does not remove any note in the wiki page.

Figure 8 shows the instance of the requirement data validation. It can also be observed that the requirement instances show the average importance, and difficulty resulting of stakeholders' votes. The stakeholders involved in this requirement, Cristobal and John, were selected from the stakeholders list, which is shown to the user when a note representing the stakeholder relationship is edited.

Requirements Internalization

Internalization is supported in ShyWiki after that stakeholders work with the wiki, and make it part of their individual knowledge. Stakeholders can use the requirements in the wiki in order to learn about the requirements of the system and can refer others to specific captured knowledge. With their new knowledge, stakeholders can analyze the previous defined requirements or can create new ones. In other words, undetected requirements might be found as a result of reflection.

In a similar way to Nonaka's Spiral Knowledge Creation Spiral, ShyWiki can be used iteratively or incrementally. For example after internalization, new requirements can be detected and captured in the wiki. The process of externalization and combination can be performed at any point.

RELATED WORK

Wang *et.al.* (2007) and Cress *et.al.* (2007) propose the use of wikis for knowledge management. They view wikis as platforms for externalization and internalization. Wiki users externalize their knowledge when they become active authors of the content, and they internalize knowledge when they act as readers of the content. They do not view wikis as platforms for combination of knowledge. However, the use of hyperlinks is a basic feature encountered in most wikis that permits the combination of different information sources. Another feature that can be used for combination is transclusion. In addition, spatial hypertext and structured wiki pages improve the combination features available in wikis.

The lack of spatial features makes externalization harder. In most wikis, the acquisition of knowledge is done using the wiki page editor. Wikis do not satisfy the requirements needed to perform collaborative interpretation or brainstorming. One of the main characteristics of collaborative interpretation is the emergence of ideas. The requirements, defined by Cox and Greenberg (2000), for systems that support the emergence of ideas are: provide a spatial visual workspace, let people express relationships between the data using spatial proximity, allow free-form annotation of the underlying space, and allow the free creation and movement of data in the space. These are supported by ShyWiki.

Oren et al. (2006) propose the use of semantic wikis for knowledge management. Semantic wikis support the combination of explicit knowledge. Semantic wikis provide semantic web knowledge description languages which allow users to annotate explicit knowledge and create structured knowledge (Schaffert *et.al.* 2008). Semantic wikis can represent structured knowledge, but they cannot represent implicit visual and spatial relations among the concepts in the semantic wiki, and neither have good support for externalization. Wen and Jiao (2009) propose the Knowledge Fusion Creation Model Wiki, which is based on the knowledge management framework of Nonaka, and is implemented using a semantic wiki.

Wikis have been widely used for capturing software engineering requirements. For example, WikiWinWin (Yang *et.al.*, 2009) is a wiki that implements the WinWin method. WikiWinWin is based on web forms, and does not have facilities for externalization based on brainstorming, which is a key element in requirements elicitation. In addition, WikiWinWin does not provide support for combination of requirements. Semantic wikis used for requirements engineering provide wiki templates, and typed relationships that permit to define the semantics of objects and relations in the domain of requirements engineering. They provide templates for stakeholders, uses cases, user stories, projects, etc. Examples of semantic wikis for requirements elicitation are SOP-wiki (Decker *et.al.*, 2007) and SmartWiki (Knauss *et.al.*, 2009). ShyWiki can also define templates and relations, and it is possible to define different conceptual models for requirements engineering. ShyWiki gives a more complete support to Nonaka's knowledge spiral than other wikis, because ShyWiki permits the collaborative creation of the different types of knowledge involved in the different knowledge conversions. In this way, ShyWiki can be considered an improved wiki solution for knowledge management.

CONCLUSION AND FURTHER WORK

ShyWiki supports the collaborative requirements elicitation process based on the knowledge creation spiral of Nonaka. Users can incrementally formalize the requirements in the wiki. They can start with an externalization process, make the requirements explicit and gradually incorporate annotations, and concept and hyperlink types

The externalization of requirements is performed by using brainstorming techniques such as the KJ method. The combination of requirements is achieved using the different knowledge representations provided. The visual and spatial characteristics make this model suitable for representing different types of explicit knowledge. Unstructured knowledge can be represented by means of the content of notes which can be grouped and moved, and by implicit visual and spatial relations among notes. Structured knowledge can be represented by means of typed concepts and typed hyperlinks. In this way, the requirements can be refined and improved in order to become specifications for further development steps. Internalization is possible because the requirements are available on line for the stakeholders to learn and consult.

The requirements elicitation process can take advantage of wikis because they provide support for the open collaboration among stakeholders, and low entry barriers. Wikis facilitate the collaborative exchange of ideas, knowledge, and can trace changes by means of versioning. ShyWiki

allows the stakeholders to manipulate spatially the requirements. They can group, relate or merge them easily. In this way, the negotiation and prioritization process can be done through the wiki pages which are virtual boards that hold hypertext card notes.

We are currently extending the ShyWiki tool for supporting synchronous communication and synchronous edition. In addition, we are performing experiments to validate the usability of ShyWiki in requirements engineering and software architecture design.

ACKNOWLEDGMENT

This work was funded by Science Foundation Ireland grant 03/CE2/I303_1 to Lero - the Irish Software Engineering Research Centre (http://www.lero.ie).

REFERENCES

Apshvalka, D., Donina, D., & Kirikova, M. (2009). Understanding the problems of Requirements elicitation process: A human perspective. In *Information Systems development challenges in practice, theory, and education*, vol. 1. (pp 211-223). Springer US.

Boehm, B. (1996). Identifying quality-requirement conflicts. *IEEE Software, 13*(2), 25–35. doi:10.1109/52.506460

Boehm, B., & Ross, R. (1989). Theory-w software project management principles and examples. *IEEE Transactions on Software Engineering, 15*(7), 902–916. doi:10.1109/32.29489

Boisot, M. H. (1998). *Knowledge assets: Securing competitive advantage in the information economy*. Oxford University Press.

Cox, D., & Greenberg, S. (2000). Supporting collaborative interpretation in distributed groupware. In Proceedings of Computer Supported Cooperative Work Conference, (pp. 289–298).

Cress, U., & Kimmerle, J. (2007). A theoretical framework of collaborative knowledge building with wikis: A systemic and cognitive perspective. In *Proceedings of the 8th International Conference on Computer Supported Collaborative Learning*, (pp.156-164).

Cunningham, W. (2006). Design principles of wiki: How can so little do so much? In *Proceedings of the International Symposium on Wikis*, (pp. 13–14).

Davis, A., Dieste, O., Hickey, A., Juristo, N., & Moreno, A. (2006). Effectiveness of requirements elicitation techniques: Empirical results derived from a systematic review. In *Proceedings of 14th IEEE International Conference of Requirements Engineering*, (pp. 179–188).

Decker, B., Ras, E., Rech, J., Jaubert, P., & Rieth, M. (2007). Wikibased stakeholder participation in requirements engineering. *IEEE Software*, *24*(2), 28–35. doi:10.1109/MS.2007.60

Francisco-Revilla, L., & Shipman, F. M. (2005). Parsing and interpreting ambiguous structures in spatial hypermedia. In *Proceedings of Hypertext and Hypermedia*, (pp. 107–116).

Gruenbacher, P. (2000). Collaborative requirements negotiation with EasyWinWin. In *Proceedings of the 11th International Workshop on Database and Expert Systems Applications*.

Hofmann, H., & Lehner, F. (2001). Requirements engineering as a success factor in software projects. *IEEE Software*, *18*(4), 58–66. doi:10.1109/MS.2001.936219

Jordan, J., & Jones, P. (1997). Assesing your company's knowledge management style. *Long Range Planning*, *30*(3), 392–398. doi:10.1016/S0024-6301(97)90254-5

Kawakita, J. (1982). *The original KJ-method*. Kawakita Research Institute.

Knauss, E., Brill, O., & Kitzmann, I. I., & Flohr, T. (2009). Smartwiki: Support for high-quality requirements engineering in a collaborative setting. In 2009 ICSE Workshop on Wikis for Software Engineering.

Leidner, D. E., & Alavi, M. (2001). Review: Knowledge management and knowledge management systems: Conceptual foundations and research issues. *MIS Quarterly: Management Information Systems*, *25*(1), 107–136.

Leuf, B., & Cunningham, W. (2001). *The wiki way: Quick collaboration on the Web*. Boston, MA: Addison-Wesley Longman.

Maiden, N., Gizikis, A., & Robertson, S. (2004). Provoking creativity: Imagine what your requirements could be like. *IEEE Software*, *21*, 68–75. doi:10.1109/MS.2004.1331305

Maiden, N., Manning, S., Robertson, S., & Greenwood, J. (2004). Integrating creativity workshops into structured requirements processes. *Proceedings of the 5th conference on Designing interactive systems*. (pp. 113–122).

Marshall, C. C., & Shipman, F. M. (1993). Searching for the missing link: Discovering implicit structure in spatial hypertext. In *Proceedings of the Conference of Hypertext and Hypermedia*, (pp. 217–230).

Marshall, C. C., & Shipman, F. M. (1995). Spatial hypertext: Designing for change. *Communications of the ACM*, *38*(8), 88–97. doi:10.1145/208344.208350

Mich, L., Anesi, C., & Berry, D. (2005). Applying a pragmatics based creativity-fostering technique to requirements elicitation. *Requirements Engineering*, *10*(4), 262–275. doi:10.1007/s00766-005-0008-3

Nonaka, I., & Takeuchi, H. (1995). *The knowledge creating company*. Oxford University Press.

Nonaka, I., Umemoto, K., & Senoo, D. (1996). From information processing to knowledge creation: A paradigm shift in business management. *Technology in Society, 18*(2), 203–218. doi:10.1016/0160-791X(96)00001-2

Oren, E., Volkel, M., Breslin, J. G., & Decker, S. (2006). Semantic wikis for personal knowledge management. *Database and Expert Systems Applications, 4080*, 509–518. doi:10.1007/11827405_50

Polanyi, M. (1967). *The tacit dimension*. Anchor Books.

Rhem, A. (2005). *UML for developing knowledge management systems*. Boston, MA: Auerbach Publications. doi:10.1201/9780203492451

Robertson, S. (2001). Requirements trawling: Techniques for discovering requirements. *International Journal of Human-Computer Studies, 55*(4), 405–421. doi:10.1006/ijhc.2001.0481

Schaffert, S., Bry, F., Baumeister, J., & Kiesel, M. (2008). Semantic wikis. *IEEE Software, 25*(4), 8–11. doi:10.1109/MS.2008.95

Schmidt, A. (2005). Knowledge maturing and the continuity of context as a unifying concept for knowledge management and e-learning. In *Proceedings of the International Conference on Knowledge Management.*

Solis, C., & Ali, N. (2008a). ShyWiki-a spatial hypertext wiki. In *Proceedings of the 2008 International Symposium on Wikis.*

Solis, C., & Ali, N. (2008b). ShyWiki-a spatial hypertext wiki prototype (demo). In *Proceedings of the 2008 International Symposium on Wikis.*

Solis, C., & Ali, N. (2010). *A spatial hypertext wiki for knowledge management*. In IEEE 2010 International Symposium on Collaborative Technologies.

Sommerville, I., & Sawyer, P. (2004). *Requirements engineering: A good practice guide*. John Wiley & Sons.

Sowa, J. F. (1991). *Principles of semantic networks*. Morgan Kaufmann.

Uren, V. S., Cimiano, P., Iria, J., Handschuh, S., Vargas-Vera, M., Motta, E., & Ciravegna, F. (2006). Semantic annotation for knowledge management: Requirements and a survey of the state of the art. *Journal of Web Semantics, 4*(1), 14–28. doi:10.1016/j.websem.2005.10.002

Wang, W., Xiong, R., & Sun, J. (2007). Design of a Web2.0-based knowledge management platform. In *Proceedings of the Seventh IFIP International Conference on e-Business, e-Services, and e-Society*, (pp. 237-245).

Wen, Y., & Jiao, Y. (2009). Knowledge fusion creation model and its implementation based on wiki platform. In *Proceedings of the International Symposium on Information Engineering and Electronic Commerce*, (pp. 495–499).

Wikipedia. (2010). *Wikipedia, the free encyclopedia*. Retrieved March 2010, from http://en.wikipedia.org

Ya, S., & Rui, T. (2006). The influence of stakeholders on technology innovation: A case study from China. In *Proceedings of the International Conference on Management of Innovation and Technology*, (pp. 295–299).

Yang, D., Wu, D., Koolmanojwong, S., Brown, A. W., & Boehm, B. (2008). WikiWinWin: A wiki based system for collaborative requirements negotiation. In *Proceedings of the Annual Hawaii International Conference on System Sciences.*

KEY TERMS AND DEFINITIONS

Explicit Knowledge: The knowledge that is articulated, codified, and can be communicated in natural or symbolic languages.

KJ Method: It is a brainstorming method used by Japanese companies to make groups externalize their tacit knowledge.

Knowledge Spiral: A dynamic and recurrent process where knowledge is created by means of knowledge conversions: socialization, externalization, combination and internalization.

Requirements Elicitation: A critical phase of requirements engineering where the requirements or the needs of a system are discovered.

Spatial Hypertext: A kind of hypermedia that is based on using visual and spatial characteristics to define relations among hypertext elements, which are seen as "sticky notes" that can hold hypermedia content.

Spatial Hypertext Wiki (ShyWiki): A kind of wiki which uses spatial hypertext for representing its content.

Tacit Knowledge: The knowledge that cannot be easily shared, and is composed of intuitions, unarticulated mental models, or technical skills.

Chapter 5
Knowledge Management in E-Commerce

Zaigham Mahmood
University of Derby, UK

ABSTRACT

Knowledge management refers to acquisition, creation, dissemination, and utilization of knowledge. Knowledge is becoming an important resource for today's organisations, and enterprises are keen to deploy this resource to improve their products, services, and processes as well as ensure delivery on demand. Through knowledge management, businesses aim to increase efficiency, reduce costs, and most importantly, retain customers. Enterprises in the electronic commerce arena are already aware of the importance of understanding customer attitudes and their buying habits and are, therefore, taking huge strides to ensure that they employ appropriate techniques to manage the information at hand. This chapter discusses the variety of approaches that business enterprises have adopted for the acquisition of customer information and its deployment and outlines the processes relevant to knowledge management in the context of electronic commerce.

INTRODUCTION

Knowledge management (KM) is the collection of processes that govern the acquisition, creation, dissemination, and utilization of knowledge. It refers to the *practice* that involves the capturing and sharing of an organization's information

DOI: 10.4018/978-1-60960-509-4.ch005

assets including the experiences of their employees. Organisations are beginning to attach huge importance to customer knowledge as customer attitudes, their purchasing habits and their becoming increasingly more knowledgeable is having a huge effect on the way the products and services are being consumed. Business organisations and enterprises that make use of such knowledge to leverage their products and services are being more successful and profitable than others. In the Electronic Commerce (EC) sector, KM can be used highly effectively for improving internal processes within organisations. Proper content representation of knowledge assets can, in turn, help to retain existing customers and gain new ones as well as provide information to others much more quickly and *on demand*.

Organisations involved in conducting trade via the Internet are employing a variety of techniques to acquire customer knowledge including: (1) surveys and questionnaires, (2) getting opinions through online communities and at the point of checkout and (3) getting customer comments through discussion forums and social networking sites. Organisations also require other forms of information e.g. information about suppliers, competitors, company's own processes, products and services as well as markets in general and global economies.

Acquiring information is relatively easy; however, management of this information with a view to deploying it to the organisations' advantage is less straight forward. This is due to the fact that KM requires satisfactory systems and controls in place to properly manage and deploy the customer and organisational information. There are two aspects to KM:

- To acquire, store, locate and update the information - for the organisation itself for the purpose of process and product improvement
- To share and disseminate contextual information and expert insight - for the benefit of the organisation's customers and partners.

This contextual information with expert insight is known as 'knowledge'. Whereas, it is imperative that business organisations follow best practices for the successful implementation of EC, it is also essential that they have appropriate strategies for the effective management of information and knowledge. In the present work, we discuss the various approaches that business enterprises have adopted for the acquisition of customer information and its deployment and outline the processes relevant to KM in the context of EC.

In the rest of this chapter, we first define, in Section 2, what knowledge is, what KM refers to and also discuss the processes associated with KM. Then, in Sections 3, 4 and 5, we discuss how knowledge is generally managed in the context of EC: referring to customer knowledge and customer relationship management (CRM). Section 6 details the various methods for acquisition of customer knowledge. In Section 7, we describe the utilization and deployment of customer information. Conclusions are briefly summarised in Section 8.

KNOWLEDGE MANAGEMENT

Knowledge Management (KM) is the process of managing corporate knowledge resources. It is the collection of processes that govern the creation, dissemination and utilization of knowledge. Lee and Yang (2000) define KM as a set of organisational principles and processes that help knowledge workers (i.e. employees involved with the processing of information and knowledge) to leverage their creativity and ability to deliver business value (Roy & Stavropoulos, 2007). It is the *practice* that involves the capturing and sharing of an organization's information assets including the experiences of their employees. According to Young (2009), KM is the discipline of enabling individuals, teams and entire organizations to collectively and systematically capture, store, create, share and apply knowledge to better achieve their objectives. In a business environment, KM refers to the management of an organisation's knowledge assets to share information to company's employees and deploy in company's processes to encourage better support and more consistent decision making (Bose and Sugumaran, 2003).

Before we discuss KM any further, it is important to note the difference between data, information and knowledge and understand what knowledge is. Spiegler (2000) defines information as *data endowed with relevance and purpose*. Data becomes information when a context is added to it. When some insight and understanding is added to information, it then transforms into what we call *knowledge* (Spiegler, 2000). Polanyi (1966) classifies knowledge as being either *tacit* or *explicit*. Tacit knowledge is subjective and hard to familiarise. It refers to expertise and skill. It is the knowledge that is held in people's minds that cannot be easily shared (Lee and Yang, 2000). Thus, such knowledge cannot be easily explicated or transferred from one person to another. On the other hand, explicit knowledge is objective and rational that is relatively easy to articulate, communicate and record in databases and archives.

Organisations create new knowledge through interactions between tacit and explicit knowledge. Although, tacit knowledge is difficult to transfer, experiences shared with others allow individuals to project themselves into each other's thinking processes (Kale et al, 2005). Thus, the knowledge transfer and creation of new knowledge takes place from individuals to teams and then it is channelled upwards towards organisations. In this context, Rowley (2002) defines KM as a philosophy that drives enterprises to optimise the utilisation of their knowledge sources, both explicit and implicit. Spender (1996) suggests that organisations possess four types of knowledge:

- **Conscious:** explicit knowledge held by individuals
- **Objectified:** explicit knowledge held by organisations
- **Automatic:** pre-conscious individual knowledge
- **Collective:** knowledge emerging from interactions between individuals and teams (Kale and Little, 2005).

It is this fourth type that may be termed as 'organisational knowledge' that is the most important asset of any organisation, whether large or small.

There are many approaches to KM. In a majority of cases, these concentrate on social and cultural aspects and ignore the role of technology. Elsewhere, such approaches are highly technology-minded but provide no appropriate solutions to cultural challenges of KM (Jansen, 2000). Thus, whereas many companies know how to acquire knowledge, there is often a difficulty when it comes to implementation, management and deployment of it. Knowledge portals provide one solution to such challenges. Knowledge portals are web-based solutions to implement Knowledge Management approaches. Jansen and Bach (2000) propose a 3-layer model for such portals:

- **Knowledge base layer:** consisting of different types of content including news, reports, services, products and procedures
- **Functions layer:** consisting of process support, teamwork, monitoring, management, personalisation and searching of information
- **User interface and navigation layer:** consisting of easy to use interlinked web pages.

However, one main issue of concern is the overflow or overload of information as clearly witnessed from consumer portals such as Yahoo and Google. Such portals do provide huge amounts of information but it is mostly irrelevant and users find it difficult to filter the relevant information. Notwithstanding this, these portals are flexible and easy to use and provide a flexible knowledge environment to a potentially large number of users. The mission of a knowledge portal is also to actively support the users in their business processes.

Galagan (1997) suggests a number of essential steps for a KM process, as shown in Figure 1. The process is reasonably universal and iterative. Here, the emphasis is on the following:

Figure 1. Steps for a KM process (adopted from Galagan, 1997)

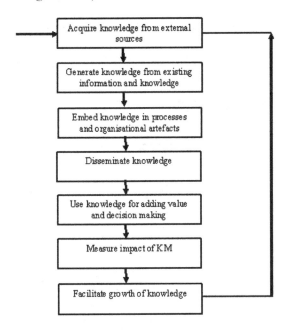

- Acquiring explicit information from customers and company employees
- Extracting tacit information about company processes
- Encouraging sharing of knowledge with company colleagues.

KNOWLEDGE MANAGEMENT IN ELECTRONIC COMMERCE

Electronic Commerce (EC) refers to conducting business via the Internet. It is about advertising and selling goods as well as providing services to customers where customers may be individual members of the public or other business organisations including global enterprises.

EC started in mid 1990's when the first 'shopping malls' appeared on the internet. By the end of the decade, EC gained such popularity that, in 1998, Amazon made an annual profit of over $1 billion and AOL generated more than $1.2 billion in just 10 weeks (Andreevskaia, 2003).

In the following decade, systems such as Customer Relationship Management (CRM) provided further effective management of relationships between the enterprises and their customers. In recent years, the amount of trade conducted via the Internet has grown extraordinarily in areas such as funds transfers, supply chain management, internet marketing, transaction processing, electronic payment and online shopping. This growth has given rise to a further development, known as Electronic Business (EB). Whereas EC refers to provision of current services and present a survival strategy, EB refers to providing new services suggesting a strategy for further growth to ensure that businesses remain agile and able to respond quickly to the changing environments. In this chapter, we do not make distinction between EC and EB and, therefore, the two terms will be used interchangeably.

In EB, customer attitudes, their purchasing habits, likes and dislikes, changing priorities and their becoming increasingly more knowledgeable is having a huge effect on the way the businesses are being conducted and the way services are being offered and consumed. Organisations that take account of these factors and accommodate change accordingly are being more successful than those who disregard such factors. 'Customer profiling' is a term that is commonly used to understand customers. For organisations that provide services and products, it is imperative that they understand and implement the scheme of operation, as shown in Figure 2 and discussed in the following sections.

A life cycle approach for customer knowledge management, as suggested by Derliyski et al (2004) and shown in Figure 3, may also be employed.

CUSTOMER INFORMATION AND CUSTOMER KM

In a business environment, there are many opportunities to collect data about customers as well as

Figure 2. Process of acquiring and utilising customer knowledge

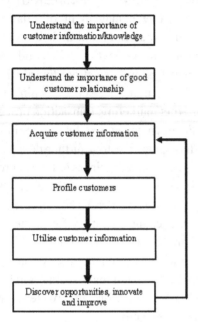

Figure 3. CKM life cycle (adopted from Deriyski, 2004)

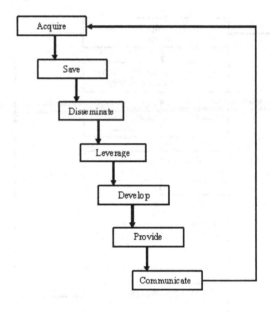

about the markets, in general. Collection of data is easy, although it often requires active participation of customers. However, extracting valid data and using it in various business processes to gain competitive advantage is far from straightforward. According to a survey by Alavi and Leidner (1999), the most important knowledge domain, especially with respect to EB, is the knowledge related to customers. The importance is due to the fact that it can be effectively exploited to increase profitability and customer satisfaction and, therefore, gain a competitive advantage over similar businesses. According to Guaspari (1998), customer knowledge refers to understanding the customers, their requirements and needs. It is essential for an enterprise to align its processes, goods and services for new product development and more appropriate provision. In general, customer KM refers to the following three aspects:

- Data/knowledge acquisition using a multitude of approaches including: conducting surveys, obtaining views from customer forums and looking at data from cookies

- Data/knowledge processing through knowledge codification, utilisation and dissemination internally and externally

- Knowledge deployment through mechanisms such as customer profiling, customer segmentation, product innovation, service improvement and targeted marketing.

Once the customer data and knowledge has been collected, it is imperative that it is appropriately managed and utilised to reap the benefits that KM promises. The term Customer Knowledge Management (CKM) has come about from the convergence of both the technology-driven and data-oriented approach in Customer Relations Management (CRM) and the people-oriented approach in KM (Chen & Su, 2006). It refers not only to the acquisition and collection of information but also to the identification and exploitation of such knowledge (Rowley, 2002; Paquette, 2006). Here, the emphasis is on the following:

- Gaining knowledge directly from customers about their experience of products and services
- Sharing knowledge with customers and further collaboration
- Retaining customers by taking into account their preferences.

According to Chen and Su (2006) and Garcia-Murrillo and Annabi (2002), CKM is the practice of extracting and exploiting two types of customer knowledge, namely knowledge about customers and knowledge from customers. However, Desouza and Awazu (2005) extend this approach and suggest three types of knowledge pertaining to customers (Roy & Stavropoulos, 2007):

- **About the customer:** This refers to information about customer characteristics, customer preferences, their purchase patterns and their socio-economic grouping. Such information is obtained using telephone and internet based surveys, customer reviews and feedback as well as through other mechanisms such as loyalty cards. However, all this requires customer participation which is often difficult to enlist. Davenport et al (2001) suggest that mixing transaction data with customer data may be the best strategy.
- **For the customer:** This refers to information such as product/service descriptions, product/service features, product/service reviews and other suggestions. Information is normally sent using emails, internet and phone; sometimes via partner organisations.
- **From the customer:** This refers to knowledge extracted from customer data to determine customer needs, their attitudes and purchase patterns which then help the organisation to profile and categorise customers. Here, tacit knowledge is also

used in such determination. A variety of data mining techniques are used for this purpose.

Darroch and McNaughton (2003) claim that Customer Knowledge can help organisations in the following ways:

- To improve innovation for the correct and appropriate provision of goods
- To discover opportunities for the introduction of new product lines
- To manage customer relationships for better interaction and liaison.

In the above context, many KM strategies have been proposed by researchers which are being effectively used by business organisations – refer to Newman (2010, online), Roseman (2000), Skyme (2010, online), Gupta (2000) and Davenport (1998).

CUSTOMER RELATIONSHIP MANAGEMENT

Collecting customer information and its management is necessarily required. However, it is also imperative that there is excellent relationship between the organisations and their customers. Customer Relationship Management (CRM) is another term that is often used for management of customer-organisation relationship in an organised manner. It is a process designed to collect data related to customers to understand their characteristics to apply these in specific marketing activities. It can serve as a tool to ensure customer satisfaction and retain customers. According to Roy and Stavropoulos (2007), it comprises three important aspects: (1) operational - referring to collection of data, (2) analytical - referring to analysis of data and (3) collaborative - referring to integration of systems and processes for greater responsiveness. Here, the emphasis is on the following:

- Keeping database of customer information and knowledge
- Extracting relevant information about customer experience and habits
- Ensuring customer satisfaction, retention and building lasting relationship.

According to Gebert et al (2003), CRM entails:

- Measuring marketing sales, service costs, revenue and profits
- Acquiring and updating knowledge on customer needs, motivation and behaviour
- Applying customer knowledge to improve performance and processes
- Integrating marketing, sales and services to achieve improvements
- Implementing controls to support customer knowledge acquisition, sharing and measuring CRM effectiveness
- Measuring and monitoring to improve and maximize profits.

ACQUISITION OF CUSTOMER KNOWLEDGE/INFORMATION

Effective Customer Knowledge Management (CKM) requires active customer involvement for the acquisition of knowledge/information and having effective and appropriate mechanisms to store, manage and disseminate this information. CKM seeks to leverage business-to-customer, customer-to-business, and customer-to-customer communication – and also, to some extent, business-to-business. Businesses and customers exchange information using a number of channels including call centres, advertising campaigns, monitoring sales/services, surveys, data mining, transaction tracking and customer feedback. Customers also exchange information between

themselves through the use of discussion forums, weblogs, social networking websites, etc.

Roy and Stavropoulos (2007), Lee et al (2006) and Rowley (2002) suggest a number of methods for acquiring customer data for EB environments, including:

- Web-based surveys – where customers provide information by filling-in questionnaires via the internet or through postal or telephone communication
- Online communities – where customers provide opinions and discuss their experiences with other customers e.g. through discussion forums
- Transactions data – where customers provide opinions and reviews directly to the commercial organisations e.g. through survey and when customers check out
- Server log file and cookies – where customers' web browsing habits, their search frequencies and search histories are analysed.

Andreevskaia (2003) has also discussed a number of traditional approaches for market research including: surveys, questionnaires (internet and postal), interviews (individual and focus groups; telephone, door-to-door and purchase intercept interview) and case studies. Other methods include getting opinions from online communities (i.e. from social networking sites), server log files and using cookies (Roy et al, 2007). Some of these are explained in the following sections.

Questionnaires

In the context of EB, customer base is widely spread and therefore internet based questionnaires are more appropriate then postal questionnaires. The advantages include: savings on printing and postal costs; ease of modification and analysis (if questionnaires are appropriately designed) and quickness of response (Andreevskaia, 2003). One drawback is that the audience may not always be correctly targeted e.g. if the questionnaire is meant for a teenager, it is possible that another adult in the household fills it in.

Purchase Intercept Interviews

This is becoming a popular method of eliciting customer feedback at the time of purchase by asking a small number of relevant questions just before 'checking out'. Here, customer targeting is much better and the review is being conducted of the 'correct' customers, although, it is possible that an adult is purchasing the item for a teenager or a child. It is important, however, that questions are no more than a few (perhaps two or three) and that they are easy to respond to. Care must be taken that the customers do not regards this as an unnecessary burden and an additional activity.

Telephone Surveys/Interviews

There can be different types of survey interviews: telephone interviews, door-to-door survey and purchase intercept interviews if the purchase is being conducted over the telephone. These interview methods are much more expensive than other types of surveys, by way of telephone costs and meeting time. Another disadvantage is that the time of interviews may not be suitable for the customers. Experience suggests that customers often hang up if they are being 'interrupted' or close the door when there appears to be a 'door-to-door salesperson'. General public do not generally wish to spend time to partake in such interviews or surveys.

Forums and Social Networking Sites

These are highly popular sites and discussion points where customers (and others) share opinions and send messages across as well as publish product reviews. Often, members share the same interests and a message sent to one can be seen by others. Business organisations can use these sites and forums, relatively easily, to collect data about customers and their opinions about products and services. Monitoring the communication that takes place on these sites can provide additional useful information for business organisations. However, it also depends on how well these communities are managed and how effective this data acquisition is, bearing in mind the data protection acts and other relevant regulations.

Server Logs and Cookies

Server logs and cookies are among the most popular means to collect data from customers. These can be analysed to determine the searching habits of customers as well as their interest in products. Cookies reside on customer computers but their data is transmitted back to the servers (of business organisations). This data refers to customers' last visit as well as customers' preferences and search histories. Much useful information can be gained that the organisations can then utilise to target their products and services. This is one of the most popular approaches employed by business organisations especially those who trade via the Internet.

Knowledge Acquisition Tools

There is an abundance of data acquisition and data mining tools that EB industry are currently employing to elicit customer knowledge. Tools that appeared in the 1980s and 1990s were mainly aimed at knowledge workers to elicit and store existing knowledge - usually static. Current tools are process and logic oriented, designed for data mining and querying the knowledge databases, able to capture dynamic knowledge e.g. changes in customer behaviours (Andreevskaia, 2003).

UTILISATION AND DEPLOYMENT OF CUSTOMER KNOWLEDGE

Once the customer data has been acquired, it needs to be converted to customer information. A model proposed by Bose et al (2003) can be effectively used. The model consists of four processes which refer to:

- Generation of knowledge i.e. identification and creation of new knowledge
- Storage of knowledge i.e. translating knowledge in machine readable form and developing suitable databases
- Distribution of knowledge - to knowledge workers within the organisations
- Utilization of knowledge - to innovate and develop new products and improve controls.

Once processed, this information needs to be made available to knowledge workers so that appropriate changes may be incorporated as customer preferences and requirements changes. The customer knowledge also needs to be made available to relevant personnel within the organisation for further processing, mainly for product innovation and process improvement. Davenport (2001) and Rowley (2005) recommend the following steps to be taken:

- Classify and Prioritise customers i.e. build customer profiles based on their purchases, frequency of purchases, etc
- Understand customers' behaviour i.e. build customer segments based on their demography, social class, etc
- Determine means to ensure customer loyalty i.e. introduce incentives such as loyalty cards, discount vouchers, etc
- Innovate existing products i.e. develop new products based on customer profiling and their changing needs and requirements

- Innovate controls; and improve processes based on customer reviews and opinions (from forums and other surveys)
- Conduct marketing and organise promotions i.e. advertise new products and service by targeting customers based on their profiles.

Personalisation of customer data has become one of the most important aspects of electronic commerce, as already mentioned in previous sections. The aim is to understand customers' preference, wants and needs so that products are correctly targeted to customers, encouraging them to return to purchase more. It is important that personalisation, also known as customer/user profiling, is dynamic so that their profiles present their changing needs and priorities. Customer profiling characterizes features of special customer groups. Better understanding through profiling can lead to better marking plans, including targeting specific groups of customers.

It should be noted that changes in profiles occur due to two main reasons: (1) changes at the EC organisation (provider of goods) and (2) changes due to customers' changing requirements. Personalisation requires a clear understanding of customer needs and requirements. Changes of the first kind refer to changes in product list, product specification, product price, discounts/incentives available, delivery modes, quality/presentation of information, service support and business practices. Changes of the later kind refer to changes due to the following: (1) changes in the first category, (2) changes in customers' circumstances, work situations, life style and interests and (3) dissatisfaction with the products or product providers.

Typically, profiling is performed with respect to the following (Rosella, 2010):

- Demographic profiling - This describes characteristics such as age, gender, race, education, income, marital status, family size, home ownership, socioeconomic status, and so on.

- Geographic variables - This describes factors such as geographic areas, climate, population, and so on.
- Psychographic profiling - This refers to customer's life style, personality, values, preferences, attitudes, and so on.
- Behavioural profiling – This includes product usage, brand royalty, benefits sought and so on - information that can be extremely useful for marketing purposes.

One method that is commonly employed for customer profiling is the RFM modelling, which is based on the following observations:

- Recency values (R) – referring to how recently any items were purchased by the customer
- Frequency values (F) – referring to how frequently the items are purchased by the customer
- Monetary values (M) – referring to how much money was spent in a given period.

Using this model, values of R, F and M are used in an expression such as x*R+y*F+z*M where x, y and z are weighting factors. A higher value of this expression signifies a 'higher-value' customer.

Customer profiling is used to determine *Customer Segmentation* which refers to dividing a customer base into groups of individuals that are similar in specific ways (e.g. the same age group, the same socio-economic class, etc). Segmentation allows companies to target similar groups more effectively.

Tesco, one of the 'big four' supermarkets in the UK, are using 'intelligent profiling' to target its customers to rank their enthusiasm for promotions, brand loyalty, purchasing habits, times of store visits, types of goods purchased, etc. Based on this information, they send promotion leaflets and discount vouchers selectively to the customers based on their purchase preferences. For example, a customer who does not drink and so does not buy alcohol will not normally receive discount vouchers for such items. The 'loyalty cards' offered by various stores all work roughly along the same lines. Another famous web retailer, Amazon. com, links their book categories so that when a customer shows interest in a particular book, the website offers a list of similar books to tempt the customer in similar purchases.

CONCLUSION

Knowledge is a hugely important resource for organisations and, therefore, business organisations, especially those in the sector of electronic commerce, are keen to collect customer knowledge (i.e. data about customers) and appropriately manage it. Knowledge Management (KM) techniques are being used highly effectively for improving internal processes within organisations as well as improving products and services quality for better customer satisfaction. Business organisations also understand that proper content representation of knowledge assets can, in turn, help to retain existing customers and gain new ones.

Businesses and customers exchange information using a number of channels including: call centres, focus groups, surveys, polling, data mining, transaction tracking and customer feedback. Customers also exchange information between themselves through the use of discussion forums, chat rooms, weblogs, social websites, etc. Once customer data is collected by enterprises, it is transformed into customer knowledge, stored, disseminated and utilised. The objective is to use such knowledge to improve processes, products and services.

In this chapter, we have discussed the processes associated with KM, mainly in the context of electronic commerce, including the various methods for acquisition of customer knowledge. We have also discussed how knowledge is generally processed, managed, utilized and deployed to the advantage of both business organisations as well as the customer community.

REFERENCES

Alavi, M., & Leidner, D. E. (1999). Knowledge management systems: Issues, challenges, and benefits. *Communications of the AIS, 1*, 7.

Andreevskaia, A. (2003). *Knowledge acquisition for dynamic personalization in e-commerce.* Thesis, Dept Computer Science, Concordia Univ., Montreal, Canada.

Bose, R., & Sugumaran, V. (2003). Application of knowledge management technology in customer relationship management. *Knowledge and Process Management, 10*(1), 3–17. doi:10.1002/kpm.163

Chen, Y., & Su, C. (2006). A Kano-CKM model for customer knowledge discovery. *Total Quality Management, 17*(5), 589–608. doi:10.1080/14783360600588158

Darroch, J., & McNaughton, R. (2003). Beyond market orientation – knowledge management and the innovativeness of New Zealand firms. *European Journal of Marketing, 37*(3/4), 572–593. doi:10.1108/03090560310459096

Dasousa, K., & Awazu, Y. (2005). What do they know? *Business Strategy Review*, Spring 2005, (pp. 42-45).

Davenport, T., Harris, J., & Kohil, A. (2001). How do they know their customers so well? *MIT Sloan Management Review*, Winter 2001.

Davenport, T., & Prusak, L. (1998). *Working knowledge: How organizations manage what they know*. Boston, MA: Harvard Business School.

Denning, S. (2000). *The springboard: How storytelling ignites action in knowledge-era organizations*. Boston, MA; London, UK: Butterworth Heinemann.

Galagan, P. (1997). Smart companies (knowledge management). *Training & Development, 51*(12).

Garcia-Murillo, M., & Annabi, H. (2002). Customer knowledge management. *The Journal of the Operational Research Society, 53*, 875–884. doi:10.1057/palgrave.jors.2601365

Gebert, H., Geib, M., Kolbe, L., & Brenner, W. (2003). Knowledge–enabled customer relationship management: Integrating customer relationship and knowledge management concepts. *Journal of Knowledge Management, 7*(5), 107–123. doi:10.1108/13673270310505421

Guaspari, J. (1998). Customer means customers. *Quality Digest*, 35-38.

Gupta, A. K., & Govindarajan, V. (2000). Knowledge management's social dimension: Lessons from Nucor Steel. *Sloan Management Review, 42*(1), 71–80.

Jansen, C. M., Bach, V., & Osterle, H. (2000). Knowledge portals: Using the Internet to enable business transactions. *Proceedings of Internet Society*, Japan, 18-21 July 2000.

Kale, D., & Little, S. (2005). Knowledge generation in developing countries: A theoretical framework for exploring dynamic learning in high–technology firms. *Electronic Journal of Knowledge Management, 3*(2), 87–96.

Lee, C. C., & Yang, J. (2000). Knowledge value chain. *Journal of Management Development, 19*(9), 783–793. doi:10.1108/02621710010378228

Lee, M. K. O., Cheung, C. M. K., Lim, K. H., & Sia, C. L. (2006). Understanding customer knowledge sharing in web-based discussion boards: An exploratory study. *Internet Research, 16*(3), 289–303. doi:10.1108/10662240610673709

Newman, B. (2010). *The knowledge management forum*. Retrieved April, 2010, from http://www.km-forum.org/htm

Paquette, S. (2006). *Customer knowledge management*. Retrieved April 2010, from www.fis.utoronto.ca/phd/paquette/documents/paquette%20%20 customer%20knowledge%20 management.pdf

Polanyi, M. (1966). *The tacit dimension*. London, UK: Routledge and Kegan.

Rosella, (2010). *Customer profiling*. Retrieved May 2010, from http://www.roselladb.com/customer-profiling.htm

Roseman, M., & Chan, R. (2000). A framework to structure knowledge for enterprise system. *Proceedings of Americas Conference on Information Systems*, 2000.

Rowley, J. (2002). Eight questions for customer knowledge management in e-business. *Journal of Knowledge Management*, 6(5), 500–511. doi:10.1108/13673270210450441

Rowley, J. (2002). Reflections on customer knowledge management in e-business. *Qualitative Market Research*, 5(4), 268–280. doi:10.1108/13522750210443227

Rowley, J. (2005). Customer knowledge management or customer surveillance. *Global Business and Economic Review*, 7(1), 100–110. doi:10.1504/GBER.2005.006923

Roy, T. K., & Stavropoulos, C. (2007). *Customer knowledge management in the e-business environment*. Master's thesis, Dept of Business Admin and Social Sciences, Lulea Univ. of Tech, Sweden.

Skyrme, D. J. (2010). *The knowledge management forum*. Retrieved April 2010, from http://www.km-forum.org/htm

Spender, J, C. (1996). Making knowledge the basis of a dynamic theory of the firm. *Strategic Management Journal*, 17, 45–62.

Spender, J. C., & Grant, R. (1996). Knowledge and the firm: Overview. *Strategic Management Journal*, 17, 45–62.

Spiegler, I. (2000). Knowledge management: A new idea or recycled concept. *Communications of the Association for Information Systems*, 3(14).

Young, R. (2009). Back to basics: Strategies for identifying, creating, storing, sharing and using knowledge: From productivity to innovation. *Proceedings of 2nd International Conference on Technology and Innovation for Knowledge Management*.

Chapter 6
Multiagent System for Supporting the Knowledge Management in the Software Process

Francisco Milton Mendes Neto
Rural Federal University of the Semi-Arid, Brazil

Marçal José de Oliveira Morais II
State University of the Ceará, Brazil

ABSTRACT

The software process consists of knowledge-intensive procedures, involving various profiles, which handle a wide range of information. The adoption of a solution that satisfies the knowledge demands related to software engineering is not a trivial task. Despite all the investment made by research institutions and software development organizations in automated environments to support the software process, the quality levels and the productivity rates they need has not been reached. In software engineering, the experience, which helps avoid mistakes of the past and improve decision making, still lies mainly in the organization collaborators. This chapter intends to contribute to software engineering by proposing a new approach to support the capture, packaging, storage, mapping, maintenance and retrieval of the knowledge related to the software process. The approach will support the software process through the creation of a knowledge management model to assist the development of intelligent agents that can (i) realize the knowledge needs, (ii) interact with the Information Systems and (iii) support executing the software developers' tasks. In other words, the chapter proposes creating a multiagent system to manage knowledge related to the execution of software development processes. This system will be the result of implementing the knowledge management models for supporting software process that will also be proposed in this chapter. It will consist of an Information System integrated with a knowledge base related to the implementation of software development processes.

DOI: 10.4018/978-1-60960-509-4.ch006

INTRODUCTION

Software Engineering (SE) involves managing a variety of knowledge about the various activities related to the software process. Moreover, each of these activities involves a set of macro actions that also involves a large number of specific knowledge themselves. Furthermore, the wide range of different knowledge assets necessary for the different collaborators involved in the software process may play, in the tasks of the process, different roles, demanding the knowledge required by each of these roles.

The amount and variety of the knowledge involved in the software process of a Software Development Organization (SDO) can grow exponentially, depending on (i) the software process model (for example, RUP – Rational Unified Process), (ii) the project management model (for example, PMBOK), (iii) the software development model, and (iv) the capacity evaluation model, like CMMI (Capability Maturity Model Integration), adopted by the SDO. Although some capacity evaluation models are proven to be efficient to improve the quality of the software process, they involve a wide range of extra information about it, many times specific to the model, which shall also be internalized and, thus, assimilated by all the people involved in the software process.

Knowledge Management (KM) solutions can be used to allow the effective use of the knowledge involved in the software process. The KM can be understood as a deliberate and explicit systematic of constructing, renovating and applying knowledge to maximize the effectiveness of the organization's business processes, producing results and ensuring the competitiveness of the organization.

However, the effective implementation of KM is not a trivial task. This is due, mainly, to the fact that most KM initiatives adopt traditional approaches, transferring to the user a large part of the responsibility to collect, pack, store, map

and recover knowledge. Inserting this extra step in the user's work process is inefficient.

In this chapter, we propose constructing an intelligent environment to support KM under the SE, that will help those involved in the software process, in a proactive way, to capture, pack, store and retrieve knowledge related to all software process activities. To achieve it, the environment will have a multiagent system, where intelligent agents are going to learn with the users' activities and suggest knowledge that can be useful to the several phases of the software process, depending on the profile of the user involved in the activity.

Among the direct benefits of the effective integration of intelligent agents with knowledge management (KM) in the software process, we can list: reach, objectivity, speed and effectiveness. How these benefits are attained is discussed in what follows.

Reach

Generally, knowledge transfer is local and fragmented. Larger the Software Development Organization (SDO), greater the demand for some required knowledge, but lesser the chance of a worker (which needs it) to know how and where find it (Davenport & Prusak, 1998; Kock, 2000). A solution to this problem is offering knowledge automatically to workers when they need it, i. e., without the need of explicit requisition of knowledge. This is important because most workers do not know which knowledge is available and, thus, they never search for it (Maurer & Tochtermann, 2002).

The effective integration of intelligent agents into KM allows releasing knowledge to software workers without the need of explicit requisition. The use of intelligent agents allows identifying and releasing automatically the proper knowledge. Automatic identification of software worker demand on particular knowledge allows greater reach in knowledge transfer.

Objectivity

It is possible to release specific knowledge for a particular demander after identifying the necessary topics for some software function or worker, as discussed before. Personalized knowledge allows more objectivity in knowledge transfer, because it avoids time and resource wasting with knowledge transfer to software workers that do not need it. Knowledge will be transferred objectively to software workers that can use it for executing their activities (right knowledge to the right person on the right time). This increases the possibility of knowledge use and adds more value to the organizational intellectual capital, which increases when knowledge is used.

Speed

The speed knowledge arrives where it can add value is an important evaluation factor on how effective the organizational intellectual capital is being used. Usually, knowledge transfer happens on demand in the SDO. When a software worker needs a specific knowledge, either he searches the knowledge database, or he interacts with specialists in the subject. In both cases, this might take precious time. Integrating intelligent agents into KM allows releasing focused knowledge as soon as the lack of a particular knowledge is detected, thus increasing the knowledge transfer speed.

Effectiveness

Knowledge transfer effectiveness, that is, the knowledge percentage that has been assimilated and applied, is influenced mainly by the method used in the transfer process (Kock, 2000). Further, richer and more tacit is the knowledge, more effort should be placed to enable software workers to share it directly.

It is possible to reach greater effectiveness in knowledge transfer through the use of mentoring. Direct interaction with a specialist (knowledge provider) during certain periods of time allows acquiring more consistent and deeper knowledge about a particular area, as well as obtaining a greater amount of knowledge. This is true because the knowledge recipient gets more detailed and implicit knowledge. The long process of trying to extract and understand specialist's knowledge by conversation, observation or interrogation provides workers with a better comprehension of the subject being learned than that acquired through learning processes based on non-interactive means (for example, searching in knowledge repositories, reading papers). Intelligent agents can efficiently identify knowledge requirements to improve software activities, as well as specialists to act as mentors in a mentoring training program.

REQUIREMENTS TO SUCCEED IN KM IN THE SOFTWARE PROCESS

Once KM is a relatively new area of research, there are not many directives about the benefits it can provide neither what kind of difficulties one must face when applying it in the software process. Despite of that, some important requirements have been identified to let KM succeed in the software process. The most important ones are the following:

1.   Improve the software workers' creativity and the innovation of software products

The encouragement to create and innovate software products in a Software Development Organization (SDO) is an important item when applicating KM in the software process is considered. It is necessary a balance between toughness and flexibility of KM applications in the software process because while toughness inhibits creativity, the flexibility excess encourages creativity but it is unable to be controlled and turned into a software product of an SDO. As a result, it is verified a tension between process and practice, that is, between the way software activities of an SDO are formally organized and the way these software activities are effectively carried through.

An aggravating factor in this process is the mentioned tension, that is different of most problems that an SDO uses to confront, which cannot be resolved or overcome. SDO must learn how to live with it and how to take advantage of it. Practice allows the coming up of new ideas and process allows controlling and putting them into effect. If balance is broken and the structure tends to a practical side, many new ideas may arise, but there will be no structure able of controlling it. This way, there is the risk it becomes useless. On the other side, if structure tends more to process side, the SDO can get a better one, but it will not be so flexible to make room to new and innovating ideas.

2.   Share essential knowledge with the software project phase that is being performed

KM intends to increase the effectiveness of a software project, and sharing knowledge is essential to reach this goal. It is necessary to share relevant knowledge that may be useful to add value to the phase of the software project that is being executed.

3.   Increase the knowledge access

A common difficulty faced by KM is how to share the essential knowledge with a software project among all the software professionals. Trying to solve the tension between thoughness and flexibility, some organizations encourage creativity only among its high-ranked professionals, such as project managers and system analysts. This way, the work of the rest of the team becomes predictable, near the structure of the process. However, because of the constant changes in development strategies of a software project imposed by demands of the market, creativity becomes a requirement in all phases. Even

during routine phases, such as software test, tasks are never performed in a precise order. This way, software workers are often compelled to improvise ways to balance differences between routine programs and the environment conditions, which is in constant change.

4.   Promote knowledge transfer

The SDO faces a common problem during the KM application: the deficit of qualified workers to structure and plan ways of sharing its knowledge. Usually, the software teams of strategic projects of an SDO do not have resources to describe what happened during the software project execution neither to display this information from a repository. Often, the few software workers with the required ability to perform these tasks do not have time to put their knowledge into a system.

5.   Increase the storage of explicit knowledge

The KM in the software process requires definition and storage of the best practices of the software projects for future reference, even if it is not a trivial task, especially considering the difference between specifying a task on a software process handbook (codified or explicit knowledge) and its practical execution. The effective execution of software tasks is full of improvisations, hardly definable for their executors. The KM needs to overcome these barriers deciding the best practices of the software project and store them as explicit knowledge.

6.   Increasing the exchange of tacit knowledge

KM needs to encourage also the exchange of tactic knowledge. Otherwise, tacit (implicit) knowledge about the software process cannot be easily articulated, formalized, communicated and codified, once it contains a personal aspect. They are deeply rooted in action, in behavior and in the involvement on a specific context.

7. Improve software workers' motivation and behavior for learning

KM faces a huge challenge: motivate software workers to pursue knowledge, because it is not interesting to provide an efficient tool for software process learning if software workers are not motivated to use it.

8. Make the execution of software tasks more efficient

Despite all the advances provided by KM, most SDO continue wasting what can be turned out in their greatest asset, that is, the value of knowledge, like ideas and insights, which are commonly dispersed in all organizations. Because of that, these SDO do not succeed in capitalizing on their intellectual resources, obstructing the use of available knowledge to improve their software activities or combine them to known software processes to make up something new. The use of organization knowledge to optimize resources and execution of software processes helps the SDO to deal with a series of new challenges, enabling them to be more efficient than their competitors.

9. Improve the quality of software products

KM should contribute for improving the intellectual capital of an SDO, to increase the quality of knowledge (organizational skills) applied to its software products. Therefore, as the intellectual capital of an SDO increases, the quality of their products is also improved.

10. Increase SDO profitability

An inherent requirement to every SDO strategy is the increase of profits. If financial results are not favorable, all the basic assertions about organizational strategies should be revised.

AGENT MODEL FOR SUPPORTING KNOWLEDGE MANAGEMENT IN THE SOFTWARE PROCESS

According to Castro (2006), the construction of Multiagents Systems (MAS) (Zambonelli et al, 2000b) is not an easy task, because it has all the problems of the traditional distributed and concurrent systems, including additional difficulties that appear related to the requirements of flexibility and sophisticated interactions. Any methodology for the Agent-Oriented Software Engineering (AOSE) should provide appropriate abstractions and tools to model not only the individual tasks, but also the agents' social tasks. In that context, several methodologies for the modelling of MAS have been proposed in the last years (Zambonelli et al, 2000a). Some examples of these methodologies are Gaia (Zambonelli et al., 2005), Multiagent Systems Engineering (MaSE) (Deloach, 2001), MAS–CommonKADS (Iglesias & Garijo, 2005) and Prometheus (Wikinoff & Padgham, 2004).

The MAS-CommonKADS methodology (Iglesias & Garijo, 2005) is an extension of the CommonKADS methodology (Schreiber et al, 2000), which includes aspects that are important for the modelling of MAS. CommonKADS is the main structured methodology for supporting knowledge engineering (Juchem & Bastos, 2001). According to Schreiber et al. (2000), several models are proposed, and the Experience Model is the main one of the CommonKADS methodology. Its objective is the modelling of the knowledge used by an agent to accomplish a task of problem solving. This model divides the knowledge of the application in three levels: domain level (declarative knowledge about the domain), inference level (a library of generic structures of inference) and task level (order of the inferences).

According to Werneck et al. (2006), the model of life cycle for the development of MAS follows the approach of project management of CommonKADS, being driven by risks. It includes the following phases: Conception, Analysis, Project,

Codification, Integration, and Operation and Maintenance. The Conception phase consists of obtaining a first description of the problem and the determination of the use cases, which can help to understand the informal requirements and to test the system. The Analysis phase determines the requirements of the system from the statement of the problem. In the Project phase, it is defined how the requirements of the analysis phase will be transformed into specifications that will be implemented. In this phase, it is determined the agent and the net architectures. In the Codification phase, each agent is implemented and tested. In the Integration phase, the complete system is tested. In the Operation and Maintenance phase, the system is installed and its operation is started, always looking for mistakes to be corrected, which were not detected in the previous phases, and also advancing in the development of the system through new functionalities.

MAS-CommonKADS defines seven models (Iglesias, 1998): Agent Model, Organization Model, Task Model, Experience Model, Communication Model, Coordination Model and Project Model. The Agent Model specifies the agent's characteristics, that is, their reasoning power, abilities, services, sensor, groups of agents they belong to and agent's class. An agent can be a human agent, a software or any entity capable of using a language for agent communication. The Organization Model is a tool to analyze the human organization in which the multiagent system will be introduced, as well to describe the agent software organization and their relationship with the environment. The Task Model describes the tasks that the agents can accomplish, the objectives of each task and their decomposition. The Experience Model describes the necessary knowledge agents demand to reach their goals. This model, as well as in CommonKADS, can reuse libraries of generic tasks. The Communication Model describes the interactions between a human agent and a software agent. It focuses in human factors for a given interaction. The Coordination Model describes the interactions among software agents. Finally, the Project Model describes the architecture and the project of a MAS as a previous step to its implementation, being the only model that doesn't deal with the Analysis. In the Figure 1, we can see the models of the MAS-CommmonKADS methodology.

This section will describe the modelling of the agents to support KM in the software process. Requirement Engineering was used as a base for creation of the agent model. The MAS –CommonKADS methodology was chosen for the agents' modelling. This methodology was selected by the following reasons:

- It explains in full detail the employed models and demonstrates how to develop its respective diagrams, besides possessing an

Figure 1. MAS-CommonKADS models (Adapted from Iglesias, 1998)

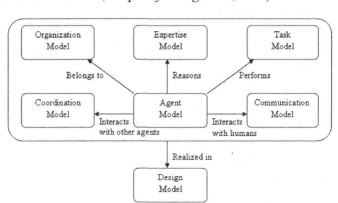

Figure 2. Generic use case diagram

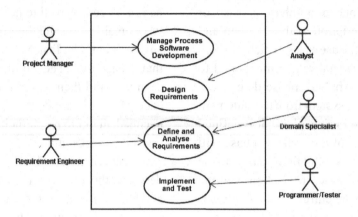

initial phase of conception in which we can easily analyze the problem to be treated;

- It uses techniques of object-oriented methodologies that favors the understanding for software programmers;
- It uses the spiral model to evaluate the existent risks in the planning of alternative strategies for the project, with the objective of not exceeding the deadlines and the costs;
- It enables the use of an independent architecture for each agent, promoting more flexibility to the development of the application;
- The methodology is an extension of CommonKADS, which is widely applied in successful projects.

Next, the application of the MAS-CommonKADS methodology will be presented for agent identification and modelling.

Conception of the System

The Conception phase has the objective of expressing the initial idea of the system by using an user centered analysis through use case techniques. In this phase, the actors and the use cases of the system should be identified and described. According to

Iglesias (1998), graphic and textual notations are usually used to describe the use cases.

Figure 2 presents the generic use case diagram of the environment, allowing a general visualization of the actor's relationships with the computational tools.

The MAS–CommonKADS methodology, as shown previously, is composed by seven models. The first model is the organization model, which has the objective of describing (i) the human organization, searching possible areas for agents' application, as well as the possible impacts caused by the introduction of a multiagent system; and (ii) the organization of the agents' society, where static relationships are demonstrated such as inheritance, aggregation, and authority relationships.

Figure 3 presents the organizational structure of the system.

Figure 3. Organizational structure of the system

In the next models, we will see if it is really possible the inclusion of agents in the environment.

Task Model

The tasks are the activities executed by the agents or of responsibility of them. It is through the accomplishment of tasks that agents usually reach their goals. This model allows presenting the functional decomposition of part of the functional areas of the organization which intend to use a multiagent system.

The tasks accomplished in the system are:

- **Task:** Register Requirements
  - **Goal:** Register the requirements obtained through communication with the business specialists.
  - **Description:** This task is accomplished to register all the requirements obtained during the phase of requirement elicitation. Always maintaining the system updated with the necessary requirements is a primordial task.
  - **Supertask:** Manage Requirements
- **Task:** Register Evolution of the Requirements
  - **Goal:** Keep the system updated considering the evolution of the requirements.
  - **Description:** This task seeks each evolution of a requirement and register it, what maintains the system updated. This way, the requirements can be traced from their elicitation to their implementation.
  - **Supertask:** Manage Requirements
- **Task:** Obtain Requirements
  - **Goal:** Capture the system's needs through communication with the customers.
  - **Description:** This task is accomplished once one can understand the customer's needs with relation to the software. To obtain the requirements, several techniques can be used, such as interviews, observation, workshops, among others.
  - **Supertask:** Manage Requirements
- **Task:** Analyze Risks
  - **Goal:** Discover risks during the project.
  - **Description:** This task has the objective of foreseeing risks that can disturb the course of the project. In this phase, the analysts and the project manager analyze each requirement and associate the risk to each one. When the risk is very high, plans are accomplished for controlling this risk.
  - **Supertask:** Manage Requirements
- **Task:** Validate Requirements
  - **Goal:** Confirm that the specification is consistent with the requirement definition.
  - **Description:** This task verifies if the specification of generated requirements is consistent with the requirements defined by the customers. After the validation phase, the project phase is begun where all the documents generated in the validation phase will be used.
  - **Supertask:** Manage Requirements
- **Task:** Create Teams
  - **Goal:** Create teams to work in several phases of the project.
  - **Description:** This task is performed by the project manager. He splits the analysts in teams based on their experiences for accomplishing the tasks that were delegated to them in each phase.
  - **Supertask:** Manage Requirements
- **Task:** Distribute Requirements to the Teams

Table 1. CRC card of the professional agent

Agent: AG 1			Class: mod_professional	
Goals	**Plans**	**Knowledge**	**Colaboration**	**Service**
Adapt professional profile	Record the user's information	The professional's data		Inform profile
Motivate	Look for and exhibit motivation	Deadlines	AG 4	Motivate

○ **Goal:** Distribute the previously validated requirements for the teams.

○ **Description:** After the validation of requirements, the project manager distributes the requirements that were validated among the teams. So that it is started the project phase of the system.

○ **Supertask:** Create Teams

Agent Model

For the specification of the agents, MAS-CommonKADS proposes the agents description through spreadsheets, which give details of the agents and their goals, and CRC cards (Class-Responsibility-Collaborators). According to Oliveira (2000), each CRC card is made to specify a certain agent. The agent's goals are listed and the plans (the actions that should be performed to reach a goal) are described. The employed knowledge in the plans, the other agents that collaborate in the execution of the plans, and the services through which happens the interaction among the agents are also identified.

Analyzing the task model and the use cases, one may find some functions accomplished by human agents that could be substituted or aided by intelligent agents. These functions are described next.

Next, the student agent goals are presented.

Agent: AG 1
Type
  Intelligent agent (software)
Description
  This agent is responsible for the direct communication with the user to motivate and capture some user's characteristics. This agent contributes to satisfy the requirements 1, 7 and 8 to succeed in KM in the software process, that is, improve the

Table 2.

Goal 1: To adapt professional profile	**Goal 2:** To motivate Team or Professionals.
Type	**Type**
Cognitive goal	Reagent goal
Input Parameters	**Input Parameters**
Information about the deadline accomplishment.	Data about deadlines for the project.
Output Parameters	**Output Parameters**
Adapted professional profile.	Motivation.
Condition of Activation	**Condition of Activation**
When the professional puts back or finishes their tasks.	When the agent notices that the team or the professional will not reach the goal.
End Condition	**End Condition**
When the profile is updated.	When an image or motivation message is sent.
Description	**Description**
The agent has as goal updating previously defined information about the professional profile of the participants of the team. This agent updates mainly the information about the execution of the goals.	The objective is providing mechanisms for motivating the team or the professional. This motivation can be accomplished in several ways, such as images or motivation phrases.

Table 3. CRC card of the manager agent teams

Agent: AG 2			Classe: mod_team	
Goals	**Plans**	**Knowledge**	**Colaboration**	**Service**
Schedule tasks	Distribute tasks to the teams	Requirements and teams	AG 2	Inform tasks
Create teams	Recognize similar profiles	Professional profile	AG1	Inform teams

software workers' creativity and the innovation of software products, improve software workers' motivation and behavior to learning and make the execution of software tasks more efficient, respectively.

In what follows, the goals of the manager agent team are presented.

Agent: AG 2
Type
　Intelligent Agent (software)
Description
　This agent is responsible for aiding the project manager in the distribution of requirements and formation of teams. This agent contributes to satisfy the requirements 8 and 9 to succeed in KM in the software process, that is, make the execution

of software tasks more efficient and improve the quality of software products, respectively.

Next, the risks manager agent goals are presented.

Agent: AG 3
Type
　Intelligent agent (software)
Description
　This agent is responsible for aiding the project manager to reuse previously defined and implemented requirements. It also verifies requirements that are pending during the project. This agent has a significant importance because the reuse of requirements allows decreasing the time and risks of the project. It also collaborates to aid the negotiation of new deadlines for the project. This

Table 4.

Goal 1: Schedule tasks	Goal 2: Create teams
Type	**Type**
Persistent reactive goal	Proactive goal
Input Parameters	**Input Parameters**
Information about the professional profiles and the requirements that should be developed.	Professional profiles.
Output Parameters	**Output Parameters**
Distribution of tasks for each team.	Created teams.
Condition of Activation	**Condition of Activation**
When all the requirements were already analyzed and validated.	When the goal of assigning tasks are activated.
End Condition	**End Condition**
When it is released to the project manager a sequence of tasks that should be developed and the teams that will accomplish them.	When the teams are generated.
Failure Condition	**Failure Condition**
The project manager does not accept the generated suggestion.	The project manager does not accept the team.
Description	**Description**
The agent has the goal of analyzing the profiles and the requirements that should be developed, and of generating a sequence of tasks based on the requirement priority and distribute it to the created teams.	This objective seeks to create teams based on the users' professional profile. To generate the team, the profile of each one is analyzed based on the requirements that should be developed, righ after the team is generated. If the project manager refuses the team, the agent should be able to keep the information to know that for some requirements those teams should not be created.

Table 5. CRC card of the risk manager agent

Agent: AG 3			Class: mod_risk	
Goals	**Plans**	**Knowledge**	**Colaboration**	**Service**
Look for similar previously developed requirements	Search requirements	Base of previously developed requirements	AG 2	To inform requirements
Inform risks	Verify the risks related to the requirements	Base of previously developed requirements		To inform risks

Table 6.

Goal 1: Look for previously developed requirements **Type** Persistent reactive goal **Input Parameters** Information about the requirements that should be developed. **Output Parameters** Similar requirements that were previously developed. **Condition of Activation** When the requirements are registered in the system. **End Condition** When similar requirements are released to the project manager. **Failure Condition** When any registered similar requirement doesn't exist. **Description** The agent has as goal to analyze the base of developed requirements and to find ones requirements by improving the reuse of requirements.	**Goal 2:** To inform risks **Type** Proactive goal **Input Parameters** Similar already developed requirements. **Output Parameters** Known risks. **Condition of Activation** When the similar requirement is found in the base of developed requirements. **End Condition** When the risks are informed. **Failure Condition** Any similar already developed requirement doesn't exist. **Description** This objective seeks to inform the risks when the requirement was developed, enabling the project manager having a previous vision of what may happen.

agent contributes to satisfy the requirements 2, 3 and 5: succeed dealing with the KM in the software process, that is, share essential knowledge with the software project phase that is being executed, increase the knowledge access and increase the storage of explicit knowledge, respectively.

In the following, the verification agent's goals are presented.

Table 7. CRC Card of the verification agent

Agent: AG 4			Classe: mod_verification	
Goals	**Plans**	**Knowledge**	**Colaboration**	**Service**
Verify idle teams	Look for and inform idle teams	None	AG 2	Inform idle teams
Verify modifications in the requirements	Notice the modified requirements and inform them	None	AG 2	Inform modifications
Verify generated artefacts	Analyze all the artefacts that were generated	Artefacts that should be generated	AG4	Informs artefacts that lack
Verify pending requirements	Analyze the requirements that are pending	None		Inform pending requirements

Agent: AG 4

Type

Intelligent Agent of Software

Description

This agent aids the project manager and the analysts to verify if in the end of each phase all the artefacts were totally generated. For this, the agent accomplishes some activities, such as verification of idle teams, modifications in the requirements and verification of pending requirements. This agent contributes to satisfy the requirements 2, 4 and 6 to succeed in KM in the software process, that is, share essential knowledge to the software project phase that is being executed, facilitate the

knowledge transfer and increasing the exchange of tacit knowledge, respectively.

Coordination Model

The coordination model was proposed in MAS-CommonKADS to develop and describe the interactions among the agents of a MAS. The main objective is to approach the risks that are directly related to the development of these interactions and to give support to the construction of MAS through a method that prevents these risks (Iglesias, 1998).

Table 8.

Goal 1: To verify idle teams **Type** Persistent reactive goal **Input Parameters** Information about the responsible teams by the requirements. **Output Parameters** Idle teams. **Condition of Activation** When a team ends all the requirements. **End Condition** When the information is released to the project manager. **Description** The agent has as goal to analyze the development of the team in each phase of the project. When the agent verifies that a team is idle, it informs to the project manager so that he can delegate new functions to this team doing with that the project be developed more quickly.	**Goal 2:** To verify modifications in the requirements. **Type** Persistent reactive goal **Input Parameters** Information about modifications in the requirements that will be developed. **Output Parameters** Modified requirements. **Condition of Activation** When the requirements are modified or are inserted new requirements. **End Condition** When the groups are informed. **Description** This goal seeks to monitor new inclusions or modifications in the requirements. The agent informs to the responsible teams for those to do the due arrangements.
Goal 3: To verify generated artefacts **Type** Proactive goal **Input Parameters** Generated artefacts. **Output Parameters** Lacking artefacts. **Condition of Activation** When the artefacts are included in the system. **End Condition** When the artefacts are informed. **Description** This goal seeks to guarantee that all the artefacts are generated and, in case a lacking artefact be identified, the agent informs the artefacts that are necessary in that phase.	**Goal 4:** To verify pending requirements **Type** Proactive goal **Input Parameters** Previously developed requirements and the requirements that should be developed in the project. **Output Parameters** Pending requirements, the requirements that depend on them and the percentage of the development. **Condition of Activation** When the project manager needs to verify the course of the development. **End Condition** When the pending requirements are informed. **Failure Condition** Any pending requirement doesn't exist. **Description** This goal seeks to inform the pending requirements to complete each phase of the development. This makes possible to the project manager to have a vision of the evolution of the development and, if necessary, to negotiate new deadlines.

The coordination model deals with the dynamic aspect of the multiagent society, offering support to the description of message exchanges among agents during the accomplishment of their goals. This model is probably one of the more complex of the MAS-CommonKADS methodology due to the great amount of generated artefacts. The main generated artefacts of this model are: spreadsheets of conversation, diagrams of message sequences (MSC - Message Sequence Charts) and diagrams of basic channels.

The conversation spreadsheets describe the existent collaborations in the system and make possible the identification of agent interventions (changes of messages among agents) that compose the conversation.

A MSC allows to describe the sequence of messages exchanged in the system during the accomplishment of a certain conversation. Among its potentialities, we can mention the support to the representation of entities (agents or any other entity of the system, for example, classes and objects), actions, messages and conditions (states of the entities). The notation still allows to represent situations where parallel and alternatives messages may happen (Oliveira, 2000).

The diagrams of basic channels are composed by boxes and nominated arrows that represent, respectively, the agents and the accomplished interventions (messages). According to Iglesias (1998), the coordination model is oriented to services, in other words, an agent can offer the accomplishment of certain tasks (services) to other agents. Each service is requested through conversations and can be associated to certain properties, such as cost and duration.

The development of the coordination model must be accomplished following some activities, such as the identification of the conversations, their description, the identification of interventions for designing the MSC and the determination of the basic communication channels.

In the first activity, the identification of the conversations must be accomplished analyzing the use cases (described in the conception phase) and the CRC cards of the agent model. The identified objectives in these cards are probable candidates to conversations. To describe the conversations, it was created an internal use case diagram that demonstrates the conversations among the agents. For better visualizing the conversations, use case diagrams were developed to represent the communications among agents, as follows.

Conversation 1: Show Motivation
Goal
Exhibit messages or images to motivate the user.
Agents
AG1 and AG4.
Initiator
AG1.
Description
When the user accesses the environment, AG1 communicates with AG4 looking for information about the pending requirements and artefacts by evaluating if the project is compliant with the expected deadlines and, if necessary, giving a motivation to the team or to the professionals.
End Condition
Exhibited message or image to the user.

Conversation 2: Form Teams
Goal

Figure 4. MSC: Schedule tasks for idle teams

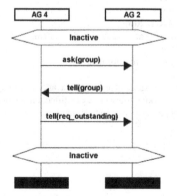

Figure 5. MSC: Form teams

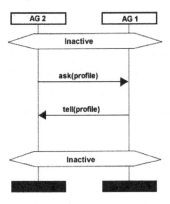

Figure 6. MSC: Send motivation

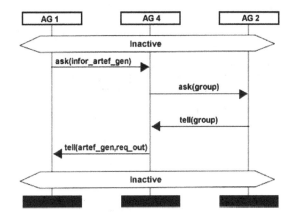

Figure 7. Collaboration Diagram: Schedule tasks for idle teams

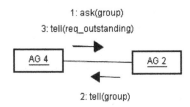

Figure 8. Collaboration Diagram: Form teams

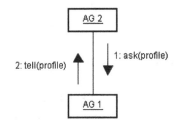

Create groups based on the users' professional profile.

Agents

AG1, AG2 and AG3.

Initiator

AG2.

Description

The AG2 is responsible for creating groups based on each analyst's professional profile. That agent communicates with the AG1 to obtain each profile. After scheduling the tasks, that agent visualizes the division of the tasks and generates teams for each task.

End Condition

A list of teams.

Conversation 3: Schedule Tasks for Idle Teams

Goal

Verify idle teams and distribute new tasks for them.

Agents

AG4 and AG2.

Initiator

AG4.

Description

AG4 communicates with AG2 to know the teams that were created. Right after, the agent verifies the requirements that are pending. Next, the AG4 sends the idle teams again to AG2, which distributes the pending requirements among the teams.

End Condition

No idle teams.

The MSCs of the conversations are shown next (Figure 4, Figure 5, Figure 6).

Figure 9. Collaboration Diagram: Send motivation

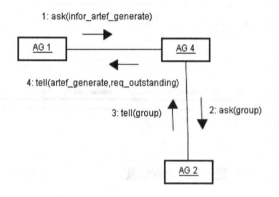

Next, the collaboration diagrams are shown (Figure 7, Figure 8, Figure 9)..

FINAL REMARKS

In this chapter, we described the project of intelligent agents for supporting knowledge management in the software process. A bibliographical revision was accomplished about the main concepts related to intelligent agents and about methodologies of the agent-oriented software engineering, which offer support for modeling MAS. For modeling the MAS it was chosen the MAS-CommonKADS methodology, an extension of the CommonKADS that is addressed to MAS. CommonKADS is an acknowledged methodology for knowledge engineering, applied in several projects.

During the development of the work, the MAS-CommonKADS methodology was very efficient for (i) the conception of the system, expressing explicitly the agents involved in the operations that will be accomplished by the MAS, (ii) representing the interactions among the agents, and (iii) identifying of the tasks accomplished by each one of them, which constitute part of their knowledge model. The MAS-CommonKADS methodology fitted very well in such activities,

because it defines precisely how to express the interactions among agents and how to integrate them inside of a tree of tasks, what constitutes part of the method of problem solving of the agents. Despite of not contemplating the implementation phase, the methodology describes in many details how the agents should be codified, facilitating the developers work.

The agent's model proposed provides more autonomy and proactive features to an environment intended for supporting the knowledge management in the software process. Although the proposed model has been elaborated based on the Requirement Engineering phase, it can be easily adapted for any other phase of the software process.

REFERENCES

Amandi, A. A. (1997). Object oriented agent programming. Porto Alegre: CPGCC/UFRGS, 1997. Unpublished doctoral thesis.

Arveson, P. (1999). *The balanced scorecard and knowledge management*. The Balanced Scorecard Institute.

Bassani, P. S., Passerino, L. M., Pasqualotti, P. R., Ritzel, M. I. (2006). Towards a methodological proposal for collaborative education software. *Novas Tecnologias na Educação Magazine, 4*(1).

Berners Lee, T., Cailiau, R., Luotonen, A., Nielsen, H. F., & Secret, A. (1994). The World Wide Web. *Communications of the ACM, 37*(8), 76–82. doi:10.1145/179606.179671

Bittencourt, G. (1998). Distributed artificial intelligence. *Proceedings of the First Workshop of Computing - ITA*.

Bontis, N., Dragonetti, N. C., Jacobsen, K., & Roos, G. (1999). The knowledge toolbox: A review of the tools available to measure and manage intangible resources. *European Management Journal, 17*(4), 391–402. doi:10.1016/S0263-2373(99)00019-5

Castro, J., Alencar, F., & Silva, C. (2006). Agent oriented software engeneering. In Breitman, K., & Anido, R. (Eds.), *Informatics upgrades* (pp. 245–282). Rio de Janeiro: PUC-Rio.

Cordeiro, A. D. (2001). *Conception and implementation of a multiagent system to manage data communication.* Master Thesis, Universidade Federal de Santa Catarina-UFSC.

Davenport, T., & Prusak, L. (1998). *Working knowledge: How organizations manage what they know.* Boston, MA: Harvard Business School Press.

Deloach, S. A. (2001). Analysis and design using MaSE and AgentTool. In *Proceedings of the 12th Midwest Artificial Intelligence and Cognitive Science Conference,* Miami University, Oxford.

Durfee, E. H., Lesser, V. V., & Corkill, D. D. (1989). Trends in cooperative distributed problem solving. *IEEE Transactions on Knowledge and Data Engineering, 1*(1), 63–83. doi:10.1109/69.43404

Feigenbaum, E., Buchanan, B., & Lederberg, J. (1971). On generality and problem solving: A case study using the dendral program. In *Machine intelligence* (*Vol. 6,* pp. 165–190). Edinburgh, UK: Edinburgh University Press.

Ferber, J. (1999). *Multi-agent system, an introduction to distributed artificial intelligence.* Addison-Wesley Publishers.

Franklin, S., & Graesse, A. (1996). Is it an agent, or just a program? A taxonomy for autonomous agents. *Proceedings of the Third International Workshop on Agents Theories, Architecture and Languages.* Springer-Verlag.

Frigo, L. B., Pozzebon, E., & Bittencout, G. (2004). *The role of intelligent agents in intelligent tutoring systems.* World Congress on Engineering and Technology Education, (pp 667-671).

Garcês, R., Freitas, P., Ferreira, N., & Freitas, F. (2006). *Knowledge representation.* Funchal: Technical Report. Madeira University.

Hanna, D. E., Glowacki Dudka, M., & Conceição Runlee, S. (2000). *147 practical tips for teaching online groups: Essentials of Web-based education.* Madison, WI: Atwood Publishing.

Hansen, M. T., Nohria, N., & Tierney, T. (1999). What's your strategy for managing knowledge? *Harvard Business Review, 77*(2), 106–116.

Hansen, M. T., & Von Oetinger, B. (2001). Introducing t-shaped managers: Knowledge management's next generation. *Harvard Business Review, 79*(3), 106–116.

Hinz, V. T. A. (2006). *Proposal for creating an ontology of ontologies.* Master Thesis, Universidade Catholic Pelotas University.

Iglesias, C. A., & Garijo, M. (2005). The agent oriented methodology MASCommonKADS. In Henderson-Sellers, B., & Giorgini, P. (Eds.), *Agented-oriented methodologies* (pp. 46–78). Hershey, PA: IDEA Group Publishing.

Iglesias, C. A. F. (1998). *Definición de uma metodología para el desarrollo de sistemas multiagente.* Tese de Doutorado – Departamento de Ingeniería de Sistemas Telemáticos, Universidad Politécnica de Madrid.

Jennings, N. R. (1996). Coordination techniques for DAI. In O'Hare, G., & Jennings, N. (Eds.), *Foundations of distributed artificial intelligence.* John Wiley and Sons.

Juchem, M., & Bastos, R. M. (2001). *Engenharia de sistemas multiagentes: Uma investigação sobre o estado da arte.* Faculdade de Informática – PUCRS. (Brazil Technical Report Series 014).

Jung, J., & Liu, C.-C. (2003). *Multi-agent system technologies and an application for power system vulnerability.* IEEE, 52-55.

Kock, N. (2000). Sharing interdepartmental knowledge using collaboration technologies: An action research study. *Journal of Information Technology Impact, 2*(1), 5–10.

Luger, G. F. (2004). *Inteligência artificial: Structures and strategies for complex problem solving.* Porto Alegre, Brazil: Bookman.

Maurer, H., & Tochtermann, K. (2002). On a new powerful model for knowledge management and its applications. *Journal of Universal Computer Science, 8*(1), 85–96.

Modro, N. R. (2000). *Intelligent system for financial managing and monitoring for little companies.* Florianópolis, Brazil: UFSC.

Mouritsen, J., Larsen, H. T., & Bukh, P. N. D. (2001). Intellectual capital and the capable firm: Narrating, visualizing and numbering for managing knowledge. *Accounting, Organizations and Society, 26*, 735–762. doi:10.1016/S0361-3682(01)00022-8

Navega, S. (2005). Techniques for knowledge computer representation. Retrieved from http://www.intelliwise.com/reports/info2005.pdf

Nery, II. de A., & Gonçalves, F. V. (2004). AORML–a laguage for modelling a multiagent application: An application on Expertcop System. In *X encontro de iniciação à pesquisa, fortaleza.*

Odell, J. D., Parunak, H. V. D., & Bauer, B. S. V. (2001). *Representing agent interaction protocols in UML.* 22nd International Conference on Software Engineering (ISCE), (pp. 121–140).

Oliveira, H. M. (2000). *Techniques for project and implementation of software agents.* (Technical report, Maringá State University).

Paraiso, E. C. (1997). *Proposal of a multagent environment for controlling and monitoring of industry processes.* Master Thesis, Cefet-PR.

Peirce, C. S. (1990). *Semiotics.*

Rezende, S. O. (2003). *Intelligent systems: Foundations and application.*

Russell, S., & Norvig, P. (1995). *Artificial intelligence: A modern approach* (2nd ed.). New Jersey: Prentice-Hall.

Schreiber, G., Akkermans, H., Anjewierden, A., de Hoog, R., Shadbolt, N., van de Velde, W., & Wielinga, B. (2000). *Knowledge engineering and management: The CommonKADS methodology.* MIT Press.

Stewart, T. A. (2002). *The case against knowledge management. Business 2.0 Magazine.* Porto Alegre, Brazil: Artes Médicas.

Sveiby, K. E. (1997). *The new organizational wealth: Managing & measuring knowledgebased assets.* San Francisco, CA: BerrettKoehler Publishers, Inc.

Werneck, V. M. B., Pereira, L. F., Silva, T. S., Almentero, E. K., & Cysneiros, L. M. (2006). *An evaluation of the MAS-CommonKADS methodology.* Second Workshop on Software Engineering for Agent-oriented Systems - SEAS.

Wikinoff, M., & Padgham, L. (2004). The Prometheus methodology. In Bergenti, F., Gleizes, M.-P., & Zambonelli, F. (Eds.), *Methodologies and software engineering for agents systems: The agent-oriented software engineering handbook.*

Wooldridge, M. (1999). Intelligent agents. In Weiss, G. (Ed.), *Multiagent systems: A modern approach to distributed artificial intelligence.* Cambridge, MA: The MIT Press.

Zambonelli, F., Jennings, N., Omicini, A., & Wooldridge, M. (2000). Agent oriented software engineering for Internet applications. In Omicini, A., Zambonelli, F., Klush, M., & Tolksdorf, R. (Eds.), *Coordination of Internet agents: Models, technologies and applications* (pp. 326–346). Springer Verlag.

Zambonelli, F., Jennings, N. R., & Wooldridge, M. (2000). Organizational abstractions for the analysis and design of multi-agent systems. In *Proceedings of the 1st International Workshop on Agent-Oriented Software Engineering*, Limerick, Ireland. (pp. 127–141).

Zambonelli, F., Jennings, N. R., & Wooldridge, M. (2005). Multi-agent systems as computational organizations: The Gaia methodology. In Henderson-Sellers, B., & Giorgini, P. (Eds.), *Agented-oriented methodologies* (pp. 136–171). Hershey, PA: IDEA Group Publishing.

Section 2
Design Patterns, Components, Services and Reuse

Chapter 7
Towards Understanding the Use of Patterns in Software Engineering

Pankaj Kamthan
Concordia University, Canada

ABSTRACT

There are a number of avenues of articulating experiential knowledge, including patterns. However, the mere availability of patterns does not lead to their suitable use, if at all. In order to establish a systematic approach for using patterns, a pattern stakeholder model and a general, process environment-neutral and domain-independent pattern usage model are proposed, and the relationships between them are underscored. The underlying essential and accidental concerns in putting patterns into practice by pattern stakeholders are highlighted and, in some cases, possible resolutions are suggested. In particular, challenges in acquisition, selection, and application of patterns are discussed.

INTRODUCTION

The reliance on the knowledge garnered from past experience can be crucial for solving problems in any development. In the past couple of decades or so, *patterns* (Buschmann, Henney, & Schmidt, 2007) have emerged as one kind of knowledge (Kamthan, 2010) that has proven to be effec-

tive. Indeed, over the years, patterns have been 'discovered' and subsequently used in a variety of domains (Rising, 2000), including software engineering.

There are both academic and industrial implications of patterns. For experts, patterns have been useful as means of reference; for novices, patterns have been useful as means for guidance. It has been suggested (Elssamadisy, 2007) that, if used appropriately, patterns contribute to business

DOI: 10.4018/978-1-60960-509-4.ch007

values such as reduction in cost and reduction in time to market.

This chapter views patterns as conceptually reusable experiential knowledge that provides value. However, the mere availability of any kind of knowledge, in itself, is not sufficient for its appropriate usage, and the same applies to patterns. The valuative aspect of patterns is also not realized automatically. Indeed, an inappropriate use of patterns can compromise the benefits of using them, and has been termed as 'pattern pathology' (LaVigne, 2009). For an objective and sustainable use of patterns, it is crucial that their usage be approached systematically.

The rest of the chapter is organized as follows. First, the background necessary for further discussion is given and related work is presented. Then, conceptual models for stakeholders of patterns and for usage of patterns are proposed, and the prospects and concerns in a commitment to patterns are analyzed. Next, directions for future research, including challenges in addressing them, are outlined. Finally, concluding remarks are given.

BACKGROUND

In this section, basic terminology related to patterns is given and related work is presented.

An Overview of the Pattern Domain

The *pattern domain* is the universe of discourse for all things related to patterns. The *pattern body of knowledge (PBOK)* is the set of fundamental concepts, activities, and results that characterize the pattern domain.

In the last two decades or so, the PBOK has grown and the scope of concepts in it has broadened. There is currently no single source, reference model, or standard for the PBOK. Therefore, to define the terminology needed for the chapter, this section relies on selected publications (Bus-

chmann, Henney, & Schmidt, 2007; Coplien, 1996; Meszaros & Doble, 1998) that can be considered as authoritative.

Basic and Ancillary Concepts in the PBOK

There are certain basic concepts in PBOK that are of interest. A *pattern* is an empirically proven solution to a recurring problem that occurs in a particular context.

A *pattern application domain* is the area of study to which a pattern corresponds to. A pattern always corresponds to some pattern application domain, even if that domain is implicit.

An *anti-pattern* suggests a 'negative' solution to a given problem. It occurs when the context of the problem is not understood or the underlying forces are not optimally balanced.

Concepts in the PBOK related to Multiple Patterns

There are certain concepts in PBOK that arise due to the existence of multiple patterns. The *patternsphere* consists of all available patterns in any medium.

A *pattern collection* is a set of patterns that are specific to some pattern application domain and correlated in some manner.

If P_1 and P_2 are two patterns in the patternsphere that address the same problem, then P_1 and P_2 are *pattern complements*. For example, the LINKS pattern, the TRANSCLUSION pattern, and the VIEWS pattern (Correia et al., 2009) are pattern complements.

It may not be feasible to provide a single solution to a 'large' problem. In such a case, the problem is considerately partitioned into a manageable collection of smaller problems. A *pattern language* is a collection of patterns that are closely related to each other through their individual contexts and contribute towards a common goal. Thus, a pattern language solves a larger problem than that possible by any individual pattern. For example, a

Figure 1. A pattern sequence that traverses through three pattern collections

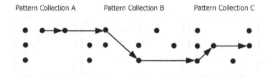

pattern language is a pattern collection; however, the converse is not necessarily the case in general.

Concepts in the PBOK related to Pattern Description

There are certain concepts in PBOK related to a pattern description. A *pattern description* is a set of indicative statements that specify a pattern.

A pattern description, if structured, typically consists of a number of *elements*. The name element of a pattern is an evocative identifier that often reflects the nature of the solution; the author element gives the identity of the pattern author(s); the context element provides the situation or pre-conditions within which the problem occurs; the forces element provides the constraints that are resolved for arriving to a solution; the solution element provides an abstract, general, and reusable solution to the problem and is shown to work in practice via an examples element; the resulting context element provides the consequences or post-conditions of applying the solution; and the related patterns element outlines any other pattern(s) to which a pattern is related to in some way. The labels of elements can vary across pattern community and other (optional) elements, such as those related to metadata, may be included to enrich a pattern description. It is this explicit structure that makes patterns more than a mere collection of problem-solution pairs, and makes them unique and more practical in their applicability among other kinds of experiential knowledge such as guidelines. A pattern is usually referred to by using its name. In this chapter, the name

of a pattern is presented in uppercase in order to distinguish it from the surrounding text.

A *pattern form* is a prescription of a specific set of pattern elements that are expected to appear in a pattern description. A number of pattern forms targeted for different pattern application domains have been proposed (Coplien, 1996).

Concepts in the PBOK related to Usage of Patterns

There are certain concepts in PBOK that are related to the usage of patterns. A *pattern thumbnail* is a succinct depiction of a pattern. For example, a pattern thumbnail could be textual or graphical. The information included in a pattern thumbnail is a proper subset of that in a pattern description.

A *pattern documentation* is a document describing how a specific pattern can (and even should) be used. It could be noted that, for the sake of this chapter, the terms 'pattern description' and 'pattern documentation' are not synonymous (and therefore not interchangeable).

A *pattern sequence* is a sequence of patterns through one or more pattern collections. Figure 1 illustrates an abstract example of a pattern sequence. A *pattern sequence map* is (usually, a two-dimensional) graphical illustration of a pattern sequence. A *pattern story* is an instance of a pattern sequence.

For example, consider the use of patterns in the elicitation of actors in use case modeling (Kamthan & Shahmir, 2009). The actors are identified using the CLEAR CAST OF CHARACTERS pattern (Adolph et al., 2003). The number of roles is kept to a minimum using the FEW ROLES pattern (Coplien & Harrison, 2005). If two (or more) actors play different roles toward a single use case, then the MULTIPLE ACTORS: DISTINCT ROLES pattern (Adolph et al., 2003) can be used. If two (or more) actors play the same role toward a use case, then this role can be reflected by a single actor inherited by the actors sharing the role using the MULTIPLE ACTORS: COMMON ROLE pattern (Adolph et al., 2003).

Figure 2. A pattern sequence map showing two pattern sequences that emanate during elicitation of actors in a pattern-oriented process for use case modeling

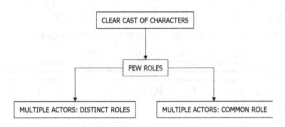

Figure 2 illustrates these two a concrete pattern sequences that traverse through two different pattern collections.

A Brief History of Patterns in Software Engineering

In this section, a short, chronological, and inevitably selective, history of patterns in software engineering is provided. A historical account of patterns in software engineering has been given on a number of occasions previously (Coplien, 1996; Gamma et al., 1995). However, these treatments have focused almost exclusively on software engineering, and disregarded its cognate disciplines such as human-computer interaction.

1970s. The development in other engineering fields, especially building engineering, has had a strong influence on software engineering, at least in the early stages of the discipline. It is therefore relatively unsurprising that the introduction of patterns for urban planning and architecture (Alexander, 1979; Alexander, Ishikawa, & Silverstein, 1977) formed an input to the inception of patterns in software engineering.

1980s. The significance of patterns in participatory design, as it applies to human-computer interaction, was known in the mid 1980s (Hooper, 1986). However, the 'formal' introduction of patterns in software engineering came in the late 1980s in the form of a pattern language consisting of five patterns for user interfaces implemented in the Smalltalk programming language (Beck & Cunningham, 1987). The original impetus for this work, as described elsewhere (Coplien, 1996), came from the fact that Kent Beck was a student at the University of Oregon at the time when Christopher Alexander used patterns to design part of that university's campus (Alexander, 1975).

1990s. The patterns for object-oriented software design (OOSD) got some attention in the early 1990s, in part, due to a doctoral dissertation on the topic (Gamma, 1991), followed by the publication of an article in a broadly read magazine (Coad, 1992). However, patterns for OOSD reached a broad audience only after the publication of a book that would become a 'classic' on the subject (Gamma et al., 1995). The book was also timely in the sense that, in the early 1990s, software engineering as discipline was undergoing a paradigm change, and there was increasing awareness of object-orientation in general and C++ in particular.

The focus on the area of OOSD was soon followed by attention on other areas including patterns for software architecture (Buschmann et al., 1996), user interface design (Coram, & Lee, 1996), and patterns for higher-level concerns beyond software design, including organizational- and process-level concerns (Coplien, 1996).

By the mid 1990s, the patterns in software engineering had reached the mainstream. The patterns and pattern languages that followed thereafter focused on different areas of the software engineering body of knowledge.

Related Work on Using Patterns in Software Engineering

In this section, a chronological account of previous work on using patterns in software engineering is given. The advantages of using patterns and, to a lesser extent, the disadvantages of using patterns have been articulated in the current literature.

In one of the earliest report on the experience of using patterns in software engineering (Riehle

& Züllighoven, 1996), it is emphasized that an appropriate use of patterns requires experience since patterns themselves emerge from experience. It has also been suggested that the approach for describing a pattern depends on the intended usage of the pattern and, to illustrate that, three pattern forms are compared.

There is an argument (Cline, 1996) in favor and against the use of patterns for OOSD (Gamma et al., 1995). It points to the lack of communicability of certain pattern names, lack of mapping pattern classification schemes to the mental models of pattern consumers, and difficulties in learning, all of which still persist. However, the focus, at times, is on accidental (for example, stating that "patterns are over hyped") rather than essential concerns regarding patterns.

It has been shown (Wendorff, 2001) by a number of examples that a lack of experience in using patterns for OOSD (Gamma et al., 1995) can lead to a sacrifice of the advantages, especially those related to flexibility, that these patterns are expected to offer. In particular, it has been pointed out that misunderstanding a pattern has the potential of misapplication of that pattern.

There are comparisons of patterns to guidelines (Wesson & Cowley, 2003). In doing so, the advantages and disadvantages of using patterns are highlighted. However, the conclusions are based on patterns for a specific domain, namely electronic commerce (e-commerce), and some statements made therein (for example, "guidelines are short, and patterns are long") are not necessarily relevant.

The difficulties faced by novices in using patterns for OOSD (Gamma et al., 1995) have been pointed out (Jalil & Noah, 2007). In particular, the difficulties faced by the students have been attributed to a lack of guidance in using patterns.

Finally, it has been advocated (Kotzé, Renaud, & van Biljon, 2008) that patterns are means for "transferring experience in a standard, understandable, and reusable way." However, this is only partially correct and not automatic.

ON FORMULATING AN UNDERSTANDING OF USING PATTERNS IN SOFTWARE ENGINEERING

In this section, a conceptual model for the possible stakeholders of a pattern, including those that are the target for using patterns, is presented. This is followed by a conceptual model for using patterns.

A Pattern Stakeholder Model

The purpose of a pattern stakeholder model (PSM) (Kamthan, 2010) is to create an understanding of stakeholders and, in doing so, that of the pattern community at-large.

Pattern Community

The *pattern community* is the group of people in society that are interested in patterns or pattern-related activities for some reason. The pattern community, as some surveys (Deng, Kemp, & Todd, 2005; Henninger & Corrêa, 2007; Kruschitz & Hitz, 2010; Manolescu et al., 2007) indicate, is burgeoning. A *pattern person* is a member of the pattern community.

The composition of the pattern community has changed over the years. In particular, the pattern community has become increasingly heterogeneous. In the 1990s, the pattern community essentially consisted of programmers, software designers, and user interface designers. In the 2000s, the pattern community expanded to include educators, other professionals and digital natives.

A *digital native* (Palfrey & Gasser, 2008; Prensky, 2001) is a person who was born at the time digital technologies were taking shape and/or has grown up with digital technologies. These digital technologies include those that underlie the current non-stationary computing devices as well as the Internet in general and the Web in particular. It can be expected that digital natives will be an integral part of the pattern community as it evolves.

The composition of the pattern community varies with respect to the pattern application domain. It appears that the 'sub-communities' of macro-architecture, micro-architecture, and interaction design patterns, and pedagogical patterns for computer science and software engineering education, are currently the most active.

Pattern Stakeholders

A *pattern stakeholder* is a person who has interest in a specific pattern for some purpose. The set of all stakeholders of a pattern is a proper subset of the set of members of the pattern community. The possible stakeholders of patterns can be identified and classified into *pattern producers* and *pattern consumers* based upon their roles with respect to a pattern. The union of the set of pattern producers and pattern consumers is equal to the set of pattern stakeholders.

Pattern Producers

There are four essential pattern producers that can be identified. A *pattern author* is a person responsible for authoring a pattern. It is expected that a pattern author typically owns the intellectual property rights (IPR) to the pattern. A *pattern evaluator* is a person responsible for evaluation and feedback on a pattern. A *pattern engineer* is a person responsible for providing means for

describing a pattern. A *pattern administrator* is a person responsible for maintenance and management of patterns.

Pattern Consumers

There are four essential pattern consumers that can be identified. A *pattern perceiver* is a person targeted for perceiving a pattern. A *pattern browser* is a person targeted for browsing a pattern. A *pattern reader* is a person targeted for reading a pattern. A *pattern user* is a person targeted for using a pattern.

The same person can take upon different roles, and the same role can be taken upon by different persons. For example, a person reading a pattern plays the role of a pattern reader but, given the write permission, can (at least in part) play the role of a pattern administrator.

The set of all stakeholders of a pattern is a proper subset of the set of members of the pattern community. For example, a pattern person may belong to the pattern community but, for any given pattern, may neither be a pattern producer, nor a pattern consumer.

Figure 3 illustrates a subset of the set of all stakeholder classes of a pattern by means of a UML Class Diagram.

Characteristics of the PSM

There are certain unique characteristics of the PSM that can be highlighted. The pattern stake-

Figure 3. A taxonomy of stakeholders of a pattern

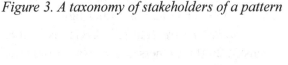
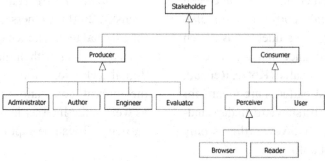

holders are not necessarily mutually exclusive. For the sake of this chapter, browsing is a form of casual scanning (of the description of a pattern) that may not have a predetermined, specific goal. Thus, browsing is a weaker form of reading. Furthermore, for information to be browsed or read, it is necessary that it be first perceived in some modality. Therefore, a pattern browser or a pattern reader is always a pattern perceiver; the converse is not necessarily true. In addition, a pattern evaluator or a pattern user is always a pattern reader; the converse is not necessarily the case.

Figure 3 provides only one view of the PSM. It is possible to make other kinds of salient relationships between pattern stakeholder classes explicit, as illustrated in Figure 4.

Extensions of the PSM

The PSM can be extended in different directions. These directions are discussed in some detail in the following.

Extending the Taxonomy of Pattern Stakeholders

The taxonomy of pattern stakeholders in Figure 3 is intentionally limited and could be extended in both 'horizontal' and 'vertical' directions by increasing the granularity of pattern stakeholder classes. For example, a person sponsoring, financing, or supervising a pattern engineering project could be considered as a producer (specifically,

Figure 4. The relationships between some of the pattern stakeholder classes

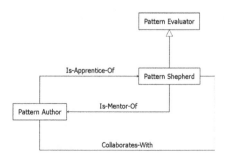

say, a *pattern manager*) but has not been included as one of the sub-classes of pattern stakeholders. Indeed, if there is a need to manage a large number of pattern stakeholders (say, multiple collaborating pattern authors) and there is a need to manage a large number of patterns (say, using a *pattern management system* (PMS)), a separate role of a pattern manager may be required. In such a case, some of the responsibilities of a pattern administrator would also be delegated to the pattern manager.

The granularity of the pattern evaluator class could be increased. The pattern evaluator class could be sub-classed, say, based on the avenue of evaluation of a pattern, into pattern shepherd and pattern Writers' Workshop participant. *A pattern shepherd* is responsible for mentoring a pattern author, and evaluating and providing feedback on a pattern. (Figure 4 illustrates the relative positioning of the pattern shepherd class with respect to other pattern stakeholder classes.) A *pattern Writers' Workshop participant* is responsible for evaluating and providing feedback on a pattern.

The granularity of the pattern user class could also be increased, say, by sub-classing it based on the user's level of knowledge and skill of usage of the pattern into *beginner pattern user* and *advanced pattern user*, or based on the user's context of usage of the pattern into *work-related pattern user* and *non-work-related pattern user*. For example, a person using a pattern for writing a program as an academic exercise at an educational institution or developing open source software (OSS) as a hobby is a non-work-related pattern user.

Creating an Understanding of Individual Pattern Stakeholders

The PSM presents the pattern stakeholders as *abstractions*. However, the concrete pattern stakeholders are heterogeneous in nature, and have individual personality traits such as abilities, goals, preferences, and so on. This information could be expressed *explicitly*.

For example, a pattern user model such as a *persona* could be useful for a pattern author in producing a pattern description; conversely, a pattern user may benefit from being aware of certain information on pattern authors such as their contact information, areas of expertise, their individual (but pattern-related) blogs, and so on.

Prospects of Using Patterns in Software Engineering

In this section, advantages emanating from a commitment to patterns are considered. The primary aspects of software engineering are project, people, process, and product. There are a variety of resources to assist in these different aspects. These resources include patterns, as illustrated in Figure 5.

Software Engineering: Patterns Everywhere

There are problems and corresponding solutions at every level, from the most general to the most specific, of each of the aspects of software engineering, namely project, people, process, and product. In other words, software engineering can be viewed as a collection of 'problem-solution' pairs. This problem solving view is a starting point for the realization of *patterns at any scale* in software engineering, as illustrated in Figure 6. It is evident that the occurrence of such problem-

solution pairs need not be symmetric across different aspects.

The problems-solutions at higher levels can give rise to, as well as constrain, the problems-solutions at lower levels. These levels could be organizational, managerial, or technical.

For example, consider an organization that needs to abide by a national law such as the Section 508 Amendment to the Rehabilitation Act of 1973 of the United States government. This need can be expressed as a relatively higher level problem-solution pair, say, (P, S). Then (P, S) will lead to the specification and realization of accessibility requirements in the underlying software system, say, in the form of relatively lower level problem-solution pairs $\{(P_1, S_1), ..., (P_n, S_n)\}$.

There can be software engineering problems, especially those in new types of software systems, for which currently there are no patterns. However, as implied by surveys (Henninger & Corrêa, 2007; Kruschitz & Hitz, 2010), the number of patterns is proliferating and therefore the patternsphere is growing.

Development of Software Systems: Opportunities for Collaboration

There are a number of approaches for *collaborative software development*, one of which is participatory design (Schuler & Namioka, 1993).

Figure 6. The pervasiveness of patterns at all scales in software engineering

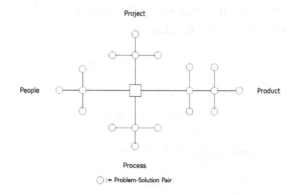

Figure 5. There are patterns to assist in project, people, process, and product aspects of software engineering

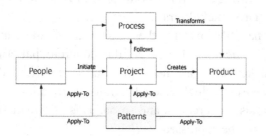

In participatory design, users are *first-class* in the sense that they are active participants in development. This involvement is especially important for parts of a software system that directly impact users such as the structure and behavior of the user interface.

It has been suggested (Coplien, 1996; Borchers, 2001) that pattern-oriented software development aims to empower *users*. Furthermore, it is acknowledged that these users may not be technically-oriented and may not be knowledgeable in the pattern application domain. Indeed, the informality of a pattern description (Alexander, Ishikawa, & Silverstein, 1977) is intended to favor the involvement of such users during development.

Development of Software Systems: Growth in Productivity

It is known that productivity is one of the attributes of people quality (Fenton & Pfleeger, 1997). The three characteristics of patterns that make them especially suitable for software projects are communicability, practicality, and reusability. There is a *potential* for improvement in productivity by using patterns, provided that the benefits of conceptual reuse outweighs the costs.

However, an improvement in productivity is contingent on a number of factors, including the following: the ability of a pattern user to understand the pattern description, especially the context of the problem and the solution; that a pattern user learns to use the pattern effectively; and that the solution suggested by the pattern be free of any errors. There is cost to any reuse (Boehm et al., 2001), including conceptual reuse, and the use of patterns is no exception.

Development of Software Systems: Availability of Empirically Proven 'Optimal' Solution

A pattern comes with a *guarantee*. It follows from the definition of a pattern that, for a given prob-

Figure 7. The difference between a pattern, an anti-pattern, and other problem-solution combinations in the sense of the resolution of high-priority forces

lem a pattern user faces in a particular context, there *is* a solution. Furthermore, this solution has been empirically proven to work in real-world situations.

It is expected that a pattern description not only provides a solution but the *rationale* behind the selection of that solution. In particular, as illustrated by Figure 7, the solution suggested by the pattern is the most optimal among the possible solutions in the sense that it resolves high-priority forces. This helps a pattern user, not merely follow, but *understand* a pattern.

A pattern reflects a *pre-defined decision* with trade-offs. It is expected that a pattern description outlines the consequences, including advantages and disadvantages, of a *commitment* to a pattern. This helps a pattern user decide if the benefits of commitment outweigh the costs, and thereby whether to commit to that pattern.

Development of Software Systems: Quality of Product

There are a number of possible views of quality in general and software quality in particular (Wong, 2006). There are also a number of quality models for general software systems such as the ISO/IEC 9126-1:2001(E) Standard and its successor the ISO/IEC 25030:2007(E) Standard. It is expected that the use of patterns aids quality. Indeed, a

Figure 8. The steps in the PUM and their temporal relationships

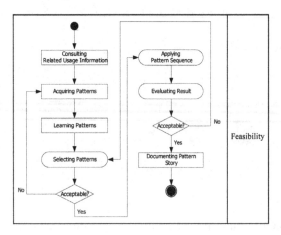

number of software systems have been developed based on this expectation (Kamthan, 2008a; Kamthan, 2008b). A pattern-based inspection method (Schmettow & Niebuhr, 2007) also assumes that interaction design patterns aid usability. There are OOSD that exude 'smells' such as resistance to change, and it has been shown (Brown et al., 1998) that patterns for OOSD can be used during the refactoring process to eradicate such smells.

However, the relationship between quality and patterns is, in general, equivocal (Kamthan, 2009b). This is due to a number of reasons, including the fact that even though the solution of a pattern resolves high-priority forces, it may not resolve other (low-priority) forces.

Software Engineering Education: Transfer of Knowledge

There are a number of reasons for describing a pattern, including pedagogy. By making implicit knowledge explicit gives the 'expert' in the field to communicate the knowledge in solving a problem to a 'novice'. Indeed, patterns have been introduced in software engineering curricula, especially in courses on software architecture and

design at a number of educational institutions over the past decade.

However, currently there is no broadly accepted pedagogical strategy for introducing patterns. It is usually the case that a selected set of patterns from a specific book on patterns are introduced in courses.

A Pattern Usage Model

A view emanating from the axiological viewpoint of a pattern (Kamthan, 2010) is that it provides some *value* to a pattern consumer. There is support for patterns in the design phase of agile methodologies such as Extreme Programming (XP), as well as, other software process environments such as the Object-oriented Process, Environment and Notation (OPEN) and the Unified Process (UP). There are a number of examples of use of patterns in the current literature such as for use case modeling (Kamthan & Shahmir, 2009), interaction design of music exhibits (Borchers, 2001), and development of distributed applications (Kamthan, 2008a; Kamthan, 2008b).

However, currently there is no conceptual model for using patterns. The details of the *process* of using patterns are often hidden or non-existent. This results in the tendency to use patterns merely as templates to mimic rather than to generate alternative solutions to a given problem (Dixon, 2009).

In this section, a domain-independent pattern usage model (PUM) is proposed. Figure 8 provides a graphical illustration of the sequence of steps underlying the PUM means of a UML Activity Diagram.

The steps of the PUM include: *[PUM-S1] Consulting Usage Information, [PUM-S2] Acquiring Patterns, [PUM-S3] Learning Patterns, [PUM-S4] Selecting Patterns, [PUM-S5] Applying Pattern Sequence, [PUM-S6] Evaluating Result,* and *[PUM-S7] Documenting Pattern Story.* These steps are elaborated in the following sections.

[PUM-S1] Consulting Usage Information

If there exists documentation on the pattern, then that could be consulted. For example, there are a number of articles and books on patterns for OOSD (Gamma et al., 1995).

There may be past projects that are similar to the one being currently pursued that may have (1) made their process documentation and/or experience reports (retrospectives) publicly available and/or (2) made use of patterns. For example, patterns for OOSD (Gamma et al., 1995) have been used in industrial software projects (Wendorff, 2001). In such an event, it could be useful to consult pattern-related information included in these resources.

The usage information could be useful in a number of ways, including the following: help elicit the names of patterns used and, if available, pattern sequences and pattern stories; learn about the difficulties, if any, in using patterns; avoid similar mistakes; and so on.

[PUM-S2] Acquiring Patterns

There are a number of patterns available in print and/or electronic mediums. There are handbooks (Rising, 2000) on patterns and surveys (Henninger & Corrêa, 2007) that provide details of distribution of patterns.

In the past decade, there has been a rise in the number of pattern repositories on the Web (Birukou & Weiss, 2009). These are often equipped with facilities for navigation and/or searching, which can be particularly helpful to a beginner pattern user. If available on these pattern repositories, pattern thumbnails can help sort through large collections of patterns.

[PUM-S3] Learning Patterns

It is evident that prior to any use, a pattern needs to be a learnt. There are a number of theories of learning (Jordan, Carlile, & Stack, 2008) and a number of definitions of learnability (Grossman, Fitzmaurice, & Attar, 2009), a topic that is beyond the scope of this chapter.

A successful learning can depend on a number of factors, including the following: the familiarity of the pattern user with the underlying domain, length of the pattern description, the structure of the pattern description, availability of pattern documentation, and so on.

[PUM-S4] Selecting Patterns

This step is the most intricate of all steps. This is because an inappropriate selection may not yield the desirable result. For example, the cost estimates based on use cases can be severely hindered by an incorrect choice of a use case pattern (Issa, Odeh, & Coward, 2006).

The need for selecting patterns arises if, for a given problem, there are two or more candidate patterns, that is, there is existence of pattern complements. The selection of a desirable pattern depends on a number of factors, including the following: the match between the quality requirements of the software system being developed and the forces of the pattern; if the pattern is the first pattern in a pattern sequence or if it is second or later pattern in a pattern sequence; if the candidate selection set is a subset of single pattern collection or if it spans multiple pattern collections; if the pattern is part of a pattern language; maturity level (rating) associated with the pattern, if any; the quality of the pattern description; the viability of the technology, if any, for implementing the pattern solution; the cost of implementing the pattern solution; and so on.

In other words, in general, there are multiple concerns in selecting a pattern. The current approaches for selecting patterns (Weiss, 2008) only consider one or two dimensions, and ignore the others. For example, none of the existing approaches for selecting patterns consider the quality of the pattern descriptions as one of the dimensions.

There are preliminary results on automating the process of selecting an appropriate pattern such as the use of multi-criteria decision making (MCDM)-based expert system (McPhail & Deugo, 2001) or the use of soft goal graphs (Gross & Yu, 2001). However, in general, selecting a pattern remains largely a manual process.

[PUM-S5] Applying Pattern Sequence

This step involves composition of patterns in some order. It is evident that, to obtain desirable result, the selected collection of patterns can not be applied in any arbitrary order. For example, consider a collection of patterns for OOSD that are used during the refactoring process to eradicate a specific design smell (Brown et al., 1998). Then, for obtaining the desirable result at the end of the process, preserving the order of patterns (and thus applying the patterns in a specific sequence) is crucial.

Indeed, certain orders of patterns may not even be possible. For example, the WIZARD pattern (Tidwell, 2005) leads a user through the interface in a stepwise manner for carrying out tasks in a prescribed order. This pattern could, for example, be used for providing a registration process. The CONTEXTUAL HELP pattern (Vora, 2009) describes means for providing context-sensitive help to a user. It is evident that the order of application of these two patterns is not commutative.

[PUM-S6] Evaluating Result

It is known that an evolutionary approach to software development involves an intermediate evaluation and, based on it, subsequent refinement of the product. Therefore, the result upon composition of patterns from [PUM-S5] needs to be evaluated internally and, if necessary, externally. For example, in case of the development of a software system, an internal evaluation could be carried out by the design team and an external evaluation could involve representative

users. In case of interactive systems, the users, for example, can be those that are interviewed for the construction of user models and elicitation of user requirements.

It is evident that the means of evaluation will vary with respect to the product that has been created using the pattern. For example, in case of requirements or design, the means of evaluation usually deployed is inspections.

[PUM-S7] Documenting Pattern Story

There are a number of reasons for documenting pattern stories. The actual use of patterns in a project, if documented, can be useful for communicating the rationale behind the decisions to appropriate stakeholders. The pattern stories can also be useful for project retrospectives and for similar, future projects by the same team, or by other teams.

Indeed, documenting pattern stories also constitutes a civic duty to the pattern community: the *benefits* of using patterns that are authored by *others* can be *reciprocated* by documenting pattern stories. In this sense, this step is related to step [PUM-S1].

In software development, the place for documenting pattern stories is the appropriate process artifact. For example, use case modeling decisions based on patterns, such as those reflected in Figure 2, should be included in the use case specification.

Feasibility

It is evident that the PUM and, by reference, the steps therein should be feasible in order to be practical.

For example, consider [PUM-S2] and [PUM-S3]. The sources of information on patterns or training in patterns are not necessarily free of cost. There is entailing cost to purchasing books or taking courses. Therefore, for the PUM to be feasible, the benefits of acquiring patterns in [PUM-S2] or learning about patterns in [PUM-S3] should outweigh the cost, say, in terms of the time, effort, or capital invested in acquiring or learning those patterns, respectively.

Characteristics of the PUM

There are certain unique characteristics of the PUM that can be highlighted. The steps [PUM-S1] – [PUM-S3] are a prerequisite to actual usage that occurs in [PUM-S4] – [PUM-S6]. The steps [PUM-S2] – [PUM-S6] are mandatory, and the steps [PUM-S1] and [PUM-S7] are optional. The step [PUM-S7] is supposed to assist similar future projects.

Relationship between the Pattern Usage Model and the Pattern Stakeholder Model

The people who use a given pattern are not all the same. In the usage of any pattern, there are different kinds of people, each having different concerns and being impacted in different ways. The knowledge of stakeholders of a pattern is a prerequisite to understanding the usage of that pattern, and thus formulation of a model such as the PUM.

Concerns in Using Patterns in Software Engineering

The apparent 'popularization' of patterns has raised unrealistic expectations (Cline, 1996) that should be addressed for their objective usage. In spite of the advantages emanating from a commitment to patterns, there are certain limitations.

In the following, salient limitations in using patterns in software engineering are highlighted. These limitations are not necessarily mutually exclusive, and impact the realization of the different steps in the PUM.

Quality of Pattern Descriptions

This is related to steps [PUM-S2] – [PUM-S5]. There are a number of patterns available in print and/or electronic mediums. However, the qual-ity of pattern descriptions varies. For example, although the definition of usability that is adopted has not been specified, a number of usability issues of interaction design patterns, such as lack of communicability of pattern names, have been pointed out (Deng, Kemp, & Todd, 2005; Segerståhl & Jokela, 2006).

The quality of the description of a pattern is a key determinant in adopting that pattern for subsequent use. There has been relatively little attention so far on the quality of pattern descriptions (Kamthan, 2009b). Furthermore, currently there is no quality model for pattern descriptions. A list of quality attributes of the solution of a pattern has been given (Lea, 1994; Taibi & Ngo, 2002); however, an examination of current literature suggests that they are not necessarily followed. Furthermore, these quality attributes focus on technical aspects and do not include the social aspects of a pattern description.

There are means for evaluating a pattern. These included, but are not limited to, submission to the Pattern Languages of Programming (or *PLoP) 'family' of conferences that leads to shepherding followed by participation in a Writers' Workshop. There have been reports of other avenues for submitting, evaluating, and subsequently revising a proto-pattern (Leacock, Malone, & Wheeler, 2005; Winters & Mor, 2008). However, currently there are no means for enforcing such an evaluation.

Challenges in Consulting Usage Information on Patterns

This is related to step [PUM-S1]. The proportion of the number of patterns currently available far exceeds the documented experience in using these patterns. For instance, there are examples of pattern stories (Elssamadisy, 2007); however, they are relatively uncommon.

There are number of challenges in locating usage information on patterns. There may not be any documentation on a given pattern for a number of reasons including novelty of the pattern, lack of popularity of the pattern, or economic infeasibility of producing documentation. This can be attributed largely to an inadequate training on pattern documentation. For example, a team may not document its decisions for a number of reasons including that the benefits of recording them are not known or are not valued, information to be recorded is not known or is unclear, and approaches of recording them are not known or are not considered feasible (the perception being that cost > benefits).

It can be expected that, for their own survivability, organizations producing commercial (for-profit) software systems need to retain their competitive advantage. The people working on corresponding projects may also be bound by contractual obligations such as confidentiality agreements. Therefore, it is unlikely that the use of patterns for such projects will ever be publicly documented to any substantial degree or depth. This is reminiscent of the lack of availability to the general public of process artifacts of commercial software systems.

Challenges in Acquiring Patterns

This is related to step [PUM-S2]. There is currently little guidance on acquiring patterns. The significance of the issue was realized early. In spite of the fact that there are 23 patterns for OOSD (Gamma et al., 1995), a relatively small number compared to other pattern collections, it is stated that "it might be hard to find the [design pattern] that addresses a particular design problem especially if the catalogue is new and unfamiliar to you."

The pattern collections are distributed over in print and/or electronic mediums without any apparent order. This can be especially challenging to those who are new or unfamiliar with the pattern collections available. The patternsphere is not static, but proliferating. However, in spite of certain isolated efforts such as PatternForge (http://www.patternforge.net/), there is an absence

of a single source or index pointing to the patterns currently available. In some cases, the existence of a pattern collection is announced (Issa, Odeh, & Coward, 2006) but is not made publicly available.

The patterns names are expected to helpful in locating the pattern descriptions, for example, by means of navigation or searching. However, that may not necessarily be the case. A pattern name may not be evocative or readily findable. For example, there is a pattern named GOOCA (Braga, Rubira, & Dahab, 1999), a not a broadly-known acronym, and may not be easily found, if at all. A pattern name may not be unique across the patternsphere. For example, there is a pattern named PROXY in two different pattern collections (Buschmann et al., 1996; Gamma et al., 1995). In some cases, the pattern name is broad to the point that a pattern name-based index may not be of much use to a beginner pattern user. For example, there are generic pattern names such as AESTHETICS (Graham, 2003), FACE-TO-FACE MEETING (Crumlish & Malone, 2009), and INDEX (B4) (Kunert, 2009). In other cases, the same pattern has been renamed later. For example, the SINGLE POINT OF ACCESS pattern (Yoder & Barcalow, 1997) is now called as the SINGLE ACCESS POINT pattern (Schumacher et al., 2006).

Challenges in Learning Patterns

This is related to step [PUM-S3]. The realization of one of the goals of describing a pattern, namely for an 'expert' to communicate past experience to a 'novice,' is *not* guaranteed a priori. Indeed, there are number of challenges in learning patterns.

A pattern description may not be targeted towards potential pattern readers (Derntl & Motschnig-Pitrik, 2008). For example, this can happen if the description of that pattern does not follow the guidance available for authoring patterns (Harrison, 2003; Meszaros & Doble, 1998). In particular, if the rationale underlying the solution is not provided, then it may be difficult for a pattern reader to obtain a thorough understanding of the pattern, thereby inhibiting learning and leading to the use of the pattern as a 'black-box.'

A pattern reader may not possess the expected level of knowledge of the pattern application domain or of the technology, if any, implementing the pattern solution. For example, the solutions of some of the patterns for OOSD (Gamma et al., 1995) are illustrated using Smalltalk, the Object Modeling Technique (OMT), and/or Message Sequence Charts (MSCs), notations that were common in the mid 1990s. It is less likely that a software engineer trained in this century is familiar with these notations; it is more likely that the engineer has been exposed to Java and the Unified Modeling Language (UML). This is especially likely for software engineers that are digital natives.

Challenges in Selecting Patterns

This is related to step [PUM-S4]. The challenges in selecting a pattern are both technical and social. The selection of an appropriate pattern is non-trivial because, in general, it is a *non-deterministic* problem involving multiple different dimensions listed in an earlier section.

It is also non-trivial to compare pattern complements across different pattern collections or patterns that are similar due to a number of reasons including the absence of a 'standard' for pattern description and the use of different pattern forms (Deng, Kemp, & Todd, 2006) by the pattern authors. The pattern forms currently being followed often vary *lexically*, *syntactically*, and/or *semantically*. For example, there are stark variations between the pattern form originally used to describe the patterns for urban planning and architecture (Alexander, Ishikawa, & Silverstein, 1977), the pattern form originally used to describe the patterns for OOSD (Gamma et al., 1995), and the pattern form originally used to describe the patterns for interaction design (Tidwell, 2005). In particular, the pattern forms in the latter two

cases are 'tied' to their respective pattern application domains.

FUTURE RESEARCH DIRECTIONS

In this section, certain directions for future research, including those directly or indirectly related to the PUM, are highlighted and, in some cases, the challenges in realizing them are given.

Empirical Studies on Using Patterns

There are a number of empirical studies on the availability and distribution of patterns (Deng, Kemp, & Todd, 2005; Henninger & Corrêa, 2007; Kruschitz & Hitz, 2010) in human-computer interaction (HCI). There have been surveys (Bennedsen, 2006) to assess the usage of pedagogical patterns and the attitudes of teachers towards them. However, currently there is a lack of similar studies on the experience in using patterns in software engineering, and constitutes an area of future research interest.

For example, it can be suggested, albeit anecdotally, that the number of documented pattern stories is disproportionately low compared to the cardinality of the patternsphere and, even though this situation is changing, the progress is slow. Furthermore, it appears that the literature on reporting successes in using patterns significantly outnumbers that reporting failures in using patterns. These assertions could be quantified by an empirical study, via interviews, surveys, or other means, organized by pattern application domain, by organization type, by geographical region, and so on.

Usability Engineering of Patterns

The *usefulness* of a software system is a necessary condition for the *acceptability* of a software system by its users and, in turn, both *utility* and *usability* of a software system are necessary for it to be perceived as useful (Grudin, 1992). In the past two decades, significant progress has been made in the usability engineering of software systems in general (Nielsen, 1993) and Web Applications in particular (Nielsen & Loranger, 2006).

It has been pointed out (Taibi & Ngo, 2002) that the usefulness of a pattern is one of its most important quality attribute. If a pattern is viewed as a product (Kamthan, 2010), then the concerns related to its usability could benefit from the literature on software usability (Sears & Jacko, 2008) including approaches for improving usability, incorporating of user feedback, creating user documentation, evaluating usability, and so on. In particular, the implications of usability on [PUM-S1], [PUM-S3], [PUM-S6], and [PUM-S7] are of research interest.

Use of Patterns in New Domains

The number of patterns is only likely to increase, and directions in which PBOK evolves are only likely to expand.

For example, there are new domains in which patterns are constantly being 'discovered.' These include interfaces for Social Web Applications (Crumlish & Malone, 2009) and gestural interfaces (Saffer, 2009). In this evolution, the need for appropriate use of patterns is likely to remain a constant.

ROI on the Use of Patterns

The allocation of finances to resources in the light of inevitable budgetary constraints is one of a number of competing business considerations in any commercial software development. A commitment to resources, such as patterns, entails costs that must therefore be justified.

However, currently there is a lack of studies addressing and calculating the return on investment (ROI) on patterns, and constitutes an area of future research interest. It is natural that a study of the ROI on patterns must take into consider-

ation the steps involved in the PUM, especially, acquisition, learning, and selection of patterns.

Use of Anti-Patterns

There are some reports on the uses (Brown et al., 1998; El-Attar & Miller, 2006) and misuses of anti-patterns (Kotzé, Renaud, & van Biljon, 2008). However, currently there is no conceptual model for using anti-patterns, and constitutes an area of future research interest.

There are a few, albeit limited, uses of anti-patterns. The solution suggested by an anti-pattern is a 'negative' form of guidance, and is therefore not generative (Coplien, 1996). In other words, an anti-pattern can not be used to build software systems. However, an anti-pattern could be used for pedagogical purposes. For example, a teacher could bring to the attention of the students that an anti-pattern is a 'symptom' of a problem that should be avoided. In this sense, a pattern and an anti-pattern can complement each other. A collection of anti-patterns could also act as a supplement to or replacement of guidelines in the conventional use of guidelines-based checklists, and serve as an instrument for software inspections.

CONCLUSION

The mere presence of knowledge is insufficient for its appropriate use. Indeed, in absence of proper guidance, the potential benefits of using available knowledge can be compromised. There is need to study the use of experiential knowledge such as patterns. In doing so, the avenues enabled by an appropriate use of patterns, and challenges along the path of realizing them, should be highlighted. The PUM introduced in this chapter is one step in the direction.

In conclusion, for patterns to remain and continue being viewed as a useful resource in software engineering, it is imperative that their use be documented and made available publicly.

The usage scenarios should include both the successes and failures in using patterns. This chapter, by means of examples from different pattern collections, provides prospective directions for using patterns and challenges in doing so.

REFERENCES

Adolph, S., Bramble, P., Cockburn, A., & Pols, A. (2003). *Patterns for effective use cases*. Addison-Wesley.

Alexander, C. (1975). *The Oregon experiment*. Oxford University Press.

Alexander, C. (1979). *The timeless way of building*. Oxford University Press.

Alexander, C., Ishikawa, S., & Silverstein, M. (1977). *A pattern language: Towns, buildings, construction*. Oxford University Press.

Beck, K., & Cunningham, W. (1987). *Using pattern languages for object-oriented programs*. OOPSLA 1987 Workshop on the Specification and Design for Object-Oriented Programming, Orlando, USA, October 4-8.

Bennedsen, J. (2006). The dissemination of pedagogical patterns. *Computer Science Education, 16*(2), 119–136. doi:10.1080/08993400600733590

Birukou, A., & Weiss, M. (2009). *Patterns 2.0: A service for searching patterns*. The Fourteenth European Conference on Pattern Languages of Programs (EuroPLoP 2009), Irsee, Germany, July 8-12.

Boehm, B. W., Abts, C., Brown, A. W., Chulani, S., Clark, B. K., & Horowitz, E. … Steece, B. (2001). *Software cost estimation with COCOMO II*. Prentice Hall. Braga, A. M., Rubira, C. M. F., & Dahab, R. (1999). *Tropyc: A pattern language for cryptographic software*. (Technical Report IC-99-03), Institute of Computing, University of Campinas, Campinas, Brazil.

Borchers, J. (2001). *A pattern approach to interaction design*. John Wiley and Sons.

Brown, W. J., Malveau, R. C., McCormick, H. W., & Mowbray, T. J. (1998). *AntiPatterns: Refactoring software, architectures, and projects in crisis*. John Wiley and Sons.

Buschmann, F., Henney, K., & Schmidt, D. C. (2007). *Pattern-oriented software architecture, vol. 5: On patterns and pattern languages*. John Wiley and Sons.

Buschmann, F., Meunier, R., Rohnert, H., Sommerlad, P., & Stal, M. (1996). *Pattern oriented software architecture, vol. 1: A system of patterns*. John Wiley and Sons.

Cline, M. P. (1996). The pros and cons of adopting and applying design patterns in the real world. *Communications of the ACM, 39*(10), 47–49. doi:10.1145/236156.236167

Coad, P. (1992). Object-oriented patterns. *Communications of the ACM, 35*(9), 152–159. doi:10.1145/130994.131006

Coplien, J. O. (1996). *Software patterns*. SIGS Books.

Coplien, J. O., & Harrison, N. B. (2005). *Organizational patterns of agile software development*. Prentice-Hall.

Coram, T., & Lee, J. (1996). *Experiences-a pattern language for user interface design*. The Third Conference on Pattern Languages of Programs (PLoP 1996), Monticello, USA, September 4-6, 1996.

Correia, F., Ferreira, H., Flores, N., & Aguiar, A. (2009). *Patterns for consistent software documentation*. The Sixteenth Conference on Pattern Languages of Programs (PLoP 2009), Chicago, USA, August 28-30, 2009.

Crumlish, C., & Malone, E. (2009). *Designing social interfaces: Principles, patterns, and practices for improving the user experience*. O'Reilly Media.

Deng, J., Kemp, E., & Todd, E. G. (2005). *Managing UI pattern collections*. The Sixth ACM SIGCHI New Zealand Chapter's International Conference on Computer-Human Interaction: Making CHI Natural, Auckland, New Zealand, July 7-8, 2005.

Deng, J., Kemp, E., & Todd, E. G. (2006). *Focusing on a standard pattern form: The development and evaluation of MUIP*. The Seventh ACM SIGCHI New Zealand Chapter's International Conference on Computer-Human Interaction: Design Centered HCI, Christchurch, New Zealand, July 6-7, 2006.

Dixon, D. (2009). Pattern languages for CMC design. In Whitworth, B., & de Moor, A. (Eds.), *Handbook of research on socio-technical design and social networking systems* (pp. 402–415). Hershey, PA: IGI Global. doi:10.4018/9781605662640. ch027

El-Attar, M., & Miller, J. (2006). *Matching antipatterns to improve the quality of use case models*. The Fourteenth International Requirements Engineering Conference (RE 2006), Minneapolis-St. Paul, USA. September 11-15, 2006.

Elssamadisy, A. (2007). *Patterns of agile practice adoption: The technical cluster*. C4Media.

Fenton, N. E., & Pfleeger, S. L. (1997). *Software metrics: A rigorous & practical approach*. International Thomson Computer Press.

Gamma, E. (1991). *Object-oriented software development based on ET++: Design patterns, class library, tools*. Unpublished doctoral thesis, University of Zürich, Zürich, Switzerland.

Gamma, E., Helm, R., Johnson, R., & Vlissides, J. (1995). *Design patterns: Elements of reusable object-oriented software*. Addison-Wesley.

Graham, I. (2003). *A pattern language for Web usability*. Addison-Wesley.

Gross, D., & Yu, E. (2001). From non-functional requirements to design through patterns. *Requirements Engineering*, *6*(1), 18–36. doi:10.1007/s007660170013

Grossman, T., Fitzmaurice, G., & Attar, R. (2009). *A survey of software learnability: Metrics, methodologies and guidelines*. The ACM CHI 2009 Conference on Human Factors in Computing Systems (CHI 2009), Boston, USA, April 4-9, 2009.

Grudin, J. (1992). Utility and usability: Research issues and development contexts. *Interacting with Computers*, *4*(2), 209–217. doi:10.1016/0953-5438(92)90005-Z

Harrison, N. (2003). *Advanced pattern writing*. The Eighth European Conference on Pattern Languages of Programs (EuroPLoP 2003), Irsee, Germany, June 25-29, 2003.

Henninger, S., & Corrêa, V. (2007). *Software pattern communities: Current practices and challenges*. The Fourteenth Conference on Pattern Languages of Programs (PLoP 2007), Monticello, USA, September 5-8, 2007.

Hooper, K. (1986). Architectural design: An analogy. In Norman, D. A., & Draper, S. W. (Eds.), *User centered system design: New perspectives on human-computer interaction*. Lawrence Erlbaum Associates.

Issa, A., Odeh, M., & Coward, D. (2006). Using use case patterns to estimate reusability in software systems. *Information and Software Technology*, *48*(9), 836–845. doi:10.1016/j.infsof.2005.10.005

Jalil, M. A., & Noah, S. A. M. (2007). *The difficulties of using design patterns among novices: An exploratory study*. The 2007 International Conference on Computational Science and its Applications (ICCSA 2007), Kuala Lumpur, Malaysia, August 26-29, 2007.

Jordan, A., Carlile, O., & Stack, A. (2008). *Approaches to learning: A guide for teachers.* McGraw-Hill.

Kamthan, P. (2008a). A situational methodology for addressing the pragmatic quality of Web applications by integration of patterns. *Journal of Web Engineering, 7*(1), 70–92.

Kamthan, P. (2008b). Towards high-quality mobile applications by a systematic integration of patterns. *Journal of Mobile Multimedia, 4*(3/4), 165–184.

Kamthan, P. (2009a). A framework for integrating the social Web environment in pattern engineering. *International Journal of Technology and Human Interaction, 5*(2), 36–62. doi:10.4018/jthi.2009092303

Kamthan, P. (2009b). *On the symbiosis between quality and patterns.* The Third International Workshop on Software Patterns and Quality (SPAQu 2009), Orlando, USA, October 25, 2009.

Kamthan, P. (2010). A viewpoint-based approach for understanding the morphogenesis of patterns. *International Journal of Knowledge Management, 6*(2), 40–65. doi:10.4018/jkm.2010040103

Kamthan, P., & Shahmir, N. (2009). *A pattern-oriented process for the realization of use case models.* The Thirteenth IBIMA Conference on Knowledge Management and Innovation in Advancing Economies, Marrakech, Morocco, November 9-10, 2009.

Kotzé, P., Renaud, K., & van Biljon, J. (2008). Don't do this–pitfalls in using anti-patterns in teaching human-computer interaction principles. *Computers & Education, 50*(3), 979–1008. doi:10.1016/j.compedu.2006.10.003

Kruschitz, C., & Hitz, M. (2010). *Analyzing the HCI design pattern variety.* The First Asian Conference on Pattern Languages of Programs (AsianPLoP 2010), Tokyo, Japan, March 16-17, 2010.

Kunert, T. (2009). *User-centered interaction design patterns for interactive digital television applications.* Springer-Verlag.

LaVigne, C. (2009). Pattern pathology. In R. Monson-Haefel (Ed.), *97 things every software architect should know: Collective wisdom from the experts.* O'Reilly Media.

Lea, D. (1994). Christopher Alexander: An introduction for object-oriented designers. *ACM SIGSOFT Software Engineering Notes, 19*(1), 39–46. doi:10.1145/181610.181617

Leacock, M., Malone, E., & Wheeler, C. (2005). *Implementing a pattern library in the real world: A Yahoo! case study.* The 2005 American Society for Information Science and Technology Information Architecture Summit (ASIS&T IA 2005), Montreal, Canada, March 3-7, 2005.

Manolescu, D., Kozaczynski, W., Miller, A., & Hogg, J. (2007). The growing divide in the patterns world. *IEEE Software, 24*(4), 61–67. doi:10.1109/MS.2007.120

McPhail, J. C., & Deugo, D. (2001). *Deciding on a pattern.* The Fourteenth International Conference on Industrial and Engineering Applications of Artificial Intelligence and Expert Systems (IEA/AIE 2001), Budapest, Hungary, June 4-7, 2001.

Meszaros, G., & Doble, J. (1998). A pattern language for pattern writing. In Martin, R. C., Riehle, D., & Buschmann, F. (Eds.), *Pattern languages of program design (Vol. 3*, pp. 529–574). Addison-Wesley.

Nielsen, J. (1993). *Usability engineering.* Morgan Kaufmann.

Nielsen, J., & Loranger, H. (2006). *Prioritizing Web usability.* New Riders Publishing.

Palfrey, J., & Gasser, U. (2008). *Born digital: Understanding the first generation of digital natives.* Basic Books.

Prensky, M. (2001). Digital natives, digital immigrants. *Horizon*, *9*(5), 1–6. doi:10.1108/10748120110424816

Riehle, D., & Züllighoven, H. (1996). Understanding and using patterns in software development. *Theory and Practice of Object Systems*, *2*(1), 3–13. doi:10.1002/(SICI)1096-9942(1996)2:1<3::AID-TAPO1>3.0.CO;2-#

Rising, L. (2000). *The pattern almanac 2000*. Addison-Wesley.

Saffer, D. (2009). *Designing gestural interfaces*. O'Reilly Media.

Schmettow, M., & Niebuhr, S. (2007). *A pattern-based usability inspection method: First empirical performance measures and future issues*. The Twenty First British HCI Group Annual Conference (HCI 2007), Lancaster, U.K., September 3-7, 2007.

Schuler, D., & Namioka, A. (1993). *Participatory design: Principles and practices*. CRC Press.

Schumacher, M., Fernandez-Buglioni, E., Hybertson, D., Buschmann, F., & Sommerlad, P. (2006). *Security patterns: Integrating security and systems engineering*. John Wiley and Sons.

Sears, A., & Jacko, J. A. (2008). *The human-computer interaction handbook: Fundamentals, evolving technologies, and emerging applications* (2nd ed.). Lawrence Erlbaum Associates.

Segerståhl, K., & Jokela, T. (2006). *Usability of interaction patterns*. The CHI 2006 Conference on Human Factors in Computing Systems, Montréal, Canada, April 22-27, 2006.

Taibi, T., & Ngo, C. L. (2002). *A pattern for evaluating design patterns*. The Sixth World Multiconference on Systemics, Cybernetics and Informatics (SCI 2002), Orlando, USA, July 14-18, 2002.

Tidwell, J. (2005). *Designing interfaces: Patterns for effective interaction design*. O'Reilly Media.

Vora, P. (2009). *Web application design patterns*. Morgan Kaufmann.

Weiss, M. (2008). *Patterns and their impact on system concerns*. The Thirteenth European Conference on Pattern Languages of Programs (EuroPLoP 2008), Irsee, Germany, July 9-13, 2008.

Wendorff, P. (2001). *Assessment of design patterns during software reengineering: Lessons learned from a large commercial project*. The Fifth European Conference on Software Maintenance and Reengineering (CSMR 2001), Lisbon, Portugal, March 14-16, 2001.

Wesson, J., & Cowley, L. (2003). *Designing with patterns: Possibilities and pitfalls*. The Second Workshop on Software and Usability Cross-Pollination, Zürich, Switzerland, September 1-2, 2003.

Winters, N., & Mor, Y. (2008). IDR: A participatory methodology for interdisciplinary design in technology enhanced learning. *Computers & Education*, *50*(2), 579–600. doi:10.1016/j.compedu.2007.09.015

Wong, B. (2006). Different views of software quality. In Duggan, E., & Reichgelt, J. (Eds.), *Measuring Information Systems delivery quality* (pp. 55–88). Hershey, PA: Idea Group.

Yoder, J., & Barcalow, J. (1997). *Architectural patterns for enabling application security*. The Fourth Conference on Pattern Languages of Programs (PLoP 1997), Monticello, USA, September 3-5, 1997.

ADDITIONAL READING

Alexander, C. (1964). *Notes on the Synthesis of Form*. Harvard University Press.

Appleton, B. A. (1997). Patterns and Software: Essential Concepts and Terminology. *Object Magazine Online, 3*(5), 20–25.

Coplien, J. O. (1998). Software Design Patterns: Common Questions and Answers. In Rising, L. (Ed.), *The Patterns Handbook: Techniques, Strategies, and Applications* (pp. 311–319). Cambridge University Press.

Derntl, M., & Motschnig-Pitrik, R. (2008). Exploring the User's View on Design Patterns for Technology-Enhanced Learning. The Sixth International Conference on Networked Learning (NLC 2008), Halkidiki, Greece, May 5-6, 2008.

Iba, T. (2007). Creation toward Quality Without a Name - Sociological Analysis of Pattern Language. The First International Workshop on Software Patterns and Quality (SPAQu 2007), Nagoya, Japan, December 3, 2007.

Kohls, C., & Panke, S. (2009). Is That True...? Thoughts on the Epistemology of Patterns. The Sixteenth Conference on Pattern Languages of Programs (PLoP 2009), Chicago, USA, August 28-30, 2009.

Kohls, C., & Uttecht, J.-G. (2009). Lessons Learnt in Mining and Writing Design Patterns for Educational Interactive Graphics. *Computers in Human Behavior, 25*(5), 1040–1055. doi:10.1016/j.chb.2009.01.004

May, D., & Taylor, P. (2003). Knowledge Management with Patterns. *Communications of the ACM, 46*(7), 94–99. doi:10.1145/792704.792705

Sharp, H., Manns, M. L., & Eckstein, J. (2006). Evolving Pedagogical Patterns: The Work of the Pedagogical Patterns Project. *Computer Science Education, 16*(2), 315–330.

Weiss, M., & Birukou, A. (2007). Building a Pattern Repository: Benefiting from the Open, Lightweight, and Participative Nature of Wikis. Wikis for Software Engineering Workshop (Wikis4SE 2007), Montreal, Canada, October 21, 2007.

KEY TERMS AND DEFINITIONS

Explicit Knowledge: A type of human knowledge that has been articulated.

Pattern: An empirically proven solution to a recurring problem that occurs in a particular context.

Pattern Description: A set of indicative statements that specify a pattern.

Pattern Documentation: A document describing how a specific pattern can (and even should) be used.

Pattern Sequence: A sequence of patterns through one or more pattern collections.

Pattern Stakeholder: A person who has interest in a specific pattern for some purpose.

Quality: The totality of attributes of an entity that bear on its ability to satisfy stated and implied needs.

Usability: The capability of a product to be understood, be learned, and be attractive to users, when used under specified conditions.

Chapter 8
Implications of Markup on the Description of Software Patterns

Pankaj Kamthan
Concordia University, Canada

ABSTRACT

The reliance on past experience is crucial to the future of software engineering. There are a number of avenues for articulating experiential knowledge, including patterns. It is the responsibility of a pattern author to ensure that the pattern is expressed in a manner that satisfies the reason for its existence. This chapter is concerned with the suitability of a pattern description for consumption by both humans and machines. For that, a pattern description model (PDM), and a pattern stakeholder model (PSM) and a pattern quality model (PQM) as necessary input to the PDM, are proposed. The relationships between these conceptual models are highlighted. The PDM advocates the use of descriptive markup for representation and suggests the use of presentation markup for presentation of information in pattern descriptions, respectively. The separation of representation of information in a pattern description from its presentation is emphasized. The potential uses of the Semantic Web and the Social Web as mediums for publishing patterns are discussed.

INTRODUCTION

There are different kinds of conceptually reusable experiential knowledge in software engineering (Garzás & Piattini, 2007). In the past few decades, *patterns* (Buschmann, Henney, & Schmidt, 2007b)

have emerged as a kind of knowledge garnered from past experience that has proven to be effective. Indeed, over the years, patterns have been 'discovered' in and applied to a variety of domains (Rising, 2000), including software engineering. For novices, patterns serve as means of guidance; for experts, they serve as means of reference.

DOI: 10.4018/978-1-60960-509-4.ch008

However, any kind of knowledge is only as useful as it is expressed, and the same applies to patterns. The usefulness of a pattern is severely hindered (Kohls & Uttecht, 2009) if it is not described properly. For example, difficulty in reading a pattern description may not be productive and poses an obstacle to any further realization; difficulty in understanding a pattern description presents a potential for its misapplication; difficulty in transforming a pattern description is a hindrance to making it available on different computing environments; and so on.

The rest of the chapter is organized as follows. First, the background necessary for further discussion is given and related work is presented. Then, conceptual models for stakeholders of patterns, quality of patterns, and description of patterns are proposed. Next, directions for future research, including challenges in addressing them, are outlined. Finally, concluding remarks are given.

BACKGROUND

In this section, a synopsis of terminology related to a pattern description and a brief introduction to the notion of markup pertaining to the scope of this chapter are given.

Basics of Patterns

The *pattern domain* is the universe of discourse for all things related to patterns. The *pattern body of knowledge (PBOK)* is the set of fundamental concepts, activities, and results that characterize the pattern domain.

There are certain basic concepts in PBOK that are of interest. A *pattern* is an empirically proven solution to a recurring problem that occurs in a particular context. A *pattern application domain* is the area of study to which a pattern corresponds to. An *anti-pattern* suggests a 'negative' solution to a given problem. A *pattern language* is a collection of patterns that are closely related to each other through their individual contexts and contribute towards a common goal.

There are other concepts in PBOK that are of interest. A *pattern description* is a set of indicative statements that specify a pattern. A pattern description, if structured, typically consists of a number of elements. A *pattern element* is a labeled placeholder for information that accentuates a certain aspect of a pattern. A *pattern form* is a prescription of a specific set of pattern elements that are expected to appear in a pattern description. A *pattern thumbnail* is a succinct depiction of a pattern. A *pattern collection* is a set of patterns that are specific to some pattern application domain and correlated in some manner. For example, a pattern language is a pattern collection; however, the converse is not necessarily the case in general. A *pattern documentation* is a document describing how a specific pattern can (and even should) be used. It could be noted that, for the sake of this chapter, the terms 'pattern description' and 'pattern documentation' are not synonymous (and therefore not interchangeable). A *pattern sequence* is a sequence of patterns through one or more pattern collections. A *pattern story* is an instance of a pattern sequence.

Significance of a Pattern Description

An appropriate pattern description is crucial for a number of reasons. These are discussed in the following.

Relationship of a Pattern Description to Pattern Acquisition

The acquisition of a pattern is one of the integral steps in pattern usage. The knowledge of mere presence of certain patterns, especially in an electronic medium, is not always sufficient for acquiring any of those patterns easily, if at all.

There are three common approaches for seeking a pattern P: (1) the address at which P is located is known and P is available, (2) P can be navigated to, and (3) P can be searched. The underlying representation of a pattern description can play an important role in the ability to search and the underlying presentation of a pattern description can play an important role in the ability to navigate.

Relationship of a Pattern Description to Pattern Learning

The learning of a pattern is one of the integral steps in pattern usage. It has been reported (Jeremić, Jovanović, & Gašević, 2008) that an inadequate structure of a pattern description can pose obstacles towards learning about that pattern.

For example, if for a given pattern, the forces that are resolved to arrive at the solution are not pointed out or are implicit, then the understanding of the reader of that pattern remains incomplete. It is known, in general, that understanding is a necessary condition for learning.

Relationship of a Pattern Description to Pattern Selection

The selection of a pattern is one of the integral steps in pattern usage. If presented with multiple choices, an effective selection of patterns depends on a number of factors including that the forces of respective patterns and the consequences of applying the patterns are explicit. This, evidently, in turn, depends on the expressiveness of the pattern description.

Relationship of a Pattern Description to Pattern Application

The application of a pattern is one of the integral steps in pattern usage. The appropriateness of the pattern description is important for an application of the corresponding pattern.

For example, to apply a pattern sequence, a pattern user must be able to remember the names of the patterns in the sequence. A lack of evocativeness of names can pose an obstacle to application of patterns in the sequence.

Related Work on Pattern Descriptions

The issue of an appropriate description of patterns has been treated previously (Buschmann, Henney, & Schmidt, 2007b; Coplien, 1996; Kohls & Panke, 2009; Kohls & Uttecht, 2009; Meszaros & Doble, 1998). However, the coverage is limited by one or more of the following issues: the relationship between a pattern description and pattern stakeholders is not studied, the relationship of a pattern description to other artifacts is not considered, the issue of the quality of a pattern description is not discussed, the treatment is usually domain-dependent, the concerns of representation and presentation are not separated, and rationale for inclusion/exclusion of pattern elements is not given.

Basics of Markup

The term markup was coined in the late 1960s, and has its origins in scholarly text processing (Coombs, Renear, & DeRose, 1987). According to the ISO 8879:1986 Standard, *markup* is text that is added to the data in order to convey information about it.

In today's computing environment, markup is ubiquitous. The ascent of the Web and especially that of the HyperText Markup Language (HTML), have played an integral role in bringing the notion of markup to the public at-large. Indeed, there is no such thing as "no markup" (Coombs, Renear, & DeRose, 1987): even when it appears that there is no markup, there is punctuational and/or presentational markup.

The term markup language was coined in the early 1970s, and has its origins in the Generalized Markup Language (GML) (Goldfarb, 1981).

Figure 1. A taxonomy of markup

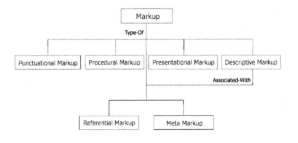

A Classification of Markup

There are different kinds of markup, each serving a certain purpose. A classification of markup has been presented (Goldfarb, 1981) and extended in (Coombs, Renear, & DeRose, 1987). The main categories are: punctuational markup, presentational markup, procedural markup, and descriptive markup. Figure 1 illustrates a taxonomy of markup.

Punctuational Markup

The purpose of punctuational markup is to create delimiters (boundaries). For example, spaces between words indicate word boundaries, commas indicate phrase boundaries, or periods indicate sentence boundaries are all manifestations of punctuational markup. The issues with punctuational markup include the fact that there is ambiguity with respect to variations in usage and appearance.

Presentational Markup

The purpose of presentational markup is to improve communicability in presentation, whether it is in visual or in aural form. For example, bolding a keyword, indenting a quote, centering the title of a book chapter, numbering a page, or emphasizing a word in spoken text by increasing its pitch relative to the others in a sentence are all manifestations of presentational markup. The issues with presentational markup include the fact that the presentation decisions are often ad hoc, and the markup process is repetitive.

Procedural Markup

The purpose of procedural markup is to instruct or provide commands to a document processing system for formatting. For example, {\rtf1\ansi\ {\b Hello World!}} in Rich Text Format (RTF) 1.0 is a directive to the processor to render "Hello World!" in bold typeface, and \parskip 0.25cm in TEX is a directive to the processor to introduce a certain space between preceding and following text. The issues with procedural markup include the fact that it is usually device dependent.

Descriptive Markup

The purpose of descriptive markup is to indicate what a text element is by declaring that a certain portion of text stream is a member of a particular class. For example, <math><ln/><ci>x</ci></math> denotes the natural logarithm function of the variable x.

It is the intention of descriptive markup to be general in its target applications (that may include formatting, say, by mapping onto procedural markup). The descriptive markup is based on a model of text known as the ordered hierarchy of content objects (OHCO) (DeRose et al., 1997) that lends a hierarchical structure to documents. This makes descriptive markup the most general in scope compared to other types of markup.

If used appropriately, the Standard Generalized Markup Language (SGML) and its simplified successor the Extensible Markup Language (XML) are exemplars of descriptive markup. SGML and XML provide machine-readable techniques and constructs for defining descriptive markup languages (Renear et al., 2002).

This chapter advocates the use of descriptive markup for representation of pattern descriptions and the use of presentation markup for presentation of pattern descriptions. The use of these markup types also has implications towards publishing patterns in electronic mediums such as the Social Web and the Semantic Web.

Related Work on Expressing Pattern Descriptions in Markup

The earliest pattern descriptions (Alexander, Ishikawa, & Silverstein, 1977) were expressed in presentation markup. For example, the pattern name is presented in small capitals, the context of a pattern is marked by an ellipsis (.. .), and the contents of problem and solution is separated from the rest of the description by a combination of asterisks (***).

In general, and for the sake of this chapter in particular, descriptive markup is the most suitable among the different types of markup. Therefore, selected notable initiatives for expressing pattern descriptions in descriptive markup are discussed chronologically in the rest of this section.

In one of the earliest efforts to represent patterns for object-oriented software design (OOSD) (Gamma et al., 1995) in SGML, a Pattern Information Markup Language (PIML) is introduced (Ohtsuki et al., 1997). The construction of an SGML DTD for PIML and means to transform the representations to HTML are discussed. However, SGML has no special implication towards dissemination over the Web, the complete grammar is not given, and the markup fragments explicitly mix presentational markup and descriptive markup.

In one of the earliest approaches to represent patterns for OOSD (Gamma et al., 1995) in XML, an XML Document Type Definition (DTD) is given (Deugo & Ferguson, 2001). However, the proposed XML DTD mixes presentational markup and descriptive markup, and is not extensible.

In one of the earliest initiatives to represent interaction design patterns in XML, a Pattern Language Markup Language (PLML) is proposed (Fincher, 2003). The use of PLML for interaction design patterns has been commonly advocated (Deng, Kemp, & Todd, 2006; Henninger & Corrêa, 2007; Kunert, 2009). However, PLML suffers from a number of technical limitations related to expressivity, grammar design, and potential for reuse that have been highlighted in detail elsewhere

(Kamthan, 2006). There have been *proposals*, such as XPLML (Kruschitz, 2009) that, based on previous work (Kamthan, 2006), aim to rectify *some* of the shortcomings of PLML. The details of elements that may contribute to XPLML have been explored (Kruschitz & Hitz, 2010). However, a specification of XPLML is yet to be seen.

ON FORMULATING AN UNDERSTANDING OF THE DESCRIPTIONS OF SOFTWARE PATTERNS

This chapter advocates a systematic approach for pattern descriptions so that they can be consumed by both humans and machines. It is based on the idea that relevant aspects of a pattern description must be identified but separated and treated separately. These aspects of a pattern description are, for example, the information contained in it; the quality of information in it; the structure of its information; the representation of its information; the presentation of its information; its stakeholders; a classification to which it may correspond to, if applicable; its avenue for publication; and its management. In some cases, an aspect is significant enough to necessitate a conceptual model.

In this section, conceptual models for patterns stakeholders and for pattern quality are presented. These are a prelude to a conceptual model for pattern descriptions that is proposed subsequently.

A Pattern Stakeholder Model

A *pattern stakeholder* is a person who has interest in a specific pattern for some purpose. The purpose of a pattern stakeholder model (PSM) (Kamthan, 2010) is to create an understanding of stakeholders and, in doing so, that of the pattern community at-large. This section provides only the essentials of PSM that are needed for this chapter.

The possible stakeholders of patterns can be identified and classified into *pattern producers* and *pattern consumers* based upon their roles with respect to a pattern. The union of the set of pattern producers and pattern consumers is equal to the set of pattern stakeholders.

Pattern Producers

There are four essential pattern producers that can be identified. A *pattern author* is a person responsible for authoring a pattern. A *pattern evaluator* is a person responsible for evaluation and feedback on a pattern. A *pattern engineer* is a person responsible for providing means for describing a pattern. A *pattern administrator* is a person responsible for maintenance and management of patterns.

Pattern Consumers

There are four essential pattern consumers that can be identified. A *pattern perceiver* is a person targeted for perceiving a pattern. A *pattern browser* is a person targeted for browsing a pattern. A *pattern reader* is a person targeted for reading a pattern. A *pattern user* is a person targeted for using a pattern.

Remarks

The same person can take upon different roles, and the same role can be taken upon by different persons. For example, a person reading a pattern plays the role of a pattern reader, however, given the write permission, can (at least in part) play the role of a pattern administrator.

It is possible to extend the PSM is different directions (Kamthan, 2010), for example, by increasing the granularity of some of the classes identified above; a topic that is beyond the scope of this chapter.

A Pattern Quality Model

The mere existence of patterns is insufficient for subsequent action. For a pattern to become open knowledge as a commons, its description needs to satisfy certain social and technical quality requirements.

In this section, a pattern quality model (PQM) is proposed. For the sake of this chapter, quality is defined using the ISO/IEC 9126-1:2001(E) as "the totality of [attributes] of an entity that bear on its ability to satisfy stated and implied needs."

Understanding Quality

It is known that quality is a multi-faceted concept. There are a number of possible viewpoints and views of quality. In one of the earliest approaches towards perceptions of quality (Garvin, 1984), five views of quality are identified: (QV1) the transcendental-based view (quality is perfective), (QV2) the product-based view (quality is measurable), (QV3) the manufacturing-based view (quality is conformance), (QV4) the economics-based view (quality is benefit for cost), and (QV5) the user-based view (quality is satisfaction).

The purpose of a quality model for an entity E is to lend an understanding of the quality of E and to provide, in a systematic manner, means for a subsequent analysis of the quality of E. The topic of quality modeling has a long history, and over the years a number of data quality models, information quality models, and software product quality models have been proposed (Dromey, 2003; Eppler, 2001; Fenton & Pfleeger, 1997). However, there is currently no quality model for patterns (Kamthan, 2009b).

The basic idea behind a quality model is the following. The definition of quality is too general to be useful. It is therefore decomposed into a manageable number of attributes (Fenton & Pfleeger, 1997) that, for the sake of this chapter, are either directly or indirectly relevant to pattern stakeholders. These quality attributes are then organized in some manner.

Related Work on Quality of Patterns

The present initiatives in the direction of addressing the quality of patterns are partial. They can be placed into one or more of the following categories: (1) *domain-specific*, (2) *quality attribute-specific*, (3) *pattern element-specific*, and (4) *pattern description-specific*.

For example, the issue of the quality of some of the elements of a pattern description, irrespective of the domain, has been raised (Meszaros & Doble, 1998; Taibi & Ngo, 2002), and belongs to (3); the issue of the quality of the solution of object-oriented design patterns has been raised (Lea, 1994), and belongs to an intersection of (1) and (3); the issue of the usability of patterns for technology-enhanced learning (TEL) has been raised (Derntl & Motschnig-Pitrik, 2008), and belongs to an intersection of (1), (2), and (4); and so on.

An Approach to Quality of a Pattern

The attention to the quality of a pattern must be addressed during the development step of the *pattern production process* (P3) (Kamthan, 2010).

In the PQM, the issue of quality of a pattern is considered at three different levels: (1) quality concerns when the view involves an individual element of a pattern, (2) quality concerns when the view involves the entire description of a pattern, and (3) quality concerns when the view involves multiple artifacts that include a pattern description. In this chapter, the interest is in the elaboration of the micro-level, namely (1), and macro-level, namely (2). This is illustrated in Figure 2.

Figure 2 suggests that, even though not comparable as such, there are similarities between the quality concerns pertaining to a pattern description and quality concerns pertaining to a software requirements specification (SRS).

Figure 2. The quality concerns of a pattern pertaining to different levels

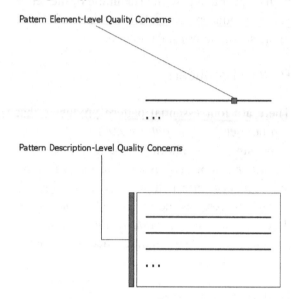

Quality of a Pattern at an Element Level

The quality of a pattern when the view involves an individual element can be considered at different basic elements such as the following:

- **Name.** At the **name** element level, the quality attributes relevant to a pattern consumer are *Evocativeness* (the name should be easy to remember), *Findability* (the name should be easy to find), and *Pronounceability* (the name should be easy to pronounce). The quality attributes relevant to a pattern producer are *Uniqueness* (the name should be unique across the associated pattern collection) and *Weavability* (the name should be such that it can be woven in narrative text). In this chapter, the name of a pattern is presented in uppercase in order to distinguish it from the surrounding text.

- **Context.** At the **context** element level, the quality attributes relevant to both a pattern consumer and to a pattern producer are *Accuracy* (the context should accurately reflect the situation of the problem) and

Completeness (the context should be as completely described as possible).

- **Problem.** At the **problem** element level, the quality attributes relevant to a pattern consumer are *Familiarity* (the problem should be familiar to the reader) and *Recurrence* (the problem should be common in the sense that it repeats). The quality attribute relevant to a pattern producer is *Context-Free-ness* (the problem should be free of specifics pertaining to the context and that context should be described separately from the problem).
- **Force.** At the **force** element level, the quality attributes relevant to a pattern consumer are *Relative Significance Emitability* (each force should be able to indicate its degree of significance relative to other forces) and *Objectivity* (the list of forces should include both the positive and the negative forces). The quality attribute relevant to a pattern producer is *Completeness* (the list of forces should be as complete as possible).
- **Solution.** At the **solution** element level, the quality attributes relevant to a pattern consumer are *Composability* (it should be possible to compose the solution of the pattern with the solutions of two or more patterns if deemed relevant), *Generativity* (the solution should be able to generate instances), and *Empirically Proven Recurrence* (the solution should be derived from actual practical experience in real-world situa-

tions). The quality attribute relevant to a pattern producer is *Abstractness* (the solution should be described at a level of abstraction so as to be general enough).
- **Example.** At the **example** element level, the quality attributes relevant to a pattern consumer are *Currency* (the solution should reflect the state-of-the-art) and *Utility* (the example should be such that it could be used). The quality attribute relevant to a pattern producer is *Demonstrability* (the example should demonstrate the solution).

The list of quality attributes indicated for each patterns element is deemed necessary; however, there is no claim of its sufficiency.

Means

There are means in form of experiential knowledge such as guidelines (Coplien, 1996; Lea, 1994) and patterns (Harrison, 2003; Meszaros & Doble, 1998), as well as, tools for addressing *most* of the quality attributes of aforementioned pattern elements.

This organization is summarized in Table 1.

Quality of a Pattern at the Description Level

For the sake of this chapter, *semiotics* (Chandler, 2007) is the field of study of signs for the purpose of communication to humans and machines. From a semiotics viewpoint (Shanks, 1999), a pattern

Table 1. The quality attributes related to specific pattern elements

Pattern Element	Quality Attribute(s)	Means	
Name	Evocativeness, Findability, Pronounceability, Uniqueness, Weavability	Experiential Knowledge, Tools	Feasibility
Context	Accuracy, Completeness		
Problem	Context-Free-ness, Familiarity, Recurrence		
Force	Completeness, Objectivity, Relative Significance Emitability		
Solution	Abstractness, Composability, Empirically Proven Recurrence, Generativity		
Example	Currency, Demonstrability, Utility		

description can be viewed on six interrelated levels, stacked on each other in the following order: *physical, empirical, syntactic, semantic, pragmatic,* and *social*. In this chapter, the interest is in the elaboration of syntactic, semantic, pragmatic, and social levels. There are different quality concerns at different semiotic levels. The quality attributes relevant to each semiotic level needs to be identified.

Means

There are means in form of experiential knowledge such as guidelines (Coplien, 1996; Lea, 1994) and patterns (Harrison, 2003; Meszaros & Doble, 1998), as well as, tools for addressing *some* of the aforementioned quality attributes.

This organization is shown in Table 2. It can be noted that Table 2 is independent of any pattern form.

Remarks

The inclusion of the quality attributes in Table 2 is based on an examination of the current literature and a number of publicly available pattern descriptions for different domains in different mediums during previous work (Kamthan, 2008; Kamthan, 2009a; Kamthan, 2010). The list of quality attributes in Table 2 is deemed necessary; however, there is no claim of its sufficiency.

In a human-machine environment, it is evident that lower semiotic levels are concerns of a machine, and the higher semiotic levels are concerns

of a human. At a pattern description level, the quality attributes relevant to a pattern consumer are *Accessibility, Attractiveness, Consistency, Syntactic Correctness, Credibility, Expressiveness, Findability, Interoperability, Learnability, Legality, Legibility, Readability, Understandability,* and *Uniguity (Unambiguousness)*, and, the quality attributes relevant to a pattern producer are *Ethics, Modifiability, Portability, Reusability,* and *Traceability*.

For considerations of space, the details, including definitions of the quality attributes in Table 2, have been suppressed. The definitions of some of these attributes can be found in quality standards from the International Organization for Standardization (ISO), the International Electrotechnical Commission (IEC), and/or the Institute of Electrical and Electronics Engineers (IEEE).

Extending the PQM

The classification of the quality attributes in Table 2 can be extended in a number of ways. It is acknowledged that certain quality attributes are relatively broad and can be decomposed further so that they can be addressed better. For example, accessibility is one such quality attribute.

The relationships between quality attributes can be made explicit in a number of ways. It is known that quality attributes could be related to each other in the sense that an attempt to address one could have a positive or negative impact on one or more of the others (Wiegers, 2003). For

Table 2. The quality attributes related to a pattern description and organized by semiotic levels

	Semiotic Level	Quality Attribute(s)		Means	
Pattern Description	Social	Credibility, Ethics, Legality		Experiential Knowledge, Tools	Feasibility
	Pragmatic	Accessibility, Attractiveness, Expressiveness, Findability, Interoperability, Learnability, Legibility, Modifiability, Portability, Readability, Reusability, Traceability, Understandability			
	Semantic	Correctness	Consistency		
			Uniguity (Unambiguousness)		
	Syntactic	Correctness			

Table 3. The steps of the pattern description model

Steps	Means	

1. Deciding the Scope of Information in a Pattern Description
2. Deciding the Structure of a Pattern Description
    (a) Deciding the Mandatory and Optional Pattern Elements
    (b) Deciding the Order and Occurrence of Pattern Elements
3. Addressing the Concerns of Representation of a Pattern Description
    (a) Selecting Means for Producing a Representation of a Pattern Description
4. Addressing the Concerns of Presentation of a Pattern Description
    (a) Selecting Means for Producing a Presentation of a Pattern Description
	PSM, PQM, Experiential Knowledge, Technologies, Tools	Feasibility

example, readability supports understandability, but accessibility and attractiveness do not necessarily support each other.

Feasibility

In order to be practical, an undertaking for tackling the issue of quality of patterns must be feasible. This is especially the case for quality attributes that can not be satisfied but only be *satisficed*. For example, from Table 1 such quality attributes are pronounceability, weavability, and utility, and from Table 2 such quality attributes are attractiveness, credibility, and uniguity.

Relationship between the Pattern Quality Model and the Pattern Stakeholder Model

The knowledge of pattern stakeholders, including their needs and preferences, is necessary towards helping create an understanding of the meaning of the quality of a pattern, and is thereby an input to the PQM.

In the PQM, the selection of human-specific quality attributes of a pattern description, and the organization of these attributes as shown in Table 1, specifically the pragmatic and social levels, are both inspired by the needs of pattern stakeholders.

A Pattern Description Model

From an epistemological viewpoint (Kamthan, 2010), a pattern is implicit knowledge made

explicit by means of a pattern description. A high-level view of a pattern description model (PDM) is given in Table 3. The PDM outlines a number steps to, with the assistance of means, to produce a pattern description.

Feasibility

In order to be practical, an undertaking for describing patterns must be feasible. There is an inevitable cost to a commitment to both representation and presentation of a pattern. For example, there is curve involved in learning a representation or a presentation language, and any tools that go with it. The cost of a commitment to XML has been explored elsewhere (Harold, 2003; Megginson, 2005).

Means

The PSM and the PQM form an input to the PDM, and the relationships between these models are discussed later. The technologies and tools for the PDM are also considered later.

There is experiential knowledge available that can help in deciding the different aspects of a pattern description. For example, there are a number of patterns for scoping the information in a pattern description, structuring a pattern description (Harrison, 2003; Meszaros & Doble, 1998), representing a pattern description (Correia et al., 2009; Rüping, 2003), and presenting a pattern description (Meszaros & Doble, 1998). However, for a given problem, a suitable pat-

Figure 3. The description of a pattern depends on the selection of patterns, and vice versa

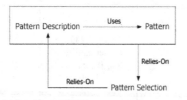

tern still needs to be selected. The selection of a suitable pattern depends on a number of factors including the quality of its description. Figure 3 illustrates this *symbiotic* relationship between a pattern description and the selection of patterns.

In the following, the steps of the PDM are discussed in detail.

Step 1. Deciding the Scope of Information in Pattern Description

This step involves deciding the information that should be internal and, by reference, deciding the information that should be external to a pattern description. A pattern description, by necessity, is a kind of social entity: it resides in an environment with other artifacts. Figure 4 illustrates a number of artifacts related to a pattern description.

For example, upon realization of the P3, a pattern description may point to the pattern author description, the pattern license description, the pattern application domain glossary and, if necessary, other pattern descriptions. Indeed, there is a GLOSSARY pattern (Meszaros & Doble, 1998; Rüping, 2003) and, to support the patterns for OOSD, a glossary for OOSD (Gamma et al., 1995). Furthermore, upon publication, a pattern description may also point to pattern feedback and, upon successful use, point to pattern story documentation. In case of a hypermedia environment, such as the Web, these ancillary descriptions could be hyperlinked. This is a realization of the TRANSCLUSION pattern (Correia et al., 2009).

Step 2. Deciding the Structure of Pattern Description

This step involves deciding an appropriate structure for a pattern description so that it can be effectively processed by both humans and machines.

Figure 4. A pattern description is related to other kinds of descriptions

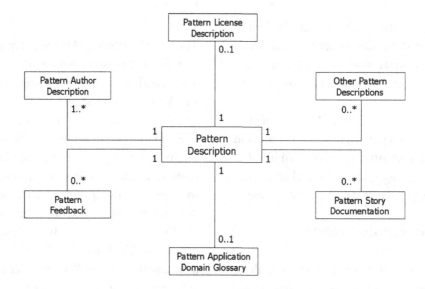

Pattern Elements

The pattern elements provide means to structure a pattern description locally. There are a number of possible pattern elements, each with a unique label assigned by a pattern author. A number of issues need to be considered in the decision to include a specific pattern element in a pattern description.

Step 2 (a). Decide the Mandatory and Optional Pattern Elements

There is no pre-determined, fixed list of pattern elements. There are some pattern elements that are indispensable to any pattern description, irrespective of the underlying pattern application domain. For example, *Name, Context, Problem, Force, Solution*, and *Example* should be mandatory elements. There are also certain pattern elements, the inclusion of which enriches a pattern description that, in turn, can be useful for a pattern consumer. For example, *Name of Pattern Classification* is not always applicable and therefore should be an optional element.

There is experiential knowledge available for deciding mandatory and optional elements. For example, the MANDATORY ELEMENTS PRESENT and OPTIONAL ELEMENTS WHEN HELPFUL patterns (Meszaros & Doble, 1998) suggest that certain pattern elements can either be mandatory or be optional, respectively.

In general, increasing the number of pattern elements in a pattern description increases the granularity of the structure and the expressiveness of the pattern description. However, increasing the number of pattern elements also increases the authoring effort and, in some cases, increases the file size of the pattern representation.

Step 2(b). Decide the Order and Occurrence of Pattern Elements

The order of pattern elements may or may not be significant. For example, to preserve the logical order of reading, the problem element *must* occur before the solution element. The order of other

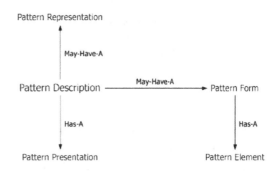

Figure 5. The relationships between a pattern description, pattern form, pattern representation, and pattern presentation

pattern elements such as the author element is relatively flexible.

Furthermore, the cardinality of a pattern element should be decided. There are some pattern elements that must occur only one time, and others that can occur one or more times. For example, a pattern name must occur only once but pattern force can occur multiple times.

Pattern Form

A pattern form reflects the global structure of a pattern description. Figure 5 shows the possible relationships between a pattern description, pattern form, pattern representation, and pattern presentation.

A pattern description may or may not correspond to any *known* pattern form. For example, the patterns included in a number of collections (Fowler et al., 2003; Morville & Callender, 2010) do not follow any known pattern form.

Characteristics of a Pattern Form

A pattern form must suggest a specific set of pattern elements. Figure 6 shows the two main constituents of a pattern form, namely the mandatory pattern elements and the optional pattern elements.

There is no universally accepted set of mandatory or optional pattern elements. It is therefore possible to have a variety of pattern forms. Indeed, a survey (Kruschitz & Hitz, 2010) has shown that

Figure 6. The constituents of a pattern form

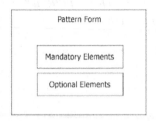

there are multiple pattern forms in use by the authors of interaction design patterns.

A pattern form may be independent of or dependent on a pattern application domain. For example, the pattern form introduced in one case (Alexander, Ishikawa, & Silverstein, 1977) is independent of its pattern application domain, namely urban planning and architecture; however, the pattern form introduced in another case (Gamma et al., 1995) is dependent on its pattern application domain, namely OOSD.

A pattern description in an electronic medium can benefit from meta-information such as information on license, version control, modification history, keywords, and so on. However, currently there is no pattern form that suggests any pattern elements related to meta-information.

Pattern Form and Pattern Stakeholders

For pattern stakeholders, the presence of a pattern form has several advantages. However, it also has a few disadvantages. These are elaborated in the following.

- **Pattern Form and Pattern Administrator.** A pattern form must include a certain number of pattern elements. This helps the machine processing of a pattern description in a variety of ways. For example, a pattern description can be manipulated for different purposes, such as, extraction of text to create a pattern thumbnail. This aids a pattern administrator.

- **Pattern Form and Pattern Author.** A pattern form *imposes* a definite structure on a pattern description. This aids a pattern author. For example, a pattern author can use a specific a pattern form as a *template* for authoring patterns. There are pattern application domain-specific pattern forms (Appleton, 1997; Buschmann, Henney, & Schmidt, 2007b; Coplien, 1996; Deng, Kemp, & Todd, 2006). In some cases, there are multiple pattern forms for the *same* pattern application domain. The presence of multiple pattern forms gives pattern authors a choice. However, a commitment to a pattern form may be perceived by pattern authors as an impediment to 'free form' authoring, and thereby limiting creativity.

- **Pattern Form and Pattern User.** A pattern form makes the 'boundaries' of the pattern solution clear. This is important in using a pattern, and therefore aids a pattern user. However, for a pattern user, the existence of pattern descriptions in different pattern forms poses obstacles towards comparison and composition of patterns, especially if a pattern element in one pattern form is not present in another pattern form or does not have an equivalent in another pattern form.

- **Pattern Form and Pattern Reader.** If adopted and applied to all the patterns in a collection, a pattern form can lend a consistent structure to the descriptions of patterns in that collection. This, in turn, contributes to familiarity of the structure on part of a pattern consumer, and it is known that familiarity aids usability. For example, upon reading different descriptions of patterns that belong to the same collection, a pattern reader can be assured that certain elements are present, in a certain order, in each pattern description.

- **Pattern Form and Pattern Browser.** A pattern form can aid browsing. For example, if presented appropriately, a pattern

Figure 7. The relationships between a pattern description, pattern representation, and pattern presentation

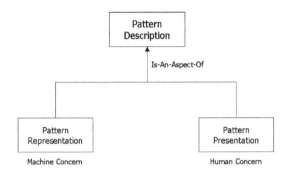

Table 4. A representation of a fragment of a pattern description and its corresponding presentation

Representation	Presentation
<xml version="1.0" encoding="UTF-8"?> <pattern> <!-- ... --> <author> <firstname>John</firstname> <lastname>Vlissides</lastname> </author> <!-- ... --> </pattern>	*John Vlissides*

description can be scanned and skipped to desirable areas, such as to specific pattern elements. This aids a pattern browser.

Step 3. Addressing the Concerns of Representation of a Pattern Description

There are number of concerns in the representation of information in a pattern description, some of which are addressed in the following.

Representation versus Presentation of a Pattern Description

For the sake of this chapter, a *representation* is some data that encodes information about resource state (Jacobs & Walsh, 2004) and a *presentation* is a rendering of an entity using some means, in some medium, and in a specific modality.

There are a number of differences between a representation and a presentation of a pattern description. In general, a pattern description may or may not have a representation but it must have a presentation. For example, a pattern description on paper is not concerned with representation. The respective aims of representation and presentation of a pattern description are different. As shown in Figure 7, a pattern representation is targeted for consumption by a machine, while a pattern presentation is targeted for consumption by a human (specifically, a pattern consumer).

An example illustrating the differences between representation and presentation of a pattern description is shown in Table 4.

Significance of Separating the Concerns of Representation and Presentation of a Pattern Description

The representation and presentation are two different views of the same entity, and need to be treated differently. There are a number of limitations of mixing representation and presentation. A mix of structure and style of information has a negative impact on readability and modifiability. For example, a pattern reader, due to visual impairment or otherwise, may wish to make adjustments to text in order to improve readability, or a pattern administrator may wish to programmatically make modifications to text at a number of places. However, these may not be readily possible if the presentation semantics is hard-coded.

For the sake of argument, let the name Christopher Alexander occur several times in text, across multiple documents in HyperText Markup Language (HTML) in the following form: <p>...<font face="Tahoma" color="Navy" size="2">Christopher Alexander</font>...</p>. If in the future any modifications to the name are to be made, such as presenting the first and last name differently, then doing so automatically or semi-automatically can be difficult, especially due to the fact that there is no 'standard' for expressing a person's name.

Remarks

The separation of structure of information from the presentation of information has been advocated in a number of contexts: it is one of the principles of Web Architecture (Jacobs & Walsh, 2004), it is advocated by the MODEL-VIEW-CONTROLLER (MVC) pattern (Buschmann et al., 1996), and it is one of the principles of descriptive markup (Goldfarb, 1981).

Step 3 (a). Selecting Means for Producing a Representation of a Pattern Description

This step involves selecting a suitable means for producing a representation of a pattern description. There are a number of means for representation of information in general. The criteria for selecting means for representation of information constitute a number of anthropological, sociological, and technical factors involving pattern producers (Kamthan, 2010). There is no a priori guarantee that a means satisfying the criteria will be available.

Natural Languages versus Formal Languages for Pattern Descriptions

In the past decade or so, as patterns become increasingly pervasive, the languages used for expressing pattern descriptions have gained attention (Taibi, 2007). The comparison between natural languages versus general- or special-purpose formal specification languages for expressing pattern descriptions is, incidentally, similar to the case of selecting a particular language for expressing software requirements (Aurum & Wohlin, 2005).

The Advantages and Limitations of Natural Languages for Pattern Descriptions. There are arguments in favor of the use of a natural language for expressing a pattern description: natural language is highly expressive that, in turn, is important as the notion of a pattern applies to any, including non-technical, domain; and natural language is a means of communication that is familiar to all stakeholders that, in turn, does not require any special training for authoring patterns and supports human-centered methodologies for collaborative development such as participatory design (Alexander, Ishikawa, & Silverstein, 1977). There are also arguments against the use of a natural language for expressing a pattern description: there is high potential for the presence of ambiguities in the information contained in the pattern description as natural languages are inherent ambiguous; and there are limits towards automatic processing.

The Advantages and Limitations of Formal Languages for Pattern Descriptions. There are arguments in favor of the use of a formal specification language for expressing a pattern description: the information contained in certain elements of a pattern description can be expressed precisely; and the information has low potential for being ambiguous. There are also arguments against the use of a formal specification language for expressing a pattern description: it is not possible and, in some cases, not recommended, to formally express the information contained in all the elements of a pattern description; the formal notation may be specific to a pattern collection for a particular domain and non-transferable to pattern collections for other domains; it may not provide any means, natively or otherwise, for managing pattern collections; and it may require special tool support that may not be mature, may not be readily available, or may not easily integrate within the daily environment of a software engineer.

Use of XML for Representing Patterns

This chapter uses descriptive markup in general and XML in particular as the basis for representing patterns. In doing so, it strikes a *balance* between natural and formal languages. However, there are both advantages and disadvantages of the use of XML for representing patterns.

The Advantages of the Use of XML for Representing Patterns. The use of XML has been advocated in a number of contexts, especially those related to the Web (Jacobs & Walsh, 2004). In this section, the inherent advantages in using XML for representing patterns (Kamthan,

& Pai, 2006a) are considered. Using XML, it is possible to semi-formalize the structure of a pattern representation and, to a certain extent, constrain the information type of a pattern representation. XML is based on Unicode. This is necessary for the support of a variety of characters including those from different natural languages and mathematical symbols. The specification of XML is open. XML has a broad support in the industry and in other contexts such as Open Source Software (OSS) development community. This has led to the development of a range of commercial and non-commercial tools for a variety of tasks including authoring, processing, and archiving XML instance documents. XML is designed for the Internet. For example, XML is not dependent on any specific device, operating system, network, or programming language. Furthermore, XML instance documents can be disseminated on the Internet and processed by tools even if these instance documents do not refer to the grammar that they correspond to. This is in contrast to SGML.

The Limitations of the Use of XML for Representing Patterns. There is a cost to a commitment to any technology, and XML is no exception. In this section, the inherent limitations in using XML for representing patterns are highlighted. The specification of XML provides little on its own, which is both its strength and weakness. (This is a direct consequence of the transition from SGML to XML, a discussion of which is beyond the scope of this chapter.) The responsibility for the aspects that are deemed necessary for the definition of (descriptive) markup languages but are not provided by XML has been relegated to other technologies. These aspects include character encoding, language support, disambiguation of elements and attributes from multiple different markup languages in a single instance document, and so on. Therefore, a commitment to XML means reliance, by necessity, on other specifications. This increases the learning time and learning curve. These ancillary technologies must work collectively. This in turn increases the

processing load. The specification of XML does not provide directions for use of markup so as to support pragmatic and social quality. Therefore, a user of XML may need to rely on other sources for an effective use of markup (Harold, 2003; Megginson, 2005). This increases the learning time and learning curve. For some, authoring XML instance documents by hand may be tedious and error-prone, and therefore tool support may be necessary. The introduction of descriptive markup in text increases the number of characters, and therefore the file size. In other words, the same text expressed in XML will always be larger than the text without the markup in XML.

Step 4. Addressing the Concerns of Presentation of a Pattern Description

There are number of concerns in the presentation of information in a pattern description, some of which are addressed in the following.

Step 4 (a). Selecting Means for Producing a Presentation of a Pattern Description

This step involves selecting a suitable means for producing a presentation of a pattern description. There are a number of means for presentation of information in general. The criteria for selecting means for presentation of information constitute a number of anthropological, sociological, and technical factors involving pattern consumers (Kamthan, 2010). There is no a priori guarantee that a means satisfying the criteria will be available.

From Representation to Presentation

It is possible to produce a presentation from a representation of a pattern description. The ability to produce multiple presentations from a single representation has a number of advantages. If carried out automatically, partially or completely, it reduces effort on part of the pattern producers towards modifying and publishing a pattern description.

Figure 8. The normative source of the representation of a pattern is transformed for the purpose of presentation onto one or more abstract targets

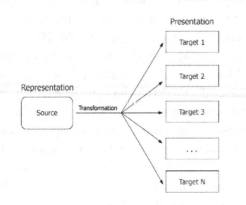

Figure 9. The representation of a pattern is transformed for the purpose of presentation onto one or more concrete targets

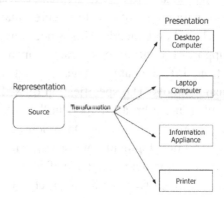

Let **R** be the set of representation sources, let **P** be the set of presentation targets, and let **T** be the set of transformers (that is, the thing that conducts a transformation such as a style sheet, a script, or a program). Then, a transformation is given by T: R → P, T(R) = P, where T is a member of **T**, R is a member of **R**, and P is a member of **P**.

There are a number of information technologies currently available for carrying out the intended transformation of a representation of a pattern R in XML (input) to a presentation P (output). The candidates for a transformer T include, for example, the Cascading Style Sheets (CSS), Extensible Stylesheet Language Transformations (XSLT), Streaming Transformations for XML (STX), and XQuery. If the output is such that none of these special-purpose options are viable, then a program in some general-purpose programming language for carrying out the intended transformation needs to be written.

The information technologies for presenting P include, for example, a profile of the Extensible HyperText Markup Language (XHTML) such as XHTML 1.1 and XHTML Basic 1.1, which are targeted for the Web and the Mobile Web, respectively; the (Wiki) Creole 1.0, which is targeted for the Social Web (Kamthan, 2009a); the Windows Help File format, which are targeted for a electronic book reader or a desktop computer;

and the Portable Document Format (PDF), which is targeted for a number of devices including a electronic book reader and a printer.

Figure 8 illustrates the relationship between a representation and an abstract presentation of a pattern.

There are a number of concrete presentation targets of interest. These target types include both stationary and non-stationary devices. For the sake of this chapter, a notebook computer is synonymous with a laptop computer and a personal digital assistant (PDA) or a smartphone is a kind of information appliance. Figure 9 illustrates some concrete presentation possibilities.

This 'one-representation-to-many-presentations' is a direct consequence of one of the principles of descriptive markup (Goldfarb, 1981). It is also a manifestation of the single source approach as suggested by the SINGLE SOURCE pattern (Correia et al., 2009) and the SINGLE SOURCE AND MULTIPLE TARGETS pattern (Rüping, 2003).

Relationship between the Pattern Description Model and the Pattern Stakeholder Model

It has been pointed out (Kunert, 2009; Meszaros & Doble, 1998; Van Welie & Van der Veer, 2003) that a pattern description should be authored from the perspective of the pattern stakeholders. It is therefore evident that the underlying stakeholders of a pattern description be identified and studied.

Relationship between the Pattern Description Model and the Pattern Quality Model

A pattern description must satisfy certain quality requirements for it to be acceptable by its stakeholders. For that, any effort for developing a pattern description needs to refer to an understanding of the quality of a pattern, that is, a pattern quality model such as the PQM.

The relationships between the quality attributes in Table 2 and three aspects of a pattern description, namely representation, presentation, and pattern form can be made explicit. There are some quality attributes that are related to the representation of a pattern description; however, others are beyond the scope of the representation of a pattern description. For example, findability and reusability are related to representation, but attractiveness, credibility, and ethics are beyond the scope of representation. There are some quality attributes that are related to the presentation of a pattern description; however, others are beyond the scope of the presentation of a pattern description. For example, attractiveness, credibility, and findability are related to presentation, but ethics and reusability are beyond the scope of presentation. Finally, there are some quality attributes that are related to a pattern form; however, others are beyond the scope of a pattern form. For example, findability is related to the type of pattern form, but attractiveness is beyond the scope of any pattern form.

FUTURE RESEARCH DIRECTIONS

In this section, certain directions for future research, including those directly or indirectly related to the PDM, are highlighted and the challenges in realizing them are given.

Towards the Specification of a Pattern Markup Language

The conceptual models presented in this chapter, especially the PSM, PQM, and PDM, can serve as an input for specifying a pattern markup language (PML) based on XML. PML is a result of a mapping from the pattern domain to XML domain (that includes a 'family' of technologies). For example, a pattern representation in the pattern domain is a PML instance document in the XML domain. To do that, an engineering approach is recommended (Kamthan, 2006), that is, requirements for PML need to be expressed, and based on that design and implementation need to be realized. The resulting PML grammar and PML instance documents should go through inspection and testing for quality evaluation.

The following is a sketch of the design process of such a PML, and constitutes an area of future research interest. The specification of PML should aim to conform to quality assurance guidelines for markup languages (Dubost et al., 2005). The structural constraints imposed by mandatory and optional pattern elements can be expressed as XML elements by appropriate grammar engineering. There are guidelines and patterns for grammar engineering that can serve as input. To directly support machine processing and indirectly support human consumption, there can be a need for PML to include other XML elements that are not necessary pattern elements. For example, certain meta-information elements can be such non-pattern elements. The properties that make an XML element unique are reflected by the attributes associated with that element. Therefore, suitable attributes need to be decided upon. To determine the final list of elements and attributes leads, inevitably, to the classical 'elements versus attributes' debate in specifying markup languages based on (SGML or) XML. The needs of a pattern representation will be one of the important factors in selecting a schema language, and a suitable grammar for PML is likely to be based on a combination of multiple schema languages. There are a number of XML schema languages including, but not limited to, Document Type Definition (DTD), XML Schema Definition Language (XSDL), and RELAX-NG. The issue of extensibility of PML should be a consideration in grammar engineering. For example, the resulting PML grammar can be made reusable-by-parts through modularization and reusable-as-a-whole by other means such as an include mechanism. The pattern elements in the PML conforming instance document will make the pattern form explicit. Finally, to provide an interface of PML to the external world, an Internet media type, a namespace name prefix, and filename extension need to be proposed.

Towards a Pattern Publishing Model

The purpose of publishing a pattern is dissemination. There are a number of concerns in formulating a pattern publishing model, and the appropriateness of the medium is one of the invariable concerns. The current commonly deployed mediums of publishing information are print and electronic, each of which has its own advantages and disadvantages.

From 1970s to about mid-1990s, the medium of choice for publishing patterns, almost exclusively, was the print medium. In the past decade or so, the medium of choice for publishing patterns has been the electronic medium, specifically the Web, in some cases in addition to and in other cases as an alternate to, the print medium.

The evolution of the Web has had an impact on publishing patterns. In particular, there are two non-mutually exclusive directions for a pattern publishing model, namely the one that uses the Semantic Web as a medium and the one that uses the Social Web as a medium.

On the Viability of the Semantic Web as a Publishing Medium for Patterns

The Semantic Web has emerged as a perceived extension of the current Web that adds technological infrastructure for better knowledge representation, interpretation, and reasoning (Hendler, Lassila, & Berners-Lee, 2001). It is a *machine-oriented extension* of the Web.

There are useful implications of the Semantic Web for patterns. For example, a formal representation of a pattern language as an ontology in the Web Ontology Language (OWL) enables better opportunities for organization and inferencing than that is possible by conventional means (Kamthan & Pai, 2006b). There are certain notable constraints of such an ontology. For example, using an OWL ontology, it is possible to declare that two patterns belong to two disjoint classes, specify the properties of relationships between two patterns, and so on.

However, ontological representation of uncertainty in relationships between patterns is non-trivial. Furthermore, the familiarity of the pattern consumers with the query language used by the ontology reasoners and the ease of formulating complex queries are among the challenges that remain.

On the Viability of the Social Web as a Publishing Medium for Patterns

The Social Web, or as it is more commonly referred to by the pseudonym Web 2.0 (O'Reilly, 2005), is the perceived evolution of the Web in a direction that is driven by 'collective intelligence,' realized by information technology, and characterized by user participation, openness, and network effects. It is a *human-oriented extension* of the Web.

There are a number of implications of Social Web for patterns (Kamthan, 2009a). It can provide a medium in which a pattern description can be produced, archived/retrieved, and modified if necessary. It can also open new vistas for publishing

Figure 10. A pattern description points, by means of hyperlinking or otherwise, to the pattern application domain glossary in a decentralized environment of the Social Web

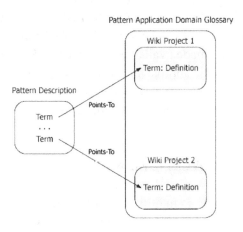

Figure 11. A tag cloud embedded in the description of the MODEL-VIEW-CONTROLLER pattern

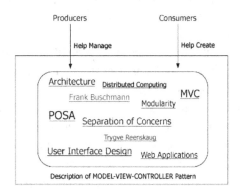

patterns. For example, in order to assist a pattern reader and to reduce ambiguity, a pattern description could be, as pointed out earlier, supplemented with a glossary in the Wiki environment. This is illustrated in Figure 10.

The term *commons* (Hess & Ostrom, 2007) refers to resources that are collectively owned. The Social Web can open new avenues for an effective use of patterns as a commons (Kamthan, 2009a). For example, it could be useful to examine the impact of blogs on the usage information on patterns, and the impact of folksonomies (generated by social tagging) on the acquisition and selection of patterns.

Figure 11 (Kamthan, 2009a) shows a tag cloud for the MODEL-VIEW-CONTROLLER (MVC) pattern (Buschmann, Henney, & Schmidt, 2007a)

Figure 12. The symbiotic relationship between patterns and the Social Web

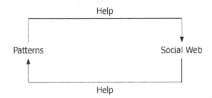

pattern. The tags in the tag cloud are aimed at different things: some are about concepts, others are about disciplines, and yet others are about people. For instance, Separation of Concerns is a software engineering principle, POSA is the acronym for Patterns for Software Architecture, Frank Buschmann is one of the authors of the book that describes MVC, and Trygve Reenskaug is the person who is ascribed for first introducing MVC.

There is a symbiotic relationship between patterns and the Social Web (Kamthan, 2008): on one hand, the Social Web presents an environment for managing patterns; on the other hand, there are patterns that can be used to develop a pattern management system based on the Social Web. Figure 12 illustrates this relationship.

Indeed, patterns for developing different Social Web applications have been introduced in recent years including that for collaborative software (Schümmer & Lukosch, 2007), mashups (Ogrinz, 2009), and Wiki systems (Mader, 2008). However, there are a number of social and technical concerns (Kamthan, 2009a; Whitworth, 2009) that must be addressed in order for the Social Web to become the medium of choice for patterns.

Description of Anti-Patterns

There is increasing literature on anti-patterns (Brown et al., 1998; El-Attar & Miller, 2006;

Kotzé, Renaud, & van Biljon, 2008). For example, an anti-pattern could be used for pedagogical purposes and as an instrument for software inspections.

An anti-pattern can be described in two different ways (Appleton, 1997): (1) a description of a negative solution to a recurring problem that occurs in a particular context, or (2) a description of the situation in (1) along with the solution that rectifies it. There are a few reports on the descriptions of anti-patterns for object-oriented design (Brown et al., 1998) and use cases (El-Attar & Miller, 2006). A description of an anti-pattern is different from that of a pattern. However, there is currently no conceptual model for the descriptions of anti-patterns, and constitutes an area of future research interest. If deemed appropriate, an anti-pattern description is yet another artifact that a pattern description could point to, thereby extending Figure 4.

CONCLUSION

It is imperative that any knowledge that is intended to be used by others should be described in a manner that it is reachable to it target audience, and patterns are no exception. In particular, a proper description of a pattern has broad implications for subsequent actions including acquisition, learning, comparison, selection, and application of the pattern.

A proper description of a pattern is a multi-dimensional concern, and a number of steps need to be carried out to address it. The relevant stakeholders of a pattern need to be identified. The quality issues, at both atomic level (namely, element level) and at the molecular level (namely, description level) that are critical to pattern stakeholders need to be considered. The concerns involving representation and presentation of a pattern description need to be separated. A pattern description needs to be structured at an adequate level of granularity. The granularity should be such that it exposes the basic elements of a pattern description that have been found useful over the years by pattern stakeholders. Finally, a description language needs to be selected.

In conclusion, in order to realize their full potential, patterns need to be described appropriately and made available subsequently. For that, a systematic approach for pattern descriptions in form of a conceptual model can be useful, and the PDM is one step in that direction.

ACKNOWLEDGMENT

The author is grateful to Terrill Fancott for early impetus and feedback, and the reviewers for suggestions on improvement.

REFERENCES

Alexander, C., Ishikawa, S., & Silverstein, M. (1977). *A pattern language: Towns, buildings, construction*. Oxford University Press.

Appleton, B. A. (1997). Patterns and software: Essential concepts and terminology. *Object Magazine Online, 3*(5), 20–25.

Aurum, A., & Wohlin, C. (2005). *Engineering and managing software requirements*. Springer-Verlag. doi:10.1007/3-540-28244-0

Brown, W. J., Malveau, R. C., McCormick, H. W., & Mowbray, T. J. (1998). *AntiPatterns: Refactoring software, architectures, and projects in crisis*. John Wiley and Sons.

Buschmann, F., Henney, K., & Schmidt, D. C. (2007a). *Pattern-oriented software architecture, volume 4: A pattern language for distributed computing*. John Wiley and Sons.

Buschmann, F., Henney, K., & Schmidt, D. C. (2007b). *Pattern-oriented software architecture, volume 5: On patterns and pattern languages*. John Wiley and Sons.

Buschmann, F., Meunier, R., Rohnert, H., Sommerlad, P., & Stal, M. (1996). *Pattern oriented software architecture, volume 1: A system of patterns*. John Wiley and Sons. Chandler, D. (2007). *Semiotics: The basics*, 2nd ed. Routledge.

Coombs, J. H., Renear, A. H., & DeRose, S. J. (1987). Markup systems and the future of scholarly text processing. *Communications of the ACM, 30*(11), 933–947. doi:10.1145/32206.32209

Coplien, J. O. (1996). *Software patterns*. SIGS Books.

Correia, F., Ferreira, H., Flores, N., & Aguiar, A. (2009). *Patterns for consistent software documentation*. The Sixteenth Conference on Pattern Languages of Programs (PLoP 2009), Chicago, USA, August 28-30, 2009.

Deng, J., Kemp, E., & Todd, E. G. (2006). *Focusing on a standard pattern form: The development and evaluation of MUIP*. The Seventh ACM SIGCHI New Zealand Chapter's International Conference on Computer-Human Interaction: Design Centered HCI, Christchurch, New Zealand, July 6-7, 2006.

Derntl, M., & Motschnig-Pitrik, R. (2008). *Exploring the user's view on design patterns for technology-enhanced learning*. The Sixth International Conference on Networked Learning (NLC 2008), Halkidiki, Greece, May 5-6, 2008.

DeRose, S. J., Durand, D. G., Mylonas, E., & Renear, A. H. (1997). What is text, really? *Journal of Computer Documentation, 21*(3), 1–24. doi:10.1145/264842.264843

Deugo, D., & Ferguson, D. (2001). *XML specification for design patterns*. The Second International Conference on Internet Computing (IC 2001), Las Vegas, USA, June 25-28, 2001.

Dromey, R. G. (2003). Software quality-prevention versus cure? *Software Quality Journal, 11*(3), 197–210. doi:10.1023/A:1025162610079

Dubost, K., Rosenthal, L., & Hazaël-Massieux, D. Henderson, L. (2005). *QA framework: Specification guidelines*. World Wide Web Consortium (W3C) Recommendation.

El-Attar, M., & Miller, J. (2006). *Matching anti-patterns to improve the quality of use case models*. The Fourteenth International Requirements Engineering Conference (RE 2006), Minneapolis-St. Paul, USA. September 11-15, 2006.

Eppler, M. J. (2001). The concept of information quality: An interdisciplinary evaluation of recent information quality frameworks. *Studies in Communication Sciences, 1*(2), 167–182.

Fenton, N. E., & Pfleeger, S. L. (1997). *Software metrics: A rigorous & practical approach*. International Thomson Computer Press.

Fincher, S. (2003). The ACM CHI 2003 Workshop Report Perspectives on HCI Patterns: Concepts and Tools (Introducing PLML). *Interfaces, 56*, 26–28.

Fowler, M., Rice, D., Foemmel, M., Hieatt, E., Mee, R., & Stafford, R. (2003). *Patterns of enterprise application architecture*. Addison-Wesley.

Gamma, E., Helm, R., Johnson, R., & Vlissides, J. (1995). *Design patterns: Elements of reusable object-oriented software*. Addison-Wesley.

Garvin, D. A. (1984). What does product quality really mean? *MIT Sloan Management Review, 26*(1), 25–43.

Garzás, J., & Piattini, M. (2007). *Object-oriented design knowledge: Principles, heuristics and best practices*. Hershey, PA: Idea Group.

Goldfarb, C. F. (1981). *A generalized approach to document markup*. The ACM SIGPLAN SIGOA Symposium on Text Manipulation, Portland, USA, June 8-10, 1981.

Harold, E. R. (2003). *Effective XML*. Addison-Wesley.

Harrison, N. B. (2003). *Advanced pattern writing*. The Eighth European Conference on Pattern Languages of Programs (EuroPLoP 2003), Irsee, Germany, June 25-29, 2003.

Hendler, J., Lassila, O., & Berners-Lee, T. (2001). The Semantic Web. *Scientific American, 284*(5), 34–43. doi:10.1038/scientificamerican0501-34

Henninger, S., & Corrêa, V. (2007). *Software pattern communities: Current practices and challenges*. The Fourteenth Conference on Pattern Languages of Programs (PLoP 2007), Monticello, USA, September 5-8, 2007.

Hess, C., & Ostrom, E. (2007). *Understanding knowledge as a commons: From theory to practice*. The MIT Press.

Jacobs, I., & Walsh, N. (2004). *Architecture of the World Wide Web, volume one*. World Wide Web Consortium (W3C) Recommendation.

Jeremić, Z., Jovanović, J., & Gašević, D. (2008). *A semantic-rich framework for learning software patterns*. The Eighth IEEE International Conference on Advanced Learning Technologies (ICALT 2008), Santander, Spain, July 1-5, 2008.

Kamthan, P. (2006). A critique of pattern language markup language. *Interfaces, 68*, 14–15.

Kamthan, P. (2008). A situational methodology for addressing the pragmatic quality of Web applications by integration of patterns. *Journal of Web Engineering, 7*(1), 70–92.

Kamthan, P. (2009a). A framework for integrating the social Web environment in pattern engineering. *International Journal of Technology and Human Interaction, 5*(2), 36–62. doi:10.4018/jthi.2009092303

Kamthan, P. (2009b). *On the symbiosis between quality and patterns*. The Third International Workshop on Software Patterns and Quality (SPAQu 2009), Orlando, USA, October 25, 2009.

Kamthan, P. (2010). A viewpoint-based approach for understanding the morphogenesis of patterns. *International Journal of Knowledge Management, 6*(2), 40–65. doi:10.4018/jkm.2010040103

Kamthan, P., & Pai, H.-I. (2006a). Knowledge representation in pattern management. In Schwartz, D. (Ed.), *Encyclopedia of knowledge management*. Hershey, PA: Idea Group. doi:10.4018/9781591405733.ch062

Kamthan, P., & Pai, H.-I. (2006b). Representation of Web application patterns in OWL. In Taniar, D., & Rahayu, J. W. (Eds.), *Web semantics and ontology*. Hershey, PA: Idea Group. doi:10.4018/9781591409052.ch002

Kohls, C., & Panke, S. (2009). *Is that true...? Thoughts on the epistemology of patterns*. The Sixteenth Conference on Pattern Languages of Programs (PLoP 2009), Chicago, USA, August 28-30, 2009.

Kohls, C., & Uttecht, J.-G. (2009). Lessons learnt in mining and writing design patterns for educational interactive graphics. *Computers in Human Behavior, 25*(5), 1040–1055. doi:10.1016/j.chb.2009.01.004

Kruschitz, C. (2009). *XPLML: A HCI pattern formalizing and unifying approach*. The ACM CHI 2009 Conference on Human Factors in Computing Systems (CHI 2009), Boston, USA, April 4-9, 2009.

Kruschitz, C., & Hitz, M. (2010). *Analyzing the HCI design pattern variety*. The First Asian Conference on Pattern Languages of Programs (AsianPLoP 2010), Tokyo, Japan, March 16-17, 2010.

Kunert, T. (2009). *User-centered interaction design patterns for interactive digital television applications*. Springer-Verlag.

Lea, D. (1994). Christopher Alexander: An introduction for object-oriented designers. *ACM SIGSOFT Software Engineering Notes*, *19*(1), 39–46. doi:10.1145/181610.181617

Mader, S. (2008). *Wikipatterns: A practical guide to improving productivity and collaboration in your organization*. John Wiley and Sons.

Manolescu, D., Kozaczynski, W., Miller, A., & Hogg, J. (2007). The growing divide in the patterns world. *IEEE Software*, *24*(4), 61–67. doi:10.1109/MS.2007.120

Megginson, D. (2005). *Imperfect XML: Rants, raves, tips, and tricks from an insider*. Addison-Wesley.

Meszaros, G., & Doble, J. (1998). A pattern language for pattern writing. In Martin, R. C., Riehle, D., & Buschmann, F. (Eds.), *Pattern languages of program design* (*Vol. 3*, pp. 529–574). Addison-Wesley.

Morville, P., & Callender, J. (2010). *Search patterns*. O'Reilly Media.

O'Reilly, T. (2005). *What is Web 2.0: Design patterns and business models for the next generation of software*. O'Reilly Network, September 30, 2005.

Ogrinz, M. (2009). *Mashup patterns: Designs and strategies for using mashups in enterprise environments*. Addison-Wesley.

Ohtsuki, M., Segawa, J., Yoshida, N., & Makinouchi, A. (1997). *Structured document framework for design patterns based on SGML*. The Twenty First International Computer Software and Applications Conference (COMPSAC 1997), Washington, D.C., USA, August 11-15, 1997.

Renear, A., Dubin, D., Sperberg-McQueen, C. M., & Huitfeldt, C. (2002). *Towards a semantics for XML markup*. The 2002 ACM Symposium on Document Engineering (DocEng 2002), McLean, USA, November 8-9, 2002.

Rising, L. (2000). *The pattern almanac 2000*. Addison-Wesley.

Rüping, A. (2003). *Agile documentation: A pattern guide to producing lightweight documents for software projects*. John Wiley and Sons.

Schümmer, T., & Lukosch, S. (2007). *Patterns for computer-mediated interaction*. John Wiley and Sons.

Shanks, G. (1999). *Semiotic approach to understanding representation in Information Systems*. The Information Systems Foundations Workshop, Sydney, Australia, September 29, 1999.

Taibi, T. (2007). *Design pattern formalization techniques*. Hershey, PA: Idea Group.

Taibi, T., & Ngo, C. L. (2002). *A pattern for evaluating design patterns*. The Sixth World Multiconference on Systemics, Cybernetics and Informatics (SCI 2002), Orlando, USA, July 14-18, 2002.

Van Welie, M., & Van der Veer, G. C. (2003). *Pattern languages in interaction design: Structure and organization*. The Ninth IFIP TC13 International Conference on Human-Computer Interaction (INTERACT 2003), Zürich, Switzerland, September 1-5, 2003.

Whitworth, B. (2009). The social requirements of technical systems. In Whitworth, B., & de Moor, A. (Eds.), *Handbook of research on socio-technical design and social networking systems* (pp. 3–22). Hershey, PA: IGI Global. doi:10.4018/9781605662640.ch001

Wiegers, K. (2003). *Software requirements* (2nd ed.). Microsoft Press.

ADDITIONAL READING

Alexander, C. (1964). *Notes on the Synthesis of Form*. Harvard University Press.

Alexander, C. (1979). *The Timeless Way of Building*. Oxford University Press.

Coplien, J. O. (1998). Software Design Patterns: Common Questions and Answers. In Rising, L. (Ed.), *The Patterns Handbook: Techniques, Strategies, and Applications* (pp. 311–319). Cambridge University Press.

Iba, T. (2007). Creation toward Quality Without a Name - Sociological Analysis of Pattern Language. The First International Workshop on Software Patterns and Quality (SPAQu 2007), Nagoya, Japan, December 3, 2007.

ISO/IEC. (2001). *ISO/IEC 9126-1:2001(E). Software Engineering -- Product Quality -- Part 1: Quality Model. The International Organization for Standardization (ISO)/The International Electrotechnical Commission*. IEC.

ISO/IEC. (2007). *ISO/IEC 25030:2007(E). Software Engineering -- Software Product Quality Requirements and Evaluation (SQuaRE) -- Quality Requirements. The International Organization for Standardization (ISO)/The International Electrotechnical Commission*. IEC.

May, D., & Taylor, P. (2003). Knowledge Management with Patterns. *Communications of the ACM, 46*(7), 94–99. doi:10.1145/792704.792705

Spinellis, D., & Louridas, P. (2008). The Collaborative Organization of Knowledge. *Communications of the ACM, 51*(8), 68–73. doi:10.1145/1378704.1378720

Weiss, M., & Birukou, A. (2007). Building a Pattern Repository: Benefiting from the Open, Lightweight, and Participative Nature of Wikis. Wikis for Software Engineering Workshop (Wikis4SE 2007), Montreal, Canada, October 21, 2007.

Wong, B. (2006). Different Views of Software Quality. In Duggan, E., & Reichgelt, J. (Eds.), *Measuring Information Systems Delivery Quality* (pp. 55–88). Idea Group.

KEY TERMS AND DEFINITIONS

Explicit Knowledge: A type of human knowledge that has been articulated.

Markup: Text that is added to the data in order to convey information about it.

Pattern: An empirically proven solution to a recurring problem that occurs in a particular context.

Pattern Description: A set of indicative statements that specify a pattern.

Pattern Stakeholder: A person who has interest in a specific pattern for some purpose.

Quality: The totality of attributes of an entity that bear on its ability to satisfy stated and implied needs.

Semantic Web: A perceived evolution of the Web that adds technological infrastructure for better knowledge representation, interpretation, and reasoning.

Social Web: A perceived evolution of the Web in a direction that is characterized by user participation, openness, and network effects; driven by 'collective intelligence;' and realized by information technology.

Chapter 9
Empowering Web Service Search with Business Know–How:
Application to Scientific Workflows

Isabelle Mirbel
Université de Nice Sophia-Antipolis, France

Pierre Crescenzo
Université de Nice Sophia-Antipolis, France

Nadia Cerezo
Université de Nice Sophia-Antipolis, France

ABSTRACT

Scientists who are not proficient in computer science and yet wish to perform in-silico experiments and harness the power of Service Oriented Architecture are presented with dozens of daunting technical solutions: scientific workflow frameworks. While these systems do take care of complex technical aspects such as Grid technologies, little is done to support transfer of service composition knowledge and know-how. The authors of this chapter believe the problem lies in the scientific workflow models which are too low-level and too anchored in the underlying technologies to allow efficient reuse and sharing. This chapter's approach, called SATIS, relies on a goal-driven model, that has proven its worth in requirement engineering, and the Semantic Web technologies to leverage the collective knowledge and know-how in order to bridge the gap between service providers and end-users.

INTRODUCTION

Service Oriented Computing (SOC) is a computing paradigm using and providing services to support the rapid and scalable development of distributed applications in heterogeneous environments. Despite its growing acceptance, we argue that it is difficult for business people to fully benefit of SOC if it remains at the software level. This is especially true for scientists looking for web services to operationalize scientific workflows. We

DOI: 10.4018/978-1-60960-509-4.ch009

claim it is required to move towards a description of services in business terms, i.e. intentions and strategies to achieve them and to organize their publication and combination on the basis of these descriptions.

Moreover, service providers and users still face many significant challenges introduced by the dynamism of software service environments and requirements. This requires new concepts, methods, models, and technologies along with flexible and adaptive infrastructure for services developments and management in order to facilitate the on-demand integration of services across different platforms and organizations. Users exploit their domain expertise and rely on previous experiences to identify relevant services to fulfill new requirements. Indeed, they develop know-how in solving software related problems (or requirements). And we claim it is required to turn this know-how into reusable guidelines or best practices and to provide means to support its capitalization, dissemination and management inside user communities.

The ability to support adequacy between service user needs and service providers' proposals is a critical factor for achieving interoperability in distributed applications in heterogeneous environments. Service final users need means to transmit their functional and non functional requirements to service designers, especially when no service is available. And service designers need means to disseminate information about available services in order to improve their acceptance by users as well as means to better handle the way final non computer scientist users combine services to fulfill their goals. Reasoning about high-level descriptions of services and know-how about final users services combination help to support bidirectional collaboration between non computer scientist users (service final users) and computer scientists (service designers).

So, from a general point of view, software engineering implies a growing need for knowledge engineering to support all aspects of software development. In this chapter, we focus on knowledge engineering to support service combination from a user perspective. And we focus on scientist needs when operationalizing scientific workflows.

We propose a framework, called SATIS, *Semantically AnnotaTed Intentions for Services* (Isabelle Mirbel & Crescenzo, 2009), to capture and organize know-how about Web Services combination. Therefore we adopt Web semantic languages and models as a unified framework to deal with user requirements, know-how about service combination as well as Web Services descriptions. Indeed, we distinguish between intentional and operational know-how. Intentional know-how captures the different goals and sub-goals the final users try to reach during his/her combination task. Intentional know-how is specified with the help of an intentional process model (Rolland, 2007). Operational know-how captures the way intentional sub-goals are operationalized by available suitable Web Services. Operational know-how is formalized as queries over Web Service descriptions.

In SATIS, users requirements, know-how about service combination as well as Web Services descriptions are resources indexed by semantic annotations (Martin et al., 2004; Ora Lassila & Ralph R. Swick, 1998; T. Version, L. Version, P. Version, & McBride, 2004) in order to explicit and formalize their informative content. Semantic annotations are stored into a dedicated memory. And information retrieval inside this memory relies on the formal manipulation of these annotations and is guided by ontologies.

Annotations of intentional and operational know-how are respectively stored as abstract and concrete rules implemented as SPARQL construct queries. When considered recursively, a set of SPARQL construct queries can be seen as a set of rules processed in backward chaining. As a result, someone looking for solutions to operationalize a business process (in our case scientific workflow) will take advantage of all the rules and all the Web Service descriptions stored in the semantic community memory at the time of his/her search. This memory may evolve over the time and therefore the Web Services descriptions retrieved by using a rule may vary as well. Business users as well as computer scientists may both take advantage of this reasoning capability to understand the way services are combined to fulfill a goal. This way, SATIS supports knowledge transfer from final expert users to novice ones as well as collaboration between users (who are not computer scientists) and computer scientists.

Beyond an alternative way to search for Web Services, we provide means to capitalize know-how about Web Service user combination. Another novelty of our approach is to operationalize goals by rules in order to promote both sharing of specifications and cross-fertilization of know-how about Web Services combinations. Therefore, we focus on scientific workflow operationalization with semantic web services. We are currently implementing our approach in the neuroscience domain where domain ontologies and semantic Web Services descriptions are already available.

In this chapter, we start by presenting a state of the art of existing approaches in the field of scientific workflows (including neuroscience workflows) (Ludascher et al., 2006; Tan, Missier, Madduri, & Foster, 2009) in order to highlight final users' needs in terms of Web Services combination. Then we discuss our SATIS approach: First, we introduce intentional process modeling for scientific workflows, focusing on web services discovery (Gomez, Rico, Garcia-Sanchez, Toma, & Han, 2006; da Silva Santos, Pires, & van Sinderen, 2008). Then, we discuss how reuse and sharing are supported by know-how fragments. Finally, we explain how relying on semantic web models and languages allows us to reason and trace web services combination know-how in order to bridge the gap between service providers and workflow users.

STATE OF THE ART OF SCIENTIFIC WORKFLOWS

Let us briefly present the current state of the art of scientific workflows research, to the best of our knowledge. We will first detail the reasons behind the creation and use of scientific workflows, then give a quick overview of the field, and then present a few well-known and very active projects and finally we will highlight the challenges left to overcome.

Motivation

First off, computational scientific experiments obviously largely pre-date the notion of workflow. The traditional way of doing things is to gather data, adapt it to whatever program you want to run it on, run said program and post-process the outputs to analyze them. If many programs have to be chained together and the process must be repeated many times over, scripting is surely the most direct solution. It has worked for a long time, but its limitations can no longer be ignored.

One of the most obvious problems with scripting is its non-existent ease-of-use: end-users need to be fully aware of technical details of both the data they want to analyze, the programs they will use and the platforms on which the programs will run, as well as every associated transfer protocol and input/output formats. Add to this appalling list the scripting language itself and you can conclude that the end-user will spend most of his or her time dealing with computer science delicacies rather than advancing his or her own research. Another aspect of accessibility is sharing, not only of scripts but of know-how. There again scripting is as bad as it gets: either the user doesn't already know the details aforementioned and the script will be cryptic to say the least, or the user already knows them and doesn't have much to learn from the script itself.

Scientific computerized experiments, like physical experiments, have to be carried out many times, either to check the consistency of results or to try different parameters and input data or new ideas. For every modification the script author had designed the script for, all is well. Problems arise with modifications the script was not designed to cope with, because they were either dismissed or not predicted at all. Such modifications happen all the time: a program is upgraded and new protocols are adopted, new data is collected that doesn't exactly fit the previous format, new algorithms are designed that need additional parameters, etc. If the modification is small and the author is around and still has a fresh memory of his or her script, it might go well. Most often, though, it is quicker to re-write a new script than to modify an existing one. Again, more time is taken from research and lost onto computer science technicalities that are essentially not re-usable.

E-sciences of late have known a small revolution: ever increasing computational costs, dataset size and process complexity have made the traditional model of one scientist running his or her programs on a single machine obsolete. To carry out one analysis, highly-distributed heterogeneous resources are needed. Scripting obviously fails to cope with such situations. Grid technologies and SOA (Service Oriented Architecture) are partial answers to the problem but they are not well-known for their ease-of-use and further alienate the typical end-user.

Scientific workflows are gaining momentum in many data-intensive research fields, e.g.:

- Bio-informatics (A. C. Jones, 2007; Lin, Peltier, Grethe, & Ellisman, 2007),
- Physics (Berriman et al., 2007; Brooke, Pickles, Carr, & Michael, 2007; Gannon et al., 2007),
- Ecology (Pennington et al., 2007),
- Disaster handling (Maechling et al., 2006).

Table 1. Criteria for scientific workflow frameworks

Name	Description
Clarity	Produce self-explanatory workflows
Well-Formedness	Help create well-formed and valid workflows
Predictability	Produce workflows whose behavior is predictable
Recordability	Record workflow execution
Reportability	Keep provenance information for all results
Reusability	Help create new workflows from existing ones
Scientific Data Modeling	Provide support for scientific data modeling
Automatic Optimization	Hide optimization concerns from users

According to (McPhillips, Bowers, Zinn, & Ludascher, 2009), a scientific workflow framework must fulfill eight criteria to be truly useful to the end-user, who is typically a scientist, with little knowledge in computer science, wishing to automate and share his or her scientific analyses.

While user needs vary greatly from a given field to another, we do believe those criteria to be of interest for most end-users.

Overview

The notion of workflow was first formally introduced in 1995 by the Workflow Management Coalition in the Workflow Reference Model (Hollingsworth, 1995). It was defined as "the computerized facilitation or automation of a business process, in whole or part". Furthermore, they explained that "a workflow is concerned with the automation of procedures where documents, information or tasks are passed between participants according to a defined set of rules to achieve, or contribute to, an overall business goal". As is obvious from the definition itself, workflows were meant solely for business uses at the time.

Table 2. Surveys we know of in a nutshell

Date	Title	Authors	Type	#SW
2005	A taxonomy of Scientific Workflow Systems for Grid Computing	J. Yu, R. Buyya,(Gridbus)	Article	12
2006	Scientific Workflows Survey	A. Slominski, G. von Laszewski (Java CoG Kit)	Wiki	32
2007	Workflows for e-science: scientific workflows for grids	I. J. Taylor et al. (Triana)	Book	10
2008	Scientific Workflow: A Survey and Research Directions	A. Barker, J. van Hemert	Article	10

The concept of a scientific workflow is much more recent than the concept of workflow itself.

It is easy to mix up the notions of scientific and business workflows. Most people who know about workflows actually know about the business version which pre-dates the scientific one. A lot of core concerns and concepts are shared by both business and scientific workflows, while some issues are specific to one domain or the other (Barga & Gannon, 2007).

Scientific Workflow systems are heavily influenced by their business counterparts, which might explain why DAG (Directed Acyclic Graphs) are the most common workflow representation in both worlds, with vertices modeling tasks and edges modeling either data or control flow. The growing need for large-scale computation, large-scale data manipulation and support for execution over highly-distributed heterogeneous resources is common to both scientific and business contexts.

In most cases, business processes are clearly defined beforehand and actual workflow building is more or less a mapping problem, whereas scientific workflow building is most often an exploratory procedure. Needs for flexibility and dynamic changes are therefore far greater for scientific workflows. While security and integrity are the top priorities in a business context, they are far outweighed by reproducibility and reusability concerns in a scientific context: a scientific experiment serves no purpose if it cannot be shared, checked (and thus, rerun) and validated by the community.

To the best of our knowledge, there have been only 4 surveys so far, detailed below, and there is no up-to-date index of existing systems. In the following table, #SW stands for the number of scientific workflows surveyed.

The sheer number and significant diversity of systems make it hard for a user to find the best-fit scientific workflow framework for his or her use. We believe an online comparison matrix of the most active projects would be highly beneficial to both researchers and end-users. Unfortunately, the typical lack of communication between projects makes maintenance of such a matrix a difficult task.

Issues

While the many scientific workflow systems share a lot, especially regarding needs and core concepts, there is no standard for either workflow, provenance or execution descriptions. Frameworks can be compared and categorized (Yu & Buyya, 2005), but interoperability is nothing short of painful in the present state of things. This can be shown simply by the sheer variety of terms in use for the most basic element of a workflow, most often the vertices in the associated graph: operations, tasks, nodes, processes, jobs, components, services, actors, transitions, procedures, thorns, activities, elements, units (Shields, 2007) and probably more. It is worth noting that BPEL (Business Process Execution Language) is often cited as a strong candidate for standard workflow description language (Addis et al., 2003; Barker

& Van Hemert, 2008; Slominski, 2006; Tan et al., 2009), surely because of its status as de facto standard business workflow description language. However, BPEL suffers many limitations and before it can be established as a standard or intermediate workflow language, it needs to be extended (Slominski, 2006).

For the results of a scientific workflow to be of any use, they need to be reproducible and therefore fully traceable: information must be kept about the conditions in which the workflow was run, the initial input data, the intermediate results as well as the chosen parameters. This concern for traceability is commonly referred to as "provenance" and has been a research subject for a while (Addis et al., 2003; Davidson et al., 2007; McPhillips et al., 2009; Oinn et al., 2004; Wroe, Stevens, Goble, Roberts, & Greenwood, 2003; J. Zhao, Goble, Greenwood, Wroe, & Stevens, 2003). Many frameworks already implement some sort of provenance tracking, but, to the best of our knowledge, a standard is yet to be established, when it is even more critical to interoperability than a common language (Deelman, 2007): indeed, without provenance description standards, it is near impossible to replay a given workflow execution on another system.

Portal-based access to scientific workflow technology is currently a hot topic. It indeed seems the best way to ensure accessibility to a maximum number of end-users. It might even turn out to be a necessary step for many projects, since users who are not knowledgeable about technology often shy away from installation instructions and would certainly prefer using thin-client technology (Barker & Van Hemert, 2008). Portals are sometimes already deployed (Allen et al., 2003; Buyya & Venugopal, 2004; Wroe et al., 2003) and often cited in Discussion and Future Works sections (Barker & Van Hemert, 2008; J. Zhao et al., 2003).

The problem of discovery, or how to retrieve existing workflows that can be reused or re-purposed for one's goals, cannot be solved directly inside the scientific workflow model, editor or enactor. It might matter little to the modeling expert, but for end-users who have little knowledge about workflows, it is a critical issue: it is not enough to store finished workflows in an open database with query functionalities. The surrounding platform must provide users with helpful discovery tools. Those are critical for knowledge sharing among users. Discovery of scientific workflows is a slightly underestimated research topic. To the best of our knowledge, the only team working on it is the Taverna (myGrid) team, through the myExperiment project (De Roure, Goble, & Stevens, 2009; Goderis et al., 2008). Note that discovery of services, however, is a rather hot topic.

While most existing systems claim to bridge the gap between computer scientists and scientists of other fields, and huge progress has certainly been made in the ease-of-use area, the impression one gets from just looking at the most basic workflows is quite different: in most cases, the underlying Web technologies are apparent. It is hard for us to picture a user with little knowledge in computer science able to make sense of concepts such as XSLT (eXtensible Stylesheet Language Transformations). Of course, such details should be neither ignored nor hidden completely. They should be left for a lower level of abstraction and higher levels need to be created between the typical user (e.g. a scientist) and the actual executable workflow, using semantic information to automate the process in the most intelligent manner possible (Gil, 2007).

In the two next sections, we present our approach SATIS which is a way to respond to the difficulty for end-users to discover adequate Web Services and for computer scientists to design and present their Web Services for a better visibility to users.

INTENTION DRIVEN PROCESS MODELING FOR SCIENTIFIC WORKFLOWS

A major interest of scientific workflows is to offer an interface to combine existing autonomous software components, like Web Services. But this is not a sufficient help for end-users. We need to give them a mean to simply express their goals and to assist them to choose the pertinent components (Web Services) to implement these goals.

One of the main objectives of SATIS is to support final users when looking for Web Services to operationalize their scientific workflow. In this paper, we focus on a neuroscientist community and we illustrate our approach on a specific kind of scientific workflow: image processing pipelines. In this section we will first discuss the role of the different actors involved in the final users community and then describe the different means we provide to support final users tasks. Our approach is illustrated on a neuroscience community.

Three core actors are identified in our framework: the *service designer*, the *community semantic memory manager* and the *domain expert*. In a neuroscientist community, computer scientists play the roles of *service designer* and *community semantic memory manager* while neuroscientists play the role of *domain expert*.

The service designer is in charge of promoting the Web Services available in the community Web Service registry. Therefore, when s/he wants to advertise a new kind of Web Service in the final users community, in addition to adding the Web Service description in the community registry, s/he writes a generic Web Service description and associates to it high-level end-user's intentional requirements to promote the services s/he is in charge from the end-user's point of view (that is to say in a non computer scientists language). Indeed, the service designer is in charge of authoring atomic reusable fragments.

The community semantic memory manager is in charge of populating the community semantic

memory with reusable pipeline fragments to help domain experts to (i) specify the image processing pipelines for which they are looking for Web Services and (ii) search for Web Service descriptions to operationalize the image processing pipelines they are interested in. Indeed, s/he provides reusable pipeline fragments useful in different image processing pipelines. Basic processes, as for instance intensity corrections, common to several image analysis pipelines, are examples of such basic fragments. Therefore, s/he may look at the fragments provided by the service designer with the aim of aggregating some of them into basic image processing pipelines. For instance in neuroscientist community, if *Image debiasing*, *Image denoising*, *Image normalization* and *Image registration* Web Service descriptions are provided in the community Web Service registry (and associated high level descriptions provided in the community semantic memory) at some point, the community semantic memory manager may put them together into a basic *Image preprocessing* pipeline. S/he may also identify recurrent needs when supporting domain experts in their authoring task and therefore provide adequate basic reusable fragments for image processing pipelines.

Finally, the domain expert (or final user) is searching for Web Service descriptions to operationalize an image processing pipeline s/he is interested in.

In our approach we clearly distinguish an authoring step and a rendering step. During the authoring step, the focus is on the elicitation of the search procedure. The domain experts think in terms of image processing pipelines (and not in terms of services). His/her search procedure is fully described, eventually with the help of the fragments already present in the community semantic memory. During the rendering step, it is the system (and not the domain expert) which tries to find Web Services corresponding to the requirements specified by the experts (by proving goals and sub-goals). Indeed, the experts don't need at all to know the content of the registry.

A pertinent subset of it will be extracted by the system and shown to the experts.

During the authoring step, s/he may first look in the community semantic memory if some existing fragments already deal with the main intention s/he is interested in. If another member of the community already authored an image processing pipeline achieving the same high-level goal, s/he may reuse it as is. The goal under consideration may also be covered by a larger image processing pipeline specified through a set of fragments already stored in the community semantic memory and correspond to one of the sub-goals of the larger pipeline. In this case also, existing fragments can be reused as is. The rendering step to operationalize the image processing pipeline under consideration is performed on the current semantic community memory content. If no high-level end-user's intentional requirements are already available, the neuroscientist specifies the image processing pipeline under consideration with the help of the community semantic memory manager. During the authoring step, for each sub-goal identified in the high-level image processing pipeline, the neuroscientist may search for existing fragments supporting their operationalization. If it is the case, then s/he can decide to rely on them and stop the authoring process. Otherwise, s/he may prefer to provide his/her own way to operationalize the sub-goals. By doing so, the domain expert enriches the semantic community memory with alternative ways to operationalize already registered goals. This will result in enriching the operationalization means of the image processing pipelines already formalized into fragments stored in the semantic community repository. In fact, when someone else looking for the sub-goals under consideration will perform a rendering process, if his/her image processing pipeline relies on the achievement of a sub-goal for which a new operationalization means has been provided, then the operationalization means previously stored in the semantic community repository as well as the new ones are exploited, increasing the number of ways to find suitable Web Service descriptions. During the authoring step, each time the domain expert, with the help of the community semantic memory manager, decides to provide new ways to operationalize a goal, s/he has to select the right level of specification of the fragment grouping a sub-goal and its operationalization means, in order to allow the reuse of the fragment under construction outside of the scope of the image processing pipeline under consideration.

From a more general point of view, domain and community semantic memory managers mainly provide fragments: Domain experts focus on high-level fragments, close to the image processing pipelines they want to operationalize. Community semantic memory managers focus on low level fragments, that is to say fragments operationalizing basic image processing pipelines. And service designers mainly focus on providing fragments to promote existing Web Services. But domain and community semantic memory managers may also provide fragments to specify their requirements in term of services. And the service designers may also provide fragments in order to show examples of use of available Web Services inside the scope of more complex examples of image processing pipelines. By providing a common goal based description for web services and user needs as well as by relying on a rule-based specification to search for operationalization means to achieve goals and sub-goals, we assist the bidirectional collaboration between non computer scientists and computer scientists inside the community.

An important objective of the SATIS project is to provide domain experts with means to better understand the characteristics of available services and how to use them in the scope of the image processing pipeline they are interested in. We support this aim by several means. The SATIS approach relies on a controlled vocabulary (domain ontology) to qualify Web Services as well as requirements, this way reducing the diversity in the labeling, especially in Web Services descriptions elements. Requirements about Web Services are described in terms of intentions (steps in the image processing pipeline) and strategies (ways to achieve intentions) that is to say a vocabulary familiar to the domain expert, making the understanding of the a Web Service purpose easier to understand by domain experts. We propose to specify required Web Service functionalities in terms of queries (i.e. generic Web Service descriptions) instead of traditional Web Service descriptions in order to provide an abstraction level supporting the categorization of available Web Services and this way an easier understanding of the content of the registry by domain experts.

In Figure 1, we can see an example of a map which is a graphical way to express and capture end-users goal. In this map, we can see two main intentions specified by a neuroscientist: *Make an image homogeneous* and *Put image in a Single reference*. *Start* and *Stop* are mandatory special intentions to delimitate the process under elicitation. Between the intentions, we discover strategies such *by normalization*, *by debiasing* or *by registration*. Strategies define the way to pass from an intention to a next one. There can be many strategies which link up the same intentions like *by normalization*, *by debiasing* and *by denoising*. Strategies may also carry information related to constraints about the kind of web services under consideration, like access rights for instance. Indeed, in a map, each set which is made up by a source intention, a strategy and a target intention is a section of the map. Let's precise that an intentional map is neither a state diagram, because there is no data structure, no object, and no assigned value, nor an activity diagram, because there is always a strong context for each section of the map: its source intention and its strategy. We can attach more information to this kind of schema (in order to help the user of the map to choose the adequate strategy, for example), but this is not the goal of this paper to fully describe the Map Model.

An intentional map may be refined. We can refine a section by giving a new map which de-

Figure 1. Map example

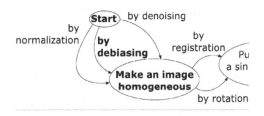

scribes how to reach a target intention in a more detailed way (by using more specific and low-level intentions and strategies). Indeed, by refining an intentional map, experts describe internal procedures to reach the target intention. When this elicitation phase is successfully completed, we have at disposal a general map and one or several level of refinements of its sections.

FRAGMENTS TO SUPPORT KNOW-HOW SHARING AND TRANSFER

SATIS relies on a fragment based approach which doesn't show to the domain expert the full set of rules exploited by the backward chaining engine to satisfy the user requirements. When rendering a search procedure, the domain expert only selects the intention characterizing his/her image processing pipeline and the system will search for the rules to use. A set of Web Services descriptions is given to the domain expert as result. But the complexity and the number of rules used to get the solution are hidden to the domain expert.

In SATIS, the process consisting in retrieving Web Services descriptions from high-level end-user's intentional requirements about image processing pipelines is viewed as a set of loosely coupled fragments expressed at different levels of granularity. A fragment is an autonomous and coherent part of a search process supporting the operationalization of part of an image processing pipeline by Web Services. Such a modular view of the process aiming at retrieving Web Service descriptions from high-level end-user's intentional requirements favors the reuse of fragments authored to deal with a specific high-level end-user's image processing pipeline in the building of other pipelines.

The fragment body captures guidelines that can be considered as autonomous and reusable. The fragment signature captures the reuse context in which the fragment can be applied.

For us, a guideline embodies know-how about how to achieve an intention in a given situation. We distinguish two types of guidelines: intentional and operational guidelines. Intentional guidelines capture high-level end-user's intentional requirements which have to be refined into more specific requirements. Operational guidelines capture generic Web Service description.

Map formalizations and queries respectively constitute the body of intentional and operational reusable fragments. The fragment signature characterizes the fragment content and let the other members of the community understand in which situation the fragment may be useful. A fragment signature aims at capturing the purpose of the fragment and its reuse situation. A fragment signature is specified by a map section. The target intention of the section indicates the goal of the reusable fragment and its source intention and strategy specify the reuse situation in which the fragment is suitable.

In a fragment signature, the target intention is mandatory to elicit the goal of the fragment. If a particular context is required to use the fragment, a source intention or a strategy may be used to specify it. Web Services retrieved by rendering a fragment which signature does not include source intention are less precise than Web Services retrieved by rendering a fragment which signature is fully described by a source intention in addition to the target intention. Similarly, to specify or not a strategy can respectively reduce or enlarge the spectrum of Web Services considered. Both means (specifying a source intention or a strategy) can be combined to obtain a signature which gener-

Figure 2. SATIS fragment model

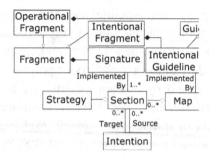

icity level actually corresponds to the guidelines proposed in the body of the fragment.

In SATIS, neuroscientist needs are captured by authoring maps as the one shown in Figure 1, and map sections are embodied into reusable fragments in order to support know-how sharing and reuse.

As shown in Figure 2, in the fragment model provided by SATIS, fragments are composed of a signature and a body. A fragment signature is specified by a map section. We distinguish operational fragments from intentional ones. Operational fragments embody generic description of web services to retrieve adequate web services in the repository. Generic descriptions of web services are implemented by query and constitute operational guidelines. Intentional fragments provide intentional guidelines specified with maps.

SEMANTIC ANNOTATION TO SUPPORT KNOW-HOW CAPITALISATION

In our approach, we adopt Web semantic languages and models as a unified framework to deal with (i) high-level end-user's intentional requirements, (ii) generic Web Service descriptions and (iii) Web Service descriptions themselves. With regards to high-level end-user's intentional requirements, we adapted the map model (Rolland, 2007) to our concern and gathered its concepts and relationships into an RDFS (T. Version et al., 2004) ontology dedicated to the representation of intentional processes: the map ontology (Corby, Faron-Zucker, & I. Mirbel, 2009). As a result, image processing pipelines annotated with concepts and relationships from this ontology can be shared and exploited by reasoning on their representations. Semantic *Web Service descriptions* are specified with the help of the OWL-S ontology (Martin et al., 2004) as well as a domain ontology. And finally, *generic Web Service descriptions* are specified with the help of the W3C standard query language for RDF (Ora Lassila & Ralph R. Swick, 1998) annotations: SPARQL (2006Prud'Hommeaux, Seaborne, & others, 2006!). Indeed, generic Web Service descriptions are formalized into graph patterns over Web Services descriptions.

Formalization of High-Level End-User's Intentional Requirements

To further formalize map elements, we rely on (Prat, 1997) proposal, which has already proved to be useful to formalize goals (Cauvet & Guzelian, 2008; Ralyté & Rolland, 2001; Rolland, 2007). According to (Prat, 1997), an intention statement is characterized by a verb and some parameters which play specific roles with respect to the verb. Among the parameters, there is the object on which the action described by the verb is processed. We gathered the concepts and relationships of the map model and this further formalization into an RDFS (T. Version et al., 2004) ontology dedicated to the representation of intentional processes: the map ontology (Corby et al., 2009).

Based on the map ontology, image processing pipelines (or fragments of image processing pipeline) are then represented by RDF annotations.

The mappings between the domain ontology and the map ontology are created when concepts of the domain ontology are selected to formalize map content. Domain concepts are then considered as instances of *AnyVerb* (subclass of *Verb*), *AnyObject* (instance of *Object*) and *AnyParameter* (instance of *Parameter*). Verb, Object and Parameter are provided by the map ontology while AnyVerb, AnyObject and AnyParameter are provided in the mappings between the domain ontology and the map ontology to support reasoning.

Let us consider again our running example and the map depicted in Figure 1. The highlighted section has a start intention as source intention, a target intention labeled "*Make an image homogeneous*" and a strategy labeled "*by debiasing*". Thanks to the domain and the map ontologies as well as the mappings between them, the target intention is described by its verb *Homogenize* and its object *Image*; the strategy is described by its parameter *Debiasing* and the source intention is described by its verb *AnyVerb* and its object *AnyObject*. The RDF dataset shown in the left part of Figure 3, where the namespace *map* refers to the map ontology and the namespace *dom* refers to a domain ontology, corresponds to the formalization of the highlighted section in the considered map.

By relying on RDF(S) which is now a widespread Web standard, we ensure the capitalization of these search procedures among community members. Beyond an alternative way to organize and to dynamically access resources in a community memory, we provide means to capitalize search procedures themselves. We take advantage of the inference capabilities provided by the RDF framework to reason on search process representations, especially to organize them and retrieve them for reuse.

Formalization of Generic Web Service Descriptions

In SATIS, we assume Web Service descriptions are expressed in OWL-S. In our current scenarios, we only use the profile and the grounding of OWL-S as well as the input and output specifications in the process description. We enrich OWL-S description by considering their content (as input and output parameters for example) as instances of domain concepts. Thanks to this additional instantiation of domain concepts, it makes it possible to reason on

Figure 3. SATIS

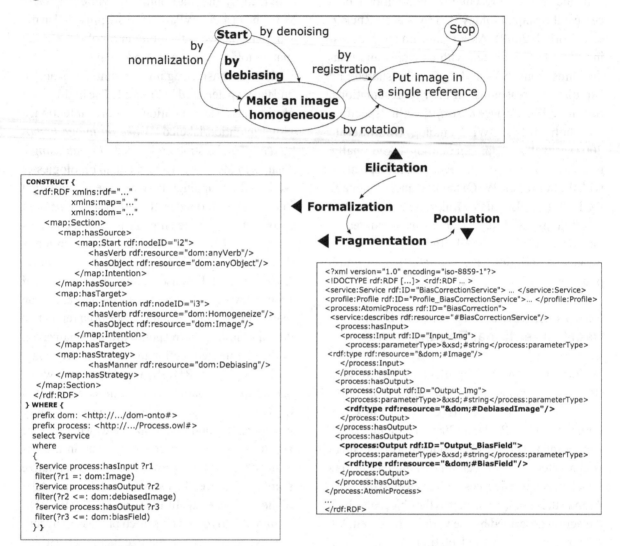

OWL-S description element types to retrieve for instance subclasses of concepts we are interested in. An example of excerpt of such an enriched OWL-S Web Service description is shown on the right side of Figure 3. This description deals with a Web Service requiring an image as input and providing a debiased image and a bias field as output.

As we don't want community members to strongly couple high-level intentional requirements to technical Web Service specifications, we introduced generic Web Service descriptions

aiming at qualifying the required features when looking for Web Services to operationalize image processing pipelines (or fragments of image processing pipeline). For instance, by looking for a Web Service which takes as input an image and provides as output a debiased image, the end-user specifies the kind of Web Service s/he is interested in without explicitly referring to one specific Web Service. The Web Service whose description is shown in Figure 3 will be retrieved by rendering the query shown on the left bottom side of Figure 3. But if other Web Services also deal with image (or a subclass) and debiased image (or a subclass), they will also be retrieved by the query under consideration. By doing so, we assume a loosely coupling between high-level end-user's intentional requirements on one hand and Web Services descriptions on the other hand: if new Web Service descriptions are added inside the community semantic memory, they can be retrieved to operationalize a high-level end-user's intentional requirement even if the requirement has been specified before the availability of the Web Services under consideration; and if Web Service descriptions are removed from the community semantic memory, the high-level end-user's intentional requirements that they satisfied are still valid and may be operationalized by other available Web Services. Web Services are dynamically selected when rendering queries associated to high-level end-user's intentional requirements.

Generic Web Service descriptions are expressed as SPARQL queries among the Web Service descriptions expressed in OWL-S. An example of such a generic Web Service description is shown in the left bottom side of Figure 3. This query aims at searching for Web Service descriptions having as input an Image (or a subclass of it) and as output a *DebiasedImage* (or a subclass of it) and a *BiasField* (or a subclass of it).

Rules

In SATIS, the process consisting in retrieving Web Services descriptions from high-level end-user's intentional requirements about image processing pipelines is viewed as a set of loosely coupled fragments expressed at different levels of granularity. The fragment body captures guidelines that can be considered as autonomous and reusable. The fragment signature captures the reuse context in which the fragment can be applied.

The RDF dataset shown on the left side of Figure 3 corresponds to a fragment signature which body is the SPARQL query shown on the left bottom side of Figure 3. The black frame depicts

a fragment. As its body contains a query, it is an operational fragment. An example of intentional fragment may be a fragment to perform image preprocessing body provides a RDF dataset formalizing the full map (i.e. all the sections) shown on top of Figure 3 and is specified by a section which target intention is finalized by the object *Image* and the verb *Preprocessing*.

This intentional fragment capitalize a know-how about how to break down an image preprocessing high-level requirement into sub-goals in order to find Web Services to operationalize an image processing pipeline.

Indeed in SATIS, fragments are implemented by backward chaining rules, which conclusions represent signatures of fragments and which premises represent bodies of fragments (either operational or intentional guidelines). We call a rule *concrete* or *abstract* depending on whether its premise encapsulates operational or intentional guidelines.

These rules are implemented as SPARQL construct queries. The CONSTRUCT part is interpreted as the head of the rule, the consequent that is proved. The WHERE part is interpreted as the body, the condition that makes the head proved. When considered recursively, a set of SPARQL construct queries can be seen as a set of rules processed in backward chaining.

CONCLUSION

The ability to support adequacy between service user needs and service providers' proposals is a critical factor for achieving interoperability in distributed applications in heterogeneous environments such as scientific workflows. The problem of discovery, or how to retrieve existing workflows that can be reused or re-purposed for one's goals, is especially important for end users who have little knowledge about workflows.

In this chapter, we focused on knowledge engineering to support service combination from an end-user perspective. We proposed SATIS, a framework to turn this know-how into reusable guidelines or best practices and to provide means to support its capitalization, dissemination and management inside business user communities.

SATIS offers a set of models to capture high-level end-user's requirements in an iterative and incremental way and to turn them into queries to retrieve Web Services descriptions. The whole framework relies on reusable and combinable elements which can be shared out inside the scope of a community of users. In our approach, we adopt Web semantic languages and models as a unified framework to deal with (i) high-level end-user's intentional requirements, (ii) generic Web Service descriptions and (iii) Web Service descriptions themselves. SATIS aims at supporting collaboration among the members of a non computer scientist community by contributing to both sharing of high-level intentional specification and cross-fertilization of know-how about Web Services search procedures among the community members.

Future works will first focus on adapting our model to a semantic Web search engine including a backward chaining mechanism in order to test our approach on examples of image processing pipelines. We also plan to develop software tools in order to automate the main tedious steps, like the transformation of the map specification into SPARQL rules and to test our approach in the context of a neuroscientist community.

We will focus on enriching the formalization step by taking into account additional information in order, for instance, to derive criteria related to quality of services. Indeed, we plan to extend our Web Service annotation model with quality of service (QoS) information and to qualify map strategies by QoS domain concepts. We will also concentrate on providing query patterns to help experts writing generic Web Service descriptions.

REFERENCES

Addis, M., Ferris, J., Greenwood, M., Li, P., Marvin, D., Oinn, T., & Wipat, A. (2003). Experiences with e-science workflow specification and enactment in bioinformatics. In *Proceedings of UK e-Science All Hands Meeting,* (pp. 459–467).

Allen, G., Goodale, T., Radke, T., Russell, M., Seidel, E., & Davis, K. (2003). Enabling applications on the Grid: A gridlab overview. *International Journal of High Performance Computing Applications, 17*(4), 449. doi:10.1177/10943420030174008

Barga, R., & Gannon, D. (2007). Scientific versus business workflows. *Workflows for e-science: Scientific workflows for Grids,* 9–16.

Barker, A., & Van Hemert, J. (2008). Scientific workflow: A survey and research directions. *Parallel Processing and Applied Mathematics,* 746–753.

Berriman, G. B., Deelman, E., Good, J., Jacob, J. C., Katz, D. S., Laity, A. C., …Prince, T. A. (2007). Generating complex astronomy workflows. *Workflows for e-science: Scientific workflows for Grids,* 19–38.

Brooke, J., Pickles, S., Carr, P., & Michael, K. (2007). Workflows in pulsar astronomy. *Workflows for e-science: Scientific workflows for Grids,* 60–79.

Buyya, R., & Venugopal, S. (2004). *The gridbus toolkit for service oriented Grid and utility computing: An overview and status report.* In 1st IEEE International Workshop on Grid Economics and Business Models, 2004. GECON 2004, (pp. 19–66).

Cauvet, C., & Guzelian, G. (2008). Business process modeling: A service-oriented approach. *Proceedings of the 41st Annual Hawaii International Conference on System Sciences,* (p. 98).

Corby, O., Faron-Zucker, C., & Mirbel, I. (2009). *Implementation of intention-driven search processes by SPARQL queries*. In International Conference on Enterprise Information Systems, Milan, Italy.

da Silva Santos, L. O., Pires, L. F., & van Sinderen, M. J. (2008). *A goal-based framework for dynamic service discovery and composition*. In International Workshop on Architectures, Concepts and Technologies for Service Oriented Computing.

Davidson, S., Cohen-Boulakia, S., Eyal, A., Ludascher, B., McPhillips, T., Bowers, S., & Freire, J. (2007). Provenance in scientific workflow systems. *A Quarterly Bulletin of the Computer Society of the IEEE Technical Committee on Data Engineering, 30*(4), 44–50.

De Roure, D., Goble, C., & Stevens, R. (2009). The design and realisation of the virtual research environment for social sharing of workflows. *Future Generation Computer Systems, 25*(5), 561–567. doi:10.1016/j.future.2008.06.010

Deelman, E. (2007). Looking into the future of workflows: The challenges ahead. *Workflows for e-science: Scientific workflows for Grids*, 475–481.

Gannon, D., Plale, B., Marru, S., Kandaswamy, G., Simmhan, Y., & Shirasuna, S. (2007). Dynamic, adaptive workflows for mesoscale meteorology. *Workflows for e-science: Scientific workflows for Grids*, 126–142.

Gil, Y. (2007). Workflow composition: Semantic representations for flexible automation. *Workflows for e-science: Scientific workflows for Grids*, 244–257.

Goderis, A., De Roure, D., Goble, C., Bhagat, J., Cruickshank, D., Fisher, P., Michaelides, D., et al. (2008). *Discovering scientific workflows: The myexperiment benchmarks*. Internal project report, submitted for publication.

Gomez, J. M., Rico, M., Garcia-Sanchez, F., Toma, I., & Han, S. (2006). *GODO: Goal oriented discovery for Semantic Web services*. 5th International Semantic Web Conference.

Hollingsworth, D. (1995). *The workflow reference model*. Workflow Management Coalition.

Jones, A. C. (2007). Workflow and biodiversity e-science. *Workflows for e-science: Scientific workflows for Grids*, 80–90.

Lassila, O. & Swick, R. R. (1998). *Resource Description Framework (RDF) model and syntax*.

Lin, A. W., Peltier, S. T., Grethe, J. S., & Ellisman, M. H. (2007). Case studies on the use of workflow technologies for scientific analysis: The biomedical informatics research network and the telescience project. *Workflows for e-science: Scientific workflows for Grids*, 109–125.

Ludascher, B., Altintas, I., Berkley, C., Higgins, D., Jaeger, E., Jones, M., & Lee, E. A. (2006). Scientific workflow management and the Kepler system. *Concurrency and Computation, 18*(10), 1039. doi:10.1002/cpe.994

Maechling, P., Deelman, E., Zhao, L., Graves, R., Mehta, G., Gupta, N., & Mehringer, J. (2006). SCEC CyberShake workflows—automating probabilistic seismic hazard analysis calculations. *Workflows for e-science*, 143–163.

Martin, D., Burstein, M., Hobbs, J., Lassila, O., McDermott, D., McIlraith, S., & Narayanan, S. (2004). *OWL-S: Semantic markup for Web services*.

McBride, B. (2004). *RDF vocabulary description language 1.0: RDF schema changes*.

McPhillips, T., Bowers, S., Zinn, D., & Ludascher, B. (2009). Scientific workflow design for mere mortals. *Future Generation Computer Systems, 25*(5), 541–551. doi:10.1016/j.future.2008.06.013

Mirbel, I., & Crescenzo, P. (2009). Improving collaborations in neuroscientist community. In *Proceedings of the 2009 IEEE/WIC/ACM International Joint Conference on Web Intelligence and Intelligent Agent Technology - Volume 03,* (pp. 567-570). IEEE Computer Society.

Oinn, T., Addis, M., Ferris, J., Marvin, D., Greenwood, M., Carver, T., & Pocock, M. R. (2004). *Taverna: A tool for the composition and enactment of bioinformatics workflows.*

Pennington, D. D., Higgins, D., Peterson, A. T., Jones, M. B., Ludascher, B., & Bowers, S. (2007). Ecological niche modeling using the Kepler workflow system. *Workflows for e-science: Scientific workflows for Grids,* 91–108.

Prat, N. (1997). Goal formalisation and classification for requirements engineering. In *Proceedings of the Third International Workshop on Requirements Engineering: Foundations of Software Quality REFSQ* (pp. 145–156).

Prud'Hommeaux, E., & Seaborne, A. (2006). *SPARQL query language for RDF.* W3C working draft, 20.

Ralyté, J., & Rolland, C. (2001). An assembly process model for method engineering. In *Advanced Information Systems engineering,* (pp. 267–283).

Rolland, C. (2007). *Conceptual modelling in Information Systems engineering.* Springer-Verlag.

Shields, M. (2007). Control-versus data-driven workflows. *Workflows for e-science: Scientific workflows for Grids,* 167–173.

Slominski, A. (2006). Adapting BPEL to scientific workflows. *Workflows for e-science,* 208–226.

Tan, W., Missier, P., Madduri, R., & Foster, I. (2009). *Building scientific workflow with Taverna and BPEL: A comparative study in caGrid.* In Service-Oriented Computing – ICSOC 2008 Workshops, (pp. 118-129).

Wroe, C., Stevens, R., Goble, C., Roberts, A., & Greenwood, M. (2003). A suite of DAML+ OIL ontologies to describe bioinformatics Web services and data. *International Journal of Cooperative Information Systems, 12*(2), 197–224. doi:10.1142/S0218843003000711

Yu, J., & Buyya, R. (2005). A taxonomy of scientific workflow systems for Grid computing. *SIGMOD Record, 34*(3), 49. doi:10.1145/1084805.1084814

Zhao, J., Goble, C., Greenwood, M., Wroe, C., & Stevens, R. (2003). Annotating, linking and browsing provenance logs for e-science. In *Proceedings of the Workshop on Semantic Web Technologies for Searching and Retrieving Scientific Data,* (pp. 158–176).

KEY TERMS AND DEFINITIONS

In-Silico Experiment: A scientific experiment performed on computer or via computer simulation.

Knowledge Transfer: Effective sharing of knowledge and know-how between people of varying proficiencies in the considered domains.

Requirement Engineering: The application of scientific knowledge to the practical problem of clearly defining issues and proposed solutions.

Scientific Workflow: The computerised facilitation or automation of an in-silico experiment, in whole or part.

Semantic Web: Latest development of the World Wide Web in which the semantics of information are exposed (formalized) for applications to use.

Software Reuse: The use of existing software parts or software knowledge to build new software with the same or a new goal.

Web Service: A functionality offered on a web server and accessible through a standardized interface.

Chapter 10
Knowledge Engineering Support for Agent-Oriented Software Reuse

Rosario Girardi
Federal University of Maranhão, Brazil

Adriana Leite
Federal University of Maranhão, Brazil

ABSTRACT

Automating software engineering tasks is essential to achieve better productivity in software development and quality of software products. Knowledge engineering can address this challenge through the representation and reuse of knowledge of how and when to perform a development task. This chapter describes a knowledge-based approach for automating agent-oriented development whose main components are a software process (MADAE-Pro) and an integrated development environment (MADAE-IDE). MADAE-Pro is an ontology-driven process for multi-agent domain and application engineering which promotes the construction and reuse of agent-oriented application families. MADAE-IDE is an integrated development environment which assists developers in the application of MADAE-Pro, allowing full or partial automation of its modeling tasks through a set of production rules that explores the semantic representation of modeling products in its knowledge base. The approach has been evaluated through the development of a multi-agent system family of recommender systems supporting alternative (collaborative, content-based and hybrid) filtering techniques. Some examples from these case studies are presented to illustrate and detail the domain analysis and application requirements engineering tasks of MADAE-Pro.

DOI: 10.4018/978-1-60960-509-4.ch010

INTRODUCTION

As well as the advent of databases allowed computers to deal with information more effectively, thus giving rise to the so called information systems, advances on knowledge representation formalisms for constructing knowledge bases have enabled the development of knowledge systems.

Knowledge representation formalisms, like ontologies, are used by modern knowledge systems, to represent and share the knowledge of an application domain. Supporting semantic processing, they allow for more precise information interpretation. Thus, knowledge systems can provide greater usability and effectiveness than traditional information systems. This is particularly the case of knowledge systems for software engineering.

Automating software engineering tasks is crucial to achieve better productivity of software development and quality of software products. Knowledge engineering approaches this challenge by supporting the representation and reuse of knowledge of how and when to perform a development task. Therefore, knowledge tools for software engineering can turn more effective the software development process by automating and controlling consistency of modeling tasks and code generation.

Knowledge systems have evolved from expert systems to agent-oriented or multi-agent systems. By supporting the properties of autonomy, sociability and learning ability of software entities, they provide a better approach to the increasing complexity of both software problems and solutions.

In the last years, many efforts have been devoted to the research on agent-oriented software engineering. The proposals have evolved from simple techniques for modeling specific applications to methodologies and software processes for supporting reuse in agent-oriented development.

This chapter describes the MADAE-Pro knowledge-based software process and its design and implementation in the MADAE-IDE software development environment.

MADAE-Pro ("Multi-agent Domain and Application Engineering Process") is a process for the development and reuse of families of multi-agent software systems. A family of software systems is defined as a set of systems sharing some commonalities but also having particular features (Czarnecki & Eisenecker, 2000). The process consists of two complementary sub-processes: Multi-agent Domain Engineering and Multi-agent Application Engineering. Multi-agent Domain Engineering is a process for the development of a family of multi-agent software systems in a problem domain using MADEM ("Multi-agent Domain Engineering Methodology"); and Multi-agent Application Engineering, the one for constructing a specific agent-oriented application by reusing one or more of those families, using MAAEM ("Multi-agent Application Engineering Methodology"). The process consolidates a long term research effort on techniques, methodologies and tools for promoting reuse on agent-oriented software development (Leite, Girardi, & Cavalcante, 2008a) (Leite, Girardi, & Cavalcante, 2008b) (Girardi & Leite, 2008) (Girardi, Marinho, & Ribeiro, 2005).

Besides providing support for reuse in multi-agent software development, through the integration of concepts of Domain Engineering and Application Engineering, MADAE-Pro is a knowledge-based process where models of requirements, agents and frameworks are represented as ontology instances. Thus, concepts are semantically related allowing effective searches and inferences, facilitating the understanding and reuse of software models during the development of specific applications in a domain. Also, the ontology-driven models of MADAE-Pro can be easily documented, adapted and integrated.

MADAE-IDE ("Multi-agent Domain and Application Engineering Integrated Development Environment") assists developers in the application of the MADAE-Pro process, allowing full or partial automation of its modeling tasks through a set of production rules that explores the semantic representation of modeling products in its knowledge base. It is currently structured as an expert system. Its main components are a user interface and a knowledge base. Through the user interface, a developer interacts with the system in all phases of MADAE-Pro. The knowledge base includes ONTORMAS ("ONTOlogy driven tool for the Reuse of Multi-Agent Systems"), an ontology representing the development knowledge of MADAE-Pro including a set of rules for reasoning about the creation and transformation of models of families or specific multi-agent applications, following the different abstraction levels of the MADAE-Pro modeling tasks.

The chapter is organized as follows. "The MADAE-Pro Software Process Model" introduces the MADAE-Pro software development process along with its lifecycle, a description of the support that the MADEM and MAAEM methodologies provide to each one of its phases, and an overview of the ONTORMAS ontology. Some examples from case studies we have conducted to evaluate MADAE-Pro are also presented in this section to illustrate and detail the domain analysis and application requirements engineering tasks of the process. In "MADAE-IDE", the MADAE-IDE environment is described. "Related Work" discusses related work on the proposed process and environment. "Concluding Remarks" concludes the paper with some considerations on ongoing work.

THE MADAE-PRO SOFTWARE PROCESS MODEL

MADAE-Pro is a knowledge-based process model which integrates an iterative, incremental and goal-driven life cycle along with methodologies for Multi-agent Domain Engineering and Multi-agent Application Engineering, respectively. The knowledge of its phases, tasks and products is represented in a knowledge-base where both multi-agent system specific applications or system families are represented as instances.

MADEM ("Multi-Agent Domain Engineering Methodology") and MAAEM ("Multi-agent Application Engineering Methodology") are the proposed methodologies for Multi-agent Domain Engineering and Multi-agent Application Engineering. Their modeling concepts and tasks are based both on techniques for Domain and Application Engineering (Arango, 1988) (Czarnecki & Eisenecker, 2000) (Pohl, Bockle & Linden, 2005) (Harsu, 2002) (Girardi, 1992) and for development of multi-agent systems (Bellifemine, Caire, Poggi, & Rimassa, 2003) (Zambonelli, Jennings, & Wooldridge, 2003) (Dileo, Jacobs, & Deloach, 2002) (Cossentino, Sabatucci, Sorace, & Chella, 2004) (Bresciani, Giorgini, Giunchiglia, Mylopoulos, & Perini, 2004).

For the specification of a problem to be solved, both methodologies focus on modeling goals, roles and interactions of entities of an organization, representing the requirements of either a multi-agent system family or a specific multi-agent application from the point of view of the organization stakeholders.

Entities have knowledge and use it to exhibit autonomous behavior. An organization is composed of entities with general and specific goals that establish what the organization intends to reach.

The achievement of specific goals allows reaching the general goal of the organization. For instance, an information system can have the general goal of "satisfying the information needs of an organization" and the specific goals of "satisfying dynamic or long term information needs".

Specific goals are reached through the performance of responsibilities in charge of particular roles with a certain degree of autonomy. Preconditions and post-conditions may need to be satisfied for/after the execution of a responsibility. Knowledge can be consumed and produced through the execution of a responsibility. For instance, an entity can play the role of "retriever" with the responsibility of executing the responsibility of satisfying the dynamic information needs of an organization. Another entity can play the role of "filter", in charge of the responsibility of satisfying the long-term information needs of the organization. Sometimes, entities have to communicate with other internal or external entities (like stakeholders) to cooperate in the execution of a responsibility. For instance, the entity playing the role of "filter" may need to interact with a stakeholder to observe his/her behavior in order to infer his/her profile of information interests.

For the specification of a design solution, roles are assigned to reactive or deliberative agents structured and organized into a particular multi-agent architectural solution according to non-functional requirements. Agents have skills related to one or a set of computational techniques that support the execution of responsibilities in an effective way. According to the previous examples, skills can be, for instance, the rules of the organization to access and structure its information sources. For the implementation, the agent design models are mapped to agents, behaviors and communication acts, concepts involved in the JADE/JESS framework (Bellifemine, Caire, Poggi, & Rimassa, 2003) (Friedman-Hill, 2003), which is the adopted implementation platform.

Goals, roles, and responsibilities are the modeling abstractions of the system requirements which are mapped to agents, behaviors and communication acts to construct an agent-oriented computational solution satisfying such requirements.

Variability modeling is a main concern on the construction of multi-agent system families. In MADAE-Pro, it is carried out in parallel with all MADEM phases to determine the common and variable parts of a family. This is done by identifying the "Variation Points" and its corresponding "Variants". A variation point is the representation of a concept subjected to variation. A variant represents the alternative or optional variations of such a concept.

The MADAE-Pro lifecycle

Figure 1 illustrates the MADAE-Pro process life cycle using the SPEM notation (SPEM, 2009). The cycle is iterative, incremental and goal-driven. Development is carried out through successive increments, looking for reducing software complexity. It is initiated with the decision of development of a new family of applications (or a specific one) by specifying a new general goal, and restarted for the development of a new specific goal or to update an existing one in evolutive and corrective maintenance, respectively ("new or existing goal' in the diamond of Figure 1). Iterations also can occur between the phases for refining modeling products. Techniques are associated to each development phase to guide the modeling tasks. Figure 1 also shows the consumed and generated products of each phase.

MADAE-Pro consists of six development phases: domain analysis, domain design and domain implementation, supported by the MADEM methodology; and application requirements engineering, application design and application implementation, guided by the MAAEM methodology.

The MADEM Phases

The domain analysis phase of MADEM approaches the construction of a domain model specifying the current and future requirements of a family of applications in a domain by considering domain knowledge and development experiences extracted from domain specialists and applications already developed in the domain, including products of the Multi-agent Application Engineering sub-process. This phase consists of the following modeling tasks: modeling of domain concepts, goal modeling, role modeling, role interaction modeling and user interface prototyping.

The product of this phase, a domain model, is obtained through the composition of the products constructed through these tasks: a concept model,

Figure 1. The MADAE-Pro lifecycle

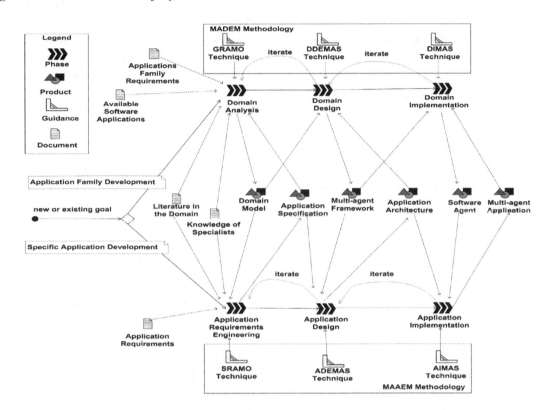

a goal model, a role model, a set of role interaction models, one for each specific goal in the goal model and a prototype of the user interface.

The domain design phase of MADEM approaches the architectural and detailed design of multi-agent frameworks providing a solution to the requirements of a family of multi-agent software systems specified in a domain model. This phase consists of two sub-phases: the architectural design sub-phase and the agent design sub-phase. In the architectural design sub-phase, an architectural model of the multi-agent society is specified, including the knowledge shared by all agents in their communication acts and their coordination and cooperation mechanisms. In the agent design sub-phase, the internal design of each reactive or deliberative agent is defined, by modeling its structure and behavior. A Multi-agent Framework Model of the Multi-agent Society is constructed as a product of this phase, composed of a Multi-

agent Society Knowledge Model, an Architectural Model and a set of Agent Models.

The domain implementation phase of MA-DEM approaches the mapping of design models to agents, behaviors and communication acts. An implementation model of the multi-agent society is constructed as a product of this phase, composed of a model of agents and behaviors and a model of communication acts.

The MAAEM Phases

MAAEM is a methodology for requirement analysis, design and implementation of multi-agent applications constructed either from scratch or through compositional reuse of software artifacts such as domain models, multi-agent frameworks, pattern systems and software agents previously developed in the MADEM Domain Engineering process.

The requirements analysis phase of MAAEM looks for identifying and specifying the requirements of a particular application by reusing requirements already specified in domain models. This phase follows a set of modeling tasks consistently uniform with the ones of the MADEM domain analysis phase for producing a set of models composing the multi-agent requirements specification of the application. The MAAEM requirements analysis phase is performed through the following modeling tasks: concept modeling, goal modeling, role modeling, role interaction modeling and user interface prototyping. The product of this phase, an application specification, is obtained through the composition of the products constructed through these tasks: a concept model, a goal model, a role model, a set of role interaction models, one for each specific goal in the goal model and a prototype of the user interface.

In the application design phase, developers reuse design solutions of a family of applications and adapt them to the specific requirements of the application under development. A set of models composing the multi-agent application architecture are produced by following a set of modeling tasks consistently uniform with the ones of the MADEM domain design phase. This phase consists of two sub-phases: the Architectural Design phase aiming at constructing a multi-agent society architectural model, and the Agent Design phase, when the internal structure of each reactive or deliberative agent in the society is defined. The Architectural Design task consists of four sub-tasks: Multi-agent Society Knowledge Modeling, Multi-Agent Society Modeling, Agent Interaction Modeling, and Coordination and Cooperation modeling. The Detailed Design task is constituted of two subtasks: Agent Knowledge Modeling and Agent Action Modeling.

In the application implementation phase, agent behaviors and interactions are identified and specified in a particular language/platform for agent development. A Behaviors Model and

Communication Acts Model are generated in this development phase.

Along all MAAEM phases, reuse is carried out by identifying variation points in MADEM products and selecting appropriate variants.

The ONTORMAS Knowledge Base

ONTORMAS (Leite, Girardi, & Cavalcante, 2008b) is an ontology representing the knowledge of the MADAE-Pro methodologies. Ontologies (Gruber, 1995) provide an unambiguous terminology that can be shared by all involved in a software development process. They can also be as generic as needed allowing its reuse and easy extension. These features turn ontologies useful for representing the knowledge of software engineering techniques and methodologies, and an appropriate abstraction mechanism for the specification of high-level reusable software artifacts like domain models, frameworks and software patterns (Girardi & Leite, 2008) (Girardi, Marinho, & Ribeiro, 2005).

The ONTORMAS knowledge base is also a software repository of agent-oriented system families and specific applications where software models in different abstraction levels of MADAE-Pro modeling tasks are represented as instances of its class hierarchy.

ONTORMAS was developed in a two phase development process: the specification and the design of the ontology. In the specification phase, the knowledge of MADEM and MAAEM were represented in a semantic network. In the design phase, concepts and relationships in the semantic network were mapped to a frame-based ontology in Protégé (Gennari et al., 2002). A graphical notation was defined for the representation of each modeling product.

The ONTORMAS ontology consists of a set of classes organized hierarchically, with the main super classes: "Variable Concepts," "Modeling Concepts," "Modeling Tasks" and "Modeling Products". The MADAE-Pro knowledge is repre-

Figure 2. Semantic network illustrating main modeling concepts of MADEM and MAAEM in ONTORMAS

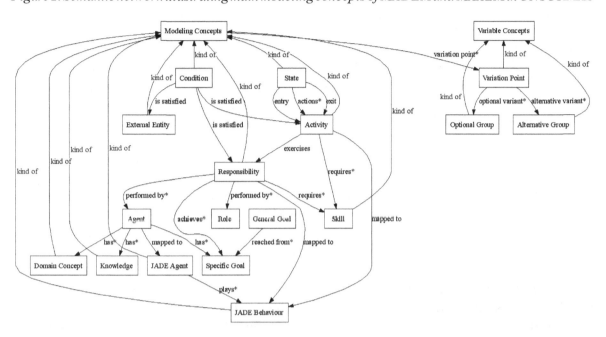

sented along these class hierarchies and semantic relations in class slots. The super class "Variable Concepts" and corresponding subclasses are used to specify the variability of a multi-agent system family. This is accomplished through the definition of "Variation Points" and "Variants" (Figure 2). A variation point is associated to a variable concept. A variant represents the alternative or optional variations of such concept which are represented as semantic relations of the of "Variation Point" class in ONTORMAS. The super class "Modeling Concepts" specifies the modeling concepts of the MADEM and MAAEM methodologies: goals, roles, responsibilities, agents, between others (Figure 2). In the super class "Modeling Tasks" and corresponding subclasses, the MADEM and MAAEM modeling tasks are defined. As an example, Figure 3 illustrates the representation of the tasks performed in the phases of Domain Analysis and Application Requirements Analysis. These tasks consist of the "Domain Engineering Tasks" and the "Application Engineering Tasks" related to the MADEM and MAAEM methodologies, respectively. Subtasks are represented

as semantic relationships of the corresponding class (e.g. "Role Modeling" is one of the sub-tasks of "Application Requirements Analysis"). The subclasses of the "Modeling Products" class represent the knowledge and structure of each software model produced by the corresponding MADEM or MAAEM modeling task. Products can be simple or composed of sub-products. For instance, Figure 4 illustrates part of the hierarchy of "Modeling Products". Sub-products are represented as semantic relationships of the corresponding class (e.g. "Goal Model" is one of the sub-products of "Domain Model").

The products of MADEM and MAAEM are represented as instances of the corresponding "Modeling Products" subclasses in the ONTORMAS class hierarchy. Modeling concepts in a product are represented as instances of the semantic relationships of the corresponding class, having each modeling concept a particular graphical notation. For instance, Figure 4 shows the semantic relationships between two instances of modeling concepts part of the "Goal Model of Infonorma".

Figure 3. Semantic Network with the representation in ONTORMAS of the tasks and subtasks of the Analysis Phase of MADEM and MAAEM

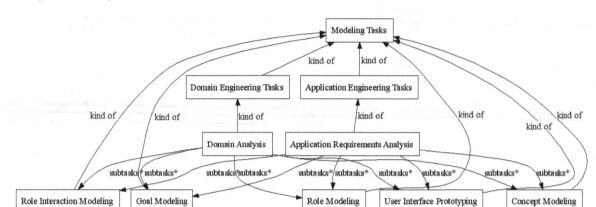

The Domain Analysis and Application Requirements Engineering Tasks

This section describes the Domain Analysis and Application Requirements Engineering tasks of MADAE-Pro showing how software artifacts of the ONTOSERS domain model (Mariano, Girardi, Leite, Drumond, & Maranhão, 2008)

are produced and reused on the development of the InfoTrib multi-agent recommender system (Mariano, 2008). ONTOSERS-DM is a domain model that specifies the common and variable requirements of recommender systems based on the ontology technology of the Semantic Web, using three information filtering approaches: content-based (CBF), collaborative (CF) and

Figure 4. Relationships between classes and instances of modeling products in ONTORMAS

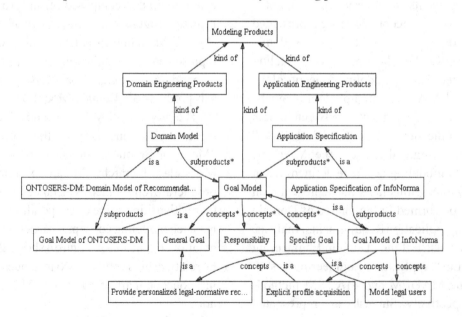

Figure 5. The Domain Analysis and Application Requirements Engineering Phases of MADAE-Pro

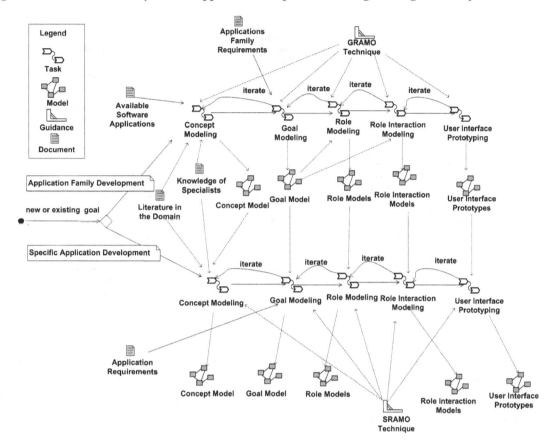

hybrid filtering (HF) (Mariano, Girardi, Leite, Drumond, & Maranhão, 2008).

InfoTrib (Mariano, 2008) is a tax law recommender system in which, based on a user profile specifying his/her interests in the diverse kind of taxes, the system provides recommendations based on new information items related with taxes.

Figure 5 shows a refinement of the MADAE-Pro lifecycle, detailing the tasks and products of the Domain Analysis and Application Requirements Engineering phases.

The Domain Analysis Tasks of MADAE-Pro

The concepts modeling task aims at just performing a brainstorming of domain concepts and their

relationships, representing them in a concept model.

The purpose of the goal modeling task is to identify the common and variant goals of the family of systems, the stakeholders with which it cooperates and the responsibilities needed to achieve them. Its product is a goal model, specifying the general and the system family hierarchy of specific goals along with the stakeholders, responsibilities and variant groups. In this task, variability modeling looks for identifying variant points in specific goals related with variant groups of responsibilities.

As an example, Figure 6 represents the goal model of ONTOSERS. The "Provide Recommendations using Semantic Web Technology" general goal is reached through the "Model Users", "Filter Information" and "Deliver Recommendations"

Figure 6. The ONTOSERS Goal Model

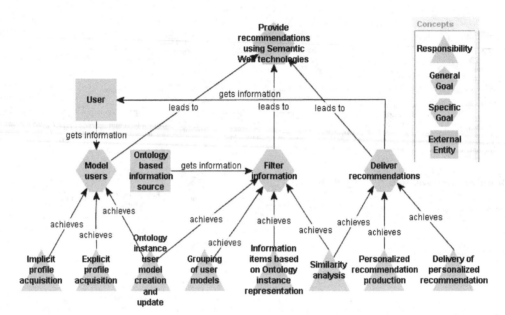

specific goals. In order to achieve the "Filter Information" specific goal, it is necessary to perform the "Ontology Instance User Model Creation and Update" responsibility, which also contributes to reach the "Model Users" specific goal. Besides that, the "Grouping of user models", "Information Items based on Ontology Instance Representation" and "Similarity Analysis" responsibilities are needed. The "Grouping of Users Models" responsibility allows for identifying groups of users with similar interests.

Figure 7 shows the variants of the specific goal "Model users" in the ONTOSERS domain model. The "Model Users" specific goal has a variation point with groups of responsibilities for user profile acquisition, being possible to choose between three alternative variants: "Implicit Profile Acquisition", "Explicit Profile Acquisition" or both. The last responsibility, "Ontology Instance User Model Creation and Update" is fixed, i.e. it is required in all the applications of the family. The "Filter Information" specific goal has a variation point that has as variant alternatives: the "Grouping of users models" responsibility, re-

quired in systems that use CF; and the "Information Items based on Ontology Instance Representation" responsibility required in the ones using CBF. The "Deliver Recommendations" specific goal does not have variation points, therefore the "Similarity Analysis", "Personalized Recommendations Production" and "Delivery of Personalized Recommendations" responsibilities are required in all the applications of the family, then belonging to the fixed part of the goal model.

The role modeling task associates the responsibilities, either common or variants, identified in the goal modeling task to the roles that will be in charge of them. The pre and post-conditions that must be satisfied before and after the execution of a responsibility are also identified. Finally, the knowledge required from other entities (roles or stakeholders) for the execution of responsibilities and the knowledge produced from their execution is identified. This task produces a set of role models, one for each specific goal or, having it one or more variation points, one role model for each variant, specifying roles,

Figure 7. The variation point of the specific goal "Model users" and the alternative groups of responsibilities variants

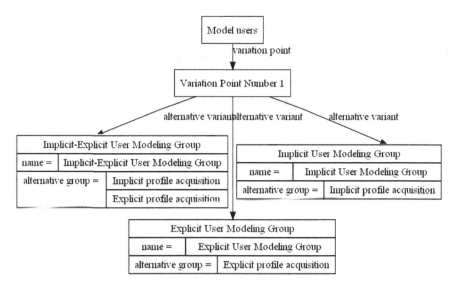

responsibilities, pre- and post-conditions, knowledge and relationships between these concepts.

The role interaction modeling task aims at identifying how external and internal entities should cooperate to achieve a specific goal. For that, responsibilities of roles are analyzed along with their required and produced knowledge specified in a role one or more variation points, one role interaction model for each variant, specifying the interactions between roles and stakeholders needed to achieve a specific goal. The interactions are numbered according to their sequencing model. A set of role interaction models is constructed as a product of this modeling task, one for each specific goal, or having it

Finally, a reusable user interface prototype is developed by identifying the interactions of users with the system family.

The Application Requirements Engineering Tasks

In this phase, reuse of domain models is supported by the MADAE-IDE software development environment. In MADAE-IDE, the selection of

software artifacts is supported by semantic retrieval, where the user inputs a query specifying the product features he/she intends to reuse and gets from the repository the available artifacts satisfying his/her query.

After the selection of the artifact that most closely matches their needs, users should check if the artifact can be integrally reused or if it needs adaptations and/or integrations with other artifacts.

The concepts modeling task aims at performing a brainstorming of the application concepts and their relationships, representing them in a concept model.

The purpose of the goal modeling task is to identify the goals of the application, the stakeholders with which it cooperates and the responsibilities needed to achieve them. Its product is a goal model, specifying the general and specific goals of the application along with the stakeholders and responsibilities. This task should be reuse-intensive. From the concept model and from a first draft of the goal model, possible terms for searching and reusing goals in already available domain models can be revealed.

Figure 8 The Goal Model of INFOTRIB

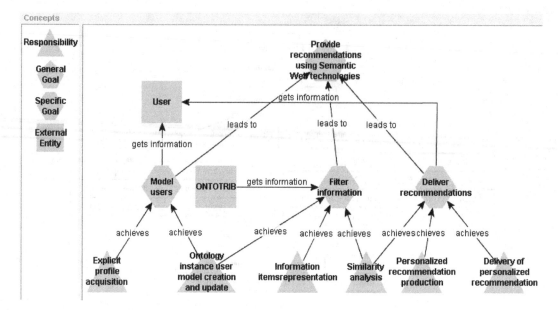

If a general goal is identified, the corresponding goal model in a domain model is selected for reuse. If a specific goal is identified, this goal, sub-goals in a possible hierarchy, related responsibilities and stakeholders in a goal model of a domain model are selected for reuse. Otherwise, the goal model is constructed from scratch.

If a selected specific goal or sub-goals in its hierarchy have associated variation points, they should be analyzed to select and possible reuse the appropriate variants of alternative or optional groups of responsibilities by considering both functional and non-functional requirements of the specific application. Only one group of responsibilities in an alternative variant can be selected for reuse. Zero or more groups of responsibilities in an optional variant can be selected for reuse.

Figure 8 illustrates the goal model of InfoTrib. To construct it, first, a search in the ONTORMAS knowledge base with the term "recommendation" was done. The general goal "Provide recommendations using semantic web technologies" was retrieved through the search. Therefore, the corresponding goal model was selected for reuse, in this case, the goal model of ONTOSERS (Figure

6), part of the ONTOSERS domain model. From the variation point of the "Model users" specific goal (Figure 7), the "Explicit profile acquisition" responsibility variant was selected in order to support just the functional requirement of explicit acquisition of user profiles. From the variation point of the "Filter Information" specific goal, the "Information Items based on Ontology Instance Representation" responsibility variant was selected for providing content-based information filtering. The name of the external entity "Ontology based information source" was specialized to "ONTOTRIB", the ontology that defines the Tax Law concepts and relationships.

The role modeling task associates the responsibilities identified in the goal modeling task to the roles that will be in charge of them. The pre and post-conditions that must be satisfied before and after the execution of a responsibility are also identified. Finally, the knowledge required from other entities (roles or stakeholders) for the execution of responsibilities and the knowledge produced from their execution is identified. A set of role models, one for each specific goal in the goal model is constructed in this task, with or without reuse.

The following rules apply for the reuse activities performed during this modeling task:

- If a similar general goal is identified during the goal modeling task, thus reusing fully or partially a goal model then, the set of role models, already available in the corresponding domain model and associated to each reused specific goal, will be reused and eventually adapted for the previously customized specific goals and selected responsibilities from groups of alternative or optional variants.

- Otherwise, if a set of similar specific goals are identified during the goal modeling task, thus reusing partially a goal model, then the set of role models already available in the corresponding domain model, associated with the similar specific goal will be reused and eventually adapted, considering selected responsibilities from groups of alternative or optional variants.

- Otherwise, if the goal model is constructed from scratch, then the set of role models will be also constructed from scratch, one for each specific goal.

Please note that, in this task, reuse is implicitly supported by the semantic relationships that associate a specific goal with a role model.

The role interaction modeling task aims at identifying how external and internal entities should cooperate to achieve a specific goal. For that, responsibilities of roles are analyzed along with their required and produced knowledge specified in a role model. A set of role interaction models is reused in this modeling task, one for each specific goal. The interactions are numbered according to their sequencing. Similar rules to the ones of the role modeling task apply for the reuse activities performed during this modeling task.

For the construction of the user interface prototype of the specific application, the generic interfaces associated to a reused external entity are selected and customized according to the specific goal with which it is related.

MADAE-IDE

MADAE-IDE is an integrated development environment which assists developers in the application of the MADAE-Pro process, allowing full or partial automation of its modeling tasks through a set of production rules that explores the semantic representation of modeling products, instances of the ONTORMAS knowledge base. It is structured as an expert system (Giarratano, & Riley, 1989) whose main components are a user interface and environment core including a knowledge base and an inference mechanism.

Through the user interface, a developer interacts with the system in all phases of MADAE-Pro. The user interface consists of a set of modeling wizards to guide the developer in the execution of each one of the tasks of MADAE-Pro.

The knowledge base includes the ONTORMAS ontology; a set of production rules for reasoning about the creation and transformation of models of families or specific multi-agent applications, following the different abstraction levels of the MADAE-Pro modeling tasks; and a working memory consisting of a set of facts (unconditional clauses) representing the knowledge introduced by the developer during his/her interaction with the system.

The system rule is composed by creating and transforming rules. Creating rules instantiate the classes that represent, in ONTORMAS, the phases, tasks, products and modeling concepts, defined in MADAE-Pro, based on the modeling information provided by the developer through his/her interactions with the environment. Transformation rules automatically generate a target model from a set of source models, based on the MADAE-Pro

Figure 9. Semantic relationships between the "Goal Model" and "Role Model" in ONTORMAS

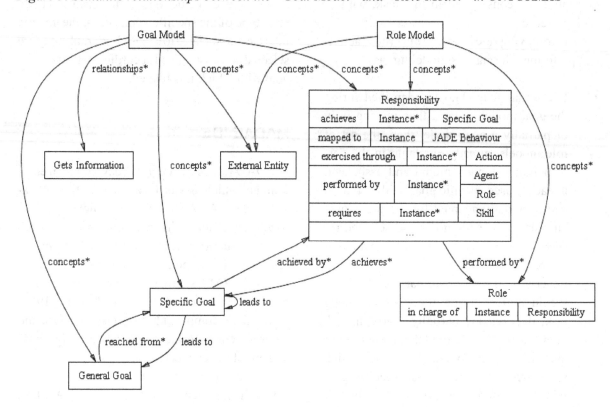

life cycle and on some user provided modeling information.

Creating Process

The creating process (P_c) of a target model is defined as the tuple $P_c = (T, U, R_c)$.

T is a target model, $T = MC_t \cup SR_t$, and $MC_t \subseteq MC$, $SR_t \subseteq SR$; $mc_i \in MC$ is a modeling concept and $sr_i \in SR$, a semantic relationship in the ONTORMAS knowledge base. For instance, in the domain analysis phase, a goal model should be created by applying a creating rule, considering the modeling concepts and semantic relationships in Figure 9: $T_{\text{"Goal Model"}} = \{$"General Goal", "Specific Goal", "Responsibility", "External Entity", "Gets Information", "Leads To", "Achieved By"$\}$.

U is the modeling information provided by users through their interactions with MADAE-IDE

using the modeling assistant associated with the respective modeling task.

R_c is the set of creating rules for generating the target model. As an example, the Jess rule (Friedman-Hill, 2003) in the example below is part of the set of creating rules for generating the ONTORMAS instances representing a "Goal Model" product.

```
(defrule GoalModelCreate
  (ModelingProduct
      (product DomainModel) (ref
?DomainModel&~nil))
  (ModelingTask
      (task GoalModeling) (ref
?GoalModeling&~nil))
  ?GoalModel <-
  (ModelingProduct
      (product GoalModel) (name
?name) (ref nil))
```

```
=>
  (bind ?ref (make-instance of "Goal
Model" (name ?name)))
  (modify ?GoalModel (ref ?ref))
  (slot-set ?GoalModeling products
?ref)
  (slot-insert$ ?DomainModel subprod-
ucts 1 ?ref))
```

Transformation Process

A transformation process (P_t) is defined as the tuple $P_t = (S_1, S_2, ..., S_n, T, U, R_t)$.

S_i is a source model and T, the target model, product of the modeling task t, having the same definition of the set T in the creating process (P_c) described above. For instance, in the "Role Modeling" task, a "Role Model" will be generated $(T_{Role\ Model})$ through a transformation of the Goal Model $(S_{Goal\ Model})$.

U is the modeling information provided by users through their interactions with MADAE-IDE using the modeling assistant associated with the respective modeling task.

R_t is the set of transforming rules for automatically generating a target model from a set of source models and the information U provided by the developer. For instance, in the domain analysis phase, a "Role model" should be partially automatically generated through a set of transforming rules which explore the semantic relationships between a "Goal Model" and a "Role Model" illustrated in Figure 9, and considering that "Responsibilities" and "External Entities" are modeling concepts of both models. The following Jess rule is part of the set of the transforming rules for generating the ONTORMAS instances representing the "Role Modeling" task and its "Role Model" product from the source "Goal Model".

```
(defrule GoalModelToRoleModel
  (ModelingProduct
        (product GoalModel) (ref
?GoalModel&~nil))
```

```
(ModelingTask
        (task RoleModeling) (ref
?RoleModeling&~nil))
  (ModelingProduct
        (product RoleModel) (name
?name) (ref ?RoleModel&~nil))
  =>
  (foreach ?concept (slot-get ?Goal-
Model concepts)
  (if (or (eq Responsibility (class
?concept))
        (eq External\ Entity (class
?concept)))
  then
    (slot-insert$ ?RoleModel concepts 1
?concept))))
```

Evaluation

Using MADAE-IDE, a case study was conducted where ADVISE, a knowledge-based system family was developed. Development efforts and quality of the generated products were compared with the ones obtained through the construction with the ONTORMAS tool, of a family with equivalent software requirements: the ONTOSERS family (Mariano, Girardi, Leite, Drumond, & Maranhão, 2008).

A reduction of more than 50% in development efforts was observed experimentally with the use of MADAE_IDE. Also, several inconsistencies detected in the ONTOSERS software models (like duplicated concept instances, non-instantiated semantic relationships, between others) were avoided in the ADVISE family, thus improving the quality of the models generated with MADAE-IDE.

RELATED WORK

Several approaches for agent-oriented software development, like GAIA (Zambonelli, Jennings, & Wooldridge, 2003), PASSI (Cossentino, Sa-

•

Table 1. A simple comparison of agent-oriented software development approaches

FEATURES	GAIA	PASSI	TROPOS	DOMAIN ENGI-NEERING PROCESS	MADAE PRO
Lifecycle	Iterative within each phase, but sequential between phases	Iterative across and within all phases and incremental	Iterative and Incremental	Iterative and Incremental	Iterative and Incremental
Coverage of the lifecycle	Analysis and design	Analysis, design and implementation	Analysis, design and implementation	Analysis, design and implementation of system families	Analysis, design and implementation of system families and specific applications
Tool Support	No	Yes	Yes	Yes	Yes
Reuse Support	Informal	Informal	Informal	Systematic (partially)	Systematic
Variability Modeling Support	No	No	No	Yes	Yes

batucci, Sorace, & Chella, 2004) and TROPOS (Bresciani, Giorgini, Giunchiglia, Mylopoulos, & Perini, 2004) and some domain engineering processes (Nunes I., Kulesza, Nunes C., & Lucena, 2009), have been already developed to increase the productivity of the software development process, the reusability of generated products, and the effectiveness of project management.

GAIA is a methodology based in human organization concepts. It supports the analysis and design phases of multi-agent system development. Tropos is an agent-oriented software development methodology supporting the complete multi-agent development process. It is based on the i* organizational modeling framework. PASSI is a process for multi-agent development integrating concepts from object-oriented software engineering and artificial intelligence approaches. It allows the development of multi-agents systems for special purposes as mobiles and robotics agents and uses an UML-based notation. In (Nunes I., Kulesza, Nunes C., & Lucena, 2009) is described a domain engineering process which focuses on system families including domain scoping and variability modeling. This process integrates a product line UML-based method, the PASSI methodology and a modeling language for developing multi-agent system product lines.

Table 1 summarizes and compares some characteristics of GAIA, PASSI, TROPOS, MADAE-Pro and the domain engineering process described above. All the approaches propose an iterative life cycle, where a software product follows several refinements during the development process. With the exception of GAIA, in all other approaches the life cycle is also incremental, where a software product is represented in several models to facilitate its understanding.

For the supported development phases, all these approaches cover analysis and design while PASSI, TROPOS and MADAE-Pro also support the implementation phase. The domain engineering process described above covers the domain engineering phases of early and late requirements, domain design and domain realization. To our knowledge, only MADAE-Pro provides support for both domain and application engineering.

For the available development tools, PASSI is supported by PTK, a Rational Rose plug-in allowing modeling in AUML and code generation. The application of TROPOS is assisted by the TAOM-Tool (Perini, & Susi, 2004), an Eclipse plug-in allowing system modeling with the i* framework. The MADAE-Pro process is supported by the MADAE-IDE integrated development environment that supports partial automatic generation of models and source code in all development phases and storage of individual applications and families of multi-agent applications as instances of the ONTORMAS ontology. GAIA does not report a tool support yet.

For reuse activities, GAIA and TROPOS allow the reuse of models and code in an informal way. PASSI permits the reuse of source code from class and activity diagrams. The domain engineering process described in (Nunes I., Kulesza, Nunes C., & Lucena, 2009) is based on the concept of feature, a system property relevant to some stakeholder, used to capture commonalities and to discriminate products in software product lines. However, this process does not offer guidelines for the selection, adaptation and integration of software artifacts. MADAE-Pro process allows reuse of both models and source code of software products giving support for their selection, adaptation and integration.

For the variability modeling support, only MADAE-Pro and the domain engineering process described in (Nunes I., Kulesza, Nunes C., & Lucena, 2009) support it. This approach uses an extension of UML for modeling variabilities (Goma, 2005) while MADAE-Pro uses MADAE-ML, an ontology-driven modeling language.

Two main features distinguish MADAE-Pro from other existing approaches. First, it provides support for manual and automatic reuse in multi-agent software development, through the integration of the concepts of Domain Engineering and Application Engineering. Second, it is a knowledge-based process where models of agents and frameworks are represented as instances of the ONTORMAS ontology. Thus, concepts are semantically related allowing effective searches and inferences thus facilitating the understanding and reuse of models during the development of specific applications in a domain. Also, the ontology-driven models of MADAE-Pro can be easily documented, adapted and integrated.

CONCLUDING REMARKS

This work described a knowledge-based approach for automating agent-oriented development whose main components are a software process (MADAE-Pro) and an integrated development environment (MADAE-IDE). MADAE-Pro is an ontology-driven process for multi-agent domain and application engineering which promotes the construction and reuse of agent-oriented application families.

The SPEM process modeling language has been used to formalize MADAE-Pro, thus providing a standard, documented and ambiguity free representation of the process. The formalization of MADAE-Pro has allowed the systematic application of its life cycle along with the MADEM and MAAEM methodologies for the construction of multi-agent system families and specific multi-agent applications as well. Also, this formal model provided a framework for automating the MADAE-Pro development tasks with the MADAE-IDE development environment.

MADAE-Pro has been evaluated with case studies approaching both the development of application families (Girardi, & Marinho, 2007) (Mariano, Girardi, Leite, Drumond, & Maranhão, 2008) and specific applications (Drumond, & Girardi, 2008) (Newton, & Girardi, 2007). The process currently supports just compositional reuse, based on the selection, adaptation and composition of software artifacts. A generative approach for reuse has been explored with the specification of the GENMADEM methodology and the ONTOGENMADEM tool (Jansen, & Girardi, 2006). ONTOGENMADEM provides support for the creation of Domain Specific Languages to be used on the generation of a family of applications in a domain. Further work will extend ONTORMAS and MADAE-IDE for supporting ONTOGENMADEM thus allowing generative reuse in Multi-agent Application Engineering.

MADAE-IDE is an integrated development environment which assists developers in the application of MADAE-Pro, allowing full or partial automation of its modeling tasks through a set of production rules that explores the semantic representation of modeling products in its knowledge base. The software artifacts produced through its modeling tasks are instantiated in the ON-TORMAS knowledge base, which it is used as a repository of reusable software artifacts. The semantic representation of software products increase reuse effectiveness, providing more precision on software retrieval.

Before MADAE-IDE, the MADAE-Pro software development process was supported by the ONTORMAS tool, composed of the ONTORMAS ontology, and a graphical language and editor for manual modeling tasks. The creation, association and retrieval of ONTORMAS instances manually revealed to be laborious and error-prone turning the ONTORMAS knowledge-base usually inconsistent.

The modeling assistants and the creating and transforming rules of MADAE-IDE encode the knowledge of the MADAE-Pro process. Thus, MADAE-IDE automates the application of MADAE-Pro improving the quality of software products. Also, modeling efforts and development times are reduced in a great extent through the automatic or semi-automatic generation of the MADAE-Pro modeling products.

REFERENCES

Arango, G. (1988). *Domain engineering for software reuse*. Unpublished doctoral thesis, Department of Information and Computer Science, University of California, Irvine.

Bellifemine, F., Caire, G., Poggi, A., & Rimassa, G. (2003). *JADE: A White Paper*. Retrieved from http://jade.tilab.com/

Bresciani, P., Giorgini, P., Giunchiglia, F., Mylopoulos, J., & Perini, A. (2004). TROPOS: An agent-oriented software development methodology. [Kluwer Academic Publishers.]. *Journal of Autonomous Agents and Multi-Agent Systems, 8*(3), 203–236. doi:10.1023/B:AGNT.0000018806.20944.ef

Cossentino, M., Sabatucci, L., Sorace, S., & Chella, A. (2004). Patterns reuse in the PASSI methodology. In *Proceedings of the Fourth International Workshop Engineering Societies in the Agents World (ESAW'03), Imperial College*, London, UK, October, (pp. 29-31).

Czarnecki, K., & Eisenecker, U. (2000). *Generative programming: Methods, tools, and applications*. New York: ACM Press/Addison-Wesley Publishing Co.

Dileo, J., Jacobs, T., & Deloach, S. (2002). Integrating ontologies into multi-agent systems engineering. *Proceedings of 4th International Bi-Conference Workshop on Agent Oriented Information Systems* (AOIS 2002), Bologna (Italy), July, (pp. 15-16).

Friedman-Hill, E. (2003). *JESS in action*. Manning Publications.

Gennari, J. (2002). *The evolution of Protégé: An environment for knowledge-based systems development*. (Technical Report SMI-2002-0943).

Giarratano, J., & Riley, G. (1989). *Expert systems: Principles and programming*. PWS-KENT Publishing Company.

Girardi, R. (1992). Application engineering: Putting reuse to work. In Tsichritzis, D. (Ed.), *Object frameworks* (pp. 137–149). Université de Geneve.

Girardi, R., & Drumond, L. (2008). Multi-agent legal recommender system. In *Artificial intelligence and law*. (pp. 175-207).

Girardi, R., & Leite, A. (2008). A knowledge-based tool for multi-agent domain engineering. *Knowledge-Based Systems Journal, 21*, 604–611. doi:10.1016/j.knosys.2008.03.036

Girardi, R., & Marinho, L. (2007). A domain model of Web recommender systems based on usage mining and collaborative filtering. [Springer-Verlag.]. *Requirements Engineering Journal*, *12*(1), 23–40. doi:10.1007/s00766-006-0038-5

Girardi, R., Marinho, L., & Ribeiro, I. (2005). A system of agent-based patterns for user model-ling based on usage mining. *Interacting with Computers*, *17*(5), 567–591. doi:10.1016/j.intcom.2005.02.003

Goma, H. (2005). *Designing software product lines with UML: From use cases to pattern-based software architectures*. Addison-Wesley Object Technology Series.

Gruber, T. (1995). Toward principles for the design of ontologies used for knowledge sharing. *International Journal of Human-Computer Studies*, *43*, 907–928. doi:10.1006/ijhc.1995.1081

Harsu, M. (2002). *A survey of domain engineering*. (Report 31, Institute of Software Systems, Tampere University of Technology).

Jansen, M., & Girardi, R. (2006). GENMADEM: A methodology for generative multi-agent domain engineering. In *Proceedings of the 9th International Conference on Software Reuse, Torino*. (LNCS 4039), (pp. 399-402). Berlin: Springer-Verlag.

Leite, A., Girardi, R., & Calvalcante, U. (2008a). MAAEM: A multi-agent application engineering methodology. *Proceedings of the 20th International Conference on Software Engineering and Knowledge Engineering*, (pp. 735-740). Redwood City, CA: Knowledge Systems Institute.

Leite, A., Girardi, R., & Cavalcante, U. (2008b). An ontology for multi-agent domain and applica-tion engineering. *Proceedings of the 2008 IEEE International Conference on Information Reuse and Integration* (IEEE IRI-08), (pp. 98-103). Las Vegas, NV: IEEE.

Mariano, R. (2008). *Development of a family of recommender systems based on the Semantic Web technology and its reuse on the recommendation of legal tax information items*. MSc dissertation.

Mariano, R., Girardi, R., Leite, A., Drumond, L., & Maranhão, D. (2008). A case study on domain analysis of Semantic Web multi-agent recom-mender systems. In *Proceedings 3th International Conference on Software and Data Technologies, Porto. Portugal*, (pp. 160-167).

Newton, E., & Girardi, R. (2007). *PROPOST: A knowledge-based tool for supporting project port-folio management*. International Conference on Systems Engineering and Modeling - ICSEM'07, (pp. 98-103).

Nunes, I., Kulesza, U., Nunes, C., & Lucena, C. A. (2009). A domain engineering process for developing multi-agent systems product lines. *Proceedings of the 8th International Conference of Autonomous Agents and Multi-agent Systems* (AAMAS 2009), Budapest, (pp. 10-15).

Perini, A., & Susi, A. (2004). Developing tools for agent-oriented visual modeling. In G. Linde-mann, J. Denzinger, I. Timm, & R. Unland (Eds.), *Proceedings of the Second German Conference* (pp. 169–182). Springer-Verlag.

Pohl, K., Bockle, G., & Linden, F. (2005). *Software product line engineering: Foundations, principles and techniques*. USA: Springer Verlag.

SPEM. (2008). Software process engineering metamodel specification. Retrieved Septem-ber 2008, from http://www.omg.org/docs/for-mal/05-01-06.pdf

Zambonelli, F., Jennings, N., & Wooldridge, M. (2003). Developing multi-agent systems: The Gaia methodology. *ACM Transactions on Software Engineering and Methodology*, 417–470.

Chapter 11
Software Reusability Estimation Model Using Metrics Governing Design Architecture

Gopalakrishnan T.R. Nair
Research and Industry Incubation Centre, Dayananda Sagar Institutions, India

Selvarani R
Research and Industry Incubation Centre, Dayananda Sagar Institutions, India

ABSTRACT

The current trend of open source development and outsourcing industry heavily banks upon the reusability of software for achieving consistency in quality and optimization of cost. Hence, software developers require excellent support in the assessment of the reusability levels of the software that they are trying to develop. This chapter introduces a method which will analyze the object oriented software design and calculate the possible reusability level of that software module. It measures the structural properties of software using design metrics and transforms those measures to reusability levels associated with that package. This scheme brings out a novel data driven-methodology, which can predict the reusability of a software system at its design phase itself and provide a feedback to the design architect to improve the design appropriately to achieve better reusable and cost effective software products.

INTRODUCTION

The industry prefers the development of software with high reusability and good maintainability for better quality and productivity. It has become necessary to optimize Object oriented (OO) paradigm

DOI: 10.4018/978-1-60960-509-4.ch011

offers the technology to create reusable classes and components. It is one of the main external quality factors of the software which is expected to produce much impact on productivity and quality. The design complexity of OO paradigm plays a major role in determining the reusability of the software. This paper proposes an effective estimation model for reusability at design stage considering the design complexity measurements in terms of Chidamber and Kemerer (Chidamber S, 1994; S.R. Chidamber, 1991) metric suite. This metric suite helps developers to understand the design complexity and is widely cited in literatures (V. Basili, 1996; Briand L. C, 1996; Bieman J, 1991; Karunanithi S, 1992; Kitchenham, B. A, 1997; Dandashi F, 1998). The six metrics in this suite indicates the internal design properties like inheritance, coupling, cohesion, class complexity, message passing and method invocation (Chidamber S, 1994; S.R Chidamber, 1991). Here, the complex functional relationship existing between the internal and external qualities of the software (Poels G, 1997; K.K. Aggarwal, 2005) is made use for estimating the reusability of fresh modules getting designed. This gives valuable information at the design phase because it can call for design changes to achieve required reusability levels at this early period saving cost and effort (J. F. Peters, 2000).

The proposed estimation model finds the intricate relationship between the internal quality attributes indicated by CK metric suite and the reusability index of software systems. This research work focuses on constructing facts having dependency on reusability and design complexity (K.K. Aggarwal, 2005; L. H. Etzkorn, 2001). We did not include the size metric because this work concentrates on the study of the influence of design properties which is independent of size metric. All the previous research work related to estimating the reusability using CK metrics deals with only a few parameters in the suite thereby covering few design aspects of OO Paradigm. In this model the complete set of metrics in the suite which represents all design features of the paradigm is considered. Most of the previous models used some statistical models but here we introduced regression approach to map the relationship between design metrics and reusability.

The organization of this paper is as follows. The section 2 discusses the background of this research work, and section three presents the properties

in CK metric suite. The section four explains the formation of reusability estimation model. The section 5 describes the empirical analysis of this model to quantify the interaction effect of these measures on software reusability. The section 6 describes the functional relationship between design metrics and reusability. In section 7, the comprehensive software reusability estimation model is explained in detail. Section 8 discusses the model evaluation and validation. In section 9 results and discussions are presented. To the best of our knowledge, this work has not been taken up in the past. Section 10 presents the conclusion and the future work.

BACKGROUND

Reusability is the external quality factor of OO software that enables it to be used again in another application, be it partial, modified or complete. In other words, software reusability is a measure of the ease with which previously acquired concepts and objects can be used in new contexts (Sommerville I., 1996; G. Caldiera, 1991). 32% reusability is reported by NASA laboratory by characteristic analysis of reusable components from existing systems (J. C. Esteva, 1991). The experimental study conducted by Selby (R. W. Selby, 1988) discussing about module design factors and module implementation factors which are the two main factors have influence on reuse in large scale systems.

The software can be planned to have reusable components for future use with extra investment in process and time (Bieman, J., 1995; Blum, 1992). Software reuse is getting considerable attention and people focus on research in methodologies, tools and techniques to promote creative reuse (C.GACEK, 2002). The object oriented design properties or internal design quality (IDQ) factors have significant influence on software reusability. This paper found out a mapping relationship between the complete set of design metrics and

Table 1. CK metrics and NASA threshold

Metric	NASA –Rosenberg Threshold (L. Rosenberg, 2001)		Description
	Optimum	Maximum	
WMC (Weigted Method for class)	20,	100	Sum of complexities of methods in a class or Count of methods of a class. High value indicates decreased Reusability and Maintainability.
RFC (Response for class)	[50, 100]	222	It measures the complexity of the class considering the number of methods and amount of communication with other classes. It is a direct indicator of design complexity and testability
LCOM (Lack of Cohesion on Method)	[0,1]	-	It is the degree to which the methods within a class are related to one another. Low value indicates good design and will increase the reusability. High value increases the complexity.
CBO (Coupling Between Objects)	5	24	It is the count of the classes to which this class is coupled. A high value indicates limited reuse and poor design.(decreased modularity)
DIT (Depth of Inheritance Trees)	3	6	It is the depth of inheritance hierarchy. High value is good for Reusability, but it will increase complexity.
NOC (Number of Children)	-	5	It is the number of immediate subclasses. High value indicates increased reusability also high maintainability, testing effort and complexity.

reusability as shown in Figure 3. The curves were created through regression properties based on the evidence as per the reference (G. Caldiera, 1991; M. F. Dunn, 1993; R.S. Arnold, 1990). The novelty of dealing the reusability is out of the successful use of regression curve with empirical data and mapping reusability based on different regions of the influence curve.

PROPERTIES IN CK METRIC SUITE

The unambiguous perspective of the definitions of CK metric suite and the assurance of their relevance to the internal design properties is the motivation to select this metric suite for representing the design characteristics. The thresholds recommended by NASA research laboratory is adopted for quantifying the influence of the design properties on reusability. Table 1 depicts the CK metric description and the adopted threshold criteria.

REUSABILITY ESTIMATION FRAMEWORK

The improvement in software quality can be achieved through software design quality measurement and implementation of the measurement driven process. Figure 1 depicts the framework for reusability estimation model. The structural design measures from design or code artifacts are obtained in terms of CK Metric data through measurement. The input to this process is the UML class diagram or the equivalent Java code. Automated tools like Understand for Java (Bieman J., 1995), Rational Rose etc. can be used to get these metric data from code artifacts.

Manual method of counting is adopted when the input for the measurement system is the class diagram. Metrics like WMC, DIT, and NOC can be calculated using static class diagrams and metrics like CBO and RFC can be calculated using dynamic sequential diagrams. According to our knowledge, there is no specific effective method to measure LCOM directly from the design diagrams; it can only be obtained through

Figure 1. Formation of reusability estimation model

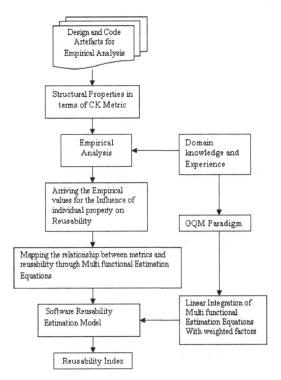

the measurement of code artifacts using the automated tools.

The empirical analysis is carried out on these metric data from selected projects. The influence of individual metrics on reusability is arrived through this analysis. The average values of these observations are shown in Table 3. The relationship between the metrics and reusability is established through multifunctional equations as shown in Figure 4. The final estimation model is arrived through the linear combination of these multifunctional estimation equations with appropriate weighted coefficients as shown in Figure 5. These coefficients are the percentage contribution of design metrics on reusability. The percentage contribution of metrics on reusability is obtained through Goal Question Metric Paradigm.

INFLUENCE OF INTERNAL DESIGN PROPERTIES ON REUSABILITY

The percentage influence of internal design quality factors on reusability is measured based on the empirical study 9Denaro, 2002; Arisholm, 2006; Sinaalto, 2006). The study is built upon framing appropriate hypotheses based on heuristic approaches, domain knowledge and the previous research work (R.S. Arnold, 1990; Bieman, J., 1995; S.R Chidamber, 1991; Krishnan, 2000). Descriptive approach is adopted to conduct the empirical study as per the guidelines suggested by Kitchenham et.al (Bieman J, 1995). It aims primarily at gathering knowledge about the nature of the internal design quality parameters on reusability factor (Denaro, 2002). The empirical measurements and observations are conducted on many medium and large scale commercial java projects in various software industries including the in-house industry. The relationship between the reusability and the design constructs is established with the thresholds (S.R Chidamber, 1991) as shown in Table 1.

Hypotheses:

H1: Classes with high DIT values are associated with higher class reusability.

H2: Classes with high LCOM have better reusability

H3: Classes with higher and lower value of RFC are associated with low reusability.

H4: Classes with high NOC are associated with a higher reusability of class

H5: Classes with higher CBO values are associated with lower reusability.

H6: Classes with high WMC values are associated with lower class reusability.

EMPIRICAL MODEL

In this section we propose an empirical model for quantifying the influence of structural properties of object oriented design on reusability. Project I consists of 265 classes out of which 96 classes are reusable, project II is having 423 classes out of which 198 classes are reusable. The heterogeneity in the empirical model analysis is controlled by accounting projects of same property and moderate complexity. Because of the intellectual property protection issues the details of the projects are not furnished here. However we had viewing admittance to the source code, design document and configuration management system during our study and the design metric data was captured. The classes in the projects are segregated and grouped according to different metric values. This process will be repeated for all the metrics in the suite. Each metric has a range of values that manifest in the design of the software. This range is split in to a few practical bins in to which classes of those values can be deposited; enabling the judgment of participatory effect of these metrics. Later investigations are carried out on the occurrence of reusability tracing to segregated classes. These counts against each parameter are noted and marked across the particular bin of classes. This is taken as the case study for generating the response curve. Figure 2 depicts the distribution with respect to metric values.

In the past, researchers have raised an argument regarding the ambiguity in the definition of the metric LCOM (Hironori Washizaki, 2003; V. Basili, 1996). It is found that the original definition of this metric pruned all values above 1 and below 0, and this pruning limits the metrics ability to fully capture the lack of cohesion. To conduct the empirical analysis, this metric is measured at code level using automated tool. It is observed that this metric value is same for all classes in a project.

The classes of the bin having metric value = N are manually checked for its properties in the industry where this research was carried out for its population ratio with respect to reusability aspect. It is to measure the contribution of all of the design metrics of particular class in support of reusability of the class. It can be seen that classes of different metric value will have different level of influence on reusability. The percentage influence on reusability by a particular metric value is given as

RuC* * 100

$$\% \text{ Influence on Reusability} = \frac{\text{RuC* * 100}}{\text{BoCR}} \rightarrow \text{Reusability Factor}$$

Where

BoCR-No. of Classes/metric (bin of classes)

RuC*-No. of classes contributed to the reusability from the bin having metric = N.

NOTE: The observation of classes shown in the column RuC* in Figure 2, has been approximated to integer values over the averages for identifying the number of classes. Hence slight difference in the percentage reusability can be present.

METHOD OF CALCULATION

For example when DIT = 3, the bin may contain 56 classes out of 265 classes in project 1 as shown in Figure 2. From this bin it is observed that 21 of them may be reusable out of 96 reusable classes of the project. Hence the percentage influence of the DIT value on reusability is 36.9. Similarly it is calculated for every metric value and shown in Figure 2 and the mean values are shown in Table 2.

Analysis of Design Properties

It is observed that the relationship between design metrics, and reusability at the class level is inherently nonlinear. Properties like inheritance will aid reusability but end up with high design complexity. It is often found that a medium level of inheritance is used in designing the components. High coupling is destined for more specialized components and it will not promote reusability. Similarly, higher number of methods in a class increases complexity and the classes will be more abstract to support reusability. If the methods are

Figure 2. Empirical model reusability

		Project - I			Project - II			
Metric Item	Metric Value N	**BoCR** No. of Classes/metric (bin of classes)	**RuC**-no. of classes contributed to the reusability from the bin having metric = N	% Influence on reusability	**BoCR** No. of Classes/metric (bin of classes)	**RuC**-no. of classes contributed to the reusability from the bin having metric = N	% Influence on reusability	Mean value
DIT	1	49	5	9.4	30	3	8.7	9.1
	2	72	16	21.9	78	16	20.4	21.2
	3	56	21	36.9	110	38	34.4	35.7
	4	41	24	57.7	105	56	53.8	55.8
	5	23	18	76.1	43	30	70.9	73.5
	6	24	24	99.9	57	54	95.3	97.6
RFC	1	60	2	2.9	54	2	3.2	3.1
	23	91	28	31.0	106	33	31.0	31.0
	45	33	18	55.8	91	51	56.3	56.1
	60	21	17	80.2	46	37	79.9	80.1
	80	12	11	90.8	35	32	90.9	90.9
	100	20	16	78.4	44	34	77.7	78.1
	120	12	7	62.0	1	1	62.1	62.1
	149	11	6	51.1	3	2	51.0	51.1
	170	2	1*	41.0	3	1	39.2	40.1
	198	2	1*	26.3	19	5	25.8	26.1
	222	1	0	6.9	21	1	7.1	7.0
NOC	0	255	0	0.0	415	0	0.0	0.0
	1	6	0	6.8	4	0	7.3	7.1
	2	1	0	29.0	1	0	29.2	29.1
	3	1	1	55.8	1	1	56.4	56.1
	4	1	1	74.1	1	1	74.2	74.2
	5	1	1	81.9	1	1	82.1	82.0
CBO	1	1	1	98.2	4	4	98.0	98.1
	3	5	5	93.0	14	13	93.2	93.1
	5	12	11	87.9	32	28	88.2	88.1
	9	14	11	80.0	52	42	80.1	80.1
	14	29	19	65.0	51	33	65.0	65.0
	19	63	28	44.2	82	36	43.9	44.1
	22	87	23	26.3	122	32	26.0	26.2
	24	54	9	16.2	66	10	15.9	16.1
WMC	1	13	1	4.9	26	1	4.9	4.9
	5	57	14	24.8	49	12	24.9	24.9
	10	39	16	41.8	56	24	42.3	42.1
	12	32	20	63.1	54	34	63.0	63.1
	16	13	10	80.2	59	47	80.0	80.1
	20	12	11	92.1	44	40	92.0	92.1
	30	14	10	71.0	31	21	69.1	70.1
	50	19	10	54.0	10	5	54.0	54.0
	60	24	10	40.2	22	9	39.9	40.1
	70	26	3	10.1	31	3	9.8	10.0
	96	18	0	1.9	41	1	2.2	2.1
	Project I : Total No. of Classes:265				Project II: Total No. of Classes: 423			
	Total No. of Reusable classes: 96				Total No. of Reusable classes: 198			

Figure 3. Response of CK metrics on reusability

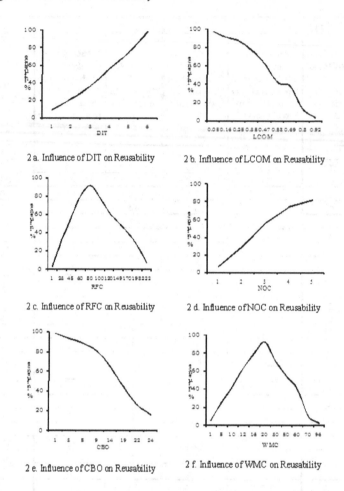

2 a. Influence of DIT on Reusability

2 b. Influence of LCOM on Reusability

2 c. Influence of RFC on Reusability

2 d. Influence of NOC on Reusability

2 e. Influence of CBO on Reusability

2 f. Influence of WMC on Reusability

of more cohesive in a class the reusability will be better and very low cohesion indicates improper design. For higher level of response in a class for a message from same class or from other classes will lead to merging of classes and increased complexity of the system. For lower level of response, the class reusability is low. No statistical studies were carried out in this respect. The data observed through empirical analysis is shown in Figure 2 and the average values in Table 2. This work leads to the formation of the functional relationship between the individual design metrics and reusability.

Functional Relationship

It has been reported widely that the influence on reusability will be 95 to 98% for a DIT value of 6, which is the maximum threshold value (S.R Chidamber, 1991). The influence of DIT on reusability is 21% for its value of 2 and 56% for its value of 4. When DIT value is zero or close to zero, the influence on reusability will also be close to zero as shown in Figure 3a. Hence it is hypothesized (H1) that classes with higher DIT values will be associated with better reusability.

It is observed from the Table 2, for a LCOM value of 0.05, its influence on reusability will be 97%. Between 0.35 and 0.47 of this metric, the

Table 2. Influence of internal design quality factors (IDQ) on reusability

I.D.Q. Factor 1		I.D.Q. Factor 2		I.D.Q. Factor 3		I.D.Q. Factor 4		I.D.Q. Factor 5		I.D.Q. Factor 6	
DIT α	% Influ-ence	LCOM β	% Influ-ence	RFC γ	% Influ-ence	NOC δ	% Influ-ence	CBO φ	% Influ-ence	WMC Ψ	% Influ-ence
1	9	0.05	97	1	3	1	7	1	98	1	5
2	21	0.16	91	23	31	2	29	3	93	5	25
3	36	0.25	87	45	56	3	56	5	88	10	42
4	56	0.35	77	60	80	4	74	9	80	12	63
5	74	0.47	62	80	91	5	82	14	65	16	80
6	98	0.58	42	100	78			19	44	2	92
		0.69	38	120	62			22	26	3	70
		0.80	13	149	51			24	16	5	54
		0.92	3	170	40					60	4
				198	26					70	1
				222	07					96	0

reusability will be 77% to 62%. For the maximum value of 1, the influence on class reusability is reported to be 0% due to low cohesion of methods in a class. Hence it is hypothesised (H2) that classes with lower LCOM values will be associated with better reusability.

It is observed that the influence on reusability is 80%, for RFC value of 60. When RFC increases merging of classes will take place and this leads to increased complexity of the system. 62 percent of reusability is reported for an RFC value of 120. With experimental results and the domain knowledge, it is observed that the reusability will be fading for an RFC value exceeding 80 as shown in Figure 3b. Hence, it is hypothesized (H3) that classes with higher and lower value of RFC are associated with low reusability.

From the set of results shown in Table 2 it is observed that classes with NOC value of 3 the influence on reusability will be 56%. It is observed as 74% for a NOC value of 4. Hence it is hypothesised (H4) that classes with higher value of NOC will increase the reusability level of classes. For a CBO value of 1 and 3, the influence on reusability is observed as 98% and 93%. The influence is reported to be 80% for a CBO value

of 9 and 16% for a CBO value of 24. Hence it is hypothesised (H5) that classes with higher value of CBO will reduce the reusability of classes.

From the empirical results shown in Figure 2, it is observed that when WMC value is 20, the influence on reusability is about 92%. For WMC value of 1, the influence on reusability is 5. The percentage influence is decreasing for values higher than 20 and for values lower than 20. This indicates the design will become more abstract if WMC is below the optimum threshold 20 (S.R Chidamber, 1991) and will become more complex if this metric value is more than the optimum value. These two scenarios are not supporting the reusability. Hence, it is hypothesized (H6) that classes with higher value of WMC will have lower reusability level of classes. In order to capture and establish the above facts, we performed multifunctional regression equations across reusability and design complexity metrics.

Estimation Model for influence Factors

It is evident from the above discussions that there is a relationship between the design quality factors

Figure 4. Multi functional reusability estimation model

$$R_\alpha = 7.8\,\alpha^{1.4} \tag{1}$$

$$R_\beta = 122.5\beta^3 - 232.4\beta^2 + 7.4\beta + 96.8 \tag{2}$$

$$R_\gamma = -0.006\gamma^2 + 1.23\gamma + 11.1 \tag{3}$$

$$R_\delta = -1.25\delta^3 + 8.6\delta^2 + 5.9\delta - 6.4 \tag{4}$$

$$R_\varphi = -0.1\varphi^2 - 1.0\varphi + 97.4 \tag{5}$$

$$R_\psi = 0.001\psi^3 - 0.16\psi^2 + 7\psi - 2.7 \tag{6}$$

Table 3. Comparison chart

Projects	The % Project Reusability Index as per Industry Data	The % Project Reusability Index as per the model SREM	The % Difference
1	32.46	31.19	1.27
2	28.03	29.31	1.28
3	30.21	29.09	1.12
4	35.16	36.12	0.96
5	45.4	43.68	1.72

and reusability. A successful model of the functional relationship between the design metric value and reusability is generated through a set of equations, fitting in to the data distribution between these metric values and the percentage influence of it. The functional estimation equations shown in Figure 4 are obtained by using various regression utilities and Matlab tools (appendix). Symbols $\pm$, β, γ, δ, φ, Ψ in the functional estimation equations represent the independent variables such as DIT, LCOM, RFC, NOC, CBO and WMC respectively.

The equation 1 is a logarithmic linear equation obtained as best fit curve for DIT and it is used to compute the sway of reusability as shown in column RuDIT of Figure 8b. Similarly, a best fit curve is obtained for the remaining five metrics in the suite. Equations 2 to 6 are the linear regression equations for LCOM, RFC, NOC, CBO and WMC respectively. These equations are used to compute the corresponding influence factors on reusability as shown in column RuLCOM (Ru_β), RuRFC (Ru_γ), RuNOC (Ru_δ), RuCBO ($Ru\varphi$) and RuWMC (Ru_ψ) of Figure 8b. It is observed that

these variables are expressing more significant contribution as linearly independent systems. The comprehensive software reusability estimation model is generated by weighted linear combination of multifunctional equations. The statistical performance analysis of these equations is out of scope of this paper.

COMPREHENSIVE SOFTWARE REUSABILITY ESTIMATION (CSRE) MODEL

This model is shown in Figure 5, equation 7. The probable dependency of all six metrics such as DIT, LCOM, RFC, NOC, CBO and WMC on Reusability Index was distributed on a unit scale with weights 0.2, 0.1, 0.3, 0.05, 0.1, and 0.25 respectively. So far no research has been carried out in analyzing and quantifying the percentage contribution of these design metrics on reusability. We assume that these six metrics together will contribute 100% towards reusability at the design stage. The weighted parameters are arrived through

Figure 5. CSRE model

$$RI = f(\alpha, \beta, \gamma, \delta, \varphi, \psi) \Rightarrow f(DIT, LCOM, RFC, NOC, CBO, WMC)$$

$$RI = 0.2(1/n)\sum_{k=1}^{n}(R_\alpha)_k + 0.1(1/n)\sum_{k=1}^{n}(R_\beta)_k + 0.3(1/n)\sum_{k=1}^{n}(R_\gamma)_k +$$

$$0.05(1/n)\sum_{k=1}^{n}(R_\delta)_k + 0.1(1/n)\sum_{k=1}^{n}(R_\varphi)_k + 0.25(1/n)\sum_{k=1}^{n}(R_\psi)_k \quad -------- (7)$$

Figure 6. Model evaluation process

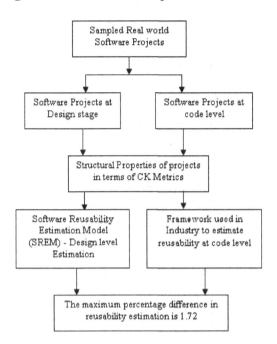

Figure 7. CSRE model performance

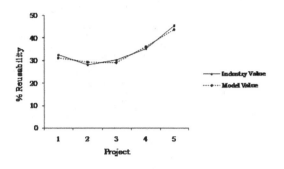

of any java projects whose structural properties of all classes are represented by CK metrics.

MODEL EVALUATION AND VALIDATION

Two commercial Java projects such as information management system and banking application are selected for model evaluation and validation as per the Figure 6. Because of the non disclosure agreements, the details of the industry and the data are not provided in this paper. We had access to design documents through configuration management system for the duration of this study and the design metric data are captured and shown in Figure 8a. These metric data are fed as input to the multifunctional estimation equations which gives the reusability factor of individual metrics as shown in Figure 8b. There is a substantial match between the values of reusability given along with the package from industry and the values calculated from our model.

The major advantage of using this method is the process managers will have an idea of reusability of their designed modules through calculations at design level rather than going for cumbersome methods of observing the codes. This estimation model was subjected to the data available from industry which contains information on the CK metric values and the estimated reusability by industry. These modules were sampled

GQM (Goal question metric) paradigm. This method provides support from the domain experts to judge and suggest the weighted parameters of individual metrics. These data are obtained by framing suitable hypotheses. The data collected are analyzed in a post-mortem fashion to assess the conformance to the goals by conducting several discussion sessions with domain experts and quality managers.

This estimation model computes the Reusability Index directly for any project from its CK metric data. Having explained this, it is possible to introduce 'k' as the number of classes varying from 1 to n, and 'RI' as the reusability Index of the software. It is defined as the percentage reusability of that class. This estimation is based on the Reusability Factor of the class. The Reusability Factor is defined as the percentage influence of individual design metric of the class on reusability.

This estimation model is evolved through the weighted linear combination of the multifunctional Estimation equations. This model can be efficiently used for automatic computation of RI

Figure 8. a. CK metric data, b. Computed data: Reusability factor

A. CK Metric Data   B. Computed Data: Reusability Factor

Project	class	DIT	LCOM	RFC	NOC	CBO	WMC	RuDIT	RuLCOM	RuRFC	RuNOC	RuCBO	RuWMC	C- RuI
	1	3	0.9	22	1	6	7	36.31	4.52	35.26	6.85	87.80	38.80	37.11
	2	2	0.9	61	1	5	22	20.58	4.52	63.80	6.85	89.90	84.51	54.17
	3	3	0.9	6	0	9	2	36.31	4.52	18.26	0.00	80.30	10.67	23.89
	4	1	0.9	6	0	5	7	7.80	4.52	18.26	0.00	89.90	38.80	26.18
	5	4	0.9	58	0	2	25	54.32	4.52	62.26	0.00	95.00	87.93	61.47
	6	4	0.9	9	0	9	4	54.32	4.52	21.68	0.00	80.30	22.80	31.55
	7	1	0.9	0	0	6	1	7.80	4.52	11.10	0.00	87.80	4.14	15.16
	8	1	0.9	3	0	12	5	7.80	4.52	14.74	0.00	71.00	28.43	20.64
	9	1	0.9	4	0	10	6	7.80	4.52	15.92	0.00	77.40	33.76	22.97
	10	4	0.9	6	0	9	5	54.32	4.52	18.26	0.00	80.30	28.43	31.93
	11	2	0.9	12	0	19	4	20.58	4.52	25.00	0.00	42.30	22.80	22.00
	12	3	0.9	13	0	13	6	36.31	4.52	26.08	0.00	67.50	33.76	30.73
	13	3	0.9	16	0	19	12	36.31	4.52	29.24	0.00	42.30	59.99	35.71
1	14	1	0.9	3	0	12	3	7.80	4.52	14.74	0.00	71.00	16.89	17.75
	15	3	0.9	5	0	19	7	36.31	4.52	17.10	0.00	42.30	38.80	26.78
	16	3	0.9	5	0	6	8	36.31	4.52	17.10	0.00	87.80	43.57	32.52
	17	3	0.9	23	0	15	10	36.31	4.52	36.22	0.00	59.90	52.30	37.64
	18	1	0.9	19	0	12	30	7.80	4.52	32.30	0.00	71.00	90.30	41.38
	19	4	0.9	31	0	16	22	54.32	4.52	43.46	0.00	55.80	84.51	51.06
	20	1	0.9	7	0	3	2	7.80	4.52	19.42	0.00	93.50	10.67	19.85
	21	3	0.9	1	0	19	1	36.31	4.52	12.32	0.00	42.30	4.14	16.68
	22	3	0.9	20	0	11	10	36.31	4.52	33.30	0.00	74.30	52.30	38.21
	23	4	0.9	23	0	15	10	54.32	4.52	36.22	0.00	59.90	52.30	41.25
	24	1	0.9	2	0	2	4	7.80	4.52	13.54	0.00	95.00	22.80	21.27
	25	3	0.9	3	0	12	2	36.31	4.52	14.74	0.00	71.00	10.67	21.90
														P- RuI
						Average		29.53	4.52	26.01	0.55	72.62	38.96	31.19
	1	1	0.86	2	0	11	1	7.80	9.20	13.54	0.00	74.30	4.14	15.01
	2	1	0.86	3	0	14	16	7.80	9.20	14.74	0.00	63.80	72.44	31.39
	3	2	0.86	4	0	9	7	20.58	9.20	15.92	0.00	80.30	38.80	27.54
	4	1	0.86	21	0	7	14	7.80	9.20	34.28	0.00	85.50	66.68	37.99
	5	3	0.86	26	0	24	10	36.31	9.20	39.02	0.00	15.80	52.30	34.54
	6	2	0.86	1	0	22	1	20.58	9.20	12.32	0.00	27.00	4.14	12.47
	7	1	0.86	25	0	16	9	7.80	9.20	38.10	0.00	55.80	48.07	31.51
	8	1	0.86	60	0	20	31	7.80	9.20	63.30	0.00	37.40	90.33	47.79
	9	1	0.86	11	0	25	4	7.80	9.20	23.90	0.00	9.90	22.80	16.34
	10	1	0.86	43	1	9	21	7.80	9.20	52.90	6.85	80.30	83.00	47.47
2	11	2	0.86	12	0	12	3	20.58	9.20	25.00	0.00	71.00	16.89	23.86
	12	2	0.86	2	0	19	2	20.58	9.20	13.54	0.00	42.30	10.67	15.99
	13	2	0.86	10	0	15	7	20.58	9.20	22.80	0.00	59.90	38.80	27.57
	14	1	0.86	5	0	16	3	7.80	9.20	17.10	0.00	55.80	16.89	17.41
	15	3	0.86	43	0	22	15	36.31	9.20	52.90	0.00	27.00	69.68	44.17
	16	2	0.86	6	0	11	2	20.58	9.20	18.26	0.00	74.30	10.67	20.61
	15	1	0.86	48	0	10	28	7.80	9.20	56.32	0.00	77.40	89.81	49.57
	18	2	0.86	3	0	12	5	20.58	9.20	14.74	0.00	71.00	28.43	23.66
	19	1	0.86	38	0	16	21	7.80	9.20	49.18	0.00	55.80	83.00	43.56
	20	3	0.86	8	0	18	3	36.31	9.20	20.56	0.00	47.00	16.89	23.27
														P- RuI
						Average		18.04	8.77	29.05	0.34	57.06	41.55	29.31

ones from a general spectrum of modules. These data are fed to the reusability estimation model to calculate the reusability.

Threat to Validity

1. There is interdependency between design properties like CBO and DIT.
2. Several other factors such as programming language specific approaches, application functionality between samples, personnel-specific influences could play a role in these findings.

We have not incorporated these factors into this estimation model.

RESULTS AND DISCUSSIONS

Figure 8a and 8b depicts the data related to the sampled two projects 1 and 2 having classes 25 and 20 respectively. The six columns of Figure 8a represent the 6 metric values of each class. The first six columns of Figure 8b represent the reusability factor of each metric and the data in the fourth column represents the calculated reusability index (RI) of the classes. The project reusability index is shown in the same table which is the weighted addition of the average value of the reusability factors of each metric involved. This model is first tested against sampled software packages taken from the industry whose reusability is already known using alternate methods. However we were given the measured data for our analysis. The comparison of estimated data from this novel estimation model with the data from industry is shown in Table 3 and Figure 7.

We found there is considerable match existing between the industry observation of reusability and the estimated value from this model. This model offers new avenues for process managers to develop a good grasp of the reusability of the

modules what they create even at design phase itself. It has two advantages; with this model the reusability level of the software projects can be measured automatically at design stage itself and the module can be redesigned to achieve the desired level of reusability.

CONCLUSION

In this chapter, we have discussed a novel approach for the estimation of reusability index of the classes at design phase of software development life cycle. Through empirical analysis we have established the validity of the hypotheses and later developed model through regression method which is capable of computing reusability index from CK metric value at design stage itself. The effects of design metrics on reusability are found to have non linear influence on reusability. This model was evaluated and found to be fairly matching with the relationship existing between the structural properties and the external quality parameters like reusability. Our future research includes the analysis of the interdependency of the design metrics and the influence of other factors like programming language specific approaches, application functionality of samples and personnel-specific influences in software development.

REFERENCES

Aggarwal, K. K., Singh, Y., Kaur, A., & Malhotra, R. (2005). *Software reuse metrics for object-oriented systems*. (pp. 48-55). Third ACIS Int'l Conference on Software Engineering Research, Management and Applications (SERA'05).

Arisholm, E. (2006). *Empirical assessment of the impact of structural properties on the changeability of object oriented software, information and software technology* (pp. 1046–1055). Elsevier.

Arnold, R. S. (1990). *Heuristics for salvaging reusable parts from Ada code.* (SPC Technical Report, ADA_REUSE_HEURISTICS-90011-N).

Basili, V., Briand, L., & Melo, W. L. (1996). A validation of object oriented design metrics as quality indicators. *IEEE Transactions on Software Engineering, 22*(10), 751–761. doi:10.1109/32.544352

Bieman, J. (1991). *Deriving measures of software reuse in object-oriented systems. (TR CS-91-112).* Colorado State University.

Bieman, J., & Xia Zhao, J. (1995). Reuse through inheritance: A quantitative study of C++ software. *Proceedings of the ACM Symposium on Software Reusability* (SSR '95), Seattle, WA, (pp. 47–52).

Blum, B. I. (1992). *Software engineering, a holistic view.* New York, NY: Oxford University Press.

Briand, L. C., Morasca, S., & Basili, V. R. (1996). Property-based software engineering. *IEEE Transactions on Software Engineering, 23*(8), 196–198.

Caldiera, G., & Basili, V. R. (1991). *Identifying and qualifying reusable software components.* IEEE Computer.

Chidamber, S. R., & Kemerer, C. (1991). Towards a metrics suite for object oriented design. *Object Oriented Programming Systems, Languages, and Applications, 26*(11), 197–211. doi:10.1145/117954.117970

Chidamber, S. R., & Kemerer, C. (1994). A metrics suite for object-oriented design. *IEEE Transactions on Software Engineering, 20*(6), 476–493. doi:10.1109/32.295895

Dandashi, F. (1998). *A method for assessing the reusability of object-oriented code using a validated set of automated measurements.* Unpublished doctoral dissertation, SITE, George Mason University, Fairfax, VA.

Denaro, G., & Pezze, G. M. (2002). An empirical evaluation of fault proneness model. *ICSE Proceedings of 24th International Conference,* (pp. 241-251).

Dunn, M. F., & Knight, J. C. (1993). Software reuse in Industrial setting: A case study. *Proceedings of the 13th International Conference on Software Engineering,* Baltimore, MD.

Esteva, J. C., & Reynolds, R. G. (1991). Identifying reusable components using induction. *International Journal of Software Engineering and Knowledge Engineering, 1*(3), 271–292. doi:10.1142/S0218194091000202

Etzkorn, L. H., Hughes, Jr., W. E., & Davis, C. G. (2001). *Automated reusability quality analysis of OO legacy software.*

Gacek, C. (Ed.). (2002). *Software reuse: Methods, techniques and tools.* 7th International Conference (ICSR7) Austin, Texas. (LNCS 2319). Springer.

Karunanithi, S., & Bieman, J. M. (1992). *Candidate reuse metrics for object-oriented and Ada software. (TR CS-92-142).* Colorado State University.

Kitchenham, B. A., Pfleeger, S. L., & Fenton, N. (1997). Comments on toward a framework for software measurement validation. *IEEE Transactions on Software Engineering, 23*(8), 189–189. doi:10.1109/TSE.1997.585507

Krishnan, M. S., Kriebel, C. H., Kekre, S., & Mukhopadhyay, T. (2000). An empirical analysis of productivity and quality in software products. *Management Science, 46,* 745–759. doi:10.1287/mnsc.46.6.745.11941

Peters, J. F., & Pedrycz, W. (2000). *Software engineering: An engineering approach.* John Wiley & Sons.

Poels, G., & Dedene, G. (1997). Comments on property-based software engineering measurement: Refining the additivity properties. *IEEE Transactions on Software Engineering, 23*(3), 190–195. doi:10.1109/32.585508

Rosenberg, L., & Hyatt, L. (2001). *Software quality metrics for object-oriented system environments.* (NASA Technical Report SATC no. 1), (pp. 11-58).

Selby, R. W. (1988). Empirically analyzing software reuse in a production environment. In Tracz, W. (Ed.), *Software reuse: Emerging technology.* IEEE Computer Society Press.

Sinaalto, M. (2006). *The impact of test driven development on design quality. Agile Software Development of Embedded Systems (Vol. 10).* ITEA.

Sommerville, I. (1996). *Software engineering* (6th ed.). Addison Wesley Publishing Company.

Washizaki, H., Yamamoto, H., & Fukazawa, Y. (2003). A metrics suite for measuring reusability of software components. *Proceedings of the 9th International Symposium on Software Metrics,* (p. 211).

Section 3
Testing, Metrics and Process Improvement

Chapter 12

Knowledge Engineering Support for Intelligent Software Test Optimization

D. Jeya Mala
Thiagarajar College of Engineering, India

ABSTRACT

Software testing is one of the most important processes in Software Development Life Cycle (SDLC) to ensure quality of software product. A large number of approaches for test data generation and optimization in software testing have been reported with varying degrees of success. In recent years, the application of artificial intelligence (AI) techniques in software testing to achieve quality software is an emerging area of research. It combines the concepts of the two domains AI and Software Engineering and yields innovative mechanisms that have the advantages of both of them. This chapter demonstrates the development of a novel software test sequence optimization framework using intelligent agents based graph searching technique. To ensure the quality, a set of test adequacy criteria such as path coverage, state coverage, and branch coverage have been applied in the approach discussed in this chapter, while achieving optimization.

INTRODUCTION

Software Testing is the process of executing a program or system with the intent of finding errors (Grottke et.al, 2007, Pressman, 2006). Since

DOI: 10.4018/978-1-60960-509-4.ch012

it typically consumes at least 50% of the total cost involved in software development; an optimization approach is required for testing without compromising quality (Rudalf et.al, 2006). As Phil McMinn briefed in his paper (McMinn, 2004), exhaustive enumeration of a programs input is infeasible for any reasonably-sized program, yet

Table 1.

Max.		
	Coverage (SUT)	(1)
	Fault Revealing (SUT)	(2)
Min.		
	Cost (Testing Process)	(3)
	Time (Testing Process)	(4)

random methods are unreliable and unlikely to exercise deeper features of software that are not exercised by mere chance.

Software testing is a dynamic activity in which test input generation and execution can be seen as optimization problems. The input domain of most of the programs is likely to be very large. A cost-surface could be formed by applying the cost function to every possible program input. It is this surface which is effectively being searched when attempting to generate test data.

Given the complexities of software systems, it is extremely unlikely that this cost surface would be linear or continuous. The size and complexity of the search space therefore limits the effectiveness of simple gradient-descent or neighborhood searches as they likely to get stuck in locally optimal solutions and hence fail to find the desired test data.

Ultimately, the cost function used for optimization is typically related to the cost and time needed for the testing process, the size of the test suite and the coverage or fault revealing capability of the test cases. The importance of software test optimization has increased in recent years due to customers need for quick delivery of quality software, reduced software development lifecycle, changing markets with global competition and rapid development of new processes and technologies.

Since software testing is a combinatorial problem in which finding solutions at a reasonable computational cost (Harman et al., 2007) is highly complex, it has been classified as NP-

complete or NP-hard, or be a problem for which a polynomial time algorithm is known to exist but is not practical. Hence, software test optimization problem is devised as a multi-objective optimization problem and the overall objective function is to minimize the total cost and time needed for the testing process and to maximize the various test adequacy criteria (coverage based, mutation score/fault revealing ability based etc.) to achieve quality. It is formally given in Table 1.

Intelligent software testing techniques support quality assurance by gathering information about the software being studied (McMinn, 2004). Meta-heuristic search techniques are high-level frameworks which utilize heuristics in order to find solutions to combinatorial problems at a reasonable computational cost (Harman, 2007).

The objective of test sequence optimization is to reduce the number of test executions. A test sequence indicates the execution of a sequence of states / blocks of statements in the given software. It usually corresponds to a test path. Assume that, a set of test cases is available in the test case repository. The intention of software testing process is to execute these test cases against the software under test to cover all the states in it. There are two cases to deal with:

1. If some of the states in a test path are infeasible, then even an exhaustive testing cannot cover them; and testing time spent on these states is merely wasted without an indication of infeasible code to the tester.

2. In looping constructs, some of the states are repeatedly exercised in different test sequences with different test cases; and testing time is simply spent without any benefit since they will not reveal any new type of errors.

If the Software under Test (SUT) is small and simple, then a human tester can identify these infeasible test sequences and repeated subsequences by applying intelligence. But, if it is large and complex, then automation is required in the testing process. Although, the testing tools available in the market provide automation, they lack human like intelligence in decision making process and they exhibit less consideration on the amount of time spent on testing process and satisfaction of the test adequacy criteria.

This leads the research on development of a testing approach that couples human like intelligence and automation like a tool. Hence, in the said approach, an intelligent agent that has these two features with autonomy, interoperability and social ability is applied to test sequence optimization. The basic reason for applying intelligent agents is that, it boils down to solve a problem that assumes intelligence by applying efficient search methods to a directed data set.

In the approach discussed here, the infeasible test sequences and the repeated subsequences are identified using heuristic guided intelligent searching performed by Intelligent Search Agent (ISA); and only the feasible and non-redundant test sequences are stored in the optimal test sequence repository with an indication of infeasible code to the tester. Now, the test cases can be exercised only on the optimal test sequences which lead to reduction in testing time. If the infeasible test sequences are corrected by the developer, then the optimal test sequences repository will be updated automatically by the agent.

BACKGROUND

Lori A.Clarke (1976) presented a system which generates test data and symbolically executes program paths to aid the selection of test data. Linear programming techniques were used in her paper, to generate input data for paths whose constraints are linear. Symbolic execution is used to generate the constraints representing the selected path and an inequality solver is used to solve the linear constraints; if the solver finds a constraint inconsistent with the previous ones, the path is marked to be non-executable.

Hedley and Hennell (1985) discussed the main causes of infeasible paths in programs and presented a classification for the causes. Frankl and Weyuker (1988) discussed the concepts related to un-executable paths and their consequences on the application of data flow testing criteria; they presented a heuristics using data flow analysis and symbolic execution techniques to determine infeasible data flow associations.

Malevris et al (1990) used the number of predicates in a path to predict infeasibility. They concluded that the greater the number of predicates in a path, the greater the probability of it being infeasible.

Korel (1990) reduced the problem of finding the input data to a sequence of sub goals; each one is associated with a path predicate. According to this approach, each sub-goal is solved by using direct search to minimize the value of the errors functions associated with the predicates.

Goldberg et al (1994) used symbolic evaluation to construct a formula that is solvable if and only if, there are input values which drive the execution down the path. A theorem-prover is invoked to test the feasibility of the formula.

Roger and Korel (1996) extended the technique proposed by Korel (1990) by including data dependence information for path selection in the test data generation process (the chaining approach). If an undesirable execution flow is observed in any branch and the search process cannot find an input value to change this execution flow, data flow analysis is applied to identify the nodes that must be executed prior to reaching the branch to increase the chance of altering the flow execution.

Paulo et al (2000) proposed a tool and techniques for test data generation and identification of a paths likely unfeasibility in structural software testing. Their tool was based on the Dynamic Technique and search using Genetic Algorithms. Their work introduced a new fitness function that combines control and data flow dynamic information to improve the process of search for test data. The unfeasibility issue was addressed by monitoring the Genetic Algorithms search progress.

Forgacs and Bertolino (1997) used control flow information and data dependencies to select feasible paths in reaching a given point in the program. The approach proposed by them minimizes the number of predicates which are essential to reach the point by reducing the number of predicates examined during the input data generation.

Bodik et al (1997) used a static branch correlation analysis to define a technique for the identification of infeasible program sub paths and infeasible def-use pairs.

Tracey et al (1998) presented a test-case data generation framework based on optimization technique called Simulated Annealing (SA) and illustrated the application of this framework to test specification failures and exception conditions.

Gupta et al (1998) suggested a method where, if the intended path is not executed, the input is iteratively refined. Two representations are computed for each predicate: the slice - a set of commands that influence the predicate along the intended path; and the predicates linear arithmetic representation as a function of input variables. The two representations are used to obtain a desired input by iteratively refining the initial input value. This technique is improved (1999) through a Unified Numerical Approach where the choice of input values is done using Least Square Errors techniques. Numerical analysis is applied to identify the infeasible paths when all the predicates in the paths are linear with respect to the input variables.

Guo et al (2005) explained an approach to generate multiple unique input/output sequences using evolutionary based search approach.

Turgut et al (2006) proposed a pair wise sequence comparison operation used in bio-informatics for fitness function evaluation in meta-heuristic based approach for structured software testing.

McMinn et al (2006) introduced the species per path approach, for search based software test data generation. In their approach, they first transformed the SUT into a version having multiple paths to the target. Then they identified test data by searching the individual path by dedicated species working in parallel. They analyzed the impact of feasible paths which gave rise to landscapes than the original landscape. The verification and validation of their study indicated the possibility of generating test data for targets using standard evolutionary method which is very troublesome.

José et al (2008) proposed a strategy for evaluating feasible and unfeasible test cases for the evolutionary testing of object-oriented software. In their paper, they provided a methodology for generating test data for the structural unit-testing of object-oriented Java programs. In their methodology, they identified feasible and unfeasible test cases based on the different paths in the SUT since they define elaborate state scenarios.

Moataz et al (2008) proposed GA based automated test data generation approach for white box testing. Their paper presented an approach to cover multiple target paths. They have designed a GA based test data generator that is able to synthesize multiple test data to cover multiple target paths.

Yan et al (2008) proposed an approach, in which a Flattened Control Flow Graph and a Flattened Control Dependence Graph for the switch-case construct are first presented, and a unified fitness calculation approach based on Alternative Critical Branches is proposed for the switch-case and other constructs. The concept of Alternative Critical Branches is extended from the single critical branch. Experiments on several large-scale open source programs demonstrate that this approach contributes a much better guidance to evolutionary search.

Minh and Hee (2008) proposed a heuristics-based approach to infeasible path detection for dynamic test data generation. Their approach is based on the observation that many infeasible program paths exhibit some common properties.

Through realizing these properties in execution traces collected during the test data generation process, infeasible paths can be detected early with high accuracy.

Willem et al (2004) developed a Java Path Finder tool for generating test paths by taking the execution traces of the given system.

Wimmel G. et al (2000) converted the specifications into prepositional logic and then fed it into a solver. Then test sequences are generated by I/O traces represented in the form of a Message Sequence Charts.

The summary of the existing approaches lead the following conclusions:

- Existing approaches are human centric.
- Manual testing is error prone and time consuming.
- Automation of the testing process lack optimization criteria and fulfillment of test adequacy criteria.
- Automated tools lack human like intelligence in decision making process.
- Automated software testing tools and techniques usually suffer from a lack of generic applicability and scalability.
- Most of the tools are language or domain dependent and human intervention is inevitable.
- The degree of automation remains at the automated test script level.
- No care / less care on optimized number of test cases.

Hence, several other research works concentrated on the application of Artificial Intelligence techniques in software testing. Further literature review shows that the research on software testing problems has centered mostly on software test optimization (Wong et al., 1999; Xiao et al., 2007; Ding et al., 2008; Chen et al., 2003, etc.); intelligent software testing techniques are extensively proposed to solve software test optimization problems; several meta-heuristic search techniques such as applying rules, meta-heuristics (like Genetic Algorithm (GA), Ant Colony Optimization (ACO), Tabu Search, Simulated Annealing, Bacteriologic Algorithm (BA), etc.), Fuzzy logic and Neural Networks (NN) and other approximation methods (Hélène et al., 2007; Díaz et al., 2008; Pargas et al., 1999; Li, 2004; Baudry et al., 2005; Meenakshi et al., 2002; Zhang et al., 2007; Eugenia et al., 2008 etc.) have been proposed for some specific types of problems in test optimization; and there is still a need for a more effective solution approach to more general problems such as test sequence, test case and test suite optimizations and there is a need for developing models and efficient algorithms to achieve these optimizations by satisfying the specified test adequacy criteria.

INTELLIGENT AGENT BASED TEST SEQUENCE OPTIMIZATION FRAMEWORK

Observations and Problems in the Existing Approaches

Software test optimization is more interesting due to several reasons: first, it reduces the total execution time of a test suite to test the SUT in limited time, secondly, to improve the turn around time required between software revisions during regression testing and finally, the generation of only effective test cases makes high likelihood of finding out errors in the SUT.

The literature study gives a lot of insight into the existing work on software test optimization problem. The observations made out of the study, have motivated this research work to propose a new framework for software test optimization. Some of the observations are given in this section.

The requirements driven test suite optimization proposed by (Beizer, 1990) cannot be generalized since requirements usually change during software development. Also, some of the requirements could have been missed and some of them may be misunderstood which leads to the assignment of wrong test cases to those requirements. When the object plus attribute combination is applied for test suite reduction, it wont produce much higher level of reduction when compared to other algorithms. If the requirements space is large, then assigning the test cases to every individual requirement is hard and requires a lot of human intervention.

In the case of BINTEST algorithm proposed by (Beydeda et al., 2003), there is no attention given for infeasible path identification. Since infeasible paths will not have any test data associated with it, if we try to identify a test data by iteratively generating them will lead to exhaustive testing only. Similarly, if a sub-path of a path P1 is already covered by some other path P2, there is no method given to avoid the generation of similar types of test cases to cover those previously covered edges.

In model based test data generation for tools testing (Ingo et al., 2007), existing tools cannot be tested with this approach, since it needs instrumentation in the software, which requires partnering with the tool vendor. When using third party generated code generators, the source models are represented in graphical representation which cannot be recognized by this model.

In program slicing based approach given by (Agrawal, 1991), if slicing cannot reduce the size of the program efficiently, the methods proposed will depress general statement, branch or path coverage. Since it requires much time and cost to slice any program, the most disadvantage of the proposed method is the low efficiency in terms of time. There is no specific approach proposed for calculating the coverage metrics of the slices. If some of the components are common to two or more slices, then overall coverage cannot be the summation of those of the subsystems.

The predicate based slicing approach proposed by (Forgacs et al., 1997), the most important observation is on deciding some predicates as influencing predicates. Since the influencing factor of the predicates is not static which may be changing dynamically, some predicates which seem to be influencing at one point of time may not influence at some later point of time. Hence the decision of slicing based on influencing predicates is really in need of a lot of training and intelligence to solve it.

In the case of Bounded Exhaustive Testing (BET) proposed by David et al (2005), have several drawbacks which have been identified by them. If the specifications themselves have faults, then this approach will not work. The approach is an incomplete work. The use of BET cannot be assessed in software systems to ensure statistical reliability. Executing the test cases is again a problem. The TestEra tool that they used has problems in generating integer based test inputs.

In the AI planning based test case generation technique proposed by Peter and Johannes (2000), the procedure can however not prevent that some manual additions have to be made such as the expected system responses have to be added to the test sequence manually to yield complete test cases; although they derived some constraints on the test inputs automatically, the concrete test data still has to be defined manually. Besides, systematic consideration should be given to other aspects of the specification, e.g. performance and frequency requirements.

In neural networks based software test optimization (Meenakshi, 2002), the drawbacks are its black-box data processing structure and, in some cases, a slow convergence speed. Thus, the data processing mechanism of a NN cannot be easily programmed, trained, understood, or verified in terms of rules. As pruning and sorting requires a lot of time for making the neural network to work properly, the other tasks such as clustering, converting from continuous to discrete and rule matching will make the approach to be highly time consuming. Also, the number of layers in the neural network is not properly specified. The rule engine has to be generated manually and is purely depending on the application under test.

Hence there is no generalization achieved in this approach. If the rules are not defined accurately, the test case selection procedure will fail. Again this approach is requirements based.

In Fuzzy Logic based test data generation (Zhang, 2007), there is no specific mechanism given for software test optimization. There is no method provided for calculating the probability which is used to handle uncertainty.

In Tabu Search based approach proposed by (Díaz et al., 2008), more amount of memory is required in terms of long term memory to avoid stuck up at local optima and short term memory to remember all the test cases in the current search. Even though this short term memory is deleted often, this will lead to a crucial problem of effective utilization of memory.

In applying Genetic Algorithms (Pargas et al., 1999), we have the risk of suboptimal solution, delayed convergence and strike up at local optima. As per Benoit Baudry et al, (2005), the experiments with genetic algorithms were not satisfactory. The mutation rate has to be increased consistently when compared to usual application of genetic algorithms (mutation rates lower than 2%). With 2% of mutation rate, the best mutation score was 80%, after a long computation. Moreover, the results are not stable, the convergence is slow and one population can be more efficient from the following, due to a non-explicit memorization.

Even though, the resultant test suite using Ant colony optimization (ACO) proposed by Li and Lam (2004) contains minimum number of test sequences, the test case within the test suite has longer sequence length which violates the optimality requirement criterion. Similar observation can be drawn when the number of ants exceeds three. The algorithm proposed by them, initially had an assumption that the two ants are started at an initial node, and during random selection of next node, they will go to the same node. The problem here is that, due to the random selection, we cannot expect that the approach will always produce the same node to be selected by two different ants at different instances of time. In our earlier works on test suite optimization, we employed multi-agent based approach in the test optimization process.

Bacteriologic algorithm based test case optimization approach proposed by Baudry et al (2005), has been applied on some test benches. Since BA doesn't have cross over operator, the further generation of test cases loses the advantage of combining the best properties of both the parents.

In the work of (Dhavachelvan & Uma, 2003), a test agent system design was proposed. In which they employed intelligent agent techniques to provide active assistance to the tester. The work concentrated on generation of test cases for the given SUT. It includes rules for construction of test cases and elimination of test cases. Even though the approach has relevant advantages, it doesn't provide any way for optimization of test cases. Hence, these observations have motivated this research work to develop a new software test optimization framework which comprises of the advantages of all of the discussed approaches and at the same time minimizes the drawbacks of them consistently.

The related work indicated the application of linear programming techniques, data and control flow analysis, data dependence analysis, static branch correlation analysis, simulated annealing and unified numerical approach to identify infeasible statements in the SUT. But each of these techniques is only partially automated and they did not provide a way to find out the feasible test paths thereby reducing the number of test runs; also, they require the guidance of a human tester during their identification process. If the test sequence selection is guided by a human tester, then by means of human intelligence it will be easier to find out the infeasible statements in the Software under Test (SUT). The problem of cost and time involved in manual software testing process implies the need for a human like intelligent approach but in an automated way.

Hence, an Intelligent Agent that couples automation and human like intelligence is applied

Figure 1. Classification of solution approaches applied in software test optimization

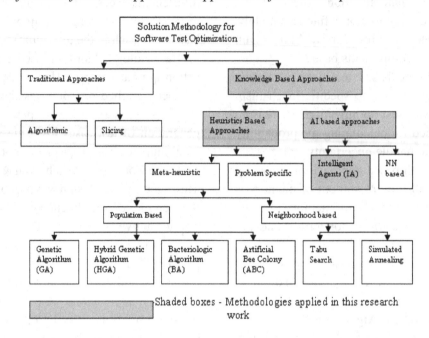

in the approach discussed here. The agent learns the Software under Test (SUT) and updates its knowledge source based on the previous decisions and current constraint satisfaction. Hence the developed agent simulates the behavior of a human tester and works in an automated way as a tool. Ultimately, a testing tool is developed that has high level of performance and selects the limited set of efficient test sequences from the SUT.

Concerning the above, the objective of the chapter is to propose a test optimization framework that can address the problems in the existing approaches and achieve software test sequence optimization using heuristics guided intelligent search approach.

Solution Methodology

A large number of approaches for test data generation and optimization in software testing have been reported with varying degrees of success. In recent years, the application of artificial intelligence (AI) techniques in software testing to achieve quality software is an emerging area of

research that brings about the cross fertilization of ideas across two domains such as AI and Software Engineering (Briand, 2002; Pedrycz et al., 1998).

The literature review shows that the research on software testing problems has centered mostly on software test optimization (Eric et al., 1999; Xiao et al., 2007; Zuohua et al., 2008; Chen et al., 2003) and intelligent software testing techniques are extensively proposed to solve software test optimization problems. Intelligent software testing techniques support quality assurance by gathering information about the software being studied (McMinn, 2004).

Figure 1 shows the classification of some of the approaches used in software test optimization. Knowledge based approaches are designed to find good approximations to the optimal solution in large complex search spaces. They are subdivided into heuristics based approaches and AI based approaches. The shaded boxes in the Figure 1 show the approaches applied in this work, which forms the intelligent agent based test optimization framework.

In traditional based approaches, algorithms and program slicing principles are applied. Algorithmic approaches include Greedy algorithm, Binary search algorithm, statistical approaches and Markov chain based algorithm (Benson, 1981; Tallam & Gupta, 2005; Richard et al., 1991; Gouraud et al., 2001; Gerlich et al., 2006; Agrawal, 1994, Banks et al., 1998). Under program slicing, many approaches have been proposed to divide the entire software into slices and then generate and select test cases to cover them (Zhenqiang et al., 2003; Forgacs & Bertolino, 1997; Hierons et al., 1999; David et al., 2005).

AI based approaches include Expert Systems, Intelligent Agents (IA), Neural Networks (NN) and Fuzzy systems. Fuzzy logic and Neural Networks (NN) and other approximation methods such as Chaotic Neural Networks have been proposed for software test optimization over the past years (Meenakshi et al., 2002; Zhang et al., 2007; Wang, 2004; Cao, 2006; Wang, 2009). Among them, the intelligent agents can be implemented with sophisticated intellectual capabilities such as the ability to reason, learn, or plan (Russell 2005). This means that the underlying agent architecture must support sophisticated reasoning, learning, planning, and knowledge representation (Russell, 2005). Intelligent Agents have been applied to various applications to achieve efficient results, and have been emerged as potential techniques to provide solutions with human like intelligence and exhibits properties such as autonomy, social ability and interoperability (Dhavachelvan et al., 2003; Mangina, 2005; Miao et al., 2007; Zhiyong et al., 2008).

Meta-heuristic search techniques are high-level frameworks which utilize heuristics in order to find solutions to combinatorial problems at a reasonable computational cost (Micheal, 1999; Harman, 2007). They have been classified into neighborhood based search approaches and population based search approaches. Several meta-heuristic search techniques such as applying rules, meta-heuristics (like Genetic Algorithm (GA),

Ant Colony Optimization (ACO), Tabu Search, Simulated Annealing, Bacteriologic Algorithm (BA), etc.), have been proposed for some specific types of problems in test optimization (Hélène et al., 2007; Pargas et al., 1999; Li & Lam, 2004; Díaz et al., 2008; Baudry et al., 2005).

Neighborhood based search approaches include Tabu Search (TS), Simulated Annealing (SA), Hill climbing Algorithm and Chaotic Simulated Annealing techniques (Aihara, 2002; Wang, 1998). Simulated Annealing is an optimization technique that has been applied for solving a wide range of combinatorial optimization problems, in which the feasible solutions represents different states of the problem. In Tabu Search based approach, two separate lists are maintained to attain near global optimal solution (Tracey, 1998). Hill Climbing is used to improve a solution, with an initial solution randomly chosen from the search space as a starting point. The neighborhood of this solution is investigated. If a better solution is found, then this replaces the current solution. This process is repeated till either the desired solution is found or the specified number of iterations is reached (McMinn, 2004).

Population based search heuristics, which belongs to the random search category, guarantees near optimal solutions in actual cases. The popularly known population based search heuristics are Genetic Algorithm (GA), Bacteriologic Algorithm (BA), Hybrid Genetic Algorithm (HGA) and Particle Swarm Optimization (PSO) such as Ant Colony Optimization (ACO) and Artificial Bee Colony Optimization (ABC). These approaches are useful for any hard optimization problem. Over the past thirty years, there has been a growing interest in problem solving systems based on the principles of evolution and heredity. Such systems maintain a population of potential solutions with selection processes based on the fitness of individuals, and some recombination operators. Among them, Hybrid Genetic Algorithm that belongs to population based approach combines the features of Genetic Algorithm with Local

Search (GA-LS). It has been applied for many hard optimization problems (José et al., 2002; Yici et al., 2005; Wappler et al., 2006; Kim et al., 2003; William et al., 2008; Zhao et al., 2009) and produces optimal or near optimal solutions. Also, Artificial Bee Colony optimization that belongs to non-pheromone based swarm intelligence algorithms is considered suitable for many optimization based problems (Karaboga et al., 2008; Mohammad et al., 2007; Alok Singh, 2009) in producing optimal results to NP-hard problems.

The above discussion indicates that, artificial intelligence based approaches and population based search heuristics are useful tools for software test optimization problem.

REPRESENTATION OF THE SEARCH SPACE: FORMAL PROBLEM DEFINITION

In the approach discussed in this chapter, the given Software under Test (SUT) is represented as a search space. Usually, search spaces are represented by graphs. This graphical representation of the Software under Test (SUT) helps to solve the testing problem which requires intelligent searching. Hence, graphs are used to visualize the given Software under Test (SUT).

A program or a software code consists of both sequential statements and control statements. During execution, the next statement in the program follows a sequential statement whereas the statement following a control statement is selected by a conditional jump (Aditya P.Mathur, 2008). The statement ordering during the execution of the program is described by an Execution Sequence Graph (ESG) similar to Control Flow Graph (CFG) derived from the State chart of the SUT.

Several research works on software testing have proposed graph-theoretic models of several types of information flows and have used them to define testing techniques (McMinn et al., 2003; Li & Lam, 2004). Hence, in this approach, the SUT is converted into a state chart which usually provides an abstract view of the software. This state chart is converted into a graph based network model, in which each state represents a block of executable statements in the software and is shown in Figure 2.

Intelligent searching is done on the converted graph using heuristics guided search process. In this thesis, the terms nodes and states are used interchangeably.

Problem Environment

The Software under Test (SUT) is given as input. Let n be the cyclomatic complexity value that

Figure 2. Sample skeleton code and network model of the SUT

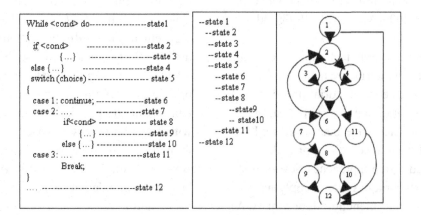

Table 2.

Min.		
	Test-cost (SUT)	(4)
	Test-time (SUT)	(5)
	Length (Test-Sequence)	(6)
Max.		
	State-Coverage (SUT)	(7)
	Branch-Coverage (SUT)	(8)
	Statement-Coverage (SUT)	(9)

indicates there are n independent test paths in the Software under Test (SUT). Each test path TP_j is the basis for generating test case TC_j, where j=1 to n. Let $TSeq_j$ is a test sequence associated with each test path.

Assumption

Software under Test (SUT) has no syntax errors (Compilation Errors). Software coding standards are followed when developing the SUT.

Objective Criterion

The objective is to generate feasible and non-redundant test sequences by identifying infeasible test sequences and redundant sub-sequences in the generated test sequences using Intelligent Search Agent that applies intelligent graph searching through the SUT.

Formal Optimization Model

The general multi-objective optimization problem for test sequence optimization is given formally as shown in Table 2.

The objective functions (4) and (5) are focusing on minimizing the cost and time associated with the testing process. The objective function (6) indicates the optimality requirement criterion in terms of length of the test sequences, stating that the length of the test sequences generated for

exercising the SUT should be less. The next set of objective functions (7), (8) and (9) enforces the quality of the software in terms of maximizing coverage based test adequacy criteria. The analysis of the different coverage measures is conducted using the survey of Horgan et al (1994).

Intelligent Agents: An Introduction

Intelligent Agents are pieces of software that are designed to make computing and other tasks easier by assisting and acting on behalf of the user. The user can interact with the agent through the user interface while the agent can sense and act according to the condition of the external environment. The agent performs its tasks by taking information from the environment in which it is working (Russel & Norvig, 1995).

Agents can be constructed with a wide range of capabilities. In agent-based approach a complex processing function can be broken into several smaller and simpler ones. An autonomous agent is a system situated within and a part of an environment that senses that environment and acts on it, over time, in pursuit of its own agenda and so as to effect, what it senses in the future (Russel & Norvig, 1995).

As in the earlier work on the application of Intelligent Agents in Software Testing (Dhavachelvan & Uma, 2003), agents can be implemented with sophisticated intellectual capabilities such as the ability to reason, learn, or plan. In addition, intelligent software agents can utilize extensive amounts of knowledge about their problem domain.

Among many type of Intelligent Agents, this approach has focused on the design of Task-Specific Software Agents to perform software testing task. Since testing activity consists of a number of uncertainties, the test agent which is used in this research work checks up all the conditions in the SUT in generating optimal test sequences.

Intelligent Search Agent (ISA) Framework

In the ISA framework shown in Figure 3, the SUT is converted into a state chart and the agent selected a very limited set of test sequences to be executed from the extreme large number (usually infinitely many) of potential ones. The approach demonstrates a way to generate few effective test sequences that are guaranteed to take less time to execute and also satisfies both state and branch coverage based test adequacy criteria using Intelligent Agents.

The Intelligent Agent namely the Intelligent Search Agent (ISA) generates the list of test sequences from the given SUT by getting the set of world states in the SUT and the transitions between them as inputs. These set of world states and the interaction between them are stored in the agents knowledge source as perception sequences. Then the action of either to include or exclude a state to or from a test sequence is done based on the two novel algorithms namely infeasible test sequence identification and repeated subsequence detection.

The agent used here is a Search Agent, which has been developed using Java. It takes the SUT as input and produces optimal few test sequences depending upon the sum of the heuristic value associated with each node and the cost associated with each edge. The objective is to cover all the feasible nodes in the SUT without the repetition of subsequences (sequence of states/nodes).

The agent learns the SUT by means of Blackboard (BB) based learning. The decision making process of the agent is guided by a novel utility function called as Happiness Value Calculation Function. The agent performs intelligent searching through the SUT by means of heuristics guided search algorithms namely Infeasible Test Sequence Identification Algorithm and Redundant Subsequence Detection Algorithm to aid the decision making process.

Figure 3. Optimized test sequence generation framework

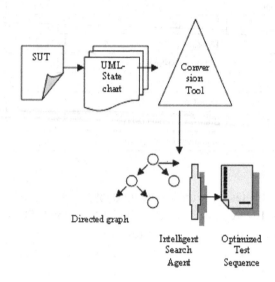

Agent Descriptor

The agent descriptions are provided by means of Prometheus Methodology (John Thangarajah et al, 2005).

- **Name:** Intelligent Search Agent (ISA)
- **Description:** Searching the states and finding the optimal test sequences by considering the heuristic values associated with each node and edge in the graph.
- **Lifetime:** Till the software became obsolete.
- **Initialization:** Based on Software Under Test (SUT).
- **Incoming and Outgoing messages:**
  - get_state(SUT → Agent)
  - Utility_calc(agent)   (or) happiness_val_calc(Agent)
  - Check_ state(Agent→Agent)
  - Opt_sel_states(agent→repository)

Learning Approach of ISA

For an intelligent agent to act according to the problem domain, a learning approach should be devised. An algorithm for learning, when the goal state is well defined involves two important design issues. One is relevance to the goal state (i.e. Measure of the adjacency, closeness) and second is relevance to the goodness criterion (i.e. Minimum distance or time). The agent learns the SUT by means of Blackboard (BB) based learning approach.

As per Nii (Nii, 1986), the purpose of the Blackboard (BB) is to hold computational and solution state data needed for the knowledge sources. The Blackboard consists of objects from the solution space. The objects on the Blackboard are hierarchically organized into levels of analysis. The objects and their properties define the vocabulary of the solution space (Grady Booch, 2003).

As shown in Figure 4, the Blackboard framework consists of three elements:

1. Blackboard (BB)
2. Multiple Knowledge Sources (KS)
3. Controller that mediates among these knowledge sources (C)

In Blackboard architectures, a central Blackboard (BB) data structure holds the entire state of a solution. The BB has computational and solution state data needed by the knowledge sources. It consists of objects from the solution space. The objects on the black board are hierarchically organized into levels of analysis. The objects and their properties define the vocabulary of the solution space.

Domain and world knowledge are represented in separate independent Knowledge Sources (KS), which hold computations that respond to changes in BB, and with direct access to it; KS interact through the BB to yield solutions. The knowledge source takes a set of current information on the blackboard and updates it as encoded on its specialized knowledge source. The knowledge sources are domain specific. They have procedures, logical rules and assertion conditions for optimal test sequence generation. They embody two elements namely Preconditions and Actions. Preconditions specify the current state of the blackboard in which the knowledge source shows its interest. Triggering a precondition causes the knowledge source to focus its attention on this part of the blackboard and then take action by processing its rules or procedural knowledge. The knowledge sources are updated through reasoning by means of forward chaining and verifying by means of backward chaining.

A Control (C) monitors the changes in BB and determines the next action to be executed, plans evaluations and activations according to a strategy that decides which KS is to be used for the next

Figure 4. Blackboard architecture

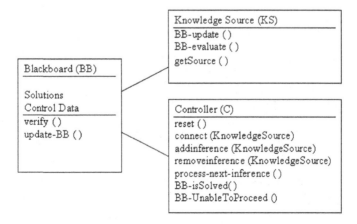

update in the BB. The controller can do the action of using the appropriate knowledge source when it has something to contribute in the processing.

The idea behind the Blackboard architecture is a collection of independent programs that work cooperatively on a common data structure. Each program is specialized for solving a particular part of the overall task, and all programs work together on the solution. These specialized programs are independent of each other. They do not call each other, nor is there a predetermined sequence for their activation. Instead, the direction taken by the system is mainly determined by the current state of progress. A central control component evaluates the current state of processing and coordinates the specialized programs.

The basic reason for applying BB based learning in the agent is that, the solution generation involves incremental learning process based on the previous state of the solution space and the current state of the problem space. The basic idea behind the solution generation of the approach is that, the solution space has several levels/layers. Initially, the solution space is empty. Then, based on the SUT, the lowest level of the solution space is formed. By means of incremental learning, the next level in the solution space is formed using the previous level of the solution space along with the current state of the system determined by constraint satisfaction. This process is continued till the solution space contains the expected solution. Since this process resembles the BB based learning, the agent learns the SUT by means of this learning approach.

As shown in Figure 5, the objects such as Blackboard, Knowledge Sources and Controller are created for Test Sequence Optimization problem. Then, identification of domain specific classes and objects is done which helps in specialization of these higher level abstractions.

Initially, the black board is empty. The knowledge sources (multiple knowledge sources namely KS1, KS2,...KSn) contain the information about the SUT like, the executable statements, states, state transitions, edge costs, node heuristics, happiness values, and similarity measures.

By using these knowledge sources, the lowest level of the BB is formed with all the executable statements in the SUT to form states. The next level in the black board is formed by combining the information from the lowest level and the knowledge sources at that level. Now, the next level in the black board is formed by grouping the block of executable statements taken from the previous level of the BB into executable states / nodes.

The knowledge sources are updated properly by the controller which monitors the activities performed in the BB. The final level in the BB is the formation of optimal test sequences. This is done by applying the infeasible test sequence identification algorithm and the repeated subsequences detection algorithm along with the current state of the progress in the BB.

Figure 5. Blackboard architecture of ISA

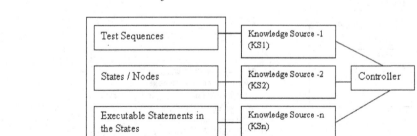

The learning process is a continuous one, till the final level in the BB is formed. Once, the solution is obtained, the agent stores all the generated optimal test sequences in the optimized test sequence repository. After that, the agent will not go into an inactive state, rather, even during maintenance, if any modifications were done in the software, the agent automatically senses the changes and by using the Controller the corresponding KS are modified to reflect the modifications.

Pruning is done by means of a user interface, which is needed only initially. Once the agent learnt the system, it will perform all the activities by its agenda and reduces the amount of user intervention.

Decision-Making by ISA

An agents preferences between world states is captured by means of an effective decision making process. The decision making process is equipped with a utility function which assigns a single number to express the desirability of a state.

As per the function used in utility value calculation, a nondeterministic action A will have possible outcome states $Result_i(A)$, where the index i ranges over the different outcomes. Prior to the execution of A, the agent calculates the Maximum Expected Utility (MEU) based on the expected utility values associated with all possible outcome states.

To calculate the utility values, the system should be represented as a complete casual model and in the approach, the SUT has been represented as a network model as shown in Figure 2. The agent in the approach takes the action of either including or excluding a state to or from a test sequence, by evaluating all possible states emerging from the current state.

The selection of the next best state to transit among the set of possible outcome states, is done based on the utility function called as Happiness Value Calculation Function. This function calculates the expected utility in terms of Happiness

Value which in turn is calculated based on the current constraint satisfaction ($h(C_k(n))$) of all the explored states and the time it takes to transit from the current state to each of the explored frontier nodes ($W_i(e)$).

Before the selection is made, the agent finds the cumulative happiness value of all the nodes along the path till the currently explored nodes have been reached. Then based on this value, the agent chooses the state with Maximum Expected Utility value (MEU) or highest cumulative happiness value. The Maximum Expected Utility value (MEU) is calculated using the formula given in Equation (10).

$$MEU\ (Result_i(A)) = \sum_i (H(\sum_k h(C_k(n)), W_i(e)))$$
(10)

Computing the utility of each state, MEU ($Result_i(A)$) often requires searching, because an agent does not know how good a state is until it knows where it can get to from that state.

Searching in ISA

Usually, simple graph searching algorithms perform blind search because they cannot provide information on where the proper solution lies in the solution space. If the solution generation is based on the minimum edge weight based graph searching technique, then the solution may lead to a wrong path and will never wind up at a goal. Hence, a more intelligent search needs to be constructed using heuristics which are general searching guidelines that guides the solution generation process.

This has indicated that, the use of Artificial Intelligence (AI) in searching the given search space is necessary to have a complete search and to gain insight into the search space in problems like Software Testing. Intelligent search methods can be mixed up with traditional methods by combining them with heuristics and sets of problem-specific rules. Application of proven Artificial Intelligence

(AI) based searching methods enables us to add power, elegance and sophistication to the testing tool development.

In this approach, the graph based searching is guided by two important heuristics for infeasible test sequence identification and repeated subsequence detection.

The domain of intelligent search algorithms for general purpose application can be classified into two primary categories: Path Finding and Constraint Satisfaction (Russel and Norvig, 1995). These divisions arise based on the type of problem that is being solved.

- Path finding problems are focused on finding the path from some initial state to some final state. When solving this type of problem, the start and end points of the search might be known in advance. Finding an efficient, and possibly optimal, path between the start and end state is the goal.

- Constraint satisfaction problems (CSP) are concerned with taking some initial state and converting it to a final state that conforms to some predefined constraints. This is the most commonly used problem category in intelligent search algorithms.

The search algorithms for the ISA are belonging to these stated categories namely path finding and constraint satisfaction. Based on constraint satisfaction, the search along the SUT is guided using the expected utility value / happiness value associated with each node. In this approach, the effective search algorithm is achieved by means of this expected utility value /happiness value which is formulated based on the identification of difference between happy and unhappy states. The distinction between happy and unhappy states is identified by means of constraint satisfaction.

Internal Architecture of Intelligent Search Agent (ISA)

In the internal architecture as in Figure 6, the ISA has a sensor, which is not a hardware sensor rather it is a software code that receives the nodes, edges, the cost associated with each edge and node heuristics along with the SUT as a directed graph. The state module consists of all the states in the system.

Starting from the initial node of the graph, the ISA explores all the frontier nodes from it, using the perception sequences available in the knowledge source. If there is a single frontier node and its constraint is satisfied, then it is assigned with a maximum happiness value. This utility value indicates that the explored node is a feasible node and so, the ISA chooses that node and append it with the current test sequence. If there are multiple frontier nodes, then the ISA decides which frontier to choose by applying the decision mak-

Figure 6. Internal architecture of intelligent search agent

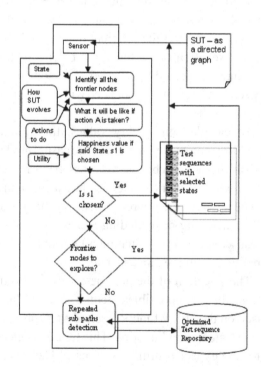

ing process based on the Maximum Expected Utility value (MEU) / cumulative happiness value.

The decision making process involves the selection or rejection of a particular node based on its associated happiness value. If the constraint associated with the current node is just a contradictory to the previously satisfied constraints, then it cannot be covered by any of the test data. Hence, the node is marked as infeasible, and its happiness value is set as zero which makes the node to be rejected and put up in the log file. If there is more than one node with same maximum happiness value, then the selection of next best node is done purely arbitrarily. Once the node is selected, it is appended with the feasible test sequence.

If the search process has revealed that the SUT has still more nodes unexplored, then the process of node exploration and selection is repeated. Once all the states in the current test sequence are completed and the agent has reached the final node in the SUT, then the test sequence is stored in the test sequence repository. The process is continued till all the nodes have been covered at least once except the infeasible nodes or till a system state of no more frontier nodes exists is reached. Then, these newly formulated test sequences are provided as input to the ISA to detect the repeated subsequences in it. Finally, the optimized test sequence repository contains only feasible and non-redundant test sequences in it.

To achieve this, two sub levels of optimizations are performed for test sequence optimization. They are,

- Infeasible test sequence identification based optimization
- Repeated subsequence detection based optimization

Here the need is to ensure that every state has been visited at least once. By using the infeasible test sequence identification algorithm, only the feasible states are included in the test sequence

repository. Since the exploration of the SUT is continued till no more frontier nodes are to be explored, the state coverage based test adequacy criteria is achieved by ensuring that all the reachable states have been covered at least once. Branch coverage criterion is achieved, by evaluating the constraints on both true and false cases through branch count measure.

The similarity measure is used to find the repetition of subsequences, thus avoiding the time spent on executing the same path again. Hence all the branches and states except the infeasible states are covered using the said approach.

Algorithms for Test Sequence Optimization

The algorithms applied in this framework are:

1. Infeasible Test Sequence Identification Algorithm
2. Repeated Subsequence Detection Algorithm

Heuristics Used in Test Sequence Optimization

- **Happiness Value:** It is associated with each constraint in the SUT. The utility function / fitness function provides the happiness value for each predicate. It is used for infeasible test sequence identification.
- **Similarity measure:** It is used to find the repetition of subsequences, thus avoiding the time spent on executing the same path again.

Infeasible Test Sequence Identification Algorithm

Infeasible Paths: An Introduction

Consider the following code:

If (a<2)

```
{ if (a>3)

{ x=x*1;}
```

Unreachable code 1

```
for(i=0; i<0;i++)

total = total +i;
```

Unreachable code 2

In the Unreachable code 1, if 'a' is less than 2, then it cannot be greater than 3, and so, x=x*1 cannot be reached. Similarly, in Unreachable code 2, i is never less than zero, and so the statement total=total +value[i] can never be reached. These statements make the path to be infeasible. And, these sorts of infeasible paths will not allow an execution path to be completed.

Functionality of Infeasible Test Sequence Identification Algorithm

In order to overcome the problem of infeasible paths, execution is not initially forced to exercise the whole test path as in the case of simple testing tools or in the case of traditional searching techniques, rather progressively one decision at a time is done. Once a set of test data has been found that executes the path up to a certain point, next decision is appended at the end of the current path and optimization process is restarted. Once a state is selected, the next state to traverse is determined by the agent automatically by means of constraint value and continue-execution-flag.

At each stage during the search, the current search point is checked to see that it satisfies all types of constraints. Only the search points or nodes which satisfy all the constraints are eligible for selection, otherwise the execution of the problem will result in run-time errors. By means of this, the infeasible paths are identified.

For example, consider the generation of test data that forms the test sequence TSEQ=$(S_1, S_2, S_3, \ldots S_n)$, Where each S_i represents a state in the state

chart. Initially, optimization is performed to find a set of test data x_1 that executes state S_1. Keeping S_1 as the initial search point, a search is then performed to find a set of test data x_2 which executes $S_1 S_2$ and the process continues until a set of test data x_n is found to execute the complete test sequence TSEQ.

If at any stage, a set of test data cannot be found to execute a current path, then it is clear that, no sets of test data will be found that will execute test sequence TSEQ and so, TSEQ becomes an infeasible test sequence; consequently the search is terminated on that sequence. Therefore, this method of step-by-step constraint satisfaction helps in the early determination of states which are not feasible.

The agent finds the infeasible test sequences by using the constraint value of each predicate in a conditional expression. The predicate is converted in the form shown below, for all the predicates of the form $<, <=, >, >=, ==$ and $! =$. The logical operators such as && and || will use the results of either of the above forms consistently. It is shown below:

If $(x==y) \rightarrow (x-y)$ // Constraint value of $(x==y)$

If $(x>y) \rightarrow (x-y)$ // Constraint value of $(x>y)$

The agent assigns a happiness value to the search point / node in which the constraint is satisfied. If the accumulated happiness value is low, then it is an indication to the tester that, some of the conditions are invalid which in turn leads to an infeasible code / dead code.

The agent selects only the set of test sequences that have the highest happiness values among the set of test sequences and stores them as the optimal test sequences. Then the Continue Execution flag will be reset to false if all the states have been visited at least once with the infeasible code are stored in the log file. If the infeasible code is corrected, the agent then adds it to the optimal test sequence set, if it is needed for the coverage of the code.

Mathematical Model for Infeasible Test Sequence Identification

The objective function is to maximize the happiness value associated with each node in the test sequence construction.

Max.

$$f(TSeq_j) = \sum_i (H(\sum_k h(C_k(X_{ij})), W_i(e))) \qquad (11)$$

Where i=1 to m; j=1 to n; k=1 to p (m- number of nodes, n-cyclomatic complexity value, p-number of predicates at constraint k)

$TSeq_j$ – Test sequence j; X_{ij}- state/node i in the test sequence j; e- edge in SUT;

$C_k = (C_1, C_2 ..., C_p)$ are the constraint values of the predicates at node X_{ij} ;

$H(\sum_k h(C_k(X_{ij})), W_i(e))$ – is the happiness function / Utility function;

$h(C_k(X_{ij}))$ - happiness value of the predicate C_k at node X_{ij};

$W_i(e)$ – Function to calculate the transition time from state x to state y

Sub. to (Box 1.)

The objective function (11) is to maximize the fitness function $H(\sum_k h(C_k(X_{ij})), W_i(e))$. Constraint (12) indicates the happiness value associated with node X_{ij} based on constraint C_k. Calculation of weight value $W_i(e)$ in terms of time taken to execute the current block is shown in constraint (13). The continuation of test sequences generation till no more frontier nodes to explore is given in constraint (14). The value of status flag associated with each node that guides the agent about the presence / absence of infeasible code is given by constraint (15). The construction of the test sequence based on the Status flag associated with each node is indicated in constraint (16). The final constraint (17) indicates the status of continuation of exploration and is based on the result of constraint (14).

Box 1.

$$h\left(C_k\left(X_{ij}\right)\right) = \begin{cases} 0 & \text{if constraint } C_k \text{ on } X_{ij} \text{ is not satisfied} \\ Max & \text{Otherwise} \end{cases} \qquad (12)$$

$$W_i(e) = \begin{cases} Max & \text{for node with minimum transition time} \\ 0 & \text{for others} \end{cases} \qquad (13)$$

$$Cover(x) = \begin{cases} false & \text{if } x \text{ is uncovered} \\ true & \text{otherwise} \end{cases} \qquad (14)$$

$$Status(x) = \begin{cases} 1 & \text{if } H(å_k h\left(C_k\left(X_{ij}\right)\right), W_i(e)) = MAX \\ 0 & \text{if } Cover(x) = false \text{ (Initialization)} \\ -1 & \text{if } H(å_k h\left(C_k\left(X_{ij}\right)\right), W_i(e)) = 0 \end{cases} \qquad (15)$$

$$Tseq_j = \begin{cases} TSeq_j + x & \text{if } Status(x) = 1 \\ TSeq_j & \text{otherwise} \end{cases} \qquad (16)$$

$$Continue-execute-flag\left(SUT\right) = \begin{cases} 1 & \text{if } Cover(x) = false \\ 0 & \text{otherwise} \end{cases} \qquad (17)$$

Based on the constraint value $(c_i(n))$, the happiness value is calculated as follows:

i. For $a > b$, $c_i(n) = (b-a)$ and if $ci(n) < 0$, $h(c_i(n)) = MAX$, otherwise $h(c_i(n)) = 0$

ii. For $a >= b$, $c_i(n) = (b-a)$ and if $ci(n) <= 0$, $h(c_i(n)) = MAX$ otherwise $h(c_i(n)) = 0$

iii. For $a < b$, $c_i(n) = (b-a)$ and if $ci(n) > 0$, $h(c_i(n)) = MAX$, otherwise $h(c_i(n)) = 0$

iv. For $a <= b$, $c_i(n) = (b-a)$ and if $ci(n) >= 0$, $h(c_i(n)) = MAX$, otherwise $h(c_i(n)) = 0$

v. For $a == b$, $c_i(n) = (b-a)$ and if $ci(n) = 0$, $h(c_i(n)) = MAX$, otherwise $h(c_i(n)) = 0$

vi. For $a != b$, $c_i(n) = (b-a)$ and if $ci(n) != 0$, $h(c_i(n)) = MAX$, otherwise $h(c_i(n)) = 0$

vii. For a OR b, $h(c_i(n)) = h(c_i(a)) + h(c_i(b))$

viii. For a AND b, $h(c_i(n)) = MIN (h(c_i(a)), h(c_i(b)))$

The happiness value associated with each state decides the next state to choose for its transition. This process is continued until a system state where no more frontier nodes to explore is reached.

Infeasible Test Sequence Identification Algorithm

1. Convert the SUT into a UML State Chart notation.
2. Translate the State Chart into an Execution Sequence Graph (ESG). This graph is a directed graph in which each node is a state in the State Chart and edge between the nodes is the state transition between the states.
3. Start from the initial node as the node to explore.
4. To identify the next best node to explore, calculate the edge weight $w(e)$ and the goodness value of each node $h(n)$.
5. The Edge Weight $(w_i(e))$ is calculated as, $w_i(e) =$ Function to calculate the time taken to traverse from the current node to the next node

6. The Goodness criterion (node heuristic) for each node is calculated as, $h(n) =$ Happiness Value associated with each constraint C_i.
7. Cumulative Happiness value $(hv (n))$ is calculated as,
8. $hv (n) =$ sum $(h (ci (n), w_i (e))$.
9. Based on this hv, the next state is selected among the set of world states and test data associated with that state is appended with the current test sequence.
10. If $h(n_i) > h(n_j)$ then $TSeq_i \leftarrow TSeq_i + n_i$
11. Else $TSeq_i \leftarrow TSeq_i + n_j$
12. If $hv (TSeq_{current}) < hv (TSeq_{rejected})$ then $TSeq_{current} \leftarrow TSeq_{rejected}$.
13. Else $TSeq_{current} \leftarrow TSeq_{current}$
14. If the final node is reached, the test sequence is stored in the optimized test sequence repository.
15. Consider the current node as the node to explore. Repeat steps 3 to 11 until we arrived at a state where we don't have any more frontier states to explore.

Repeated Subsequence Detection Algorithm

Repeated Subsequences: An Introduction

For the graph shown in Figure 7, the possible test sequences are derived and are listed as below:

- TSeq1: $A \rightarrow C \rightarrow F$
- TSeq2: $A \rightarrow B \rightarrow E \rightarrow F$
- TSeq3: $A \rightarrow D \rightarrow C \rightarrow F$
- TSeq4: $A \rightarrow B \rightarrow E \rightarrow A \rightarrow C \rightarrow F$
- TSeq5: $A \rightarrow B \rightarrow E \rightarrow A \rightarrow B -> E \rightarrow F$
- TSeq6: $A \rightarrow B \rightarrow E \rightarrow B \rightarrow E \rightarrow F$
- TSeq7: $A \rightarrow B \rightarrow E \rightarrow A \rightarrow D \rightarrow C \rightarrow F$
- TSeq8: $A \rightarrow B \rightarrow E \rightarrow A \rightarrow B \rightarrow E \rightarrow B \rightarrow E \rightarrow F$
- TSeq9: $A \rightarrow B \rightarrow E \rightarrow B \rightarrow E \rightarrow A \rightarrow D \rightarrow C \rightarrow F$

Etc…

Figure 7. Sample graph with loops

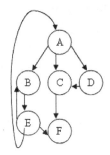

Among the generated test sequences, some of the test sequences are simply the combination of other test sequences thus leads to repeated subsequences. These test sequences should be identified and marked so that, they will not be included in the optimal test sequences set.

Functionality of Repeated Subsequence Detection Algorithm

For identifying the repeated subsequences in a test sequence, the agent breaks the given test sequence into a number of subsequences. Where, if there is a repetition for ensuring a branch coverage, then the said sequence is broken in such a way that, a sub sequence before the branch, a subsequence with a branch and a subsequence after the branch is obtained for all the set of available paths. The repeated subsequences are removed and marked as visited since they won't produce a new coverage factor.

To detect the repeated subsequences, the approach applies Hamming Distance as a measure to find the similarity value. The Hamming distance between two strings of equal length is the number of positions for which the corresponding symbols are different. It has been applied in network security based problems. Its functionality has been extended in this approach to detect the positions in which two test sequences exactly differing from each other and matching each other.

The repeated subsequences are identified by finding the similarity measure based on Hamming distance between the generated test sequences. If two test sequences/paths are of the same length, then the difference between them is calculated. It is the number indicating the places where the test sequences are differing from each other.

If it is zero, then the test sequences are repeating exactly and one of them should be rejected. If they are differing in one or more places, then find the subsequences in it which are simply a repetition of other test sequences. Only the test sequences which are not yet traversed or not repeated are added to the list.

Mathematical Model of Repeated Subsequence Detection

The optimization problem is given as,
   Min.

$$f(TSeq_x, TSeq_y) = \sum Similarity(TSeq_x, TSeq_y) \quad (16)$$

Where $TSeq_x$, $TSeq_y$ – Test sequences x and y respectively.
   Sub. to (Box 2.)
   The objective function (16) is to minimize the similarity between two test sequences $TSeq_x$ and $TSeq_y$. Constraint (17) represents the similarity value calculation based on the Hamming-Distance between two test sequences $TSeq_x$ and $TSeq_y$. The

Box 2.

$$Similarity\left(TSeq_x,\ TSeq_y\right) = \begin{cases} 0 & if\ Hamming-Dist\left(TSeq_x,\ TSeq_y\right)\ =\ 0 \\ >0 & otherwise \end{cases} \quad (17)$$

Hamming distance between two strings of equal length is the number of positions for which the corresponding symbols are different.

Repeated Subsequence Detection Algorithm

For each generated test sequence a similarity measure is calculated which is acting as a fitness value to find the repeated subsequences.

- Take two test sequences $TSeq_i$ and $TSeq_j$.
- Represent the given sequences in terms of 1s and 0s based on the presence or absence of states in the test sequences.
- Break the test sequences based on the occurrence of branches.
- Calculate the Fitness Function $f(x)$ = similarity ($TSeq_i$, $TSeq_j$), where similarity ($TSeq_i$, $TSeq_j$) finds the distance between two test sequences $TSeq_i$ and $TSeq_j$ which extends the functionality of Hamming distance.
- For the given two test sequences $TSeq_i$ and $TSeq_j$, the similarity between them is calculated, based on the comparison of n-order sets of ordered and even the cascaded branches (subsequences) of each test sequence.
- Normalize the symmetric difference between the subsequences. Then the similarity measure is calculated by subtracting a value 1 from the calculated value if there is a repetition of a subsequence.
- Finally, the total similarity between the two test sequences is calculated as the sum of similarities of all n-order sets. It is the measure indicating the number of places in which the two test sequences are differing with each other.
- If the similarity measure is zero, then the two test sequences are not differing in any of the places and are exactly the same and so, one of them should be rejected.

Otherwise, the value of similarity measure is used to find the number of places and the locations in which the two test sequences are differing and resembling each other because of the absence or presence of repeated subsequences respectively

Case Study: Temperature Monitoring System

Here as a case study, a Temperature monitoring system is taken and the optimal test sequences are identified for it. The agent ISA converted the given SUT into the state chart and its corresponding graphical notation.

Step 1: Construction of State Chart

The given SUT is analyzed and a corresponding state chart is built and was checked against the given scenarios. The final one looks as shown in Figure 8.

At the end of step 1, the given SUT has been converted into a state chart using UML notation.

Step 2: Conversion of State Chart into a Directed Graph Notation with Edges Assigned with Weights Calculated in Terms of their Transition Times as Shown in Figure 9

In the Figure 9, the following conventions are used: N1 – node1, N2-node2, N3-node3, N4-node4, N5-node5 and N6-node6.

Step 3: Generating All Possible Independent Test Sequences, with the Total Cost Required for Each Test Sequence

Then by applying the infeasible test sequence detection algorithm, ISA generated all the feasible paths from the SUT as shown in Table 3.

Figure 8. State chart of temperature monitoring system

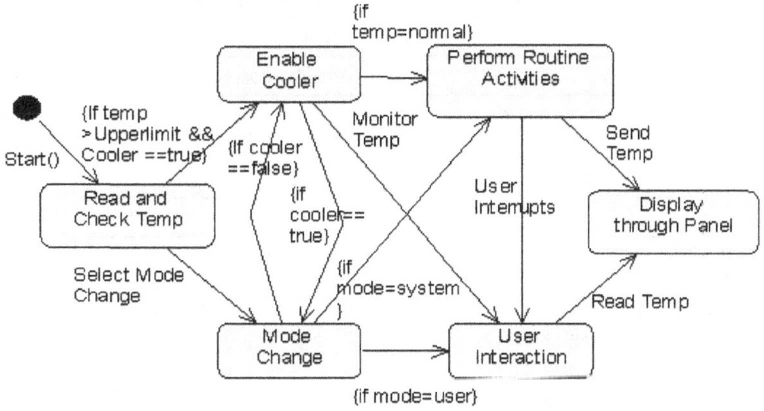

The Generated Test Sequences

Feasible Test Sequences

1. Read and Check Temp → Mode Change → User Interaction → Display Thru Panel (8)
2. Read and Check Temp → Mode Change → Perform Routine Activities → Display Thru Panel (9)
3. Read and Check Temp → Enable Cooler → User Interaction → Display Thru Panel (12)
4. Read and Check Temp → Enable Cooler → Perform Routine Activities → Display Thru Panel (13)

5. Read and Check Temp → Enable Cooler → Mode Change → User Interaction → Display Thru Panel (14)
6. Read and Check Temp → Mode Change → Perform Routine Activities→ User Interaction → Display Thru Panel (15)
7. Read and Check Temp → Enable Cooler → Perform Routine Activities → User Interaction → Display Thru Panel (16)
8. Read and Check Temp → Enable Cooler → Mode Change → Perform Routine Activities → Display Thru Panel (20)
9. Read and Check Temp → Enable Cooler → Mode Change → Perform Routine Activities → User Interaction → Display Thru Panel (22)

Infeasible Test Sequences

10. Read and Check Temp → Enable Cooler → Mode Change → Enable Cooler → Perform Routine Activities→ User Interaction → Display Thru Panel
11. Read and Check Temp → Mode Change → Enable Cooler → Perform Routine Activities → Display Thru Panel

Figure 9. Graphical representation of the state chart with edge cost

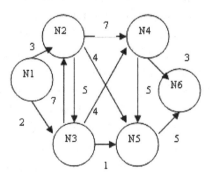

Table 3. The generated feasible paths

Test Sequences	Cost	Included Edges	Excluded Edges	Other Sequences
node1->node3->node5 ->node6	8	None	None	
		None	<node5,node6>	node1,node3,node4,node6 = 9
		<node5,node6>	<node3,node5>	node1, node2,node3,node6=12
		<node3,node5><node5, node6>	<node1,node3>	node1,node2,node3,node5,node6=14
node1->node3->node4->node6	9	None	<node5,node6>	
		None	<node4,node6><node5,node6>	∞
		<node4,node6>	<node3,node4><node5, node6>	node1,node2,node4,node6=13
		<node3,node4><node4,node6>	<node1,node3><node5,node6>	node1,node2,node3,node4,node6=15
node1->node2->node5->node6	12	<node5,node6>	<node3,node5>	
		<node5,node6>	<node2,node5><node3,node5>	node1,node3,node4,node5,node6=16
		<node2,node5><node5,node6>	<node1,node2><node3,node5>	∞

12. Read and Check Temp → Mode Change → Enable Cooler → Perform Routine Activities → User Interaction → Display Thru Panel
13. Read and Check Temp → Mode Change → Enable Cooler → User Interaction → Display Thru Panel
14. Read and Check Temp → Enable Cooler → Mode Change → Enable Cooler → Perform Routine Activities → Display Thru Panel
15. Read and Check Temp → Enable Cooler → Mode Change → Enable Cooler → Perform Routine Activities → User Interaction → Display Thru Panel
16. Read and Check Temp → Enable Cooler → Mode Change → Enable Cooler → User Interaction → Display Thru Panel

Step 4: Rule for inclusion and exclusion of paths

From the above list of all test sequences, the feasible test sequences are identified by means of constraint satisfaction. By applying the infeasible test sequence identification algorithm it has been identified that; the test sequences from 10 to 16 are infeasible. The reason is, to enable cooler, the constraint cooler=true should be satisfied. Once it is satisfied, the Enable Cooler state has been appended to the current test sequence. Then, it explores all the frontier states from Enable Cooler state. The agent then calculates the happiness values of all the frontier nodes. Consider the Mode Change state which is one of the frontier states of Enable Cooler state. This state has been further explored in which, it has a constraint, cooler=false for making the system to transit to the same Enable Cooler state. Since the constraint cooler=true is already satisfied, it cannot be false (contradictory), to go to the same state. Since the cooler variable cannot be true as well as false in the same sequence, this leads to an infeasible test sequence. Hence, all the transitions going through the states Enable Cooler → Mode Change→Enable Cooler and Mode Change→Enable Cooler, lead to infeasible test sequences and their corresponding happiness values are zero. So, the test sequences from 10 to 16 are named as infeasible and they have been removed from the test sequence repository and only the test sequences from 1 to 9 are stored in the feasible test sequence repository.

From the identified set of feasible test sequences, the redundant subsequence detection algorithm is applied to find out repeated subsequences. By applying the similarity measure heuristic, it has been identified that, the test sequences 8 and 9 have repeated subsequences which have been already covered by other test sequences. Hence, these two test sequences have been removed and the remaining test sequences from 1 to 7 are stored in the optimal test sequence repository. It has also been verified that, all the states and branches have been covered at least once except the infeasible states.

Step 5: The Optimized Test Sequences Which Require only Less Cost are Given in Ascending Order of their Cost Associated

1. Read and Check Temp → Mode Change → User Interaction → Display Thru Panel (8)
2. Read and Check Temp → Mode Change → Perform Routine Activities → Display Thru Panel (9)
3. Read and Check Temp → Enable Cooler → User Interaction → Display Thru Panel (12)
4. Read and Check Temp → Enable Cooler → Perform Routine Activities → Display Thru Panel (13)
5. Read and Check Temp → Enable Cooler → Mode Change → User Interaction → Display Thru Panel (14)
6. Read and Check Temp → Mode Change → Perform Routine Activities→ User Interaction → Display Thru Panel (15)
7. Read and Check Temp → Enable Cooler → Perform Routine Activities → User Interaction → Display Thru Panel (16)

Table 4.

Path	Cost
node1→node3→node5→node6 -	8
node1→node3→node4→node6 -	9
node1→node2→node5→node6 -	12
node1→node2→node4→node6 -	13
node1→node2→node3→node5→node6 -	14
node1→node2→node3→node4→node6 -	15
node1→node3→node4→node5→node6 -	16

From the set of all generated test sequences, ISA applied the redundancy detection algorithm and generated the optimal test sequences. They are listed in Table 4.

Result of Case Study: Test Adequacy Criteria vs. Optimization

The first study with the Temperature Monitoring System validates the test adequacy criteria of branch and state coverage with reduced length of the test sequences. The approach generates the feasible and non-redundant test sequences based on the infeasible test sequences identification and redundant subsequences detection algorithms. Among the total number of feasible test sequences, two test sequences have been excluded due to the coverage of them by other sequences.

Hence, with a fitness function based on path, state and branch coverage, the ISA algorithms optimized the test sequences. By using these test sequences, one can ensure that a test suite composed of seven test cases (each for one test sequence) covers 96.4% of the code (by excluding infeasible code).

FUTURE RESEARCH DIRECTIONS

The book is based on the application of knowledge based approaches in Software Development Life Cycle. This chapter focused on the most important life cycle phase Testing Phase and provides a framework for optimization in the testing process. In this work, a novel Test Sequence Optimization framework which applies the working of an Intelligent Agent (IA) to develop an Intelligent Search Agent (ISA). In which, two novel optimization algorithms namely Infeasible Test Sequence Identification and Repeated Subsequence Detection are developed to generate optimal test sequences by identifying infeasible and repeated test sequences in the SUT to reduce the number of test runs. To achieve this, the intelligent search process is guided by two important heuristics namely Happiness Value and Similarity Measure.

Some of the future research directions are:

- This research work concentrates on optimization based on test adequacy criteria such as coverage and fault revealing capability of the test cases. In the future research work, this can be done based on other test adequacy criteria such as data flow based and LCSAJ based measures.
- For test sequence optimization, a Utility based agent is employed to do the task. As a future work, the other types of agents can be applied to this process and the performance of them can be compared in achieving test sequence optimization.

CONCLUSION

This chapter describes the application of Intelligent Agents in test sequence optimization. The developed agent namely the Intelligent Search Agent (ISA), couples human like intelligence and automation as a tool in selection and optimization of test sequences in the SUT. In the approach discussed in this chapter, two mathematical models have been formulated, for infeasible test sequence identification and repeated subsequence detection to achieve test sequence optimization. During this optimization, the search process is equipped

with two important heuristics namely Happiness Value and Similarity Measure to guide intelligent searching.

The results of the approach using Intelligent Search Agent (ISA) have been compared with Ant Colony Optimization (ACO) based approach with respect to time, cost and length of the test sequences. Since ACO has been a proven technique when compared to other techniques, this thesis compared the approach with ACO only; and by transitivity it proves that ISA is better than all other approaches.

The evaluation results show that, the test sequences generated by ISA are sufficient for covering the states and branches in the SUT. ACO does not take into consideration the branch coverage criterion and the sequences are simply the repetition of previously visited states. Also, from the evaluations, it is clear that ISA consumes less time and cost and also generates lesser length (reduction of up to 50%) test sequences when compared to ACO based on several bench mark problems. Hence, the developed test sequence optimization approach proved that, ISA is better in test sequence optimization when compared to ACO.

Even though the initial learning time taken by the agent is high; later on, the agent takes only less time to learn and plan any modifications made in the SUT. Thus the reduced set of test sequences using ISA consumes only less time and cost when compared to ACO and saves tremendous amount of resources needed in software testing process. Hence, a novel software test sequence optimization paradigm equipped with intelligent agent based search approach has been developed to be capable of reducing the length of the test sequences (up to 50% approx. based on coverage).

The previous works of the author on the application of Intelligent Agents, Hybrid Genetic Algorithm and Artificial Bee Colony Optimization to achieve test sequence, test case and test suite optimizations have provided better results in software test optimization. (Jeya Mala et al, 2007, 2008, 2009 and 2010).

REFERENCES

Agrawal, H. (1994). Dominators, super blocks, and program coverage. *Proceedings of the 21st ACM SIGPLAN-SIGACT Symposium on Principles of Programming Languages*, (pp. 25-34).

Agrawal, H., Demillo, R. A., & Spafford, E. H. (1991). Dynamic slicing in presence of unconstrained pointers. *Proceedings of the ACM SIGSOFT91 Symposium On Software Testing, Analysis and Verification*, (pp. 60-73).

Banks, D., Dashiell, W., Gallagher, L., Hagwood, C., Kacker, R., & Rosenthal, L. (1998). *Software testing by statistical methods preliminary success estimates for approaches based on binomial models, coverage designs, mutation testing, and usage models*. Technical Report – NIST.

Baudry, B., Fleurey, F., Le Traon, Y., & Jézéquel, J. M. (2005). An original approach for automatic test cases optimization: A bacteriologic algorithm. *IEEE Software, 22*(2), 76–82. doi:10.1109/MS.2005.30

Beizer, B. (1990). *Software testing techniques* (2nd ed.). Thomson Computer Press.

Benson, J. P. (1981). Adaptive search techniques applied to software testing. *Proceedings of the 1981 ACM Workshop/Symposium on Measurement and Evaluation of Software Quality*, (pp. 109-116).

Beydeda, S., & Gruhn, V. (2003). *Test case generation according to the binary search strategy*. (LNCS 2869), (pp. 1000-1007).

Bodik, R., Gupta, R., & Mary, L. S. (1997). *Refining data flow information using infeasible paths*. (pp. 361-377). FSE-1997, Springer.

Briand, L. C. (2002). On the many ways software engineering can benefit from knowledge engineering. *Proceedings of the 14th SEKE Conference*, Italy, (pp. 3-6).

Bueno, P. M. S., & Jino, M. (2000). *Identification of potentially infeasible program paths by monitoring the search for test data*. 15th IEEE International Conference on Automated Software Engineering (ASE00), 209.

Chen, T. Y., & Lau, M. F. (2003). On the divide-and-conquer approach towards test suite reduction. *Information Sciences: An International Journal, 152*(1), 89–119.

Clarke, L. A. (1976). A system to generate test data and symbolically execute programs. *IEEE Transactions on Software Engineering, 2*(3), 915–1222. doi:10.1109/TSE.1976.233817

Coppit, D., Yang, J., Khurshid, S., Le, W., & Sullivan, K. (2005). Software assurance by bounded exhaustive testing. *IEEE Transactions on Software Engineering, 31*(4), 328–339. doi:10.1109/TSE.2005.52

Dhavachelvan, P., & Uma, G. V. (2003). *Multi-agent based integrated framework for intra-class testing of object-oriented software*. (LNCS 2869).

Díaz, E., Tuya, J., & Blanco, R. (2008). A Tabu search algorithm for structural software testing. *Computers & Operations Research, 35*(10), 3052–3072. doi:10.1016/j.cor.2007.01.009

Eric, W.W., Joseph, R.H., & Aditya, P., Mathur & Alberto P. (1999). Test Set Size Minimization and Fault Detection Effectiveness: A Case Study in a Space Application. *Journal of Systems and Software, 48*(2), 79–89. doi:10.1016/S0164-1212(99)00048-5

Forgacs, I., & Bertolino, A. (1997). Feasible test path selection by principal slicing. In *Proceedings of 6th European Software Engineering Conference*.

Frankl, P. G., & Weyuker, E. J. (1988). An applicable family of data flow testing criteria. *IEEE Transactions on Software Engineering, 14*(10), 1483–1498. doi:10.1109/32.6194

Frolich, P., & Link, J. (2000). *Automated test case generation from dynamic models*. (LNCS 1850), (pp. 472-491).

Gerlich, R., Boll, Th., & Chevalley, Ph. (2006). *Improving test automation by deterministic methods in statistical testing. Proceedings of Data Systems In Aerospace* (DASIA 2006), *European Space Agency*, (p. 630).

Goldberg, A. T. C., Wang, T. C., & Zimmerman, D. (1994). *Applications of feasible path analysis to program testing*. In International Symposium on Software Testing and Analysis, (pp. 80-94).

Gonçalves, J. F., & Resende, M. G. C. (2002). *A hybrid genetic algorithm for manufacturing cell formation*. Technical Report, AT and T Lab.

Gouraud, S. D., Denise, A., Gaudel, M. C., & Marre, B. (2001). A new way of automating statistical testing methods. *Proceedings of the 16th IEEE International Conference On Automated Software Engineering*, (p. 5).

Grottke, M., & Trivedi, K. S. (2007). Fighting bugs: Remove, retry, replicate, and rejuvenate. *IEEE Computer*, *40*(2), 107–109.

Grottke, M., & Trivedi, K. S. (2007). Fighting Bugs: Remove, Retry, Replicate, and Rejuvenate. *IEEE Computer*, *40*(2), 107–109.

Guo, Q., Hierons, R. M., Harman, R. M., & Derderian, K. (2005). Constructing multiple unique input/output sequences using evolutionary optimization techniques. *IEE Proceedings. Software*, *152*(3), 127–140. doi:10.1049/ip-sen:20045001

Gupta, N., Mathur, A. P., & Soffa, M. L. (1998). Automated test data generation using an iterative relaxation method. *Foundations of Software Engineering*, *11*, 231–244.

Harman, M. (2007). The current state and future of search based software engineering. *Future of Software Engineering*, *2007*, 342–357. doi:10.1109/FOSE.2007.29

Harman, M., Hassoun, Y., Lakhotia, K., Mcminn, P., & Wegener, J. (2007). The impact of input domain reduction on search-based test data generation. *Proceedings of the ACM SIGSOFT Symposium on the Foundations of Software Engineering*.

Harman, M., & Jones, B. F. (2001). Search based software engineering. *Information and Software Technology*, *43*(14), 833–839. doi:10.1016/S0950-5849(01)00189-6

Hedley, D., & Hennell, M. A. (1985). The causes and effects of infeasible paths in computer programs. In *Proceedings of 8th ICSE - 1985*, (pp. 259-266).

Hélène, W., Pascale, T. F., & Olfa, A. K. (2007). Simulated annealing applied to test generation: Landscape characterization and stopping criteria. *Empirical Software Engineering*, *12*(1), 35–63. doi:10.1007/s10664-006-7551-5

Hierons, R. M., Harman, M., & Danicic, S. (1999). Using program slicing to assist in the detection of equivalent mutants. *Software Testing. Verification and Reliability*, *9*(4), 233–262. doi:10.1002/(SICI)1099-1689(199912)9:4<233::AID-STVR191>3.0.CO;2-3

Horgan, J., London, S., & Lyu, M. (1994). Achieving software quality with testing coverage measures. *IEEE Computer*, *27*(9), 60–69.

Ingo, S., Mirko, C., Heiko, D. R., & Peter, P. (2007). Systematic testing of model-based code generators. *IEEE Transactions on Software Engineering*, *33*(9), 622–634. doi:10.1109/TSE.2007.70708

John, T., Lin, P., & Michael, W. (2005). Prometheus Design Tool. *AAMAS*, *2005*, 1–2.

José C.B.R., Mário Z.R. and Francisco F.D.V. (2008), *A Strategy For Evaluating Feasible And Unfeasible Test Cases For The Evolutionary Testing Of Object-Oriented Software*, ASE-2008, 85-92.

José F. Gonçalves, Mauricio G.C. & Resende (2002), *A Hybrid Genetic Algorithm for Manufacturing Cell Formation*, Technical Report, AT and T Lab.

Karaboga, D., & Bahriye, B. (2008). On the performance of Artificial Bee Colony (ABC) algorithm. *Applied Soft Computing*, 8(1), 687–697. doi:10.1016/j.asoc.2007.05.007

Kim, K. J., & Han, I. (2003). Application of a hybrid genetic algorithm and neural network approach in activity-based costing. *Expert Systems with Applications*, 24(1), 73–77. doi:10.1016/S0957-4174(02)00084-2

Korel, B. (1990). Automated software test data generation. *IEEE Transactions on Software Engineering*, 16(8), 870–879. doi:10.1109/32.57624

Li, H., & Lam, C. P. (2004). Optimization of state-based test suites for software systems: An evolutionary approach. *International Journal of Computer and Information Science*, 5(3), 212–223.

Malevris, N., Yates, D. F., & Veevers, A. (1990). Predictive metric for likely feasibility of program paths. *Information and Software Technology*, 32(2), 115–118. doi:10.1016/0950-5849(90)90110-D

Mangina, E. (2005). Intelligent agent-based monitoring platform for applications in engineering. *International Journal of Computer Science and Applications*, 2(1), 38–48.

Mathur, A. P. (2008). *Foundations of software testing* (2nd ed.). Pearson Education.

Mcminn, P. (2004). Search-based software test data generation: A survey. *Software Testing. Verification and Reliability*, 14(2), 105–156. doi:10.1002/stvr.294

Mcminn, P., Harman, M., Binkley, D., & Tonella, P. (2006). *The species per path approach to search based test data generation*. ISSTA-2006, (pp. 13-24).

Mcminn, P., & Holcombe, M. (2003). The state problem for evolutionary testing. *Proceedings of GECCO 2003*, (LNCS 2724), (pp. 2488-2500).

Meenakshi, V., Last, M., & Kandel, A. (2002). Using a neural network in the software testing process. *International Journal of Intelligent Systems*, 17(1), 45–62. doi:10.1002/int.1002

Micheal, C. C., & Mcgraw, G. (1999). *Automated software test data generation for complex programs*. Technical Report, Reliable Software Technologies.

Moataz, A. A., & Irman, H. (2008). GA-based multiple paths test data generator. *Computers & Operations Research*, 35(10), 3107–3124. doi:10.1016/j.cor.2007.01.012

Mohammad, F., Babak, A., & Ali, M. (2007). Application of honey-bee mating optimization algorithm on clustering. *Applied Mathematics and Computation*, 190(2), 1502–1513. doi:10.1016/j.amc.2007.02.029

Nii, P. (1986). The blackboard model of problem solving. *AI Magazine*, 7(2), 38–53.

Pargas, R. P., Harrold, M., & Peck, R. (1999). Test-data generation using genetic algorithms. *Software Testing. Verification and Reliability*, 9(4), 263–282. doi:10.1002/(SICI)1099-1689(199912)9:4<263::AID-STVR190>3.0.CO;2-Y

Paulo, M. S. B., & Mario, J. (2000*), Identification of Potentially Infeasible Program Paths by Monitoring the Search for Test Data*, 15th IEEE International Conference on Automated Software Engineering (ASE00), 209.

Pedrycz, W., & Peters, J. F. (1998). *Computational intelligence in software engineering* (*Vol. 16*). World Scientific Publishers.

Peter, F., & Johannes, L. (2000). Automated Test Case Generation From Dynamic Models. *Lecture Notes in Computer Science, 1850/2000*, 472–491.

Pressman, R. S. (2005). *Software engineering-a practitioners approach* (6th ed.). McGraw Hill.

Ribeiro, J. C. B., Rela, M. Z., & de Vega, F. F. (2008). *A strategy for evaluating feasible and unfeasible test cases for the evolutionary testing of object-oriented software.* ASE-2008, (pp. 85-92).

Russel, S., & Norvig, P. (1995). *Artificial intelligence: A modern approach* (2nd ed.). Prentice-Hall Publications.

Singh, A. (2009). An Artificial Bee Colony Algorithm for the Leaf-Constrained Minimum Spanning Tree Problem. *Applied Soft Computing, 9*(2), 625–631. doi:10.1016/j.asoc.2008.09.001

Singh, A. (2009). An artificial bee colony algorithm for the leaf-constrained minimum spanning tree problem. *Applied Soft Computing, 9*(2), 625–631. doi:10.1016/j.asoc.2008.09.001

Tallam, S., & Gupta, N. (2005). *A concept analysis inspired greedy algorithm for test suite minimization.*

Thangarajah, J., Padgham, L., & Winikoff, M. (2005). Prometheus design tool. *AAMAS, 2005*, 1–2.

Tracey, N., Clark, J., & Mander, K. (1998). Automated program flaw finding using simulated annealing. *Proceedings of the 1998 ACM SIGSOFT International Symposium on Software Testing and Analysis*, (pp. 73-81).

Willem, V., Corina, S. P., & Sarfraz, K. (2004). Test input generation with Java path finder. *Proceedings of the 2004 ACM SIGSOFT International Symposium on Software Testing and Analysis.*

Wimmel, G., Läotzbeyer, H., Pretschner, A., & Slotosch, O. (2000). Specification based test sequence generation with propositional logic. *Journal Software Testing, Validation, And Reliability, 10*(4), 229–248. doi:10.1002/1099-1689(200012)10:4<229::AID-STVR213>3.0.CO;2-O

Wong, E., Horgan, J. R., Mathur, A. P., & Pasquini, A. (1999). Test set size minimization and fault detection effectiveness: A case study in a space application. *Journal of Systems and Software, 48*(2), 79–89. doi:10.1016/S0164-1212(99)00048-5

Xiao, M., Mohamed, E. A., Marek, R., & James, M. (2007). Empirical evaluation of optimization algorithms when used in goal-oriented automated test data generation techniques. *Empirical Software Engineering, 12*(2), 183–239. doi:10.1007/s10664-006-9026-0

Zhang, Z., & Zhou, Y. (2007). Fuzzy logic based approach for software testing. *International Journal of Pattern Recognition and Artificial Intelligence*, 709–722. doi:10.1142/S0218001407005636

Zhao, F., Sun, J., Li, S., & Liu, W. (2009). A hybrid genetic algorithm for the traveling salesman problem with pickup and delivery. *International Journal of Automation and Computing, 6*(1), 97–102. doi:10.1007/s11633-009-0097-4

Zhenqiang, C., Baowen, X., William, C. C., Hongji, Y., & Jianjun, Z. (2003). *Partial slicing for large programs.* SEKE-2003, (pp. 204-207).

Zhiyong, Z., John, T., & Lin, P. (2008). *Automated unit testing intelligent agents in PDT.* International Conference on Autonomous Agents, (pp. 1673-1674).

Zuohua, D., Kao, Z., & Jueliang, H. (2008). A rigorous approach towards test case generation. *Information Sciences: An International Journal, 178*(21), 4057–4079.

ADDITIONAL READING

Christopher, R. (2003). Testing and Monitoring Intelligent Agents. *Lecture Notes in Computer Science, 2564*, 155–164. doi:10.1007/978-3-540-45173-0_12

Jeremy, B., & Azim, E. (2002). Enhancing Intelligent Agent Collaboration for Flow Optimization of Railroad Traffic. *Transportation Research Part A, Policy and Practice, 36*(10), 919–930. doi:10.1016/S0965-8564(02)00002-2

Jeya Mala, D., Kamalapriya, M., Shobana, M. K., & Mohan, V. (2009), *A Non-Pheromone based Intelligent Swarm Optimization Technique in Software Test Suite Optimization*, International Conference on Intelligent Agents and Multi Agents (IAMA)-2009, IEEExplore DOI No.: 10.1109/IAMA.2009.5228012, pp.1-15.

Jeya Mala, D., & Mohan, V. (2007*), Intelligent Test Sequence Optimization using Graph based Intelligent Search Agent*, 22-25, IEEExplore - Vol. No. 0-7695-3050-8/07 DOI 10.1109 / ICCIMA 2007.109.

Jeya Mala, D., & Mohan, V. (2007). *Intelligent Test Sequence Optimization using Graph based searching technique, ICISTM 2007* (pp. 10–19). Book on Information Systems, Technology and Management, Allied Publishers Pvt.Ltd.

Jeya Mala, D., & Mohan, V. (2008). Hybrid Tester - An Automated Hybrid Genetic Algorithm Based Test Case Optimization Framework for Effective Software Testing. *International Journal of Computational Intelligence: Theory and Practice, 3*(2), 81–94.

Jeya Mala, D., & Mohan, V. (2008). Intelligen-Tester –Test Sequence Optimization framework using Multi-Agents. *Journal of Computers, 3*(6), 39–46.

Jeya Mala D. and Mohan V.(2008), *ABC Model based Software Test Optimization Framework for effective software testing*, ICONSO-2008.

Jeya Mala, D., & Mohan, V. (2009). On the Use of Intelligent Agents to Guide Test Sequence Selection and Optimization. *International Journal of Computational Intelligence and Applications, 8*(2), 155–179. doi:10.1142/S1469026809002515

Jeya Mala, D., & Mohan, V. (2009). ABC Tester - Artificial Bee Colony Based Software Test Suite Optimization Approach. *International Journal of Software Engineering, 2*(2), 15–43.

Jeya Mala D. and Mohan V.(2009), *Software Test Optimization Using Artificial Bee Colony Based Approach*, CSIE-2009, organized by World Research Institutes (WRI) and IEEE –USA.

Jeya Mala, D., & Mohan, V. (2009), *An Effective Software Test Suite Optimization Framework Using Intelligent Agents with Black Board Architecture Based Learning*, Proceedings of ICOREM-2009.

Jeya Mala D., Prasanna Nagarjunan S., Ruby Elizabeth S. and V.Mohan,(2008), *Intelligent Tester – Intelligent Test Sequence Optimization Framework To Achieve Quality In Highly Reliable Systems*, ICRSQE 2008, Book on Advances in Performance and Safety of Complex Systems, Macmillan Publications, ISBN No. 0230-63441-9, pp.669 – 778.

Jeya Mala, D., Ruby Elizabeth, S., & Mohan, V. (2008). Intelligent Test Case Optimizer – Test Case optimization using Hybrid Genetic Algorithm. *International Journal of Computer Science and Applications, 1*(1), 51–55.

Jeya Mala, D., Ruby Elizabeth, S., & Mohan, V. (2008), *Intelligent Test Case Optimization Using Hybrid Genetic Algorithm*, Proceedings of INCRUIS 2K8, 2008.

Jeya Mala D., Ruby Elizabeth S. and Mohan V. (In Press), *A Hybrid Test Optimization Framework– Coupling Genetic Algorithm with Local Search Technique*, Computing and Informatics - an International Journal, 29(1), 133-164.

Ken Koster and David Kao. (2007), *State coverage: a structural test adequacy criterion for behavior checking*, Foundations of Software Engineering, The 6th Joint Meeting on European software engineering conference and the ACM SIGSOFT symposium on the foundations of software engineering.

Kung, D. (2004). *An Agent-Based Framework for Testing Web Applications*. Annual International Computer Software and Applications Conference N°28.

Lin Padgham and Michael Winikoff. (1995), *Prometheus: A Pragmatic Methodology for Engineering Intelligent Agents*, 2002, Proceedings of the OOPSLA 2002 Workshop on Agent-Oriented Methodologies

Lueven & Belgium J.N.R. (2001). An Agent-Based Approach for Building Complex Software Systems. *Communications of the ACM, 44*(4), 35–41. doi:10.1145/367211.367250

Miao, H., Chen, S., & Qian, Z. (2007). *A Formal Open Framework Based On Agent For Testing Web Applications*. International Conference On Computational Intelligence And Security, 15(19), 281-285.

Myres, (1995), *Art of Software Testing*, 1995, 2nd Edition Taylor, B.J. and Cukic.B, (2000), *Evaluation of regressive methods for automated generation of test trajectories*, Software Reliability Engineering, 2000. ISSRE 2000, 97 - 109

Paolo, B., Ralph, R., Andrew, H., & Andrew, L. (1999). *Using Java for Artificial Intelligence and Intelligent Agent Systems*. Melbourne, Australia: Agent Oriented Software Pty. Ltd.

Rem, W. C., Gregory, M. P. O., & Rooney, C. (2004). A UML-Based Software Engineering Methodology for Agent Factory. *SEKE, 2004*, 25–30.

Shoham, Y. (1993). Agent-Oriented Programming. *Artificial Intelligence, 60*(1), 51–92. doi:10.1016/0004-3702(93)90034-9

Zhiyong, Z., John, T., & Lin, P. (2008), *Automated Unit Testing Intelligent Agents in PDT*. International Conference on Autonomous Agents, pp. 1673-1674.

Zhu, Y. P., Li, S., & Juanyue, E. (2008). Application of the Agent in Agricultural Expert System Inspection Software. *Agricultural Sciences in China, 7*(1).

KEY TERMS AND DEFINITIONS

Software Testing: It is defined as the process of operating a system or component under specified conditions, observing or recording the results, and making an evaluation of some aspect of the system or component (IEEE Standard 610.12-1990).

Execution Sequence Graph of a Program: The Execution Sequence graph of a program, $ESG = \langle S; E; S_0; S_e \rangle$, is a directed graph $\langle S;E \rangle$ in which the nodes S represent the block of executable statements and the edges E indicate the conditional transfer of control between the blocks. There is a path from node S_0 belongs to S to other nodes, and all paths end with node S_e belongs to S. S_0 is called the initial node and S_e is called the terminal node.

Test Sequence: A sequence of test data in the ESG traversing nodes S_i, e.g., $\{S_1; S2; \_ \_ \_; S_k\}$ is called a test sequence. Since each state/node is associated with a test data; the sequence of states represents the test sequence that covers a particular test path.

Test Case: A test case is a triplet, which can be represented as, {I/P, Actual O/P, and Expected

O/P}. It can be exercised for each test sequence identified from the control flow graph.

Test Adequacy Criterion: It is a predicate that defines what properties of a program must be exercised to constitute a thorough test, i.e., one whose successful execution implies no errors in a tested program. There are several coverage based test adequacy criterion available. In our approach, we used, State Coverage, Code Coverage and Branch Coverage criterion.

State Coverage: Unlike other coverage-based criteria, state coverage measures the extent of checks of program behavior. Let Ni be the set of output-defining nodes of SUT subject to test ti, and Vi be the set of covered output defining nodes

of CUT subject to test ti. The optimistic state coverage of test suite T is $\dfrac{|Vi|}{|Ni|}$

Code Coverage: In code testing, criteria based on coverage of the building blocks of programs can be used to determine the adequacy of tests. Code coverage is a measure used in software testing. It describes the degree to which the source code of a program has been tested. It is a form of testing that inspects the code directly and is therefore a form of white box testing.

Branch Coverage: Branch coverage adequacy criterion verifies whether each control structure (such as an if statement) is evaluated both to true and false conditions. Branch Coverage % = No. of Branches covered / Total No. of branches

Chapter 13
A Framework for Internet Security Assessment and Improvement Process

Muthu Ramachandran
Leeds Metropolitan University, UK

Zaigham Mahmood
University of Derby, UK

ABSTRACT

Internet security is paramount in today's networked systems, especially when they provide wireless application access and enable personal and confidential data to be transmitted across the networks. Numerous tools and technologies are available to ensure system security, however, external threats to computer systems and applications are also becoming more and more sophisticated. This chapter presents a framework that consists of two components: (1) an assessment model to look at the existing security infrastructure of an organisation to determine its security maturity level; and (2) a process improvement maturity model to suggest an improvement mechanism for the organisation to progress from one maturity level to the next higher level. The intention is to provide a framework to improve the organisation's Internet and network security so that it becomes more efficient and effective than before. The improvement process model is a 5-stage framework, which has the potential to be established as a standard maturity model for assessing and improving security levels in a manner similar to other software process improvement framework such as CMMI. Preliminary results, based on looking at the existing security measures of one particular organisation, reveal that there is indeed a need for an appropriate model such as the one being proposed in this chapter.

INTRODUCTION

In the information society of the 21st century, the information and communication technologies have revolutionised human lives. Wireless

DOI: 10.4018/978-1-60960-509-4.ch013

telephony, electronic commerce and online transactions are now common place and within easy reach of general public. All this has become possible through the proliferation of computing technologies and use of the Internet. There is no doubt that World Wide Web, or the Internet, is the binding and enabling force behind all this.

Since the use of the Internet is growing, the demand for the associated products, applications and services is also growing. As a bi-product, the concerns with respect to the security of information, confidentiality of data and reliability of services are also growing. Previously, when the computing systems were used as standalone devices, the security concerns amounted to only the physical security (i.e. fear of getting it damaged, getting it stolen, etc). Now, however, because of interconnectivity of computing equipment on a global basis, there are serious concerns with respect to security of networks (including the Internet), theft of data, cyber terrorism and so on. Although, network managers and security experts are doing their best to ensure that transactions are safe, networks are secure and malicious damage to data, services, applications and equipment is eliminated, hackers and cyber terrorists are also becoming more intelligent and finding new ways of breaking and getting into computing systems. The technologies that exist for the benefit of citizens are, ironically, the same technologies that hackers are using for their malicious acts. To ensure the security of internet applications and the use of internet, many approaches has been employed including systems such as the following:

- Intrusion detection mechanisms
- Intrusion prevention schemes
- Firewalls and Filters
- Virus detection and removal software

However, these mechanisms have limitations. In this context, the biggest challenge is to develop and apply appropriate internet security strategies consistently and uniformly across the entire network and ultimately to individual nodes of a network.

The aim of the current study is to suggest a framework for the Internet security and the security of an organisation's use of Internet - along the lines similar to software process improvement frameworks such as CMMI (SEI, 2005).

The framework being proposed has two aspects to it:

- **Internet security assessment model:** Here, the intention is to understand the current security situation of an organisation to identify the strengths and weaknesses of the existing security practices in the organisation .
- **Internet security improvement model:** Here, the intention is to assess the security maturity level of the organisation and recommend ways for improving the security posture of the organisation and methods of implementing it.

In the rest of this chapter, we first discuss various aspects of internet security in "Internet Security." Then, we present the internet security assessment process in some detail in "Security Assessment and Improvement Process" and "Proposed Framework for Security Improvement." In "Preliminary Results", we summarise results of a simple experiment. That follows the conclusions in "Conclusion."

INTERNET SECURITY

Types of Security Threats

With the proliferation of computing, internet and wireless devices as well as their connection to the World Wide Web, security has become an issue of serious concern with respect to the following three core areas:

- **Confidentiality:** ensuring that data and information resident on computing systems and being transmitted over the networks are protected from access by unauthorised persons
- **Integrity:** ensuring that data and information resident on computing systems and

being transmitted over the networks do not get altered through unauthorised access or by unauthorised persons

- **Authentication:** ensuring that data and information resident on computing systems and being transmitted over the networks are available only to those authorised to receive or access it.

In a broader context, there are several aspects to security, including:

- Physical security
- Procedural and system security
- Network security
- Internet security

Physical security refers to ensuring that the system does not get stolen or physically damaged. This type of security is not the topic for discussion in this chapter. Procedural and system security refers to ensuring that access and authentication controls and access privileges are not compromised in any way and that monitoring and control procedures do not get modified by unauthorised persons. Network security refers to protecting the entire network (including nodes, connections, systems, storage, data, services and other relevant resources) from unwanted intruders i.e. from unauthorised modification, destruction or disclosure.

Use of a firewall between the individual computer systems (or Intranet) and the Internet is a common approach to implement network security. This, coupled with virus detection and removal software, is normally considered sufficient for such security.

Different types of network threats and attacks can be categorised as follows:

- **Email-based Service Attacks:** these are carried out using emails which then infect the system by transferring viruses, worms and Trojans. Much guidance exists as to how to deal with such emails, including not opening the emails if they have attachments with file extension of .exe.

- **Denial of Service (DoS) attacks:** these attacks are probably the most dangerous and difficult to address. They cause such serious malfunction of the system that it is often taken out of action to repair the damage - thus disrupting or even blocking the service that the system provides, until the problem is sorted out. For big organisations, it can result in huge financial losses – not to mention the loss of face and credibility. Methods used to prevent such attacks include keeping up-to-date with security related patches and using packet filtering to prevent 'unauthorised' packets from entering the system (Curtin, 1997).

- **Unauthorised Access:** this refers to unauthorised persons being able to access organisation's resources including data, information and files as well as access to services. These attacks result in confidentiality breaches and can result in the theft of data, unplanned changes made to files (including deletions) as well as undesired modifications to existing services. It can be highly damaging even in case of a single personal computer on the network. Protecting systems using passwords is one common approach to restrict unauthorised access.

- **Viruses, Worms and Trojans:** here, malicious software programmes known as viruses, worms and Trojans, get installed on the host systems. These programmes then cause damage to the data and files residing on the system as well as to the system devices. Firewalls can, in most cases, block such programmes, but not always.

- **Wireless-specific Breaches:** in this case, signals being transmitted between devices can be picked up by hackers using intelligent receiving devices and thus the messages arriving possibly at incorrect and unintended addresses.

Internet security refers to protecting websites and associated files (including data) from hackers and malicious programmes (viruses, worms and Trojans). It is the practice of protecting and preserving private resources and information on the Internet. The Internet is, by definition, a huge network so, in what follows, we will use the terms network security and Internet security interchangeably.

It should be noted that whereas an Intranet may be a controlled and secure network, the Internet is an uncontrolled network, although, Internet Service Providers do have some responsibility to control. Any computer linked to the Internet is open to attacks and any data while in transmission from one node to another, or a copy of it, is open to be redirected to an unauthorised destination. Encryption techniques and use of secure socket layers are commonly applied for the protection of data packets.

Security Approaches and Mechanisms

Hackers and unauthorised persons who try to breach network or internet security can be regarded as belonging to two groups: those who break the system with intent and those who monitor the traffic and take the opportunity when it offers itself. The first group will break the system and do everything possible to penetrate the security mechanism e.g. a firewall. The second group are opportunists, rather than vandals, who will try to find the required information (e.g. password or authentication key) and then enter or access the system posing as a valid user of the system.

It should also be noted that the attacks may be intentional or unintentional but the harm caused is the same – also that attacks may be from outside the organisation (e.g. from another node on the network) or from inside (e.g. from disgruntled employees). So the security measures have to take into consideration all these different varieties of threats.

Network administrators and security experts have come up with a number of approaches to protect networks, various systems on the networks and information and data existing on these systems. Software vendors have also developed tools and toolkits to address the concerns due to malicious attacks. Commonly used security approaches include:

- **Authentication:** for the integrity and protection of data
- **Firewalls:** to enforces network policies on the users
- **Intrusion Detection Systems:** to detect and prevent computer worms and malwares
- **Encryption techniques:** to maintain privacy.

As the methods to safeguard a network's security are getting better, the ways of breaking into the security mechanisms are also increasing. The ever growing need for faster data transmission, and availability of wireless technology, are bringing their own sets of security related concerns. Today's hacker is far more intelligent and smarter than before. A casual attitude towards a network/Internet security policy (i.e. by not following it strictly) and anti-virus and firewall software (i.e. not updating it on a regular basis) are making it rather easy for the attackers to succeed. So, for any network in a company to run successfully it needs to be protected against hackers and intruders. There is, thus, a dire need for network administrators and Internet security specialists to continuously evolve better and more effective security mechanism. For any network in a company to run successfully, it needs to be protected against hackers and intruders. This, in turn, suggests that each organisation on the Internet, or linked to an outside network, needs to do the following:

- First, assess their current situation with respect to security policies, mechanisms and tools used for this purpose
- Secondly, determine their security maturity level
- Then, suggest an improvement mechanism to make the existing mechanism much more robust
- And finally, implement the improvement strategy and continue to monitor and update the improvement mechanism for even better network/Internet security.

"Security Assessment and Improvement Process" and "Proposed Framework for Security Improvement," address the way forward in terms of the above four bullet points.

SECURITY ASSESSMENT AND IMPROVEMENT PROCESS

In the software industry, numerous process improvement models have been proposed and successfully employed e.g. Capability Maturity Model - CMM/CMMI (SEI, 2005), Software Process And Capability dEtermination - SPICE (SQI, 2010; Kuvaja, 2004) and BOOTSTRAP (Kuvaja, 1994). These are recognized as having the potential to improve competitiveness by: (1) increasing productivity; reducing costs, defects and reworking; and (2) improving time to market as well as customer satisfaction. In the current study, it is suggested that we apply similar concepts of a stage-wise approach to internet assessment and improvement which then acts as a device for measuring and improving the effectiveness of key security practices within the organisations.

Assessment requires looking into the following core aspects:

- Analysis of the current security policies, tools, technologies and techniques employed

- Determination of the effectiveness of such policies, tools, technologies and techniques
- Preparing lists of inherent weaknesses in the use of such policies, tools, technologies and techniques
- Determination of the maturity level of the organisation's security policies

Improvement process, then, suggests the following:

- Providing guidelines on the correct use of tools, technologies and techniques
- Suggesting better security policies based on good practices employed by other organisations that are already at a higher security maturity level
- Suggesting mechanisms to minimize the security risks and monitoring and measuring the effectiveness of improved mechanisms
- Implementing appropriate changes and ensuring that assessment and improvement continues.

It is important that best practices followed by other organisations also become part of the framework. There is no doubt that security breaches are rising in frequency and cost and targeted attacks are threatening businesses as never before. Insiders can also pose a threat to organisational data and processes. Often, there is ignorance as to the extent to which networked systems can be exposed to malicious attacks. Compliance processes are also generally inadequate. Even if the security policies are in place, complexity of the physical systems undermines the security efforts. Organisations have adopted their own ways of dealing with the security situations and a huge amount of advice is available. Scott Schnoll (2003), president of NOBUG, provides the following guidance:

- Establish a security policy and ensure its maintenance, dissemination and enforcement bearing in mind that technology is always changing

- Ensure the protection of all systems at all levels including data, information, applications, services and networked physical devices using techniques such as authentication as well as intrusion detection/prevention techniques and tools
- Implement firewall and anti-virus software and install latest service packs and system patches
- Understand the extent of system vulnerabilities with respect to existing devices including operation systems
- Understand the nature of possible security threats and attacks e.g. viruses, Trojans, malware, spoofing, phishing and their effects including denial of service, loss of data, loss of integrity, etc
- Understand that attack can happen from outside as well as from inside the organisations e.g. from disgruntled workers

- Block all incoming traffic during installation and maintenance
- Establish teams to handle security incidents whose role also includes ensuring that company personnel have the necessary awareness and understand and know how to deal with relevant incidents.

The entire process of assessment and improvement is shown in Figure 1. The first three steps refer to the assessment process and the last four refer to the improvement process. The *best practices* component is fed into both processes.

The approach being suggested for the assessment of the current situation is to conduct a questionnaire survey. It is suggested that the questionnaire be designed as a checklist referring to the network security policies, techniques, tools and approaches commonly applied by organisations – each question to have a number of possible options for choosing a response. The questions to be answered by people at different level

Figure 1. Internet security assessment and improvement processes

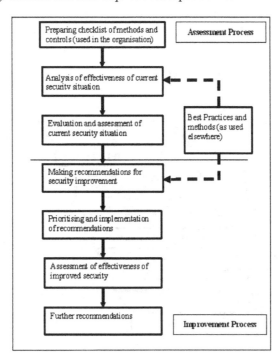

of responsibility working within the organisation: some of these persons will be security experts or network administrative; other will be the users of the network. Survey can also include interviews with the relevant members of staff to gather further information. Refer to the first three steps of Figure 1. It is also suggested that good practices employed by other successful organisations (in terms of effective security) also provide an input when designing the questionnaire or conducting the interviews. Here, the following aspects are also considered and taken into account:

•   Organisational security policies
•   Training and educational aspects
•   Implementation of security strategies
•   Security tools and technologies used.

Analysis of the information gathered determines the security maturity level and recommendations for improvement. The list of best practices, considered at this point, provides further guidance for appropriate suggestions. It is recognised that it may not be possible to implement all required improvement recommendations due to various reasons including the time, budget and resource constraints. Thus, prioritisation becomes neces-

sary in which case the improvement process becomes iterative. At this stage of the entire process, the organisational priorities enter in the process to provide a practical and achievable solution. Certain metrics may also be usefully employed e.g. security threat level (low, medium, high), security threat frequency, impact of security breaches, perceived or possible risks to the business and other organisational policies such as those with respect to the use of email system, use of Internet etc.

Analysis of the responses, as a result of the questionnaire survey and interviews form the basis for the evaluation, which, in turn, determines the scope for improvement after discussions with the relevant personnel in the organisation. The analysis helps to determine the security maturity level of the organisation, which then helps to suggest possible improvements for a much better network/Internet security. The prioritisation of improvements is also built into the process. Refer to the last four steps of Figure 1 which is expanded in Figure 2 and further explained in "Proposed Framework for Security Improvement".

Figure 2. Internet security process improvement maturity model

PROPOSED FRAMEWORK FOR SECURITY IMPROVEMENT

Every organisation needs to follow an appropriate set of procedures to ensure that their networks, and therefore, their processes and data are always secure. These procedures need to be designed in a way that they guide the organisations to tackle all the threats, external and internal, that a network faces with regards to security and further improve the security. The proposed improvement process model, as shown in Figure 2, is designed with this requirement in mind. It is a 5-stage model and similar to CMMI (SEI, 2005). The stages being: *Ad hoc*, *Acceptable*, *Satisfactory*, *Complete* and *Improving*. Each stage refers to a certain maturity level of an organisation, with reference to its Internet/network security. The assessment process, as outlined above, helps to determine an organisation's current maturity level. Guidance provided within each stage informs the organisation as to what it needs to do to achieve an improved higher maturity level.

It is suggested that the improvement process be formally defined as a 5 stage maturity model as shown in Figure 2. The stages are termed and defined as follows:

- **Ad-hoc:** where there are no real policies in place and the security is by means of commonly used standard devices such as firewalls, virus scanners etc which may or may not be fit for purpose.
- **Acceptable:** in which case, there are some established security policies including frequent updating of standard devices such as firewalls, virus scanners etc, however, the full awareness with respect to detection and prevention of security may be lacking.
- **Satisfactory:** where security is considered as important as any other function of the organisation, policies are implemented as required, the personnel are fully aware and

there is full commitment from the senior management.
- **Complete:** where the security aspects of the system are continuously monitored and performance measured, technologies and mechanisms for further investment in security are in place and a complete set of policies enacted as necessary.
- **Improving:** where proactive measures are taken to continuously improve the existing security including any further investment as required. This is the highest level of security which can serve as an exemplar for other organisations to follow.

The five stages also serve as maturity levels with respect to an organisation's Internet security. The assessment exercise will establish the maturity level for the organisation and the improvement model will help to determine how the organisation can move upwards to the next higher maturity level. Once the maturity level of the organisation's security is determined, our framework provides the following suggestions for moving upwards from one level to another.

Level 1 to Level 2 - This requires:

- Establishing a basic level of security by employing standard methods and techniques
- Identifying and establishing a need for a tighter security
- Conducting cost-benefit analysis of a much tighter security
- Developing security awareness
- Obtaining management commitment and support
- Understanding customers' concerns and fears.

Level 2 to Level 3 - This requires:

- Conducting security assessment processes on a regular basis

- Delivering awareness training programmes on a regular basis
- Implementing a much tighter security based on needs of the organisation
- Establishing security incident-response-action systems
- Establishing plans for security contingency and data recovery
- Creating an environment of trust and mechanisms for threat management
- Identifying key security improvement metrics for monitoring performance
- Prioritising areas for further improvement.

Level 3 to Level 4 - This requires:

- Implementing awareness and training schemes for relevant personnel
- Implementing incident-response-action systems and mechanisms for disaster recovery
- Implementing contingency plans
- Developing and implementing metrics for measurement of security systems and performance
- Monitoring security performances and quantifying effects of improvements
- Establishing and implementing network/Internet security maintenance management.

Level 4 to Level 5 - This requires:

- Measuring security performances and quantifying effects of improvements
- Ensuring management commitment to further investment, as need arises
- Developing and implementing improvement process, including investment in new technologies and resources
- Disseminating good practices within and outside the organisation's boundaries

PRELIMINARY RESULTS

Based on the security assessment approach, as mentioned in previous sections, the authors have carried out a preliminary investigation to determine the existing security situation in the case of one particular organisation. A questionnaire survey was conducted with the following aims: (1) to identify the most commonly and often used security techniques and (2) to identify the security guidelines and mechanisms in place to monitor the performance for the purpose of eventual recommendations for improvements.

It was a very basic survey: the questionnaire asked questions with respect to the following:

- Top security threats to network's security
- Types of security tools and technologies used
- Types of firewalls used in the organisation.

There were also questions such as:

- How frequently were the users/employees required to change their passwords?
- How strong were the password encryption keys?
- What were the data authentication techniques?
- Was there an event log and was it properly maintained?

It should be noted that no further investigation was carried out as this required detailed investigation of the security procedures which was not easily possible and no suggestions were provided regarding the improvement of the security of the organisation. Also, no performance monitoring was carried out and there was no attempt to determine the organisation's Internet security maturity level. The exercise required just the collection of some preliminary data for basic analysis. The outcome of the survey is shown in Table 1 and summarised in Figure 3.

Table 1. Assessment results

Questions	Answers	Collected Responders
Most dreaded security threat?	Intrusion	10 out of 10
Cause of main network breaches in the past 12 months?	Hacker attack	4 out of 10
Most popular/effective system security technology?	Firewall	8 out of 10
Best way of avoiding insider attack?	Implement strict password and account management policies	8 out of 10
Formal training for employees regarding security techniques?	Very important with routine assessments	5 out of 10

The analysis suggests that eradication of intrusion detection and elimination of system breaches appears to be a key priority for the organisation in question. Whereas, this seems crucial to the business, there appears to be a lack of policies on virus protection and identity theft. This is often one of the main reasons why phishing is still being a successful practice for security attackers. It is also clear that all 100% of the IT staff believe that their network is constantly under the threat of intrusion or breach of computer system. The two most dreaded security threats are:

- Denial of service attacks in which a network can become paralysed by repeated authentication and association requests. This is because of the overwhelming RF signals from the attacker that jams or saturates the network resulting in eventual shut down
- Misuse of computing systems by the employees. Nearly half the respondents were of this opinion. The least significant threat is considered to be a computer virus attack or information theft. Approximately 37.5% of staff surveyed was of this opinion.

Figure 3. Major security threats in the organization

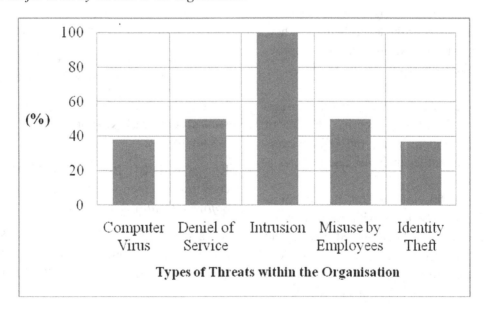

CONCLUSION

Today's information society is becoming increasingly reliant on the information and communications technologies and the Internet. Wireless telephony, electronic banking, electronic commerce, internet transactions and social networking are becoming a vital part of our lives. With this, the general public are revealing confidential and personal information to others via the Internet. Organisations are also exchanging huge amounts of similar information to partner and other organisations. Although, network specialists and security experts are implementing necessary applications and software to ensure security of data and equipment, Internet security is becoming a concern of paramount importance.

With the passing of time, cyber crimes in the form of threats to networks via Internet, and breaches of confidentiality, are on the increase. This suggests a need not only for better security products and policies, but also for appropriate assessment and improvement frameworks to improve the products and policies. In this chapter, we have proposed such a framework.

The framework has two components: (1) an assessment model for determination of existing security situation and (2) a process improvement maturity model which is a staged model consisting of five maturity levels; the levels being: Ad hoc, Acceptable, Satisfactory, Complete and Improving. The entire framework works as follows:

- The first component refers to the assessment of the existing security situation of an organisation. Here, the effectiveness of the current technologies and policies is determined.
- Based on this information, the organisation's maturity level with respect to its Internet security is determined. The second component then suggests ways of improving the existing security with a view to increasing the organisation's maturity level.

We believe that the suggested framework has the potential to become a standard process improvement model along the same lines as other process improvement models such as CMMI (SEI, 2005).

REFERENCES

AirTight Networks. (2005). *Best practices for securing your enterprise wireless perimeter* (pp. 1–6). AirTight Networks.

Christopher, L. (2005). *APC legendary reliability physical security of data centres and network rooms* (pp. 4–10). Fundamental Principles of Network Security.

Curtin, M. (1997). *Introduction to network security*. Kent Information Services, UK, March 1997. Retrieved April 2010, from http://www.interhack. net/pubs/network-security/

House of Lords. (2007). *Personal Internet security, vol 1*. House of Lords Science and Technology Committee, (pp. 13-27). Retrieved April 2010, from www.publications.parliament. uk/pa/ ld200607/ldselect/ldsctech/165/165i.pdf

Joshua, C. (2003). *Defining the rules for pre-emptive host protection: Multi-layered strategy* (pp. 5–7). Internet Security Systems.

Karanjit, S., & Chris, H. (1994). *Internet firewall and network security*. New Riders Publishing.

Kizza, J. M. (2009). *A guide to computer network security*. London, UK: Springer. doi:10.1007/978-1-84800-917-2

Kuvaja, P. (2004). BOOTSTRAP 3.0–a SPICE1 conformant process assessment methodology. *Software Quality Journal, 8*(1).

Kuvaja, P., & Bicego, A. (1994). BOOTSTRAP– a European assessment methodology. *Software Quality Journal, 3*(3). doi:10.1007/BF00402292

Merritt, M., & David, P. (2002). *Wireless security.*

Papadimitriou, D., et al. (2009). *The future of Internet.* Retrieved April 2010, from http://www.future-internet.eu/fileadmin/documents/reports/Cross-ETPs_FI_Vision_Document_v1_0.pdf

Randall, N. K., & Panos, L. C. (2002). *Wireless security model threads solutions.* McGraw-Hill Telecom.

Schnoll, S. (2003). *Internet security best practices, presentation.* NOBUG, June 2003.

Schweitzer, D. (2003). *Incident response: Computer forensics toolkit.* USA: Wiley.

SEI. (2005). *CMMI.* Retrieved April 2010, from http://www.sei.cmu.edu/cmmi/

SQI. (2010). *What is SPICE?* Retrieved April 2010, from http://www.sqi.gu.edu.au/spice/

Stallings, W. (1999). *SNMP, SNMPv2, SNMPv3 and RMON 1 and 2.* Harlow, UK: Addison Wesley.

Stallings, W. (2003). *Network security essentials* (2nd ed.). Pearson Education Inc.

Chapter 14
Software Metrics and Design Quality in Object Oriented Paradigm

Gopalakrishnan T.R. Nair
Research and Industry Incubation Centre, Dayananda Sagar Institutions, India

Selvarani R
Research and Industry Incubation Centre, Dayananda Sagar Institutions, India

ABSTRACT

As the object oriented programming languages and development methodologies moved forward, a significant research effort was spent in defining specific approaches and building models for quality based on object oriented measurements. Software metrics research and practice have helped in building an empirical basis for software engineering. Software developers require objectives and valid measurement schemes for the evaluation and improvisation of product quality from the initial stages of development. Measuring the structural design properties of a software system such as coupling, inheritance, cohesion, and complexity is a promising approach which can lead to an early quality assessment. The class codes and class diagrams are the key artifacts in the development of object oriented (OO) software and it constitutes the backbone of OO development. It also provides a solid foundation for the design and development of software with a greater influence over the system that is implemented. This chapter presents a survey of existing relevant works on class code / class diagram metrics in an elaborate way. Here, a critical review of the existing work is carried out in order to identify the lessons learnt regarding the way these studies are performed and reported. This work facilitates the development of an empirical body of knowledge. The classical approaches based on statistics alone do not provide managers and developers with a decision support scheme for risk assessment and cost reduction. One of the future challenges is to use software metrics in a way that they creatively address and handle the key objectives of risk assessment and the estimation of external quality factors of the software.

DOI: 10.4018/978-1-60960-509-4.ch014

INTRODUCTION

Though the management of software development is an integral part of the industry today, most software houses face significant barriers in this activity. One of the important determinants of success in software process improvement is the measurement of properties of software to determine the quality of the software by methods that can capture, control and improve the process and products. It is widely accepted in software engineering that the quality of a software system should be assured from the initial phases of its life cycle and it will help the managers for arriving at an early assessment on the level of quality that they are heading to. Quality assurance methods are most effective when they are applied at initial phases and least effective when the system is already implemented. As Boehm [Shull F, 2002] remarks, problems in the artifacts produced in the initial stages of software system development generally propagate to the artifacts produced in later stages, which increases the maintenance cost of the product. Quality measures of the artifacts of object-oriented code or design usually involve analyzing the structure of these artifacts with respect to the internal quality aspects such as coupling, cohesion, association and interdependencies of classes and components. These measures can be used as objective measures to predict various external quality aspects of the design artifacts such as functionality, maintainability, reliability, reusability, risk assessment and portability. Such predictions can then be used to help decision-making during development. A large number of quality measures have been defined in the literature. A critical review of existing work was performed in order to identify the lessons learned regarding the way those studies were carried out and reported. This has facilitated the development of an empirical body of knowledge. Measuring quality of the design allows OO software designers to identify weak design spots in the early stage (design stage) which cost less to repair rather than detecting it as defects at implementation phases. The measurement at an early stage provides appropriate guidelines to choose between design alternatives in an objective way, to predict external quality characteristics and to improve resource allocation based on these predictions.

SOFTWARE METRICS

"You can neither predict nor control what you cannot measure" – Norman E. Fenton

Software metrics are defined to be a measure to quantify attributes in software processes, products and projects. Quality is a phenomenon, which involves a number of variables that depend on human behavior which cannot be controlled easily. The metrics approach can measure and quantify these kinds of variables. The most common definition according to R.S Pressman and L. Rosencrance (Fenton N, 1997; Dandashi F, 1998) "Software metrics is a method to quantify attributes in software processes, products and projects. Measurement finds a numerical value for software product attributes or software process attributes. These values can be compared against the standards applicable in an organization to quantify the quality of the product or quality of the software process".

Measurable characteristics of the analysis and design model of an OO system assists the project manager in planning and tracking activities and also provide information about the level of effort required to implement the system (Dandashi F, 1998). Somerville (Li, 1998) classifies metrics in two categories:

i. Control metrics, generally associated with software process.
ii. Predict metrics, normally associated with software product.

Predict metrics are useful in predicting the static and dynamic characteristics of the software [Li Li., 1998]. These predicted variables are the indicators of complexity of the code, instability, coupling, cohesion, inheritance etc. An attribute analysis can be conducted to assess the quality of the products in early stage of software development (Dandashi F., 1998). Here, software metrics play an important role in better planning, assessment of improvements, reduction of unpredictability, early identification of potential problems and productivity evaluation. These managerial aspects of the software development process using object oriented technology have to be carefully addressed. Metrics are independent of the adopted paradigm, although the latter deeply influences the set of metrics to choose, as its concepts and corresponding abstractions are either disjointed or implemented differently (Dandashi F., 1998).

At high maturity organizations, metrics are expected to play a key role in overall process management as well as in managing the process of a project. In a software organization, metrics data finds application in project planning, monitoring and controlling a project. It also helps in, overall process management and improvement (quality of the product). Figure 1 depicts the uses of metrics in software industry at process level.

GENERAL OO METRICS

There have been numerous studies on software metrics. This section looks at some of the metrics that are relevant to object oriented software measurement.

Li and Henry's Metrics

Li and Henry's metrics (Li W., 1993) has proposed the following metrics which measure different internal attributes such as coupling, cohesion and design complexity.

DAC: The number of attributes in a class that have another class as their type

DAC': The number of different classes that are used as types of attributes in a class.

NOM: The number of local methods

SIZE2: Number of Attributes + Number of local methods

Theoretical Validation

Briand *et al.* (Briand, L., 1999) have found that DAC and DAC' do not fulfill all the properties for coupling measures proposed by Briand et al. (Briand L., 1997). This means that neither DAC nor DAC' metrics can be classified according to Briand *et al.*'s framework, which defines the set of properties like length, size, coupling, complexity and cohesion.

Figure 1. Uses of metrics in software organizations

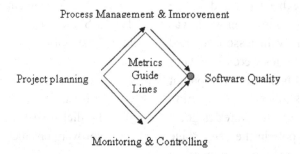

Empirical Validation

Li and Henry (Li W., 1993) have applied these metrics to two real systems developed using Classic-ADA. They found that the maintenance effort (measured by the number of lines changed per class in its maintenance history) could be predicted from the values of DAC and NOM metrics.

MOOD Metrics

The original proposal of MOOD metrics (Brito, E., 1994) was improved in (Brito, E., 1996) and extended to MOOD2 metrics (Thibodaux P, 2002) which consider metrics defined at different levels of granularity, not only at class diagram level. Brito e Abreu (Brito, E., 1996) also presented a formal definition of MOOD2 metrics using the Object Constraint Language (OCL) (Warmer J, 1999).

MHF: The Method Hiding Factor is defined as a quotient between the sum of the invisibilities of all methods defined in all of the classes and the total number of methods defined in the system under consideration. The invisibility of a method is the percentage of the total classes from which the method is not visible. Where, TC = total number of classes in the system under consideration, $M_d(C_i) = M_v(C_i) + M_h(C_i)$ is the methods defined in class C_i. $M_v(C_i)$ is the visible methods in class C_i (public methods), $M_h(C_i)$ is the hidden methods in class C_i (private and protected methods).

AHF: The Attribute Hiding Factor is defined as a quotient between the sum of the invisibilities of all attributes defined in all of the classes and the total number of attributes defined in the system under consideration. The invisibility of an attribute is the percentage of total classes from which the attribute is not visible. Where, $A_d(C_i) = A_v(C_i) + A_h(C_i)$ is the attributes defined in class C_i, $A_v(C_i)$ is the visible attributes in class C_i, $A_h(C_i)$ is the hidden attributes in class C_i (public attributes), $M_h(C_i)$ is the hidden attributes in class Ci (private and protected attributes).

MIF: The Method Inheritance Factor is defined as a quotient between the sum of inherited methods in all classes of the system under consideration and the total number of available methods (locally defined and include those inherited) for all classes. Where, $M_a(Ci) = M_d(Ci) + M_i(C_i)$ is the available methods in class C_i (those that can be invoked in association with class C_i), $M_d(C_i) = M_n(Ci) + M_o(C_i)$ is the methods defined in class C_i (those declared in C_i), $M_n(C_i)$ is the new methods in class Ci (those declared within Ci that do not override inherited ones), $M_o(C_i)$ is the overriding methods in class Ci (those declared within class Ci that override (redefine) inherited ones, $M_i(Ci)$ is the inherited methods in class C_i (those inherited but not overridden in class C_i).

AIF: The Attribute Inheritance Factor is defined as a quotient between the sum of inherited attributes in all classes of the system under consideration and the total number of available attributes (locally defined plus inherited) for all classes.

Where, $A_a(Ci) = A_d(C_i) + A_i(C_i)$ is the attributes available in class C_i (those that can be manipulated in association with class C_i), $A_d(C_i) = A_n(C_i) + A_o(C_i)$ is the attributes defined in class C_i (those declared in class C_i), $A_n(C_i)$ is the new attributes in class Ci (those declared within class C_i that do not override inherited ones), $A_o(C_i)$ is the overriding attributes in class C_i (those declared within class C_i that override (redefine) inherited ones), $A_i(C_i)$ is the attributes inherited in class Ci (those inherited but not overridden in class C_i).

PF: The Polymorphism Factor is defined as the quotient between the actual number of different possible polymorphic situations, and the maximum number of possible distinct polymorphic situations for class Ci. Where,$M_o(C_i)$ is the overriding methods in class C_i, $M_n(C_i)$ is the new methods in class C_i, $DC(C_i)$ is the number of descendants of class C_i. They were defined to measure the use of OO design mechanisms such as inheritance (MIF and AIF) metrics, information hiding (MHF and AHF metrics), and polymorphism (PF metric) and the consequent relation with software quality and development productivity.

Theoretical Validation

Harrison et al. (Harrison R., 2000) demonstrated that all but the PF metric hold all the properties for valid metrics proposed in Kitchenham's framework (Kitchenham B., 2002). The PF metric is not valid, as in a system without inheritance the value of PF is not defined, being discontinuous.

Empirical Validation

Brito e Abreu *et al.* (Brito E., 1996) applied MOOD metrics to 5 class libraries written in the C++ language. They gave design heuristics based on the metric values to help novice designers. They suggested that AHF is lower bounded; this means that there is a lower limit for this metric. If it goes below that limit, it is a hindrance to the resulting quality of the software. On the other hand, MHF, MIF, AIF, PF are upper bounded. It means that if the metric value exceeds the upper limit, it indicates poor design of the software.

Brito e Abreu and Melo (Brito, E., 1996) applied the MOOD metrics to three class libraries written in C++. They provided the following comments:

- When the value of MHF or MIF increases, the density of defects and the effort required to correct them should decrease. Ideally, the value of the AHF metric should be 100%, i.e., all attributes would be hid-

den and only accessed by the corresponding class methods.

- Excessive reuse through inheritance makes the system more difficult to understand and maintain.

In relation to the PF metric in some cases, overriding methods could contribute to reducing complexity, thus making the system more understandable and easier to maintain. A work similar to that described above was carried out in Brito e Abreu *et al.* (Linda H. Rosenberg) where the metrics were applied to seven classes written in the Eiffel language. Harrison *et al.* (Harrison R., 2000) applied MOOD metrics to nine commercial systems. They concluded that MOOD metrics provide an overall quality assessment of systems.

Lorenz and Kidd's Metrics

Lorenz and Kidd's (Lorenz M., 1994) metrics are classified into Class size metrics, Class inheritance metrics and Class internals metrics. These metrics were defined to measure the static characteristics of software design, such as the usage of inheritance and the amount of responsibilities in a class.

Class Size Metrics

PIM: This metric counts the total number of public instance methods in a class. Public methods are those that are available as services to other classes.

NIM: These metric counts all the public, protected and private methods defined for class instances.

NIV: This metric counts the total number of instance variables in a class. Instance variables include private and protected variables available to the instances.

NCM: This metric counts the total number of class methods in a class. A class method is a method that is global to its instances.

NCV: This metric counts the total number of class variables in a class.

Class Inheritance Metrics

NMO: This metric counts the total number of methods overridden by a subclass. A subclass is allowed to define a method of the same name as a method in one of its super-classes. This is called overriding the method.

NMI: 'The Number of Methods Inherited' metric is the total number of methods inherited by a subclass.

NMA: This metric count the total number of methods defined in a subclass.

Class Internals

APPM: The Average Parameters per Method Metric.

Theoretical Validation

No significant work related to the theoretical validation of these metrics has been published and those published have not had any significant impact.

Empirical Validation

After applying these metrics to 5 real projects (written in Smalltalk and C++), Lorenz and Kidd (Lorenz M., 1994) have provided the following recommendations,

1. No instance methods or too many instance methods can indicate non-optimal allocation of responsibility (related to the NIM metric).
2. Large numbers of instance variables can indicate too much coupling with other classes and reduce reuse (related to the NIV metric).
3. The average number of class variables should be low. In general, there should be fewer class variables than instance variables.
4. Too many class methods indicate inappropriate use of classes to do work instead of instances (related to the NCM metric).
5. Overriding methods, especially deeper in the hierarchy, can indicate poor sub classing (related to the NMO metric).
6. Specialization index has done a good job on identifying classes worth looking at, for their placement in the inheritance hierarchy and for design problems.
7. They also suggest an upper threshold of 0.7 parameters per method (related to the APPM metric).
8. An inheritance hierarchy that is too shallow or too deep has quality repercussions.

Briand et al.'s Metrics

ACAIC, OCAIC, DCAEC, OCAEC, ACMIC are the metrics of Briand *et al* (Briand L., 1997). The first letter indicates the relationship (A: coupling to ancestor classes, D: Descendants, O: Others, i.e. none of the other relationships). The next two letters indicate the type of interaction.

CA: There is a Class-attribute interaction between class c and d, if c has an attribute of type 'd'.

CM: There is a Class-Method interaction between class's c and d, if class c has a method with a parameter of type class d. The last two letters indicate the locus of impact.

IC: The Import Coupling (IC) measure counts for a class c all interactions where c is using another class.

EC: The Export Coupling (EC) is defined at the class level by Briand *et al.*'s metric [Briand L., 1997]. It is the counts of interactions between classes. These measures distinguish the relationship between classes, different type of interactions and the locus of impact of the interaction. These metrics are used for the measurement of the coupling between classes.

Theoretical Validation

Briand *et al.* (Briand, L., 1999) have demonstrated that all of these measures fulfill the properties for coupling measures (Briand L., 1997).

Empirical Validation

Briand *et al.* have carried out two case studies (Briand L., 1997) applying the metrics to real systems. After both studies they conclude that if one intends to build quality models of OO designs coupling will be an important structural dimension to consider. More specifically the impact of export coupling on fault-proneness is weaker than that for import coupling. El-Emam *et al.* (Briand, L., 1999) have applied these metrics to a system implemented in C++ in which they found that the metrics OCAEC, ACMIC and OCMEC tend to be associated with fault-proneness. A similar study applying the metrics to a Java system concluded that the metrics OCAEC, OCMEC and OCMIC seem to be associated with fault-proneness.

Marchesi's Metrics

Marchesi's metrics for single classes (Marchesi, 1998) and measure the system complexity.

$$CL1 = NC_i + K_a NA_i + K_r \sum_{hb^i} NC_h$$

$$CL2 = \sum_{k=1}^{N_c} [d_{ik}]^{kd} + K_e \sum_{jb^{[i]}} [d_{jk}]^{kd}$$

CL1: It is the weighted number of responsibilities of a class, inherited or not. It is defined as "Where NC_i is the number of concrete responsibilities of class C_i, NA_i is the number of abstract responsibilities of class C_i, $b^{(i)}$ is an array whose elements are the indexes of all super classes of class C_i". Responsibili-

ties can be abstract, if they are specified in subclasses. It is concrete, if they are detailed in the class where they are defined.

CL2: Is the weighted number of dependencies of a class. Specific and inherited dependencies are weighted differently. It is defined as "Where the exponent $K_d < 1$, N_c is the total number of classes, NCxNC is the dependency matrix and an element d_{ik} is the number of dependencies between class C_i (client) and class C_k (server), $b_{(i)}$ is an array whose elements are the indexes of all superclasses of class C_i. A dependency between a class C_i (client class) and a class Ck (server class), indicates that the class C_i will use one or more of the services offered by the C_k."

Empirical Validation

Marchesi (Marchesi, 1998) applied the metrics for three real projects developed in Smalltalk. It is observed that the value of the metrics obtained is related to the required man-months to develop the systems. They concluded that, it is possible to develop 14 to 20.5 responsibilities in a man-month. Marchesi also remarks that for small to medium-sized projects Smalltalk productivity are very high compared to that of other programming languages.

Harrison et al.'s Metrics

The authors have proposed the metric Number of Associations (NAS), which is defined as the number of associations of each class, counted by the number of association lines emanating from a class in a class diagram. The NAS metric measures the inter-class coupling.

Empirical Validation

Harrison *et al.* (Harrison R., 1998) have applied this metric to five systems developed in C++. No relationships were found for any of the systems between class understandability and the metric NAS. The authors partly attributed this fact to the way in which the subjective understandability metric was evaluated by the developer. Only limited evidence was found to support the hypothesis linking increase coupling (measured by the metric NAS) to increase error density. In this study Harrison *et al.* (Harrison R., 1998) also found a strong relationship between CBO (Linda H. Rosenberg) and NAS metrics, implying that one of these is needed to assess the level of coupling at design time. Moreover, NAS is available at a high-level design in contrast to CBO metric and it could be used by managers to obtain early coupling estimates.

Bansiya et al.'s Metrics

These metrics were defined by Bansiya and Davis (Bansiya J., 2002) for assessing design properties such as encapsulation (DAM), coupling (DCC), cohesion (CACM), composition (MOA) and inheritance (MFA) at class level.

DAM: The Data Access metric is the ratio of the number of private (protected) attributes to the total number of attributes declared in the class.

DCC: The Direct Class Coupling metric is a count of the different number of classes that a class is directly related to. The metric includes classes that are directly related by attribute declarations and message passing (parameters) in methods.

CAMC: The Cohesion Among Methods of Class metric computes the relatedness among methods of a class based upon the parameter list of methods. The metric is computed using the summation of the intersection of parameters of a method with the maximum independent set of all parameter types in the class.

MOA: The Measure of Aggregation metric is a count of the number of data declarations whose types are user defined classes.

MFA: The Measure of Functional Abstraction metric is the ratio of the number of methods inherited by a class to the total number of methods accessible by member.

Empirical Validation

As part of the empirical validation study, CAMC was statistically correlated with the metric Lack of Cohesion in Method (LCOM) (Hayes, M., 2003), which has been shown to effectively predict cohesiveness of classes in several studies (Li W., 1993; Chidamber, S., 1994; Basili, V., 1996; Etzkorn L., 1998; Bansiya J., 2002). In this study a high correlation between CAMC and LCOM was found, which has the advantage that CAMC can be used earlier in the development process to evaluate the cohesion characteristic of classes. The authors have observed that CAMC values greater than 0.35 indicate classes that are reasonably cohesive. Classes with a CAMC measure of 0.35 and below are the most likely to be separate.

Bansiya and Davis

Bansiya and Davis (Bansiya J., 2002) have used the following metrics from the literature for evaluating the overall quality of an OO design based on its internal design properties.

DSC: This metric counts the total number of classes in the design.

NOH: The metric counts the total number of class hierarchies in the design.

ANA: The Average Number of Ancestors metric is computed by determining the number of classes along all paths from the 'root' class or classes to all classes in an inheritance structure.

NOP: This metric counts the total number of polymorphic methods.

This hierarchical model called QMOOD has the lower-level design metrics well defined in terms of design characteristics, and quality is assessed as an aggregation of the model's individual high-level quality attributes. The high-level attributes are assessed using a set of empirically identified and weighted OO design properties, which measure the lowest-level structural, functional and relational details of a design such as design size (DSC), Hierarchies(NOH), Abstraction (ANA), Encapsulation (DAM), Coupling(DCC), Cohesion(CAMC), Composition (MOA), Inheritance (MFA), Polymorphism (NOP), Messaging(CIS), Complexity(NOM). The effectiveness of the initial model in predicting design quality attributes has been validated against numerous real-world projects. The quality predicted by the model shows good correlation with the assessment of project designs and predicts implementation qualities.

Genero et al.'s Metrics

These metrics were grouped as Class-scope metrics and Class-diagram scope metrics [Genero M., 2001]. Class diagram-scope metrics for UML class diagram structural complexity [Chidamber, S.R., 1991] are defined to measure class diagram complexity, due to the use of different kinds of relationships, such as associations, generalizations, aggregations and dependencies, in relation with their impact on external quality attributes such as class diagram maintainability.

Class-Diagram Scope Metrics

NAssoc: 'The Number of Association' metric is defined as the total number of associations within a class diagram. This is a generalization of the NAS (Number of Associations) to the class diagram level.

NAgg: The Number of Aggregation' metric is defined as the total number of aggregation relationships within a class diagram (each whole-part pair in an aggregation relationship).

NDep: The Number of Dependencies metric is defined as the total number of dependency relationships within a class diagram.

NGen: The Number of Generalization metric is defined as the total number of generalization relationships within a class diagram (each parent-child pair in a generalization relationship).

NGenH: The Number of Generalization Hierarchies metric is defined as the total number of generalization hierarchies within a class diagram.

NAggH: The Number of Aggregation Hierarchies metric is defined as the total number of aggregation hierarchies within a class diagram.

MaxDIT: The Maximum DIT metric is defined as the maximum between the DIT values obtained for each class of the class diagram. The DIT value for a class within a generalization hierarchy is the length of the longest path from the class to the root of the hierarchy [Linda H. Rosenberg].

Class-Scope Metrics for UML Class Diagram Structural Complexity (Genero M., 2001)

NOA: The Number of Association per Class metric is defined as the total number of associations a class has with other classes or with itself.

HAgg: The height of a class within an aggregation hierarchy is defined as the length of the longest path from the class to the leaves.

NODP: The Number of Direct Parts metric is defined as the total number of 'direct part' classes which compose a composite class.

NP: The Number of Parts metric is defined as the number of 'part' classes (direct and indirect) of a 'whole' class.

NW: The Number of Wholes metric is defined as the number of 'whole' classes (direct or indirect) of a 'part' class.

MAgg: The Multiple Aggregation metric is defined as the number of direct 'whole' classes that a class is part-of, within in an aggregation hierarchy.

NDepIn: The Number of Dependencies In metric is defined as the number of classes that depend on a given class.

NDepOut: The Number of Dependencies Out metric is defined as the number of classes on which a given class depends.

Theoretical Validation

These metrics were validated using a property-based approach (Briand L., 1996), aiming to classify them as complexity, size, length, coupling or cohesion metrics (Genero M., 2002). A Measurement theory-based approach (Basili, V., 1996; Cartwright M., 1998) was also used, thereby justifying that the metrics are constructively valid and characterized by the ratio scale (Genero M., 2002).

Empirical Validation

Two controlled experiments to empirically validate class diagram-scope metrics were carried out. A controlled experiment (Genero M., 2001) was carried out with the aim of building a prediction model for the UML class diagram maintainability based on the values of the class diagram-scope measures (traditional metrics were also considered such as the number of classes, attributes and methods within a class diagram). To build the prediction model, an extension of the original Knowledge Discovery in Databases (KDD) the Fuzzy Prototypical Knowledge Discovery (Delgado M., 2001) was used. The authors of these metrics also demonstrated by statistical analysis that these metrics are strongly correlated with the subject's rating of class diagram maintainability characteristics (understandability, modifiability and analyzability) (Genero M., 2002).

In Genero *et al.* (Genero M., 2001) a controlled experiment was carried out with the following two goals:

1. To ascertain if any relationship exists between the class diagram-scope metrics (also considering traditional metrics, such as the number of classes, attributes and operations within a class diagram) and the UML class diagram maintainability.
2. To build a prediction model for the UML class diagram maintainability. An approach based on fuzzy regression and classification trees was used (Delgado M., 2001) for these purposes. They concluded that the NAssoc, NDep and MaxDIT metrics do not seem to be related with maintenance time. However, they argued, this may be due to the design of the experiments, in which the value of those metrics did not take a great range of values.

It is found that all class diagram-scope measures (except NDep) seem to be highly correlated to the maintenance time of class diagrams (Genero M., 2003). Through a controlled experiment and prediction models were built to predict the time a subject spent on understanding and modifying UML class diagrams (Genero M., 2003). This study reveals that in some sense most of the proposed metrics have influence in maintenance activities.

OO Design-Specific CK Metrics

Chidamber and Kemerer (Chidamber S., 1994) proposed a first version of Design metrics and later the definition of some of them were improved and presented in (Chidamber, S.R., 1991). CK metric suit can target all the essential attributes of OO software .These metrics are used to explore different structural dimensions of a class. The OO design metrics are primarily used to measure the internal quality attributes such as complexity

(Gui, 2007; Selby, R.W., 1988), coupling, cohesion, inheritance, association, etc. These attributes can be measured by examining the product on its own, separate from its behaviour (Fenton N., 1997). These measurements are used to define the design complexity in relation to their impact on external quality attributes such as maintainability, reusability, etc. External quality attributes are those that can be measured only with respect to how the product relates to its environment. Here the behaviour of the product is more important than the product itself.

WMC: Weighted Methods per Class is a class level metric. A class is a template from which objects can be created. This set of objects share a common structure and a common behaviour manifested by a set of methods. The WMC is a count of the methods implemented within a class or the sum of complexities of the methods (method complexity is measured by cyclomatic complexity). Consider a class K_1 with methods $M_1, M_2, M_3, M_4, M_5, M_6, ... M_n$. Let $C_1 ... C_n$ be the static complexity of methods. Where 'n' is the number of methods in that class.

$$WMC = \sum_{i=1}^{n} C_i$$

RFC: Response for a Class metric is meant for class level which looks at methods and messages within a class. A message is a request that an object makes of another object to perform an operation. The operation executed as a result of receiving a message is called a method. The RFC is a set of all methods (internal, external) that can be invoked in response to a message sent to an object of the class or by some method in the class.

LCOM: Lack of Cohesion of Methods is a metric that deals with extension of information hiding in terms of cohesion [Linda H. Rosenberg]. It is defined as the degree to which methods within a class are related to

one another and work together to provide a well-bounded behaviour.

CBO: Coupling between Object is a measure of the strength of association established by a connection from one entity to another (Linda H. Rosenberg). Classes (objects) are said to be coupled when a message is passed between objects when methods declared in one class use methods or attributes from the other classes. CBO is a count of the number of other classes to which a class is coupled (Linda H. Rosenberg).

DIT: Depth of Inheritance Tree is a type of metric that deals with the relationship among classes that enables programmers to reuse previously defined objects, including variables and operators. The depth of inheritance hierarchy is the number of classes (nodes) connected to the main class (root of the tree).

NOC: Number of Children (NOC) of a class is the number of immediate sub-classes subordinated to a class in the class hierarchy.

Theoretical Validation

Chidamber and Kemerer (Chidamber S., 1994; Chidamber, S.R., 1991) substantiate that DIT and NOC both accomplish Weyuker's axioms for complexity measures (Weyuker, E., 1988). Briand et al. (Briand L., 1996) classified the DIT metric as a length measure, and the NOC metric as a size measure. Poels and Dedene (Poels G., 1999) have demonstrated by means of the DISTANCE framework that they can be characterized at ratio the scale level.

Empirical Validation

Several empirical studies have been carried out to validate these metrics, Li and Henry (Li W., 1993) showed that CK metrics appeared to be adequate in predicting the frequency of changes across classes during the maintenance phase. Chidamber and Kemerer (Chidamber S.,1994) have applied these metrics to two real projects and observed that designers may tend to keep the inheritance hierarchies shallow, forsaking reusability through inheritance for simplicity of understanding. These metrics were useful for detecting possible design flaws or violations of design philosophy and for allocating testing resources. Basili et al. (Briand L., 1996) have put the DIT metric under empirical validation, concluding that the larger the DIT value, the greater the probability of fault detection. Also they observed that larger the NOC, the lower the probability of fault detection. Daly et al. (Daly J., 1996) found that the time taken to perform maintenance tasks was significantly lower in systems with three levels of inheritance depth as compared to systems with no use of inheritance.

Cartwright (Cartwright M., 1998) performed a small replication of Daly et al. (Daly J., 1996). The results of that replication indicate that the three levels of inheritance depth have a significant positive effect on the time taken to make a change and a significant negative effect upon the size of a change in lines of code. The experiment carried out by Unger and Prechelt (Prechelt L., 2003) worked based on that of Daly et al.'s experiment (Daly J., 1996). But they changed certain parameters in order to increase external validity. The results obtained indicate that the deeper inheritance hierarchies did not generally speed up maintenance nor did they result in superior quality. Thus concluding that inheritance depth in itself was not an important factor for maintenance effort.

Chidamber et al. (Chidamber S., 1998) have carried out studies on three medium commercial systems to examine the relationships between CK metrics and productivity, rework effort, design effort etc. None of the three systems showed significant use of inheritance, so DIT and NOC tended to have minimal values. He suggested that low values of DIT and NOC indicate that the reuse opportunities (via inheritance) were perhaps compromised in favour of comprehensibility of the overall architecture of the applications. Tang et al. [Tang M., 1998] have investigated the cor-

relation between CK metrics and the likelihood of the occurrence of OO faults, using three industrial real-time systems (implemented in VISUAL C++). The results suggest that WMC can be a good indicator for faulty classes. After carrying about two case studies Briand et al. (Briand L., 1998; 2000) have concluded that inheritance measures (DIT, NOC, etc.) appear to be inconsistent indicators of class-fault proneness but they suggested that the use of inheritance is an important topic for further research.

Harrison et al. (Harrison R., 2000) which was a replication of Daly et al.'s experiment (Daly J., 1996) used the DIT metric in an empirical study, demonstrating that systems without inheritance are easier to understand and modify than systems with three or five levels of inheritance. Poels and Dedene (Genero M., 2003) used the DIT metric in an empirical study, demonstrating that the extensive use of inheritance leads to models that are more difficult to modify. Briand et al. (Briand L., 1998; 2000), used the metrics NOC, DIT and CBO metric in an empirical study demonstrating that the use of design principles leads to OO designs that are easier to maintain. Prechelt et al. (Prechelt L., 2003) in two controlled experiments compared the performance on code maintenance tasks for three equivalent programs with 0, 3 and 5 levels of inheritances. They concluded that for the given tasks which focus on understanding effort more than change effort programs with less inheritance were faster to maintain. They also found that code maintenance effort is hardly correlated with inheritance depth but depends on other factors like the number of relevant methods.

CONCLUSION

The observations of analysis of each proposal indicate that there is great need for further theoretical validation of the metrics. Even though some of the metrics have been theoretically validated, each author follows different frameworks considering

Table 1. Summary of empirical literature on OO metrics

Source	Objective	Metric	Validation		Summary of results
			Theoretical	**Empirical**	
Li and Henry's Metrics (Li W.,1993)	Coupling, cohesion and design complexity	DAC,DAC' NOM, SIZE2	Briand *et al.* (Briand, L., 1999)	Li and Henry (Li W., 1993)	Two real systems were studied and found that DAC and NOM metric can be used for maintenance effort prediction.
MOOD Metrics (Brito, E., 1994)	Inheritance, Polymorphism Method hiding Attribute hiding	MHF, AHF MIF, AIF PF	Harrison et al. (Harrison R., 2000)	Brito e Abreu *et al.* (Brito, E., 1994)	Applied to seven classes written in Eiffel language and also on nine commercial systems. It is found that this metric can provide overall quality assessment of system
Lorenz and Kidd's Metrics (Lorenz M., 1994)	Class Size Inheritance information hiding polymorphism	PIM, NIM NIV, NCM NCV, NMO NMI, NMA	--	Lorenz and Kidd (Lorenz M., 1994)	Applied to five real projects. Found the relevance of these metrics in quality prediction
Briand *et al.*'s Metrics [Briand L., 1997]	Static characteristics of a design	ACAIC, OCAIC, DCAEC, OCAEC, ACMIC	Briand *et al.* (Briand, L., 1999)	Briand *et al.* (Briand L., 1997) El-Emam *et al.* (Briand, L., 1999)	Applied to two real systems. Found that these metrics are associated with fault proneness.
Marchesi's Metrics (Marchesi, 1998)	coupling inheritance	CL1, CL2	-	Marchesi (Marchesi, 1998)	Applied to three real projects developed in Small talk. It is observed that the value of the metrics obtained is related to the required man-months to develop the systems.
Harrison *et al.*'s metrics (Harrison R., 1998)	System complexity, balancing of responsibilities and coupling	NAS	-	-	Applied to five systems developed in C++. Found that it is for high level design used by managers to obtain early coupling estimates.
Bansiya *et al.*'s metrics (Bansiya J., 2002)	Inter-class coupling Encapsulation Cohesion inheritance composition	DAM, DCC, CAMC MOA, MFA	-	(Hayes, M., 2003; Li W. 1993; Chidamber, S. 1994; Basili, V., 1996; Etzkorn L., 1998).	It effectively predict cohesiveness of classes in several studies
Bansiya and Davis (Bansiya J., 2002)	Encapsulation, coupling,	DSC, NOH, ANA NOP	-	-	The quality predicted by the model shows good correlation with the assessment of project designs and predicts implementation qualities.

continued on following page

Table 1. continued

Genero *et al.*'s metrics (Genero M., 2001)	Class diagram structural complexity due to UML relationship	NAssoc, NAgg NDep, NGenH NAggH, MaxDIT NOA, HAgg NODP, NP, NW,MAgg, NDepIn NDepOut	(Briand L., 1996; Basili, V., 1996; Cartwright M., 1998; Genero M., 2002)	(Genero M., 2001; Genero M., 2002; Delgado M., 2001), Genero *et al.* (Genero M., 2001)	Two experiments to empirically validate class diagram-scope metrics were carried out. These metrics are correlated with class diagram maintainability characteristics.
Chidamber and Kemerer (Chidamber, S., 1994; Chidamber, S.R., 1991)	Class diagram structural complexity Inheritance Coupling Message Passing cohesion	WMC, RFC DIT, CBO LCOM, NOC	Chidamber and Kemerer (Chidamber, S., 1994; Chidamber, S.R., 1991)	Li and Henry (Li W.,1993), Chidamber et al. (Chidamber S., 1998)	CK metric suit can target all the essential attributes of OO software .These metrics are used to explore different structural dimensions of a class.

different properties or axioms. Some use property-based approaches like Briand *et al.*'s properties (Briand L., 1997) or Weyuker's axioms (Weyuker, E., 1988), while others use measurement theory-based approaches like Zuse's framework (Zuse, H., 1998) or DISTANCE framework (Poels G.,1999; Poels G., 2000). This fact reveals that there is no concrete standard, or accepted way of theoretically validating a measure. As Van den Berg and Van den Broek (Van Den Berg, 1996) said that a standard on theoretical validation issues in software measurement is immediately required. Even though CK metrics are shown overall to be empirically the most thoroughly investigated, the arguments relating to the DIT metric, prove to be contradictory. In summary, evidence regarding the impact of inheritance depth on fault-proneness proves to be rather ambiguous. Further research is necessary to identify this confounding effect and disentangle it from inheritance depth in order to assess the effect of inheritance depth by itself. This paper presents the methods of defining and applying the metrics in the software engineering industry at the design level of object oriented software development. Yet, it remains to be one of the challenging areas which require quality research for identifying better rationality to assess the quality of the system early in the development life cycle. This will enable better managerial decisions for improved methods and resource allocation. The main contribution of this paper is to provide a comprehensive survey of the relevant works related to metrics for class diagrams and class code artifacts at initial stages of development.

Finally, it is observed that despite all efforts put forward and new developments realized in research and international standardization, there is still a long way to realize clear concepts and terminology used in this field. With the goal of contributing to the harmonization of the different software measurement standards and research proposals, Garcia *et al.* have proposed a thorough and comparative analysis of the concepts and terms used within each. This in turn may serve as a basis for further research.

REFERENCES

Bansiya, J., & Davis, C. (2002). A hierarchical model for object-oriented design quality assessment. *IEEE Transactions on Software Engineering*, *28*(1), 4–17. doi:10.1109/32.979986

Basili, V., Briand, L., & Melo, W. (1996). A validation of object oriented design metrics as quality indicators. *IEEE Transactions on Software Engineering*, *22*, 751–761. doi:10.1109/32.544352

Briand, L., Daly, J., & Wüst, J. (1999). A unified framework for coupling measurement in object-oriented systems. *IEEE Transactions on Software Engineering, 25*(1), 91–121. doi:10.1109/32.748920

Briand, L., Devanbu, W., & Melo, W. (1997). *An investigation into coupling measures for C++*. 19th International Conference on Software Engineering (ICSE 97), Boston, USA, (pp. 412-421).

Briand, L., Morasca, S., & Basili, V. (1996). Property-based software engineering measurement. *IEEE Transactions on Software Engineering, 22*(6), 68–86. doi:10.1109/32.481535

Briand, L., Wüst, J., Daly, J., & Porter, V. (2000). Exploring the relationships between design measures and software quality in object-oriented systems. *Journal of Systems and Software, 51*, 245–273. doi:10.1016/S0164-1212(99)00102-8

Briand, L., Wüst, J., & Lounis, H. (1998). *Investigating quality factors in object-oriented designs: An industrial case study*. (Technical report ISERN 98-29, version 2).

Brito, E., Abreu, F., & Carapuça, R. (1994). *Object-oriented software engineering: Measuring and controlling the development process*. 4th International Conference on Software Quality, McLean, VA, USA.

Brito, E., Abreu, F., & Melo, W. (1996). *Evaluating the impact of object-oriented design on software quality*. 3rd International Metric Symposium, (pp. 90-99).

Cartwright, M. (1998). An empirical view of inheritance. *Information and Software Technology, 40*(4), 795–799. doi:10.1016/S0950-5849(98)00105-0

Chidamber, S., Darcy, D., & Kemerer, C. (1998). Managerial use of metrics for object-oriented software: An exploratory analysis. *IEEE Transactions on Software Engineering, 24*(8), 629–639. doi:10.1109/32.707698

Chidamber, S., & Kemerer, C. F. (1994). A metrics suite for object-oriented design. *IEEE Transactions on Software Engineering, 20*(6), 476–493. doi:10.1109/32.295895

Chidamber, S. R., & Kemerer, C. F. (1991). Towards a metrics suite for object oriented design. *Proceedings of the Conference on Object Oriented Programming Systems, Languages, and Applications (OOPSLA'91), 26*(11), 197-211.

Daly, J., Brooks, A., Miller, J., Roper, M., & Wood, M. (1996). An empirical study evaluating depth of inheritance on maintainability of object-oriented software. *Empirical Software Engineering, 1*(2), 109–132. doi:10.1007/BF00368701

Dandashi, F. (1998). *A method for assessing the reusability of object-oriented code using a validated set of automated measurements*. Unpublished doctoral dissertation, SITE, George Mason University, Fairfax, VA

Delgado, M., Gómez Skarmeta, A., & Jiménez, L. (2001). A regression methodology to induce a fuzzy model. *International Journal of Intelligent Systems, 16*(2), 169–190. doi:10.1002/1098-111X(200102)16:2<169::AID-INT20>3.0.CO;2-L

Etzkorn, L., Davis, C., & Li, W. (1998). A practical look at the lack of cohesion in methods metrics. *Journal of Object-Oriented Programming, 11*(5), 27–34.

Fenton, N., & Pfleeger, S. (1997). *Software metrics: A rigorous approach* (2nd ed.). London, UK: Chapman & Hall.

Genero, M. (2002). *Defining and validating metrics for conceptual models*. Unpublished doctoral thesis, University of Castilla-La Mancha.

Genero, M., Manso, M. E., Piattini, M., & Cantone, G. (2003). Building UML class diagram maintainability prediction models based on early metrics. *Proceedings IEEE Computer Society 9th International Symposium on Software Metrics*, (pp. 263-275).

Genero, M., Olivas, J., Piattini, M., & Romero, F. (2001). *Using metrics to predict OO Information Systems maintainability*. (LNCS 2068), (pp. 388-401).

Genero, M., Olivas, J., Romero, F., & Piattini, M. (2003). Assessing OO conceptual models maintainability. In Olive, et al. (Eds.), *International Workshop on Conceptual Modeling Quality* (IWCMQ'02), Tampere, Finland, (pp. 288-299). (LNCS 2784), Springer-Verlag.

Genero, M., Piattini, M., & Calero, C. (2001). Early measures for UML class diagrams. [Hermes Science Publications.]. *L'Objet*, 6(4), 489–515.

Gui, G., & Scott, P. D. (2007). Ranking reusability of software components using coupling metrics. *Journal of Systems and Software*, 1450–1459. doi:10.1016/j.jss.2006.09.048

Harrison, R., Counsell, S., & Nithi, R. (1998). *Coupling metrics for object-oriented design*. 5th International Software Metrics Symposium Metrics, (pp. 150-156).

Harrison, R., Counsell, S., & Nithi, R. (2000). Experimental assessment of the effect of inheritance on the maintainability of object-oriented systems. *Journal of Systems and Software*, 52, 173–179. doi:10.1016/S0164-1212(99)00144-2

Hayes, M. (2003). *Precious connection* (pp. 34–50). Information Week.

Kitchenham, B., Pfleeger, S., Pickard, L., Jones, P., & Hoaglin, D., El- Emam, K., & Rosenberg, J. (2002). Preliminary guidelines for empirical research in software engineering. *IEEE Transactions on Software Engineering*, 28(8), 721–734. doi:10.1109/TSE.2002.1027796

Li, L. (1998). *Change impact analysis for object-oriented software*. Unpublished doctoral dissertation, George Mason University, Virginia, USA.

Li, W., & Henry, S. (1993). Object-oriented metrics that predict maintainability. *Journal of Systems and Software*, 23(2), 111–122. doi:10.1016/0164-1212(93)90077-B

Lorenz, M., & Kidd, J. (1994). *Object-oriented software metrics: A practical guide*. Englewood Cliffs, NJ: Prentice Hall.

Marchesi, M. (1998). OOA metric for the unified modeling language. *Proceedings of the 2nd Euro Micro Conference on Software Maintenance and Reengineering*.

Poels, G., & Dedene, G. (1999). *DISTANCE: A framework for software measure construction*. (Research Report DTEW9937), Dept. Applied Economics, Katholieke Universiteit Leuven, Belgium.

Poels, G., & Dedene, G. (2000). Distance-based software measurement: Necessary and sufficient properties for software measures. *Information and Software Technology*, 42(1), 35–46. doi:10.1016/S0950-5849(99)00053-1

Prechelt, L., Unger, B., Philippsen, M., & Tichy, W. (2003). A controlled experiment on inheritance depth as a cost factor for code maintenance. *Journal of Systems and Software*, 65, 115–126.

Pressman, R. S. (1997). *Software engineering: A practitioner's approach* (4th ed.). New York, NY: McGraw-Hill.

Rosenberg, L. H., & Hyatt, L. A. (2000). *Software quality metrics for object-oriented environments*. Unisys Government Systems, Software Assurance technology Center.

Selby, R. W. (1988). Empirically analyzing software reuse in a production environment. In Tracz, W. (Ed.), *Software reuse: Emerging technology*. IEEE Computer Society Press.

Shull, F., Basili, V., Carver, J., & Maldonado, J. (2002). *Replicating software engineering experiments: Addressing the tacit knowledge problem.* 1st International Symposium on Empirical Software Engineering (ISESE 2002*),* Nara, Japan, (pp. 7-16). IEEE Computer Society.

Tang, M., Kao, M., & Chen, M. (1998). *An empirical study on object-oriented metrics.* 6th IEEE International Symposium on Software Metrics.

Thibodeau, P., & Rosencrance, L. (2002). Users losing billions due to bugs. *Computerworld, 36,* 1–2.

Van Den Berg, K. G., & Van Den Broek, P. M. (1996). Axiomatic validation in the software metric development process. In Melton, A. (Ed.), *Software measurement.* Thomson Computer Press.

Warmer, J., & Kleppe, A. (1999). *The object constraint language: Precise modeling with UML.* Addison Wesley Publishing Company.

Weyuker, E. (1988). Evaluating software complexity measures. *IEEE Transactions on Software Engineering, 14*(9), 1357–1365. doi:10.1109/32.6178

Zuse, H. (1998). *A framework of software measurement.* Berlin, Germany: Walter de Gruyter.

Chapter 15
Knowledge Management in Software Process Improvement:
A Case Study of Very Small Entities

Shuib Bin Basri
Lero, Dublin City University, Ireland & Universiti Teknologi PETRONAS, Malaysia

Rory V. O'Connor
Lero, Dublin City University, Ireland

ABSTRACT

This chapter discusses knowledge management (KM) aspects of how software process and software process improvement (SPI) is practiced within very small entities (VSEs) in the context of Irish software development industry. In particular, this study is concerned with the process of software development knowledge management in supporting the SPI. In order to understand the support process, the authors of this chapter have studied how KM processes are practiced within VSEs which includes communication, learning, sharing, and documentation process. This study also focuses in detail on the issues of the knowledge atrophy problem in VSEs. The findings explain how KM has been practiced and influenced the software development process and process improvement in VSEs. This result indicates that KM processes in VSEs are being undertaken in a very informal manner and also in indirect way. This is due to a small team size, autonomous working and macro-management style and caused VSEs to be more informal in their KM processes specifically and SPI generally. In addition, the results have indicated that the informal environment and culture helped VSEs to easily create and share knowledge between staff members and also assisted VSEs to mitigate the knowledge atrophy problem in their organization.

INTRODUCTION

Small and very small companies are the fundamental growth of many national economies. It is important to notice that the contribution from the small companies should be seen as important and significant as compare to the large one. The majority of software companies are small (Richardson & Von Wangenheim, 2007) and for example in Ireland the majority of the Irish indigenous software firms are employed between 10 to 99 employees (Crone, 2002) and average size is about

DOI: 10.4018/978-1-60960-509-4.ch015

16 employees (Coleman & O'Connor, 2008). The same scenario occurs in many other countries especially in Europe, Brazil and Canada (Laporte et al, 2008a), where Very Small Entities (VSEs), which employed less than 25 people (Laporte et al, 2006) are the majority software companies in the respective country. Therefore in order to be always relevance in software industry, small companies need to maintains and enhances their products and for that they need to improve their development process (Valtanen & Sihvonen, 2008; Reed & Kelly, 2002). Even though several methods and guidelines (e.g. Moprosoft and CMMI) have been produced in order to enhance software companies' development process, there are still a lot of challenges and obstacles have to manage (Laporte et al, 2008b). Hence, small companies whose have limited resources; particularly in financial and human resources; and practicing unique processes in managing their business have influenced their business style compare to large companies which are very formal and well documented (Sapovadia, 2006; Mtigwe, 2005).

Therefore consider to the above characteristics and situations, have shows that most of the management processes activities (e.g. decision-making, communication and problem solving) are done in informally way (e.g. orally and less documented) and more towards to human-oriented and communication factors (Valtanen & Sihvonen, 2008; Laporte et al, 2008b). Therefore it is belief that these issues will also influence software development VSEs in organized their software development knowledge. Furthermore the influence of well organized software development knowledge is seen could assist small companies or VSEs in maintain their product relevancy in market. This process also could mitigate from knowledge atrophy problem from affecting their company.

BACKGROUND

Software Process and SPI

The software process is all the stages and activities that are followed by organization to develop a software product (Zahran, 1998). The software process has four distinct roles; (i) to present a guidance as the guideline of the activities to be undertaken; (ii) to specify the artefact that should be developed and when; (iii) to direct the task of the development team; and (iv) to offer ways of monitoring and measuring a project progress and output (Kruchten, 2000). Moreover based on the first role, (Sommerville, 2004) has claimed that development process must be update, improve and maintain in order to meet current business and customer requirement. In addition, the issues SPI has gained increasing importance in software engineering area. The main aims of SPI are to understand the software process used in the organization and to guide the implementation of changes of that process in order to achieve specific goals such as to improve software development time, on budget and with the desired functionality. According to several authors, SPI has a close link between the quality of the development process and the quality of the product developed using the process (Kruchten, 2000; Olsen et al, 1989). In regards to small companies, improving software process is like improving a business process and both are related (Sanders, 1998; Ward & Aurum, 2004). In addition 4 categories; economic, people, organization and implementation; are believed as SPI influencing factors in an organization (Hall et al, 2002).

Moreover, SPI also goes through a lifecycle as exist in software development process (Cook & Wolf, 1998). The SPI lifecycle is constantly changing software processes and it consists of two phases; (i) analysing process phase and (ii) changing process phase (Stelzer & Mellis, 1998) and this process will be continuously as depicted in Figure 1.

Figure 1. SPI change process

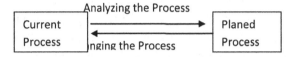

Knowledge Management (KM)

Knowledge can be divided into two classes, explicit and tacit (Polanyi, 1966). Explicit knowledge is easier to communicate, transmit and reuse across an organization (Desouza, 2003). While tacit knowledge is highly personal knowledge that is gained through experience and deeply rooted in action, commitment and involved in a specific context (Argesti, 2000). In software engineering, individuals are the most important actor in KM, who perform tasks for achieving goal that been set by the organizational level. Through social and collaborative work among the people in an organization, process knowledge is created, shared, amplified, enlarged and justified on organizational setting (Nonaka & Takeuchi, 1995). Moreover knowledge is about action-outcome and the effects of the firm environment (Weick, 1995) and was created through a conversion between tacit knowledge and explicit knowledge (Nonaka et al, 2000).

KM is a discipline that crosses many areas such as economics, informatics, psychology and technology. KM is seen as a strategy that creates, acquires, transfers, consolidates, shares and enhances the use of knowledge in order to improve organizational performance and survival in a business environment (Zhang & Zao, 2006). This scenario becomes a challenge to the companies in managing their organizational knowledge (Kvale, 2007). Therefore specific plans and suitable tools will guide the knowledge management process (Dingsoyr & Conradi, 2002). This plans and tools must be promoted in applying the old knowledge to new situations in an organization (Kukko et al, 2008).

In KM, knowledge creation and sharing is a continuous process whereby individuals and groups within the organization and between the organizations share tacit and explicit knowledge. The organization capability to create knowledge is important in order to sustainable competitive advantage (Nonaka et al, 2000; Parent et al, 2000). Knowledge creation process is believed started when an individual recognize the related and useful data and information and then able to transform it into a new knowledge that brings a future value to an organization. Organizational knowledge is not only created within the organization but also can be acquired externally and this can be done through knowledge sharing (Grant, 1996; Awazu, 2004; Nonaka & Takeuchi, 1995). The important of knowledge sharing and knowledge creation in any organization will help organization to continuously innovate and help organization to sustain their competitiveness (Rhodes et al, 2008). These activities are usually supported by a social network within an organization and through the development between departments in an organization link (Szulanski, 1996). In addition, Turner and Makhija added that in sharing and creating knowledge, trust and organizational control plays an important role in how individual transferring and sharing their knowledge with others in an organization (Turner & Makhija, 2006). Moreover, (Dingsoyr & Conradi, 2002) have investigated knowledge management approaches in eight case studies; proposed with a framework of knowledge management program that must exist in the companies, as depicted in Figure 2.

Figure 2. A framework of the components of a knowledge management

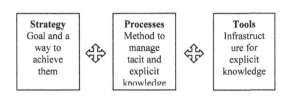

Knowledge Loss Issues

Knowledge is vital for every organization because it is needed to perform a work in an organization. According to (Hendricks & Vriens, 1999) an organization cannot survive and sustain their competitiveness without knowledge. Therefore knowledge needs to be managed to ensure that the right knowledge gets into the right place. This also will increase the innovation power of organization and its knowledge worker. In addition knowledge in organization also will be eroding over the time and will contribute to loss of knowledge in organization. This condition is often implicit and its loss is often not recognizing until too late. According to (Shaw et al, 2003) knowledge erosion is referred as the loss of knowledge resulting from people leaving an organization or changing jobs within it. Several author claimed that knowledge erosion became one of the main problems as the organization expanding over the time (Litern, 2002). The lacking of resource and time in small company in implement knowledge management will introduce a knowledge erosion situation through employee retirement and resignation (Bjorson & Dingsoyr, 2008). In addition, 4 important criteria in organization; the staff development, team building, communication of role and function, and formal continuous process improvement; was believed could help organization in mitigated this issue (Shaw et al, 2003).

KM and SPI

Software process is not standardized in all software projects (Borges & Falbo, 2002). Software process must be updated and improved frequently in order to cope with any environment changes. Such environment required KM in supporting software process definition and activities (Sirvio et al, 2002). (Hansen & Kautz, 2004) explained that SPI could strengthen KM abilities for software development organization. In term of small organization, (Meehan & Richardson, 2002;

Kettunen, 2003), argues that KM is core to a software process improvement model and that the relationship between SPI and organizational learning are very strong. They points out that people in an organization will create, acquire and share knowledge continuously in order to improve software development practices. Moreover, in nowadays business environment where software development project becoming more complex, the greater reliance upon the knowledge processes to resolves problems are really important (Aurum et al, 2003; Bjornson & Dingsoyr, 2005). (Bjornson & Dingsoyr, 2008) stated in their review that proper managing of organizational knowledge is important in SPI efforts and it is a major factor for success. (Mathiassen & Pourkomeylian, 2003) in their survey on practical usage of KM to support innovation in a software organization claims that KM and SPI are very close related. They added that knowledge management is used to update practices within software organization generally and SPI specifically. According to (Sirvio et al, 2002) software organization needs to improve their practices in order to cope with market changes. These situations have lead to considerable interest in how organization can effectively respond to changing environment or agile environment (Aaen et al, 2007) (Sirvio et al, 2002). Therefore KM is seen as critical to SPI process.

Therefore, based on the above discussion we proposed a study model as depicted in Figure 3. From the diagram, it shown that the SPI and software development KM are related to each other. This relationship is vital in preventing knowledge atrophy and process erosion problems. In addi-

Figure 3. The study model

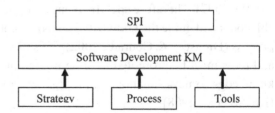

tion, a proper KM process could help software teams become more effective in performing team task and making a decision (Salas et al, 2000; Kettunen, 2003). (Aaen et al, 2002) added with an appropriate knowledge creation and sharing process could provide team members with clear SPI goals and sustain their interest.

METHODOLOGY

Data collection consisted of two complimentary methods, individual and focus group interviews. These processes are done almost simultaneously. For the interview and focus group purposes, we have been guide by an interview guide and focus group question guide (Taylor & Bodgan, 1984). The individual interview approach was used in this study in order to discuss the research issues in depth, to get respondents' candid discussion on the topic and to be able to get the depth of information of the study situation for the research context (Kvale, 2007). A semi-structured interview includes the open-ended and specific question. It been designed to gather not only the information foreseen, but also unexpected type of information (Li, 2006). The respondents for this individual interview session are the managers from the identified Irish Software VSEs. The interview session happened approximately 40 to 90 minutes. In overall, we have interviewed 4 managers from various software VSEs; which their main activities is software development; around Dublin, Ireland at their respective company.

The second interview method is the focus group interview. The focus group interview approached was used in this study in order to get a detail explanation and viewed from the development team which involved directly with the development process. Moreover, the existence of team interactions in this activity could help to release inhibitions amongst the team members. Furthermore, this method could activate forgotten details of experiences and also could generate more data through wide range of responses. Focus group interviews were also chosen because it was the most appropriate method to study attitudes and experiences; to explore how opinion were constructed (Kitzinger, 1995) and to understand behaviours, values and feelings (Patton, 2002). According to (Valtanen & Sihvonen, 2008; Powell & Single, 1996), the advantage of focus group is the ability to help the researcher in identifying quickly a full range of perspectives held by respondents. They added that focus groups expand the details that might have been left out in an in-depth interview. The focus group participants for this activity are from the same company as the individual interviews participants. 14 development people have been involved in this activity and have been conducted at their respective companies'. In analysing all data we have followed the qualitative contents analysis method (Elo & Kyngas, 2008) and adopted the Grounded Theory (GT) (Strauss & Corbin, 1998) data coding process in order to have a systematic data coding activities. In this part all qualitative data that gathered from individual interviews and focus group interviews were analyzed and coded. This process involves the development of the codes, code-categories and inter-relationship of categories which is based on the GT process and coding strategy (Strauss & Corbin, 1998). The *Atlas.Ti* software also was used to help us to code the interview transcript and linking these codes to produce the semantic network diagrams, which are illustrated later in the chapter.

FINDINGS AND DISCUSSIONS

Based on the analysis process we have identified 7 main related categories that shape up the SPI environment in VSEs. Figure 4 illustrates all the categories that influence VSEs SPI initiatives. In additional these categories are the main categories and variables that gave an influence to the software development process environments in VSEs. The details of the main categories are

Figure 4. The overall main category diagram

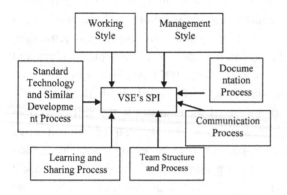

presented below, which grouped and listed out in details the important variable that gathered from the analysis process.

Team Structure and Process

The analysis result shows that the team environment in VSEs could be divided into 2 categories as tabulated in Table 1. The organizational and team structure category indicates that due to small number of people working in the organization, the team size also small and this lead to a flat team and organizational structure. From the interviews analysis results indicates that all interviewees admitted that the companies having no real team structure or team structure is only exist occasionally and it depends to the company project. For example, one company says of its team structure *"Since we are 3 people in development plus the*

manager we have very direct contact with each other and with the manager".

In additional we also found that due to the small number employee, flat organization and team structure and informal environment, interviewees are perceived that all peoples in the companies or department are in the same level. In addition the analysis show that they have the same level of working experience, skills and very much depends to each others in performing their task. Beside that the close working space or area and high frequent and informal communication are also influence this perception. All these criteria have lead VSEs in narrow down the gap between the management and the team development, as illustrated by this interview extract:

"The management and staff relationship is very close, it is probably we are in the similar age and similar interest. No body works in this company that not interested what we do in this company.".

The second category have indicates the team role, team involvement and team culture issues. The analysis shown that the staff role which includes the role in team and the task they perform in development process is very informal and very general. This could apply that the development staff could worked or assigned as different role in one time in organization development project. In addition they also can work with others or different people and different position as and when they are required. These situations have explained

Table 1. Team structure and process

Sub Category	Category	Main Category
Team Size - Small	Organizational and Team Structure	Team Structure and Process
Organizational and Team Flat Structure -		
Team Role - informal	Team process	
Team Involvement - direct		
Team Culture – informal		

that team involvement process in VSEs is direct and informal in development activities.

Working and Management Style

The analysis has shown that the team structure and process category gave an impact on VSEs working and management style. It is indicates that staffs have autonomy on their work which make them more self dependent, self responsibility, work independently and self learning as in Table 2.

The result from the analysis emphasises that people in VSEs working style is more toward individually or been assigned task according to their expertise. This situation has been defined as 'team of one' by one of the interviewee. The formal interactions of between the team member is more on the strategic area only such as problem solving or knowledge sharing in particular issue that related with the software development issues. But most of other interaction or communication are more indirect, casual and very informal. This situation gave researcher an indication that notion of team work in VSEs only appears or happened in informal way or periodic basis. The following interview quotes represents this situation: *"It depends and because we are small company sometime we have big project but most of it is small. It depend the scope of the project if big we might do it in team and again most of it is individual basis. Basically people work quite autonomous and specific."*

In relation to autonomous work, the analysis also indicates that, the people in VSEs also exercise an autonomous communication style in performed their works. Informal communication, less structure and direct communication, self learning and explore, frequent informal guidance, and informal meeting code that produce from the analysis indicates the autonomous communication process happened in VSEs. Several interviewed quotes below explain the autonomous communication issues in VSEs, such as this: *"They tend to communicate when they want a problem answered. They are very autonomous and everybody helps to solve a problem"*. The analysis process also indicates that there are similar management styles adopted within VSEs. During the study, it shows that the small team size elements in VSEs are also gave an impact on the management style in the companies. Table 3 indicates how the management style has been adopted in VSEs.

Trust, relationships, flexible environment and loose project management are the subcategories that indicate the based management style in VSEs. This type of management approaches is defined as 'Embrace and Empower' (Coleman and O' Connor, 2008) regime as similar to 'Theory Y' management style (McGregor, 1985). In this context the idea and opinion from all subordinate have a values and been adopted in the development process and policy. There are also indicators that the element of trust in development team and their ability to carry task with less direction. This

Table 2. Working Style

Sub Category	Category	Main Category
Autonomous work		
Autonomous Communication		
Work independently		
Strategic area	Working Style	
Sole Responsibility		
Self Learning		
'Team of One'		

Table 3. Management style

Sub Category	Category	Main Category
Trust		
Family and Flexible Environment	Management Style	
Loose PM		
Open Environment		

could be identified in Table 3 which identifies the working style on how the development staffs perform their task. For example, this extract clearly shows a flat management structure, which is representative of these study VSE participants: *"Is very informal, very flat structure not huge hierarchy and have a freedom to implement what they think is working to the task. We just control very loosely over time."*

Standard Technology and Similar Development Process

The analysis also indicates 2 subcategories appear in this category as list in Table 4.

We found that type of development tools and development process being used and adopted are varies in VSEs. These are depends on companies main technology platform and framework in developing their software product. The analysis has indicates that VSEs are adopted similar development technology, tools and method in developing company software product, as illustrated by this interview extract: *"Yes, the development processes are quite identical and small changes depend to situation but overall the development process is same."*.

The analysis of the interviews data also indicates that developers in VSEs adopting the agile development philosophy and approaches in developing systems. This could be identified with the method and process they are adopting in performing software development task. The details of this process will be explained in later parts that related with this issue. In overall this part explains the issue of development technology and method that have been adopted in VSEs. The analysis has explained that VSEs are using the same development tools and method in developing the system. This is due to a few reasons that have been stated above. The analysis has indicates that the combination of both issues has given an impact to the others processes.

SPI Process

In this main category, we could be detailed into 2 categories as illustrates in Table 5.

The first subcategory that exists in process status category is process loss and focus subcategory. The results indicate the SPI process started when the process loss and/or process focus happened. Process loss happened when the technology change, customer requirement creeps, software function creep, and a new idea or sug-

Table 4. Standard technology and similar development process

Sub Category	Category	Main Category
Standard Technology	Applied standard technology and similar development method	
Similar development Process		

Table 5. SPI process

Sub Category	Category	Main Category
Team Structure and Process		
Informal/Indirect		
Small Scale	Process status	Improvement Development Process
Process Loss and Focus		
'Agile' Development Style	Development method	

gestion from the staffs exist in their business activities. Meanwhile, process focus happened when new customer requirements, market changes, business procedure and requirement upgrade, software module or product update and expert/staff suggestion and idea occurred in their business environment. In addition, the analysis also indicates that VSEs are work very close with the customer in improving the software product and process.

The second subcategories are the small scale and informal or indirect subcategory. The analysis indicates that the SPI process in VSEs has been done in a small scale but very frequent. This process could be identify the analysis code such as organic, natural change, reactive vs. proactive, try and error, module orientation, minor changes and profitable orientate that extract from the interviews quotes represents the scale of SPI process in VSEs. Meanwhile from the analysis axial code such as RAD development, frequent change, direct and rapid change, and 'agile' process are reflected the frequent level of changes in SPI. This point is illustrated in this interview extract: *"we doing it little by little and that way we going to do we going to improve the process kind of and we open the discuss ask about what to do next, what is the basic/biggest problem of current process and what we could do to address that"*

Beside smalls scale and high frequent changes in SPI process, the analysis also indicates that the improvement process in software development is performed in informal or indirect process. Not following any standard and guideline, not structure improvement process and informal post mortem process are the indicator that the SPI process are being performed in informal and indirect way. Meanwhile the development method category indicates that VSEs are more likely to follow an agile development approach in their software development process than the other developments method This could be identified in the communication process, documentation process, change process and customer collaboration which have been identified and explained above indicates that VSEs have fulfilled the 4 main general characteristic as in Agile Manisfesto (Fowler & Highsmith, 2001).

KM PROCESS

In order to understand VSEs KM process, we have combines 3 main categories into one section as follows:

Communication Process

From the analysis, we could divide the communication process in VSEs in 2 categories namely open and informal communication category and online communication category. It also shows that the communication processes in VSEs are influence by the companies team structure and process and the working and management style Table 6 shows the details communication process categories produced from the analysis.

Table 6. Communication process

Sub Category	Category	Main Category
Team Structure and Process Working and Management Style		Communication Process
Open Communication	Open and Informal Communication	
Informal Communication		
Communication tools	Online and Electronic Communication	
Internet/ Electronically		

In the open and informal category, we have identified several interviews quotations that indicate the communication process where people are more towards informal and direct/casual communication. This could be identifies in the way of meeting have been conducted which are more informal, 'stand up', periodic and individual. This is due to the working environment, team size and working style in their company. Furthermore relationship between staffs in the company also influences the communication process in VSE. The family and flexible environment, frequent socialize between staff; flat organization structure and closeness working space have given an impact on communication process in VSEs.

The analysis also shows that the use of communication tools such as email, phone, blog and internet are very active in VSEs. This communication tools is more vital to the company that have a staff who works outside Ireland or having others offices in different locations. The use of these tools is believed could close the gap between remote and collocate staff and allow staffs to share and document all work related information or knowledge in informal way.

The following interview extract summarises a typical study participants communications processes: *"Formal meeting are not held very often because we always communicate each other... so a formal meeting isn't required... we do might have a kick off project meeting and generally people discuss the work all of the time"*.

Learning and Sharing Process

The analysis has shows the learning and sharing process in VSEs as in Table 7.

In self learning category, the analysis shows at in VSEs there are no formal trainings are given or provides to employees in enhancing their

Table 7. Learning and sharing process

Sub Category	Category	Main Category
Communication Process Working and Management Style Team Structure and Process		Learning and Sharing Process (Knowledge Management)
Training	Self Learning	
Self Learning		
Continuous Guidance		
Internal Training	Sharing	
Meeting		
Document		

knowledge or skills. The analysis also has explained that people in VSEs are more depends to self learning in mastering the technology or process that used in the organization. Besides self learning, the analysis also shows on the job training, self exploring and continues guidance from expert within the companies are the main process that frequently been practised in enhanced staff knowledge and skills.

The second category in this part is sharing category. The analysis shows that in VSEs knowledge sharing process happened in informal training, informal meeting and document sharing. Informal training happened through informal and guidance from expert, peer to peer programming process, shared books and others material, internal training, high frequent open and direct discussion with team member and online sharing with others. Meanwhile the informal meeting process happened through an informal stand-up meeting, direct and open discussion and online meeting via email, Skype and blog. In relation, the analysis results indicate that the learning and sharing process in VSEs is been influenced and shaped by 3 existing main factors which are VSEs team size and process which are small team size and flat organization structure; working and management style which are more toward autonomous work and macro management process and, communication process which are indirect and informal process. In additional from the interviews data analysis shows that in general knowledge sharing activities either via electronic or personal are important in main-

taining and evolving the current VSEs software development process. The following interview extract is typical of VSE who participated in this study: *"We shared books and we talk… Generally it is informal process just asking questions, maybe grab someone and talk to them"*.

Documentation Process

The results have indicates 2 category that falls in main documentation activities as in Table 8.

The analysis has indicates the documentation processes are very informal process and individual initiatives. In additional, in VSEs documentation process are not given high priority because of time constraints and small team size. The results from the analysis also indicate in VSEs most of the information is documented in an electronic format rather than a paper format. The interviewees also admit due to similar technology and development method applied in all development projects, details documentation process is not necessary and important. They claimed that the staffs are more focused to software development activities rather than the documentation process. In additional from the analysis indicates that due to the autonomous work culture in VSEs, which based on person experience and skills, most of the documentation process in VSEs is individual and personal basis. Besides that, the analysis also shows that programming codes, technical issues and business procedures are the

Table 8. Documentation process

Sub Category	Category	Main Category
Working and Management Style Team Structure and Process		
Informal documentation	Informal and Individual Documentation	Documentation Process (Knowledge Management)
Individual Documentation		
Technical Business related document	Specific Information and Procedure	
Client related Document		

main documentation in the VSEs which fall under specific information and procedure category.

The following two interview extracts best represent the documentation process: *"We haven't clearly defined and documented it yet. We considered our process to be evolving and is not finished. We started of with formal old style model then we change continuously until we happy on it. We can improve it anymore, so that kind of project of itself"* and *"The documentation is only for our internal need, so means there no general standard how we documented it everyone who is participate just preparing it in the future".*

Knowledge Loss Issues

In conjunction of the above, the knowledge loss issues also have been explore in order to understand the interviewees views and companies actions in order to mitigate this problems. From the analysis indicates that due to economy situation nowadays, the use standard technology and similar development process in every company project, and company nature in VSEs, indicates that knowledge loss problem is not an important and serious issues in VSEs. In additional, the interviewees' claimed that with the informal and autonomous work environments will create an atmosphere that people in the company are more willing to share and work closely each others.

The following interview extracts are representative of typical VSE approach to this issue: *"Really knowledge is secure by the process, the development process, the tools and framework. We put in place we follow the same tool and process and framework. So if anyone left could company would be loss of knowledge to them"* and *"Sometime we make people working together and ensure that no one exclusively work in one project. But sometimes it hard to apply due to our size."*

OVERALL THEORITICAL MODEL

From the overall discussion above, a theoretical and relational model is illustrated as in figure 5. This illustrates that the software process and process improvement strategy which started from process loss or process focus which was influences by several variables which has been discuss above. The process formation is created and will indicate the process that need to improve, change or upgrade. As discussed above the software development process in VSEs are done in informal, indirect and small scale at one time but in a high frequent. The analysis in this part also shows that VSEs followed or adopted the agile development approaches which involved a lot of interaction or communication either with the customers or the developers, high focus of the development process and having minimal documentation process the organization. Due to small team size, flat team and organization structure, staffs or management geographical location, autonomous working style and macro project management the communication process are more become informal and autonomous. Beside that the uses of the com-

Figure 5. Overall theoretical diagram

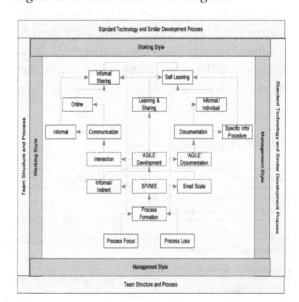

munication tools are also being used extensively among peoples in communicate and shared their knowledge. In term of documentation process, the analysis indicate that in VSEs the documentation process have been practiced either informal or individual. The analysis also shows that due to macro project management style, autonomous working style and influence standard technology and similar development process have lead to the these situation. Moreover the interviewees admitted that only the issue related to business procedure and technical specification are being formally documented. Moreover the analysis also indicated that due to the informal communication, informal documentation and autonomous work have created the informal and personal organization learning and sharing process. Therefore from learning and sharing process a new idea and weakness of the area that need to improved, change and upgrade. This process will start back at the process formation and iterative.

CONCLUSION AND CONTRIBUTION

It was collectively agreed by the respondents that the documentation process in VSEs is done very informally, individually and specifically. In term of knowledge management issues, the result showed that all respondents claimed that they have a clear KM strategy in the organization. However the analysis showed that this process are done informally and is not organised. In addition the result show that even though the KM was done informally either in communication, management, working style and team structure in VSEs, 90% of the respondents believed that this environment have lead them to mitigate the knowledge and process loss problem in their organization. Moreover the results also indicated that in overall the size of the company given an impact to all the process that have discussed above.

The main contribution of this study is an expanded understanding of SPI research area by merging the issues of KM from both a general and VSE specific perspective. Our results indicate that KM factor gave indirect influences to the process of improving current software process and process improvement activities in software development companies. Others contribution of this research is providing an additional knowledge to the SPI research area focused more on VSEs, which have been least explored by current literature. The research has found the variables that influence the software process and process improvement issues that could be explored individually in further detail in future. The last contribution is the type of strategies used to carry out research methodology work, especial in analyzing the qualitative data which was the output from the interviews (interview and focus groups) activities. If survey questionnaire approach is a familiar approach and was often used in the software engineering field, the interviews data analysis research technique which adopted qualitative contents data analysis and GT coding approach, is rarely been used in the analysis of the software process improvement and in software engineering research in general. Therefore we believe that we are adding to the body of knowledge associated with suitability of the GT research method to software engineering area.

ACKNOWLEDGMENT

This work were supported, between Science Foundation Ireland grant 03/CE2/I303_1 to Lero - The Irish Software Engineering Research Centre (www.lero.ie) and Universiti Teknologi PETRONAS, Malaysia (www.utp.edu.my).

REFERENCES

Aaen, I., Arent, J., Mathiassen, L., & Ngwenyama, O. (2002). A conceptual map of software process improvement. *Scandinavian Journal of Information Systems, 13*(13), 81–101.

Aaen, I., Börjesson, A., & Mathiassen, L. (2007). SPI agility: How to navigate improvement projects. *Software Process Improvement and Practice, 12*(3), 267. doi:10.1002/spip.309

Agresti, W. (2000). Knowledge management. *Advances in Computers, 53*(5), 171–283. doi:10.1016/S0065-2458(00)80006-6

Aurum, A., Jeffery, R., Wohlin, C., & Handzic, M. (2003). *Managing software engineering knowledge*. Germany: Springer.

Awazu, Y. (2004). Knowledge management in distributed environments: Roles of informal network players. *Proceedings of the 37th Annual Hawaii International Conference on System Sciences*, (p. 6).

Bjornson, F. O., & Dingsoyr, T. (2005). *A study of a mentoring program for knowledge transfer in a small software consultancy company. (LNCS 3547)*. Berlin / Heidelberg, Germany: Springer.

Bjørnson, F. O., & Dingsøyr, T. (2008). Knowledge management in software engineering: A systematic review of studied concepts, findings and research methods used. *Information and Software Technology, 50*(11), 1055–1068. doi:10.1016/j.infsof.2008.03.006

Borges, L. M. S., & Falbo, R. A. (2002). Managing software process knowledge. *Proceedings of the International Conference on Computer Science, Software Engineering, Information Technology, e-Business, and Applications* (CSITeA'2002), (pp. 227–232).

Coleman, G., & O'Connor, R. V. (2008). The influence of managerial experience and style on software development process. *International Journal of Technology. Policy and Management, 8*(1), 91–109.

Coleman, G., & O'Connor, R. V. (2008). Investigating software process in practice: A grounded theory perspective. *Journal of Systems and Software, 81*(5), 772–784. doi:10.1016/j.jss.2007.07.027

Cook, J. E., & Wolf, A. L. (1998). Discovering models of software process from event-based data. [TOSEM]. *ACM Transactions on Software Engineering and Methodology, 7*(3), 215–249. doi:10.1145/287000.287001

Crone, M. (2002). *A profile of software Irish industry. Northern Ireland Economic Research Center (NIERC)*. Belfast NI.

Desouza, K. C. (2003). Facilitating tacit knowledge exchange. *Communications of the ACM, 46*(6), 6. doi:10.1145/777313.777317

Dingsoyr, T., & Conradi, R. (2002). A survey of case studies of the use of knowledge management in software engineering. *International Journal of Software Engineering and Knowledge Engineering, 12*(4), 391–414. doi:10.1142/S0218194002000962

Elo, S., & Kyngäs, H. (2008). The qualitative content analysis process. *Journal of Advanced Nursing, 62*(1), 107–115. doi:10.1111/j.1365-2648.2007.04569.x

Fowler, M., & Highsmith, J. (2001). The agile manifesto. *Software Development, 9*(8), 28–35.

Grant, R. M. (1996). Prospering in dynamically-competitive environments: Organisational capability as knowledge integration. *Organization Science, 7*(4), 375–387. doi:10.1287/orsc.7.4.375

Hall, T., Rainer, A., & Baddoo, N. (2002). Implementing software process improvement: An empirical study. *Software Process Improvement and Practice, 7*(1), 3–15. doi:10.1002/spip.150

Hansen, B. H., & Kautz, K. (2004). *Knowledge mapping: A technique for identifying knowledge flows in software organisations. (LNCS 3281)*. Springer.

Hendricks, P. H. J., & Vriens, D. J. (1999). Knowledge-based systems and knowledge management: Friends or foe. *Information and Management Journal, 35*, 113–125. doi:10.1016/S0378-7206(98)00080-9

Kettunen, P. (2003). Managing embedded software project team knowledge. *IEEE Software, 1*(6), 359–366.

Kitzinger, J. (1995). Introducing focus groups. *British Medical Journal, 311*, 299–302.

Kruchten, P. (2000). *The rational unified process*. Reading, MA: Addison Wesley.

Kukko, M., Helander, N., & Virtanen, P. (2008). Knowledge management in renewing software development processes. *Proceedings of the 41st Annual Hawaii International Conference on System Sciences*, (pp. 332-332).

Kvale, S. (2007). *Doing interviews: The Sage qualitative research kit*. Thousand Oaks, CA: Sage.

Laporte, C. Y., Alxender, S., & O'Connor, R. V. (2008). A software engineering lifecycle standard for very small enterprise. *Proceeding of the 15th European Conference, EuroSPI 2008 Industrial Proceeding*, (pp. 10.33-10.41).

Laporte, C. Y., Alxender, S., & Renault, A. (2008). Developing international standards for very small enterprises. *Journal of Computer, 41*(3), 98. doi:10.1109/MC.2008.86

Laporte, C. Y., & April, A. (2006). *Applying software engineering standards in small setting: Recent historical perspectives and initial achievements*. International Research Workshop in Small Setting, Software Engineering Institue, Pittsburgh, Oct 19-20.

Li, J. Y. (2006). *Process improvement and risk management in off-the shelf componenet-based development*. Unpublished doctoral dissertation, Norwegian University science and Technology.

Litern, G., Diedrich, F. J., & Serfaty, D. (2002). Engineering the community of practice for maintenance of organizational knowledge. *Proceedings IEEE 7th Conference on Human Factors and Power Plants*, (pp. 7-13).

Mathiassen, L., & Pourkomeylian, P. (2003). Managing knowledge in a software organization. *Journal of Knowledge Management, 7*(2), 63–80. doi:10.1108/13673270310477298

McGregor, D. (1985). *The human side of enterprise: 25th anniversary printing*. McGraw-Hill/Irwin.

Meehan, B., & Richardson, I. (2002). Identification of software process knowledge management. *Software Process Improvement and Practice, 7*(2), 47–55. doi:10.1002/spip.154

Mtigwe, B. (2005). The entrepreneurial firm internationalization process in Southern African context: A comparative approach. *International Journal of Entrepreneurial Behaviour and Research, 11*(5), 358–377. doi:10.1108/13552550510615006

Nonaka, I., & Takeuchi, H. (1995). *The knowledge creating company*. New York, NY: Oxford University Press.

Nonaka, I., Toyama, R., & Konno, N. (2000). SECI, Ba and leadership: A unified model of dynamic knowledge creation. *Long Range Planning, 33*(1), 5–34. doi:10.1016/S0024-6301(99)00115-6

Olsen, T., Humphrey, W. S., & Kitson, D. (1989). *Conducting SEI-assisted software process assessments*. Pittsburgh, PA: Software Engineering Institute. (Technical Report CMU/SEI-89-TR-07).

Parent, M., Gallupe, R. B., Salisbury, W. D., & Handelman, J. M. (2000). Knowledge creation in focus group: Can group technologies help? *Information & Management, 38*(1), 47–58. doi:10.1016/S0378-7206(00)00053-7

Patton, M. Q. (2002). *Qualitative evaluation and research methods* (3rd ed.). Newbury Park, CA: Sage Publications, Inc.

Polanyi, M. (1966). *The tacit dimension*. London, UK: Routledge.

Powell, R. A., & Single, H. M. (1996). Focus groups. *International Journal for Quality in Health Care, 8*(5), 499–504. doi:10.1093/intqhc/8.5.499

Reed, T. F., & Kelly, D. (2002). The skill gap in the Irish software industry. *Irish Journal of Management, 23*(2), 95–110.

Rhodes, J., Hung, R., Lok, P., Lien, B. Y., & Wu, C. M. (2008). Factors influencing organizational knowledge transfer: Implication for corporate performance. *Journal of Knowledge Management, 12*(3), 84. doi:10.1108/13673270810875886

Richardson, I., & von Wangenheim, C. G. (2007). Guest editors introduction: Why are small software organizations different? *IEEE Software, 24,* 18–22. doi:10.1109/MS.2007.12

Salas, E., Burke, C. S., & Cannon-Bowers, J. A. (2000). Teamwork: Emerging principles. *International Journal of Management Reviews, 2*(4), 339–356. doi:10.1111/1468-2370.00046

Sanders, M. (1998). *The Spire handbook: Better, faster, cheaper software development in small organization.* Dublin, Ireland: Centre for Software Engineering.

Sapovadia, V. K. (2006). *Micro finance: The pillars of a tool to socio-economic development.* Development Gateway. Retrieved on October 9, 2008, from http://ssrn.com/abstract=955062

Shaw, D., Edward, J. S., Baker, B., & Collier, P. M. (2003). Achieving closure through knowledge management. *Electronic Journal of Knowledge Management, 1*(2), 197–204.

Sirvio, K. S., Mantyniemi, A., & Seppanen, V. (2002). Toward a practical solution for capturing knowledge for software projects. *IEEE Software, 19*(3), 60–62. doi:10.1109/MS.2002.1003457

Sommerville, I. (2004). *Software engineering* (7th ed.). Reading, MA: Addison Wesley.

Stelzer, D., & Mellis, W. (1998). Success factors of organizational change in software process improvement. *Software Process Improvement and Practice, 4*(4), 227–250. doi:10.1002/(SICI)1099-1670(199812)4:4<227::AID-SPIP106>3.0.CO;2-1

Strauss, A., & Corbin, J. (1998). *Basics of qualitative research: Techniques and procedures for developing grounded theory* (2nd ed.). Thousand Oaks, CA: Sage.

Szulanski, G. (1996). Exploring internal stickiness: Impediments to the transfer of best practice within firm. *Journal of Strategic Management, 17*(2), 27–43.

Taylor, S. J., & Bodgan, R. (1984). *Introduction to qualitative research method.* John Wiley & Sons.

Turner, K., & Makhija, M. (2006). The role of organizational controls in managing knowledge. *Academy of Management Review, 31*(1), 197–217.

Valtanen, A., & Sihvonen, H. M. (2008). Employees' motivation for SPI: Case study in a small Finnish software company. *Proceeding of the 15th European Conference, EuroSPI 2008,* (pp. 152-163). Berlin/Heildelberg, Germany: Springer–Verlag.

Ward, J., & Aurum, A. (2004). *Knowledge management in software engineering-describing the process.* Australian Software Engineering Conference (ASWEC'04), (pp. 137-146).

Weick, K. E. (1995). *Sense making in organization.* Thousand Oak, CA: Sage Publication.

Zahran, S. (1998). *Software process improvement: Practical guidelines for business success.* Boston, MA: Addison Wesley.

Zhang, D., & Zao, L. (2006). Knowledge management in organization. *Journal of Database Management, 17*(1), 1–8.

Chapter 16
Software Process Model using Dynamic Bayesian Networks

Thomas Schulz
Robert Bosch GmbH, Germany

Łukasz Radliński
University of Szczecin, Poland

Thomas Gorges
Robert Bosch GmbH, Germany

Wolfgang Rosenstiel
University of Tübingen, Germany

ABSTRACT

This chapter describes a methodology to support the management of large scale software projects in optimizing product correction effort versus initial development costs over time. The Software Process Model (SPM) represents the implementation of this approach on a level of detail explicitly developed to meet project manager's demands. The underlying technique used in this approach is based on Dynamic Bayesian Networks (DBNs). The use of Bayesian Networks (BNs) enables the representation of causal relationships among process and product key performance indicators elicited either by data or expert knowledge. DBNs provide an insight into various aspects of SPM over time to assess current as well as predicting future model states. The objective of this chapter is to describe the practical approach to establish SPM as state of the art decision support in an industrial environment.

INTRODUCTION

The most common way inserting defects into a software product is by applying changes to it. In every software release, hundreds of changes are applied to the software product. Every change has its unique characteristic based on process and product factors. With regard to these factors, every change has its own probability of injecting a defect. This chapter presents a methodology to estimate the amount of defects for a specific software product. It includes a goal oriented model design, detailed description of the process measurement framework including corresponding data mining

DOI: 10.4018/978-1-60960-509-4.ch016

concepts. The approach is based on process and product data combined with expert knowledge from one of the leading companies in the field of embedded applications in automotive industries. The resulting model is called the *Software Process Model* (SPM). SPM is built based on an extended version of the software process V-Model which itself is derived from the waterfall model. Process and product measurement frameworks combined with the knowledge of experts describe every phase of the V-Model and hereby enable the representation as a consistent model on the complete engineering process. SPM is mainly designed to optimize product quality and development effort over time. It enables to assess measures of the process influencing product quality. Due to the dynamic capabilities of the model, it further allows to analyze the impact of possible process and product changes over time. These capabilities give various views to project managers on the current and future software product that are discussed at the end of the chapter to highlight the practical benefit of the model. Details on *automotive software engineering* are part of the background section.

SPM is a Dynamic Bayesian Network (DBN) with capabilities to represent multiple change characteristics of a specific software release. It enables project managers to oversee the impact of every change made within this software release taking these individual change characteristics into account. Bayesian Networks (BNs), the base element for every DBN, are part of modern techniques of artificial intelligence (AI). Although a fundamental theorem on conditional probability was introduced by *The Reverend Thomas Bayes* back in XVIII century (Bayes, 1763), the term "Bayesian network" and its concepts were introduced in the 1980's in pioneering work of Judea Pearl (Pearl, 1985; Pearl, 1988). Experienced researchers have recently put strong statements in the review of one of the books (Darwiche, 2009) on BNs: "Bayesian Networks are as important to AI Artificial Intelligence (AI) and Machine Learn-

ing as Boolean circuits are to computer science", "Bayesian networks have revolutionized AI". A BN can be perceived from two perspectives: (1) as a graph where the nodes represent random variables and the arcs represent the relationships between variables; (2) as a formal mathematical model definition where variables are expressed as conditional probability distributions. A DBN is a model forming a sequence of individual BNs where each individual BN reflects the state of the system at a specific point of time. BNs can be built by applying a learning algorithm to the dataset that enables learning a structure, parameters or both. The greatest potential of BNs lies in the ability to combine expert knowledge with empirical data. Other benefits of BNs include the ability to reflect causal relationships, to run the model with incomplete data, to forward and backward reasoning, explicit modeling of uncertainty as well as combining quantitative and qualitative data. An *introduction to BNs and DBNs* is given as part of the background section.

SPM's structure and data as well as determination of usability, based on expert knowledge, are based on a certified industrial engineering process, focusing on high quality products. Databases on historical and current projects are used to validate the results. Process and project experts have assessed the resulting model for predictive accuracy and usability. All details on how SPM is built are part of the *software process model* section.

BACKGROUND

Automotive Software Engineering

The demand for software products in the automotive industry has been exponentially increasing over the last decades, making software engineering one of its critical success factors (Lee, 2007). The intensive use of *electronic control units* (ECUs) in vehicles today has already lead to an average of 20 ECUs in smaller and even more than 70

ECUs in upper class cars (Hauser, 2004). Complex features with short time to market and minimal engineering costs at very high quality are the challenges to be met. Besides functional complexity, embedded software is subject to domain specific characteristics, especially

- *Code efficiency* due to limitations of processor and memory resources.
- *Code portability* to ensure further development and variant handling.
- *High availability* and *reliability* to support safety critical applications.
- *Real-time operation.*
- *Network operation.*

Given these aspects, the estimation of software defects already plays a major role in the domain of automotive engineering.

Software Engineering

Standardized engineering processes are crucial to continuously improve and adapt to the markets demands. The engineering process, underlying the model presented here, is based on the *V-Model* (IABG, 2009), an international standard for developing information technology systems. V-Model is an enhancement of the common waterfall model and is intended for planning and executing interdisciplinary projects, combining hardware and software as well as high level system engineering activities within a single framework. For decades, the V-Model has been enhanced to reflect the needs of the automotive industry to develop high quality, failsafe products. The V-Model describes different phases of a software release life cycle and focuses on high level system specification and testing as well as on implementation level, module testing respectively. On management level, every phase of the V-Model is supported by specific methods to ensure a seamless integrated engineering environment.

Figure 1 illustrates the V-Model phases. Starting with System Requirements Engineering & Design, high level functions are specified according to the desired product functionality. They are further specified and assigned to specific software components according to their functionality. These components contain software modules building the code base of the product. The assessed product consists of approximately 50 high level functions, 15 components and 100 modules. Detailing requirements and testing is continued from the highest level of function definition down to the module level where mod-

Figure 1. V-Model engineering process phases

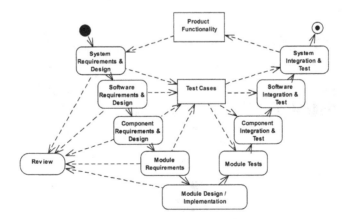

ule reviews and tests are performed. The right side of the V-Model is related to integration and testing. Modules are integrated into components and components are integrated into the overall software. Software engineers assess the software on a more detailed, software related perspective. After software testing, the overall software is integrated in the system forming an ECU as part of a vehicle's functionality. System engineers review and test high level product functionality from the customer's perspective.

Introduction to Bayesian Networks

BN consists of two main representations: graphical and numerical. In a graphical representation a BN is a directed acyclic graph in which the nodes correspond to random variables and the links between pairs of nodes indicate relationships between variables. Numerically a BN consists of a set of probability distributions which define the variables. A node which does not have a link directed from another node is called a root node and it is therefore defined by an unconditional probability distribution. In contrast, a node for which there is at least one incoming link from another node is called a child node and it is defined by a conditional probability distribution.

The inference process in a BN extensively uses a Bayes' Theorem:

$$P(A \mid B) = \frac{P(B \mid A) \cdot P(A)}{P(B)}$$

where:

- $P(A)$ is prior probability of event A,
- $P(B)$ is prior probability of event B,
- $P(B|A)$ is conditional probability of event B given event A,
- $P(A|B)$ is conditional probability of event A given event B.

In the more complex real-life BN models that we use, it is impossible to perform the Bayesian inference calculations manually. Fortunately, there are various efficient algorithms implemented in BN toolkits to do this. They can be either "exact" (e.g.: variable elimination, clique tree propagation, recursive conditioning, enumeration) or "approximate" (e.g.: direct sampling, Markov chain sampling, variational methods, loopy propagation). More on theoretical aspects of BNs can be found in various books (Darwiche, 2009; Jensen, 1996; Neapolitan, 2004; Pearl, 1998, Russel and Norvig, 2003, Winkler, 2003).

Figure 2 illustrates a simple example of a BN consisting of three variables related to software projects. This model assumes that *fast delivery* de-

Figure 2. BN example

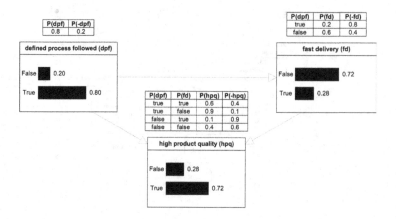

pends on *defined process followed* – i.e. following a defined process requires additional effort apart from pure development effort and thus reduces the ability of fast delivery of a software product. Both *defined process followed* and *fast delivery* influence *high product quality* – having a good process, gives a greater confidence in the quality of a developed product and rushing a project may cause a decrease in product quality. All variables are Boolean, i.e. a value "true" indicates high level of intensity of a given feature and a value "false" indicates low level of intensity of this feature.

One very useful feature of BNs is their ability to run with an incomplete set of observations. This means, the user does not need to provide observations to all predictors in the model, as is required for example in a model represented with an equation. In fact, a BN does not have a separate fixed list of predictors and a separate fixed list of dependant variables. The role of a variable as either a predictor or a dependant variable depends on the scenario of model usage. When the variable has an observation assigned, it becomes the predictor which is used to predict the posterior distribution of variable(s) for which no observation is assigned.

Another important feature of BNs is the ability of forward and backward reasoning. The direction of a link between the nodes represents a direction of statistical influence between this pair of variables, which in many cases also corresponds to their causal relationship. However, this direction does not determine the only way of reasoning.

These features are explained in Figure 3. Let us assume we do not have any information on the state of the nodes in the model. In this case no observation is entered in the model and it is calculated using prior distributions only. In our example, this means the probability of fast product delivery is 0.28 and achieving high product quality is around 0.72. But let us assume that due to some special conditions we do not have a process defined for the project under consideration. After entering such an observation, the model predicts that we will be able to deliver a product faster (*P(fast delivery)*=0.6) but it will be of very low quality (*P(high product quality)*=0.22) (Figure 3, left). To demonstrate the ability of backward reasoning let us assume that *high product quality* becomes a constraint. The model, using an appropriately adopted Bayes' Theorem, predicts that more time has to be spent on the project and it will be less likely to deliver it fast (*P(fast delivery)*≈0.28) (Figure 3, right).

An important problem building a BN is related to obtaining reliable prior distributions. These distributions can be assessed using objective approach by observing the frequencies of features in a system in the past or based on physical aspects of components. In a subjective (Bayesian) approach probability is a measure of personal degree of belief. Thus, it may vary among

Figure 3. Propagation of evidence

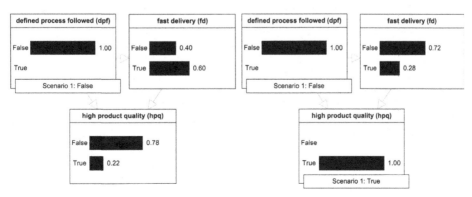

individuals and the whole model may give different predictions depending on whose expert knowledge it is based on.

Depending on the aim of an experiment and the availability of empirical data and expert knowledge four main structures of BNs are used in modeling software engineering issues as illustrated in Figure 4:

- *Naive Bayesian classifier* has a structure of a diverging star with the single dependant variable in the middle and all links directed from the dependant variable to each of the predictors. Such models are usually built automatically, based on empirical data. Experts only need to select appropriate predictors which should be independent of each other.

- *Converging star* has a similar topology to the naive Bayesian classifier with the difference in having reversed directions of links – from each predictor to a single dependant variable. The complexity of the definition of the dependant variable causes such models, even with only very few

predictors, only being built automatically based on collected data.

- *Causal Bayesian net* contains causal relationships between variables. In software engineering they are built automatically on empirical data (both structure and parameters), using a mixture of expert knowledge and empirical data (structure by expert knowledge, parameters using a learning algorithm based on data), or both structure and parameters using expert knowledge only.

- *Dynamic Bayesian net* is a sequence of causal BNs linked sequentially. Each instance represents the system state at a particular point of time and the whole model representing the dynamics of the system.

Both some of the existing models and our new model, proposed in later sections extensively use the notion of ranked nodes (Fenton et al., 2007a). Ranked nodes are used to define qualitative variables which can be expressed on a ranked scale that is where the states can be ordered depending on the degree of intensity of a given feature. Most

Figure 4. Common structures of BNs used in software engineering

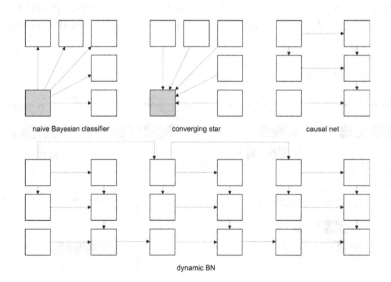

often we use either 5 point scale (from 'very low' to 'very high').

In a ranked node the whole range of possible values is internally defined as the interval [0, 1]. This range is divided in as many equal-width intervals as there are labeled states. Each interval has a label assigned. Users refer to node states by their labels (e.g. 'very low', 'very high'), not by intervals.

During the calculation process the ranked nodes are treated as continuous nodes – their intervals are used. This enables various arithmetic expressions, such as sum, multiplication, etc. and statistics such as mean, median, standard deviation etc. to be calculated. The ability to use various weighted expressions, such as weighted mean, weighted max, weighted min (Fenton et al., 2007a) drastically simplifies the process of defining probability tables.

SOFTWARE PROCESS MODEL

The SPM has been developed to estimate defect correction effort in relation to development effort for a specific feature of a software product, e.g. a Human Machine Interface as part of an ECU. SPM is intended to be used in a number of analyses to support project managers planning or assessing their software project. The major advantage of SPM is its capability to incorporate product, project and process information in form of objective data (e.g. metrics) and subjective data (e.g. expert knowledge) in a causal relationship. Furthermore it takes Key Performance Indicators (KPIs) into account having a significant influence on the estimation variables *development effort* and *defect correction effort*. Figure 5 depicts the process of effort estimation as part of the software release planning. After analyzing the product requirements for a specific feature a task list is built up to define the work packages for the specific release. This task list is used by project managers for planning and tracking as well as by developers assigned to implement specific tasks. For every task of the task list KPIs are considered to estimate engineering effort as a sum of development effort as well as defect correction effort.

Defect Cost Factor

Defect costs can be derived from the rework needed to complete a product. Rework is necessary where a released part of the product needs to be corrected because it does not meet the specified requirements. The amount of rework sometimes is expressed in defects found in a product. Nevertheless the number of defects is only a qualitative description of a product's error rate. As a single indicator it does not characterize the impact of a defect e.g. what is its influence on customer satisfaction or effort needed to correct this defect.

Figure 5. Effort estimation

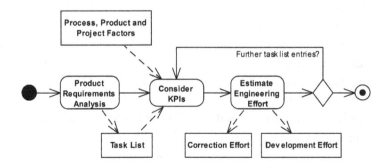

A defect detected in a system and integration test leading to an architectural change is much more cost intensive than an implementation error in a software module especially if the implementation error is detected by a module test. Further categorization with the goal to describe its impact on a project's effort estimation leads to the potential effort needed to fix this defect category. SPM uses the potential defect correction effort as indicator to describe a product's error rate. Furthermore defect correction effort needs to be related to a reference value to indicate its relevance, e.g. 10 hours of defect correction effort in relation to 1000 hours of development effort represents a low defect rate, whereas 10 hours of defect correction effort for a feature with only 5 hours of development indicates a very high defect rate. This leads to the definition of the *defect cost factor* (DCF) representing SPM's measure for an error rate:

$$DCF = \frac{defect\ correction\ effort}{development\ effort}$$

where:

- *DCF* represents the defect cost factor,
- *Defect correction effort* is the effort used to fix a deviation to the requirements,
- *Development effort* represents the effort needed for implementation.

This implies with increasing development effort the potential effort needed for later fixing increases proportionally. In SPM every product feature has a different DCF. Features are different concerning their requirement complexity and volatility, resulting code complexity and finally their testability leading to different DCFs for different features, e.g. it is easier to implement parameter changes ideally supported by a tool taking advantage of code generation compared to

implementing a complex state machine used to realize Human Machine Interface logic.

Methodology

SPM is a DBN representing the successive development tasks being part of a software release life cycle. For every task a single BN is created to estimate development and defect correction effort needed for its finalization. KPIs used in SPM can be devided into five categories:

- *Process activities* represent the influence of process activities, such as process maturity grade and its degree of implementation.
- *Product factors* such as quality of documentation and further engineering artifacts, e.g. if source code is complex and undocumented, there is a high chance that making changes results in a fault-prone implementation.
- *Project factors* are project constraints which may vary over time, e.g. a project's deadline pressure has major influence on a task's error proneness.
- *Change factors* are related to the feature to be developed. Some features are easier to implement than others, resulting in different DCFs for different features.
- *Test activities* incorporate the amount of tests carried out as well as how effective tests are.

These factors form the core parameters of SPM. They are identified to have major influence on a task's error-proneness and consequently to the error-proneness of the overall software product.

Define the Problem

Building the SPM is a challenging task. Figure 6 illustrates the methodology according to (Weiss, 1984) that has been used to build SPM supporting decision makers and project managers in SPM's context respectively. Essential to every expert system is the definition of the problem to be assessed and the important indicators related to it. Following the Goal Question Metric (GQM) approach (Basili, 1988) the definition of the problem includes the purpose of the model, the object of interest, the issue to be modeled and the viewpoint from which the model will be used. This leads to the following problem definition: *Estimate the defect correction effort of every task for a specific feature in a specific software development process from a project manager's point of view.*

Identify KPIs and Relationships

KPIs are indentified together with their relationships among each other. SPM uses statistical data to represent KPIs in their context. These KPIs are described in detail later in this section because they have major influence on SPM's performance. KPIs can be obtained from various sources but it is crucial to consider only data from a similar statistical context (Druzdzel, 2003) otherwise combining these sources on a higher context error

propagation might lead to inaccurate predictions. SPM uses data from

- *Internal process data* from databases, e.g. from change management system where every change to the software is tracked with most of the attributes needed by SPM. Internal data form a major part of SPMs data base also for adding significance to statements made based on a specific model state.
- *Expert Knowledge* from project managers or stakeholders being experts for specific process domains is used where no internal data is available. Sometimes it is not possible to get all necessary data in a productive environment, e.g. usually there is no data on how process maturity and process activity influence defect correction effort.
- *External Data*, e.g. from other companies or the research community should be used very carefully to ensure the model's validity. However it is possible to combine external data with expert knowledge. SPM

Figure 6. SPM's research procedure

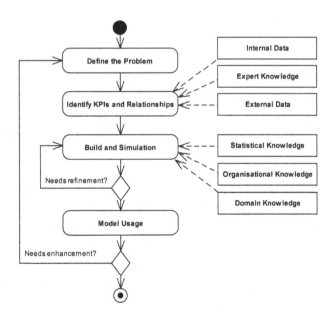

uses external data for the ideal amount of effort spent on testing compared to effort spent on development. Although research results give exact numbers it still needs to be confirmed that these results apply to the context of SPM.

KPIs are derived from the problem definition which is broken down into its major components for further characterization. Questions are used for this refinement. Questions which also project managers might ask to understand the problem to be assessed. For every question there is a set of metrics characterizing it. Metrics represent a model to measure properties of any engineering artifact, KPIs in SPM respectively. Table 1 holds a set of questions along with their metrics characterizing the goal of SPM. Metric type might be numeric or ranked where numeric is an actual value or probability distribution of the correspondent metric and ranked expresses a quantitative description where no qualitative description is available. All questions are related to a single task implementing a specific feature.

Setup the Task Model

The actual build and test stages require expertise from multiple fields of knowledge, which is the main reason making SPM's setup so challenging. On the one hand the model designer has to be a statistician knowing how to collect data and how to represent these data in a cause and effect chain within a BN. On the other hand he has to be fully aware of the problem to be solved by the model. In case of SPM being an expert in software engineering means someone to describe how defect correction effort is influenced by a software engineering process. Furthermore the model designer needs to know the organizational structure in detail. How is the implemented software engineering process established, what kind of data is available and where to acquire it? For every KPI a mapping of real world data to model

data has to be done. The model designer needs to know what is the meaning of the data and which relevance has it for SPM.

SPM offers the possibility to assess characteristics of a feature's defect correction effort in relation to its influencing factors. It is even possible to calculate different what-if scenarios to compare alternatives to the current model settings. The task model in form of a BN illustrated in Figure 7 represents the central part of SPM. It depicts causal relationships represented by the arcs among key performance indicators represented by its nodes. Strong borders indicate the nodes, being calibration nodes, used by the simulation environment to calibrate the model according to the simulation conditions. Model data is elicited based on internal data, expert knowledge and external data whereas data has been made anonymous due to their confidentiality. All KPIs and relations described in the previous section provide the basis for building the model. There are five main category groups in the task model: change factors, test activities, product factors, process activities and project factors described throughout the following sections.

Change Factors

Change factors describe relations among task specific KPIs. The complexity of a feature is influenced by feature specific factors *feature difficulty* and *feature volatility*. It describes the complexity of requirements and its impact on the difficulty to realize the feature. In SPM it is possible to distinguish between three different levels of feature volatility and feature difficulty, from low to high. These nodes are merged with their weighted average to node *feature complexity* with levels from low to high complexity. Feature volatility and complexity are elicited from internal data. They are acquired from the requirements management system used. Feature complexity also influences the DCF due to different error rates for different features. Some features are much easier to realize

Table 1. KPIs and relations

Question	Metric			
	Symbol	**Name**	**Description**	**Type**
What is the difficulty of a feature?	feat_dif	feature difficulty	How difficult is it to realize?	Ranked
	feat_vol	feature volatility	How often are requirements changed?	Ranked
	feat_com	feature complexity	How complex are the requirements of a specific feature?	Ranked
What is the engineering effort?	eng_effort	engineering effort	Effort used to develop a single task including effort spent on test activities.	Numeric
	task_type	type of task	Category of a specific task describing its complexity.	Ranked
What is the potential defect correction effort?	corr_effort	defect correction effort	Potential effort used to fix a deviation according to the requirements.	Numeric
	dev_effort	development effort	Effort to implement a single task in hours.	Numeric
	cost_factor	defect cost factor	Factor indicating a feature's error-proneness.	Numeric
	corr_final	defect correction effort after testing	Residing defect correction effort after finishing a task.	Numeric
What is the testing effectiveness?	test_effect	testing effectiveness	How many defects can be found by testing activities?	Numeric
	test_effort	effort spent on testing	Effort used for testing after implementation.	Numeric
	test_ratio	test ratio	Amount of testing as a proportion of development effort.	Ranked
	test_payoff	test payoff	Defect detection potential. How good are test activities established?	Ranked
	defects_found	defects found	Reduction of potential defect correction effort.	Numeric
What are product factors?	prod_fact	product factor	Existing product as base for further development.	Ranked
	prod_docq	documentation quality	Understandability of the product base.	Ranked
	prod_codq	code quality	Ease of understanding, changing, enhancing the existing code base.	Ranked
What are project activities?	dead_pres	deadline pressure	Amount of pressure put on the engineering team to finish a task within a specific time frame.	Ranked
What are process activities?	proc_act	process activities	Supporting measure for less error-prone engineering.	Ranked
	proc_org	process organization	Maturity level of the organizational process definition.	Ranked
	proc_app	process application	Implementation of maturity level.	Ranked

resulting in a low DCF whereas other features, e.g. with a high volatility and complexity have much higher DCFs. Furthermore it is influenced by process activities and project factors indicating the engineering environment quality. The higher the quality of these influencing factors the lower the DCF. SPM is calibrated as illustrated in Table 2.

Figure 7. Task model BN

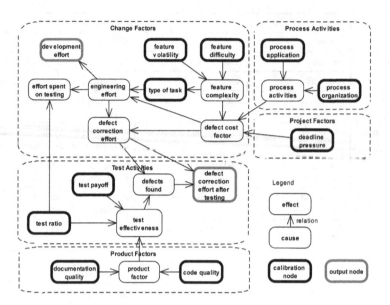

Based on feature complexity the *type of task* is determined. It holds a distribution defining the amount of task categories used for a specific feature complexity, e.g. a feature with low complexity responsible for parameter maintenance within the product are developed by mostly smaller tasks consuming only a small amount of effort because in the majority of cases only parameters would be changed. Whereas features with higher complexity, e.g. a human machine interface development are realized mainly by larger tasks consuming more effort. The average *engineering effort* needed for development is elicited based on the type of task. It includes all activities for a task including requirements and design, implementation and testing. Engineering effort spent without testing is expressed in node *development effort*. It is dependant on effort spent

on testing as a result of the test activities. SPM is calibrated based on the following data set illustrated in Table 3. It has been elicited based on internal process data derived from the change management system used.

The potential *defect correction effort* results from the average engineering effort needed for a specific type of task in combination with a feature's DCF. It estimates how much defect correction effort will be needed after task implementation. It is the basis for the potential amount of defects to be found by all test activities.

Process Activities, Product and Project Factors

Process organization and *process application* represent the maturity level and its application of

Table 2. Features

	Feature 1	Feature 2	Feature 3	Feature 4	Feature 5
Volatility	Medium	High	Low	Low	Low
Complexity	Medium	High	Low	Low	Low
DCF	0,08	0,10	0,04	0,00	0,01

Table 3. Type of task distribution

Type of Task	Feature Complexity			Engineering Effort
	Low	Medium	High	
Category A	1,08%	8,23%	14,29%	7.15
Category B	74,19%	60,13%	45,71%	3.84
Category C	7,73%	25,32%	22,86%	19.58
Category D	3,09%	0,00%	5,71%	53.9
Category E	13,91%	6,33%	11,43%	5.31

Table 4. Deadline pressure

Effort	Process Activities and Project Factors		
	Low	Medium	High
corr_effort	100%	350%	500%
eng_effort	100%	50%	37.5%

an organization. It is a measure of how capable process activities are to continuously ensure the development of high quality products. Both process organization and process application are merged to *process activities* by their weighted minimum. The *deadline pressure* of a project influences the DCF of a feature as well as all process activities. With higher deadline pressure and low process activities it is possible to lower the average engineering effort to realize a specific task down to 50% of its origin effort. The consequences lead up to 350% more defects compared to ideal engineering conditions. Further pressure in combination with low process activities reduce the average engineering effort down to 37.5% with the effect to increase the potential amount of defects up to 500%. Data leading to Table 4 has been acquired based on a design of experiment carried out to calibrate this node (Wuchenauer, 2009).

Product factors *documentation quality* and *code quality* represent a software product's testability. They have a major influence on a feature's error rate after the tests. The better these product factors the more effective testing is possible leading to higher defect detection rates. These nodes are defined by expert knowledge and merged in node *product factors* by their weighted minimum.

Test Activities

The better the test process is established, assuming the product is testable and there is enough effort spent on testing, the fewer defects reside in the final product. *Test payoff* and *test ratio* influence the *test effectiveness*. Test payoff is the amount of defects that can be found by test activities as a proportion of the estimated defect correction effort. Test ratio is the relative amount of engineering effort spent on testing. The higher the test ratio the more effort is spent on testing as illustrated in Table 5.

Both test payoff and test ratio are merged by their weighted average in node test effectiveness.

Table 5. Effort spent on testing

test_ratio	test_effort / eng_effort
Low	10%
Medium	20%
High	40%

Table 6. Defect detection rates

Test Effectiveness		Detection Rate
Test Payoff	**Test Ratio**	
Low	Low	1%
Low	Medium	30%
Low	High	40%
Medium	Low	5%
Medium	Medium	37%
Medium	High	53%
High	Low	10%
High	Medium	75%
High	High	87%

Table 6 illustrates different detection rates for all combinations of test ratio and test payoff levels. Detection rates are elicited based on external data (Jones, 2000) indicating how successful test activities can be.

Defects found and *defect correction effort after testing* are arithmetical nodes combing estimated defect correction effort from change factors with test activities.

Measurement Concept

For all data a measurement concept has to be established to continuously supply SPM with fresh data. Figure 8 illustrates the measurement concept for eliciting the following nodes:

- Feature volatility indicated by a feature's requirements change rates.
- Type of task as the category for changes.
- Effort needed for every type of task, change, defect and defect correction.

Figure 8. Measurement concept

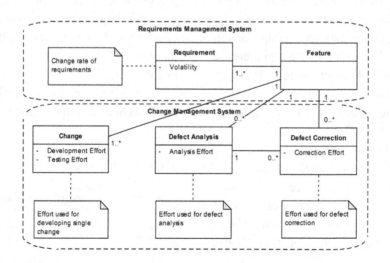

Figure 9. Setup SPM

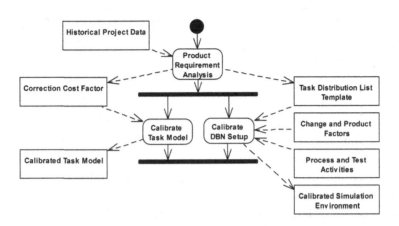

- Defect analysis and defect correction as specific type of tasks.

This data is collected in two different management systems, one for managing and developing requirements, the other for managing tasks and changes respectively. In this measurement concept every node has a relation to the feature it describes. A feature has at least one requirement related to it whereas every requirement is related to exactly one feature. Changes, defect analysis and correction nodes also relate to exactly one feature. There is at least one change related to a feature in the sense that the measurement concept needs at least one data point to be applied to. Features might have zero defects and therefore no defect correction nodes related to it. But if a feature has defects there is always one defect analysis node describing the defect and, in case it can be fixed, a defect correction node describing what needs to be fixed to solve the defect.

Simulation

After building the model it can be used for test runs. Typically models like SPM need calibration until they perform as expected. Finally the model is validated against its initial requirements whether it fulfils the solution of the problem definition derived from the first stage.

From simulation perspective Figure 9 shows how the SPM is set up. It is crucial to every form of effort estimation to calibrate the KPIs influencing the development effort of a specific product feature. Therefore *product requirement analysis* acts as entry point to SPM's setup to categorize the feature to be assessed according to its feature complexity. In *calibrate task model* and *calibrate DBN setup* SPM is calibrated according to the results of the product requirement analysis. SPM uses five different features along with its DCFs according to building the task model from the previous section. Product features are assigned to one of the predefined complexity and volatility levels where DCF is based on. Based on this analysis, the task distribution template illustrated in Table 7 and correspondent DCFs are determined. Every task in the task distribution list is calibrated according to its KPIs enabling SPM to vary product, process and project factors over time.

In typical engineering environments these data can be derived from historical project data but could also be obtained based on expert judgment. If a feature already has been developed in another project the former distribution of tasks can be taken as basis for the current estimation and

Table 7. Task distribution list template

Task Number	Feature Complexity	Type of Change	Product Factors	Process Activities	Project Factors	Testing Effectiveness
Number	Ranked	List	Ranked	Ranked	Ranked	Ranked

adjusted by an expert according to their degree of belief. The feature might also be similar to another feature already implemented in the past. In this case the former distribution could be taken for the current task distribution list and adjusted according to its new characteristics. For calibration correspondent DCFs and a task distribution list template with 206 data points are elicited according to the measurement concept from the previous section.

After SPM is calibrated, the final DBN is built using the simulation environment and the task model shown in Figure 10. The simulation environment holds information for every task about the feature to be developed. Iterating over these tasks it *creates separate BN sub models*, each for every task and updates the task model with task specific evidence. The sub model is *joined to the DBN* accordingly. Finally SPM is ready to run its *calculations* according to the evidence that

has been entered to it. Calculation takes place for every BN sub model taking previously calculated models into account if required. Results are stored back in the simulation environment explicitly for every BN sub model, for every task and for every related KPI. This enables project managers to assess the characteristics of KPIs developing over time. *Analyzing results* according to the definition of the problem, the calibration of features, tasks and KPIs are discussed in the following section.

Model Usage

The final step for SPM is its validation regarding the problem statement. In the case of SPM it is the estimation of defect correction effort of every task for a specific feature in the software release cycle from a project manager's viewpoint. The following scenario is used to verify how SPM performs with regard to estimation. Five features

Figure 10. SPM execution

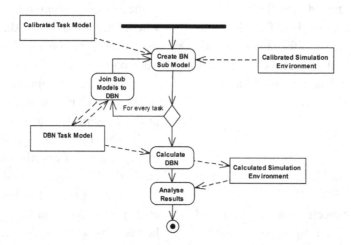

along with their volatility and complexity are defined from the requirements management system. They are related to 412 data points from change management system and split into calibration and validation data, each of the 206 data points randomly selected. In combination with expert knowledge in areas where no data is available it is used to calibrate

- feature volatility, complexity and DCF,
- task distribution template,
- task model,
- change and product factors,
- process and test activities.

Validation results after simulation are presented in Table 8 in form of the median of the resulting probability distribution. For Feature 1 SPM predicted 246 hours of engineering effort and 23 hours for defect correction effort. Prediction accuracy is calculated in relation to the reference data set. SPM achieves an accuracy of 95% for engineering effort and 97% for defect correction effort. Similar to Feature 2, 3 and 4 prediction accuracy is over 75%. For Feature 5 prediction accuracy is lower, 63% for engineering effort and 14% for defect correction effort. Deviation in prediction accuracy for feature 5 compared to the other features could be a result of only a small amount of reference data available for model calibration.

Complex DBNs are very processor time consuming, depending on processor speed, amount of tasks to be estimated and BN specific algorithmic features, e.g. does the BN engine use dynamic discretization or not. In the case of SPM simulation takes about 120 minutes on a 2GHz dual core processor.

To demonstrate SPM's analyzing capabilities two scenarios are compared. In both scenarios feature 1 and 2 are developed, distributed over 93 tasks according to the feature's correspondent type of task distribution. Scenario 1 represents a project under normal development conditions of a mature organization, medium deadline pressure, high process application, high defect detection potential with a high amount of testing. In contrast to this, scenario 2 represents a project where deadlines are close, low process and test activities with focus to reducing the development effort to a minimum. Table 9 illustrates the main differences between scenarios 1 and 2.

Table 8. Prediction accuracy

Feature	Prediction		Reference		Accuracy	
	eng_effort	corr_effort	eng_effort	corr_effort	eng_effort	corr_effort
Feature 1	246	23	260	22	95%	97%
Feature 2	257	32	258	35	100%	92%
Feature 3	126	4	143	3	88%	77%
Feature 4	186	2	218	2	85%	84%
Feature 5	81	1	51	0	63%	14%

Table 9. Project scenarios

	Deadline Pressure	**Process Application**	**Defect Detection Potential**	**Amount of Testing**
Scenario 1	Medium	High	High	High
Scenario 2	High	Low	Low	Low

Figure 11. Development effort

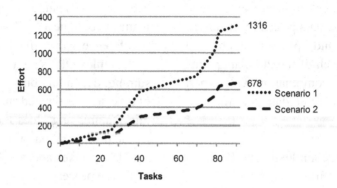

Figure 11 illustrates the results. Calculated values represent the median of the resulting probability distribution. SPM estimates 1316 hours of development effort for scenario 1 and 678 hours for scenario 2. The development effort needed to realize the features is reduced down to 50% where scenario 2 meets the target to reduce development effort to a minimum.

Due to the missing quality and testing measures there is a higher amount of hidden defect correction effort in scenario 2. Figure 12 illustrates this. In scenario 1 with normal deadline pressure and established quality measures support the development of robust software leading to a very small amount of potential defect correction effort (41 hours). In contrast, scenario 2 has 1119 hours of

potential defect correction effort still pending at the end of the project.

Table 10 depicts the overall effort needed to get a product at a similar quality level. In scenario 1 SPM estimates 1316 hours of development effort and 41 hours of potential defect correction effort. The resulting overall effort is 1357 hours. Scenario 2 has 678 hours of development effort and 1119 hours of defect correction effort resulting in 1797 hours overall effort. Thus scenario 2 working at high deadline pressure with supposed low overall effort overruns scenario 1 by 440 hours, 24% respectively.

Based on such a scenario analysis, arguing for any scenario is well-founded, based not only on the knowledge of a single expert but incorporat-

Figure 12. Defect correction effort

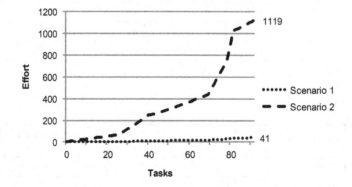

Table 10 Simulation results

Scenario 1	Development Effort1316	Defect Correction Effort41	Overall Effort1357
Scenario 2	678	1119	1797

ing knowledge from multiple experts possibly from different domains, e.g. project management, development or testing. Furthermore the argumentation is based on empirical data from various sources of the implemented engineering process and hereby further supports a decision in this specific context.

FUTURE RESEARCH DIRECTIONS

A further step to enhance the estimation of a software product's potential defect correction effort is to represent every engineering phase separately at a higher level of detail. SPM in its current version estimates the total defect correction effort over all phases of the engineering process. The design of a model incorporating explicitly the KPIs of every single engineering phase offers a wider range of optimization possibilities regarding effort estimation. This improvement enables not only to estimate the potential defect correction effort per engineering phase but also to consider the flow of defects from one phase to another. The resulting model is called the *Defect Cost Flow Model* (DCFM) where a defect's origin is assessed in relation to the place where it is detected. DCFM takes the variation of effort, costs respectively, over multiple process phases into account. From this it follows that not only project managers but also process responsible could have a benefit of DCFM.

CONCLUSION

Even though there are many metric and related effort estimation programs established for a long period of time (Ordonez, 2008) the final breakthrough and commitment to metric based software quality assessment is still missing. These metric programs form the basis for further effort estimation methods such as SPM. SPM shows that based on accurate data it is possible to handle complex structures as well as incomplete and changing data. To achieve the goal of building a decision support system based on BNs it is crucial to have data representing the real world. It is essential to have a positive way of managing errors in order that employees as well as project managers use a defect tracking system that potentially has negative influence on their reputation. Furthermore employees need to belief that continuous improvement programs alleviate daily work. With the commitment to such programs the results of SPM show that it is possible to predict defect correction effort at high accuracy.

SPM demonstrates the potential of using a system based on BNs to support decisions in the context of software effort estimation. Even though it is very challenging to build such complex models, BNs include a wide range of benefits. BNs offer the possibility to support decision makers based on objective process and product data as well as on expert knowledge. Using BNs project managers could not only monitor the current situation of a project but also estimate and predict project behavior under specific circumstances. BNs enable decision makers to justify and document their decisions. Based on the graphical representation of cause and effect it is easy to communicate even complex problems and identify weaknesses or even new aspects in such complex domains as software effort estimation.

REFERENCES

Basili, V. R., & Rombach, H. D. (1988). The TAME project. Towards improvement-oriented software environments. *IEEE Transactions on Software Engineering, 14*(6), 758–773. doi:10.1109/32.6156

Bayes, T. (1763). An essay towards solving a problem in the doctrine of chances. *Philosophical Transactions of the Royal Society of London, 53*, 370–418. doi:10.1098/rstl.1763.0053

Bibi, S., & Stamelos, I. (2004). Software process modeling with Bayesian belief networks. *Proceedings of 10th International Software Metrics Symposium*, Chicago.

Cockram, T. (2001). Gaining confidence in software inspection using a Bayesian belief model. *Software Quality Journal, 9*(1), 31–42. doi:10.1023/A:1016600602423

Dabney, J. B., Barber, G., & Ohi, D. (2006). Predicting software defect function point ratios using a Bayesian belief network. *Proceedings of 2nd International Workshop on Predictor Models in Software Engineering*, Philadelphia, PA.

Darwiche, A. (2009). *Modeling and reasoning with Bayesian networks*. Cambridge University Press.

Druzdzel, M. J., & Dez, F. J. (2003). Combining knowledge from different sources in causal probabilistic models. *Journal of Machine Learning Research, 4*, 295–316. doi:10.1162/jmlr.2003.4.3.295

Fenton, N., Hearty, P., Neil, M., & Radliński, Ł. (2009). Software project and quality modelling using Bayesian networks. In Meziane, F., & Vadera, S. (Eds.), *Artificial intelligence applications for improved software engineering development: New prospects* (pp. 1–25). Hershey, PA: IGI-Global.

Fenton, N., Marsh, W., Neil, M., Cates, P., Forey, S., & Tailor, M. (2004). Making resource decisions for software projects. *Proceedings of the 26th International Conference on Software Engineering*, Washington, DC, IEEE Computer Society, (pp. 397–406).

Fenton, N. E., Neil, M., & Caballero, J. G. (2007). Using ranked nodes to model qualitative judgements in Bayesian networks. *IEEE Transactions on Knowledge and Data Engineering, 19*(10), 1420–1432. doi:10.1109/TKDE.2007.1073

Fenton, N. E., Neil, M., Marsh, W., Krause, P., & Mishra, R. (2007). Predicting software defects in varying development lifecycles using Bayesian nets. *Information and Software Technology, 43*(1), 32–43. doi:10.1016/j.infsof.2006.09.001

Hauser, H. M. (2004). *The growing importance of embedded software: Managing hybrid hardware-software business*. (Technical report, The Boston Consulting Group, Inc).

Hearty, P., Fenton, N., Marquez, D., & Neil, M. (2009). Predicting project velocity in XP using a learning dynamic Bayesian network model. *IEEE Transactions on Software Engineering, 37*(1), 124–137. doi:10.1109/TSE.2008.76

IABG. (2009). *V-model*. Retrieved December 14, 2009, from http://v-modell.iabg.de/

Jensen, F. V. (1996). *An introduction to Bayesian networks*. London, UK: UCL Press.

Jones, C. (2000). *Software quality: Analysis and guidelines for success*. International Thomson Computer Press.

Lee, I., Leung, J. Y. T., & Son, S. H. (2007). *Handbook of real-time and embedded systems*. Chapman & Hall/CRC.

Neapolitan, R. E. (2004). *Learning Bayesian networks*. Upper Saddle River, NJ: Pearson Prentice Hall.

Ordonez, M. J., & Haddad, H. M. (2008). *The state of metrics in software industry*. Information Technology: New Generations.

Pai, G., Bechta-Dugan, J., & Lateef, K. (2005). Bayesian networks applied to software IV&V. *Proceedings of 29th Annual IEEE/NASA Software Engineering Workshop*, IEEE Computer Society, Washington, DC, (pp. 293-304).

Pai, G. I., & Dugan, J. B. (2007). Empirical analysis of software fault content and fault proneness using Bayesian methods. *IEEE Transactions on Software Engineering, 33*(10), 675–686. doi:10.1109/TSE.2007.70722

Pearl, J. (1985). Bayesian networks: A model of self-activated memory for evidential reasoning. (UCLA Technical Report CSD-850017). *Proceedings of the 7th Conference of the Cognitive Science Society*, University of California, Irvine, CA. (pp. 329–334).

Pearl, J. (1988). *Probabilistic reasoning in intelligent systems: Networks of plausible inference*. San Francisco, CA: Morgan Kaufmann.

Radlinski, L. (2008). *Improved software project risk assessment using Bayesian nets*. Unpublished doctoral dissertation, Queen Mary, University of London, London.

Radliński, Ł. (2009). Predicting defect types in software projects. *Polish Journal of Environmental Studies, 18*(3B), 311–315.

Radliński, Ł., Fenton, N., Neil, M., & Marquez, D. (2007). Improved decision-making for software managers using Bayesian networks. *Proceedings of 11th IASTED International Conference Software Engineering and Applications*, Cambridge, MA. (pp. 13–19).

Russell, S., & Norvig, P. (2003). *Artificial intelligence: A modern spproach* (2nd ed.). Upper Saddle River, NJ: Pearson Education, Inc.

Stewart, B. (2002). Predicting project delivery rates using the naive–Bayes classifier. *Journal of Software Maintenance and Evolution: Research and Practice, 14*, 161–179. doi:10.1002/smr.250

Weiss, S. M., & Kulikowsky, C. A. (1984). *A practical guide to designing expert systems*. Yourdon Press.

Winkler, R. L. (2003). *An introduction to Bayesian inference and decision* (2nd ed.). Gainsville, FL: Probabilistic Publishing.

Wooff, D. A., Goldstein, M., & Coolen, F. P. A. (2002). Bayesian graphical models for software testing. *IEEE Transactions on Software Engineering, 28*(5), 510–525. doi:10.1109/TSE.2002.1000453

Wuchenauer, V. (2009). *Ein empirisches Vorgehen zur Prognostizierung von Softwarefehlern auf Basis ausgewählter Entwicklungsprozessgrößen eingebetteter Software im Automobilbereich*. Unpublished master's thesis, University of Stuttgart, Stuttgart.

Zhou, Y., Würsch, M., Giger, E., Gall, H. C., & Lü, J. (2008). A Bayesian network based approach for change coupling prediction. *Proceedings of the 15th Working Conference on Reverse Engineering*, Washington, DC, IEEE Computer Society, (pp. 27–36).

ADDITIONALREADING

Table 11 summarizes recently developed BNs for various issues in the area of software engineering. Most of them enable the prediction of software development effort or various aspects of software quality. Some of those with causal topology enable both effort and quality prediction.

Table 11. Summary of existing BNs for software engineering

Author	Main problem analyzed	BN topology
Radliński, 2009	types of defects	naive Bayesian classifier
Stewart, 2002	effort, productivity	naive Bayesian classifier
Pai et al., 2005	maturity of requirements	converging star
Zhou et al., 2008	change coupling	converging star
Cockram, 2001	effectiveness of inspections	causal
Dabney, 2006	defect rate	causal
Fenton et al., 2004	trade-off between: functionality, effort, quality	causal
Fenton et al., 2008; Fenton et al., 2007b	defects, partly: effort	causal/dynamic BN
Pai and Dugan, 2007	fault content, fault proneness	causal
Radliński et al., 2007; Radlinski, 2008	trade-off between: functionality, effort, quality	causal
Wagner, 2009	various aspects of software quality	causal
Woof et al., 2002	testing process	causal
Bai et al., 2005	failures	dynamic BN
Bibi, 2004	effort	dynamic BN
Fenton et al., 2009; Radlinski, 2008	defects	dynamic BN
Hearty, 2009	project velocity (functionality)	dynamic BN

Compilation of References

Aaen, I., Arent, J., Mathiassen, L., & Ngwenyama, O. (2002). A conceptual map of software process improvement. *Scandinavian Journal of Information Systems*, *13*(13), 81–101.

Aaen, I., Börjesson, A., & Mathiassen, L. (2007). SPI agility: How to navigate improvement projects. *Software Process Improvement and Practice*, *12*(3), 267. doi:10.1002/spip.309

Abrial, J. R. (1996). *The B book-assigning programs to meanings*. Cambridge, UK: Cambridge University Press. doi:10.1017/CBO9780511624162

Addis, M., Ferris, J., Greenwood, M., Li, P., Marvin, D., Oinn, T., & Wipat, A. (2003). Experiences with e-science workflow specification and enactment in bioinformatics. In *Proceedings of UK e-Science All Hands Meeting*, (pp. 459–467).

Adolph, S., Bramble, P., Cockburn, A., & Pols, A. (2003). *Patterns for effective use cases*. Addison-Wesley.

Aggarwal, K. K., Singh, Y., Kaur, A., & Malhotra, R. (2005). *Software reuse metrics for object-oriented systems*. (pp. 48-55). Third ACIS Int'l Conference on Software Engineering Research, Management and Applications (SERA'05).

Agrawal, H. (1994). Dominators, super blocks, and program coverage. *Proceedings of the 21st ACM SIGPLAN-SIGACT Symposium on Principles of Programming Languages*, (pp. 25-34).

Agrawal, H., Demillo, R. A., & Spafford, E. H. (1991). Dynamic slicing in presence of unconstrained pointers. *Proceedings of the ACM SIGSOFT91 Symposium On Software Testing, Analysis and Verification*, (pp. 60-73).

Agresti, W. (2000). Knowledge management. *Advances in Computers*, *53*(5), 171–283. doi:10.1016/S0065-2458(00)80006-6

AirTight Networks. (2005). *Best practices for securing your enterprise wireless perimeter* (pp. 1–6). AirTight Networks.

Akbiyik, E. K. (2008). Service oriented system design through process decomposition. MS thesis, Computer Engineering Department, Middle East Technical University, Ankara, Turkey.

Alavi, M., & Leidner, D. E. (1999). Knowledge management systems: Issues, challenges, and benefits. *Communications of the AIS*, *1*, 7.

Albinet, A., Begoc, S., Boulanger, J.-L., et al. (2008). *The MeMVaTEx methodology: From requirements to models in automotive application*. ERTS 2008, Toulouse, France.

Albinet, A., Boulanger, J.-L., Dubois, H., et al. (2007). Model-based methodology for requirements traceability in embedded systems. In *Proceedings of ECMDA*, June 2007.

Alexander, I. F., & Stevens, R. (2002). *Writing better requirements*. Addison-Wesley.

Alexander, C. (1975). *The Oregon experiment*. Oxford University Press.

Alexander, C. (1979). *The timeless way of building*. Oxford University Press.

Alexander, C., Ishikawa, S., & Silverstein, M. (1977). *A pattern language: Towns, buildings, construction*. Oxford University Press.

Allen, G., Goodale, T., Radke, T., Russell, M., Seidel, E., & Davis, K. (2003). Enabling applications on the Grid: A gridlab overview. *International Journal of High Performance Computing Applications, 17*(4), 449. doi:10.1177/10943420030174008

Altintas, N. I., Cetin, S., & Dogru, A. (2007). Industrializing software development: The factory automation way. *LNCS, 4473,* 54–68.

Amandi, A. A. (1997). Object oriented agent programming. Porto Alegre: CPGCC/UFRGS, 1997. Unpublished doctoral thesis.

Ambriola, V., & Gervasi, V. (1997). Processing natural language requirements. *Proceedings of the 12th IEEE Conference on Automated Software Engineering (ASE '97).*

André, C., Malet, F., & Peraldi-Frati, M.-A. (2007). A multiform time approach to real-time system modeling: Application to an automotive system. In *Proceedings of IEEE Industrial Embedded Systems,* July 2007.

Andreevskaia, A. (2003). *Knowledge acquisition for dynamic personalization in e-commerce.* Thesis, Dept Computer Science, Concordia Univ., Montreal, Canada.

Appleton, B. A. (1997). Patterns and software: Essential concepts and terminology. *Object Magazine Online, 3*(5), 20–25.

Apshvalka, D., Donina, D., & Kirikova, M. (2009). Understanding the problems of Requirements elicitation process: A human perspective. In *Information Systems development challenges in practice, theory, and education,* vol. 1. (pp 211-223). Springer US.

Arango, G. (1988). *Domain engineering for software reuse.* Unpublished doctoral thesis, Department of Information and Computer Science, University of California, Irvine.

Arisholm, E. (2006). *Empirical assessment of the impact of structural properties on the changeability of object oriented software, information and software technology* (pp. 1046–1055). Elsevier.

Arnold, R. S. (1990). *Heuristics for salvaging reusable parts from Ada code.* (SPC Technical Report, ADA_REUSE_HEURISTICS-90011-N).

Arveson, P. (1999). *The balanced scorecard and knowledge management.* The Balanced Scorecard Institute.

Aurum, A., & Wohlin, C. (2005). *Engineering and managing software requirements.* Springer-Verlag. doi:10.1007/3-540-28244-0

Aurum, A., Jeffery, R., Wohlin, C., & Handzic, M. (2003). *Managing software engineering knowledge.* Germany: Springer.

Awazu, Y. (2004). Knowledge management in distributed environments: Roles of informal network players. *Proceedings of the 37th Annual Hawaii International Conference on System Sciences,* (p. 6).

Banks, D., Dashiell, W., Gallagher, L., Hagwood, C., Kacker, R., & Rosenthal, L. (1998). *Software testing by statistical methods preliminary success estimates for approaches based on binomial models, coverage designs, mutation testing, and usage models.* Technical Report – NIST.

Bansiya, J., & Davis, C. (2002). A hierarchical model for object-oriented design quality assessment. *IEEE Transactions on Software Engineering, 28*(1), 4–17. doi:10.1109/32.979986

Barga, R., & Gannon, D. (2007). Scientific versus business workflows. *Workflows for e-science: Scientific workflows for Grids,* 9–16.

Barker, A., & Van Hemert, J. (2008). Scientific workflow: A survey and research directions. *Parallel Processing and Applied Mathematics,* 746–753.

Basili, V., Briand, L., & Melo, W. L. (1996). A validation of object oriented design metrics as quality indicators. *IEEE Transactions on Software Engineering, 22*(10), 751–761. doi:10.1109/32.544352

Basili, V. R., & Rombach, H. D. (1988). The TAME project. Towards improvement-oriented software environments. *IEEE Transactions on Software Engineering, 14*(6), 758–773. doi:10.1109/32.6156

Bassani, P. S., Passerino, L. M., Pasqualotti, P. R., Ritzel, M. I. (2006). Towards a methodological proposal for collaborative education software. *Novas Tecnologias na Educação Magazine, 4*(1).

Baudry, B., Fleurey, F., Le Traon, Y., & Jézéquel, J. M. (2005). An original approach for automatic test cases optimization: A bacteriologic algorithm. *IEEE Software, 22*(2), 76–82. doi:10.1109/MS.2005.30

Bayes, T. (1763). An essay towards solving a problem in the doctrine of chances. *Philosophical Transactions of the Royal Society of London, 53*, 370–418. doi:10.1098/rstl.1763.0053

Beck, K., & Cunningham, W. (1987). *Using pattern languages for object-oriented programs*. OOPSLA 1987 Workshop on the Specification and Design for Object-Oriented Programming, Orlando, USA, October 4-8.

Beizer, B. (1990). *Software testing techniques* (2nd ed.). Thomson Computer Press.

Bellifemine, F., Caire, G., Poggi, A., & Rimassa, G. (2003). *JADE: A White Paper*. Retrieved from http://jade.tilab.com/

Bennedsen, J. (2006). The dissemination of pedagogical patterns. *Computer Science Education, 16*(2), 119–136. doi:10.1080/08993400600733590

Benson, J. P. (1981). Adaptive search techniques applied to software testing. *Proceedings of the 1981 ACM Workshop/Symposium on Measurement and Evaluation of Software Quality*, (pp. 109-116).

Berners Lee, T., Cailiau, R., Luotonen, A., Nielsen, H. F., & Secret, A. (1994). The World Wide Web. *Communications of the ACM, 37*(8), 76–82. doi:10.1145/179606.179671

Berriman, G. B., Deelman, E., Good, J., Jacob, J. C., Katz, D. S., Laity, A. C., …Prince, T. A. (2007). Generating complex astronomy workflows. *Workflows for e-science: Scientific workflows for Grids*, 19–38.

Berry, D. M., Kamsties, E., & Krieger, M. M. (2003). *From contract drafting to software specification: Linguistic sources of ambiguity–a handbook (version 1.0). Technical report*. Ontario, Canada: University of Waterloo – Computer Science Department.

Beydeda, S., & Gruhn, V. (2003). *Test case generation according to the binary search strategy*. (LNCS 2869), (pp. 1000-1007).

Bibi, S., & Stamelos, I. (2004). Software process modeling with Bayesian belief networks. *Proceedings of 10th International Software Metrics Symposium*, Chicago.

Bieman, J. (1991). *Deriving measures of software reuse in object-oriented systems. (TR CS-91-112)*. Colorado State University.

Bieman, J., & Xia Zhao, J. (1995). Reuse through inheritance: A quantitative study of C++ software. *Proceedings of the ACM Symposium on Software Reusability* (SSR '95), Seattle, WA, (pp. 47–52).

Birukou, A., & Weiss, M. (2009). *Patterns 2.0: A service for searching patterns*. The Fourteenth European Conference on Pattern Languages of Programs (EuroPLoP 2009), Irsee, Germany, July 8-12.

Bittencourt, G. (1998). Distributed artificial intelligence. *Proceedings of the First Workshop of Computing - ITA*.

Bjornson, F. O., & Dingsoyr, T. (2005). *A study of a mentoring program for knowledge transfer in a small software consultancy company. (LNCS 3547)*. Berlin / Heidelberg, Germany: Springer.

Bjørnson, F. O., & Dingsøyr, T. (2008). Knowledge management in software engineering: A systematic review of studied concepts, findings and research methods used. *Information and Software Technology, 50*(11), 1055–1068. doi:10.1016/j.infsof.2008.03.006

Bleul, S., Weise, T., & Geihs, K. (2006). *Large-scale service composition in semantic service discovery*. The 8th IEEE International Conference on e-Commerce Technology and The 3rd IEEE International Conference on Enterprise Computing, E-Commerce, and E-Services (CEC/EEE'06), (p. 64).

Blum, B. I. (1992). *Software engineering, a holistic view*. New York, NY: Oxford University Press.

Bodik, R., Gupta, R., & Mary, L. S. (1997). *Refining data flow information using infeasible paths*. (pp. 361-377). FSE-1997, Springer.

Boehm, B. (1981). *Software engineering economics*. Englewood Cliffs, NJ: Prentice-Hall.

Boehm, B., & Basili, V. R. (2001). Software defect reduction top 10 list. *IEEE Computer, 34*(1), 135–137.

Boehm, B. (1996). Identifying quality-requirement conflicts. *IEEE Software, 13*(2), 25–35. doi:10.1109/52.506460

Boehm, B., & Ross, R. (1989). Theory-w software project management principles and examples. *IEEE Transactions on Software Engineering, 15*(7), 902–916. doi:10.1109/32.29489

Bois, P. D., Dubois, E., & Zeippen, J. M. (1997). On the use of a formal RE language-the generalized railroad crossing problem. *Proceedings of the Third IEEE International Symposium on Requirements Engineering*, (pp. 128–137).

Boisot, M. H. (1998). *Knowledge assets: Securing competitive advantage in the information economy*. Oxford University Press.

Bon, P., Boulanger, P.-L., & Mariano, G. (2003). *Semi formal modeling and formal specification: UML & B in simple railway application*. ICSSEA 2003, December 2-4 2003.

Bontis, N., Dragonetti, N. C., Jacobsen, K., & Roos, G. (1999). The knowledge toolbox: A review of the tools available to measure and manage intangible resources. *European Management Journal*, *17*(4), 391–402. doi:10.1016/S0263-2373(99)00019-5

Borchers, J. (2001). *A pattern approach to interaction design*. John Wiley and Sons.

Borges, L. M. S., & Falbo, R. A. (2002). Managing software process knowledge. *Proceedings of the International Conference on Computer Science, Software Engineering, Information Technology, e-Business, and Applications* (CSITeA'2002), (pp. 227–232).

Bose, R., & Sugumaran, V. (2003). Application of knowledge management technology in customer relationship management. *Knowledge and Process Management*, *10*(1), 3–17. doi:10.1002/kpm.163

Boulanger, J.-L., Bon, P., & Mariano, G. (2004). From UML to B-a level crossing case study. [May. Dresden, Germany.]. *Oral Presentation to COMPRAIL*, *2004*, 17–19.

Boulanger, J.-L. (2009). Requirements engineering in a model-based methodology for embedded automotive software. In Ramachandran, M., & Atem de Carvalho, R. (Eds.), *Handbook of software engineering research and productivity technologies: Implications of globalization*.

Boulanger, J.-L., Rasse, A., & Idani, A. (2009). Models oriented approach for developing railway safety-critical systems with UML. In Ramachandran, M., & Atem de Carvalho, R. (Eds.), *Handbook of software engineering research and productivity technologies: Implications of globalization*.

Boulanger, J.-L. (2008). RT3-TUCS: How to build a certifiable and safety critical railway application. 17th International Conference on Software Engineering and Data Engineering, SEDE-2008, June 30-July 2, 2008, Los Angeles, (pp. 182-187).

Boulanger, J.-L., & Dao, V. Q. (2007). A requirement-based methodology for automotive software development. In *Proceedings of MCSE*, July 2007.

Boulanger, J.-L., & Dao, V. Q. (2008a). *An example of requirements engineering in a model-based methodology for embedded automotive software*. 17th International Conference on Software Engineering and Data Engineering, SEDE-2008, June 30-July 2 2008, Los Angeles, (pp. 130-137).

Boulanger, J.-L., & Dao, V. Q. (2008b). *Requirements engineering in a model-based methodology for embedded automotive software*. July 13-17, 2008, IEEE RIVF 2008, IEEE International Conference on Research, Innovation and Vision for the Future, Ho Chi Minh City, Vietnam, (pp. 263-268).

Boulanger, J.-L., & Schön, W. (2007). Certification and safety assessment in railway domain. LT 2007, Sousse, Tunisie, 18-20 November 2007.

Breitman, K. K., Leite, J. C. S. P., & Finkelstein, A. (1999). The world's stage: A survey on requirements engineering using a real-life case study. *Journal of the Brazilian Computer Society*, *6*(1), 13–37. doi:10.1590/S0104-65001999000200003

Bresciani, P., Giorgini, P., Giunchiglia, F., Mylopoulos, J., & Perini, A. (2004). TROPOS: An agent-oriented software development methodology. [Kluwer Academic Publishers.]. *Journal of Autonomous Agents and Multi-Agent Systems*, *8*(3), 203–236. doi:10.1023/B:AGNT.0000018806.20944.ef

Briand, L. C., Morasca, S., & Basili, V. R. (1996). Property-based software engineering. *IEEE Transactions on Software Engineering*, *23*(8), 196–198.

Briand, L., Daly, J., & Wüst, J. (1999). A unified framework for coupling measurement in object-oriented systems. *IEEE Transactions on Software Engineering*, *25*(1), 91–121. doi:10.1109/32.748920

Briand, L., Morasca, S., & Basili, V. (1996). Property-based software engineering measurement. *IEEE Transactions on Software Engineering*, *22*(6), 68–86. doi:10.1109/32.481535

Briand, L., Wüst, J., Daly, J., & Porter, V. (2000). Exploring the relationships between design measures and software quality in object-oriented systems. *Journal of Systems and Software*, *51*, 245–273. doi:10.1016/S0164-1212(99)00102-8

Briand, L. C. (2002). On the many ways software engineering can benefit from knowledge engineering. *Proceedings of the 14th SEKE Conference*, Italy, (pp. 3-6).

Briand, L., Devanbu, W., & Melo, W. (1997). *An investigation into coupling measures for C++*. 19th International Conference on Software Engineering (ICSE 97), Boston, USA, (pp. 412-421).

Briand, L., Wüst, J., & Lounis, H. (1998). *Investigating quality factors in object-oriented designs: An industrial case study*. (Technical report ISERN 98-29, version 2).

Brito, E., Abreu, F., & Carapuça, R. (1994). *Object-oriented software engineering: Measuring and controlling the development process*. 4th International Conference on Software Quality, McLean, VA, USA.

Brito, E., Abreu, F., & Melo, W. (1996). *Evaluating the impact of object-oriented design on software quality*. 3rd International Metric Symposium, (pp. 90-99).

Brooke, J., Pickles, S., Carr, P., & Michael, K. (2007). Workflows in pulsar astronomy. *Workflows for e-science: Scientific workflows for Grids*, 60–79.

Brown, W. J., Malveau, R. C., McCormick, H. W., & Mowbray, T. J. (1998). *AntiPatterns: Refactoring software, architectures, and projects in crisis*. John Wiley and Sons.

Bueno, P. M. S., & Jino, M. (2000). *Identification of potentially infeasible program paths by monitoring the search for test data*. 15th IEEE International Conference on Automated Software Engineering (ASE00), 209.

Buschmann, F., Henney, K., & Schmidt, D. C. (2007a). *Pattern-oriented software architecture, volume 4: A pattern language for distributed computing*. John Wiley and Sons.

Buschmann, F., Henney, K., & Schmidt, D. C. (2007b). *Pattern-oriented software architecture, volume 5: On patterns and pattern languages*. John Wiley and Sons.

Buschmann, F., Meunier, R., Rohnert, H., Sommerlad, P., & Stal, M. (1996). *Pattern oriented software architecture, vol. 1: A system of patterns*. John Wiley and Sons.

Buyya, R., & Venugopal, S. (2004). *The gridbus toolkit for service oriented Grid and utility computing: An overview and status report*. In 1st IEEE International Workshop on Grid Economics and Business Models, 2004. GECON 2004, (pp. 19–66).

Caldiera, G., & Basili, V. R. (1991). *Identifying and qualifying reusable software components*. IEEE Computer.

Cartwright, M. (1998). An empirical view of inheritance. *Information and Software Technology*, *40*(4), 795–799. doi:10.1016/S0950-5849(98)00105-0

Castro, J., Alencar, F., & Silva, C. (2006). Agent oriented software engeneering. In Breitman, K., & Anido, R. (Eds.), *Informatics upgrades* (pp. 245–282). Rio de Janeiro: PUC-Rio.

Cauvet, C., & Guzelian, G. (2008). Business process modeling: A service-oriented approach. *Proceedings of the 41st Annual Hawaii International Conference on System Sciences,* (p. 98).

CEI 61025. (1990). *Fault Tree Analysis (FTA)*. (International Electrotechnical Commission Std. 61025).

CEI 61508. (2000). *Functional safety of electrical/electronic/programmable electronic safety-related systems*. (International Electrotechnical Commission Std. 61508).

CENELEC EN 50126. (1999). *Railways application–the specification and demonstration of Reliabilty, Availibility, Maintenabiliy and Safety* (RAMS).

CENELEC EN 50128. (2001). Railways application–communication, signaling and processing systems–software for railway control and protection systems.

CENELEC EN 50129. (2000). *Railways application–safety related electronic systems for signaling*. dSPACE. (2007). *ECU testing with hardware-in-the-loop simulation*.

Chen, Y., & Su, C. (2006). A Kano-CKM model for customer knowledge discovery. *Total Quality Management*, *17*(5), 589–608. doi:10.1080/14783360600588158

Chen, T. Y., & Lau, M. F. (2003). On the divide-and-conquer approach towards test suite reduction. *Information Sciences: An International Journal*, *152*(1), 89–119.

Chidamber, S. R., & Kemerer, C. (1991). Towards a metrics suite for object oriented design. *Object Oriented Programming Systems, Languages, and Applications*, *26*(11), 197–211. doi:10.1145/117954.117970

Chidamber, S. R., & Kemerer, C. (1994). A metrics suite for object-oriented design. *IEEE Transactions on Software Engineering*, *20*(6), 476–493. doi:10.1109/32.295895

Chidamber, S., Darcy, D., & Kemerer, C. (1998). Managerial use of metrics for object-oriented software: An exploratory analysis. *IEEE Transactions on Software Engineering*, *24*(8), 629–639. doi:10.1109/32.707698

Chidamber, S. R., & Kemerer, C. F. (1991). Towards a metrics suite for object oriented design. *Proceedings of the Conference on Object Oriented Programming Systems, Languages, and Applications (OOPSLA'91)*, *26*(11), 197-211.

Christopher, L. (2005). *APC legendary reliability physical security of data centres and network rooms* (pp. 4–10). Fundamental Principles of Network Security.

Chung, L., Nixon, B., Yu, E., & Mylopoulos, J. (2000). *Non-functional requirements in software engineering*. Dordrecht, The Netherlands: Kluwer Academic Publications.

Clarke, L. A. (1976). A system to generate test data and symbolically execute programs. *IEEE Transactions on Software Engineering*, *2*(3), 915–1222. doi:10.1109/TSE.1976.233817

Cleland-Huang, J., Setimi, R., Zou, X., & Solc, P. (2007). Automated classification of non-functional requirements. *Requirements Engineering*, *12*, 103–120. doi:10.1007/s00766-007-0045-1

Cline, M. P. (1996). The pros and cons of adopting and applying design patterns in the real world. *Communications of the ACM*, *39*(10), 47–49. doi:10.1145/236156.236167

Coad, P. (1992). Object-oriented patterns. *Communications of the ACM*, *35*(9), 152–159. doi:10.1145/130994.131006

Cockburn, A. (2000). *Writing effective use cases*. Boston, MA: Addison-Wesley.

Cockram, T. (2001). Gaining confidence in software inspection using a Bayesian belief model. *Software Quality Journal*, *9*(1), 31–42. doi:10.1023/A:1016600602423

Coleman, G., & O'Connor, R. V. (2008). The influence of managerial experience and style on software development process. *International Journal of Technology. Policy and Management*, *8*(1), 91–109.

Coleman, G., & O'Connor, R. V. (2008). Investigating software process in practice: A grounded theory perspective. *Journal of Systems and Software*, *81*(5), 772–784. doi:10.1016/j.jss.2007.07.027

Cook, J. E., & Wolf, A. L. (1998). Discovering models of software process from event-based data. [TOSEM]. *ACM Transactions on Software Engineering and Methodology*, *7*(3), 215–249. doi:10.1145/287000.287001

Coombs, J. H., Renear, A. H., & DeRose, S. J. (1987). Markup systems and the future of scholarly text processing. *Communications of the ACM*, *30*(11), 933–947. doi:10.1145/32206.32209

Coplien, J. O. (1996). *Software patterns*. SIGS Books.

Coplien, J. O., & Harrison, N. B. (2005). *Organizational patterns of agile software development*. Prentice-Hall.

Coplien, J. O. (1996). *Software patterns*. SIGS Books.

Coppit, D., Yang, J., Khurshid, S., Le, W., & Sullivan, K. (2005). Software assurance by bounded exhaustive testing. *IEEE Transactions on Software Engineering*, *31*(4), 328–339. doi:10.1109/TSE.2005.52

Coram, T., & Lee, J. (1996). *Experiences-a pattern language for user interface design*. The Third Conference on Pattern Languages of Programs (PLoP 1996), Monticello, USA, September 4-6, 1996.

Corby, O., Faron-Zucker, C., & Mirbel, I. (2009). *Implementation of intention-driven search processes by SPARQL queries*. In International Conference on Enterprise Information Systems, Milan, Italy.

Cordeiro, A. D. (2001). *Conception and implementation of a multiagent system to manage data communication.* Master Thesis, Universidade Federal de Santa Catarina-UFSC.

Correia, F., Ferreira, H., Flores, N., & Aguiar, A. (2009). *Patterns for consistent software documentation.* The Sixteenth Conference on Pattern Languages of Programs (PLoP 2009), Chicago, USA, August 28-30, 2009.

Correia, F., Ferreira, H., Flores, N., & Aguiar, A. (2009). *Patterns for consistent software documentation.* The Sixteenth Conference on Pattern Languages of Programs (PLoP 2009), Chicago, USA, August 28-30, 2009.

Cossentino, M., Sabatucci, L., Sorace, S., & Chella, A. (2004). Patterns reuse in the PASSI methodology. In *Proceedings of the Fourth International Workshop Engineering Societies in the Agents World (ESAW'03), Imperial College*, London, UK, October, (pp. 29-31).

Cox, D., & Greenberg, S. (2000). Supporting collaborative interpretation in distributed groupware. In Proceedings of Computer Supported Cooperative Work Conference, (pp. 289–298).

Cress, U., & Kimmerle, J. (2007). A theoretical framework of collaborative knowledge building with wikis: A systemic and cognitive perspective. In *Proceedings of the 8th International Conference on Computer Supported Collaborative Learning*, (pp.156-164).

Crone, M. (2002). *A profile of software Irish industry. Northern Ireland Economic Research Center (NIERC).* Belfast NI.

Crumlish, C., & Malone, E. (2009). *Designing social interfaces: Principles, patterns, and practices for improving the user experience.* O'Reilly Media.

Cunningham, W. (2006). Design principles of wiki: How can so little do so much? In *Proceedings of the International Symposium on Wikis*, (pp. 13–14).

Curtin, M. (1997). *Introduction to network security.* Kent Information Services, UK, March 1997. Retrieved April 2010, from http://www.interhack.net/pubs/network-security/

Cysneiros, L. M., Leite, J. C. S. P., & Neto, J. M. S. (2001). A framework for integrating non-functional requirements into conceptual models. *Requirements Engineering, 6*, 97–115. doi:10.1007/s007660170008

Czarnecki, K., & Eisenecker, U. (2000). *Generative programming: Methods, tools, and applications.* New York: ACM Press/Addison-Wesley Publishing Co.

da Silva Santos, L. O., Pires, L. F., & van Sinderen, M. J. (2008). *A goal-based framework for dynamic service discovery and composition.* In International Workshop on Architectures, Concepts and Technologies for Service Oriented Computing.

Dabney, J. B., Barber, G., & Ohi, D. (2006). Predicting software defect function point ratios using a Bayesian belief network. *Proceedings of 2nd International Workshop on Predictor Models in Software Engineering*, Philadelphia, PA.

Daly, J., Brooks, A., Miller, J., Roper, M., & Wood, M. (1996). An empirical study evaluating depth of inheritance on maintainability of object-oriented software. *Empirical Software Engineering, 1*(2), 109–132. doi:10.1007/BF00368701

Dandashi, F. (1998). *A method for assessing the reusability of object-oriented code using a validated set of automated measurements.* Unpublished doctoral dissertation, SITE, George Mason University, Fairfax, VA.

Dardenne, A., van Lamsweerde, A., & Fickas, S. (1993). Goal directed requirements acquisition. *Science of Computer Programming, 20*, 3–50. doi:10.1016/0167-6423(93)90021-G

Darroch, J., & McNaughton, R. (2003). Beyond market orientation – knowledge management and the innovativeness of New Zealand firms. *European Journal of Marketing, 37*(3/4), 572–593. doi:10.1108/03090560310459096

Darwiche, A. (2009). *Modeling and reasoning with Bayesian networks.* Cambridge University Press.

Dasousa, K., & Awazu, Y. (2005). What do they know? *Business Strategy Review*, Spring 2005, (pp. 42-45).

Davenport, T., & Prusak, L. (1998). *Working knowledge: How organizations manage what they know.* Boston, MA: Harvard Business School Press.

Davenport, T., Harris, J., & Kohil, A. (2001). How do they know their customers so well? *MIT Sloan Management Review*, Winter 2001.

Davidson, S., Cohen-Boulakia, S., Eyal, A., Ludascher, B., McPhillips, T., Bowers, S., & Freire, J. (2007). Provenance in scientific workflow systems. *A Quarterly Bulletin of the Computer Society of the IEEE Technical Committee on Data Engineering*, *30*(4), 44–50.

Davis, A., Dieste, O., Hickey, A., Juristo, N., & Moreno, A. (2006). Effectiveness of requirements elicitation techniques: Empirical results derived from a systematic review. In *Proceedings of 14th IEEE International Conference of Requirements Engineering*, (pp. 179–188).

De Roure, D., Goble, C., & Stevens, R. (2009). The design and realisation of the virtual research environment for social sharing of workflows. *Future Generation Computer Systems*, *25*(5), 561–567. doi:10.1016/j.future.2008.06.010

Decker, B., Ras, E., Rech, J., Jaubert, P., & Rieth, M. (2007). Wikibased stakeholder participation in requirements engineering. *IEEE Software*, *24*(2), 28–35. doi:10.1109/MS.2007.60

Deelman, E. (2007). Looking into the future of workflows: The challenges ahead. *Workflows for e-science: Scientific workflows for Grids*, 475–481.

Delgado, M., Gómez Skarmeta, A., & Jiménez, L. (2001). A regression methodology to induce a fuzzy model. *International Journal of Intelligent Systems*, *16*(2), 169–190. doi:10.1002/1098-111X(200102)16:2<169::AID-INT20>3.0.CO;2-L

Deloach, S. A. (2001). Analysis and design using MaSE and AgentTool. In *Proceedings of the 12th Midwest Artificial Intelligence and Cognitive Science Conference*, Miami University, Oxford.

Denaro, G., & Pezze, G. M. (2002). An empirical evaluation of fault proneness model. *ICSE Proceedings of 24th International Conference*, (pp. 241-251).

Deng, J., Kemp, E., & Todd, E. G. (2005). *Managing UI pattern collections*. The Sixth ACM SIGCHI New Zealand Chapter's International Conference on Computer-Human Interaction: Making CHI Natural, Auckland, New Zealand, July 7-8, 2005.

Deng, J., Kemp, E., & Todd, E. G. (2006). *Focusing on a standard pattern form: The development and evaluation of MUIP*. The Seventh ACM SIGCHI New Zealand Chapter's International Conference on Computer-Human Interaction: Design Centered HCI, Christchurch, New Zealand, July 6-7, 2006.

Denning, S. (2000). *The springboard: How storytelling ignites action in knowledge-era organizations*. Boston, MA; London, UK: Butterworth Heinemann.

Derntl, M., & Motschnig-Pitrik, R. (2008). *Exploring the user's view on design patterns for technology-enhanced learning*. The Sixth International Conference on Networked Learning (NLC 2008), Halkidiki, Greece, May 5-6, 2008.

DeRose, S. J., Durand, D. G., Mylonas, E., & Renear, A. H. (1997). What is text, really? *Journal of Computer Documentation*, *21*(3), 1–24. doi:10.1145/264842.264843

Desouza, K. C. (2003). Facilitating tacit knowledge exchange. *Communications of the ACM*, *46*(6), 6. doi:10.1145/777313.777317

Deugo, D., & Ferguson, D. (2001). *XML specification for design patterns*. The Second International Conference on Internet Computing (IC 2001), Las Vegas, USA, June 25-28, 2001.

Dhavachelvan, P., & Uma, G. V. (2003). *Multi-agent based integrated framework for intra-class testing of object-oriented software*. (LNCS 2869).

Díaz, E., Tuya, J., & Blanco, R. (2008). A Tabu search algorithm for structural software testing. *Computers & Operations Research*, *35*(10), 3052–3072. doi:10.1016/j.cor.2007.01.009

Dileo, J., Jacobs, T., & Deloach, S. (2002). Integrating ontologies into multi-agent systems engineering. *Proceedings of 4th International Bi-Conference Workshop on Agent Oriented Information Systems* (AOIS 2002), Bologna (Italy), July, (pp. 15-16).

Dingsoyr, T., & Conradi, R. (2002). A survey of case studies of the use of knowledge management in software engineering. *International Journal of Software Engineering and Knowledge Engineering*, *12*(4), 391–414. doi:10.1142/S0218194002000962

Dixon, D. (2009). Pattern languages for CMC design. In Whitworth, B., & de Moor, A. (Eds.), *Handbook of research on socio-technical design and social networking systems* (pp. 402–415). Hershey, PA: IGI Global. doi:10.4018/9781605662640.ch027

Dobson, G., Lock, R., & Sommerville, I. (2005, August). *QoSOnt: A QoS ontology for service-centric systems*. In Proceedings of the 31st EUROMICRO Conference on Software Engineering and Advanced Applications, (pp. 80-87).

Dogru, A. H. (2006). *Component oriented software engineering*. Grandbury, TX: The Atlas Publishing.

Dogru, A. H., & Tanik, M. M. (2003). A process model for component-oriented software engineering. *IEEE Software*, *20*(2), 34–41. doi:10.1109/MS.2003.1184164

Dromey, R. G. (2003). Software quality-prevention versus cure? *Software Quality Journal*, *11*(3), 197–210. doi:10.1023/A:1025162610079

Druzdzel, M. J., & Dez, F. J. (2003). Combining knowledge from different sources in causal probabilistic models. *Journal of Machine Learning Research*, *4*, 295–316. doi:10.1162/jmlr.2003.4.3.295

Dubost, K., Rosenthal, L., & Hazaël-Massieux, D. Henderson, L. (2005). *QA framework: Specification guidelines*. World Wide Web Consortium (W3C) Recommendation.

Dunn, M. F., & Knight, J. C. (1993). Software reuse in Industrial setting: A case study. *Proceedings of the 13th International Conference on Software Engineering*, Baltimore, MD.

Durfee, E. H., Lesser, V. V., & Corkill, D. D. (1989). Trends in cooperative distributed problem solving. *IEEE Transactions on Knowledge and Data Engineering*, *1*(1), 63–83. doi:10.1109/69.43404

Einer, S., Schrom, H., Slovák, R., & Schnieder, E. (2002). A railway demonstrator model for experimental investigation of integrated specification techniques. In Ehrig, H., & Grosse-Rhode, M. (Eds.), *ETAPS 2002-integration of software specification techniques* (pp. 84–93).

El-Attar, M., & Miller, J. (2006). *Matching antipatterns to improve the quality of use case models*. The Fourteenth International Requirements Engineering Conference (RE 2006), Minneapolis-St. Paul, USA. September 11-15, 2006.

Elo, S., & Kyngäs, H. (2008). The qualitative content analysis process. *Journal of Advanced Nursing*, *62*(1), 107–115. doi:10.1111/j.1365-2648.2007.04569.x

Elssamadisy, A. (2007). *Patterns of agile practice adoption: The technical cluster*. C4Media.

Eppler, M. J. (2001). The concept of information quality: An interdisciplinary evaluation of recent information quality frameworks. *Studies in Communication Sciences*, *1*(2), 167–182.

Eric, W. W., Joseph, R. H., & Aditya, P., Mathur & Alberto P. (1999). Test Set Size Minimization and Fault Detection Effectiveness: A Case Study in a Space Application. *Journal of Systems and Software*, *48*(2), 79–89. doi:10.1016/S0164-1212(99)00048-5

Esteva, J. C., & Reynolds, R. G. (1991). Identifying reusable components using induction. *International Journal of Software Engineering and Knowledge Engineering*, *1*(3), 271–292. doi:10.1142/S0218194091000202

Etzkorn, L., Davis, C., & Li, W. (1998). A practical look at the lack of cohesion in methods metrics. *Journal of Object-Oriented Programming*, *11*(5), 27–34.

Etzkorn, L. H., Hughes, Jr., W. E., & Davis, C. G. (2001). *Automated reusability quality analysis of OO legacy software*.

Fabbrini, F., Fusani, M., Gervasi, V., Gnesi, S., & Ruggieri, S. (1998a). Achieving quality in natural language requirements. *Proceedings of the 11th International Software Quality Week*.

Fabbrini, F., Fusani, M., Gervasi, V., Gnesi, S., & Ruggieri, S. (1998b). On linguistic quality of natural language requirements. *Proceedings of 4th International Workshop on Requirements Engineering: Foundations of Software Quality (REFSQ'98)*.

Fabbrini, F., Fusani, M., Gnesi, S., & Lami, G. (2000). Quality evaluation of software requirement specifications. *Proceedings of Software & Internet Quality Week*.

Fabbrini, F., Fusani, M., Gnesi, S., & Lami, G. (2001a). An automatic quality evaluation for natural language requirements. *Proceedings of the 7th International Workshop on Requirements Engineering: Foundation for Software Quality (REFSQ'01)*, 2001.

Fabbrini, F., Fusani, M., Gnesi, S., & Lami, G. (2001b). The linguistic approach to the natural language requirements quality: Benefits of the use of an automatic tool. *Proceedings of 26th Annual IEEE Computer Society - NASA Goddard Space Flight Center Software Engineering Workshop.*

Fantechi, A., Fusani, M., Gnesi, S., & Ristori, G. (1997). *Expressing properties of software requirements through syntactical rules. (Technical Report. IEI-CNR).* Italy: Pisa.

Fantechi, A., Gnesi, S., Ristori, G., Carenini, M., Vanocchi, M., & Moreschini, P. (1994). Assisting requirement formalization by means of natural language translation. *Formal Methods in System Design, 4*(3), 243–263. doi:10.1007/BF01384048

Feigenbaum, E., Buchanan, B., & Lederberg, J. (1971). On generality and problem solving: A case study using the dendral program. In *Machine intelligence* (Vol. 6, pp. 165–190). Edinburgh, UK: Edinburgh University Press.

Fensel, D., & Bussler, C. (2002). *Semantic Web enabled Web services.* International Semantic Web Conference (ISWC'2002), vol. 2342.

Fenton, N. E., & Pfleeger, S. L. (1997). *Software metrics: A rigorous & practical approach.* International Thomson Computer Press.

Fenton, N. E., Neil, M., & Caballero, J. G. (2007). Using ranked nodes to model qualitative judgements in Bayesian networks. *IEEE Transactions on Knowledge and Data Engineering, 19*(10), 1420–1432. doi:10.1109/TKDE.2007.1073

Fenton, N. E., Neil, M., Marsh, W., Krause, P., & Mishra, R. (2007). Predicting software defects in varying development lifecycles using Bayesian nets. *Information and Software Technology, 43*(1), 32–43. doi:10.1016/j.infsof.2006.09.001

Fenton, N., Hearty, P., Neil, M., & Radliński, Ł. (2009). Software project and quality modelling using Bayesian networks. In Meziane, F., & Vadera, S. (Eds.), *Artificial intelligence applications for improved software engineering development: New prospects* (pp. 1–25). Hershey, PA: IGI-Global.

Fenton, N., Marsh, W., Neil, M., Cates, P., Forey, S., & Tailor, M. (2004). Making resource decisions for software projects. *Proceedings of the 26th International Conference on Software Engineering*, Washington, DC, IEEE Computer Society, (pp. 397–406).

Ferber, J. (1999). *Multi-agent system, an introduction to distributed artificial intelligence.* Addison-Wesley Publishers.

Fincher, S. (2003). The ACM CHI 2003 Workshop Report Perspectives on HCI Patterns: Concepts and Tools (Introducing PLML). *Interfaces, 56*, 26–28.

Finkelstein, A., & Dowell, J. A. (1996). Comedy of errors: The London ambulance service case study. *Proceedings of the Eighth International Workshop on Software Specification and Design*, (pp. 2–5).

Firesmith, D. (2003). Specifying good requirements. *Journal of Object Technology, 2*(4), 77–87. doi:10.5381/jot.2003.2.4.c7

Forgacs, I., & Bertolino, A. (1997). Feasible test path selection by principal slicing. In *Proceedings of 6th European Software Engineering Conference.*

Fowler, M., Rice, D., Foemmel, M., Hieatt, E., Mee, R., & Stafford, R. (2003). *Patterns of enterprise application architecture.* Addison-Wesley.

Fowler, M., & Highsmith, J. (2001). The agile manifesto. *Software Development, 9*(8), 28–35.

Francisco-Revilla, L., & Shipman, F. M. (2005). Parsing and interpreting ambiguous structures in spatial hypermedia. In *Proceedings of Hypertext and Hypermedia*, (pp. 107–116).

Frankl, P. G., & Weyuker, E. J. (1988). An applicable family of data flow testing criteria. *IEEE Transactions on Software Engineering, 14*(10), 1483–1498. doi:10.1109/32.6194

Franklin, S., & Graesse, A. (1996). Is it an agent, or just a program? A taxonomy for autonomous agents. *Proceedings of the Third International Workshop on Agents Theories, Architecture and Languages.* Springer-Verlag.

Friedman-Hill, E. (2003). *JESS in action.* Manning Publications.

Frigo, L. B., Pozzebon, E., & Bittencout, G. (2004). *The role of intelligent agents in intelligent tutoring systems.* World Congress on Engineering and Technology Education, (pp 667-671).

Frolich, P., & Link, J. (2000). *Automated test case generation from dynamic models.* (LNCS 1850), (pp. 472-491).

Gacek, C. (Ed.). (2002). *Software reuse: Methods, techniques and tools.* 7th International Conference (ICSR7) Austin, Texas. (LNCS 2319). Springer.

Galagan, P. (1997). Smart companies (knowledge management). *Training & Development, 51*(12).

Gamma, E., Helm, R., Johnson, R., & Vlissides, J. (1995). *Design patterns: Elements of reusable object-oriented software.* Addison-Wesley.

Gamma, E. (1991). *Object-oriented software development based on ET++: Design patterns, class library, tools.* Unpublished doctoral thesis, University of Zürich, Zürich, Switzerland.

Gannon, D., Plale, B., Marru, S., Kandaswamy, G., Simmhan, Y., & Shirasuna, S. (2007). Dynamic, adaptive workflows for mesoscale meteorology. *Workflows for e-science: Scientific workflows for Grids,* 126–142.

Garcês, R., Freitas, P., Ferreira, N., & Freitas, F. (2006). *Knowledge representation.* Funchal: Technical Report. Madeira University.

Garcia-Murillo, M., & Annabi, H. (2002). Customer knowledge management. *The Journal of the Operational Research Society, 53,* 875–884. doi:10.1057/palgrave.jors.2601365

Garvin, D. A. (1984). What does product quality really mean? *MIT Sloan Management Review, 26*(1), 25–43.

Garzás, J., & Piattini, M. (2007). *Object-oriented design knowledge: Principles, heuristics and best practices.* Hershey, PA: Idea Group.

Gause, D. C., & Weinberg, G. M. (1989). *Exploring requirements: Quality before design.* New York, NY: Dorset House Publishing.

Gebert, H., Geib, M., Kolbe, L., & Brenner, W. (2003). Knowledge–enabled customer relationship management: Integrating customer relationship and knowledge management concepts. *Journal of Knowledge Management, 7*(5), 107–123. doi:10.1108/13673270310505421

Genero, M., Piattini, M., & Calero, C. (2001). Early measures for UML class diagrams. [Hermes Science Publications.]. *L'Objet, 6*(4), 489–515.

Genero, M. (2002). *Defining and validating metrics for conceptual models.* Unpublished doctoral thesis, University of Castilla-La Mancha.

Genero, M., Manso, M. E., Piattini, M., & Cantone, G. (2003). Building UML class diagram maintainability prediction models based on early metrics. *Proceedings IEEE Computer Society 9th International Symposium on Software Metrics,* (pp. 263-275).

Genero, M., Olivas, J., Piattini, M., & Romero, F. (2001). *Using metrics to predict OO Information Systems maintainability.* (LNCS 2068), (pp. 388-401).

Genero, M., Olivas, J., Romero, F., & Piattini, M. (2003). Assessing OO conceptual models maintainability. In Olive, et al. (Eds.), *International Workshop on Conceptual Modeling Quality* (IWCMQ'02), Tampere, Finland, (pp. 288-299). (LNCS 2784), Springer-Verlag.

Gennari, J. (2002). *The evolution of Protégé: An environment for knowledge-based systems development.* (Technical Report SMI-2002-0943).

Gerlich, R., Boll, Th., & Chevalley, Ph. (2006). *Improving test automation by deterministic methods in statistical testing. Proceedings of Data Systems In Aerospace* (DASIA 2006), *European Space Agency,* (p. 630).

Gervasi, V., & Nuseibeh, B. (2002). Lightweight validation of natural language requirements. *Software, Practice & Experience, 32,* 113–133. doi:10.1002/spe.430

Giarratano, J., & Riley, G. (1989). *Expert systems: Principles and programming.* PWS-KENT Publishing Company.

Gil, Y. (2007). Workflow composition: Semantic representations for flexible automation. *Workflows for e-science: Scientific workflows for Grids,* 244–257.

Girardi, R., & Leite, A. (2008). A knowledge-based tool for multi-agent domain engineering. *Knowledge-Based Systems Journal*, *21*, 604–611. doi:10.1016/j.knosys.2008.03.036

Girardi, R., & Marinho, L. (2007). A domain model of Web recommender systems based on usage mining and collaborative filtering. [Springer-Verlag.]. *Requirements Engineering Journal*, *12*(1), 23–40. doi:10.1007/s00766-006-0038-5

Girardi, R., Marinho, L., & Ribeiro, I. (2005). A system of agent-based patterns for user modelling based on usage mining. *Interacting with Computers*, *17*(5), 567–591. doi:10.1016/j.intcom.2005.02.003

Girardi, R. (1992). Application engineering: Putting reuse to work. In Tsichritzis, D. (Ed.), *Object frameworks* (pp. 137–149). Université de Geneve.

Girardi, R., & Drumond, L. (2008). Multi-agent legal recommender system. In *Artificial intelligence and law*. (pp. 175-207).

Goderis, A., De Roure, D., Goble, C., Bhagat, J., Cruickshank, D., Fisher, P., Michaelides, D., et al. (2008). *Discovering scientific workflows: The myexperiment benchmarks.* Internal project report, submitted for publication.

Goldberg, A. T. C., Wang, T. C., & Zimmerman, D. (1994). *Applications of feasible path analysis to program testing*. In International Symposium on Software Testing and Analysis, (pp. 80-94).

Goldfarb, C. F. (1981). *A generalized approach to document markup*. The ACM SIGPLAN SIGOA Symposium on Text Manipulation, Portland, USA, June 8-10, 1981.

Goma, H. (2005). *Designing software product lines with UML: From use cases to pattern-based software architectures.* Addison-Wesley Object Technology Series.

Gomez, J. M., Rico, M., Garcia-Sanchez, F., Toma, I., & Han, S. (2006). *GODO: Goal oriented discovery for Semantic Web services*. 5th International Semantic Web Conference.

Gonçalves, J. F., & Resende, M. G. C. (2002). *A hybrid genetic algorithm for manufacturing cell formation.* Technical Report, AT and T Lab.

Gouraud, S. D., Denise, A., Gaudel, M. C., & Marre, B. (2001). A new way of automating statistical testing methods. *Proceedings of the 16th IEEE International Conference On Automated Software Engineering*, (p. 5).

Graham, I. (2003). *A pattern language for Web usability*. Addison-Wesley.

Grant, R. M. (1996). Prospering in dynamically-competitive environments: Organisational capability as knowledge integration. *Organization Science*, *7*(4), 375–387. doi:10.1287/orsc.7.4.375

Gross, D., & Yu, E. (2001). From non-functional requirements to design through patterns. *Requirements Engineering*, *6*(1), 18–36. doi:10.1007/s007660170013

Grossman, T., Fitzmaurice, G., & Attar, R. (2009). *A survey of software learnability: Metrics, methodologies and guidelines.* The ACM CHI 2009 Conference on Human Factors in Computing Systems (CHI 2009), Boston, USA, April 4-9, 2009.

Grottke, M., & Trivedi, K. S. (2007). Fighting bugs: Remove, retry, replicate, and rejuvenate. *IEEE Computer*, *40*(2), 107–109.

Grottke, M., & Trivedi, K. S. (2007). Fighting Bugs: Remove, Retry, Replicate, and Rejuvenate. *IEEE Computer*, *40*(2), 107–109.

Gruber, T. (1995). Toward principles for the design of ontologies used for knowledge sharing. *International Journal of Human-Computer Studies*, *43*, 907–928. doi:10.1006/ijhc.1995.1081

Grudin, J. (1992). Utility and usability: Research issues and development contexts. *Interacting with Computers*, *4*(2), 209–217. doi:10.1016/0953-5438(92)90005-Z

Gruenbacher, P. (2000). Collaborative requirements negotiation with EasyWinWin. In *Proceedings of the 11th International Workshop on Database and Expert Systems Applications*.

Guaspari, J. (1998). Customer means customers. *Quality Digest*, 35-38.

Gui, G., & Scott, P. D. (2007). Ranking reusability of software components using coupling metrics. *Journal of Systems and Software*, 1450–1459. doi:10.1016/j.jss.2006.09.048

Guo, Q., Hierons, R. M., Harman, R. M., & Derderian, K. (2005). Constructing multiple unique input/output sequences using evolutionary optimization techniques. *IEE Proceedings. Software, 152*(3), 127–140. doi:10.1049/ip-sen:20045001

Gupta, A. K., & Govindarajan, V. (2000). Knowledge management's social dimension: Lessons from Nucor Steel. *Sloan Management Review, 42*(1), 71–80.

Gupta, N., Mathur, A. P., & Soffa, M. L. (1998). Automated test data generation using an iterative relaxation method. *Foundations of Software Engineering, 11*, 231–244.

Hall, T., Rainer, A., & Baddoo, N. (2002). Implementing software process improvement: An empirical study. *Software Process Improvement and Practice, 7*(1), 3–15. doi:10.1002/spip.150

Hanks, K. S., Knight, J. C., & Strunk, E. A. (2001a). Erroneous requirements: A linguistic basis for their occurrence and an approach to their reduction. *Proceedings of Software Engineering Workshop - NASA Goddard Space Flight Center*.

Hanks, K. S., Knight, J. C., & Strunk, E. A. (2001b). *A linguistic analysis of requirements errors and its application.* (Technical Report CS-2001-30), University of Virginia Department of Computer Science.

Hanna, D. E., Glowacki Dudka, M., & Conceição Runlee, S. (2000). *147 practical tips for teaching online groups: Essentials of Web-based education.* Madison, WI: Atwood Publishing.

Hansen, M. T., Nohria, N., & Tierney, T. (1999). What's your strategy for managing knowledge? *Harvard Business Review, 77*(2), 106–116.

Hansen, M. T., & Von Oetinger, B. (2001). Introducing t-shaped managers: Knowledge management's next generation. *Harvard Business Review, 79*(3), 106–116.

Hansen, B. H., & Kautz, K. (2004). *Knowledge mapping: A technique for identifying knowledge flows in software organisations. (LNCS 3281).* Springer.

Harman, M. (2007). The current state and future of search based software engineering. *Future of Software Engineering, 2007*, 342–357. doi:10.1109/FOSE.2007.29

Harman, M., & Jones, B. F. (2001). Search based software engineering. *Information and Software Technology, 43*(14), 833–839. doi:10.1016/S0950-5849(01)00189-6

Harman, M., Hassoun, Y., Lakhotia, K., Mcminn, P., & Wegener, J. (2007).The impact of input domain reduction on search-based test data generation. *Proceedings of the ACM SIGSOFT Symposium on the Foundations of Software Engineering*.

Harold, E. R. (2003). *Effective XML.* Addison-Wesley.

Harrison, R., Counsell, S., & Nithi, R. (2000). Experimental assessment of the effect of inheritance on the maintainability of object-oriented systems. *Journal of Systems and Software, 52*, 173–179. doi:10.1016/S0164-1212(99)00144-2

Harrison, N. (2003). *Advanced pattern writing.* The Eighth European Conference on Pattern Languages of Programs (EuroPLoP 2003), Irsee, Germany, June 25-29, 2003.

Harrison, N. B. (2003). *Advanced pattern writing.* The Eighth European Conference on Pattern Languages of Programs (EuroPLoP 2003), Irsee, Germany, June 25-29, 2003.

Harrison, R., Counsell, S., & Nithi, R. (1998). *Coupling metrics for object-oriented design.* 5th International Software Metrics Symposium Metrics, (pp. 150-156).

Harsu, M. (2002). *A survey of domain engineering.* (Report 31, Institute of Software Systems, Tampere University of Technology).

Hauser, H. M. (2004*). The growing importance of embedded software: Managing hybrid hardware-software business.* (Technical report, The Boston Consulting Group, Inc).

Hayes, M. (2003). *Precious connection* (pp. 34–50). Information Week.

Hearty, P., Fenton, N., Marquez, D., & Neil, M. (2009). Predicting project velocity in XP using a learning dynamic Bayesian network model. *IEEE Transactions on Software Engineering, 37*(1), 124–137. doi:10.1109/TSE.2008.76

Hedley, D., & Hennell, M. A. (1985). The causes and effects of infeasible paths in computer programs. In *Proceedings of 8th ICSE* - 1985, (pp. 259-266).

Hélène, W., Pascale, T. F., & Olfa, A. K. (2007). Simulated annealing applied to test generation: Landscape characterization and stopping criteria. *Empirical Software Engineering, 12*(1), 35–63. doi:10.1007/s10664-006-7551-5

Hendler, J., Lassila, O., & Berners-Lee, T. (2001). The Semantic Web. *Scientific American, 284*(5), 34–43. doi:10.1038/scientificamerican0501-34

Hendricks, P. H. J., & Vriens, D. J. (1999). Knowledge-based systems and knowledge management: Friends or foe. *Information and Management Journal, 35*, 113–125. doi:10.1016/S0378-7206(98)00080-9

Henninger, S., & Corrêa, V. (2007). *Software pattern communities: Current practices and challenges.* The Fourteenth Conference on Pattern Languages of Programs (PLoP 2007), Monticello, USA, September 5-8, 2007.

Henninger, S., & Corrêa, V. (2007). *Software pattern communities: Current practices and challenges.* The Fourteenth Conference on Pattern Languages of Programs (PLoP 2007), Monticello, USA, September 5-8, 2007.

Hess, C., & Ostrom, E. (2007). *Understanding knowledge as a commons: From theory to practice.* The MIT Press.

Hierons, R. M., Harman, M., & Danicic, S. (1999). Using program slicing to assist in the detection of equivalent mutants. *Software Testing. Verification and Reliability, 9*(4), 233–262. doi:10.1002/(SICI)1099-1689(199912)9:4<233::AID-STVR191>3.0.CO;2-3

Hinz, V. T. A. (2006). *Proposal for creating an ontology of ontologies.* Master Thesis, Universidade Catholic Pelotas University.

Hofmann, H., & Lehner, F. (2001). Requirements engineering as a success factor in software projects. *IEEE Software, 18*(4), 58–66. doi:10.1109/MS.2001.936219

Hollingsworth, D. (1995). *The workflow reference model.* Workflow Management Coalition.

Hooks, I. F., & Kristin, A. F. (2001). *Customer-centered products: Creating successful products through smart requirements management.* New York, NY: AMACOM.

Hooks, I. (1993). Writing good requirements. *Proceedings of the 3rd International Symposium of International Council of Systems Engineering.*

Hooper, K. (1986). Architectural design: An analogy. In Norman, D. A., & Draper, S. W. (Eds.), *User centered system design: New perspectives on human-computer interaction.* Lawrence Erlbaum Associates.

Horgan, J., London, S., & Lyu, M. (1994). Achieving software quality with testing coverage measures. *IEEE Computer, 27*(9), 60–69.

House of Lords. (2007). *Personal Internet security, vol 1.* House of Lords Science and Technology Committee, (pp. 13-27). Retrieved April 2010, from www.publications.parliament. uk/pa/ld200607/ldselect/ldsctech/165/165i.pdf

Hull, E., Jackson, K., & Dick, J. (2005). *Requirement engineering.* Springer Verlag.

IABG. (2009). *V-model.* Retrieved December 14, 2009, from http://v-modell.iabg.de/

Idani, A., Boulanger, J.-L., & Philippe, L. (2009). *Linking paradigms in safety critical systems.* Revue ICSA.

Iglesias, C. A. F. (1998). *Definición de uma metodología para el desarrollo de sistemas multiagente.* Tese de Doutorado – Departamento de Ingeniería de Sistemas Telemáticos, Universidad Politécnica de Madrid.

Iglesias, C. A., & Garijo, M. (2005). The agent oriented methodology MASCommonKADS. In Henderson-Sellers, B., & Giorgini, P. (Eds.), *Agented-oriented methodologies* (pp. 46–78). Hershey, PA: IDEA Group Publishing.

Ingo, S., Mirko, C., Heiko, D. R., & Peter, P. (2007). Systematic testing of model-based code generators. *IEEE Transactions on Software Engineering, 33*(9), 622–634. doi:10.1109/TSE.2007.70708

Institute of Electrical and Electronics Engineers. (1993). *IEEE Std 830-1993: Recommended practice for software requirements specifications.* Piscataway, NJ: IEEE Standards Association.

International Organization for Standardization. (2001). *ISO/IEC 9126-1-2001. Software engineering–product quality.* Geneva, Switzerland: ISO Publications.

Issa, A., Odeh, M., & Coward, D. (2006). Using use case patterns to estimate reusability in software systems. *Information and Software Technology, 48*(9), 836–845. doi:10.1016/j.infsof.2005.10.005

Jacobs, I., & Walsh, N. (2004). *Architecture of the World Wide Web, volume one*. World Wide Web Consortium (W3C) Recommendation.

Jalil, M. A., & Noah, S. A. M. (2007). *The difficulties of using design patterns among novices: An exploratory study*. The 2007 International Conference on Computational Science and its Applications (ICCSA 2007), Kuala Lumpur, Malaysia, August 26-29, 2007.

Jansen, C. M., Bach, V., & Osterle, H. (2000). Knowledge portals: Using the Internet to enable business transactions. *Proceedings of Internet Society*, Japan, 18-21 July 2000.

Jansen, L., & Schneider, E. (2000). *Traffic control systems case study: Problem description and a note on domain-based software specification*. Institute of Control and Automation Engineering, Technical University of Braunschweig, 2000.

Jansen, M., & Girardi, R. (2006). GENMADEM: A methodology for generative multi-agent domain engineering. In *Proceedings of the 9th International Conference on Software Reuse, Torino*. (LNCS 4039), (pp. 399-402). Berlin: Springer-Verlag.

Jennings, N. R. (1996). Coordination techniques for DAI. In O'Hare, G., & Jennings, N. (Eds.), *Foundations of distributed artificial intelligence*. John Wiley and Sons.

Jensen, F. V. (1996). *An introduction to Bayesian networks*. London, UK: UCL Press.

Jeremić, Z., Jovanović, J., & Gašević, D. (2008). *A semantic-rich framework for learning software patterns*. The Eighth IEEE International Conference on Advanced Learning Technologies (ICALT 2008), Santander, Spain, July 1-5, 2008.

John, T., Lin, P., & Michael, W. (2005). Prometheus Design Tool. *AAMAS, 2005*, 1–2.

Jones, C. (2000). *Software quality: Analysis and guidelines for success*. International Thomson Computer Press.

Jones, A. C. (2007). Workflow and biodiversity e-science. *Workflows for e-science: Scientific workflows for Grids*, 80–90.

Jordan, J., & Jones, P. (1997). Assesing your company's knowledge management style. *Long Range Planning, 30*(3), 392–398. doi:10.1016/S0024-6301(97)90254-5

Jordan, A., Carlile, O., & Stack, A. (2008). *Approaches to learning: A guide for teachers*. McGraw-Hill.

José C.B.R., Mário Z.R. and Francisco F.D.V. (2008), *A Strategy For Evaluating Feasible And Unfeasible Test Cases For The Evolutionary Testing Of Object-Oriented Software*, ASE-2008, 85-92.

José F. Gonçalves, Mauricio G.C. & Resende (2002), *A Hybrid Genetic Algorithm for Manufacturing Cell Formation*, Technical Report, AT and T Lab.

Joshua, C. (2003). *Defining the rules for pre-emptive host protection: Multi-layered strategy* (pp. 5–7). Internet Security Systems.

Juchem, M., & Bastos, R. M. (2001). *Engenharia de sistemas multiagentes: Uma investigação sobre o estado da arte*. Faculdade de Informática – PUCRS. (Brazil Technical Report Series 014).

Jung, J., & Liu, C.-C. (2003). *Multi-agent system technologies and an application for power system vulnerability*. IEEE, 52-55.

Kale, D., & Little, S. (2005). Knowledge generation in developing countries: A theoretical framework for exploring dynamic learning in high–technology firms. *Electronic Journal of Knowledge Management, 3*(2), 87–96.

Kamthan, P. (2008a). A situational methodology for addressing the pragmatic quality of Web applications by integration of patterns. *Journal of Web Engineering, 7*(1), 70–92.

Kamthan, P. (2008b). Towards high-quality mobile applications by a systematic integration of patterns. *Journal of Mobile Multimedia, 4*(3/4), 165–184.

Kamthan, P. (2010). A viewpoint-based approach for understanding the morphogenesis of patterns. *International Journal of Knowledge Management, 6*(2), 40–65. doi:10.4018/jkm.2010040103

Kamthan, P. (2006). A critique of pattern language markup language. *Interfaces, 68*, 14–15.

Kamthan, P. (2008). A situational methodology for addressing the pragmatic quality of Web applications by integration of patterns. *Journal of Web Engineering, 7*(1), 70–92.

Kamthan, P. (2009a). A framework for integrating the social Web environment in pattern engineering. *International Journal of Technology and Human Interaction*, *5*(2), 36–62. doi:10.4018/jthi.2009092303

Kamthan, P. (2010). A viewpoint-based approach for understanding the morphogenesis of patterns. *International Journal of Knowledge Management*, *6*(2), 40–65. doi:10.4018/jkm.2010040103

Kamthan, P., & Pai, H.-I. (2006a). Knowledge representation in pattern management. In Schwartz, D. (Ed.), *Encyclopedia of knowledge management*. Hershey, PA: Idea Group. doi:10.4018/9781591405733.ch062

Kamthan, P., & Pai, H.-I. (2006b). Representation of Web application patterns in OWL. In Taniar, D., & Rahayu, J. W. (Eds.), *Web semantics and ontology*. Hershey, PA: Idea Group. doi:10.4018/9781591409052.ch002

Kamthan, P. (2009b). *On the symbiosis between quality and patterns*. The Third International Workshop on Software Patterns and Quality (SPAQu 2009), Orlando, USA, October 25, 2009.

Kamthan, P. (2009b). *On the symbiosis between quality and patterns*. The Third International Workshop on Software Patterns and Quality (SPAQu 2009), Orlando, USA, October 25, 2009.

Kamthan, P., & Shahmir, N. (2009). *A pattern-oriented process for the realization of use case models*. The Thirteenth IBIMA Conference on Knowledge Management and Innovation in Advancing Economies, Marrakech, Morocco, November 9-10, 2009.

Karaboga, D., & Bahriye, B. (2008). On the performance of Artificial Bee Colony (ABC) algorithm. *Applied Soft Computing*, *8*(1), 687–697. doi:10.1016/j.asoc.2007.05.007

Karanjit, S., & Chris, H. (1994). *Internet firewall and network security*. New Riders Publishing.

Kardas, K., & Senkul, P. (2007). *Enhanced semantic operations for Web service composition*. International Symposium on Computer and Information Sciences, Ankara, November 2007.

Karunanithi, S., & Bieman, J. M. (1992). *Candidate reuse metrics for object-oriented and Ada software. (TR CS-92-142)*. Colorado State University.

Kasser, J. (2002). A prototype tool for improving the wording of requirements. *Proceedings of the International Symposium of Systems Engineering*.

Kawakita, J. (1982). *The original KJ-method*. Kawakita Research Institute.

Kaya, O., Hashemikhabir, S. S., Togay, C., & Dogru, A. H. (2010). *A rule-based domain specific language for fault management*. SDPS 2010: Transformative Systems Conference, Dallas Texas, June 6-11.

Kettunen, P. (2003). Managing embedded software project team knowledge. *IEEE Software*, *1*(6), 359–366.

Kim, K. J., & Han, I. (2003). Application of a hybrid genetic algorithm and neural network approach in activity-based costing. *Expert Systems with Applications*, *24*(1), 73–77. doi:10.1016/S0957-4174(02)00084-2

Kitchenham, B. A., Pfleeger, S. L., & Fenton, N. (1997). Comments on toward a framework for software measurement validation. *IEEE Transactions on Software Engineering*, *23*(8), 189–189. doi:10.1109/TSE.1997.585507

Kitchenham, B., Pfleeger, S., Pickard, L., Jones, P., & Hoaglin, D., El- Emam, K., & Rosenberg, J. (2002). Preliminary guidelines for empirical research in software engineering. *IEEE Transactions on Software Engineering*, *28*(8), 721–734. doi:10.1109/TSE.2002.1027796

Kitzinger, J. (1995). Introducing focus groups. *British Medical Journal*, *311*, 299–302.

Kizilca, H., & Yilmaz, A. E. (2008). Natural language requirement analysis methods and their applicability for Turkish. *Proceedings of the First Software Quality and Software Development Tools Symposium (YKGS 2008)*, (pp. 69–77).

Kizza, J. M. (2009). *A guide to computer network security*. London, UK: Springer. doi:10.1007/978-1-84800-917-2

Klaus, P., Günter, B., & van der Linden, F. (2005). *Software product line engineering: Foundations, principles, and techniques*. Berlin: Springer-Verlag.

Knauss, E., Brill, O., & Kitzmann, I. I., & Flohr, T. (2009). Smartwiki: Support for high-quality requirements engineering in a collaborative setting. In 2009 ICSE Workshop on Wikis for Software Engineering.

Kock, N. (2000). Sharing interdepartmental knowledge using collaboration technologies: An action research study. *Journal of Information Technology Impact, 2*(1), 5–10.

Kohls, C., & Uttecht, J.-G. (2009). Lessons learnt in mining and writing design patterns for educational interactive graphics. *Computers in Human Behavior, 25*(5), 1040–1055. doi:10.1016/j.chb.2009.01.004

Kohls, C., & Panke, S. (2009). *Is that true...? Thoughts on the epistemology of patterns.* The Sixteenth Conference on Pattern Languages of Programs (PLoP 2009), Chicago, USA, August 28-30, 2009.

Korel, B. (1990). Automated software test data generation. *IEEE Transactions on Software Engineering, 16*(8), 870–879. doi:10.1109/32.57624

Kotzé, P., Renaud, K., & van Biljon, J. (2008). Don't do this–pitfalls in using anti-patterns in teaching human-computer interaction principles. *Computers & Education, 50*(3), 979–1008. doi:10.1016/j.compedu.2006.10.003

Krishnan, M. S., Kriebel, C. H., Kekre, S., & Mukhopadhyay, T. (2000). An empirical analysis of productivity and quality in software products. *Management Science, 46*, 745–759. doi:10.1287/mnsc.46.6.745.11941

Kruchten, P. (2000). *The rational unified process.* Reading, MA: Addison Wesley.

Kruschitz, C. (2009). *XPLML: A HCI pattern formalizing and unifying approach.* The ACM CHI 2009 Conference on Human Factors in Computing Systems (CHI 2009), Boston, USA, April 4-9, 2009.

Kruschitz, C., & Hitz, M. (2010). *Analyzing the HCI design pattern variety.* The First Asian Conference on Pattern Languages of Programs (AsianPLoP 2010), Tokyo, Japan, March 16-17, 2010.

Kruschitz, C., & Hitz, M. (2010). *Analyzing the HCI design pattern variety.* The First Asian Conference on Pattern Languages of Programs (AsianPLoP 2010), Tokyo, Japan, March 16-17, 2010.

Kukko, M., Helander, N., & Virtanen, P. (2008). Knowledge management in renewing software development processes. *Proceedings of the 41st Annual Hawaii International Conference on System Sciences*, (pp. 332-332).

Kunert, T. (2009). *User-centered interaction design patterns for interactive digital television applications.* Springer-Verlag.

Kuvaja, P. (2004). BOOTSTRAP 3.0–a SPICE1 conformant process assessment methodology. *Software Quality Journal, 8*(1).

Kuvaja, P., & Bicego, A. (1994). BOOTSTRAP–a European assessment methodology. *Software Quality Journal, 3*(3). doi:10.1007/BF00402292

Kvale, S. (2007). *Doing interviews: The Sage qualitative research kit.* Thousand Oaks, CA: Sage.

Lami, G. (2009). Analytic effectiveness evaluation of techniques for natural language software requirements testability. *International Journal of Computer Systems Science and Engineering, 29*(2).

Lami, G. (1999). *Towards an automatic quality evaluation of natural language software specifications.* (Technical Report B4-25-11-99: IEI-CNR), Pisa, Italy.

Lami, G. (2005). (QuARS: A tool for analyzing requirements). (Technical Report CMU/SEI-2005-TR-014 ESC-TR-2005-014), Carnegie Mellon University Software Engineering Institute, Software Engineering Measurement and Analysis Initiative.

Lami, G., Gnesi, S., Fabbrini, F., Fusani, M., & Trentanni, M. (2001). An automatic tool for the analysis of natural language requirements. *Proceedings of the 7th International Workshop on RE: Foundation for Software Quality (REFSQ'2001).*

Laporte, C. Y., Alxender, S., & Renault, A. (2008). Developing international standards for very small enterprises. *Journal of Computer, 41*(3), 98. doi:10.1109/MC.2008.86

Laporte, C. Y., & April, A. (2006). *Applying software engineering standards in small setting: Recent historical perspectives and initial achievements.* International Research Workshop in Small Setting, Software Engineering Institue, Pittsburgh, Oct 19-20.

Laporte, C. Y., Alxender, S., & O'Connor, R. V. (2008). A software engineering lifecycle standard for very small enterprise. *Proceeding of the 15th European Conference, EuroSPI 2008 Industrial Proceeding,* (pp. 10.33-10.41).

Lassila, O. & Swick, R. R. (1998). *Resource Description Framework (RDF) model and syntax.*

LaVigne, C. (2009). Pattern pathology. In R. Monson-Haefel (Ed.), *97 things every software architect should know: Collective wisdom from the experts.* O'Reilly Media.

Lea, D. (1994). Christopher Alexander: An introduction for object-oriented designers. *ACM SIGSOFT Software Engineering Notes, 19*(1), 39–46. doi:10.1145/181610.181617

Leacock, M., Malone, E., & Wheeler, C. (2005). *Implementing a pattern library in the real world: A Yahoo! case study.* The 2005 American Society for Information Science and Technology Information Architecture Summit (ASIS&T IA 2005), Montreal, Canada, March 3-7, 2005.

Lee, C. C., & Yang, J. (2000). Knowledge value chain. *Journal of Management Development, 19*(9), 783–793. doi:10.1108/02621710010378228

Lee, M. K. O., Cheung, C. M. K., Lim, K. H., & Sia, C. L. (2006). Understanding customer knowledge sharing in web-based discussion boards: An exploratory study. *Internet Research, 16*(3), 289–303. doi:10.1108/10662240610673709

Lee, I., Leung, J. Y. T., & Son, S. H. (2007). *Handbook of real-time and embedded systems.* Chapman & Hall/CRC.

Leidner, D. E., & Alavi, M. (2001). Review: Knowledge management and knowledge management systems: Conceptual foundations and research issues. *MIS Quarterly: Management Information Systems, 25*(1), 107–136.

Leite, A., Girardi, R., & Calvalcante, U. (2008a). MAAEM: A multi-agent application engineering methodology. *Proceedings of the 20th International Conference on Software Engineering and Knowledge Engineering,* (pp. 735-740). Redwood City, CA: Knowledge Systems Institute.

Leite, A., Girardi, R., & Cavalcante, U. (2008b). An ontology for multi-agent domain and application engineering. *Proceedings of the 2008 IEEE International Conference on Information Reuse and Integration* (IEEE IRI-08), (pp. 98-103). Las Vegas, NV: IEEE.

Leuf, B., & Cunningham, W. (2001). *The wiki way: Quick collaboration on the Web.* Boston, MA: Addison-Wesley Longman.

Li, H., & Lam, C. P. (2004). Optimization of state-based test suites for software systems: An evolutionary approach. *International Journal of Computer and Information Science, 5*(3), 212–223.

Li, W., & Henry, S. (1993). Object-oriented metrics that predict maintainability. *Journal of Systems and Software, 23*(2), 111–122. doi:10.1016/0164-1212(93)90077-B

Li, J. Y. (2006). *Process improvement and risk management in off-the shelf component based development,* Unpublished doctoral dissertation, Norwegian University science and Technology.

Li, L. (1998). *Change impact analysis for object-oriented software.* Unpublished doctoral dissertation, George Mason University, Virginia, USA.

Li, X., Liu, Z., & He, J. (2001). Formal and use-case driven requirement analysis in UML. *Proceedings of the 25th Annual International Computer Software and Applications Conference (COMPSAC2001),* (pp. 215–224).

Lin, A. W., Peltier, S. T., Grethe, J. S., & Ellisman, M. H. (2007). Case studies on the use of workflow technologies for scientific analysis: The biomedical informatics research network and the telescience project. *Workflows for e-science: Scientific workflows for Grids,* 109–125.

Litern, G., Diedrich, F. J., & Serfaty, D. (2002). Engineering the community of practice for maintenance of organizational knowledge. *Proceedings IEEE 7th Conference on Human Factors and Power Plants,* (pp. 7-13).

Liu, D., Subramaniam, K., Eberlein, A., & Far, B. H. (2004). *Natural language requirements analysis and class model generation using UCDA.* (LNCS 3029), (pp. 295–304).

Lorenz, M., & Kidd, J. (1994). *Object-oriented software metrics: A practical guide.* Englewood Cliffs, NJ: Prentice Hall.

Ludascher, B., Altintas, I., Berkley, C., Higgins, D., Jaeger, E., Jones, M., & Lee, E. A. (2006). Scientific workflow management and the Kepler system. *Concurrency and Computation, 18*(10), 1039. doi:10.1002/cpe.994

Luger, G. F. (2004). *Inteligência artificial: Structures and strategies for complex problem solving.* Porto Alegre, Brazil: Bookman.

Macias, B., & Pulman, S. G. (1993). Natural language processing for requirement specifications. In Redmill, F., & Anderson, T. (Eds.), *Safety-critical systems: Current issues, techniques and standards*. London, UK: Chapman-Hall.

Mader, S. (2008). *Wikipatterns: A practical guide to improving productivity and collaboration in your organization*. John Wiley and Sons.

Maechling, P., Deelman, E., Zhao, L., Graves, R., Mehta, G., Gupta, N., & Mehringer, J. (2006). SCEC CyberShake workflows—automating probabilistic seismic hazard analysis calculations. *Workflows for e-science*, 143–163.

Maiden, N., Gizikis, A., & Robertson, S. (2004). Provoking creativity: Imagine what your requirements could be like. *IEEE Software*, *21*, 68–75. doi:10.1109/MS.2004.1331305

Maiden, N., Manning, S., Robertson, S., & Greenwood, J. (2004). Integrating creativity workshops into structured requirements processes. *Proceedings of the 5th conference on Designing interactive systems*. (pp. 113–122).

Malevris, N., Yates, D. F., & Veevers, A. (1990). Predictive metric for likely feasibility of program paths. *Information and Software Technology*, *32*(2), 115–118. doi:10.1016/0950-5849(90)90110-D

Mangina, E. (2005). Intelligent agent-based monitoring platform for applications in engineering. *International Journal of Computer Science and Applications*, *2*(1), 38–48.

Manolescu, D., Kozaczynski, W., Miller, A., & Hogg, J. (2007). The growing divide in the patterns world. *IEEE Software*, *24*(4), 61–67. doi:10.1109/MS.2007.120

Manzer, A., & Dogru, A. H. (2007). Process integration through hierarchical decomposition. In Lam, W., & Shankararaman, V. (Eds.), *Enterprise architecture and integration: Methods, implementation, and technologies*. New York: Information Science Reference. doi:10.4018/9781591408871.ch005

Marchesi, M. (1998). OOA metric for the unified modeling language. *Proceedings of the 2nd Euro Micro Conference on Software Maintenance and Reengineering*.

Mariano, R. (2008). *Development of a family of recommender systems based on the Semantic Web technology and its reuse on the recommendation of legal tax information items*. MSc dissertation.

Mariano, R., Girardi, R., Leite, A., Drumond, L., & Maranhão, D. (2008). A case study on domain analysis of Semantic Web multi-agent recommender systems. In *Proceedings 3th International Conference on Software and Data Technologies, Porto. Portugal*, (pp. 160-167).

Marshall, C. C., & Shipman, F. M. (1995). Spatial hypertext: Designing for change. *Communications of the ACM*, *38*(8), 88–97. doi:10.1145/208344.208350

Marshall, C. C., & Shipman, F. M. (1993). Searching for the missing link: Discovering implicit structure in spatial hypertext. In *Proceedings of the Conference of Hypertext and Hypermedia*, (pp. 217–230).

Martin, D., Burstein, M., McDermott, D., McIlraith, S., Paolucci, M., & McGuinness, D. (2007). Bringing semantics to Web services with OWL-S. *World Wide Web (Bussum)*, *10*(3), 243–277. doi:10.1007/s11280-007-0033-x

Martin, D., Burstein, M., Hobbs, J., Lassila, O., McDermott, D., McIlraith, S., & Narayanan, S. (2004). *OWL-S: Semantic markup for Web services*.

Mathiassen, L., & Pourkomeylian, P. (2003). Managing knowledge in a software organization. *Journal of Knowledge Management*, *7*(2), 63–80. doi:10.1108/13673270310477298

Mathur, A. P. (2008). *Foundations of software testing* (2nd ed.). Pearson Education.

Maurer, H., & Tochtermann, K. (2002). On a new powerful model for knowledge management and its applications. *Journal of Universal Computer Science*, *8*(1), 85–96.

McBride, B. (2004). *RDF vocabulary description language 1.0: RDF schema changes*.

McGregor, D. (1985). *The human side of enterprise: 25th anniversary printing*. McGraw-Hill/Irwin.

McIlraith, S., Son, T. C., & Zeng, H. (2001). Semantic Web services. *IEEE Intelligent Systems*, *16*(2), 46–53. doi:10.1109/5254.920599

Mcminn, P. (2004). Search-based software test data generation: A survey. *Software Testing. Verification and Reliability, 14*(2), 105–156. doi:10.1002/stvr.294

Mcminn, P., & Holcombe, M. (2003). The state problem for evolutionary testing. *Proceedings of GECCO 2003*, (LNCS 2724), (pp. 2488-2500).

Mcminn, P., Harman, M., Binkley, D., & Tonella, P. (2006). *The species per path approach to search based test data generation*. ISSTA-2006, (pp. 13-24).

McPhail, J. C., & Deugo, D. (2001). *Deciding on a pattern*. The Fourteenth International Conference on Industrial and Engineering Applications of Artificial Intelligence and Expert Systems (IEA/AIE 2001), Budapest, Hungary, June 4-7, 2001.

McPhillips, T., Bowers, S., Zinn, D., & Ludascher, B. (2009). Scientific workflow design for mere mortals. *Future Generation Computer Systems, 25*(5), 541–551. doi:10.1016/j.future.2008.06.013

Medjahed, B., Bouguettaya, A., & Elmagarmid, A. K. (2003). Composing Web services on the Semantic Web. *Very Large Data Bases Journal, 12*(4), 333–351. doi:10.1007/s00778-003-0101-5

Meehan, B., & Richardson, I. (2002). Identification of software process knowledge management. *Software Process Improvement and Practice, 7*(2), 47–55. doi:10.1002/spip.154

Meenakshi, V., Last, M., & Kandel, A. (2002). Using a neural network in the software testing process. *International Journal of Intelligent Systems, 17*(1), 45–62. doi:10.1002/int.1002

Megginson, D. (2005). *Imperfect XML: Rants, raves, tips, and tricks from an insider*. Addison-Wesley.

MeMVaTEx. (2008). *Méthode de modélisation pour la validation et la traçabilité des exigences, Continental AG and ANR*. Retrieved from www.memvatex.org

Merritt, M., & David, P. (2002). *Wireless security*.

Meszaros, G., & Doble, J. (1998). A pattern language for pattern writing. In Martin, R. C., Riehle, D., & Buschmann, F. (Eds.), *Pattern languages of program design (Vol. 3*, pp. 529–574). Addison-Wesley.

Mich, L., Franch, M., & Inverardi, P. N. (2004). Market research for requirements analysis using linguistic tools. *Requirements Engineering, 9*, 40–56. doi:10.1007/s00766-004-0195-3

Mich, L., Anesi, C., & Berry, D. (2005). Applying a pragmatics based creativity-fostering technique to requirements elicitation. *Requirements Engineering, 10*(4), 262–275. doi:10.1007/s00766-005-0008-3

Micheal, C. C., & Mcgraw, G. (1999). *Automated software test data generation for complex programs*. Technical Report, Reliable Software Technologies.

Mirbel, I., & Crescenzo, P. (2009). Improving collaborations in neuroscientist community. In *Proceedings of the 2009 IEEE/WIC/ACM International Joint Conference on Web Intelligence and Intelligent Agent Technology - Volume 03*, (pp. 567-570). IEEE Computer Society.

Moataz, A. A., & Irman, H. (2008). GA-based multiple paths test data generator. *Computers & Operations Research, 35*(10), 3107–3124. doi:10.1016/j.cor.2007.01.012

Modro, N. R. (2000). *Intelligent system for financial managing and monitoring for little companies*. Florianópolis, Brazil: UFSC.

Mohammad, F., Babak, A., & Ali, M. (2007). Application of honey-bee mating optimization algorithm on clustering. *Applied Mathematics and Computation, 190*(2), 1502–1513. doi:10.1016/j.amc.2007.02.029

Morville, P., & Callender, J. (2010). *Search patterns*. O'Reilly Media.

Mouritsen, J., Larsen, H. T., & Bukh, P. N. D. (2001). Intellectual capital and the capable firm: Narrating, visualizing and numbering for managing knowledge. *Accounting, Organizations and Society, 26*, 735–762. doi:10.1016/S0361-3682(01)00022-8

Mtigwe, B. (2005). The entrepreneurial firm internationalization process in Southern African context: A comparative approach. *International Journal of Entrepreneurial Behaviour and Research, 11*(5), 358–377. doi:10.1108/13552550510615006

Mylopoulos, J., Chung, L., Yu, E., & Nixon, B. (1992). Representing and using non-functional requirements: A process-oriented approach. *IEEE Transactions on Software Engineering, 18*(6), 483–497. doi:10.1109/32.142871

Nattoch Dag, J., Regnell, B., Carlshamre, P., Andersson, M., & Karlsson, J. (2001). Evaluating automated support for requirements similarity analysis in market-driven development. *Proceedings of the Seventh International Workshop on Requirements Engineering: Foundation for Software Quality.*

Navega, S. (2005). Techniques for knowledge computer representation. Retrieved from http://www.intelliwise.com/reports/info2005.pdf

Neapolitan, R. E. (2004). *Learning Bayesian networks.* Upper Saddle River, NJ: Pearson Prentice Hall.

Nery, H. de A., & Gonçalves, F. V. (2004). AORML–a laguage for modelling a multiagent application: An application on Expertcop System. In *X encontro de iniciação à pesquisa, fortaleza.*

Newman, B. (2010). *The knowledge management forum.* Retrieved April, 2010, from http://www.km-forum.org/htm

Newton, E., & Girardi, R. (2007). *PROPOST: A knowledge-based tool for supporting project portfolio management.* International Conference on Systems Engineering and Modeling - ICSEM'07, (pp. 98-103).

Nielsen, J. (1993). *Usability engineering.* Morgan Kaufmann.

Nielsen, J., & Loranger, H. (2006). *Prioritizing Web usability.* New Riders Publishing.

Nii, P. (1986). The blackboard model of problem solving. *AI Magazine, 7*(2), 38–53.

Noh, S.-Y., & Gadia, S. K. (2003). *RAST: Requirement analysis support tool based on linguistic information.* (Technical Report 03-08), Iowa State University Department of Computer Science.

Nonaka, I., & Takeuchi, H. (1995). *The knowledge creating company.* Oxford University Press.

Nonaka, I., Umemoto, K., & Senoo, D. (1996). From information processing to knowledge creation: A paradigm shift in business management. *Technology in Society, 18*(2), 203–218. doi:10.1016/0160-791X(96)00001-2

Nonaka, I., & Takeuchi, H. (1995). *The knowledge creating company.* New York, NY: Oxford University Press.

Nonaka, I., Toyama, R., & Konno, N. (2000). SECI, Ba and leadership: A unified model of dynamic knowledge creation. *Long Range Planning, 33*(1), 5–34. doi:10.1016/S0024-6301(99)00115-6

Nunes, I., Kulesza, U., Nunes, C., & Lucena, C. A. (2009). A domain engineering process for developing multi-agent systems product lines. *Proceedings of the 8th International Conference of Autonomous Agents and Multi-agent Systems* (AAMAS 2009), Budapest, (pp. 10-15).

O'Reilly, T. (2005). *What is Web 2.0: Design patterns and business models for the next generation of software.* O'Reilly Network, September 30, 2005.

Odell, J. D., Parunak, H. V. D., & Bauer, B. S. V. (2001). *Representing agent interaction protocols in UML.* 22nd International Conference on Software Engineering (ISCE), (pp. 121–140).

Ogrinz, M. (2009). *Mashup patterns: Designs and strategies for using mashups in enterprise environments.* Addison-Wesley.

Ohtsuki, M., Segawa, J., Yoshida, N., & Makinouchi, A. (1997). *Structured document framework for design patterns based on SGML.* The Twenty First International Computer Software and Applications Conference (COMPSAC 1997), Washington, D.C., USA, August 11-15, 1997.

Oinn, T., Addis, M., Ferris, J., Marvin, D., Greenwood, M., Carver, T., & Pocock, M. R. (2004). *Taverna: A tool for the composition and enactment of bioinformatics workflows.*

Oliveira, H. M. (2000). *Techniques for project and implementation of software agents.* (Technical report, Maringá State University).

Olsen, T., Humphrey, W. S., & Kitson, D. (1989). *Conducting SEI-assisted software process assessments.* Pittsburgh, PA: Software Engineering Institute. (Technical Report CMU/SEI-89-TR-07).

OMG SysML. (2006). *The Systems Modeling Language, Object Modeling Group std.* July 2006. Retrieved from http://www.sysml.org

OMG. (2004). *Unified Modelling Language version 2.0.* Report 2004.

OMG. (2006). Unified Modeling Language: Infrastructure, version 2.0, March 2006, (OMG document formal/05-07-05).

Ordonez, M. J., & Haddad, H. M. (2008). *The state of metrics in software industry*. Information Technology: New Generations.

Oren, E., Volkel, M., Breslin, J. G., & Decker, S. (2006). Semantic wikis for personal knowledge management. *Database and Expert Systems Applications, 4080*, 509–518. doi:10.1007/11827405_50

OWL-S. (2004). *Semantic markup for Web services*. Retrieved in October 2009, from http://www.w3.org/Submission/OWL-S/

Pai, G. I., & Dugan, J. B. (2007). Empirical analysis of software fault content and fault proneness using Bayesian methods. *IEEE Transactions on Software Engineering, 33*(10), 675–686. doi:10.1109/TSE.2007.70722

Pai, G., Bechta-Dugan, J., & Lateef, K. (2005). Bayesian networks applied to software IV&V. *Proceedings of 29th Annual IEEE/NASA Software Engineering Workshop*, IEEE Computer Society, Washington, DC, (pp. 293-304).

Palfrey, J., & Gasser, U. (2008). *Born digital: Understanding the first generation of digital natives*. Basic Books.

Paolucci, M., Kawamura, T., Payne, T. R., & Sycara, K. (2002). *Importing the Semantic Web in UDDI*. International Semantic Web Conference, (pp. 225-236).

Paolucci, M., Kawamura, T., Payne, T. R., & Sycara, K. (2002a). *Semantic matching of Web services capabilities*. International Semantic Web Conference, (pp. 333-347).

Papadimitriou, D., et al. (2009). *The future of Internet*. Retrieved April 2010, from http://www.future-internet.eu/fileadmin/documents/reports/Cross-ETPs_FI_Vision_Document_v1_0.pdf

Paquette, S. (2006). *Customer knowledge management*. Retrieved April 2010, from www.fis.utoronto .ca/phd/paquette/documents/paquette%20%20customer%20knowledge%20management.pdf

Paraiso, E. C. (1997). *Proposal of a multagent environment for controlling and monitoring of industry processes*. Master Thesis, Cefet-PR.

Parent, M., Gallupe, R. B., Salisbury, W. D., & Handelman, J. M. (2000). Knowledge creation in focus group: Can group technologies help? *Information & Management, 38*(1), 47–58. doi:10.1016/S0378-7206(00)00053-7

Pargas, R. P., Harrold, M., & Peck, R. (1999). Test-data generation using genetic algorithms. *Software Testing. Verification and Reliability, 9*(4), 263–282. doi:10.1002/(SICI)1099-1689(199912)9:4<263::AID-STVR190>3.0.CO;2-Y

Patton, M. Q. (2002). *Qualitative evaluation and research methods* (3rd ed.). Newbury Park, CA: Sage Publications, Inc.

Paulo, M. S. B., & Mario, J. (2000*), Identification of Potentially Infeasible Program Paths by Monitoring the Search for Test Data*, 15th IEEE International Conference on Automated Software Engineering (ASE00), 209.

Pearl, J. (1988). *Probabilistic reasoning in intelligent systems: Networks of plausible inference*. San Francisco, CA: Morgan Kaufmann.

Pearl, J. (1985). Bayesian networks: A model of self-activated memory for evidential reasoning. (UCLA Technical Report CSD-850017). *Proceedings of the 7th Conference of the Cognitive Science Society*, University of California, Irvine, CA. (pp. 329–334).

Pedrycz, W., & Peters, J. F. (1998). *Computational intelligence in software engineering* (*Vol. 16*). World Scientific Publishers.

Peirce, C. S. (1990). *Semiotics*.

Pennington, D. D., Higgins, D., Peterson, A. T., Jones, M. B., Ludascher, B., & Bowers, S. (2007). Ecological niche modeling using the Kepler workflow system. *Workflows for e-science: Scientific workflows for Grids*, 91–108.

Perini, A., & Susi, A. (2004). Developing tools for agent-oriented visual modeling. In G. Lindemann, J. Denzinger, I. Timm, & R. Unland (Eds.), *Proceedings of the Second German Conference* (pp. 169–182). Springer-Verlag.

Peter, F., & Johannes, L. (2000). Automated Test Case Generation From Dynamic Models. *Lecture Notes in Computer Science, 1850 /2000*, 472–491.

Peters, J. F., & Pedrycz, W. (2000). *Software engineering: An engineering approach*. John Wiley & Sons.

Poels, G., & Dedene, G. (1997). Comments on property-based software engineering measurement: Refining the additivity properties. *IEEE Transactions on Software Engineering, 23*(3), 190–195. doi:10.1109/32.585508

Poels, G., & Dedene, G. (2000). Distance-based software measurement: Necessary and sufficient properties for software measures. *Information and Software Technology, 42*(1), 35–46. doi:10.1016/S0950-5849(99)00053-1

Poels, G., & Dedene, G. (1999). *DISTANCE: A framework for software measure construction.* (Research Report DTEW9937), Dept. Applied Economics, Katholieke Universiteit Leuven, Belgium.

Pohl, K. (1994). The three dimensions of requirements engineering: A framework and its application. *International Journal of Information Systems, 19*(3), 243–258.

Pohl, K., Bockle, G., & Linden, F. (2005). *Software product line engineering: Foundations, principles and techniques.* USA: Springer Verlag.

Polanyi, M. (1966). *The tacit dimension.* London, UK: Routledge and Kegan.

Powell, R. A., & Single, H. M. (1996). Focus groups. *International Journal for Quality in Health Care, 8*(5), 499–504. doi:10.1093/intqhc/8.5.499

Prasad, B. E., Tolety, S. P., Uma, G., & Umarani, P. (1994). An expert system shell for aerospace applications. *IEEE Expert, 9*(4). doi:10.1109/64.336148

Prat, N. (1997). Goal formalisation and classification for requirements engineering. In *Proceedings of the Third International Workshop on Requirements Engineering: Foundations of Software Quality REFSQ* (pp. 145–156).

Prechelt, L., Unger, B., Philippsen, M., & Tichy, W. (2003). A controlled experiment on inheritance depth as a cost factor for code maintenance. *Journal of Systems and Software, 65*, 115–126.

Prensky, M. (2001). Digital natives, digital immigrants. *Horizon, 9*(5), 1–6. doi:10.1108/10748120110424816

Pressman, R. S. (1997). *Software engineering: A practitioner's approach* (3rd ed.). McGraw Hill.

Pressman, R. S. (2005). *Software engineering-a practitioners approach* (6th ed.). McGraw Hill.

Pressman, R. S. (1997). *Software engineering: A practitioner's approach* (4th ed.). New York, NY: McGraw-Hill.

Prud'Hommeaux, E., & Seaborne, A. (2006). *SPARQL query language for RDF.* W3C working draft, 20.

Radliński, Ł. (2009). Predicting defect types in software projects. *Polish Journal of Environmental Studies, 18*(3B), 311–315.

Radlinski, L. (2008). *Improved software project risk assessment using Bayesian nets.* Unpublished doctoral dissertation, Queen Mary, University of London, London.

Radliński, Ł., Fenton, N., Neil, M., & Marquez, D. (2007). Improved decision-making for software managers using Bayesian networks. *Proceedings of 11th IASTED International Conference Software Engineering and Applications,* Cambridge, MA. (pp. 13–19).

Ralyté, J., & Rolland, C. (2001). An assembly process model for method engineering. In *Advanced Information Systems engineering,* (pp. 267–283).

Randall, N. K., & Panos, L. C. (2002). *Wireless security model threads solutions.* McGraw-Hill Telecom.

Reed, T. F., & Kelly, D. (2002). The skill gap in the Irish software industry. *Irish Journal of Management, 23*(2), 95–110.

Renear, A., Dubin, D., Sperberg-McQueen, C. M., & Huitfeldt, C. (2002). *Towards a semantics for XML markup.* The 2002 ACM Symposium on Document Engineering (DocEng 2002), McLean, USA, November 8-9, 2002.

Rezende, S. O. (2003). *Intelligent systems: Foundations and application.*

Rhem, A. (2005). *UML for developing knowledge management systems.* Boston, MA: Auerbach Publications. doi:10.1201/9780203492451

Rhodes, J., Hung, R., Lok, P., Lien, B. Y., & Wu, C. M. (2008). Factors influencing organizational knowledge transfer: Implication for corporate performance. *Journal of Knowledge Management, 12*(3), 84. doi:10.1108/13673270810875886

Ribeiro, J. C. B., Rela, M. Z., & de Vega, F. F. (2008). *A strategy for evaluating feasible and unfeasible test cases for the evolutionary testing of object-oriented software.* ASE-2008, (pp. 85-92).

Richardson, I., & von Wangenheim, C. G. (2007). Guest editors introduction: Why are small software organizations different? *IEEE Software*, *24*, 18–22. doi:10.1109/MS.2007.12

Riehle, D., & Züllighoven, H. (1996). Understanding and using patterns in software development. *Theory and Practice of Object Systems*, *2*(1), 3–13. doi:10.1002/(SICI)1096-9942(1996)2:1<3::AID-TAPO1>3.0.CO;2-#

Rising, L. (2000). *The pattern almanac 2000*. Addison-Wesley.

Robertson, S. (2001). Requirements trawling: Techniques for discovering requirements. *International Journal of Human-Computer Studies*, *55*(4), 405–421. doi:10.1006/ijhc.2001.0481

Rolland, C. (2007). *Conceptual modelling in Information Systems engineering*. Springer-Verlag.

Rolland, C., & Proix, C. (1992). A natural language approach for requirements engineering. *Proceedings of the 4th International Conference on Advanced Information Systems Engineering*.

Rosella, (2010). *Customer profiling*. Retrieved May 2010, from http://www.roselladb.com/ customer-profiling.htm

Roseman, M., & Chan, R. (2000). A framework to structure knowledge for enterprise system. *Proceedings of Americas Conference on Information Systems*, 2000.

Rosenberg, L. H., & Hyatt, L. A. (2000). *Software quality metrics for object-oriented environments*. Unisys Government Systems, Software Assurance technology Center.

Rowley, J. (2002). Eight questions for customer knowledge management in e-business. *Journal of Knowledge Management*, *6*(5), 500–511. doi:10.1108/13673270210450441

Rowley, J. (2002). Reflections on customer knowledge management in e-business. *Qualitative Market Research*, *5*(4), 268–280. doi:10.1108/13522750210443227

Rowley, J. (2005). Customer knowledge management or customer surveillance. *Global Business and Economic Review*, *7*(1), 100–110. doi:10.1504/GBER.2005.006923

Roy, T. K., & Stavropoulos, C. (2007). *Customer knowledge management in the e-business environment*. Master's thesis, Dept of Business Admin and Social Sciences, Lulea Univ. of Tech, Sweden.

Rumbaugh, J., Jacobson, I., & Booch, G. (1999). *The unified modeling language reference manual*. Boston, MA: Addison-Wesley.

Rüping, A. (2003). *Agile documentation: A pattern guide to producing lightweight documents for software projects*. John Wiley and Sons.

Russel, S., & Norvig, P. (1995). *Artificial intelligence: A modern approach* (2nd ed.). Prentice-Hall Publications.

Saffer, D. (2009). *Designing gestural interfaces*. O'Reilly Media.

Salas, E., Burke, C. S., & Cannon-Bowers, J. A. (2000). Teamwork: Emerging principles. *International Journal of Management Reviews*, *2*(4), 339–356. doi:10.1111/1468-2370.00046

Sanders, M. (1998). *The Spire handbook: Better, faster, cheaper software development in small organization*. Dublin, Ireland: Centre for Software Engineering.

Sapovadia, V. K. (2006). *Micro finance: The pillars of a tool to socio-economic development*. Development Gateway. Retrieved on October 9, 2008, from http://ssrn.com/abstract=955062

Schaffert, S., Bry, F., Baumeister, J., & Kiesel, M. (2008). Semantic wikis. *IEEE Software*, *25*(4), 8–11. doi:10.1109/MS.2008.95

Schmettow, M., & Niebuhr, S. (2007). *A pattern-based usability inspection method: First empirical performance measures and future issues*. The Twenty First British HCI Group Annual Conference (HCI 2007), Lancaster, U.K., September 3-7, 2007.

Schmidt, A. (2005). Knowledge maturing and the continuity of context as a unifying concept for knowledge management and e-learning. In *Proceedings of the International Conference on Knowledge Management*.

Schnoll, S. (2003). *Internet security best practices, presentation*. NOBUG, June 2003.

Schreiber, G., Akkermans, H., Anjewierden, A., de Hoog, R., Shadbolt, N., van de Velde, W., & Wielinga, B. (2000). *Knowledge engineering and management: The CommonKADS methodology*. MIT Press.

Schuler, D., & Namioka, A. (1993). *Participatory design: Principles and practices*. CRC Press.

Schumacher, M., Fernandez-Buglioni, E., Hybertson, D., Buschmann, F., & Sommerlad, P. (2006). *Security patterns: Integrating security and systems engineering*. John Wiley and Sons.

Schümmer, T., & Lukosch, S. (2007). *Patterns for computer-mediated interaction*. John Wiley and Sons.

Schweitzer, D. (2003). *Incident response: Computer forensics toolkit*. USA: Wiley.

Sears, A., & Jacko, J. A. (2008). *The human-computer interaction handbook: Fundamentals, evolving technologies, and emerging applications* (2nd ed.). Lawrence Erlbaum Associates.

Segerståhl, K., & Jokela, T. (2006). *Usability of interaction patterns*. The CHI 2006 Conference on Human Factors in Computing Systems, Montréal, Canada, April 22-27, 2006.

SEI. (2005). *CMMI*. Retrieved April 2010, from http://www.sei.cmu.edu/cmmi/

Selby, R. W. (1988). Empirically analyzing software reuse in a production environment. In Tracz, W. (Ed.), *Software reuse: Emerging technology*. IEEE Computer Society Press.

Shanks, G. (1999). *Semiotic approach to understanding representation in Information Systems*. The Information Systems Foundations Workshop, Sydney, Australia, September 29, 1999.

Shaw, D., Edward, J. S., Baker, B., & Collier, P. M. (2003). Achieving closure through knowledge management. *Electronic Journal of Knowledge Management*, *1*(2), 197–204.

Shields, M. (2007). Control-versus data-driven workflows. *Workflows for e-science: Scientific workflows for Grids*, 167–173.

Shull, F., Basili, V., Carver, J., & Maldonado, J. (2002). *Replicating software engineering experiments: Addressing the tacit knowledge problem*. 1st International Symposium on Empirical Software Engineering (ISESE 2002), Nara, Japan, (pp. 7-16). IEEE Computer Society.

Siemens. (2006). (Introduction to future ISO 26262, Siemens VDO internal presentation).

Sinaalto, M. (2006). *The impact of test driven development on design quality. Agile Software Development of Embedded Systems* (*Vol. 10*). ITEA.

Singh, A. (2009). An Artificial Bee Colony Algorithm for the Leaf-Constrained Minimum Spanning Tree Problem. *Applied Soft Computing*, *9*(2), 625–631. doi:10.1016/j.asoc.2008.09.001

Sirin, E., Hendler, J., & Parsia, B. (2003). *Semi automatic composition of Web services using semantic descriptions*. In Web Services: Modeling, Architecture and Infrastructure Workshop in conjunction with ICEIS.

Sirvio, K. S., Mantyniemi, A., & Seppanen, V. (2002). Toward a practical solution for capturing knowledge for software projects. *IEEE Software*, *19*(3), 60–62. doi:10.1109/MS.2002.1003457

Sivashanmugam, K., Miller, J., Sheth, A., & Verma, K. (2004). Framework for Semantic Web process composition. *International Journal of Electronic Commerce*, *9*(2), 71–106.

Skoutas, D., Sacharidis, D., Kantere, V., & Sellis, T. (2008). *Efficient Semantic Web service discovery in centralized and P2P environments*. 7th International Semantic Web Conference (ISWC), (pp. 583-598), Karlsruhe, Germany, October 26-30.

Skyrme, D. J. (2010). *The knowledge management forum*. Retrieved April 2010, from http://www.km-forum.org/htm

Slominski, A. (2006). Adapting BPEL to scientific workflows. *Workflows for e-science*, 208–226.

Solis, C., & Ali, N. (2008a). ShyWiki-a spatial hypertext wiki. In *Proceedings of the 2008 International Symposium on Wikis*.

Solis, C., & Ali, N. (2008b). ShyWiki-a spatial hypertext wiki prototype (demo). In *Proceedings of the 2008 International Symposium on Wikis*.

Solis, C., & Ali, N. (2010). *A spatial hypertext wiki for knowledge management*. In IEEE 2010 International Symposium on Collaborative Technologies.

Sommerville, I., & Sawyer, P. (2004). *Requirements engineering: A good practice guide*. John Wiley & Sons.

Sommerville, I. (1996). *Software engineering* (6th ed.). Addison Wesley Publishing Company.

Sommerville, I. (2004). *Software engineering* (7th ed.). Reading, MA: Addison Wesley.

Sowa, J. F. (1991). *Principles of semantic networks*. Morgan Kaufmann.

SPEM. (2008). Software process engineering metamodel specification. Retrieved September 2008, from http://www.omg.org/docs/formal/05-01-06.pdf

Spender, J, C. (1996). Making knowledge the basis of a dynamic theory of the firm. *Strategic Management Journal, 17*, 45–62.

Spender, J. C., & Grant, R. (1996). Knowledge and the firm: Overview. *Strategic Management Journal, 17*, 45–62.

Spiegler, I. (2000). Knowledge management: A new idea or recycled concept. *Communications of the Association for Information Systems, 3*(14).

Spivey, J. M. (1992). *The Z notation: A reference manual*. London, UK: Prentice-Hall.

SQI. (2010). *What is SPICE?* Retrieved April 2010, from http://www.sqi.gu.edu.au/spice/

Stallings, W. (1999). *SNMP, SNMPv2, SNMPv3 and RMON 1 and 2*. Harlow, UK: Addison Wesley.

Stallings, W. (2003). *Network security essentials* (2nd ed.). Pearson Education Inc.

Standish Group. (1995). *Chaos report*. Boston, MA: The Standish Group International Inc.

Stelzer, D., & Mellis, W. (1998). Success factors of organizational change in software process improvement. *Software Process Improvement and Practice, 4*(4), 227–250. doi:10.1002/(SICI)1099-1670(199812)4:4<227::AID-SPIP106>3.0.CO;2-1

Stewart, T. A. (2002). *The case against knowledge management. Business 2.0 Magazine*. Porto Alegre, Brazil: Artes Médicas.

Stewart, B. (2002). Predicting project delivery rates using the naive–Bayes classifier. *Journal of Software Maintenance and Evolution: Research and Practice, 14*, 161–179. doi:10.1002/smr.250

Strauss, A., & Corbin, J. (1998). *Basics of qualitative research: Techniques and procedures for developing grounded theory* (2nd ed.). Thousand Oaks, CA: Sage.

Sveiby, K. E. (1997). *The new organizational wealth: Managing & measuring knowledgebased assets*. San Francisco, CA: BerrettKoehler Publishers, Inc.

Szulanski, G. (1996). Exploring internal stickiness: Impediments to the transfer of best practice within firm. *Journal of Strategic Management, 17*(2), 27–43.

Szyperski, C. (2002). *Component software: Beyond object oriented programming*. New York: Addison-Wesley.

Taibi, T. (2007). *Design pattern formalization techniques*. Hershey, PA: Idea Group.

Taibi, T., & Ngo, C. L. (2002). *A pattern for evaluating design patterns*. The Sixth World Multiconference on Systemics, Cybernetics and Informatics (SCI 2002), Orlando, USA, July 14-18, 2002.

Tallam, S., & Gupta, N. (2005). *A concept analysis inspired greedy algorithm for test suite minimization*.

Tan, W., Missier, P., Madduri, R., & Foster, I. (2009). *Building scientific workflow with Taverna and BPEL: A comparative study in caGrid*. In Service-Oriented Computing – ICSOC 2008 Workshops, (pp. 118-129).

Tang, M., Kao, M., & Chen, M. (1998). *An empirical study on object-oriented metrics*. 6th IEEE International Symposium on Software Metrics.

Taylor, S. J., & Bodgan, R. (1984). *Introduction to qualitative research method*. John Wiley & Sons.

Tekkalmaz, M., Gurler, E., & Dursun, M. (2009). *Görev Kritik ve Gömülü Sistemler için T5D Uyumlu Bir Hata Yönetimi Altyapısı Tasarımı ve Gerçeklemesi*. Ulusal Yazılım Mühendisliği Sempozyumu (UYMS – Turkish National Software Engineering Symposium), İstanbul, October 2009.

Thangarajah, J., Padgham, L., & Winikoff, M. (2005). Prometheus design tool. *AAMAS, 2005*, 1–2.

Thibodeau, P., & Rosencrance, L. (2002). Users losing billions due to bugs. *Computerworld, 36*, 1–2.

Tidwell, J. (2005). *Designing interfaces: Patterns for effective interaction design*. O'Reilly Media.

Tracey, N., Clark, J., & Mander, K. (1998). Automated program flaw finding using simulated annealing. *Proceedings of the 1998 ACM SIGSOFT International Symposium on Software Testing and Analysis*, (pp. 73-81).

Turner, K., & Makhija, M. (2006). The role of organizational controls in managing knowledge. *Academy of Management Review, 31*(1), 197–217.

U. S. Department of Defense. (1985). *DOD MIL-STD-490A specification practices*. Washington, DC: United States Federal Government.

Uren, V. S., Cimiano, P., Iria, J., Handschuh, S., Vargas-Vera, M., Motta, E., & Ciravegna, F. (2006). Semantic annotation for knowledge management: Requirements and a survey of the state of the art. *Journal of Web Semantics, 4*(1), 14–28. doi:10.1016/j.websem.2005.10.002

Valtanen, A., & Sihvonen, H. M. (2008). Employees' motivation for SPI: Case study in a small Finnish software company. *Proceeding of the 15th European Conference, EuroSPI 2008,* (pp. 152-163). Berlin/Heildelberg, Germany: Springer–Verlag.

Van Den Berg, K. G., & Van Den Broek, P. M. (1996). Axiomatic validation in the software metric development process. In Melton, A. (Ed.), *Software measurement*. Thomson Computer Press.

Van Welie, M., & Van der Veer, G. C. (2003). *Pattern languages in interaction design: Structure and organization*. The Ninth IFIP TC13 International Conference on Human-Computer Interaction (INTERACT 2003), Zürich, Switzerland, September 1-5, 2003.

Verma, K., Sivashanmugam, K., Sheth, A., Patil, A., Oundhakar, S., & Miller, J. (2005). METEOR-S WSDI: A scalable infrastructure of registries for semantic publication and discovery of Web services. *Journal of Information Technology Management, 6*(1), 17–39. doi:10.1007/s10799-004-7773-4

Vora, P. (2009). *Web application design patterns*. Morgan Kaufmann.

Wang, W., Xiong, R., & Sun, J. (2007). Design of a Web2.0-based knowledge management platform. In *Proceedings of the Seventh IFIP International Conference on e-Business, e-Services, and e-Society*, (pp. 237-245).

Ward, J., & Aurum, A. (2004). *Knowledge management in software engineering-describing the process*. Australian Software Engineering Conference (ASWEC'04), (pp. 137-146).

Warmer, J., & Kleppe, A. (1999). *The object constraint language: Precise modeling with UML*. Addison Wesley Publishing Company.

Washizaki, H., Yamamoto, H., & Fukazawa, Y. (2003). A metrics suite for measuring reusability of software components. *Proceedings of the 9th International Symposium on Software Metrics*, (p. 211).

Weick, K. E. (1995). *Sense making in organization*. Thousand Oak, CA: Sage Publication.

Weiss, S. M., & Kulikowsky, C. A. (1984). *A practical guide to designing expert systems*. Yourdon Press.

Weiss, M. (2008). *Patterns and their impact on system concerns*. The Thirteenth European Conference on Pattern Languages of Programs (EuroPLoP 2008), Irsee, Germany, July 9-13, 2008.

Wen, Y., & Jiao, Y. (2009). Knowledge fusion creation model and its implementation based on wiki platform. In *Proceedings of the International Symposium on Information Engineering and Electronic Commerce*, (pp. 495–499).

Wendorff, P. (2001). *Assessment of design patterns during software reengineering: Lessons learned from a large commercial project*. The Fifth European Conference on Software Maintenance and Reengineering (CSMR 2001), Lisbon, Portugal, March 14-16, 2001.

Werneck, V. M. B., Pereira, L. F., Silva, T. S., Almentero, E. K., & Cysneiros, L. M. (2006). *An evaluation of the MAS-CommonKADS methodology*. Second Workshop on Software Engineering for Agent-oriented Systems - SEAS.

Wesson, J., & Cowley, L. (2003). *Designing with patterns: Possibilities and pitfalls*. The Second Workshop on Software and Usability Cross-Pollination, Zürich, Switzerland, September 1-2, 2003.

Weyuker, E. (1988). Evaluating software complexity measures. *IEEE Transactions on Software Engineering, 14*(9), 1357–1365. doi:10.1109/32.6178

Whitworth, B. (2009). The social requirements of technical systems. In Whitworth, B., & de Moor, A. (Eds.), *Handbook of research on socio-technical design and social networking systems* (pp. 3–22). Hershey, PA: IGI Global. doi:10.4018/9781605662640.ch001

Wiegers, K. (2003). *Software requirements* (2nd ed.). Microsoft Press.

Wikinoff, M., & Padgham, L. (2004). The Prometheus methodology. In Bergenti, F., Gleizes, M.-P., & Zambonelli, F. (Eds.), *Methodologies and software engineering for agents systems: The agent-oriented software engineering handbook.*

Wikipedia. (2010). *Wikipedia, the free encyclopedia.* Retrieved March 2010, from http://en.wikipedia.org

Willem, V., Corina, S. P., & Sarfraz, K. (2004). Test input generation with Java path finder. *Proceedings of the 2004 ACM SIGSOFT International Symposium on Software Testing and Analysis.*

Wilson, W. M., Rosenberg, L. H., & Hyatt, L. E. (1997). Automated analysis of requirement specifications. *Proceedings of the 19th International Conference on Software Engineering.*

Wimmel, G., Läotzbeyer, H., Pretschner, A., & Slotosch, O. (2000). Specification based test sequence generation with propositional logic. *Journal Software Testing, Validation, And Reliability, 10*(4), 229–248. doi:10.1002/1099-1689(200012)10:4<229::AID-STVR213>3.0.CO;2-O

Winkler, R. L. (2003). *An introduction to Bayesian inference and decision* (2nd ed.). Gainsville, FL: Probabilistic Publishing.

Winters, N., & Mor, Y. (2008). IDR: A participatory methodology for interdisciplinary design in technology enhanced learning. *Computers & Education, 50*(2), 579–600. doi:10.1016/j.compedu.2007.09.015

Wong, E., Horgan, J. R., Mathur, A. P., & Pasquini, A. (1999). Test set size minimization and fault detection effectiveness: A case study in a space application. *Journal of Systems and Software, 48*(2), 79–89. doi:10.1016/S0164-1212(99)00048-5

Wong, B. (2006). Different views of software quality. In Duggan, E., & Reichgelt, J. (Eds.), *Measuring Information Systems delivery quality* (pp. 55–88). Hershey, PA: Idea Group.

Wooff, D. A., Goldstein, M., & Coolen, F. P. A. (2002). Bayesian graphical models for software testing. *IEEE Transactions on Software Engineering, 28*(5), 510–525. doi:10.1109/TSE.2002.1000453

Wooldridge, M. (1999). Intelligent agents. In Weiss, G. (Ed.), *Multiagent systems: A modern approach to distributed artificial intelligence.* Cambridge, MA: The MIT Press.

Wroe, C., Stevens, R., Goble, C., Roberts, A., & Greenwood, M. (2003). A suite of DAML+ OIL ontologies to describe bioinformatics Web services and data. *International Journal of Cooperative Information Systems, 12*(2), 197–224. doi:10.1142/S0218843003000711

Wuchenauer, V. (2009). *Ein empirisches Vorgehen zur Prognostizierung von Softwarefehlern auf Basis ausgewählter Entwicklungsprozessgrößen eingebetteter Software im Automobilbereich.* Unpublished master's thesis, University of Stuttgart, Stuttgart.

Xiao, M., Mohamed, E. A., Marek, R., & James, M. (2007). Empirical evaluation of optimization algorithms when used in goal-oriented automated test data generation techniques. *Empirical Software Engineering, 12*(2), 183–239. doi:10.1007/s10664-006-9026-0

Ya, S., & Rui, T. (2006). The influence of stakeholders on technology innovation: A case study from China. In *Proceedings of the International Conference on Management of Innovation and Technology,* (pp. 295–299).

Yang, D., Wu, D., Koolmanojwong, S., Brown, A. W., & Boehm, B. (2008). WikiWinWin: A wiki based system for collaborative requirements negotiation. In *Proceedings of the Annual Hawaii International Conference on System Sciences.*

Yeniaras, E., Navkar, N., Syed, M. A., & Tsekos, N. V. (2010). *A computational system for performing robot assisted cardiac surgeries with MRI guidance.* Presented in the SDPS Conference, June 6-10, 2010, Dallas, Texas.

Yilmaz, A. E., & Kizilca, H. (2009). A tool for improvement of the software requirement quality. *Proceedings of the 2nd Engineering and Technology Symposium*, (pp. 270–276).

Yilmaz, I. B. (2010). *Quality improvement of the software requirements written in natural language by means of linguistic analysis techniques*. MSc Thesis, Ankara University, Turkey.

Yoder, J., & Barcalow, J. (1997). *Architectural patterns for enabling application security*. The Fourth Conference on Pattern Languages of Programs (PLoP 1997), Monticello, USA, September 3-5, 1997.

Young, R. R. (2001). *Effective requirements practices*. Boston, MA: Addison-Wesley.

Young, R. (2009). Back to basics: Strategies for identifying, creating, storing, sharing and using knowledge: From productivity to innovation. *Proceedings of 2nd International Conference on Technology and Innovation for Knowledge Management*.

Yu, J., & Buyya, R. (2005). A taxonomy of scientific workflow systems for Grid computing. *SIGMOD Record*, *34*(3), 49. doi:10.1145/1084805.1084814

Zahran, S. (1998). *Software process improvement: Practical guidelines for business success*. Boston, MA: Addison Wesley.

Zambonelli, F., Jennings, N., & Wooldridge, M. (2003). Developing multi-agent systems: The Gaia methodology. *ACM Transactions on Software Engineering and Methodology*, 417–470.

Zambonelli, F., Jennings, N. R., & Wooldridge, M. (2005). Multi-agent systems as computational organizations: The Gaia methodology. In Henderson-Sellers, B., & Giorgini, P. (Eds.), *Agented-oriented methodologies* (pp. 136–171). Hershey, PA: IDEA Group Publishing.

Zambonelli, F., Jennings, N., Omicini, A., & Wooldridge, M. (2000). Agent oriented software engineering for Internet applications. In Omicini, A., Zambonelli, F., Klush, M., & Tolksdorf, R. (Eds.), *Coordination of Internet agents: Models, technologies and applications* (pp. 326–346). Springer Verlag.

Zambonelli, F., Jennings, N. R., & Wooldridge, M. (2000). Organizational abstractions for the analysis and design of multi-agent systems. In *Proceedings of the 1st International Workshop on Agent-Oriented Software Engineering*, Limerick, Ireland. (pp. 127–141).

Zhang, Z., & Zhou, Y. (2007). Fuzzy logic based approach for software testing. *International Journal of Pattern Recognition and Artificial Intelligence*, 709–722. doi:10.1142/S0218001407005636

Zhang, D., & Zao, L. (2006). Knowledge management in organization. *Journal of Database Management*, *17*(1), 1–8.

Zhao, F., Sun, J., Li, S., & Liu, W. (2009). A hybrid genetic algorithm for the traveling salesman problem with pickup and delivery. *International Journal of Automation and Computing*, *6*(1), 97–102. doi:10.1007/s11633-009-0097-4

Zhao, J., Goble, C., Greenwood, M., Wroe, C., & Stevens, R. (2003). Annotating, linking and browsing provenance logs for e-science. In *Proceedings of the Workshop on Semantic Web Technologies for Searching and Retrieving Scientific Data*, (pp. 158–176).

Zhenqiang, C., Baowen, X., William, C. C., Hongji, Y., & Jianjun, Z. (2003). *Partial slicing for large programs*. SEKE-2003, (pp. 204-207).

Zhiyong, Z., John, T., & Lin, P. (2008). *Automated unit testing intelligent agents in PDT*. International Conference on Autonomous Agents, (pp. 1673-1674).

Zhou, Y., Würsch, M., Giger, E., Gall, H. C., & Lü, J. (2008). A Bayesian network based approach for change coupling prediction. *Proceedings of the 15th Working Conference on Reverse Engineering*, Washington, DC, IEEE Computer Society, (pp. 27–36).

Zuohua, D., Kao, Z., & Jueliang, H. (2008). A rigorous approach towards test case generation. *Information Sciences: An International Journal*, *178*(21), 4057–4079.

Zuse, H. (1998). *A framework of software measurement*. Berlin, Germany: Walter de Gruyter.

About the Contributors

Muthu Ramachandran is currently a Principal Lecturer in Computing and Information Systems Group, The Faculty of Arts, Environment and Technology, Leeds Metropolitan University, Leeds, UK. Previously, he spent nearly eight years in industrial research (Philips Research Labs and Volantis Systems Ltd, Surrey, UK) where he worked on software architecture, reuse, and testing. Prior to that, he was teaching at Liverpool John Moores University and received his PhD from Lancaster University. His first career started as a research scientist from India Space Research Labs where he worked on real time systems development projects. Muthu is an author of a book called Software Components: Guidelines and Applications, (Nova Publishers, NY, USA, 2008). He is also an edited co-author of a book on Handbook of research in software engineering, (IGI, 2010). He has also widely published articles on journals, chapters, and conferences on various advanced topics on software engineering and education. He did his Masters degrees from Indian Institute of Technology, Madras and from Madurai Kamaraj University, Madurai, India. Muthu is also a member of various professional organisations and computer societies: IEEE, ACM, BCS, Fellow of HEA.

* * *

Nour Ali is a research fellow at Lero, Ireland. She has graduated in Computer Science from Bir-Zeit University-Palestine, and has obtained her PhD at the Polytechnic University of Valencia, Spain. She has been a member of several research projects such as the Microsoft Research Cambridge Project: "PRISMA Model Compiler of aspect-oriented component-based software architectures" and others. Her research interests are related to software engineering, specifically knowledge management, software architectures, distributed and mobile systems, aspect-oriented software development, and automatic code generation.

Shuib Bin Basri is a lecturer in Computer and Information Science at the Universiti Teknologi PETRONAS and a researcher with Lero, the Irish Software Engineering Research Centre. He received a PhD in Software Engineering from Dublin City University for his work in the role of knowledge management in software process evolution and maintenance in small software companies. His earned his Master in Software System Engineering from University of Melbourne, Australia in 2001. His main area of research interest is software engineering, specifically software process, and quality standards.

Nadia Cerezo started in 2009 and is currently carrying out a PhD at the I3S Laboratory, University of Nice Sophia-Antipolis (France), supervised by Isabelle Mirbel and Pierre Crescenzo, on the subject "From user needs to Web services: top-down approach driven by intentions." Before that, she completed a Master of Engineering degree in Computer Science at the ENSIMAG engineering school, did a 6-months research training under Hideaki Takeda at the National Institute of Informatics, Tokyo (Japan), and participated in the 07-08 edition of the Junior Year Program in English at Tohoku University, Sendai (Japan) in which she joined Takao Nishizeki's research team for a 1-year Introduction to Research course.

Pierre Crescenzo is Assistant Professor at Université de Nice Sophia-Antipolis (France) since September 2002. He received a PhD in Computer Science from this University in December 2001. The main theme of this work was meta-modelling and meta-programming of object-oriented languages, with a particular attention on inter-classes relationships like inheritance, generalisation, aggregation, composition, et cetera. Since his PhD, he developed more contributions about this theme: he worked on the definition about new kinds of relationships like pure generalisation or reverse inheritance and their integration in existing object-oriented languages (Java for example). He continued his studies to a more extensive way by applying these ideas in the field of the separation of concerns, especially aspect-oriented or subject-oriented programming. Then, he made a redeployment to model-driven engineering and need-driven engineering. Since 2009, he works with Isabelle Mirbel on the SATIS Project in order to assist non-computer-scientist users to search and retrieve Web services which are adequate to their needs. He is co-director, with Isabelle Mirbel, of the current PhD Thesis of Nadia Cerezo.

Ali Dogru is currently an associate professor in the Computer Engineering Department of METU. After his PhD in Computer Science from SMU in 1992, he has been publishing books, chapters and numerous articles, organizing and refereeing conferences, and similar activities. Also actively involved in the industry projects, he has participated in the large-scale software development activities, besides consulting and training for big enterprises in the US and Turkey. Dr. Dogru has developed and coordinated the Software Engineering masters program in METU, took part in the development of similar programs in University of Texas and Texas Tech University. His current research interests are focused on methodologies and specification formalisms for compositional approaches.

Rosario Girardi, Doctor (Computer Science), University of Geneva, Switzerland, 1996. Master in Computer Science, UFRGS, Brazil, 1991. Engineer in Computer Science, UdelaR, Uruguay, 1982. Associate Professor (Computer Science Department at Federal University of Maranhão). She acts as lecturer, researcher, and advisor on the Graduate course in Electric Engineering (Computer Science area) and on the Undergraduate course in Computer Science. Her specialization areas are: software engineering, artificial intelligence and information engineering. Since 2001, she coordinates research projects with support of the CNPq federal funding agency and receives a CNPq research productivity grant since 2008. Dr. Girardi has orientated more than 90 final degree, research works, and teaching apprenticeships at the graduate and undergraduate level. She has produced more than 100 publications in books, book chapters, journals and proceedings of events related with her research activities. She has been participating as member of program committees, lecturer, and moderator in several national and international events related with her specialties.

Thomas Gorges started working as software engineer within telecommunication industries in 1989. At Alcatel SEL, he acted as project leader in numerous software projects. Since 2004, he is working at the driver assistance division within the Robert Bosch GmbH. Here he is responsible for all testing aspects in product development. Since 2007, he is supervising the PhD of Thomas Schulz.

Pankaj Kamthan has been teaching in academia and industry for several years. He has also been a technical editor, participated in standards development, served on program committees of international conferences, and is on the editorial board of a number of journals, including the International Journal of Technology Enhanced Learning and the Information Resources Management Journal. His research interests include conceptual modeling, software quality, and knowledge representation.

Ozgur Kaya is a PhD student in the Computer Engineering Department of METU. Serving as the systems administrator, he also took part in industry projects, such as fault management for mission critical systems and software product line reference architectures. Mr. Kaya has presented a few conference articles and is actively involved in continuing research and development.

Adriana Leite Master's at Electric Engineering (Computer Science area) from Federal University of Maranhão, UFMA, Brazil. Expert in Systems Analysis and Design from the Federal University of Maranhão, 2006, and at Graduate in Computer Technology from University Center of Maranhão, 2004. Has experience in Computer Science, focusing on software engineering, acting on the following subjects: software process, software reuse, domain engineering, application engineering and ontologies.

Zaigham Mahmood is a Principal Researcher, Reader in Applied Computing and Operations Coordinator for DISYS (Distributed and Intelligent Systems Research Group) in the School of Computing, University of Derby, UK. He is also a Chartered Engineer of the Engineering Council, UK and a member of the British Computer Society. Dr. Mahmood has in excess of 50 publications in proceedings of international conferences and referred internal journals as well as chapters in books. Dr. Mahmood is also Editor-in-Chief of Journal of E-Government Studies and Best Practices as well as a member of editorial boards of several international conferences and journals. His research interests are in the areas of Information Systems, enterprise computing, software engineering, project management, and e-government studies.

Francisco Milton Mendes Neto received a PhD in Electrical Engineering from Federal University of Campina Grande. He received the MSc degree in Informatics from Federal University of Campina Grande and received the Bachelor's degree in Computer Science from State University of Ceará. He was Software Development Project Manager for Federal Service of Data Processing for several years. In 2006, after an excursion in industry, he joined the Rural Federal University of the Semi-Arid, Brazil, where he is currently an associate professor of the Graduate Program in Computer Science and of the Post Graduate Program in Computer Science and coordinator of both the Research Group in Software Engineering and the Technology Center of Software Engineering. His main research areas are in knowledge engineering, software engineering, multiagent systems, and computer-supported collaborative learning. Dr. Mendes Neto is a member of the Brazilian Computing Society.

Isabelle Mirbel is associate professor at the University of Nice Sophia-Antipolis since 1998. Her research interests include Information Systems design, method engineering, and requirement engineering. She has published papers at international level, and she participated in the WIDE ESPRIT project (Workflow on Intelligent Distributed database Environment) and Chorochronos on the European projects: spatio-temporal databases (Training and Mobility of Researchers program). She has been part of the program committee in several international conferences, among which CAISE and ICEIS, and referee for several international journals. She is member of the IFIP 8.1 Working Group.

Rory O'Connor is a Senior Lecturer in Software Engineering at Dublin City University and a Senior Researcher with Lero, the Irish Software Engineering Research Centre. He received a PhD in Computer Science from City University (London) and a MSc in Computer Applications from Dublin City University. He has previously held research positions at both the National Centre for Software Engineering and the Centre for Teaching Computing, and has also worked as a software engineer and consultant for several Irish and European technology organisations. His research interests are centred on the processes whereby software intensive systems are designed, implemented, and managed. He is also interested in technology adoption issues and the process whereby Information Technology tools and techniques are evaluated and selected in a commercial setting.

Marçal José de Oliveira Morais II has degrees in Computer Science from State University of Rio Grande do Norte (2006) and specialization in Applied Computer Science by the State University of Rio Grande do Norte (2008). He is currently Professor of the Federal Institute of Education, Science and Technology of Rio Grande do Norte. He is currently receiving his master degree by State University of the Ceará. He has experience in computer science, with emphasis on computer methods and techniques.

Łukasz Radliński currently is an Assistant Professor at the Institute of Information Technology in Management, University of Szczecin in Poland where he has been working since 2000. In 2008, he obtained a PhD degree from Queen Mary, University of London, UK. His research interests include applications of Bayesian networks, project and risk management, process modeling, and general software engineering.

Wolfgang Rosenstiel is University Professor and holds the Chair for Computer Engineering. He is also Managing Director of the Wilhelm Schickard Institute at Tübingen University, and Director for the Department for System Design in Microelectronics at the Computer Science Research centre (FZI). Furthermore he is Chairman of the German edacentrum. His research areas include embedded system design, electronic design automation, computer architecture, multi-media, and artificial neural networks.

Pinar Senkul is an assistant professor at Middle East Technical University (METU), Computer Engineering Department. She received her PhD from Middle East Technical University, Computer Engineering Department. During her thesis work, she has worked as a visiting researcher at State University of New York at Stony Brook. She is the author/co-author of publications presented and published at international conferences and journals including VLDB Conference and Information Systems Journal. She serves as PC member and reviewer for several journals and conferences such as IET Software, VLDB Journal, ISCIS, and EDBT. Her research interests include Semantic Web services, Web services discovery and composition, workflow modeling and scheduling, and data mining.

Thomas Schulz has been working at the Robert Bosch GmbH division driver assistance since 2004. He carried out multiple projects mainly in the area of software management and engineering for embedded applications. In same fields, he started to pursue his PhD since 2007 with focus on software quality assessment.

Carlos Solis is a research fellow in Lero, the Irish Software Engineering Research Centre. He received his PhD from the Polytechnic University of Valencia, Spain in 2008. His research interest are hypermedia, computer supported collaborative work, and knowledge management.

Asim Egemen Yilmaz received his BSc degrees in Electrical-Electronics Engineering and Mathematics from the Middle East Technical University in 1997. He received his MSc and PhD degrees in Electrical-Electronics Engineering from the same university in 2000 and 2007, respectively. For more than 10 years, he has been involved in various software-intensive defense projects where he held different technical and administrative positions. He is currently with the Department of Electronics Engineering in Ankara University, where he is an Assistant Professor. His research interests include optimization, knowledge-based systems; more generally, he is interested in software development processes and methodologies.

Ibrahim Berk Yilmaz received his BSc degree in Electrical-Electronics Engineering from the Middle East Technical University in 1998. He received his MSc degrees in Business Administration from Yeditepe University in 2003, and Electronics Engineering from Ankara University in 2010. For more than 10 years, he has been involved in various military projects at different technical and administrative positions.

Index

A

agent-oriented software engineering (AOSE) 100

agglutination 29

Amazon 87, 93

ant colony optimization (ACO) 215, 217, 219, 236

anti-virus software 249

AOL 87

artificial intelligence (AI) 2, 3, 5, 6, 7, 8, 211, 216, 218, 219, 225, 226, 239, 290

attribute hiding factor (AHF) 259, 260, 268

attribute inheritance factor (AIF) 259, 260, 268

automotive safety integrity levels (ASIL) 38, 66

automotive software engineering 290

auxiliary verbs 25

average parameters per method metric (APPM) 261

B

backward chaining 162, 169, 173, 174

bacteriologic algorithm (BA) 215, 217, 219

bayesian networks (BNs) 289, 290, 292, 293, 294, 296, 298, 300, 304, 305, 307, 310

Bayes' Theorem 292, 293

bee colony optimization (ABC) 219, 239, 241

BN sub models 304

boolean circuits 290

bounded exhaustive testing (BET) 216

business process execution language (BPEL) 165, 166, 176

C

C++ 118

candidate requirement databases 25

capability maturity model (CMM or CMMI) 244, 245, 248, 251, 254, 255

causal bayesian net 294

central processing unit (CPU) 2, 12, 14, 15, 16

class-attribute (CA) 261

class-method (CM) 260, 261

class-responsibility-collaborators (CRC) 104, 105, 106, 107

class-responsibility-collaborators (CRC) cards 104, 105, 106, 108

.code quality 299, 301

cohesion 256, 257, 258, 263, 265, 266, 268, 269, 270

cohesion among methods of class (CAMC) 263, 264, 268

collaborative filtering (CF) 184, 186

collective knowledge 161

communication model 101

community semantic memory managers 167, 168

component orientation 2

comprehensive software reusability estimation (CSRE) 204, 205

computer-aided software engineering 47

computer science (CS) 2, 3

computer scientists 162, 163, 166, 167, 168

computing devices 119

constraint satisfaction problems (CSP) 226

content-based filtering (CBF) 184, 186

control flow graph (CFG) 220